New Perspectives on

THE INTERNET
2nd EDITION

Comprehensive

The Internet Tutorials

JAMES T. PERRY
University of San Diego

GARY P. SCHNEIDER
University of San Diego

HTML Brief Tutorials

PATRICK CAREY
Carey Associates, Inc.

COURSE
TECHNOLOGY

Thomson Learning™

ONE MAIN STREET, CAMBRIDGE, MA 02142

Australia • Canada • Mexico • Singapore • Spain • United Kingdom • United States

New Perspectives on The Internet—Comprehensive, 2nd Edition is published by Course Technology.

Managing Editor	Greg Donald
Senior Editor	Donna Gridley
Senior Product Manager	Rachel Crapser
Product Manager	Karen Shortill
Product Manager	Catherine Donaldson
Associate Product Manager	Melissa Dezotell
Editorial Assistant	Jill Kirn
Developmental Editor	Catherine Skintik
Production Editor	Jennifer Goguen
Text Designer	Meral Dabcovich
Cover Art Designer	Douglas Goodman

For more information contact:

Course Technology
1 Main Street
Cambridge, MA 02142
Or find us on the World Wide Web at: http://www.course.com.

For permission to use material from this text or product, contact us by
- Web: www.thomsonrights.com
- Phone: 1-800-730-2214
- Fax: 1-800-730-2215

ISBN 0-619-01938-7

Printed in the United States of America

2 3 4 5 6 7 8 9 10 BM 04 03 02 01 00

New Perspectives on

THE INTERNET
2nd EDITION

Comprehensive

The Internet Tutorials

JAMES T. PERRY
University of San Diego

GARY P. SCHNEIDER
University of San Diego

HTML Brief Tutorials

PATRICK CAREY
Carey Associates, Inc.

COURSE
TECHNOLOGY

Thomson Learning™

ONE MAIN STREET, CAMBRIDGE, MA 02142

Australia • Canada • Mexico • Singapore • Spain • United Kingdom • United States

New Perspectives on The Internet—Comprehensive, 2nd Edition is published by Course Technology.

Managing Editor	Greg Donald
Senior Editor	Donna Gridley
Senior Product Manager	Rachel Crapser
Product Manager	Karen Shortill
Product Manager	Catherine Donaldson
Associate Product Manager	Melissa Dezotell
Editorial Assistant	Jill Kirn
Developmental Editor	Catherine Skintik
Production Editor	Jennifer Goguen
Text Designer	Meral Dabcovich
Cover Art Designer	Douglas Goodman

For more information contact:

Course Technology
1 Main Street
Cambridge, MA 02142
Or find us on the World Wide Web at: http://www.course.com.

For permission to use material from this text or product, contact us by
- Web: www.thomsonrights.com
- Phone: 1-800-730-2214
- Fax: 1-800-730-2215

ISBN 0-619-01938-7

Printed in the United States of America

2 3 4 5 6 7 8 9 10 BM 04 03 02 01 00

PREFACE

The New Perspectives Series

About New Perspectives

Course Technology's **New Perspectives Series** is an integrated system of instruction that combines text and technology products to teach computer concepts, the Internet, and microcomputer applications. Users consistently praise this series for innovative pedagogy, use of interactive technology, creativity, accuracy, and supportive and engaging style.

How is the New Perspectives Series different from other series?

The **New Perspectives Series** distinguishes itself by **innovative technology**, from the renowned Course Labs to the state-of-the-art multimedia that is integrated with our Concepts texts. Other distinguishing features include **sound instructional design, proven pedagogy,** and **consistent quality**. Each tutorial has students learn features in the context of solving a realistic case problem rather than simply learning a laundry list of features. With the **New Perspectives Series,** instructors report that students have a complete, integrative learning experience that stays with them. They credit this high retention and competency to the fact that this series incorporates critical thinking and problem-solving with computer skills mastery. In addition, we work hard to ensure accuracy by using a multi-step quality assurance process during all stages of development. Instructors focus on teaching and students spend more time learning

Choose the coverage that's right for you

New Perspectives applications books are available in the following categories:

Brief: approximately 150 pages long, two to four "Level I" tutorials, teaches basic application skills.

Introductory: approximately 300 pages long, four to seven tutorials, goes beyond the basic skills. These books often build out of the Brief book, adding two or three additional "Level II" tutorials.

Comprehensive: approximately 600 pages long, eight to twelve tutorials, all tutorials included in the Introductory text plus higher-level "Level III" topics. The book you are holding is a Comprehensive book.

Advanced: approximately 600 pages long, cover topics similar to those in the Comprehensive books, but offer the highest-level coverage in the series. Advanced books assume students already know the basics, and therefore go into more depth at a more accelerated rate than the Comprehensive titles. Advanced books are ideal for a second, more technical course.

Office: approximately 800 pages long, covers all components of the Office suite as well as integrating the individual software packages with one another and the Internet.

Custom Books The New Perspectives Series offers you two ways to customize a New Perspectives text to fit your course exactly: *CourseKits*™—two or more texts shrinkwrapped together. We offer significant price discounts on *CourseKits*™. *Custom Editions*® offer you flexibility in designing your concepts, Internet, and applications courses. You can build your own book by ordering a combination of topics bound together to cover only the subjects you want. There is no minimum order, and books are spiral bound. Contact your Course Technology sales representative for more information.

Brief

2-4 tutorials

Introductory

6 or 7 tutorials, or Brief + 2 or 3 more

Comprehensive

Introductory + 4 or 5 more tutorials. Includes Brief Windows tutorials and Additional Cases

Advanced

Quick Review of basics + in-depth, high-level coverage

Office

Office suite components + integration + Internet

Custom Editions

Choose from any of the above to build your own Custom Editions or CourseKits

What course is this book appropriate for?

New Perspectives on The Internet— Comprehensive, 2nd Edition can be used in any course in which you want students to learn all the most important topics of using the internet, including the history of the internet, getting connected, basic e-mail and integrated browser e-mail software, and advanced Internet topics. It is particularly recommended for a full semester course on internet concepts. This book assumes that students have learned basic Windows navigation and file management skills from Course Technology's *New Perspectives on Microsoft Windows 95—Brief, New Perspectives on Microsoft Windows NT Workstation 4.0—Introductory,* or an *equivalent* book.

Proven Pedagogy

CASE

Tutorial Case Each tutorial begins with a problem presented in a case that is meaningful to students. The case turns the task of learning how to use an application into a problem-solving process.

45-minute Sessions Each tutorial is divided into sessions that can be completed in about 45 minutes to an hour. Sessions allow instructors to more accurately allocate time in their syllabus, and students to better manage their own study time.

1.
2.
3.

Step-by-Step Methodology We make sure students can differentiate between what they are to *do* and what they are to *read*. Through numbered steps – clearly identified by a gray shaded background – students are constantly guided in solving the case problem. In addition, the numerous screen shots with callouts direct students' attention to what they should look at on the screen.

TROUBLE?

TROUBLE? Paragraphs These paragraphs anticipate the mistakes or problems that students may have and help them continue with the tutorial.

"Read This Before You Begin" Page Located opposite the first tutorial's opening page for each level of the text, the Read This Before You Begin Page helps introduce technology into the classroom. Technical considerations and assumptions about software are listed to save time and eliminate unnecessary aggravation. Notes about the Student Disks help instructors and students get the right files in the right places, so students get started on the right foot.

QUICK CHECK

Quick Check Questions Each session concludes with meaningful, conceptual Quick Check questions that test students' understanding of what they learned in the session. Answers to the Quick Check questions are provided at the end of each tutorial.

RW

Reference Windows Reference Windows are succinct summaries of the most important tasks covered in a tutorial and they preview actions students will perform in the steps to follow.

TASK REFERENCE

Task Reference Located as a table at the end of the book, the Task Reference contains a summary of how to perform common tasks using the most efficient method, as well as references to pages where the task is discussed in more detail.

End-of-Chapter Review Assignments, Case Problems, Internet Assignments and Lab Assignments Review Assignments provide students with additional hands-on practice of the skills they learned in the tutorial using the same case presented in the tutorial. These Assignments are followed by three to four Case Problems that have approximately the same scope as the tutorial case but use a different scenario. In addition, some of the Review Assignments or Case Problems may include Exploration Exercises that challenge students, encourage them to explore the capabilities of the program they are using, and/or further extend their knowledge. Each tutorial also includes instructions on getting to the text's Student Online Companion page, which contain the Internet Assignments and other related links for the text. Internet Assignments are additional exercises that integrate the skills the students learned in the tutorial with the World Wide Web. Finally, if a Course Lab accompanies a tutorial, Lab Assignments are included after the Case Problems.

New Perspectives on The Internet—Comprehensive, 2ⁿᵈ Edition Instructor's Resource Kit for this title contains:

- Instructor's Manual in Word 97 format
- Sample Syllabus
- Data Files
- Solution Files
- Course Labs
- Course Test Manager Testbank
- Course Test Manager Engine
- Figure files

These supplements come on CD-ROM. If you don't have access to a CD-ROM drive, contact your Course Technology customer service representative for more information.

The New Perspectives Supplements Package

Electronic Instructor's Manual Our Instructor's Manuals include tutorial overviews and outlines, technical notes, lecture notes, solutions, and Extra Case Problems. Many instructors use the Extra Case Problems for performance-based exams or extra credit projects. The Instructor's Manual is available as an electronic file, which you can get from the Instructor Resource Kit (IRK) CD-ROM or download it from **www.course.com.**

Data Files Data Files contain all of the data that students will use to complete the tutorials, Review Assignments, and Case Problems. A Readme file includes instructions for using the files. See the "Read This Before You Begin" page for more information on Data Files.

Solution Files Solution Files contain every file students are asked to create or modify in the tutorials, Tutorial Assignments, Case Problems, and Extra Case Problems. A Help file on the Instructor's Resource Kit includes information for using the Solution files.

Course Labs: Concepts Come to Life These highly interactive computer-based learning activities bring concepts to life with illustrations, animations, digital images, and simulations. The Labs guide students step-by-step, present them with Quick Check questions, let them explore on their own, test their comprehension, and provide printed feedback. Lab icons at the beginning of the tutorial and in the tutorial margins indicate when a topic has a corresponding Lab. Lab Assignments are included at the end of each relevant tutorial. The Labs available with this book and the tutorials in which they appear are:

E-mail

Tutorial 2

The Internet: World Wide Web

Tutorial 3

Multimedia

Tutorial 5

Web Pages & HTML

HTML
Tutorial 1

Figure Files Many figures in the text are provided on the IRK CD-ROM to help illustrate key topics or concepts. Instructors can create traditional overhead transparencies by printing the figure files. Or they can create electronic slide shows by using the figures in a presentation program such as PowerPoint.

Course Test Manager: Testing and Practice at the Computer or on Paper   Course Test Manager is cutting-edge, Windows-based testing software that helps instructors design and administer practice tests and actual examinations. Course Test Manager can automatically grade the tests students take at the computer and can generate statistical information on individual as well as group performance.

Online Companions: Dedicated to Keeping You and Your Students Up-To-Date   Visit our faculty sites and student sites on the World Wide Web at www.course.com. Here instructor's can browse this text's password-protected Faculty Online Companion to obtain an online Instructor's Manual, Solution Files, Student Files, and more. Students can also access this text's Student Online Companion, which contains Data files other useful links.

More innovative technology

Course CBT   Enhance your students' Office 2000 classroom learning experience with self-paced computer-based training on CD-ROM. Course CBT engages students with interactive multimedia and hands-on simulations that reinforce and complement the concepts and skills covered in the textbook. All the content is aligned with the MOUS (Microsoft Office User Specialist) program, making it a great preparation tool for the certification exams. Course CBT also includes extensive pre- and post-assessments that test students' mastery of skills. These pre- and post-assessments automatically generate a "custom learning path" through the course that highlights only the topics students need help with.

Skills Assessment Manager (SAM)   How well do your students really know Microsoft Office? SAM is a performance-based testing program that measures students' proficiency in Microsoft Office 2000. SAM is available for Office 2000 in either a live or simulated environment. You can use Course Assessment to place students into or out of courses, monitor their performance throughout a course, and help prepare them for the MOUS certification exams.

CyberClass   CyberClass is a web-based tool designed for on-campus or distance learning. Use it to enhance how you currently run your class by posting assignments and your course syllabus or holding online office hours. Or, use it for your distance learning course, and offer mini-lectures, conduct online discussion groups, or give your mid-term exam. For more information, visit our Web site at: www.course.com/products/cyberclass/index.html

Acknowledgments

Creating a quality textbook is a collaborative effort between author and publisher. We work as a team to provide the highest quality book possible. The authors want to acknowledge the work of the seasoned professionals at Course Technology. We thank Mac Mendelsohn, Vice President of Product Development, for his initial interest in and continual support of our work on this book. It was Mac's vision for a book focused on the Internet, rather than on a specific software application, that motivated us to take on this project. We offer a special thank you to Martha Wagner, our former Course Technology sales representative, for introducing us to Mac. For the many years we have known Martha, she has always been an enthusiastic and committed professional—devoted to her business and her customers. In addition we thank Rachel Crapser, Senior Product Manager; Karen Shortill, Product Manager; Jennifer Goguen, Production Editor; and John Bosco's team of Quality Assurance testers for being terrific, positive, and supportive members of a great publishing team. We also thank our Developmental Editor, Cat Skintik. Her sharp eyes caught all the small (and sometimes not-so-small) mistakes and made the manuscript better. We offer our heartfelt thanks to the Course Technology organization as a whole. The people at Course Technology have been, by far, the best publishing team with which we have ever worked.

We want to thank the following reviewers for their insightful comments and suggestions at various stages of the book's development: Cathy Fothergill, Kilgore College; Don Lopez, The Clovis Center; Suzanne Nordhaus, Lee College; Sorel Reisman, California State University, Fullerton; T. Michael Smith, Austin Community College; and Bill Wagner, Villanova University. Margaret Beeler and Pamela Drotman provided helpful comments on early drafts of the outline for this book.

Finally, we want to express our deep appreciation for the continuous support and encouragement of our spouses, Nancy Perry and Cathy Cosby. They demonstrated remarkable patience as we worked both ends of the clock to complete this book on a very tight schedule. Without their support and cooperation, we would not have attempted to write this book. We also thank our children for tolerating our absences while we were busy writing.

James T. Perry
Gary P. Schneider

Dedication

To my oldest daughter, Jessica Perry
 Finally, you have learned to soar. Keep giving life your best. — J.T.P.

To the memory of my brother, Bruce Schneider. — G.P.S.

TABLE OF CONTENTS

Reference **Window List**

Tutorial Tips

These tutorials will help you learn about Internet concepts. The tutorials are designed to be worked through at a computer. Each tutorial is divided into sessions. Watch for the session headings, such as Session 1.1 and Session 1.2. Each session is designed to be completed in about 45 minutes, but take as much time as you need. It's also a good idea to take a break between sessions.

Before you begin, read the following questions and answers. They will help you use the tutorials.

Where do I start?

Each tutorial begins with a case, which sets the scene for the tutorial and gives you background information to help you understand what you will be doing. Read the case before you go to the lab. In the lab, begin with the first session of a tutorial.

How do I know what to do on the computer?

Each session contains steps that you will perform on the computer to learn how to use the Internet. Read the text that introduces each series of steps. The steps you need to do at a computer are numbered and are set against a shaded background. Read each step carefully and completely before you try it.

How do I know if I did the step correctly?

As you work, compare your computer screen with the corresponding figure in the tutorial. Don't worry if your screen display is somewhat different from the figure. The important parts of the screen display are labeled in each figure. Check to make sure these parts are on your screen.

What if I make a mistake?

Don't worry about making mistakes—they are part of the learning process. Paragraphs labeled "TROUBLE?" identify common problems and explain how to get back on track. Follow the steps in a TROUBLE? paragraph only if you are having the problem described. If you run into other problems:

- Carefully consider the current state of your system, the position of the pointer, and any messages on the screen.

- Complete the sentence, "Now I want to…" Be specific, because identifying your goal will help you rethink the steps you need to take to reach that goal.

- If you are working on a particular piece of software, consult the Help system.

- If the suggestions above don't solve your problem, consult your technical support person for assistance.

How do I use the Reference Windows?

Reference Windows summarize the procedures you will learn in the tutorial steps. Do not complete the actions in the Reference Windows when you are working through the tutorial. Instead, refer to the Reference Windows while you are working on the assignments at the end of the tutorial.

How can I test my understanding of the material I learned in the tutorial?

At the end of each session, you can answer the Quick Check questions. The answers for the Quick Checks are at the end of that tutorial.

After you have completed the entire tutorial, you should complete the Review Assignments and Case Problems. They are carefully structured so that you will review what you have learned and then apply your knowledge to new situations.

What if I can't remember how to do something?

You should refer to the Task Reference at the end of the book; it summarizes how to accomplish tasks using the most efficient method.

Before you begin the tutorials, you should know the basics about your computer's operating system. You should also know how to use the menus, dialog boxes, Help system, and My Computer.

Now that you've read Tutorial Tips, you are ready to begin.

New Perspectives on

THE
INTERNET

2ⁿᵈ Edition

Read This Before You Begin

To the Student

Data Disks

To complete the Level I tutorials, Review Assignments, and Case Problems in this book, you need two Data Disks. Your instructor will either provide you with Data Disks or ask you to make your own.

If you are making your own Data Disks, you will need two blank, formatted, high-density disks. You will need to copy onto your disks a set of folders from a file server, a standalone computer, or the Web. Your instructor will tell you which computer, drive letter, and folders contain the files you need. You could also download the files by going to www.course.com, clicking Data Disk Files, and following the instructions on the screen.

The following table shows you which folders go on your disks, so that you will have enough disk space to complete all the tutorials, Review Assignments, and Case Problems:

Data Disk 1

Write this on the disk label:
Data Disk 1: Tutorial 2

Put this folder on the disk:
Tutorial.02

Data Disk 2

Write this on the disk label:
Data Disk 2: Tutorial 3

Put this folder on the disk:
Tutorial.03

When you begin each tutorial, be sure you are using the correct Data Disk. See the inside back cover of this book for more information on Data Disk files, or ask your instructor or technical support person for assistance.

Course Labs

The tutorials in this book feature two interactive Course Labs to help you understand e-mail and multimedia concepts. There are Lab Assignments at the end of Tutorials 2 and 3 that relate to these Labs.

To start a Lab, click the **Start** button on the Windows taskbar, point to **Programs**, point to **Course Labs**, point to **New Perspectives Applications**, and click the name of the Lab you want to use.

Using Your Own Computer

If you are going to work through this book using your own computer, you need:

- **Computer System** Netscape Navigator 4.0 or higher OR Microsoft Internet Explorer 4.0 or higher and Windows 95 or higher must be installed on your computer. This book assumes a complete installation of the Web browser software and its components, and that you have an existing e-mail account and an Internet connection. Because your Web browser may be different from the ones used in the figures or the book, your screens may differ slightly at times.

- **Data Disks** You will not be able to complete the tutorials or exercises in this book using your own computer until you have Data Disks.

- **Course Labs** See your instructor or technical support person to obtain the Course Lab software for use on your own computer.

Visit Our World Wide Web Site

Additional materials designed especially for you are available on the World Wide Web.

Go to http://www.course.com.

To the Instructor

The Data files and Course Labs are available on the Instructor's Resource Kit for this title. Follow the instructions in the Help file on the CD-ROM to install the programs to your network or standalone computer. For information on creating Data Disks, see the "To the Student" section above. To complete the tutorials in this book, students must have a Web browser, an e-mail account, and an Internet connection.

You are granted a license to copy the Data Files to any computer or computer network used by students who have purchased this book.

INTRODUCTION
TO THE INTERNET AND THE WORLD WIDE WEB

History, Potential, and Getting Connected

CASE

Tropical Exotics Produce Company

Lorraine Tomassini, the owner of the Tropical Exotics Produce Company (TEPCo), is concerned about the firm's future. She started TEPCo 10 years ago to import organically grown exotic fruits and vegetables from South America, Africa, and Asia to the U.S. market. The TEPCo product line includes items such as babaco, cherimoya, feijoa, African horned melon, malanga, and tamarillo. The business has grown rapidly and thrived financially, but Lorraine is worried that TEPCo is failing to use technology effectively. She already knows that this weakness has caused TEPCo to lose customers and suppliers to competitors.

You started work as an intern at TEPCo six months ago to learn more about international business while you attend college. Justin Jansen and Arti Rao have been with the firm for about five years and are Lorraine's key assistants. During this week's meeting with you, Justin, and Arti, Lorraine expressed concern that TEPCo has become internally focused and might be missing major trends that affect its worldwide suppliers. She worries that reading newspapers for market information and staying in touch with suppliers by telephone are time-consuming, ineffective strategies. She recalled the events of the last year, when bad weather in Costa Rica destroyed most of their suppliers' sapote crop and TEPCo received the reports too late to change its customer price schedule.

Justin mentioned that he knew some people who followed weather reports from all over the world using the Internet, which he explained was a worldwide collection of computers, connected together to allow communication. He also suggested that TEPCo might be able to attract new customers by creating a World Wide Web site on a computer connected to the Internet. Arti looked worried as she noted that TEPCo's five computers were not even connected to each other, much less to a worldwide network of computers. Lorraine knew that colleges and universities had been involved in the Internet for years and asked you to do some research on ways that TEPCo might use the Internet. You agreed to undertake the project so you could learn more about international business in general.

SESSION 1.1

The Internet offers anyone connected to it a vast array of communication tools and information resources. This session explains what the Internet and World Wide Web are, describes how they have grown from their beginnings in the military and research communities, and outlines some of the resources available on them.

Internet and World Wide Web: Amazing Developments

The **Internet**—a large collection of computers all over the world that are connected to one another in various ways—is one of the most amazing technological developments of the twentieth century. Using the Internet, you can communicate with other people throughout the world through **electronic mail** (or **e-mail**); read online versions of newspapers, magazines, academic journals, and books; join discussion groups on almost any conceivable topic; participate in games and simulations; and obtain free computer software. In recent years, the Internet has allowed commercial enterprises to connect. Today, all kinds of businesses provide information about their products and services on the Internet. Many of these businesses use the Internet to market and sell their products and services. The part of the Internet known as the **World Wide Web** (or the **Web**), is a subset of the computers on the Internet that are connected to each other in a specific way that makes those computers and their contents easily accessible to all computers in that subset. The Web has helped to make Internet resources available to people who are not computer experts. Figure 1-1 shows some of the tools and resources available on the Internet today.

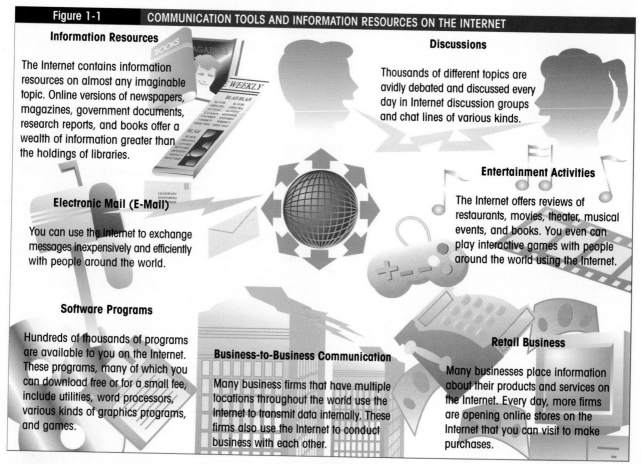

Figure 1-1   COMMUNICATION TOOLS AND INFORMATION RESOURCES ON THE INTERNET

Information Resources

The Internet contains information resources on almost any imaginable topic. Online versions of newspapers, magazines, government documents, research reports, and books offer a wealth of information greater than the holdings of libraries.

Discussions

Thousands of different topics are avidly debated and discussed every day in Internet discussion groups and chat lines of various kinds.

Entertainment Activities

The Internet offers reviews of restaurants, movies, theater, musical events, and books. You even can play interactive games with people around the world using the Internet.

Electronic Mail (E-Mail)

You can use the Internet to exchange messages inexpensively and efficiently with people around the world.

Software Programs

Hundreds of thousands of programs are available to you on the Internet. These programs, many of which you can download free or for a small fee, include utilities, word processors, various kinds of graphics programs, and games.

Business-to-Business Communication

Many business firms that have multiple locations throughout the world use the Internet to transmit data internally. These firms also use the Internet to conduct business with each other.

Retail Business

Many businesses place information about their products and services on the Internet. Every day, more firms are opening online stores on the Internet that you can visit to make purchases.

As you begin Lorraine's research project, you remember Arti's comment that TEPCo does not have its computers connected to each other. You decide to learn more about what computer networks are and how to connect computers to each other to form those networks.

Computer Networks

After talking with Adolfo Segura, the director of your school's computer lab, you realize that you will have some good news for Arti. Adolfo explained to you that he linked the lab computers to each other by inserting a network interface card into each computer and connecting cables from each card to the lab's main computer, called a server. Adolfo told you that a **network interface card** (**NIC**) is a card or other device used to connect a computer to a network of other computers. A **server** is a general term for any computer that accepts requests from other computers that are connected to it and shares some or all of its resources, such as printers, files, or programs, with those computers.

Client/Server Local Area Networks

The server runs software that coordinates the information flow among the other computers, which are called **clients**. The software that runs on the server computer is called a **network operating system**. Connecting computers this way, in which one server computer shares its resources with multiple client computers, is called a **client/server network**. Client/server networks commonly are used to connect computers that are located close together (for example, in the same room or building). Because the direct connection from one computer to another through NICs only works over relatively short distances (no more than a few thousand feet), this kind of network is called a **local area network** (**LAN**). Figure 1-2 shows a typical client/server LAN.

| Figure 1-2 | A CLIENT/ SERVER LAN |

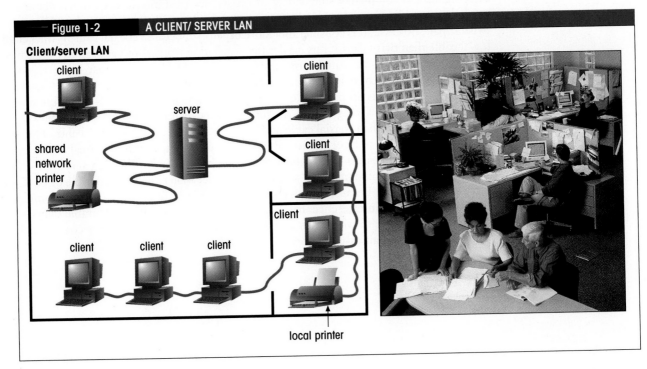

The good news for Arti is that both the NICs and the cable that connects them are fairly inexpensive. Arti's first step is to select one of TEPCo's more powerful computers to be the server. A server can be a powerful personal computer (PC) or a larger computer such as a minicomputer or a mainframe computer. **Minicomputers** and **mainframe computers** are larger, more expensive computers that businesses and other organizations use to process large volumes of work at high speeds. For many years, even the largest PCs were not powerful enough to be servers, but this has changed in the past few years.

Next, Arti will need to buy the network operating system software and have a network technician install it on the server. This software is more expensive than the operating system software for a standalone computer; however, you find that having the computers connected in a client/server network offers TEPCo some potential cost savings. For example, by connecting each computer to the server, each computer now has its own printer and its own tape drive for backups because a client/server network lets computers on the network share printers and tape drives.

Connecting Computers to a Network

As you talk with Adolfo, you learn more about computer networks. You find that not all LANs use the same kind of cables to connect their computers. The oldest cable type is called **twisted-pair**, which is the type of cable that telephone companies have used for years to wire residences and businesses. Twisted-pair cable has two or more insulated copper wires that are twisted around each other and enclosed in another layer of plastic insulation. The wires are twisted to reduce interference from other nearby current-carrying wires. The type of twisted-pair cable that telephone companies have used for years to transmit voice signals is called **Category 1** cable. Category 1 cable transmits information more slowly than the other cable types, but it is also much less expensive. **Coaxial cable** is an insulated copper wire that is encased in a metal shield that is enclosed with plastic insulation. The signal-carrying wire is completely shielded, so it resists electrical interference much better than twisted-pair cable. Coaxial cable also carries signals about 20 times faster than Category 1 twisted-pair; however, it is considerably more expensive. Because coaxial cable is thicker and less flexible than twisted-pair, it is harder for installation workers to handle and thus is more expensive to install. You might recognize coaxial cable because most cable television connections still use coaxial cable. In the past 20 years, cable manufacturers have developed better versions of twisted-pair cable. The current standard for twisted-pair cable used in computer networks is **Category 5**. Category 5 twisted-pair cable carries signals between 10 and 100 times faster than coaxial cable and is as easy to install as Category 1 cable. The most expensive cable type is **fiber-optic cable**, which does not use an electrical signal at all. Fiber-optic cable transmits information by pulsing beams of light through very thin strands of glass. Fiber-optic cable transmits signals much faster than either coaxial cable or Category 5 twisted-pair cable. Because it does not use electricity, fiber-optic cable is completely immune to electrical interference. Fiber-optic cable is lighter and more durable than coaxial cable, but it is harder to work with and much more expensive than either coaxial cable or Category 5 twisted-pair cable. Figure 1-3 shows these three types of cable.

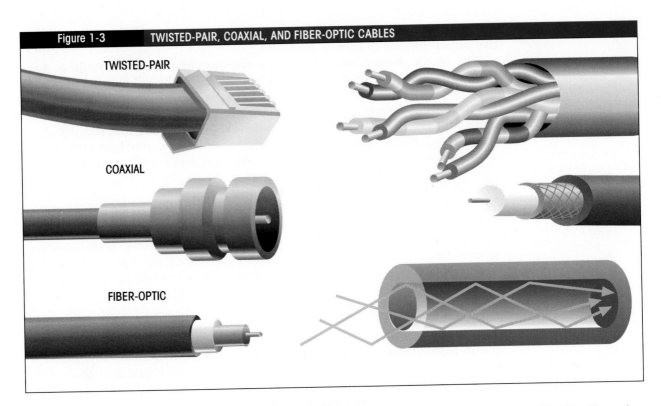

| Figure 1-3 | TWISTED-PAIR, COAXIAL, AND FIBER-OPTIC CABLES |

Perhaps the most intriguing way to connect computers in a LAN is to avoid cable all together. **Wireless networks** are becoming more common as the cost of the wireless transmitters and receivers that plug into NICs continues to drop. Wireless LANs are especially welcome in organizations that occupy old buildings. Many cities have structures that were built before electricity and telephones were widely available. These buildings have no provision for running wires through walls or between floors, so a wireless network can be the best option for connecting resources.

Wide Area Networks

You know that your school has several computer labs in different buildings, so you ask Adolfo whether the individual labs are connected to each other as a larger LAN. Adolfo explains that each computer lab is its own client/server LAN, but that these individual networks are connected to each other as part of the school's **wide area network (WAN)**. Adolfo remembers that you came to him with questions about the Internet and tells you that **internet** (lowercase "i") is short for **interconnected network**. The computer lab LANs are networks, and the school's WAN is a network of networks, or an internet. You look a little puzzled, so Adolfo continues to explain that *any* network of networks is called an internet. However, the school's WAN is connected to an internet called the Internet (capital "I"). The **Internet** is a specific worldwide collection of interconnected networks whose owners have voluntarily agreed to share resources and network connections with each other. You decide that your project is starting to become interesting and head toward the campus library to find out more about this huge interconnected network called the Internet.

How the Internet Began

In the early 1960s, the U.S. Department of Defense (DOD) became very concerned about the possible effects of nuclear attack on its computing facilities. The DOD realized that the weapons of the future would require powerful computers for coordination and control. The powerful computers of that time were all large mainframe computers, so the DOD began examining ways to connect these computers to each other and also to weapons installations that were distributed all over the world.

The agency charged with this task was the **Advanced Research Projects Agency**. (During its lifetime, this agency has used two acronyms, ARPA and DARPA; this book uses its current acronym, **DARPA**.) DARPA hired many of the best communications technology researchers and, for many years, funded research at leading universities and institutes to explore the task of creating a worldwide network. DARPA researchers soon became concerned about computer networks' vulnerability to attack and worked hard to devise ways to eliminate the need for network communications to rely on a central control function.

Circuit Switching vs. Packet Switching

The early models for networked computers were the telephone companies; most early WANs used leased telephone company lines for their connections. In telephone company systems of that time, a telephone call established a single connection between sender and receiver. Once the connection was established, all data then traveled along that single path. The telephone company's central switching system selected specific telephone lines, or **circuits**, that would be connected to create the single path. This centrally controlled, single-connection method is called **circuit switching**.

DARPA researchers turned to a different method of sending information, packet switching. In a **packet switching** network, files and messages are broken down into packets that are labeled electronically with codes for their origin and destination. The packets travel from computer to computer along the network until they reach their destination. The destination computer collects the packets and reassembles the original data from the pieces in each packet. Each computer that an individual packet encounters on its trip through the network determines the best way to move the packet forward to its destination. Computers that perform this function on networks are often called **routers**, and the programs they use to determine the best path for packets are called **routing algorithms**.

By 1967, DARPA researchers had published their plan for a packet switching network and in 1969, they connected the first computer switches at the University of California at Los Angeles, SRI International, the University of California at Santa Barbara, and the University of Utah. This experimental WAN, called the **ARPANET**, grew over the next three years to include over 20 computers and used the **Network Control Protocol (NCP)**. A **protocol** is a collection of rules for formatting, ordering, and error-checking data sent across a network.

Open Architecture Philosophy

As more researchers connected to the ARPANET, interest in the network grew in the academic community. The next several years saw many technological developments that increased the speed and efficiency with which the network operated. One reason for the project's success was its adherence to an **open architecture** philosophy; that is, each network could continue using its own protocols and data-transmission methods internally. Conversion to NCP occurred only when the data moved out of the local network and onto the ARPANET. The original purpose of the ARPANET was to connect computers in the field that were controlling a wide range of diverse weapons systems, so the ARPANET could not force its protocol or structure onto those individual component networks. This open approach was quite different from the closed architecture designs that companies such as IBM and Digital Equipment Corporation were using to build networks for their customers during this period. The open architecture philosophy included four key points:

- Independent networks should not require any internal changes to be connected to the Internet.
- Packets that do not arrive at their destinations must be retransmitted from their source network.
- The router computers do not retain information about the packets they handle.
- No global control will exist over the network.

One of the new developments of this time period that was rapidly adopted throughout the ARPANET was a set of new protocols developed by Vincent Cerf and Robert Kahn. These new protocols were the **Transmission Control Protocol** and the **Internet Protocol**, which usually are referred to by their combined acronym, **TCP/IP**. TCP includes rules that computers on a network use to establish and break connections; IP includes rules for routing of individual data packets. These two protocols were technically superior to the NCP that ARPANET had used since its inception and gradually replaced that protocol. TCP/IP continues to be used today in LANs and on the Internet. The term *Internet* was first used in a 1974 article about the TCP protocol written by Cerf and Kahn. The importance of the TCP/IP protocol in the history of the Internet is so great that many people consider Vincent Cerf to be the Father of the Internet.

ARPANET's successes were not lost on other network researchers. Many university and research institution computers used the UNIX operating system. When TCP/IP was included in a version of UNIX, these institutions found it easier to create networks and interconnect them. A number of TCP/IP-based networks—independent of the ARPANET—were created in the late 1970s and early 1980s. The National Science Foundation (NSF) funded the **Computer Science Network** (**CSNET**) for educational and research institutions that did not have access to the ARPANET. The City University of New York started a network of IBM mainframes at universities, called the **Because It's Time** (originally, "**There**") **Network** (**BITNET**).

Birth of E-Mail: A New Use for Networks

Although the goals of ARPANET were still to control weapons systems and transfer research files, other uses for this vast network began to appear in the early 1970s. In 1972, an ARPANET researcher named Ray Tomlinson wrote a program that could send and receive messages over the network. E-mail had been born and became widely used very quickly; in 1976, the Queen of England sent an e-mail message over the ARPANET. By 1981, the ARPANET had expanded to include over 200 networks and was continuing to develop faster and more effective network technologies; for example, ARPANET began sending packets via satellite in 1976.

More New Uses for Networks Emerge

The number of network users in the military and education research communities continued to grow. Many of these new participants used the networking technology to transfer files and access computers remotely. The TCP/IP suite included two tools for performing these tasks. **File Transfer Protocol** (**FTP**) enabled users to transfer files between computers, and **Telnet** let users log in to their computer accounts from remote sites. Both FTP and Telnet still are widely used on the Internet today for file transfers and remote logins, even though more advanced techniques facilitate multimedia transmissions such as realtime audio and video clips. The first e-mail mailing lists also appeared on these networks. A **mailing list** is an e-mail address that takes any message it receives and forwards it to any user who has subscribed to the list.

Although file transfer and remote login were attractive features of these new TCP/IP networks, their improved e-mail and other communications facilities attracted many users in the education and research communities. For example, BITNET would run mailing list software (called **LISTSERV**) on its IBM mainframe computers that provided automatic control and maintenance for the mailing lists. In 1979, a group of students and programmers at Duke University and the University of North Carolina started **Usenet**, an acronym for **User's News Network**. Usenet allows anyone that connects with the network to read and post articles on a variety of subjects.

Usenet survives on the Internet today, with over a thousand different topic areas, called **newsgroups**. Going even farther from the initial purpose of TCP/IP networks, researchers at the University of Essex wrote a program that allowed users to assume character roles and play an adventure game. This adventure game let multiple users play at the same time and interact with each other. These games continue on the Internet today and are called **MUDs**, which originally stood for **multiuser dungeon**, although many users now consider the term an acronym for **multiuser domain**, or **multiuser dimension**.

Although the people using these networks were developing many creative applications, the number of persons who had access to the networks was limited to members of the research and academic communities. The decade from 1979 to 1989 would be the time in which these new and interesting network applications were improved and tested with an increasing number of users. The TCP/IP set of protocols would become more widely used as academic and research institutions realized the benefits of having a common communications network. The explosion of PC use during that time also would help more people become comfortable with computing.

Interconnecting the Networks

The early 1980s saw continued growth in the ARPANET and other networks. The **Joint Academic Network (Janet)** was established in the United Kingdom to link universities there. Traffic increased on all of these networks and, in 1984, the Department of Defense (DOD) split the ARPANET into two specialized networks: ARPANET would continue its advanced research activities, and **MILNET** (for **Military Network**) would be reserved for military uses that required greater security. That year also saw a new addition to CSNET, named the **National Science Foundation Network (NSFnet)**. By 1987, congestion on the ARPANET caused by a rapidly increasing number of users on the limited-capacity leased telephone lines was becoming severe. To reduce the government's traffic load on the ARPANET, the NSFnet merged with BITNET and CSNET to form one network. The resulting NSFnet awarded a contract to Merit Network, Inc., IBM, Sprint, and the State of Michigan to upgrade and operate the main NSFnet backbone. A **network backbone** includes the long-distance lines and supporting technology that transports large amounts of data between major network nodes. The NSFnet backbone connected 13 regional WANs and six supercomputer centers. By the late 1980s, many other TCP/IP networks had merged or established interconnections. Figure 1-4 summarizes how the individual networks described in this section combined to become the Internet as we know it today.

Figure 1-4   NETWORKS THAT BECAME THE INTERNET

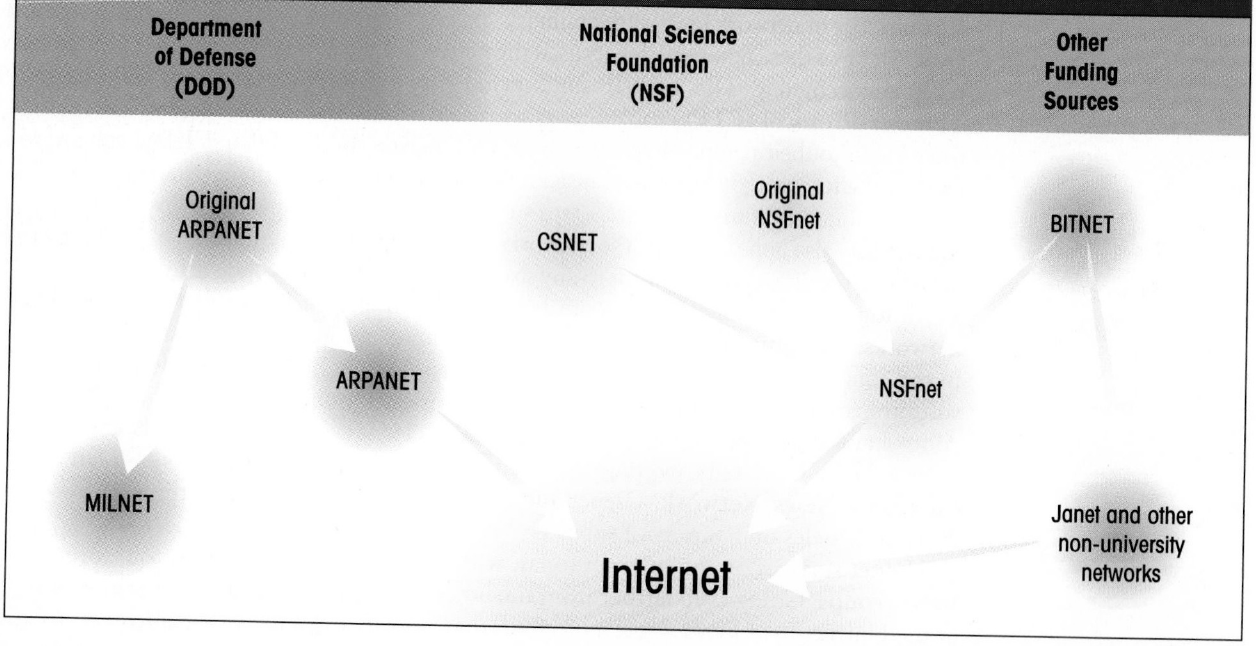

Commercial Interest Increases

As PCs became more powerful, affordable, and available during the 1980s, firms increasingly used them to construct LANs. Although these LANs included e-mail software that employees could use to send messages to each other, businesses wanted their employees to be able to communicate with people outside their corporate LANs. The National Science Foundation (NSF) prohibited commercial network traffic on the networks it funded, so businesses turned to commercial e-mail services. Larger firms built their own TCP/IP-based WANs that used leased telephone lines to connect field offices to corporate headquarters. Today, we use the term **intranet** to describe LANs or WANs that use the TCP/IP protocol but do not connect to sites outside the firm. In 1989, the NSF permitted two commercial e-mail services, MCI Mail and CompuServe, to establish limited connections to the Internet that allowed their commercial subscribers to exchange e-mail messages with the members of the academic and research communities who were connected to the Internet. These connections allowed commercial enterprises to send e-mail directly to Internet addresses and allowed members of the research and education communities on the Internet to send e-mail directly to MCI Mail and CompuServe addresses. The NSF justified this limited commercial use of the Internet as a service that would primarily benefit the Internet's noncommercial users.

People from all walks of life—not just scientists or academic researchers—started thinking of these networks as a global resource that we now know as the Internet. Information systems professionals began to form volunteer groups such as the **Internet Engineering Task Force (IETF)**, which first met in 1986. The IETF is a self-organized group that makes technical contributions to the engineering of the Internet and its technologies. IETF is the main body that develops new Internet standards.

Just as the world was coming to realize the value of these interconnected networks, however, it also became aware of the threats to privacy and security posed by these networks. In 1988, Robert Morris launched a program called the **Internet Worm** that used weaknesses in e-mail programs and operating systems to distribute itself to over 6,000 of the 60,000 computers that were then connected to the Internet. The Worm program created multiple copies of itself on the computers it infected. The large number of program copies consumed the processing power of the infected computer and prevented it from running other programs. This event brought international attention and concern to the Internet.

Although the network of networks that is now known as the Internet had grown from four computers on the ARPANET in 1969 to over 300,000 computers on many interconnected networks by 1990, the greatest growth in the Internet was yet to come.

Growth of the Internet

A formal definition of Internet, which was adopted in 1995 by the Federal Networking Council, appears in Figure 1-5.

Figure 1-5	THE FEDERAL NETWORKING COUNCIL'S OCTOBER 1995 RESOLUTION TO DEFINE THE TERM INTERNET

RESOLUTION: The Federal Networking Council (FNC) agrees that the following language reflects our definition of the term "Internet." "Internet" refers to the global information system that—

(i) is logically linked together by a globally unique address space based on the Internet Protocol (IP) or its subsequent extensions/follow-ons;

(ii) is able to support communications using the Transmission Control Protocol/Internet Protocol (TCP/IP) suite or its subsequent extensions/follow-ons, and/or other IP-compatible protocols; and

(iii) provides, uses or makes accessible, either publicly or privately, high level services layered on the communications and related infrastructure described herein.

Source: http://www.fnc.gov/Internet_res.html

Many people find it interesting to note that a formal definition of the term did not appear until 1995. The Internet was a phenomenon that surprised an unsuspecting world. The researchers who had been so involved in the creation and growth of the Internet accepted it as part of their working environment. People outside the research community were largely unaware of the potential offered by a large interconnected set of computer networks.

From Research Project to Information Infrastructure

By 1990, the Internet had become a well-functioning grid of useful technology. Much of the funding for these networks had come from the U.S. government, through its DOD and the NSF. The NSFnet alone consumed over $200 million from 1986 to 1995 on research and development. Realizing that the Internet was no longer a research project, the DOD finally closed the research portion of its network, the ARPANET. The NSF also wanted to turn over the Internet to others so it could return its attention and funds to other research projects.

In 1991, the NSF further eased its restrictions on Internet commercial activity and began implementing plans to privatize much of the Internet eventually. The first parts of the NSFnet on which it encouraged commercial activity were the local and regional nodes, which allowed time for private firms to develop long-haul network capacity similar to that of the NSFnet national network backbone. Businesses and individuals connected to the Internet in ever-increasing numbers. Figure 1-6 shows the number of Internet host computers from 1991 through 1999. As you can see, the growth has been dramatic.

Figure 1-6	GROWTH OF THE NUMBER OF INTERNET HOSTS 1991–1999

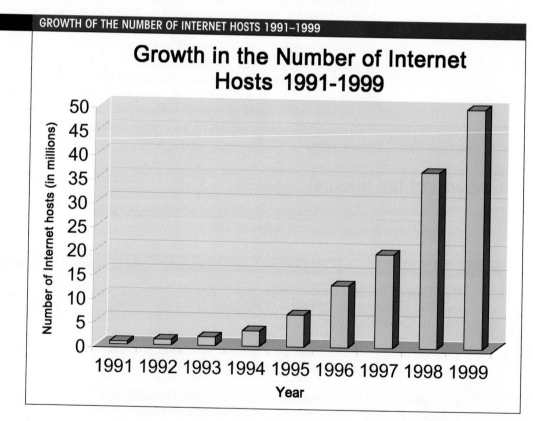

The numbers in Figure 1-6 probably understate the true growth of the Internet in recent years for two reasons. First, the number of hosts connected to the Internet includes only directly connected computers. In other words, if a LAN with 100 PCs is connected to the

Internet through only one host computer, those 100 computers appear as one host in the count. Because the number and size of LANs has increased steadily in recent years, the host count probably is understated. Second, the number of computers is only one measure of growth. Internet traffic now carries more files that contain graphics, sound, and video, so Internet files have become larger. A given number of users sending video clips will use much more of the Internet's capacity than the same number of users will use by sending e-mail messages or text files. Many people are surprised to learn that no one knows how many users are on the Internet. The Internet has no central management or coordination, and the routing computers do not maintain records of the packets they handle. Therefore, no one has the capability to know how many individual e-mail messages or files travel on the Internet.

New Structure for the Internet

As NSFnet converted the main traffic-carrying backbone portion of its network to private firms, it organized the network around the four network access points (NAPs) shown in Figure 1-7. A different company now operates each of these NAPs, as shown in Figure 1-7.

| Figure 1-7 | NETWORK ACCESS POINTS ON THE INTERNET BACKBONE |

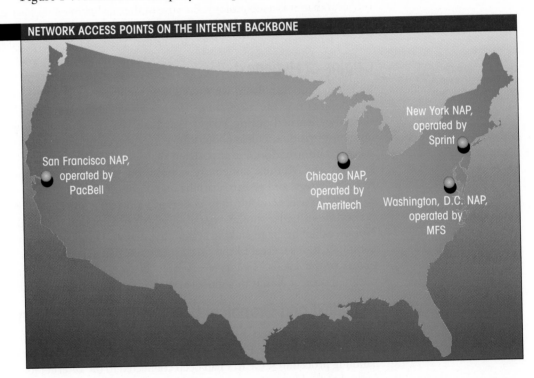

These four companies sell access to the Internet through their NAPs to organizations and businesses. The NSFnet still exists for government and research use, but it uses these same NAPs for long-range data transmission.

With over 20 million connected computers and an estimate of between 50 and 150 million worldwide Internet users, the Internet faces some challenges. The firms that sell network access have enough incentive to keep investing in the network architecture because they can recoup their investments by attracting new Internet users. However, the existing TCP/IP numbering system that identifies users will run out of addresses in a few years if the Internet continues its current rate of growth. Groups like the IETF are working on a new addressing scheme that will allow existing users to continue accessing the Internet while the new system is implemented.

In less than 30 years, the Internet has become one of the most amazing technological and social accomplishments of the century. Millions of people use a complex, interconnected network of computers that run thousands of different software packages. The computers are located in almost every country of the world. Over one billion dollars changes hands over the Internet in exchange for all kinds of products and services. All of this activity occurs with no central coordination point or control. Even more interesting is that the Internet began as a way for the military to maintain control while under attack.

The opening of the Internet to business enterprise helped increase its growth dramatically in recent years. However, another development worked hand-in-hand with the commercialization of the Internet to spur its growth. That development was the technological advance known as the World Wide Web.

World Wide Web

The World Wide Web (the Web) is more a way of thinking about information storage and retrieval than it is a technology. Because of this, its history goes back many years. Two important innovations played key roles in making the Internet easier to use and more accessible to people who were not research scientists: hypertext and graphical user interfaces (GUIs).

Origins of Hypertext

In 1945, Vannevar Bush, who was Director of the U.S. Office of Scientific Research and Development, wrote an *Atlantic Monthly* article about ways that scientists could apply the skills they learned during World War II to peacetime applications. The article included a number of visionary ideas about future uses of technology to organize and facilitate efficient access to information. He speculated that engineers eventually would build a machine that he called the **Memex**, a memory extension device that would store all of a person's books, records, letters, and research results on microfilm. Bush's Memex would include mechanical aids to help users consult their collected knowledge quickly and flexibly. In the 1960s, Ted Nelson described a similar system in which text on one page links to text on other pages. Nelson called his page-linking system **hypertext**. Douglas Englebart, who also invented the computer mouse, created the first experimental hypertext system on one of the large computers of the 1960s. Twenty years later, Nelson published *Literary Machines*, in which he outlined project **Xanadu**, a global system for online hypertext publishing and commerce.

Hypertext and Graphical User Interfaces Come to the Internet

In 1989, Tim Berners-Lee and Robert Calliau were working at CERN-The European Laboratory for Particle Physics and were trying to improve the laboratory's research document-handling procedures. CERN had been connected to the Internet for two years, but its scientists wanted to find better ways to circulate their scientific papers and data among the high-energy physics research community throughout the world. Independently, they each proposed a hypertext development project.

Over the next two years, Berners-Lee developed the code for a hypertext server program and made it available on the Internet. A **hypertext server** is a computer that stores files written in the hypertext markup language and lets other computers connect to it and read those files. **Hypertext markup language (HTML)** is a language that includes a set of codes (or **tags**) attached to text. These codes describe the relationships among text elements. For example, HTML includes tags that indicate which text is part of a header element, which text is part of a paragraph element, and which text is part of a numbered list element. One important type of tag is the hypertext link tag. A **hypertext link**, or **hyperlink**, points to another location in the same or another HTML document. You can use several different types of software to read HTML documents, but most people use a Web browser such as Netscape Navigator or Microsoft Internet Explorer. A **Web browser** is software that lets users read (or browse) HTML documents and move from one HTML document to another through the text formatted with hypertext link tags in each file. If the HTML documents are on computers connected to the Internet, you can use a Web browser to move from an HTML document on one computer to an HTML document on any other computer on the Internet. HTML is based on **Standard Generalized Markup Language** (**SGML**), which organizations have used for many years to manage large document-filing systems.

An HTML document differs from a word-processing document because it does not specify *how* a particular text element will appear. For example, you might use word-processing software to create a document heading by setting the heading text font to Arial, its font size to 14 points, and its position to centered. The document would display and print these exact settings whenever you opened the document in that word processor. In contrast, an HTML document would simply include a heading tag with the text. Many different programs can read an HTML document. Each program recognizes the heading tag and displays the text in whatever manner each program normally displays headers. Different programs might display the text differently.

A Web browser presents an HTML document in an easy-to-read format in its graphical user interface. A **graphical user interface (GUI)** is a way of presenting program output to users that uses pictures, icons, and other graphical elements instead of just displaying text. Almost all PCs today use a GUI such as Microsoft Windows or the Macintosh user interface.

Berners-Lee and Calliau called their system of hyperlinked HTML documents the World Wide Web. The Web caught on quickly in the scientific research community, but few people outside that community had software that could read the HTML documents. In 1993, a group of students led by Marc Andreessen at the University of Illinois wrote **Mosaic**, the first GUI program that could read HTML and use HTML documents' hyperlinks to navigate from page to page on computers anywhere on the Internet. Mosaic was the first Web browser that became widely available for PCs.

The Web and Commercialization of the Internet

Programmers quickly realized that a functional system of pages connected by hypertext links would provide many new Internet users with an easy way to locate information on the Internet. Businesses quickly recognized the profit-making potential offered by a worldwide network of easy-to-use computers. In 1994, Andreessen and other members of the University of Illinois Mosaic team joined with James Clark of Silicon Graphics to found Netscape Communications. Their first product, the Netscape Web browser program based on Mosaic, was an instant success. Netscape became one of the fastest growing software companies ever. Microsoft created its Internet Explorer Web browser and entered the market soon after Netscape's success became apparent. A number of other Web browsers exist, but these two products dominate the market today.

The number of **Web sites**, which are computers connected to the Internet that store HTML documents, has grown even more rapidly than the Internet itself to nearly 8 million sites. Each Web site might have hundreds, or even thousands, of individual Web pages, so the amount of information on the Web is astounding. Figure 1-8 shows the phenomenal growth in the Web during its short lifetime.

As more people obtain access to the Web, commercial uses of the Web and a variety of nonbusiness uses will greatly increase. Although the Web has grown rapidly, many experts believe that it will grow at an increasing rate for the foreseeable future.

| Figure 1-8 | GROWTH OF THE WORLD WIDE WEB |

Growth of the World Wide Web

A bar chart titled "Growth of the World Wide Web" with the y-axis labeled "Estimated number of Web sites (millions)" ranging from 0 to 8, and the x-axis labeled "Year" showing years 1993 through 1999. The bars show minimal values from 1993-1995, small growth in 1996, about 1 million in 1997, 5 million in 1998, and 8 million in 1999.

Session 1.1 QUICK CHECK

1. Name three resources that computers connected to a client/server LAN can share.

2. The fastest and most expensive way to connect computers in a network is _____ cable.

3. Telephone companies use centrally controlled circuit switching to connect telephone callers and transmit data. Name and briefly describe the switching method used by the Internet.

4. What is the technical term for the collection of rules that computers follow when formatting, ordering, and error-checking data sent across a network?

5. The networks that became the Internet were originally designed to transmit files; however, early in its history, people found other uses for the Internet. Name three of those uses.

6. What is an intranet?

7. Name and briefly describe two key factors that contributed to the Internet's rapid growth in the 1990s.

8. What type of software can network users run on their computers to access HTML documents that are stored on other computers?

You have obtained a good background for your report on how TEPCo might use the Internet and the Web by learning about their histories. You are convinced that the Internet can help Lorraine and her assistants manage the company better, identify new customers, and stay in contact with suppliers. You decide that the next logical step in your research is to identify ways that TEPCo can connect to the Internet. In the next session, you will learn how to evaluate Internet connection options.

SESSION 1.2

You can connect your computer to the Internet in several different ways. This session presents an overview of connection options and explains how you can choose the one that is right for you.

Connection Options

Remember that the Internet is a set of interconnected networks. Therefore, you cannot become a part of the Internet unless you are part of a communications network, whether it is a LAN, an intranet, or through a telephone connection. Each network that joins the Internet must accept some responsibility for operating the network by routing message packets that other networks pass along. As you consider your project for TEPCo, you become concerned that Justin and Arti are not going to want to become involved in something this complex. After all, they are exotic-produce experts—not computer wizards!

Business of Providing Internet Access

As you continue your research, you learn more about the NAPs (network access points) that maintain the core operations and long-haul backbone of the Internet. You find that they do not offer direct connections to individuals or small businesses. Instead, they offer connections to large organizations and businesses that, in turn, provide Internet access to other businesses and individuals. These firms are called **Internet access providers (IAPs)** or **Internet service providers (ISPs)**. Most of these firms call themselves ISPs because they offer more than just access to the Internet. ISPs usually provide their customers with the software they need to connect to the ISP, browse the Web, send and receive e-mail messages, and perform other Internet-related functions such as file transfer and remote login to other computers. ISPs often provide network consulting services to their customers and help them design Web pages. Some ISPs have developed a full range of services that include network management, training, and marketing advice. Some larger ISPs not only sell Internet access to end users, but also market Internet access to other ISPs, which then sell access and service to their own business and individual customers. This hierarchy of Internet access appears in Figure 1-9.

Figure 1-9   THE HIERARCHY OF INTERNET SERVICE OPTIONS

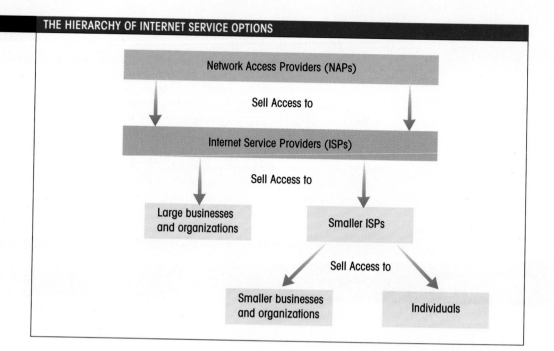

Connection Bandwidth

Of the differences that exist among service providers at different levels of the access hierarchy, one of the most important is the connection bandwidth that an ISP can offer. **Bandwidth** is the amount of data that can travel through a communications circuit in one second. The bandwidth that an ISP can offer you depends on the type of connection it has to the Internet and the kind of connection you have to the ISP.

The bandwidth for a network connection between two points always is limited to the narrowest bandwidth that exists in any part of the network. For example, if you connect to an ISP through a regular telephone line, your bandwidth is limited to the bandwidth of that telephone line, regardless of the bandwidth connection that the ISP has to the Internet. Bandwidth is measured in multiples of **bits per second (bps)**. Discussions of Internet bandwidth often use the terms **kilobits per second (Kbps)**, which is 1,024 bps; **megabits per second (Mbps)**, which is 1,048,576 bps; and **gigabits per second (Gbps)**, which is 1,073,741,824 bps. Most LANs run either an Ethernet network, which has a bandwidth of 10 Mbps, or Fast Ethernet, which operates at 100 Mbps. When you extend your network beyond a local area, the speed of the connection depends on what type of connection you use.

One way to connect computers or networks over longer distances is to use regular telephone service (sometimes referred to as **POTS**, or **plain old telephone service**). Regular telephone service to most U.S. residential and business customers provides a maximum bandwidth of between 28.8 Kbps and 56 Kbps. These numbers vary because the United States has a number of different telephone companies that do not all use the same technology. Some telephone companies offer a higher grade of service that uses one of a series of protocols called **Digital Subscriber Line** or **Digital Subscriber Loop (DSL)**. The first technology that was developed using a DSL protocol is called **Integrated Services Digital Network (ISDN)**. ISDN service has been available in various parts of the United States since 1984. Although considerably more expensive than regular telephone service, ISDN offers bandwidths of up to 128 Kbps. ISDN is much more widely available in Australia, France, Germany, Japan, and Singapore than in the United States because the regulatory structure of the telecommunications industries in these countries encouraged rapid deployment of this new technology. All technologies based on the DSL protocol require the implementing telephone company to install modems at its switching stations, which can be very expensive. New technologies that use the DSL protocol are currently being implemented around the world. One of those, **Asymmetric Digital Subscriber Line**

(**ADSL**, also abbreviated **DSL**), offers transmission speeds ranging from 16 to 640 Kbps from the user to the telephone company and from 1.5 to 9 Mbps from the telephone company to the user.

Larger firms can connect to an ISP using higher-bandwidth telephone company connections called **T1** (1.544 Mbps) and **T3** (44.736 Mbps) connections. These connections are much more expensive than POTS or ISDN connections; however, organizations that must link hundreds or thousands of individual users to the Internet require the greater bandwidth of T1 and T3 connections. The NAPs currently operate the Internet backbone using a variety of connections. In addition to T1 and T3 lines, the NAPs use newer **Asynchronous Transfer Mode (ATM)** connections that have bandwidths of up to 622 Mbps. Improved ATM methods are being developed that will provide bandwidths exceeding 1 Gbps. NAPs also use satellite and radio communications links to transfer data over long distances. The NAPs are working with a group of universities and the National Science Foundation (NSF) to develop a network called **Internet 2** that will have backbone bandwidths that exceed 1 Gbps.

A new connection option that is available in parts of the United States is to connect to the Internet through a cable television company. The cable company transmits data in the same cables it uses to provide television service. Only a few cable operators around the country currently have the necessary cable installed to offer this service; however, many cable operators are planning to upgrade their facilities during the next few years. Cable can deliver up to 10 Mbps to an individual user and can accept up to 768 Kbps from an individual user. These speeds far exceed those of existing POTS and ISDN connections and are comparable to speeds provided by the ADSL technologies currently being implemented by telephone companies.

An option that is particularly appealing to users in remote areas is connecting via satellite. Using a satellite-dish receiver, you can download at a bandwidth of approximately 400 Kbps. Unfortunately, you cannot send information to the Internet using a satellite dish, so you must also have an ISP account to send files or e-mail. Figure 1-10 summarizes the bandwidths for various types of connections currently in use on the Internet.

Figure 1-10	BANDWIDTHS FOR VARIOUS TYPES OF INTERNET CONNECTIONS	
TYPE OF SERVICE	**SPEED**	**TYPICAL USES**
Regular telephone service	28.8 Kbps to 56 Kbps	Individual and small business users connecting to ISPs
Integrated Services Digital Network (ISDN)	128 Kbps	Individual and small business users connecting to ISPs
Asymmetric Digital Subscriber Line (ADSL or DSL)	16 Kbps to 640 Kbps (upload) 1.5 Mbps to 9 Mbps (download)	Individual and small business users connecting to ISPs
Cable modem	Up to 768 Kbps (upload) Up to 10 Mbps (download)	Individual and small business users connecting to ISPs
T1 leased line	1.544 Mbps	Large businesses and other organizations connecting to ISPs and ISPs connecting to other ISPs
T3 leased line	44.736 Mbps	Large businesses and other organizations connecting to ISPs, ISPs connecting to other ISPs, ISPs connecting to NAPs, and portions of the Internet backbone
Asynchronous Transfer Mode (ATM) Line	622 Mbps	Internet backbone

As you evaluate the information you have gathered about ways Lorraine might connect TEPCo to the Internet, you realize that there are four ways that individuals or small businesses can link to the Internet. The first way, which is only for individuals, is a connection through your school or employer. The second option is to connect through an ISP. The third option is to connect through a cable television company. The fourth option is to use a combination of satellite download and an upload method. Next, you will learn about some of the advantages and disadvantages of each connection method that you have identified for your analysis and report to Lorraine.

Connecting Through Your School or Employer

One of the easiest ways to connect to the Internet is through your school or employer, if it already has an Internet connection. The connection is either free or very reasonably priced. However, by using your school or employer to connect to the Internet, you must comply with its rules. In some cases, this can outweigh the cost advantage.

Connecting Through Your School

Most universities and community colleges are connected to the Internet, and many offer Internet access to their students, faculty members, and other employees. In most schools, you can use computers in computing labs or in the library to access the Internet. Many schools provide a way to connect your own computer through the school's network to the Internet. The form of connection will depend on what your school offers. An increasing number of schools have dormitory rooms wired with LAN connections so students can connect using their own computers. Some schools even provide the computers as part of their tuition or housing charge.

Dialing in

Most schools or businesses, whether or not they have LANs in their buildings, provide telephone numbers that you can call and connect your computer through a modem. **Modem** is short for **modulator-demodulator**. When you connect your computer, which communicates using digital signals, to another computer through a telephone line, which uses analog signals, you must perform a signal conversion. Converting a digital signal to an analog signal is **modulation**; converting that analog signal back into digital form is called **demodulation**. A modem performs both functions; that is, it acts as a modulator-demodulator. If you use a modem to connect to the Internet, you will need to install software that implements a protocol that makes your modem connection appear to be a TCP/IP connection. Two of the most frequently used software packages are the **serial line Internet protocol** (**SLIP**) and the **point-to-point protocol** (**PPP**). Usually, this software automatically chooses the correct protocol (either SLIP or PPP) when you install it, based on your description of the connection you are making.

Connecting Through Your Employer

Your employer might offer you a connection to the Internet through the computer you use in your job. This computer might be connected through a LAN to the Internet, or you might have to use a modem to connect it. Before you attempt to connect to the Internet this way, make sure that your employer permits personal use of company computing facilities. Remember, your employer owns the computers you use as an employee. In most of the world, this gives your employer the right to examine any e-mail or files that you transmit or store using those computers. A number of schools retain similar rights under the law or through policies they publish in their student handbooks.

Acceptable Use Policies

Most schools and employers have an **acceptable use policy** (**AUP**) that specifies the conditions under which you can use their Internet connections. Some organizations require you to sign a copy of the AUP before they permit you to use their computing facilities; others simply include it as part of your student or employee contract. AUPs often include provisions that require you to respect copyright laws, trade secrets, the privacy of other users, and standards of common decency. Many AUPs expressly prohibit you from engaging in commercial activities, criminal activities, or specific threat-making or equipment-endangering practices.

Many provisions in AUPs are open to honest misunderstanding or disagreement in interpretation. It is extremely important for you to read and understand any AUP with which you must comply when you use computing facilities at your school or employer. AUPs often include punitive provisions that include revocation of user accounts and all rights to use the network. Some AUPs state that a user can be expelled or fired for serious violations.

Advantages and Disadvantages

Although accessing the Internet through your school or employer might be the least expensive option, you might decide that the restrictions on your freedom of expression and actions are too great. For example, if you wanted to start a small business on the Web, you would not want to use your school account if its AUP has a commercial-activity exclusion. An important concern when using your employer's computing facilities to connect to the Internet is that the employer generally retains the right to examine any files or e-mail messages that you transmit through those facilities. Carefully consider whether the limitations placed on your use of the Internet are greater than the benefits of the low cost of this access option.

Connecting Through an Internet Service Provider

Depending on where you live, you might find that an ISP is the best way for you to connect to the Internet. In major metropolitan areas, many ISPs compete for customers and, therefore connection fees often are reasonable. Smaller towns and rural areas have fewer ISPs and, thus might be less competitive. When you are shopping for an ISP, you will want to find information such as:

- The monthly base fee and number of hours it provides
- The hourly rate for time used over the monthly base amount
- Whether the telephone access number is local or long distance
- Which specific Internet services are included
- What software is included
- What user-support services are available

Advantages and Disadvantages

ISPs are the best option for many Internet users, in part because they usually provide reliable connectivity at a reasonable price. The terms of their AUPs often are less restrictive than those imposed by schools on their students or employers on their employees. You should examine carefully the terms of the service agreement, and you always should obtain references from customers who use an ISP before signing any long-term contract.

Some ISPs limit the number of customers they serve, whereas others guarantee that you will not receive a busy signal when you dial in. These are significant factors in the quality of service you will experience. Remember, each ISP has a limited amount of bandwidth in its connection to the Internet. If your ISP allows more new customers to subscribe to its service than leave each month, each remaining user will have proportionally less bandwidth available. Be especially wary of ISPs that offer a large discount if you sign a long-term agreement. The quality of service might deteriorate significantly over time if the ISP adds many new customers without expanding its bandwidth.

You also should find out whether the ISP has an AUP and, if so, you should examine its terms carefully. Some ISPs have restrictive policies. For example, an ISP might have an entirely different fee structure for customers who use their Internet access for commercial purposes. Carefully outline how you plan to use your Internet connection and decide what services you want before signing any long-term contract with an ISP.

Connecting Through Your Cable Television Company

One of the more recent developments in the Internet access business is the cable modem. A **cable modem** performs a function similar to that of a regular modem; that is, it converts digital computer signals to analog signals. However, instead of converting the digital signals into telephone-line analog signals, a cable modem converts them into radio-frequency analog signals that are similar to television transmission signals. The converted signals travel to and from the cable company on the same lines that carry your cable television service. The cable company maintains a connection to the Internet and otherwise operates much like the ISPs discussed previously, which deliver an Internet connection through telephone lines.

To install a cable modem, the cable company first installs a **line-splitter**, a device that divides the combined cable signals into their television and data components, and then connects the television (or televisions) and the cable modem to the line-splitter. Most cable companies that offer this service rent the required line-splitter and cable modem to each customer.

Advantages and Disadvantages

The main advantage of a cable television connection to the Internet is its high bandwidth. A cable connection can provide very fast downloads to your computer from the Internet, as much as 170 times faster than a telephone line connection. Although upload speeds are not as fast, they are still about 14 times faster than a telephone line connection. The cost usually is higher than—and often more than double—what competing ISPs charge. However, if you consider that the cable connection might save you the cost of a second telephone line, the net benefit can be significant. The greatest disadvantage for most people right now is that the cable connection is simply not available in their area yet. Because cable companies must invest in expensive upgrades to offer this service, it might not become available in many parts of the U.S. for many years. You should remember that, other than the nature of the connection, a cable company is the same as any other ISP. Therefore, all of the issues outlined in the previous section about contracting with ISPs apply equally to dealing with your cable company.

Connecting Via Satellite

Many rural areas in the United States do not have cable television service and never will because their low population density makes it too expensive: A cable company cannot afford to run miles of cable to reach one or two isolated customers. People in these areas often buy satellite receivers to obtain television signals. Recently, Internet connections via satellite became available. The satellite connection is downlink only, so you also must have another connection through an ISP that uses telephone lines to handle the uplink half of the connection.

Advantages and Disadvantages

The major advantage of a satellite connection is speed. Although the speeds are not as great as those offered by cable modems, they are about five to ten times greater than telephone connections. The speed increase is in one direction only, so you still send information to the Internet through a modem and telephone lines to an ISP. An ISP still is involved in this connection option, so all of the advantages and disadvantages outlined earlier also apply to a satellite connection. The cost of the satellite dish antenna and receiver still is fairly high, but prices are slowly dropping as more people become aware of this connection option. For users in remote areas, this technology often offers the best connection solution.

Session 1.2 QUICK | CHECK

1. To connect to the Internet, your computer must be part of a(n) _____.
2. What services do ISPs usually offer their customers?
3. How much greater bandwidth does ISDN offer over telephone service?
4. The Internet backbone today uses a combination of technologies to transmit data over long distances. Name and briefly describe three of these technologies.
5. Explain briefly how a modem enables a computer to transmit information over regular telephone lines.

6. Many schools and businesses have adopted acceptable use policies (AUPs). Describe the purpose of an AUP.

7. What conditions would lead you to consider connecting to the Internet via satellite?

You now have collected a great deal of information about the origins and history of the Internet and the Web. As you conducted your research project for TEPCo, you learned about some of the information and tools that exist on the Internet. You also gathered information about ways to connect to the Internet. Now you are ready to prepare your report for Lorraine and recommend a plan of action for connecting TEPCo to the Internet.

PROJECTS

1. *Diagramming School Networks* Your school probably has a number of computer networks. At most schools, you can find information about computing facilities from the department of academic computing or the school library. Identify what LANs and WANs you have on your campus, and determine whether any or all of them are interconnected. Draw a diagram that shows the networks, their connections to each other, and their connection to the Internet.

2. *DARPA Alternatives* The DARPA researchers that laid the foundation for the Internet were conducting research on ways to coordinate weapons control. They chose to develop a computer network that could operate without a central control mechanism. Think about alternative directions that the DARPA researchers might have taken to achieve their objective. Select one of these alternative directions, and discuss whether you think that approach would have given birth to something like the Internet. Describe how you think it would differ from the Internet and Web that exist today.

3. *School Cabling Choices* Select two or three buildings on your campus that have computers in offices, dormitory rooms, or computing labs. Find out from the appropriate office administrator, dormitory official, or lab supervisor what kind of computer cable the school uses to connect the computers. Evaluate the school's cabling choices. Would you make the same decisions? Why or why not?

4. *Using the Web and E-Mail* Describe three ways in which you might use the Web or e-mail to identify part-time job and internship opportunities that relate to your major.

5. *Acceptable Use Policy Evaluation* Obtain a copy of your school's or employer's acceptable use policy (AUP). Outline the main restrictions it places on student (or employee) activities. Compare those restrictions with the limits it places on faculty (or employer) activities. Analyze and evaluate any differences in treatment. If there are no differences, discuss whether the policy should be rewritten to include differences. If your school or employer has no policy, outline the key elements that you believe should be included in such a policy for your school or employer.

6. *Commercialization of the Internet* Many people who have been involved with the Internet for many years believe that the National Science Foundation (NSF) made a serious mistake when it opened the Internet to commercial traffic. Discuss the advantages and disadvantages of this policy decision. Do you think that the Internet would be as successful as it is today if no commercial activity were allowed?

7. *The Web and the Memex Machine* Vannevar Bush died before the Web came into existence. Speculate on what he would have thought about the Web. Would he have seen it as the embodiment of his Memex machine? Why or why not?

8. *Evaluating ISPs* Contact three ISPs in your area and obtain information about their Internet access and related services. You can find ISPs in your local telephone directory (try headings such as "Internet Services," "Computer Networks," or "Computer On-Line Services"), or look for advertisements in your local or student newspaper. Summarize the services and the charges for each service by ISP. Which ISP would you recommend for an individual? Why? Which ISP would you recommend for a small business? Why?

QUICK | CHECK ANSWERS

Session 1.1

1. Printers, scanners, digital cameras, data files, programs, and so forth.

2. fiber-optic

3. The Internet uses packet switching, a method in which files and messages are broken down into packets that are labeled electronically with codes for their origin and destination. The packets travel along the network until they reach the destination computer, which collects the packets and reassembles the original data from the pieces in each packet.

4. protocol

5. e-mail, mailing lists, Usenet newsgroups, and adventure gaming

6. A LAN or WAN that uses the TCP/IP protocol but does not connect to sites outside a particular business firm or other organization.

7. Commercialization and the development of the WWW. Commercialization opened the Internet's potential to persons outside the academic and research communities, and the WWW graphical user interface (GUI) helped these new participants effectively use and add value to the Internet.

8. Web browser software

Session 1.2

1. network

2. Software to connect to the ISP, browse the Web, send and receive e-mail messages, transfer files, and log in to remote computers. Also, some ISPs provide network-consulting services and network management, training, and marketing advice.

3. two to four times

4. Leased telephone lines, satellite links, and radio communications links. Leased telephone lines include T1 lines, T3 lines, and Asynchronous Transfer Mode (ATM) connections. Satellite and radio links are used for the parts of the Internet that cross oceans and connect to remote locations.

5. A modem converts a computer's digital signals into analog signals that will travel over regular telephone lines (modulation). When the analog signal arrives at its destination, another modem converts the analog signals back into digital signals (demodulation).

6. An AUP specifies the conditions under which you can use your school's or your employer's Internet connection. AUPs often prohibit users from engaging in commercial activities, criminal activities, or specific threat-making or equipment-endangering practices.

7. Persons who live in remote areas that are not served by cable television providers would consider connecting to the Internet via satellite if they desired a faster connection than that available through regular telephone lines.

BASIC E-MAIL:
INTEGRATED BROWSER E-MAIL SOFTWARE

Evaluating E-Mail Alternatives

CASE

Sidamo's Carpets

Sidamo's Carpets is a large retail store that has been selling fine Oriental rugs since 1930. Ifram Sidamo opened his store on one floor of a large department store in Syracuse, New York. In the early days, Sidamo's sold all of its rugs to walk-in customers. Most new customers learned about Sidamo's through other customers who raved about Sidamo's high quality and variety of handmade rugs from Iran, India, Pakistan, and China.

Sidamo's Carpets has grown considerably over the years, both in size and sales volume. Today, Sidamo's boasts of customers from all over the United States as well as from many other countries. No longer a regional company, Sidamo's is now housed in a single, large store on the outskirts of Syracuse. With over 7,000 Oriental rugs in stock, Sidamo's offers a complete line of Oriental rugs that range in size from small mat and scatter rugs to large carpets. Over the past three years, Sidamo's has used extensive advertising campaigns to broaden its visibility. Barbara Goldberg, Sidamo's vice president of marketing, estimates that more than half of Sidamo's sales are from customers who have never visited Sidamo's showroom. Interestingly, 42 percent of all sales are to repeat customers.

Typically, a customer would see a Sidamo's advertisement in a magazine and then call the toll-free number to inquire about available rugs. This system has worked well so far, but Barbara believes that Sidamo's could serve a growing number of customers better—especially repeat customers—if it provided e-mail as an alternative way of contacting the Sidamo's sales staff. Barbara has hired you to put the new e-mail system in place. Your job includes evaluating available e-mail systems and overseeing the software's installation. Eventually, you will train the sales staff so they can use the new e-mail system efficiently and effectively.

SESSION 2.1

In this session, you will learn what e-mail is, how it travels to its destination, and the parts of a typical e-mail message. You will find out about signature files and how to use them. You will set up an e-mail client program to send, receive, print, delete, file, forward, reply to, and respond to e-mail messages. Finally, you will use an address book to manage your e-mail addresses.

What Is E-Mail and How Does It Work?

E-mail

Electronic mail, or **e-mail**, is one of the most prevalent forms of business communication and the most popular use of the Internet. In fact, many people view the Internet as an electronic highway that transports e-mail messages, without realizing that the Internet provides a wide variety of services. E-mail travels across the Internet to its destination and is deposited in the recipient's electronic mailbox. While similar to other forms of correspondence, including letters and memos, e-mail has the added advantage of being fast and inexpensive. Instead of traveling through a complicated, expensive, and frequently slow mail delivery service such as a postal system, e-mail travels quickly, efficiently, and inexpensively to its destination across the city or around the world. You can send a message any time you want, without worrying about when the mail is picked up or delivered or adding any postage. In business and recreation today, people rely on e-mail as an indispensable way of sending messages and data to each other. Businesses today depend on e-mail to deliver mission-critical and time-sensitive information to other businesses, customers, and employees internal to the organization.

E-mail travels across the Internet like other forms of information—that is, in small packets, which are reassembled at the destination and delivered to the addressee, whose address you specify in the message. When you send an e-mail message to its addressee, the message is sent to a **mail server**, which is a hardware and software system that determines from the recipient's address one of several electronic routes to send your message. When you send an e-mail message to another person, the message is routed from one computer to another and is passed through several mail servers. Each mail server determines the next leg of the journey for your message until it finally arrives at the recipient's electronic mailbox.

Sending e-mail employs one of the many technologies used on the Internet. Special **protocols**, or rules that determine how the Internet handles message packets flowing on it, are used to interpret and transmit e-mail. **SMTP (Simple Mail Transfer Protocol)** decides which paths your e-mail message takes on the Internet. SMTP handles outbound mail; another protocol called **POP (Post Office Protocol)** takes care of incoming messages. POP is a standard, extensively used protocol that is part of the Internet suite of recognized protocols. Other protocols used to deliver mail include **IMAP (Internet Message Access Protocol)** and **MIME (Multipurpose Internet Mail Extensions)**. IMAP is a protocol for retrieving mail messages from a server, and MIME protocol specifies how to encode nontext data, such as graphics and sound, so they can travel over the Internet.

When an e-mail message arrives at its destination mail server, the mail server's software handles the details of distributing the e-mail locally, much like a mail-room worker unbundles a bag of mail and places letters and packages into individual departmental or personal mail slots. When the server receives a new message, it is not saved directly on the recipient's individual computer, but rather, it is held on the mail server. When you check for new e-mail messages, you use a program stored on your personal computer (PC) to request the mail server to deliver any stored mail to your PC. The software that requests mail delivery from the mail server to your PC is known as **mail client software**. You will learn about two popular e-mail client programs—Netscape Messenger and Microsoft Outlook Express—in Sessions 2.2 and 2.3, respectively.

Anatomy of an E-Mail Message

An e-mail message consists of two major parts: the message header and the message body. The **message header** contains all the information about the message, and the **message body** contains the actual message. A message header contains the recipient's e-mail address (To), the sender's e-mail address (From), and a subject line (Subject), which indicates the topic of the message. In addition, the message header can contain a carbon copy (or courtesy copy) address (Cc), a blind carbon copy (or blind courtesy copy) address (Bcc), and, sometimes, an attachment filename. Normally, your name automatically appears in the From line when you send a message. When you receive an e-mail message, the date and time it was sent and other information is added to the message automatically.

Figure 2-1 shows a message that Barbara Goldberg wrote to Ifram Sidamo, the company president. The memo contains an attached file named 800LineSale.xls. This file is a spreadsheet composed using a spreadsheet program and then attached to the message. Notice that Ifram's e-mail address appears in the To line. When Ifram receives Barbara's message, Barbara's name and e-mail address will appear in the From line. Following good e-mail etiquette, Barbara included a short Subject line so Ifram can quickly determine the content of the message. The Cc line indicates that the marketing department will receive a copy of the message. Sylvia Sidamo, Ifram's vice president of sales, will also receive a copy of the message, but Sylvia's e-mail address is on the Bcc line, so neither Ifram nor the marketing department will know that she also received a copy of the message. Each of the message parts is described next.

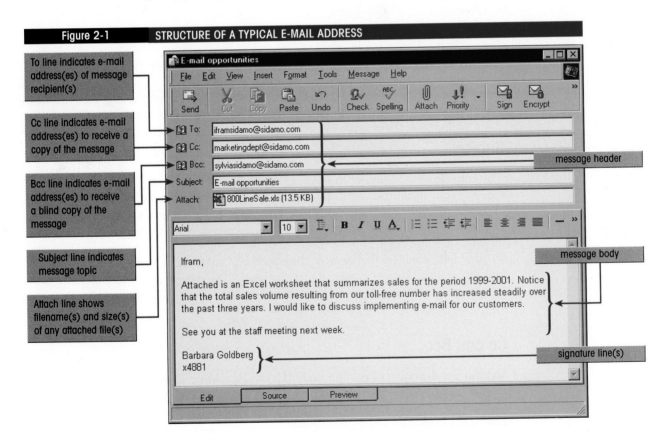

Figure 2-1   STRUCTURE OF A TYPICAL E-MAIL ADDRESS

To line indicates e-mail address(es) of message recipient(s)

Cc line indicates e-mail address(es) to receive a copy of the message

Bcc line indicates e-mail address(es) to receive a blind copy of the message

Subject line indicates message topic

Attach line shows filename(s) and size(s) of any attached file(s)

message header

message body

signature line(s)

To

You type the recipient's full e-mail address in the **To line** of an e-mail header. Usually, the To line is at the top of the header. Be careful to type the address correctly; otherwise, the e-mail cannot be delivered. You can send mail to multiple people by typing a comma between the individual e-mail addresses. There is no real limit on the number of addresses you can type in the To line or in the other parts of the e-mail header that require an address. Figure 2-2 shows the message header for a message that Barbara is sending to three people.

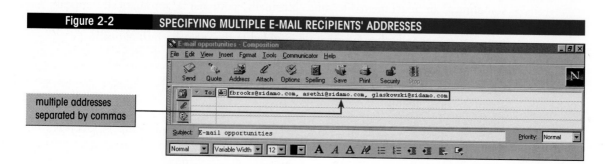

Figure 2-2 SPECIFYING MULTIPLE E-MAIL RECIPIENTS' ADDRESSES

multiple addresses separated by commas

Sometimes, the To address contains one physical mailing address that is not one person's address, but rather, a message to a special service called a **mailing list**. In a mailing list, the single e-mail address contains dozens or even thousands of individual e-mail addresses.

From

The **From line** of an e-mail message includes the sender's e-mail address. Most e-mail programs automatically insert the sender's e-mail address into all messages. Even if you don't insert your e-mail address in an outgoing message, the recipient *always* sees the sender's e-mail address in the message—in other words, you cannot send anonymous e-mail.

Subject

The content of the **Subject line** is very important. Often, the person receiving your message will scan an abbreviated display of incoming messages, looking for the most interesting or important messages based on the contents of the Subject line. If the Subject line is blank, then the recipient might not read the associated message immediately. It is always best to include a message subject so the reader has a hint of the message's contents and importance. For example, a subject line such as "Just checking" is far less informative and certainly less interesting than "Urgent: new staff meeting time." The e-mail message shown in Figure 2-1, for example, contains the subject "E-mail opportunities" and thus indicates that the message concerns e-mail.

Cc and Bcc

You can use the optional **carbon copy (Cc)** and the **blind carbon copy (Bcc)** header lines to send mail to people who should be aware of the e-mail message but who are not the message's main addressees. When an e-mail message is delivered, every recipient can see the addresses of other recipients, except for those who receive a blind carbon copy. Neither the primary recipient (in the To line) nor those recipients on the carbon copy list are aware of those recipients on the blind carbon copy list because Bcc addresses are hidden from messages sent to people on the To and Cc lists. Recipients on the Bcc list are unaware of others who receive blind copies. For example, if you send a thank you message to a salesperson for performing a task especially well, you might consider sending a blind carbon copy to that person's supervisor. That way, the supervisor knows a customer is happy and that the praise was unsolicited.

Attachments

Because of the way the messaging system is set up, you can send only plain-text messages using SMTP—the protocol that handles outgoing e-mail. When you need to send a more complex document, such as a Word document or an Excel worksheet, you send it along as an attachment. An **attachment** is encoded so that it can be carried safely over the Internet, to "tag along" with the message. Frequently, the attached file is the most important part of the e-mail message, and the message body contains a brief statement such as "The worksheet you requested is attached." Barbara's e-mail message contains an attachment whose location and filename (on Barbara's computer) appear in the Attach line in the header. The attachment is stored on Barbara's computer on drive C with the filename 800LineSale.xls. You can attach more than one file to an e-mail message, and files can be delivered to more than one recipient at the same time. E-mail attachments provide a convenient way of transmitting electronic documents of various types to a colleague down the hall or on the other side of the world.

When you receive an e-mail message with an attached file, you can preview it within the message or save it and review it later. E-mail programs differ in how they handle and display attachments. Several e-mail programs identify an attached file with an icon that represents the program associated with that file type. In addition to an icon, several programs also display an attached file's size in kilobytes (a **kilobyte** is approximately 1,000 characters) and indicate the attached file's name. Other e-mail programs display an attached file in a preview window when they recognize the attached file's format and can start a program to display the file. In any case, you can always save the file and later execute a program associated with the file type.

With most e-mail client programs, you can easily detach an attached file, examine the file, and save it. An icon representing an attached file accompanies the file. To open the attached file, you click the icon. If a worksheet is attached to an e-mail message, for example, a spreadsheet program on your computer starts and opens the worksheet. Similarly, a Word file opens inside the Word program when you click the icon representing the Word file inside your e-mail message. Saving an open attachment is simple. Usually, you click File on the menu bar, and then click Save or Save As in the program displaying the attached file. Then, you indicate the disk and folder into which you want to save the attached file.

Message Body and Signature Files

Most often, people use e-mail to write short, quick messages. However, e-mail messages can be dozens or hundreds of pages long, although the term *pages* has little meaning in the e-mail world. Few people using e-mail think of a message in terms of page-sized chunks; e-mail is more like an unbroken scroll with no physical page boundaries.

Frequently, an e-mail message includes an optional **signature** that identifies more detailed information about the sender. You can sign a message by typing your name and other information at the end of the message for each message you send, or you can create a signature file. A **signature file** contains the information you routinely type at the end of your e-mail messages. You can instruct your e-mail program to insert the signature file into every message automatically to save a lot of time. The signature usually contains the sender's name, title, and company name. Signature files often contain a complete nonelectronic address, facsimile telephone number, and a voice phone number. Periodically, signature files include graphics, such as a company logo, or the sender's favorite quotation or saying. Enclosing a signature file in an e-mail message ensures that e-mail recipients can contact you in a variety of ways besides using your e-mail address. For example, in Figure 2-1, Barbara's signature file contains her full name and her internal company phone extension.

Signatures can be either formal or informal, or a hybrid. A **formal signature** typically contains the sender's name, title, company name, company address, telephone and fax numbers, and e-mail address. **Informal signatures** can contain graphics or quotations that express a more casual style found in correspondence between friends and acquaintances. Most e-mail software programs automatically include a signature at the end of each e-mail message you send. You can easily modify your signature or choose not to include it in selected messages. Most e-mail programs allow you to create multiple signature files so you can choose which one to include when sending a message.

When you create a signature, don't overdo it. A signature that is extremely long is in bad taste—especially if it is much longer than the message. It is best to keep a signature to a few lines that identify alternative ways to contact you. Figure 2-3 shows two examples of signatures. The top signature is informal and typical of one you might send to a friend. The bottom signature is Barbara's formal signature that she uses for all external business correspondence to identify herself, her title, and her mailing and telephone information.

Figure 2-3	EXAMPLES OF INFORMAL AND FORMAL SIGNATURES

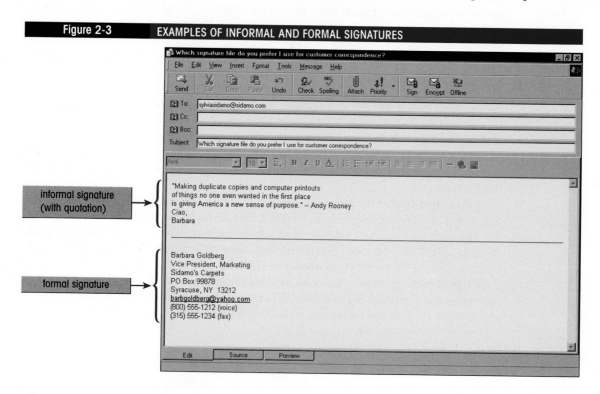

informal signature (with quotation)

"Making duplicate copies and computer printouts of things no one even wanted in the first place is giving America a new sense of purpose." -- Andy Rooney
Ciao,
Barbara

formal signature

Barbara Goldberg
Vice President, Marketing
Sidamo's Carpets
PO Box 99878
Syracuse, NY 13212
barbgoldberg@yahoo.com
(800) 555-1212 (voice)
(315) 555-1234 (fax)

E-Mail Addresses

E-mail addresses, also called Internet addresses, uniquely identify an individual or organization that is connected to the Internet. They are like telephone numbers—when you want to call anyone in the world, you dial a series of numbers that route your call through a series of switchboards until your call reaches its destination. For example, calling a friend in San Diego from another country requires you to dial the country code for the United States first (the country code varies according to the country from which you are calling). Then, you must know the area code for the part of San Diego in which your friend lives, and dial that three-digit number. Finally, you dial the last seven digits of your friend's local number. Like telephone numbers, e-mail addresses consist of a series of numbers. Usually, addresses consist of three or four groups of numbers that are separated by periods. For instance, the number 192.55.87.1 is an **Internet Protocol address**, or more commonly an **IP address**, which corresponds to a single computer connected to the Internet. The IP address uniquely identifies the computer at the organization you want to contact. To route an e-mail message to an *individual* whose mail is stored on a particular computer, you must identify that person by his or her account name, or **user name**, and also by the computer on which mail is stored. The two parts of an e-mail address—the user name and the computer name—are separated by an "at" sign (@). Barbara Goldberg, for example, uses the user name *barbgoldberg* to access her e-mail. If her account were stored on a Sidamo computer whose address is 194.206.126.204, then one form of her e-mail address would be barbgoldberg@194.206.126.204.

Fortunately, you rarely have to use numeric IP addresses. Instead, you use **host names**, which are unique names that are equivalent to IP addresses. Barbara Goldberg's address using a host name is simply *barbgoldberg@sidamo.com*, which is much easier to remember and certainly less error prone. A full e-mail address consists of your user name, followed by an @ sign, followed by the host name (or address). A user name usually specifies a person within an organization, although it can sometimes refer to an entire group. Sometimes, you can select your own user name, but frequently the organization through which you obtain an e-mail account has rules about acceptable user names. Some organizations insist that the user name consist of a person's first initial followed by up to seven characters of the person's last name. Other institutions prefer that your user name contain your full first and last names separated by an underscore character (for example, Barbara_Goldberg). Occasionally, you can pick a nick-name such as "ziggy" or "bigbear" as your user name. When typing e-mail addresses, the usage of upper- and lower-case letters does matter, and the *spelling* is important. When mail cannot be delivered, the electronic postmaster sends the mail back to you and indicates the addressee is unknown—just like conventional mail.

The host name (or host address) is the second part of an e-mail address. The host name specifies the computer to which the mail is to be delivered on the Internet. Host names contain periods, which are usually pronounced "dot," to divide the host name. The most specific part of the host name appears first in the host address followed by more general destination names. Barbara's host name, sidamo.com (and pronounced "sidamo dot com"), contains only two names separated by a period. The suffix *com* in the address indicates that this company falls into the large, general class of commercial locations.

Host names can consist of more than two parts. For example, Figure 2-4 shows that the host name *condor.cs.missouri.edu* contains four parts. Clusters of related computers are sometimes given related names such as earth, wind, and fire. In this address, *condor* is one of several related computers. Where is this computer located? The second name, *cs*, is a common abbreviation for computer science. In all likelihood, the computer belongs to a computer science department. Judging by the third part of the host name, *missouri*, it's a good bet that the institution is located in Missouri or at the University of Missouri. The *edu* host name suffix indicates the organization is an educational institution of some sort. Taken together, the host name parts strongly point to the University of Missouri's computer science department. With a little imagination and experience, you can decipher most host names and determine the location of the computers to which the names refer.

| Figure 2-4 | HOST NAME ELEMENTS |

E-Mail Programs

Several programs for managing e-mail are available today because no single program works on all computers. The good news is that you can use any e-mail program to send mail to people with different e-mail clients. The recipient will be able to read your mail and you will be able to read mail from other people, regardless of which e-mail programs are used. If you have an Internet service provider (ISP) with a PPP or SLIP connection, then you can choose from a large selection of e-mail client programs that run on your PC and periodically check the mail server for incoming mail. On the other hand, you might have to use the e-mail program provided by your college or university if you have a dial-up connection that does not provide access to the Internet. Some e-mail programs—called **shareware**—are free or very inexpensive, and others are not. Some e-mail programs are software clients that run on your computer and receive mail from the mail server. Other e-mail programs run strictly on a server machine that you access from your personal computer, which acts as a dumb terminal. A **dumb terminal** is an otherwise "smart" computer that passes all your keystrokes to another computer to which you are connected and does not attempt to do anything else during the e-mail session. Examples of popular e-mail clients operating in the Windows environment are Netscape Messenger, Microsoft Outlook Express, and Eudora. A widely used e-mail program running on larger, multiuser computers is Pine. Especially popular on university campuses, Pine is a simple system that accepts and displays only plain-text messages. In your future personal and professional life, chances are good that you will encounter a different system from the one you are currently using, so it's a good idea to learn about different e-mail clients.

Free E-Mail Clients

Several free e-mail programs are available on the Internet. Some free programs require you to access e-mail through the Web, and others have a proprietary program that you install on your computer. Examples of free e-mail programs that you access from any Web browser include Yahoo!Mail, ExciteMail, and HotMail. Another program is Juno, which is an example of a free proprietary e-mail program that was one of the earliest free e-mail services. One advantage that these e-mail services share is that you can have e-mail service without being affiliated with an organization. Before these free e-mail services came to the Internet, many people who were not students or employees of a company could not use e-mail. Now, anyone with an Internet connection can use these services to send and receive e-mail messages.

To use e-mail provided by HotMail, ExciteMail, or Yahoo!Mail, you apply for an e-mail account. In order to apply for an e-mail account, you visit the Web site of the company offering free e-mail with your Web browser. (You will learn about Web browsers in Tutorial 3.) When you apply for free e-mail, you will probably be asked to supply a small amount of information about yourself. Then, you choose a user name and secret password. Next, the e-mail service checks to see that no one else has applied for the same user name you requested. If the user name is available, then you are immediately enrolled in the e-mail service. On the other hand, if someone already has the user name you selected, the service will ask you to try a different user name or change the one you chose slightly by adding digits to the end of it.

Once you have one of the Web-based e-mail accounts, such as Yahoo!Mail, you can send and receive e-mail. A big advantage of Web-based e-mail accounts is that you can get your e-mail from any computer with a Web browser and Internet access. In other words, you can access your e-mail account in Mexico City, Hong Kong, or any other place where there is public access to a Web browser. This is an advantage for people who travel a lot and do not want to incur long-distance telephone charges when accessing their own e-mail server from another city or country.

Juno and other similar services offer a different type of free e-mail service. First, you must install its free software on your computer, and then you activate a Juno e-mail account. The program automatically dials the Juno computer and establishes an e-mail account with a user name and password of your choosing—subject to the user name not being assigned already. Subsequently, you can access your e-mail from the same computer on which you installed it. The big disadvantage of Juno and systems like it is that you must install the Juno program on any computer on which you want to access your e-mail, which is sometimes impractical for people who travel a lot and use different computers to access their e-mail.

You might wonder how these companies can provide free e-mail—after all, nothing is free! The answer is advertising. With each e-mail message you receive, you also receive some sort of advertisement—either large or small—in the message itself or stored on your computer. Advertising revenues pay for free e-mail, so you must decide whether you are willing to put up with a little advertising for the free e-mail service. Most users of these free services agree that seeing some ads is a small price to pay for the great convenience e-mail provides.

Setting Up and Using Your E-Mail Client

Many ISPs support POP (Post Office Protocol) or SMTP (Simple Mail Transfer Protocol), whereby the mail server receives mail and stores it until you use your mail client software to request the mail server to deliver mail to your computer. Similarly, when you send e-mail from your computer, that mail is forwarded across the Internet until it reaches its destination. Once e-mail reaches the mail server at the addressee's location, it is stored. Subsequently, e-mail is downloaded from the server to a user on request. In either case—sending or receiving and reading e-mail—a client program must notify the mail server to deliver the mail or accept outgoing mail.

Your message might not be sent to the mail server immediately, depending on how the e-mail client is configured on your computer. A message can be **queued**, or temporarily held with other messages, and sent when you either exit the program or check to see if you received any new e-mail.

Remember, e-mail correspondence can be formal or informal, but you should still follow the rules of good writing and grammar. After typing the content of your message—even a short message—it is always a good idea to check your typing and spelling. Most mail systems do not allow you to retract mail after you send it, so you should examine your messages carefully *before* sending them. Always exercise politeness and courtesy in your messages. Don't write anything in an e-mail message that you wouldn't want someone else to post on a public bulletin board.

Receiving Mail

The mail server is always ready to process mail; in theory, it never sleeps. That means that when you receive e-mail, it is held on the mail server until you start the e-mail client on your PC and ask the server to retrieve your mail. Most clients allow you to save delivered mail in any of several standard or custom mailboxes or folders on your PC. However, the mail server is a completely different story. Once the mail is delivered to your PC, one of two things can happen to it on the server: either the server's copy of your mail is deleted, or it is preserved and marked as delivered or read. Marking mail as **delivered** or **read** is the server's way of identifying new mail from mail that you have read. For example, when Barbara receives mail on the Sidamo mail server, she might decide to save her accumulated mail—even after she reads it—so she has an archive of all of her received e-mail messages. On the other hand, Barbara might want to delete old mail to save space on the mail server. Both methods have advantages. Saving old mail on the server lets you access your mail from any PC that can connect to your mail server. On the other hand, if you automatically delete mail after reading it, you don't have to worry about storing and organizing messages that you don't need, which requires less effort.

Printing a Message

Reading mail on the computer is fine, but there are times when you will need to print a copy of some or all of your messages. Other times, you need to file your mail in an appropriate mailbox and deal with it later or simply file it for safekeeping. You also might find that you don't need to keep or file certain messages, so you can read and immediately delete them. Most client programs provide these facilities to help you manage your electronic correspondence.

The majority of programs let you print a message during or after you compose it or after mail has been received or sent. The Print command usually appears on the File menu in a GUI program, or there is a Print button on the toolbar. In a character-based program, the Print command is usually a key combination, such as Ctrl + P.

Filing a Message

Most clients let you create separate mailboxes or folders in which to store related messages. You can create new mailboxes or folders when needed, rename existing mailboxes and folders, or delete folders and their contents when you no longer need them. You can move mail from the incoming mailbox or folder to any other mailbox or folder to file it. Some programs let you use a **filter** to move incoming mail into one or several mailboxes or folders automatically based on the content of the message. If your client does not allow the use of filters, you can filter the messages manually by reading them and filing them in the appropriate folder.

Forwarding a Message

You can forward any message that you receive to one or more recipients. When you **forward** a message to another recipient, a copy of the original message is sent to the new recipient you specify, without the original sender's knowledge. You can forward a misdirected message to another recipient, or you can forward a message to someone who was not included in the original message routing list.

For example, suppose you receive a message intended for someone else, or the message requests information that you do not have but you know a colleague who does know the information. In either case, you can forward the message you received to the person who can deal with the request best. When you forward a message, your e-mail address and name appear automatically on the From line, and most e-mail clients amend the Subject line with the text "Fwd," "Forward," or something similar to indicate that the message is being forwarded. You simply fill in the To line and then send the message. Optionally, the message you received is quoted. A **quoted** message is a copy of the sender's original message that is returned to the sender with your comments added. Each line of the quoted message is preceded by a special mark (usually the greater than symbol, >). When you respond to a message someone sent to you, it is a good idea to include parts of the sender's message, or the quoted message. That way, the receiver can recall his or her original statement or question and therefore better understand your "yes, I agree with you" response.

Replying to a Message

When you **reply** to a message, the e-mail client automatically formats a new, blank message and addresses it to the sender. Replying to a message is a quick way of sending a response to someone who sent a message to you. When you reply to a message, the client automatically addresses a new message to the sender of the original message. Most clients will copy the entire message from the original message and place it in the response window. Usually, a special mark, such as >, appears at the beginning of each line of the response to indicate the text of the original message. When you are responding to more than one question, it is a good idea to type your responses below the original questions. That way, the recipient can better understand the context of your responses. When you respond to a message that has been sent to a number of people—perhaps some people received the message as a carbon copy—be careful about responding. You can choose to respond to all the original recipients or just to the sender.

Deleting a Message

On most e-mail clients, deleting a message is a two-step process in order to avoid accidental deletions of important messages. First, you temporarily delete a message by placing it in a "trash" folder or by marking it for deletion. Then, you permanently delete the trash or marked messages by emptying the trash or by indicating to the client to delete the messages. It is a good idea to delete unneeded mail.

Maintaining an Address Book

E-mail addresses are sometimes difficult to remember and type, especially when you send many e-mail messages to the same recipients. You can use an **address book** to save e-mail addresses and convenient nicknames to remember them by. The features of an e-mail address book vary by e-mail client. Usually, you can organize information about individuals or companies. Each entry in the address book can contain an individual's full e-mail address (or a group e-mail address that represents several individual addresses), a person's real name, and the person's complete contact information. In addition, some e-mail clients allow you to include notes for each address book entry. You can assign a unique nickname to each entry so it is easier to refer to e-mail addresses when you need them.

After saving entries in your address book, you can refer to them at any point while you are composing, replying to, or forwarding a message. You can review your address book and sort the entries in alphabetical order by nickname, or you can view them in last name order. Of course, you can switch between several sort orders any time you want—even as you are creating a message.

Creating a Multi-Address Entry

What happens if you need to send the same e-mail message to different recipients? You could send the message to all recipients by typing their nicknames in the To line and separating them with a comma. But what if you need to send a message to an entire department or the entire sales staff? You can create a handy address entry called a distribution list. A **distribution list**, or a **group mailing list**, is a single nickname that represents more than one individual e-mail address. For example, you might use the nickname "Web Site" to save the e-mail addresses of your partners on a Web site project. When you need to send a message to your partners, you just type "Web Site" in the To line, and then the client will send the same message to each individual's e-mail address.

Session 2.1 QUICK CHECK

1. True or False: E-mail travels across the Internet in small clusters.

2. The special rules governing how information is handled on the Internet are collectively called _____.

3. An e-mail message consists of two parts: the message _____ and the message _____.

4. Explain why it is a good practice to include a Subject line in your e-mail messages.

5. True or False: You use the Bcc line in an e-mail message to send copies of a message to others without the principal addressee knowing who received a copy.

6. Can you send a spreadsheet file over the Internet? If so, how?

7. The four-part number comprising an Internet address is known as a(n) _____ address.

8. Why is it important to include part of the sender's message in your reply?

9. What advantage(s) does a distribution list or mailing list provide when sending a message to many recipients?

Now that you understand some basic information about e-mail and e-mail client software, you are ready to start using your e-mail client. If you are using Netscape Messenger, your instructor will assign Session 2.2; if you are using Microsoft Outlook Express, your instructor will assign Session 2.3. The authors recommend, however, that you read both sessions in order to be familiar with both e-mail clients. In the future, you might encounter a different e-mail client on a public or employer's computer, so it is important to be familiar with both clients. Fortunately, most e-mail clients work the same, so it is easy to use other programs once you master the basics.

SESSION 2.2

In this session you will learn how to use Netscape Messenger to send and receive e-mail. You will learn how to print, file, save, delete, respond to, and forward e-mail messages. Finally, you will organize your e-mail addresses in an address book.

Netscape **Messenger Client**

You continue to express your enthusiasm for your newly assigned task of evaluating e-mail software. **Netscape Messenger**, or simply **Messenger**, is the e-mail client that is an integral part of the Netscape Communicator suite. You installed Netscape Communicator and are anxious to start using Messenger. Barbara stopped by to ask you a few questions about the program and wants you to use Messenger to e-mail items, such as the weekly marketing meeting agenda, to members of the marketing department staff. You start Messenger by using the Start menu or by double-clicking a desktop icon, if one is installed. Figure 2-5 shows the Message List window. When you open Messenger, a window opens containing mailbox folders in the left pane, message summary lines in the upper-right panel, and the selected message's contents in the lower-right panel. (Your Message List window might look different from the one shown in Figure 2-5.)

Figure 2-5	MESSENGER MESSAGE LIST WINDOW

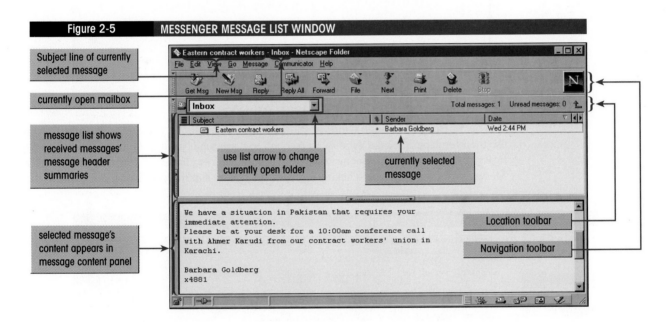

Messenger uses four different windows to furnish the tools you need to manage your e-mail: the Message List, Netscape Message Center, Netscape Message, and Composition windows. When you start Messenger, the Message List window shown in Figure 2-5 opens. The Message List window opens the **Inbox**, which is one of several mailboxes, and displays its contents in two panels. The top panel shows a summary of messages, called **message header summaries**. The lower panel, or the **message content panel**, shows the contents of a selected message header summary.

The **Netscape Message Center** window contains a list of your mailboxes, mail folders, and discussion groups. You open the Netscape Message Center window by clicking Communicator on the menu bar and then clicking Messenger. When you open the Netscape Message Center window, you can see the mailboxes on your computer (see Figure 2-6). Mailboxes in the list shown in Figure 2-6 include Inbox, Unsent Messages, Drafts, Sent, Trash, and Samples. News, another item on the Local Mail list, contains mail from **newsgroups**, which are Internet discussion groups on a specified topic. The Inbox contains your incoming mail messages.

Figure 2-6   NETSCAPE MESSAGE CENTER WINDOW

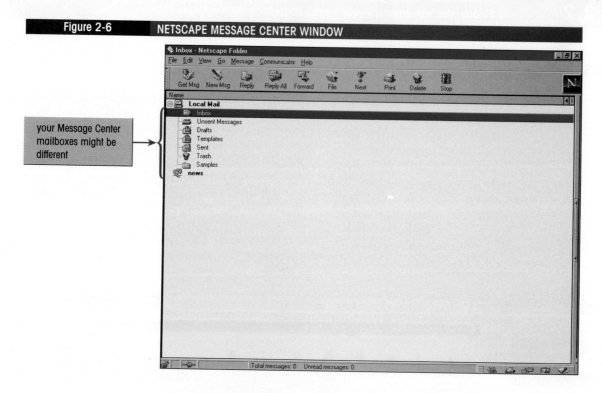

The **Netscape Message window**, shown in Figure 2-7, shows your individual messages. You use the Netscape Message window to respond to a message, file it in one of several mailboxes, forward a message to someone else, print a message, or delete it. You open the Netscape Message window by double-clicking any message header summary in the Message List window.

Figure 2-7   NETSCAPE MESSAGE WINDOW

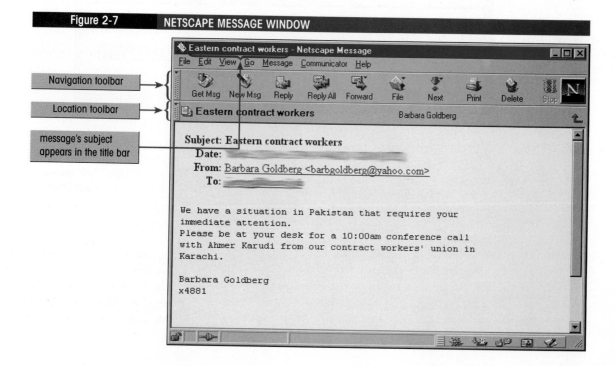

You use the **Composition window**, shown in Figure 2-8, to create messages. You open the Composition window by clicking the New Message button on the Navigation toolbar in the Message List or Netscape Message windows. The Composition window toolbar contains buttons to send e-mail, quote (paste) information from another person's e-mail message, use the address book to find someone's e-mail address, attach files, check spelling, save an e-mail message as a draft, or stop a current message after sending it. When you start a new message, you will see the To, From, Cc, and Bcc lines in the Composition window.

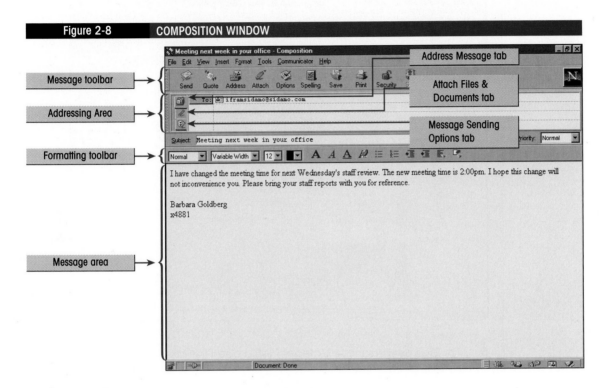

Figure 2-8   COMPOSITION WINDOW

Setting Up E-Mail

You are eager to start using Messenger to see if Sidamo's customers can use it to contact sales representatives. Cost is not a consideration because the Netscape Communicator suite—including Netscape Messenger—is free. Your first step is to start and configure Messenger so it fetches and sends *your* e-mail.

To start and initialize Messenger for use on a public computer:

1. Click the **Start** button on the Windows taskbar, point to **Programs**, point to **Netscape Communicator**, and then click **Netscape Messenger** to start the program. The Message List window opens (see Figure 2-5).

2. Click the **New Msg** button on the Navigation toolbar to open the Composition window (see Figure 2-8). If necessary, click the **Maximize** button on the Composition window title bar so the window fills the desktop.

3. Click **Edit** on the menu bar, and then click **Preferences**. The Preferences window opens and shows the preferences for the Mail & Newsgroups category.

4. If necessary, click the **plus sign** to the left of the Mail & Newsgroups category to show the different settings that you can change. (After you click the plus sign, it changes to a minus sign.) To set up your e-mail information, you will change the settings in the Mail Servers category. See Figure 2-9.

Figure 2-9	PREFERENCES DIALOG BOX

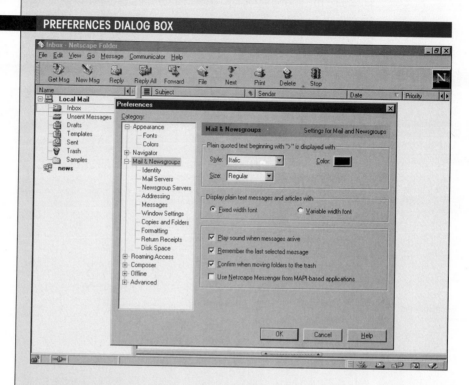

5. Click **Mail Servers** in the Category list to open the Mail Servers settings on the right side of the window.

TROUBLE? If you (or someone else) already set up your account, then go to Step 4 in the next set of steps ("To change your e-mail name").

6. If the Incoming Mail Servers text box is empty, then click the **Add** button. Otherwise, click the **Edit** button. In either case, type the name of the server that processes your incoming mail. (Your instructor or lab manager will provide you with this name.) Usually, your incoming mail server name is POP, POP3, or IMAP followed by a domain name.

7. Click the **Server Type** list arrow and select the server type (ask your instructor).

8. Type your e-mail user name in the User Name text box (see Figure 2-10) and click the **OK** button.

Figure 2-10	CONFIGURING MESSENGER FOR BARBARA GOLDBERG

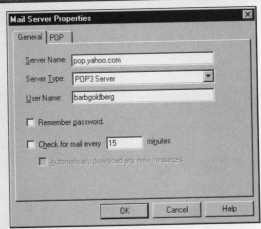

9. In the Outgoing mail (SMTP) server text box, type the name of the server that processes your outgoing mail. Your instructor or technical support person will provide you with this name. Usually, your outgoing mail server name is either SMTP or MAIL followed by a domain name. Press the **Tab** key to move to the Outgoing mail server user name text box.

10. Type your e-mail address (or login name) in the Mail server user name text box.

11. Click the **Choose** button. The Directory dialog box opens. Select drive A and click the **OK** button.

If you want your mail to remain on the mail server so you can read it from any computer, then check the Leave messages on server after retrieval check box. (In the Preferences dialog box, click the Mail & Newsgroups plus sign, click Mail Servers, and then click the Edit button. In the Mail Server Properties dialog box, click the POP tab and check the Leave messages on the server check box.) Otherwise, the server will delete your e-mail messages from the mail server after you retrieve your e-mail. You aren't finished configuring Messenger yet—you still need to set up the way that your e-mail is identified to its recipients.

To change your e-mail name:

1. Click **Identity** in the Category list to open the Identity settings in the right side of the window.

2. If necessary, click in the Your name text box, and then type your first and last names. Type your name the way you want it to appear in the message summary header when recipients receive your messages.

3. Press the **Tab** key to move the insertion point to the Email address text box, and then type your full e-mail address. Figure 2-11 shows the Identity tab for Barbara Goldberg. The values you enter in the Identity panel have no affect on your ability to send or receive e-mail; these text boxes only identify a name and associated address in the From text box of your outgoing e-mail messages.

Figure 2-11   ADDING YOUR IDENTITY INFORMATION

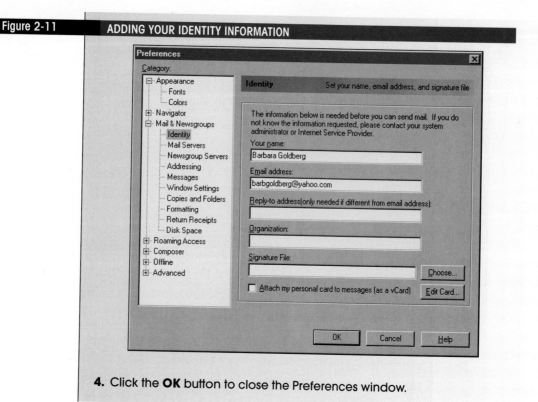

4. Click the **OK** button to close the Preferences window.

Now your copy of Messenger is set up to send and receive messages, so you are ready to send a message to Barbara.

Note: In this tutorial, you will send messages to a real mailbox with the address barbgoldberg@yahoo.com. Follow the instructions carefully so you use the correct address. Messages sent to this mailbox are deleted without being opened or read, so do not send important messages to this address.

Sending a Message Using Messenger

You decide to use Messenger to send a message with an attached file to Barbara. You will send a carbon copy of the message to your own e-mail address to make sure that the message and attached file are sent correctly. The Composition window is open, so you are ready to start typing Barbara's e-mail address.

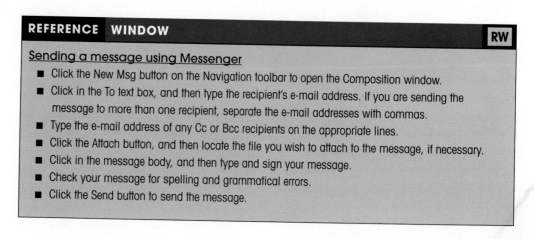

REFERENCE WINDOW   **RW**

Sending a message using Messenger

- Click the New Msg button on the Navigation toolbar to open the Composition window.
- Click in the To text box, and then type the recipient's e-mail address. If you are sending the message to more than one recipient, separate the e-mail addresses with commas.
- Type the e-mail address of any Cc or Bcc recipients on the appropriate lines.
- Click the Attach button, and then locate the file you wish to attach to the message, if necessary.
- Click in the message body, and then type and sign your message.
- Check your message for spelling and grammatical errors.
- Click the Send button to send the message.

To send a message with an attachment:

1. Click in the To text box, and then type **barbgoldberg@yahoo.com**.

   TROUBLE? Make sure that you use the address barbgoldberg@yahoo.com, instead of barbgoldberg@sidamo.com. If you type Barbara's e-mail address incorrectly, your message will be returned with an error message attached.

2. Click the empty box below the To button in the message header. When the second To button appears (below the first one), click it to show a list of alternate text boxes, and then click **Cc:** in the list. A Cc button replaces the To button on the second line of the message header.

3. Type your full e-mail address in the Cc text box so you will receive a copy of your own message. It is a good idea to save a copy of all electronic correspondence as a reference. Most e-mail programs allow you to choose whether to save a copy of the messages you send.

   TROUBLE? If you make a typing mistake on a previous line, use the arrow keys or click the insertion point to return to a previous line so you can correct your mistake. If the arrow keys do not move the insertion point backward or forward in the header block, then press Shift + Tab or the Tab key to move backward or forward, respectively.

4. Click in the **Subject** text box, and then type **Test message**.

5. Click the **Attach** button on the Message toolbar, and then click **File** in the drop-down list. The Enter file to attach dialog box opens.

6. Make sure your Data Disk is in drive A. Click the **Look in** list arrow, and select **3½ Floppy (A:)** to display the list of folders on your Data Disk.

7. Double-click the **Tutorial.02** folder to open it, and then double-click the file named **Market.wri** to close the dialog box. The Attach Files & Documents tab changes color, and the filename appears on the first line of the Addressing Area. The color change indicates one or more files are attached to the message.

8. Click the **Address Message** tab to see the message recipients' addresses again.

9. Click in the message body, and then type **Please let me know that this message arrived safely and that you are able to read it and the attached file with no difficulty. I'm testing Netscape Messenger and want to make sure that it is working properly.**

10. Press the **Enter** key twice, and then type your first and last name to sign your message. See Figure 2-12.

| Figure 2-12 | SENDING A TEST MESSAGE USING MESSENGER |

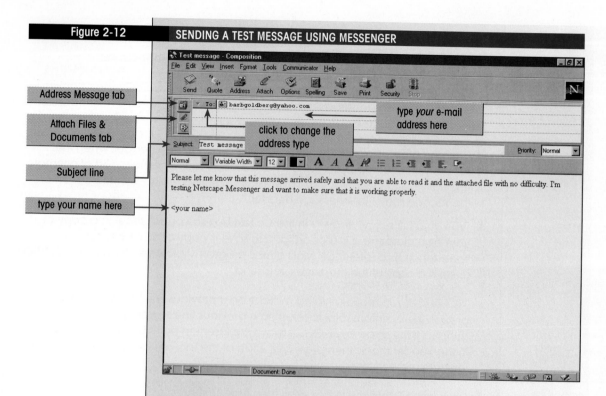

11. Click the **Spelling** button on the Message toolbar to check your spelling before sending the message. If necessary, correct any typing errors. When you are finished, click the Done button to close the Check Spelling dialog box.

12. Click the **Send** button on the Message toolbar to send the message. The Composition window closes, and the message is sent to the mail server for delivery to Barbara. The Message List window reappears.

TROUBLE? If you see a message that says "No SMTP server has been specified in the Mail & Newsgroups Preferences," then you did not provide enough information about your mail server and your login name. Return to the Composition window, click Edit on the menu bar, click Preferences, click the Mail & Newsgroups category, click the Mail Servers category, and then ask your instructor or technical support person for the correct mail server user name, outgoing mail (SMTP) server name, and incoming mail server. After entering this information, click the OK button and repeat Step 12 to continue.

Depending on your system configuration, Messenger might not send your message immediately. Instead, it might queue (hold) the message until you connect to your Internet service provider (ISP). When you are ready to send your messages, you can send all the queued messages at once when you connect to your ISP.

Receiving and Reading a Message

When you receive new mail, messages that you have not opened have a closed envelope with a downward-pointing green arrow to their left in the message list summaries, and messages that you have opened have a closed envelope next to them. Messages that have an attached file have a paperclip icon attached to the envelope in their message summaries. Next, you will check your e-mail to see if you received the Cc copy of the message you sent to Barbara.

REFERENCE WINDOW   **RW**

Using Messenger to receive and read an e-mail message
- Click the Get Msg button on the Navigation toolbar.
- Type your password in the text box, and then click the OK button.
- Double-click the summary line of any received message to read it.

To check for incoming mail:

1. Click the **Get Msg** button on the Navigation toolbar in the Message List window. The Password Entry dialog box opens.

2. Type your password in the text box, and then click the **OK** button. Depending on your system configuration, you might have to connect to your ISP to get your new mail. Within a few moments, your mail server transfers all new mail to your Inbox. You should see the Cc message that you sent to yourself when you mailed the test message to Barbara.

   TROUBLE? If you do not see any incoming messages in your Inbox, then you either did not receive any new mail or you might be looking in the wrong mailbox. If necessary, click the list arrow next to the mailbox name on the Location toolbar, which is just above the message summary list, and then click Inbox. If you still don't have any mail messages, wait a few moments and then repeat Steps 1 and 2 until you receive a message. Sometimes mail delivery slows down at peak times during the day.

3. Click the summary line for the copy of the test message that you just received in the message list. The Netscape Message window opens and shows the full message, including the header lines. The paperclip icon to the right of the sender's name indicates that the message contains an attached file. See Figure 2-13.

Figure 2-13   REVIEWING NEW E-MAIL

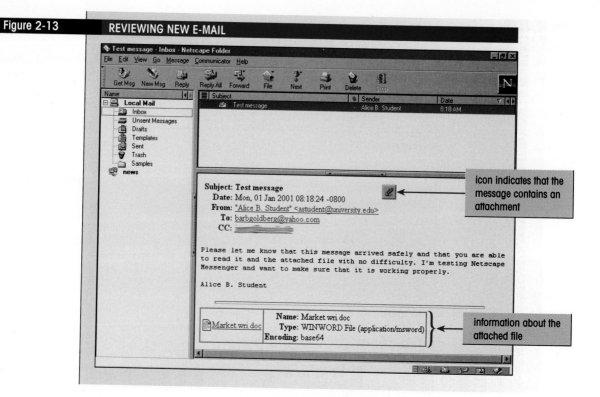

You received your Cc copy of the test message that you sent to Barbara, and the paperclip icon indicates that you received an attached file with the message. Now you can open the attachment in a preview window, or save it for viewing later. Open the attachment next.

Saving an Attached File

You want to make sure that your attached file was sent properly, so you decide to open it in the preview window. After you are finished looking at an attached file, you can decide whether to save or delete it from your system.

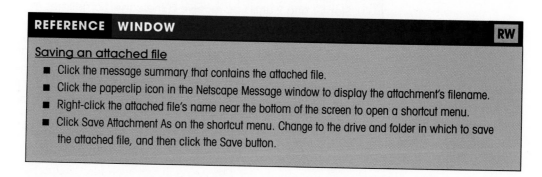

REFERENCE   WINDOW   **RW**

Saving an attached file
- Click the message summary that contains the attached file.
- Click the paperclip icon in the Netscape Message window to display the attachment's filename.
- Right-click the attached file's name near the bottom of the screen to open a shortcut menu.
- Click Save Attachment As on the shortcut menu. Change to the drive and folder in which to save the attached file, and then click the Save button.

To save an e-mail attachment:

1. Click the paperclip icon in the Netscape Message window to show the attachment's filename.

2. Right-click the attachment name **Market.wri** icon near the bottom of the screen. (You might need to scroll down the window to see the icon.) A shortcut menu opens.

3. Click **Save Attachment As** on the shortcut menu to open the Save As dialog box.

4. Click the **Save in** list arrow, and then select the drive that contains your Data Disk.

5. Double-click the **Tutorial.02** folder to open it. Change the suggested filename to **Memo1.wri** (see Figure 2-14).

Figure 2-14	SAVING AN ATTACHED FILE

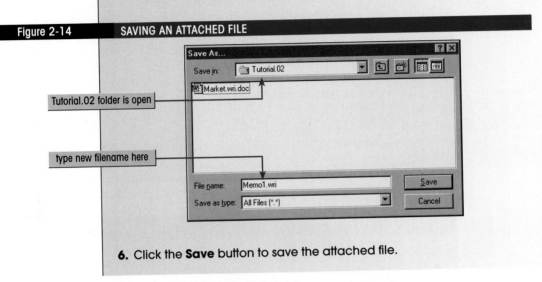

Tutorial.02 folder is open

type new filename here

6. Click the **Save** button to save the attached file.

Replying to and Forwarding Messages

You can forward any message you receive to someone else. Similarly, you can respond to the sender of a message quickly and efficiently to respond to a sender's message. You will reply to and forward messages extensively as you use e-mail.

Replying to an E-Mail Message

To reply to a message, select the message summary line in the Message List window and click the Reply to sender only button—it is labeled Reply—on the Navigation toolbar to respond to the sender. To reply to all the recipients, click the Reply All button. Messenger opens a Composition window and places the original sender's address in the message header To text box. You can leave the Subject line as is or modify it. Most systems, including Messenger, will copy the entire body from the original message and place it in the response window. Usually, a special mark in one edge of the response indicates what part is the original message. After typing your response, you click the Composition window Send button to send your response to the original message's author.

If you are responding to a question, it is a good idea to intersperse your responses below each question from the original message so the recipient can better understand the context of your responses. When you respond to a message that was sent to a number of people—perhaps some people received the message as a carbon copy—be careful how you respond. You can choose to respond to all the original recipients or just to the sender. Figure 2-15 shows the Composition window that opens when you reply to a message sent by Alice B. Student.

Figure 2-15	REPLYING TO A MESSAGE

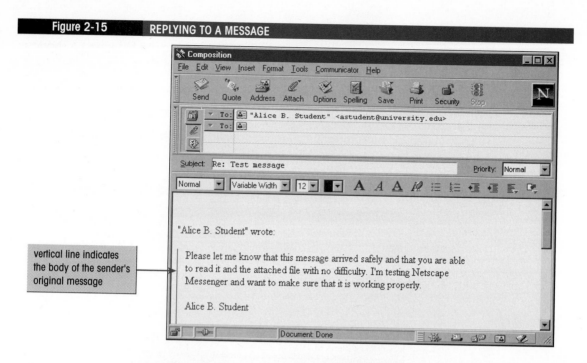

vertical line indicates the body of the sender's original message

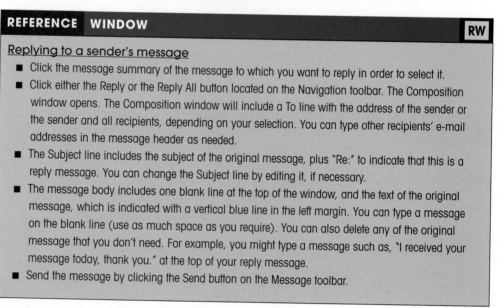

REFERENCE WINDOW   RW

Replying to a sender's message

- Click the message summary of the message to which you want to reply in order to select it.
- Click either the Reply or the Reply All button located on the Navigation toolbar. The Composition window opens. The Composition window will include a To line with the address of the sender or the sender and all recipients, depending on your selection. You can type other recipients' e-mail addresses in the message header as needed.
- The Subject line includes the subject of the original message, plus "Re:" to indicate that this is a reply message. You can change the Subject line by editing it, if necessary.
- The message body includes one blank line at the top of the window, and the text of the original message, which is indicated with a vertical blue line in the left margin. You can type a message on the blank line (use as much space as you require). You can also delete any of the original message that you don't need. For example, you might type a message such as, "I received your message today, thank you." at the top of your reply message.
- Send the message by clicking the Send button on the Message toolbar.

Forwarding an E-Mail Message

When you forward a message, it is copied from your Inbox folder and travels to the person to whom you are forwarding the message. To forward an existing mail message to another user, open the folder containing the message (usually, the Inbox folder) in the Message List window, double-click the message summary to open a full Message window, click Message on the menu bar, click Forward As, and then click Quoted. The Composition window opens and displays the message to forward along with a full message header. The forwarded message is marked with a line to the left side. You can include your own comments along with the message itself. Figure 2-16 shows the Composition window for forwarding a message. You can forward a message to more than one person by including each e-mail address in the To, Cc, or Bcc text boxes as necessary.

Figure 2-16	FORWARDING A MESSAGE

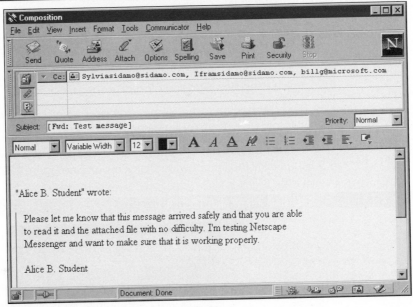

REFERENCE WINDOW   **RW**

Forwarding an e-mail message

- Click the message summary for the message that you want to forward to another person.
- Click the Forward button on the Navigation toolbar to open the Composition window.
- The Subject line changes to include "Fwd:" and the original message's subject so the recipient knows that this is a forwarded message.
- Click in the To text box, and then type the e-mail address of the recipient. You can forward one message to multiple recipients or Cc and Bcc recipients by including the recipients' e-mail addresses on these lines.
- The message body includes one blank line at the top of the window and the text of the original message, if you are sending a quoted message, which is indicated with a vertical blue line in the left margin. You can type a message on the blank line (use as much space as you require). You can also delete any part of the original message that you don't need. For example, you might type a message such as, "I thought you might be interested in this message that I received." at the top of your forwarded message. If you do not see in your reply the message you received, then click the Quote button on the Message toolbar. The message will appear.
- Send the message by clicking the Send button on the Message toolbar.

Filing and Printing an E-Mail Message

You can use Messenger mail folders to file your e-mail messages by category. When you file a message, you move it from the Inbox to another folder. You can also make a *copy* of a message in the Inbox and save it in another folder. You will make a copy of your Cc message and save it in a folder named "Marketing" for safekeeping. You can create other folders to suit your individual working style.

To create a new folder:

1. Click **File** on the menu bar in the Message List window, and then click **New Folder**. The New Folder dialog box opens.

2. Type **Marketing** in the Name text box to name the new folder. You will create this folder as a sub-folder of the Inbox folder.

3. Make sure that the Create as a subfolder of list box shows the Inbox. If it doesn't, then click the list arrow and click **Inbox**. See Figure 2-17.

| Figure 2-17 | CREATING A NEW MAIL FOLDER |

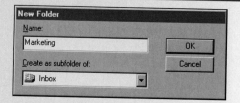

4. Click the **OK** button to create the new folder.

After you create the Marketing folder, you can transfer messages to it. Besides copying or transferring mail from the Inbox, you can select any other mail folder's messages for transfer to another folder.

To send a copy of a message to another folder:

1. Click the message summary for your Cc message in the Message List window in order to select it.

2. Click **Message** on the menu bar, point to **Copy Message**, point to **Inbox**, and then click **Marketing**. Your Cc message still appears in the Inbox. Now, make sure that you have copied and filed your Cc message correctly.

   TROUBLE? If you make a mistake and move or copy messages to the wrong folder, click Edit on the menu bar, and then click Undo to cancel the action.

3. Click the **list arrow** on the Location toolbar, and then click **Marketing** to open that mailbox. Your Cc message appears in the Marketing mailbox.

When you need to file a message, you follow a similar procedure.

To file a message in another folder:

1. Select the message summary for your Cc message in the Marketing folder.

2. Click the **File** button on the Navigation toolbar, and then click **Trash**. The message is removed from the Marketing folder and is transferred to the Trash folder.

Moving or copying several messages at once is a snap. Hold down the Ctrl key and click each message summary in the Message List window that you want to move. Then click Message on the menu bar. Next, point to either Move Message or Copy Message, and then click the folder to which you want to move or copy the group of messages.

You might need to print important messages in the future, so you want to make sure that you can print and file messages in a safe place.

To print an e-mail message:

1. Click the **Inbox** to return to that folder.

2. Right-click the message summary for your Cc message in the Inbox window to open the shortcut menu that shows the actions you can take.

3. Click **Print Message** on the shortcut menu, and then click the **OK** button in the Print dialog box to send the message to the printer.

You can print a message at any time—when you receive it, before you send it, or after you file it.

Deleting an E-Mail Message

You saved and printed your Cc message, so now you can delete the message and the Marketing folder that you created. Deleting messages in the Inbox mailbox and other mailboxes is easy. When you delete a message, you are really just moving it to the Trash mailbox. To remove messages permanently, click File on the menu bar, and then click Empty Trash on Local Mail. If you are using a public PC in a university computer laboratory, it is always a good idea to delete all your messages and then empty the trash before you leave the computer. Otherwise, the next person who uses Messenger will be able to access and read your messages.

REFERENCE WINDOW	RW

Deleting an e-mail message
- Right-click the message summary to delete, and then click Delete Message on the shortcut menu.
- To delete the message permanently, click File on the menu bar, and then click Empty Trash on Local Mail.

To delete a message and empty the trash:

1. Right-click the message summary line for your Cc message. See Figure 2-18.

Figure 2-18 DELETING A MESSAGE

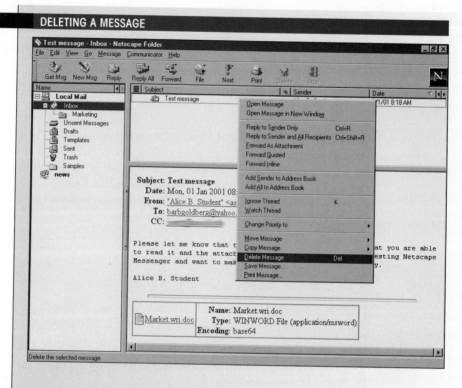

2. Click **Delete Message** on the shortcut menu to delete the message. The message is moved from the Inbox to the special folder named Trash.

   TROUBLE? If you deleted a message you wanted to keep, you can recover it by clicking Edit on the menu bar and then clicking Undo. To remove the message completely, you must empty the contents of the Trash folder.

3. Click **File** on the menu bar, and then click **Empty Trash on Local Mail**. Any deleted messages or folders are permanently removed.

To delete a folder, you follow the same process.

To delete a user-created folder:

1. Click the **Marketing** folder and then right-click the **Marketing** folder.

2. Click **Delete Folder** on the shortcut menu.

3. The dialog box appears asking if you want to move the selected folders into the Trash. Click **OK**. The folder moves to the Trash folder.

   TROUBLE? If you deleted a folder you wanted to keep, you can recover it by clicking Edit on the menu bar and then clicking Undo.

4. To remove the folder completely, click **File** on the menu bar, and then click **Empty Trash on Local Mail**. Any deleted messages or folders are permanently removed.

Maintaining an Address Book

As you send e-mail to different people, you will probably find it burdensome and sometimes errorprone to type their e-mail addresses, especially long and difficult ones. As you use e-mail to contact business associates and friends, you will want to save their addresses in an address book.

Adding an Address to the Address Book

You can access the address book by clicking Communicator on the menu bar and then clicking Address Book. To create a new address, you open the address book and then click the New Card button so you can enter information into the text boxes in the New Card dialog box for each person, including the person's first and last names and complete e-mail address information. If you enter a short name in the Nickname text box, then you can use that name to address a new message. After you click the OK button in the New Card dialog box, Messenger adds the new contact information to your address book.

You are eager to add information to your address book. Begin by entering Barbara Goldberg's contact information into your Messenger address book.

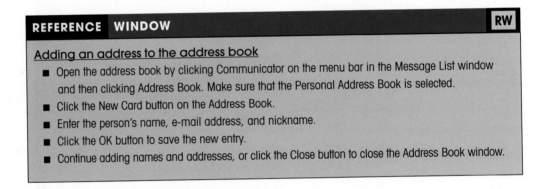

REFERENCE WINDOW   **RW**

<u>Adding an address to the address book</u>
- Open the address book by clicking Communicator on the menu bar in the Message List window and then clicking Address Book. Make sure that the Personal Address Book is selected.
- Click the New Card button on the Address Book.
- Enter the person's name, e-mail address, and nickname.
- Click the OK button to save the new entry.
- Continue adding names and addresses, or click the Close button to close the Address Book window.

To add an e-mail address to the address book:

1. Click **Communicator** on the menu bar in the Message List window, and then click **Address Book** to open the Address Book window. See Figure 2-19.

Figure 2-19   ADDRESS BOOK WINDOW

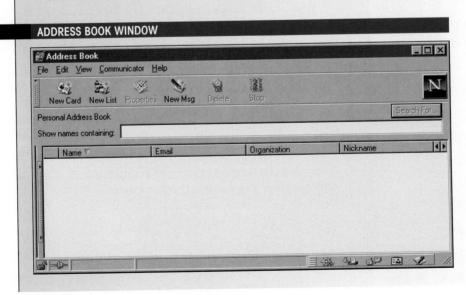

2. Click the **New Card** button on the Address Book toolbar. The New Card dialog box opens. You use this dialog box to add addresses to your address book. The Name tab stores information about a person's e-mail address. You can use the Contact tab to store postal mail address information and other personal information.

3. Make sure that the **Personal Address Book** is selected in the list box that appears at the top of the New Card dialog box. If it is not selected, click the list arrow and then click Personal Address Book.

4. Type **Barbara** in the First Name text box, and then press the **Tab** key to go to the Last Name text box.

5. Type **Goldberg**, and then press the **Tab** key two times to go to the Email text box.

6. Type **barbgoldberg@yahoo.com**, press the **Tab** key to go to the Nickname text box, and then type **Barbara**. Your New Card dialog box looks like Figure 2-20.

Figure 2-20	ENTERING A NEW ADDRESS IN THE ADDRESS BOOK

make sure that this list box displays *Personal Address Book*

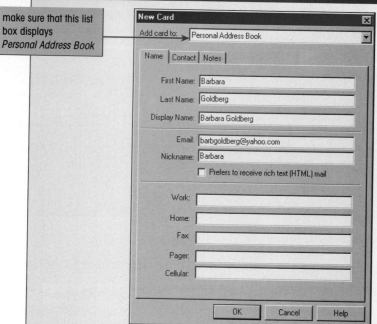

7. Click the **OK** button to store your new address entry.

8. Repeat Steps 3 through 7 to create address cards for the following members of the marketing department:

First Name	Last Name	E-mail Address	Nickname
Gary	Kildare	gkildare@sidamo.com	Gary
Faye	Borthman	fborthman@sidamo.com	Faye
Fran	Brooks	fbrooks@sidamo.com	Fran

9. When you are finished adding the addresses, click the **Close** button on the Address Book window title bar to close it.

With these entries now in your address book, you can easily insert even the most complicated e-mail address in any of the message text boxes as you compose a message. To insert an e-mail address into a new message's address line, open the address book, select the address, and then click the To, Cc, or Bcc buttons as needed. You can edit an address book entry while viewing the address book by either double-clicking the name or right-clicking the name and then clicking Properties. Another handy facility lets you easily add new names to your address book. Whenever you receive mail from someone not in your address book, right-click the message summary line in the Message List window, and then click Add Sender to Address Book on the shortcut menu to add the sender's e-mail address to your address book.

Creating a Multi-Address Entry

You can use Messenger to create a distribution list, or a **mailing list**, which is an address entry consisting of more than one e-mail address in a single group. A mailing list is helpful when you want to send one message to several people simultaneously.

Barbara frequently sends messages to each member of the marketing department. She asks you to create a mailing list entry in her address book so she can type one nickname for the group of e-mail addresses, instead of typing each address separately.

REFERENCE **WINDOW**   **RW**

Creating a mailing list
- Click Communicator on the menu bar in the Message List window, and then click Address Book to open the Address Book window.
- Click the New List button on the Address Book toolbar.
- Enter the mailing list's name in the List Name text box.
- Enter the mailing list's nickname in the List Nickname text box.
- Enter the individual nicknames or e-mail address information of the individual group members.
- Click the OK button to create the list.

To create a mailing list address entry:

1. Click **Communicator** on the menu bar in the Message List window, and then click **Address Book** to open the Address Book window. Maximize the Address Book window, if necessary.

2. Click the **New List** button on the Address Book toolbar. The Mailing List dialog box opens. You will add a group name, a nickname, and the individual e-mail addresses for the group to your mailing list entry.

3. Type **Marketing List** in the List Name text box, and then press the **Tab** key to go to the List Nickname text box.

4. Type **mkt** in the List Nickname text box. Now, when Barbara needs to send a message to every member of the marketing department, she can type "mkt" on the To line.

5. Click **OK** to create the list. The Address Book window reappears. Next, add the individual e-mail addresses to the mailing list.

6. Double-click the **Marketing List** entry in the address book to open the list.

7. Press the **Tab** key three times to move to the address list, and then type **Fran**. You already added Fran's address to the address book. After you start typing Fran's name, Messenger recognizes it. Press the **Enter** key to add Fran's address to the list.

8. Repeat Step 5 to add Faye Borthman and Gary Kildare to the mailing list. Press the **Enter** key after entering each name to add the name to the mailing list and to move to the next line in the address list. Figure 2-21 shows the marketing list after three names have been entered.

Figure 2-21   CREATING A MAILING LIST

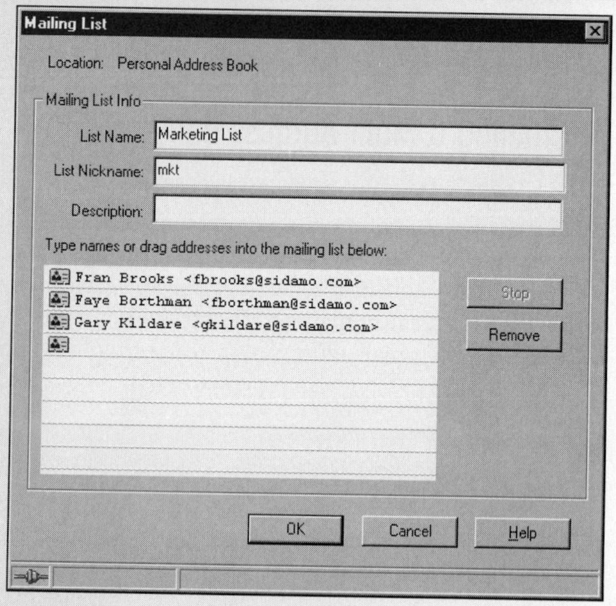

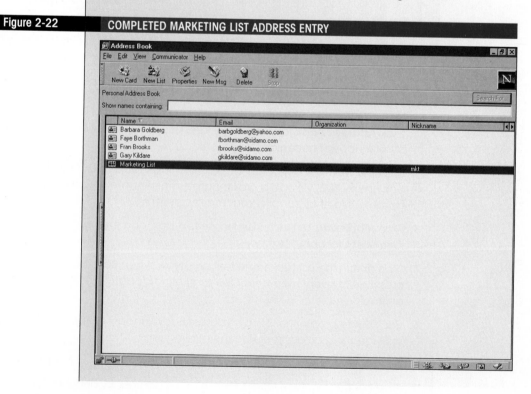

9. Click the **OK** button to close the Mailing List dialog box. Now, the Marketing List entry appears in the Address Book window. See Figure 2-22.

Figure 2-22   COMPLETED MARKETING LIST ADDRESS ENTRY

10. Close the Address Book by clicking the **Close** button.

11. Close all open Netscape windows, and then close your dial-up connection, if necessary.

When you need to modify a mailing list, you can delete one or more members from the group by opening the address book, double-clicking the list name, and then deleting a member's name by selecting it and clicking the Remove button. You can add members to an existing list by opening the mailing list and typing the new member's name.

Session 2.2 QUICK CHECK

1. Netscape Messenger is known as an e-mail _____ because it runs on a PC and it sends requests for mail delivery to the mail server.

2. What is perhaps the most important potential disadvantage of using mail programs such as Netscape Messenger? *Hint:* What happens when you read mail in another location?

3. When you delete an e-mail message in a mail program, are the messages deleted immediately? If not, then how do you delete mail messages permanently?

4. You can organize mail by placing messages into _____.

5. Discuss whether or not it is important to include parts of the original message when replying to the sender.

6. If you store people's e-mail addresses in an address book, then you can type a(n) _____ in place of a person's e-mail address and Netscape Messenger will automatically fill in the correct e-mail address.

7. When you assemble several e-mail addresses under a single address book entry, you are creating a(n) _____ list.

If your instructor assigns Session 2.3, continue reading. Otherwise, complete the Review Assignments at the end of this tutorial.

SESSION 2.3

In this session you will learn how to use Microsoft Outlook Express to send and receive e-mail. You will learn how to print, file, save, delete, respond to, and forward e-mail messages. Finally, you will organize your e-mail addresses in an address book.

Microsoft Outlook Express Client

Microsoft Outlook Express, or simply **Outlook Express**, is an e-mail client that supports all the standard e-mail functions you learned about in Session 2.1 to send and receive mail. You can access Outlook Express from within a Web browser or from any Microsoft Office program.

You are eager to continue your evaluation of e-mail software. You start Outlook Express by double-clicking its icon on the Windows desktop or by using the Start menu. Figure 2-23 shows the Outlook Express Inbox window.

| Figure 2-23 | OUTLOOK EXPRESS INBOX WINDOW |

toolbar

your Folder list might be different

Preview pane

Message list

Three panels appear on the screen: the Folder list on the left side, the Message list in the upper-right pane, and the Preview pane in the lower-right pane. The **Folder list** displays a list of folders for receiving, saving, and deleting mail messages. Your folders might be different from those that appear in Figure 2-23. The **Inbox** folder holds messages you have received, the **Outbox** folder holds messages waiting to be sent, the **Sent Items** folder contains copies of messages you sent, and the **Deleted Items** folder contains messages you deleted from other folders.

The Message list contains summary information for each message that you receive, including the message priority, an indication for an attached file, the sender's name, and the message's subject. The message summary that is selected in the Message list appears in the Preview pane. The Preview pane is normally located below the message list and reveals part of the message's contents. You can customize each of the panels to display different information, so Figure 2-23 might be slightly different from what you see in your copy of Outlook Express.

Setting Up E-Mail

You are eager to get started using Outlook Express. These steps assume that Outlook Express is already installed on your computer. First, you want to set up Outlook Express so it will retrieve your mail from a publicly accessible computer. Cost is not a consideration because the Microsoft Outlook Express program is free. Your first step is to start and configure Outlook Express so it fetches and sends *your* e-mail.

To start and initialize Outlook Express for use on a public computer:

1. Click the **Start** button on the Windows taskbar, point to **Programs**, point to **Internet Explorer**, and then click **Outlook Express** to start the program. The Inbox folder opens (see Figure 2-23).

TROUBLE? If a graphic Microsoft Outlook Express screen appears when you start Outlook Express, click the Read Mail icon to go directly to your Inbox.

TROUBLE? If a Browse for Folder dialog box opens when you first try to start Outlook Express, click the Outlook Express folder, and then click the OK button.

TROUBLE? If the Internet Connection Wizard starts, click the Cancel button.

TROUBLE? If you cannot find the Outlook Express program on your computer, ask your instructor or technical support person for assistance.

2. Click **Tools** on the menu bar, click **Accounts**, and then, if necessary, click the **Mail** tab so you can set up your mail account settings.

TROUBLE? If you (or someone else) already set up your account, then click the Close button in the Internet Accounts dialog box and skip the remainder of these steps.

3. Click the **Add** button in the Internet Accounts dialog box, and then click **Mail**, if necessary. The Internet Connection Wizard starts. You use the Wizard to identify yourself and the settings for your mail server and user name. See Figure 2-24.

| Figure 2-24 | INTERNET CONNECTION WIZARD DIALOG BOX |

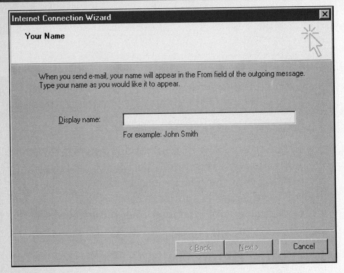

4. Type your first and last name in the Display name text box, and then click the **Next** button to go to the next dialog box, where you enter your e-mail address.

5. Type your full e-mail address (such as student@university.edu) in the E-mail address text box, and then click the **Next** button. The next dialog box asks you for your incoming and outgoing mail server names.

6. Enter the name of your incoming and outgoing mail servers in the text boxes where indicated. Your instructor or technical support person will provide you with this information. Usually, your outgoing mail server name is either SMTP or MAIL followed by a domain name. Your incoming mail server name is typically POP, POP3, or IMAP followed by a domain name. When you are finished, click the **Next** button to continue.

7. In the Account name text box type your Internet mail logon, as supplied by your instructor or technical support person. Make sure that you type only your login name and not your domain name. Enter your password in the Password text box.

8. Clear the **Remember password** check box and click the **Next** button.

9. Click the **Finish** button to save the mail account information and close the Internet Connection Wizard. The Internet Accounts dialog box reappears, and your account is listed on the Mail tab. Figure 2-25 shows Barbara Goldberg's information.

Figure 2-25   INTERNET ACCOUNTS INFORMATION FOR BARBARA GOLDBERG

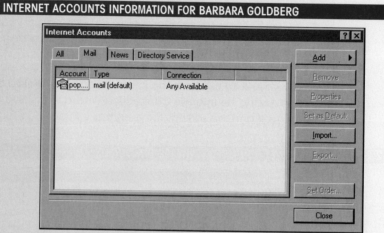

10. Click the **Close** button in the Internet Accounts dialog box to close it.

Now, your copy of Outlook Express is set up to send and receive messages, so you are ready to send a message to Barbara. *Note:* In this tutorial, you will send messages to a real mailbox with the address barbgoldberg@yahoo.com. Follow the instructions carefully so you use the correct address. Messages sent to this mailbox are deleted without being opened or read, so do not send important messages to this address.

Sending a Message Using Outlook Express

You decide to use Outlook Express to send a message with an attached file to Barbara. You will send a carbon copy of the message to your own e-mail address to make sure that the message and attached file are sent correctly.

Sending a message using Outlook Express

- Click the New Mail button on the toolbar to open the New Message window.
- Click in the To text box, and then type the recipient's e-mail address. If you are sending the message to more than one recipient, separate the e-mail addresses with commas. If necessary, click the View menu in the New Message window and then click the All Headers selection to display the Bcc line in your New Message window.
- Type the e-mail address of any Cc of Bcc recipients on the appropriate lines.
- Click the Attach button on the toolbar, and then locate the file to attach to the message, if necessary.
- Click in the message body, and then type and sign your message.
- Check your message for spelling and grammatical errors.
- Click the Send button to send the message.

To send a message:

1. Make sure that the Inbox is selected in the Folder list, and then click the **New Mail** button on the toolbar to open the New Message window. If necessary, click the **Maximize** button on the New Message window. See Figure 2-26. The New Message window contains its own menu bar, toolbar, message display area, and text boxes in which you enter address and subject information.

Figure 2-26   **NEW MESSAGE WINDOW**

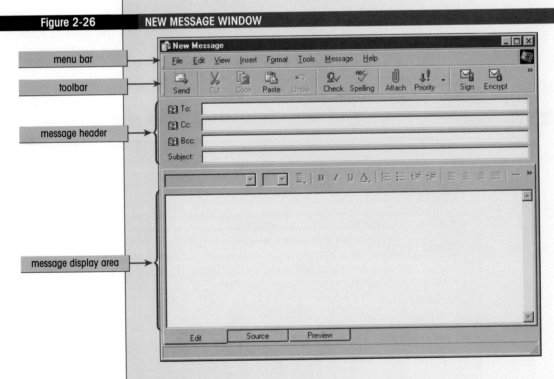

2. Type **barbgoldberg@yahoo.com** in the To text box, and then press the **Tab** key to move to the Cc line.

TROUBLE? Make sure that you use the address barbgoldberg@yahoo.com, instead of barbgoldberg@sidamo.com. If you type Barbara's e-mail address incorrectly, your message will be returned with an error message attached.

3. Type your full e-mail address on the Cc line in order to receive a copy of your own message. It is a good idea to save a copy of all electronic correspondence as a reference.

TROUBLE? If you make a typing mistake on a previous line, use the arrow keys or click the insertion point to return to a previous line so you can correct your mistake. If the arrow keys do not move the insertion point backward or forward in the header block, then press Shift + Tab or the Tab key to move backward or forward, respectively.

4. Press the **Tab** key to move the insertion point to the Subject line, and then type **Test message**. Notice that the title bar now shows "Test message" as the window title.

5. Click the **Attach** button on the New Message window toolbar. The Insert Attachment dialog box opens.

6. Make sure your Data Disk is in drive A. Click the **Look in** list arrow, and then click **3½ Floppy (A:)** to display the contents of your Data Disk.

7. Double-click **Tutorial.02** to open that folder, and then double-click the **Market.wri** file. The Insert Attachment dialog box closes, and the attached file's icon appears in the Attach box.

8. Click the insertion point in the message display area, and then type **Please let me know that this message arrived safely and that you are able to read it and the attached file with no difficulty. I'm testing Outlook Express and want to make sure that it is working properly.**

9. Press the **Enter** key twice, and then type your first and last name. See Figure 2-27.

Figure 2-27   SENDING AN E-MAIL MESSAGE

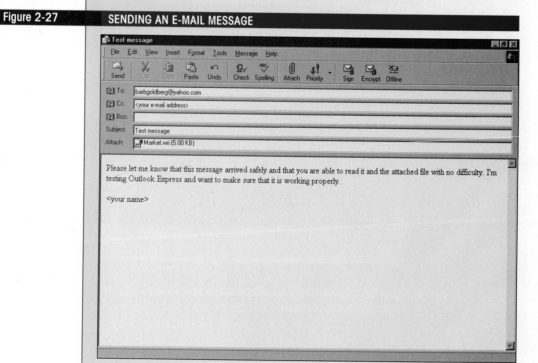

10. Click **Tools** on the menu bar, and then click **Spelling** to check your spelling before sending the message. If necessary, correct any typing errors. When you are finished, click the **OK** button to close the Check Spelling dialog box.

   TROUBLE? If the Spelling command is dimmed on the Tools menu, then your computer does not have the spelling feature installed. Press the Esc key to close the menu, and then continue with Step 11.

11. Click the **Send** button on the toolbar to mail the message. The Test message window closes and the message is placed in the Outbox. The Outlook Express window reappears.

Depending on your system configuration, Outlook Express might not send your message(s) immediately. It might queue (hold) the message(s) until you connect to your Internet service provider (ISP). If you want to examine the setting and change it, click Tools on the menu bar, and then click Options. Select the Send tab. If the Send messages immediately check box has a check mark, then mail goes out as soon as you click the Send button on the toolbar. Otherwise, the message is held and sent when you connect again.

Receiving and Reading a Message

When you receive new mail, messages that you have not opened have a closed envelope to their left in the Message list, and messages that you have opened have an open envelope next to them. You will check for new mail next.

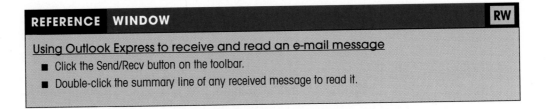

REFERENCE   WINDOW   RW

Using Outlook Express to receive and read an e-mail message
- Click the Send/Recv button on the toolbar.
- Double-click the summary line of any received message to read it.

To check for incoming mail:

1. Click the **Send/Recv** button on the toolbar. Depending on your system configuration, you might have to connect to your ISP to get your new mail. Within a few moments, your mail server transfers all new mail to your Inbox. You should see the Cc message that you sent to yourself. Notice that the Inbox folder in the Folder list is bold, but other folders are not. A bold folder indicates that it contains unread mail. Unread messages have a closed envelope to their left in the Message list, whereas read messages have an open envelope next to them.

   TROUBLE? If an Outlook Express message box opens and tells you that it could not find your host, click the Hide button to close the message box, click Tools on the menu bar, click Accounts, and then click the Properties button. Verify that your incoming and outgoing server names are correct, and then repeat Step 1. If you still have problems, ask your instructor or technical support person for help.

TROUBLE? If you do not see any incoming messages in your Inbox, then you either did not receive any new mail or you might be looking in the wrong mailbox. If necessary, click the Inbox folder in the Folder list. If you still don't have any mail messages, wait a few moments, and then repeat Step 1 until you receive a message.

2. Click the message summary for your Cc message in the Message list pane to open it in the Preview pane. See Figure 2-28.

Figure 2-28 **RECEIVING A NEW MESSAGE**

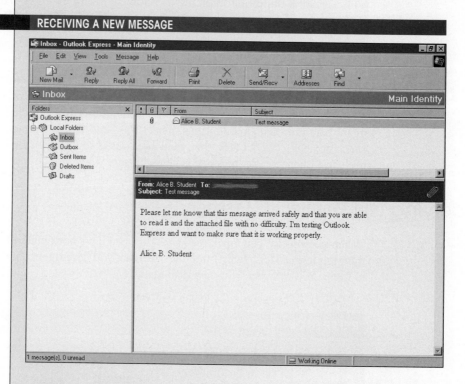

3. Now, double-click the message summary for your Cc message in the Message list to open the Test message window with the full message content.

4. Click the **Close** button on the Test message title bar to close the window. You return to the Inbox window.

You received your Cc copy of the test message that you sent to Barbara, and the paperclip icon indicates that you received an attached file with the message. Either open the attachment in a preview window or save it for viewing later. Open the attachment next.

Saving an Attached File

You want to make sure that your attached file was sent properly, so you decide to open it in the preview window. After you are finished looking at an attached file, you can decide whether to save or delete it from your system.

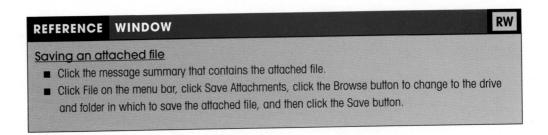

REFERENCE WINDOW   RW

Saving an attached file
- Click the message summary that contains the attached file.
- Click File on the menu bar, click Save Attachments, click the Browse button to change to the drive and folder in which to save the attached file, and then click the Save button.

To save an e-mail attachment:

1. Click the message summary for your Cc message in the Message list.

2. Click **File** on the menu bar, and then click **Save Attachments**.

3. Click the **Browse** button and move to the top of the Browse for Folder dialog box, if necessary. Double-click the drive icon that contains your Data Disk.

4. Select the **Tutorial.02** folder, if necessary, and click **OK**. See Figure 2-29.

| Figure 2-29 | SAVING AN ATTACHED FILE |

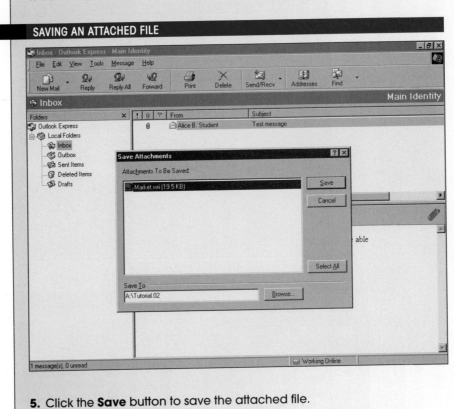

5. Click the **Save** button to save the attached file.

Replying to and Forwarding Messages

You can forward any message you receive to someone else. Similarly, you can respond to the sender of a message quickly and efficiently by replying to a message. You will use both extensively as you use e-mail.

Replying to an E-Mail Message

To reply to a message, select the message in the message summary list (or from any folder), and then click the Reply button on the toolbar. Outlook Express will open a new message window and place the original sender's address in the To text box. You can leave the Subject line as is or modify it. Most systems, including Outlook Express, will copy the entire body from the original message and place it in the response window. Usually, a special mark in one edge of the response indicates what part is the original message. You click the Send button in the Re: window to send the message to the original author.

If you are responding to a question, it is a good idea to type your responses below each question from the original message to help the recipient better understand the context of your responses. When you respond to a message that was sent to a number of people—perhaps some people received the message as a carbon copy—be careful how you respond. You can choose to respond to all the original recipients or just to the sender. Figure 2-30 shows the window that you would use to reply to a message sent by Alice B. Student.

Figure 2-30	REPLYING TO A MESSAGE

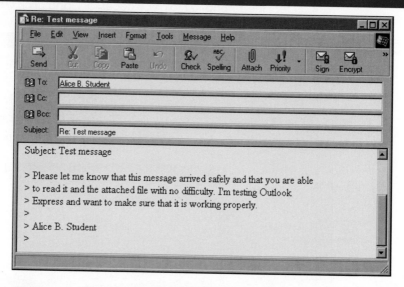

REFERENCE WINDOW **RW**

Replying to a message

- Click the message summary of the message to which you want to reply.
- Click the Reply button on the toolbar. A new message window opens. The message window will include a To line with the address of the sender or the sender and all recipients, depending on your selection. You can type other recipients' e-mail addresses in the message header as needed. Maximize the window, if necessary.
- The Subject line includes the subject of the original message plus "Re:" to indicate that this is a reply message. You can change the Subject line by editing it, if necessary.
- The message body includes one blank line at the top of the window, and the text of the original message contains either a vertical black line to its left or greater than (>) symbols next to each original line. You can type a message on the blank line (and use as much space as you require). You can delete any of the original message that you don't need. For instance, you might type a message such as, "I thought you might be interested in this message that I received." at the top of your message.
- Send the message by clicking the Send button on the toolbar.

Forwarding an E-Mail Message

When you forward a message, it is copied from your Inbox folder and travels to the person to whom you are forwarding the message. To forward an existing mail message to another user, open the folder containing the message (the Inbox folder usually), select the message in the Message list, and then click the Forward button on the toolbar. The Fw: window opens. Type the address of the recipient in the To text box. If you want to forward the message to several people, type their addresses in the To text box (or Cc text box) and separate each e-mail address with a semicolon or comma. Finally, click the Send button on the toolbar to send the message. Figure 2-31 shows the window that you use to forward a message.

Figure 2-31	FORWARDING A MESSAGE

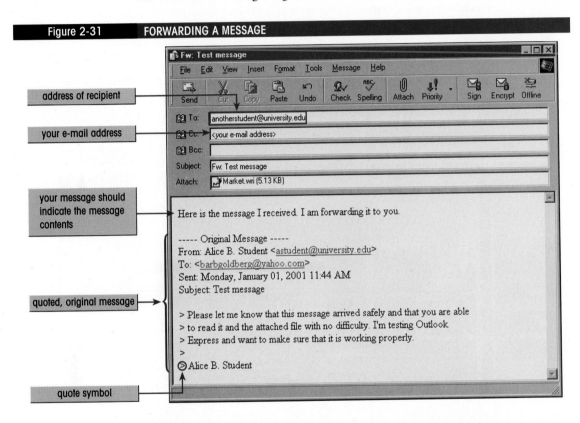

- address of recipient
- your e-mail address
- your message should indicate the message contents
- quoted, original message
- quote symbol

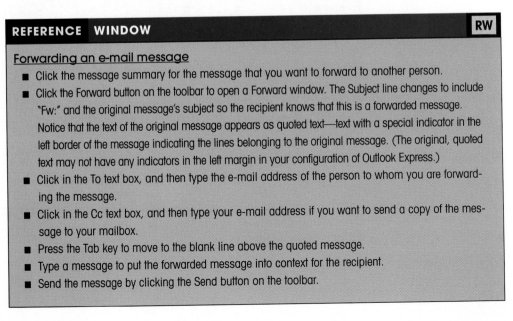

REFERENCE WINDOW   **RW**

Forwarding an e-mail message

- Click the message summary for the message that you want to forward to another person.
- Click the Forward button on the toolbar to open a Forward window. The Subject line changes to include "Fw:" and the original message's subject so the recipient knows that this is a forwarded message. Notice that the text of the original message appears as quoted text—text with a special indicator in the left border of the message indicating the lines belonging to the original message. (The original, quoted text may not have any indicators in the left margin in your configuration of Outlook Express.)
- Click in the To text box, and then type the e-mail address of the person to whom you are forwarding the message.
- Click in the Cc text box, and then type your e-mail address if you want to send a copy of the message to your mailbox.
- Press the Tab key to move to the blank line above the quoted message.
- Type a message to put the forwarded message into context for the recipient.
- Send the message by clicking the Send button on the toolbar.

Occasionally, you will receive important messages, so you want to make sure that you print them and then file them in a safe place.

Filing and Printing an E-Mail Message

You can use the Outlook Express mail folders to file your e-mail messages by category. When you file a message, you move it from the Inbox to another folder. You can also make a *copy* of a message in the Inbox and save it in another folder. You will make a copy of Barbara's message and save it in a folder named "Marketing" for safekeeping. Later, you can create other folders to suit your style and working situation.

To create a new folder:

1. Click **File** on the menu bar, point to **Folder**, and then click **New**. The Create Folder dialog box opens.

2. Type **Marketing** in the Folder name text box. See Figure 2-32.

Figure 2-32	CREATING A NEW FOLDER

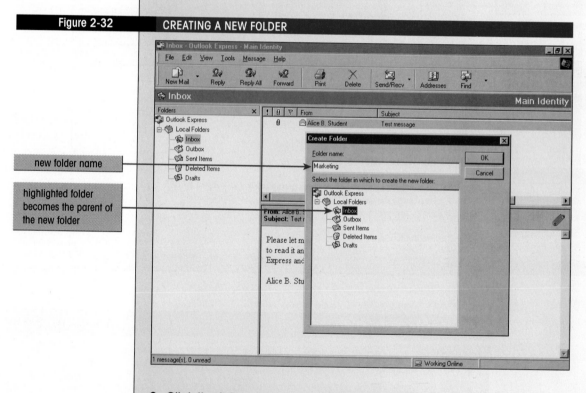

new folder name

highlighted folder becomes the parent of the new folder

3. Click the **Inbox** folder in the Select the folder in which to create the new folder list box. You will create the new Marketing folder below the Inbox folder.

4. Click the **OK** button to create the folder and close the Create Folder dialog box. The new Marketing folder appears in the Folder list.

After you create the Marketing folder, you can transfer messages to it. Besides copying or transferring mail from the Inbox, you can select messages in any other folder and then transfer them to another folder.

To send a copy of a message to another folder:

1. Click the message summary for Barbara's message in the Message list in order to select it, if necessary.

2. Click **Edit** on the menu bar, click **Copy to Folder**, click **Marketing**, and then click the **OK** button. Your Cc message still appears in the Inbox. Now, make sure that you copied and filed your Cc message correctly.

3. Click the **Marketing** folder in the Folder list to open that folder. Your Cc message appears in the Marketing folder.

When you need to move a message to another folder, you follow a similar procedure.

To move a message to another folder:

1. Click the message summary for your Cc message in the Message list.

2. Click and hold down the mouse button, and then drag the message summary for your Cc message from the Marketing folder to the **Deleted Items** folder. When the message summary is on top of the Deleted Items folder, release the mouse button. The message moves from the Inbox to the Deleted Items folder. (That is equivalent to deleting the message.)

Moving or copying several messages at once is a snap. Hold down the Ctrl key, and click each message summary in the Message list that you want to move. Then drag the selected messages to the correct folder, or use the menu commands to copy the messages and save them in a folder.

You might need to print important messages in the future, so you want to make sure that you can print and file messages in a safe place.

To print an e-mail message:

1. Open the Inbox, and then right-click your Cc message summary in the Message list to open the shortcut menu that shows the actions you can take, such as moving messages to folders, replying to a message, and other similar tasks.

2. Click **Print** on the shortcut menu. The Print dialog box opens. Click the **OK** button. The message prints within a few seconds.

You can print a message at any time—when you receive it, before you send it, or after you file it.

Deleting an E-Mail Message

When you don't need a message any longer, select the message and then click the Delete button on the toolbar. You can select multiple messages using the Ctrl key and delete them simultaneously. Also, you can delete a folder by selecting it in the Folder list and then clicking the Delete button. When you delete a message, you are simply moving it to the Deleted Items folder. To remove messages permanently, delete them from the Deleted Items folder using the same procedure. When you delete a folder, the deletion is permanent, but you receive a warning dialog box, giving you a chance to cancel your proposed folder deletion. If you are using a public PC in a university computer laboratory, it is always a good idea to delete all your messages from the Inbox and then delete them again from the Deleted Items folder before you leave the computer. Otherwise, the next person who uses Outlook Express will be able to access and read your messages.

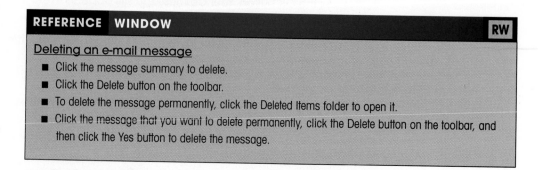

REFERENCE WINDOW **RW**

Deleting an e-mail message

- Click the message summary to delete.
- Click the Delete button on the toolbar.
- To delete the message permanently, click the Deleted Items folder to open it.
- Click the message that you want to delete permanently, click the Delete button on the toolbar, and then click the Yes button to delete the message.

To delete a message permanently:

1. Select the message summary for the message you received as a carbon copy.

2. Click the **Delete** button on the toolbar. The message is moved to the Deleted Items folder.

3. Click the **Deleted Items** folder to open it.

4. Click the message summary for the message you received that is now in the Deleted Items folder. You can press Ctrl and click more than one message summary to delete them permanently. Click the **Delete** button on the toolbar. A dialog box opens warning you that the deletion will be permanent (see Figure 2-33).

Figure 2-33   **DELETING A MESSAGE**

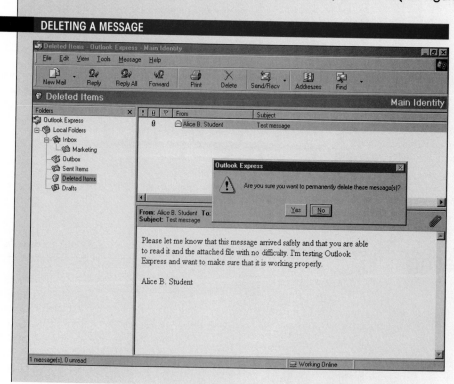

5. Click the **Yes** button to confirm your deletion.

To delete a folder, you follow the same process.

To delete a user-created folder:

1. Right-click the **Marketing** folder in the Folder list.

2. Click **Delete** from the shortcut list of commands. A dialog box opens and asks you to confirm that it is okay to move the folder to the Deleted Items folder.

3. Click the **Yes** button.

4. Select the Marketing folder in the Deleted Items folder. (You may have to click the plus icon to open the Deleted Items folder to reveal the Marketing folder.)

5. Click the **Delete** button on the toolbar. A dialog box opens and warns you that the deletion will be permanent.

6. Click **Yes** to permanently delete the Marketing folder.

7. Click the **Inbox** folder to re-display your list of mail folders, message summary, and preview panels.

Maintaining **an Address Book**

As you send e-mail to different people, you will probably find it burdensome and sometimes errorprone to type their e-mail addresses, especially long and difficult ones. As you use e-mail to contact business associates and friends, you will want to save their addresses in an address book.

Adding an Address to the Address Book

You can access the address book by clicking the Addresses button on the toolbar. To create a new address, you open the address book, click the New button on the toolbar, click New Contact from the drop-down list, and then enter information into the Properties dialog box for that contact. You can enter first and last names and e-mail address information. If you enter a short name in the Nickname text box, then you can use that shortened name when you create a new message.

You are eager to add information to your address book. Begin by entering Barbara Goldberg's contact information into your Outlook Express address book.

REFERENCE   WINDOW   **RW**

Entering a new e-mail address in the address book
- Click the Addresses button on the toolbar to open the Address Book window.
- Click the New button on the toolbar.
- Click New Contact from the drop-down list.
- Enter the person's name, e-mail address, and other information, as necessary.
- Click the OK button to add the entry to the address book.
- Repeat the steps to add more addresses, or click the Close button to close the Address Book window.

To create an address book entry:

1. Open the Address Book window by clicking the **Addresses** button on the toolbar.

2. Click the **New** button on the toolbar and click **New Contact** from the drop-down menu to open the Properties window.

3. Type **Barbara** in the First text box, and then press the **Tab** key twice to go to the Last text box.

4. Type **Goldberg** in the Last text box, and then press the **Tab** key three times to go to the Nickname text box.

5. Type **Barbara** in the Nickname text box, and then press the **Tab** key to go to the E-mail Addresses text box.

6. Type **barbgoldberg@yahoo.com** in the E-mail Addresses text box. See Figure 2-34.

Figure 2-34 ENTERING A NEW ADDRESS IN THE ADDRESS BOOK

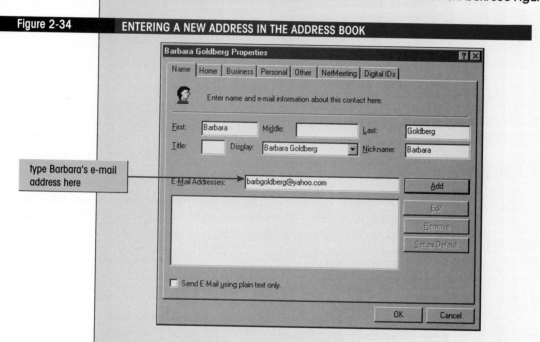

type Barbara's e-mail address here

7. Click the **Add** button and then click the **OK** button to close the Properties dialog box and return to the Address Book window.

8. Repeat Steps 2 through 7 to create address cards for the following members of the marketing department:

First Name	Last Name	E-mail Address	Nickname
Gary	Kildare	gkildare@sidamo.com	Gary
Faye	Borthman	fborthman@sidamo.com	Faye
Fran	Brooks	fbrooks@sidamo.com	Fran

9. When you are finished adding the addresses, click the **Close** button on the Address Book window title bar to close it.

With these entries in your address book, you can easily insert even the most complicated e-mail address in any of the message text boxes as you compose a message by typing the first few letters of the addressee's e-mail address. As you type one, two, or three of the first letters of the e-mail address, full addresses from the address book appear in the address text box. Edit a name by either double-clicking the name or clicking the name and clicking Properties. Another handy facility lets you easily add new names to your address book. Whenever you receive mail from someone who is not in your address book, double-click the message to display it in a window, and then right-click the "From" name. Finally, click the Add to Address Book command on the shortcut menu. The sender's e-mail address is added to your address book.

Creating a Multi-Address Entry

You can use Outlook Express to create a distribution list, or a **group**, which is an address entry consisting of more than one e-mail address in a single group. A distribution list is helpful when you want to send one message to several people simultaneously.

Barbara frequently sends messages to each member of the marketing department. She asks you to create a distribution list entry in her address book so she can type one nickname for the group of e-mail addresses, instead of having to type each address separately.

REFERENCE   WINDOW   **RW**

Creating a group address entry
- Click the Addresses button on the toolbar to open the Address Book window.
- Click the New button on the toolbar.
- Click New Group from the drop-down menu.
- Type the group's name in the Group Name text box.
- Click the Select Members button to add existing entries to the group.
- Add each group member's address to the group list, and then click the OK button.
- Click the OK button to finish creating the group.

To create a group address entry:

1. Click the **Addresses** button on the toolbar to open the address book.

2. Click the **New** button on the toolbar and then click New Group from the drop-down menu to open the New Group dialog box.

3. Type **mkt** in the Group Name text box to establish the group's name.

4. Click the **Select Members** button to add existing entries to the group. The Select Group Members dialog box opens so you can choose which names to add to the marketing group list.

5. Select Faye's name in the left panel, and then click the **Select** button to add it to the Members panel.

6. Repeat Step 5 to select Fran and Gary to add them to the group list. Remember to click the **Select** button after selecting each name. Figure 2-35 shows the completed group.

Figure 2-35   CREATING AN ADDRESS GROUP

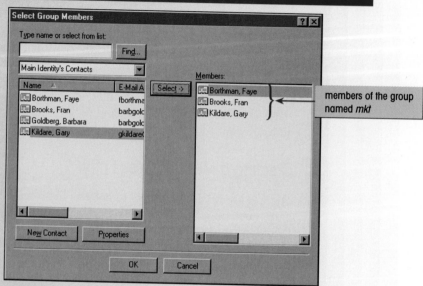

7. Click the **OK** button to close the Select Group Members dialog box.

8. Click the **OK** button to close the mkt Properties dialog box. Notice the new group, mkt, appears in the address book, sorted alphabetically by the Name column.

9. Close the Address Book by clicking the **Close** button.

10. Close Outlook Express, and close your dial-up connection, if necessary.

When you need to modify a group's members, you can delete one or more members from the group by opening the address book, double-clicking the group name, and then deleting a member's name by clicking the Remove button. Similarly, you can add members by clicking the Select Members button on the group's Properties dialog box. Now, whenever Barbara Goldberg wants to send mail to the marketing department members, she can select the group name *mkt* from the address book for any of a message's address text boxes (To, Cc, or Bcc for example). Clearly, group addresses are very convenient.

Session 2.3 QUICK CHECK

1. True or False: It is good etiquette to include a Subject line in your e-mail message so the recipient has a summary of a message's contents before reading it.

2. You use the _____ line to send copies of a message to other recipients without the principal addressee's knowledge.

3. When you want to send a complex document, such as a spreadsheet, it should be included in the message as a(n) _____.

4. What should you include in a message so that the receiver can contact you nonelectronically?

5. Discuss the advantages of using an electronic address book.

6. When you send the same group of people e-mail messages frequently, you can create a(n) _____ list by which you can refer to the group with a single nickname.

Now you are ready to complete the Review Assignments using the e-mail client of your choice.

REVIEW ASSIGNMENTS

You have explored two different e-mail clients, so you are ready to make a recommendation and send it to your instructor. Your status report will give an overview of either Netscape Messenger or Microsoft Outlook Express (or both programs, depending on your instructor's preferences), and then you will use your e-mail client to send the report, as a blind carbon copy, to three classmates. You will send a carbon copy of the report to yourself and then print it for your records. Finally, you will delete the message.

1. Start Messenger or Outlook Express and set up yourself as a user, if necessary.

2. Add your instructor's name and full e-mail address to the address book. Use an appropriate nickname that will be easy for you to remember.

3. Add a distribution list that consists of three classmates' e-mail addresses. Enter your classmates' full names and e-mail addresses, and assign each individual a unique nickname.

4. Create a new message.

5. Type "E-mail evaluation status report 1" on the Subject line.

6. Click the To line, and then type your instructor's nickname.

7. Click the Cc line, and then type your full e-mail address.

8. Click the Bcc line, and then type the nickname of your distribution list for your classmates so they also receive a copy of the report. (If the Bcc line is not visible, then select All Headers from the View menu.)

9. Select the message area, and then type three or more sentences describing your overall impressions about Messenger and/or Outlook Express.

10. Attach the file named Security.wri from the Tutorial.02 folder on your Data Disk to the message.

11. Leave a blank line after the end of your message, and then type your name, class name, class section, and e-mail address on four separate lines.

12. Check your spelling before you send the message and correct any mistakes.

13. Carefully proofread your message for errors, make sure that the correct recipients are indicated, and then correct any problems.

14. Send the message.

15. Wait about 15 to 30 seconds, and then manually check for new mail to see if your message arrived on the server. Retrieve your new mail, and open the new message.

16. Print the new message.

17. Permanently delete the new message from your program.

18. Exit the e-mail client.

CASE PROBLEMS

Case 1. Grand American Appraisal Company You work as an office manager for Grand American Appraisal Company, which is a national real-estate appraisal company with its corporate headquarters in Los Angeles. Grand American handles real-estate appraisal requests from all over the United States and maintains a huge inventory of approved real-estate appraisers located throughout the country. When an appraisal request is phoned into any regional office, an office staff member phones or faxes the national office to start the appraisal process. The appraisal order desk in Los Angeles receives the request and is responsible for locating a real-estate appraiser in the community in which the target property (i.e., the one to be appraised) is located. After the Los Angeles office identifies and contacts an appraiser by phone, the appraiser has two days to perform the appraisal and either phone or fax the regional office with a preliminary estimate of value for the property. The entire process of phoning the regional office and then phoning or faxing the national office is both cumbersome and expensive.

Your supervisor asks you to investigate alternatives to reduce the number of phone calls necessary to complete the appraisal cycle. You discover that Grand American requires all independent appraisers to have e-mail access and addresses. Nearly every Grand American employee has a PC connected on a LAN that ties into the larger computer on the Internet. Your job is to reduce the number of phone calls needed to set up an appraisal. You think e-mail is the solution, and you will be working with the existing e-mail system at Grand American to experiment with feasible alternatives.

Do the following:

1. Start Messenger or Outlook Express and ensure that the e-mail program has the correct settings for your mail server, your e-mail address, and your user name.

Explore ▶ 2. Use the Help system to learn how to create a signature file. (Netscape Messenger users: Create a text file in Notepad and save it. Then, click Edit, Preferences, select Identity in the Mail & Newsgroups category, and type the absolute path in the Signature File text box. Outlook Express Users: Click Tools, Options, click the Signatures tab, click the New button, and type the signature information in the Edit Signature text box.) Create a personal signature file that has three lines: your first and last name (line 1), your class and section (line 2), and your e-mail address (line 3).

3. Find a classmate and get his or her e-mail address. Your classmate will play the role of the Los Angeles order desk. Enter your classmate's nickname, full name, and e-mail address in the address book.

4. Enter your instructor's nickname, full name, and e-mail address in the address book.

5. Compose a message to your classmate. Type your classmate's nickname on the To line, type your e-mail address and your instructor's nickname on the Cc line, and then type "Request for appraisal" on the Subject line.

6. Type a short message that requests the assignment of an appraiser. Include your street address and the request date in the message.

Explore ▶ 7. Include your signature file in the message you are about to send.

8. Send the message immediately, without queuing it.

9. Wait a few seconds, and then retrieve the message that you sent to yourself.

10. Print a copy of your message, and then delete it permanently from the server and the PC.

11. Remove the signature file you created. Exit the e-mail client.

Case 2. Bridgefield Engineering Company Bridgefield Engineering Company (BECO) is a small engineering firm in Somerville, New Jersey, that manufactures and distributes heavy industrial machinery for factories worldwide. Because BECO has trouble reaching its customers around the world in different time zones, the company decided to implement an e-mail system to facilitate contact between BECO employees and their customers. BECO hired you to help employees set up and use their e-mail system to reach their customers. Your first task is to compile a list of typical industrial machines that BECO can manufacture and send it to several of BECO's marketing staff located throughout the country.

Do the following:

1. Start Messenger or Outlook Express and ensure that the e-mail program has the correct settings for your mail server, your e-mail address, and your user name.

2. Add your instructor and two classmates to the address book. Use an appropriate nickname for each person.

3. Start a new message. Use the To line to address the message to three people: yourself, your instructor, and to one of the classmates that you added to the address book in Step 2.

4. Send a blind carbon copy of the message to the second classmate that you added to the address book in Step 2.

5. In the message body, type "Bridgefield manufactures machines to your specifications. We can build borers, planers, horn presses, and a variety of other machines. E-mail us for further information."

6. Send the message to yourself.

Explore ➤ 7. Save the message in the Tutorial.02 folder on your Data Disk as BECO.txt.

8. Create a mail folder or mailbox named BECO on your client, in which you will store all mail for BECO.

9. Save the message you mailed to yourself in the BECO mail folder.

10. Create a distribution list address book entry using only the nicknames of the people that you added to the address book in Step 2. The nickname for the distribution list is classinfo.

11. Close and save the changes to your address book.

12. Delete the BECO folder and its contents from your PC.

13. Exit the e-mail client.

Case 3. Recycling Awareness Campaign You are an assistant in the mayor's office in Cleveland. The mayor has asked you to help with the recycling awareness campaign. Your job is to use e-mail to increase awareness of the recycling centers throughout the city and to encourage Cleveland's citizens and businesses to participate in the program. As it happens, you know that over 45 percent of the city's registered voters have subscribed to a particular television cable service. Of those, over 8 percent have e-mail addresses and cable modems. You decide to send an e-mail message to several key businesspeople with an invitation to help increase awareness of the program by forwarding the recycle message to their employees and colleagues. Your message includes an attached file that explains the program in detail and how to use it.

Do the following:

1. Start Messenger or Outlook Express, and ensure that the e-mail program has the correct settings for your mail server, your e-mail address, and your user name.

2. You will use the e-mail addresses of five classmates to act as the city's key businesspeople. Obtain and add the nicknames, full names, and e-mail addresses of five classmates as a distribution list named "council" in your address book. Then add the nickname, full name, and e-mail address of your instructor as a single-entry address.

3. Create a new message. Type the distribution list nickname on the To line, your e-mail address on the Cc line, and your instructor's nickname on the Bcc line. Add an appropriate subject on the Subject line.

Explore

4. Create a signature file. Your signature should include your name on line 1, your new title of "Assistant to the mayor" on line 2, and your real e-mail address on line 3.

5. Write a two- or three-line message urging the council members to encourage recycling in their districts by forwarding the attached file to their local business contacts. Thank them for reading your e-mail.

6. Attach the file named Recycle.wri that is saved in the Tutorial.02 folder on your Data Disk to the message.

7. Make sure that your signature file is added automatically to the outgoing message, proofread and spellcheck your message, and then send your message.

8. After a few moments, retrieve your e-mail message from the server and print it.

9. Forward the message to any one of the classmates in your address book. Add a message to the forwarded message that asks the recipient to forward the message to appropriate business leaders per your program objectives.

10. Save a copy of your message in a new folder named "Recycling," and then delete the original message.

11. Delete the Recycling folder and your message.

12. Remove the signature file you created. Exit the e-mail client.

Case 4. Student Birds-of-a-Feather Group In two weeks, you have a midterm exam and you want to organize a study group with your classmates. Everyone in your class has an e-mail account on the university's computer. You want to contact some classmates to find out when they might be available to get together in the next week to study for the exam. To reach these students to create a study group, you decide to use e-mail.

Do the following:

1. Start Messenger or Outlook Express and ensure that the e-mail program has the correct settings for your mail server, your e-mail address, and your user name.

2. Type the e-mail addresses of at least four group members—people in your class or friends' e-mail addresses who won't mind getting an e-mail message from you—on the To line of the new message.

3. Type your e-mail address on the Bcc line and your instructor's e-mail address on the Cc line.

4. In the message body, tell your classmates about your study group. Ask your recipients to respond to you through e-mail by a specified date so you can see who is interested.

5. Sign the message at the bottom with your full name, your course name and section number, and your e-mail address.

6. Send the message.

7. Create a new mailbox or folder named "Studygroup."

8. Check your mail for a copy of your message. When the message arrives, file a copy of the message in the Studygroup folder, and then delete the original message.

9. Print a copy of the message.

10. Delete the Studygroup folder and your message.

11. Exit the e-mail client.

Case 5. *Jacopini's Student Survey*   During breaks from school, you work for a local company that surveys student opinions about various topics of interest to college students. The director of research, Lisa Giancone, has asked you to e-mail a short survey to three students at your university. She wants to know the name of three of their favorite music CDs, where they prefer to shop, and how much time they spend listening to music per week. Lisa asks you to create a survey using any word processing program—Word 2000, WordPad, or WordPerfect, for example—and attach the survey to the brief e-mail message. She would like to have the survey results compiled within three weeks, so you are to ask the respondents to e-mail back their answers within 15 days.

Do the following:

1. Using a word processor, create a survey that asks: 1) Name your three favorite music CDs, 2) List the names of two of your favorite stores to shop for music (online stores or not), and 3) How much time do you spend per week listening to music: 1 hour, 5 hours, or more than 5 hours. Print out the word processed document and be prepared to turn it in to your instructor.

2. Save the word processed document to your Data Disk in the Tutorial.02 folder. Call it Survey (let the word processing program assign its default extension to the file). Close your word processing program.

3. Start Messenger or Outlook Express and ensure that the e-mail program has the correct settings for your mail server, your e-mail address, and your user name.

4. Start a new e-mail message. In the To line, list the e-mail addresses of three other students in your class to whom you can mail the survey.

5. Place your e-mail address in the Cc line.

6. Also send a Cc copy of the message to barbgoldberg@yahoo.com.

7. In the Subject line enter "Music survey."

8. In the message body, write a short message indicating that the survey is part of your class assignment and that you would appreciate a quick response. Tell the student respondents that they are to detach and read the survey. Indicate that they can respond to the three questions by sending an e-mail response with the answers numbered 1 through 3 without using an attached document. They can simply indicate their answers in the e-mail response itself, in other words.

9. Type your name to sign your e-mail message.

10. Attach the word processed survey to the e-mail message.

11. Send the message.

12. When you receive the message back, print it and be prepared to turn it in to your instructor.

13. Exit the e-mail client program.

LAB ASSIGNMENTS

E-Mail E-mail that originates on a local area network with a mail gateway can travel all over the world. That's why it is so important to learn how to use it. In this Lab, you will use an e-mail simulator, so even if your school's computers don't provide you with e-mail service, you will learn the basics of reading, sending, and replying to electronic mail. See the Read This Before You Begin page for information on installing and starting this Lab.

1. Click the Steps button to learn how to work with e-mail. As you proceed through the Steps, answer all of the Quick Check questions that appear. After you complete the Steps, you will see a Quick Check summary report. Follow the instructions on the screen to print this report.

2. Click the Explore button. Write a message to re@films.org. The subject of the message is "Picks and Pans." In the body of your message, describe a movie you have recently seen. Include the name of the movie, briefly summarize the plot, and give it a thumbs up or a thumbs down. Print the message before you send it.

3. Look in your In Basket for a message from jb@music.org. Read the message, then compose a reply indicating that you will attend. Carbon copy mciccone@music.org. Print your reply, including the text of JB's original message before you send it.

4. Look in your In Basket for a message from leo@sports.org. Reply to the message by adding your rating to the text of the original message as follows:

Equipment:	Your rating:
Rollerblades	2
Skis	3
Bicycle	1
Scuba gear	4
Snowmobile	5

Print your reply before you send it.

5. Go into the lab with a partner. You should each log into the E-mail Lab on different computers. Look at the Addresses list to find the user ID for your partner. You should each send a short e-mail message to your partner. Then, you should check your mail message from your partner. Read the message and compose a reply. Print your reply before you send it. *Note:* Unlike a full-featured mail system, the e-mail simulator does not save mail in mailboxes after you log off.

QUICK CHECK ANSWERS

Session 2.1

1. True
2. protocols
3. header, body
4. A recipient can quickly prioritize messages by reading the Subject line and decide when or if to read the message.
5. True
6. Yes; you can send it as an attachment to an e-mail message.
7. IP or Internet Protocol
8. so the receiver has a context for your responses
9. It is easier and faster to type a short distribution list name than several individual e-mail addresses.

Session 2.2

1. client
2. Mail messages are (optionally) deleted from the mail server and downloaded to the PC where you are located, so unless you save the messages on a disk, you won't be able to retrieve them from the server.
3. No. Most mail clients simply put the deleted messages in a special "trash" folder where they remain on the computer until the user empties the trash.
4. folders or mailboxes
5. Yes, it is important so your recipient has a context for your message.
6. nickname
7. distribution or mailing

Session 2.3

1. True
2. Bcc or blind carbon copy
3. attachment
4. a signature file with a phone number or an address
5. It makes entering e-mail addresses faster and more error-free. It also serves as a repository for address and phone information, which is another form of electronic organizer.
6. distribution or mailing

LABS

The Internet: World Wide Web

BROWSER BASICS

Introduction to Netscape Navigator and Microsoft Internet Explorer

CASE

Sunset Wind Quintet

The Sunset Wind Quintet is a group of five musicians who have played together for eight years. At first, the group began by playing free concerts for local charitable organizations. As more people heard the quintet and its reputation grew, the musicians were soon in demand at art gallery openings and other functions.

Each member of the quintet is an accomplished musician. The instruments in a wind quintet include flute, oboe, clarinet, bassoon, and French horn, which are all orchestral instruments. Each quintet member has experience as a player in a symphony orchestra as well. Three quintet members—the flutist, bassoonist, and the French horn player—currently hold positions with the local orchestra. The other two quintet members—the clarinetist and the oboist—teach classes in their respective instruments at the local university.

This past summer, a booking agent asked the quintet to do a short regional tour. Although the tour was successful, the quintet members realized that none of them had any business-management skills. Marianna Rabinovich, the clarinetist, handles most of the business details for the group. The quintet members realized that business matters related to the tour were overwhelming Marianna and that they wanted to do more touring, so they hired you as their business manager.

One of your tasks will be to help market the Sunset Wind Quintet. To do this, you must learn more about how other wind quintets operate and sell their services. At one of your early meetings with the group, you found that each member of the quintet had different priorities. In addition to marketing the quintet's performances, some members felt it would be a good idea to record and sell CDs, whereas others were concerned about finding instrument-repair facilities on the road when tours extended beyond the local area.

As you discussed these issues with the quintet members, you started thinking of ways to address their concerns. Your first idea was to find trade magazines and newspapers that might describe what other small classical musical ensembles were doing. As you considered the time and cost of this alternative, you realized that the Internet and World Wide Web might offer a better way to get started.

SESSION 3.1

In this session, you will learn how Web pages and Web sites make up the World Wide Web. You will find out about things to consider when you select and use a specific software tool to find information on the Web. Finally, you will learn about some basic browser concepts.

Web Browsers

The Internet:
World Wide
Web

As you start to consider how you might use the Web to gather information for the Sunset Wind Quintet, you remember that one of your college friends, Maggie Beeler, earned her degree in library science. You met with Maggie at the local public library, where she is working at the reference desk. She is glad to assist you.

Maggie begins by explaining that the Web is a collection of files that reside on computers, called **Web servers**, that are located all over the world and are connected to each other through the Internet. Most computer files connected to the Internet are private; that is, only the computer's users can access them. The owners of the files that make up the Web have made their files publicly available so you can obtain access to them if you have a computer connected to the Internet.

Client/Server Structure of the World Wide Web

When you use your Internet connection to become part of the Web, your computer becomes a **Web client** in a worldwide client/server network. A **Web browser** is the software that you run on your computer to make it work as a Web client. The Internet connects many different types of computers running different operating system software. Web browser software lets your computer communicate with all of these different types of computers easily and effectively.

Computers that are connected to the Internet and contain files that their owners have made available publicly through their Internet connections are called **Web servers**. Figure 3-1 shows how this client/server structure uses the Internet to provide multiple interconnections among the various kinds of client and server computers.

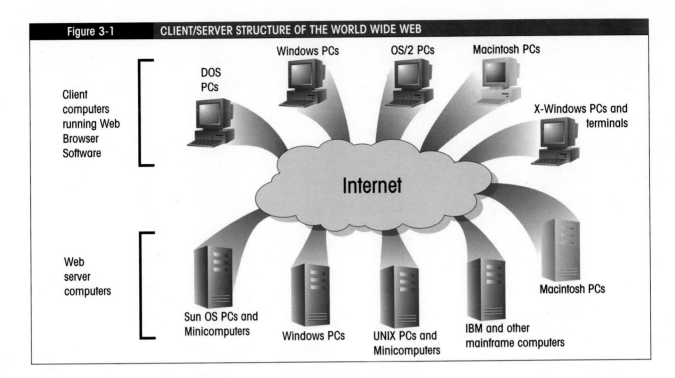

Figure 3-1 | **CLIENT/SERVER STRUCTURE OF THE WORLD WIDE WEB**

Hypertext, Links, and Hypermedia

The public files on Web servers are ordinary text files, much like the files used by word-processing software. To allow Web browser software to read them, however, the text must be formatted according to a generally accepted standard. The standard used on the Web is **Hypertext Markup Language (HTML)**. HTML uses codes, or **tags**, to tell the Web browser software how to display the text contained in the document. For example, a Web browser reading the following line of text:

<B>A Review of the Book <I>Wind Instruments of the 18th Century</I></B>

recognizes the <B> and </B> tags as instructions to display the entire line of text in bold and the <I> and </I> tags as instructions to display the text enclosed by those tags in italics. Different Web clients that connect to this Web server might display the tagged text differently. For example, one Web browser might display text enclosed by bold tags in a blue color instead of displaying the text as bold.

HTML provides a variety of text formatting tags that you can use to indicate headings, paragraphs, bulleted lists, numbered lists, and other useful text formats in an HTML document. The real power of HTML, however, lies in its anchor tag. The **HTML anchor tag** enables you to link multiple HTML documents to each other. When you use the anchor tag to link HTML documents, you create a **hypertext link**. Hypertext links also are called **hyperlinks**, or **links**. Figure 3-2 shows how these hyperlinks can join multiple HTML documents to create a web of HTML text across computers on the Internet.

| Figure 3-2 | USING HYPERLINKS TO CREATE A WEB OF HTML TEXT ACROSS MULTIPLE FILE LOCATIONS |

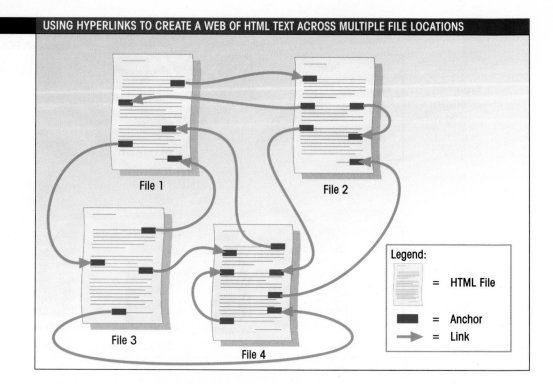

Most Web browsers display hyperlinks in a color different from other text and underline them so they are easily distinguished in the HTML document. When a Web browser displays an HTML document, people usually call the file a Web page. Maggie shows you the Web page that appears in Figure 3-3 and suggests that it might be interesting to the Sunset Wind Quintet. The hyperlinks on this Web page are easy to identify because the Web browser software that displayed this page shows the hyperlinks as red, underlined text.

| Figure 3-3 | WEB PAGE WITH HYPERLINKS |

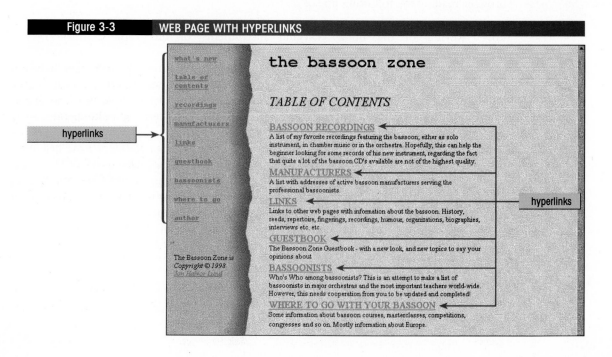

Each of the hyperlinks on the Web page shown in Figure 3-3 allows the user to connect to another Web page. In turn, each of those Web pages contains hyperlinks to other pages, including one hyperlink that leads back to the Web page shown in Figure 3-3. Hyperlinks usually connect to other Web pages; however, they can lead to other media, including graphic image files, sound clips, and video files. Hyperlinks that connect to these types of files often are called **hypermedia links**. You are especially interested in learning more about these hypermedia links, but Maggie suggests you first need to understand a little more about how people organize the Web pages on their servers.

Maggie tells you that the easiest way to move from one Web page to another is to use the hyperlinks that the authors of Web pages have embedded in their HTML documents. Web page authors often use a graphic image as a hyperlink. Sometimes, it is difficult to identify which objects and text are hyperlinks just by looking at a Web page displayed on your computer. Fortunately, when you move the mouse pointer over a hyperlink in a Web browser, the pointer changes to 👆. For example, when you move the pointer over the Reservations hyperlink shown in Figure 3-4, it changes shape to indicate that if you click the Reservations text, the Web browser will open the Web page to which the hyperlink points.

| Figure 3-4 | MOUSE POINTER ON THE RESERVATIONS HYPERLINK |

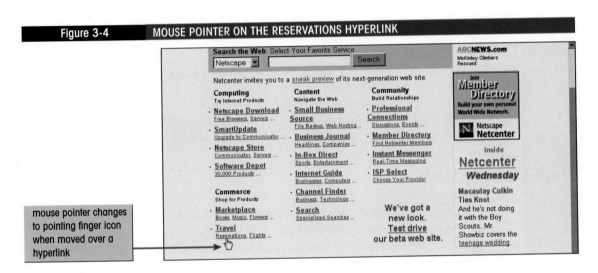

mouse pointer changes to pointing finger icon when moved over a hyperlink

You might encounter an error message when you click on a hyperlink. Two common messages that appear in dialog boxes are the "server busy" and the "DNS entry not found" messages. Either of these messages means that your browser was unable to communicate successfully with the Web server that stores the page you requested. The cause for this inability might be temporary—in which case, you will be able to use the hyperlink later—or the cause might be permanent. The browser has no way of determining the cause of the connection failure, so it provides the same error messages in both cases. Another error message that you might receive displays as a Web page and includes the text "File not Found." This error message usually means that the Web page's location has changed permanently or that the Web page no longer exists.

Web **Pages and Web Sites**

Maggie explains that people who create Web pages usually have a collection of pages on one computer that they use as their Web server. A collection of linked Web pages that has a common theme or focus is called a **Web site**. The main page that all of the pages on a particular Web site are organized around and link back to is called the site's **home page**.

Home Pages

Maggie warns you that the term *home page* is used at least three different ways on the Web and that it is sometimes difficult to tell which meaning people intend when they use the term. The first definition of home page indicates the main page for a particular site: This home page is the first page that opens when you visit a particular Web site. The Bassoon Zone Table of Contents page shown in Figure 3-3 is a good example of this use. All of the hyperlinks on that page lead to pages in the Bassoon Zone site. Each page in the site links back to the Table of Contents page. The second definition of home page is the first page that opens when you start your Web browser. This type of home page might be an HTML document on your own computer. Some people create such home pages and include hyperlinks to Web sites that they frequently visit. If you are using a computer on your school's or employer's network, its Web browser might be configured to open the main page for the school or firm. The third definition of home page is the Web page that a particular Web browser loads the first time you use it. This page usually is stored at the Web site of the firm or other organization that created the Web browser software. Home pages that fall within the second or third definitions are sometimes called **start pages**.

Web Sites

Most people who create Web sites store all of the site's pages in one location, either on one computer or on one LAN. Some large Web sites, however, are distributed over a number of locations. In fact, it is sometimes difficult to determine where one Web site ends and another begins. Many people consider a Web site to be any group of Web pages that relates to one specific topic or organization, regardless of where the HTML documents are located.

Addresses on the Web

Maggie reminds you that there is no centralized control over the Internet. Therefore, no central starting point exists for the Web, which is a part of the Internet. However, each computer on the Internet does have a unique identification number, called an **IP (Internet Protocol) address**.

IP Addressing

The IP addressing system currently in use on the Internet uses a four-part number. Each part of the address is a number ranging from 0 to 255, and each part is separated from the previous part by a period, such as 106.29.242.17. You might hear a person pronounce this address as "one hundred six dot twenty-nine dot two four two dot seventeen." The combination of these four parts provides 4.2 billion possible addresses ($256 \times 256 \times 256 \times 256$). This number seemed adequate until 1998, when the accelerating growth of the Internet pushed the number of host computers from 5 to 30 million. Members of various Internet task forces are working to develop an alternative addressing system that will accommodate the projected growth; however, all of their working solutions require extensive hardware and software changes throughout the Internet.

Domain Name Addressing

Although each computer connected to the Internet has a unique IP address, most Web browsers do not use the IP address to locate Web sites and individual pages. Instead, they use domain name addressing. A **domain name** is a unique name associated with a specific IP address by a program that runs on an Internet host computer. This program, which coordinates the IP addresses and domain names for all computers attached to it, is called **DNS (domain name system) software**, and the host computer that runs this software is called a **domain name server**. Domain names can include any number of parts separated by periods; however, most domain names currently in use have only three or four parts. Domain names follow a hierarchical model that you can follow from top to bottom, if you read the name from right to left. For example, the domain name gsb.uchicago.edu is the computer connected to the Internet at the Graduate School of Business (gsb), which is an academic unit of the University of Chicago (uchicago), which is an educational institution (edu). No other computer on the Internet has the same domain name.

The last part of a domain name is called its **top-level domain**. For example, DNS software on the Internet host computer that is responsible for the "edu" domain keeps track of the IP address for all of the educational institutions in its domain, including "uchicago." Similar DNS software on the "uchicago" Internet host computer would keep track of the academic units' computers in its domain, including the "gsb" computer. Figure 3-5 shows the seven currently used top-level domain names.

Figure 3-5	TOP-LEVEL INTERNET DOMAIN NAMES

DOMAIN NAME	DESCRIPTION
com	Businesses and other commercial enterprises
edu	Postsecondary educational institutions
gov	U.S. government agency, bureau, or department
int	International organizations
mil	U.S. military unit or agency
net	Network service provider or resource
org	Other organizations, usually charitable or not-for-profit

In addition to these top-level domain names, Internet host computers outside the United States often use two-letter country domain names. For example, the domain name uq.edu.au is the domain name for the University of Queensland (uq), which is an educational institution (edu) in Australia (au). Recently, state and local government organizations in the United States have started using an additional domain name, "us." The "us" domain is also being used by U.S. primary and secondary schools as they begin to create Web presences because the "edu" domain is reserved for postsecondary educational institutions. Figure 3-6 shows 10 of the most frequently accessed country domain names.

| Figure 3-6 | FREQUENTLY ACCESSED INTERNET COUNTRY DOMAIN NAMES |

DOMAIN NAME	COUNTRY
au	Australia
ca	Canada
de	Germany
fi	Finland
fr	France
jp	Japan
nl	Netherlands
no	Norway
se	Sweden
uk	United Kingdom

The large increase in the number of host computers on the Internet has taxed the capacity of the existing top-level domain name structure, especially that of the "com" domain. A proposal to expand the available top-level domain names is currently under consideration by the Internet Policy Oversight Committee. The seven additional top-level domain names are shown in Figure 3-7.

| Figure 3-7 | PROPOSED ADDITIONAL TOP-LEVEL INTERNET DOMAIN NAMES |

DOMAIN NAME	DESCRIPTION
firm	Business firms
shop	Businesses that offer goods for sale
web	Entities that engage in World Wide Web-related activities
arts	Entities that engage in cultural and entertainment activities
rec	Entities that engage in recreational and entertainment activities
info	Entities that provide information services
nom	Individuals

Uniform Resource Locators

The IP address and the domain name each identify a particular computer on the Internet, but they do not indicate where a Web page's HTML document resides on that computer. To identify a Web page's exact location, Web browsers rely on Uniform Resource Locators. A **Uniform Resource Locator (URL)** is a four-part addressing scheme that tells the Web browser:

- What transfer protocol to use when transporting the file
- The domain name of the computer on which the file resides
- The pathname of the folder or directory on the computer on which the file resides
- The name of the file

The **transfer protocol** is the set of rules that the computers use to move files from one computer to another on an internet. The most common transfer protocol used on the Internet is the hypertext transfer protocol (HTTP). You can indicate the use of this protocol by typing http:// as the first part of the URL. People do use other protocols to transfer files on the Internet, but most of these protocols were used more frequently before the Web became part of the Internet. Two protocols that you still might see on the Internet are the file transfer protocol (FTP), which is indicated in a URL as ftp://, and the Telnet protocol, which is indicated in a URL as telnet://. FTP is just another way to transfer files, and Telnet is a set of rules for establishing a remote terminal connection to another computer.

The domain name is the Internet address of the computer described in the preceding section. The pathname describes the hierarchical directory or folder structure on the computer that stores the file. Most people are familiar with the structure used on Windows and DOS PCs, which uses the backslash character (\) to separate the structure levels. URLs follow the conventions established in the UNIX operating system that use the forward slash character (/) to separate the structure levels. The forward slash character works properly in a URL, even when it is pointing to a file on a Windows or DOS computer.

The filename is the name that the computer uses to identify the Web page's HTML document. On most computers, the filename extension of an HTML document is either .html or .htm. Although many PC operating systems are not case-sensitive, computers that use the UNIX operating system *are* case-sensitive. Therefore, if you are entering a URL that includes mixed-case and you do not know the type of computer on which the file resides, it is safer to retain the mixed-case format of the URL.

Not all URLs include a filename. If a URL does not include a filename, most Web browsers will load the file named index.html. The **index.html** filename is the default name for a Web site's home page. Figure 3-8 shows an example of a URL annotated to show its four parts.

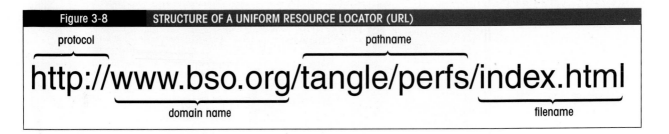

Figure 3-8 STRUCTURE OF A UNIFORM RESOURCE LOCATOR (URL)

protocol pathname

http://www.bso.org/tangle/perfs/index.html

domain name filename

The URL shown in Figure 3-8 uses the HTTP protocol and points to a computer that is connected to the Web (www) at the Boston Symphony Orchestra (bso), which is a not-for-profit organization (org). The Boston Symphony's Web page contains many different kinds of information about the orchestra. The path shown in Figure 3-8 includes two levels. The first level indicates that the information is about the orchestra's summer home at Tanglewood (tangle), and the second level indicates that the page will contain information about the orchestra's performances (perfs) at Tanglewood. The filename (index.html) indicates that this page is the home page in the Tanglewood performances folder or directory.

You tell Maggie how much you appreciate all of the help she has given you by explaining how you can use Internet addresses to find information on the Web. Now you understand that the real secret to finding good information on the Web is to know the right URLs. Maggie tells you that you can find URLs in many places; for example, newspapers and magazines often publish URLs of Web sites that might interest their readers. Friends who know about the subject area in which you are interested also are good sources. The best source, however, is the Web itself.

You are eager to begin learning how to use a Web browser, so Maggie explains some elements common to all Web browsers. Most Web browsers have similar functions, which make it easy to use any Web browser after you have learned how to use one.

Main Elements of Web Browsers

Now that you know a little more about Web sites, you start to wonder how you can make your computer communicate with the Internet. Maggie tells you that there are many Web browsers that turn your computer into a Web client that communicates through an Internet service provider (ISP) or a network connection with the Web servers. Two popular browsers are **Netscape Navigator**, or simply **Navigator**, and **Microsoft Internet Explorer**, or simply **Internet Explorer**. Each browser has been released in different versions; however, the steps in this book should work for most browsers.

Maggie reminds you that most Windows programs use a standard graphical user interface (GUI) design that includes a number of common screen elements. Figures 3-9 and 3-10 show the main elements of the Navigator and Internet Explorer program windows. These two Web browsers share common Windows elements: a title bar at the top of the window, a scroll bar on the right side of the window, and a status bar at the bottom of the window.

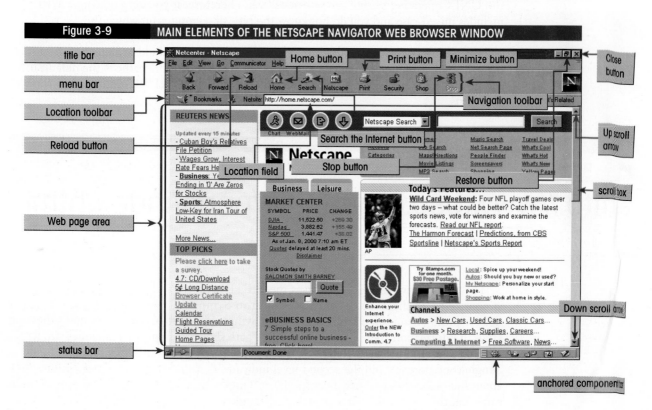

Figure 3-9   **MAIN ELEMENTS OF THE NETSCAPE NAVIGATOR WEB BROWSER WINDOW**

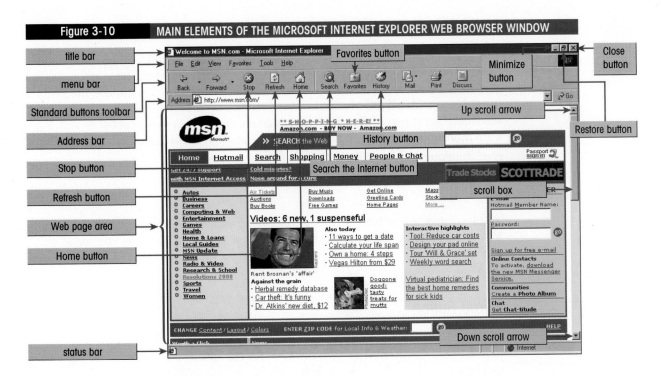

Figure 3-10 MAIN ELEMENTS OF THE MICROSOFT INTERNET EXPLORER WEB BROWSER WINDOW

The menu bar appears below the title bar. Many of the toolbar button functions in Navigator and Internet Explorer are similar, too. Next, Maggie describes each of these elements.

Title Bar

A Web browser's **title bar** shows the name of the open Web page and the Web browser's program name. As in all Windows programs, you can double-click the title bar to resize the window quickly. The title bar contains the Minimize, Restore, and Close buttons when the window is maximized to fill the screen. To restore a resized window to its original size, click the Maximize button.

Scroll Bars

A Web page can be much longer than a regular-sized document, so you often need to use the **scroll bar** at the right side of the program window to move the page up or down through the document window. You can use the mouse to click the **Up scroll** arrow or the **Down scroll** arrow to move the Web page up or down through the window's **Web page area**. Although most Web pages are designed to resize automatically when loaded into different browser windows with different display areas, some Web pages might be wider than your browser window. When this happens, the browser places another scroll bar at the bottom of the window and above the status bar, so you can move the page horizontally through the browser. You can also click and drag the scroll box in the scroll bar to move the Web page through the window.

Status Bar

The **status bar** at the bottom of the browser window includes information about the browser's operations. Each browser uses the status bar to deliver different information, but generally, the status bar indicates the name of the Web page that is loading, the load status (partial or complete), and important messages, such as "Document: Done." Some Web sites send messages as part of their Web pages that are displayed in the status bar as well. You will learn more about the specific functions of the status bar in Navigator and Internet Explorer in Sessions 3.2 and 3.3, respectively.

Menu Bar

The browser's **menu bar** provides a convenient way for you to execute typical File, Edit, View, and Help commands. In addition to these common Windows command sets, the menu bar also provides specialized command sets for the browser that allow you to navigate the Web.

Home Button

Clicking the **Home** button in Navigator or in Internet Explorer displays the home (or start) page for your browser. Most Web browsers let you specify a page that loads automatically every time you start the program. You might not be able to do this if you are in your school's computer lab because schools often set the start page for all browsers on campus and then lock that setting. If you are using your own computer, you can choose your own start page. Some people like to use a Web page that someone else has created and made available for others to use. One example of a start page is the My Virtual Reference Desk Web page, shown in Figure 3-11.

Figure 3-11   **MY VIRTUAL REFERENCE DESK WEB PAGE**

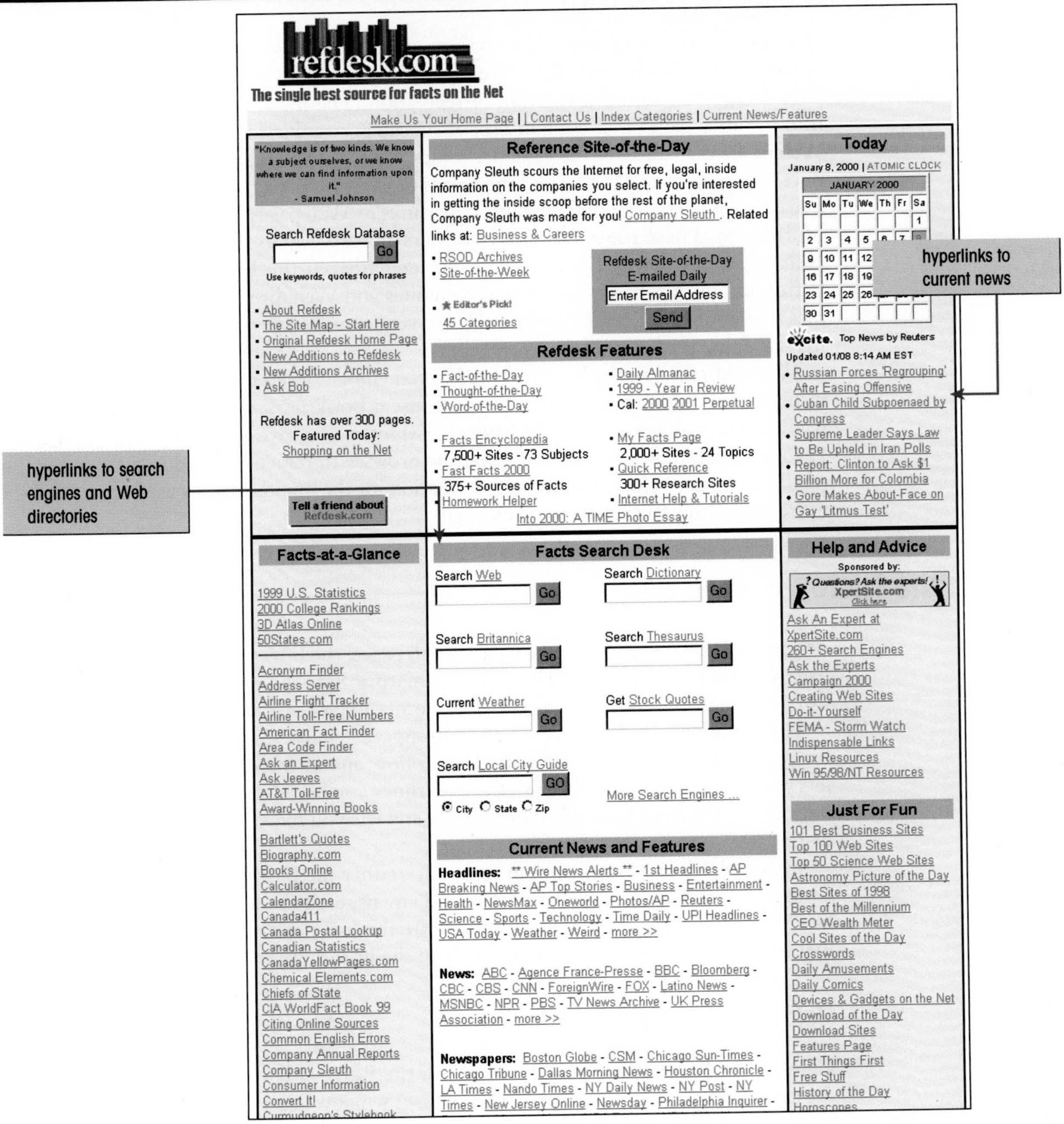

hyperlinks to search engines and Web directories

hyperlinks to current news

Pages such as the one shown in Figure 3-11 offer links to pages that many Web users frequently visit. The people and organizations that create these pages often sell advertising space on their pages to pay the cost of maintaining their sites.

Quick Access to Web Page Directories and Guides

You are starting to understand how to use the Internet to gather information about wind quintets. Maggie explains that a **Web directory** is a Web page that contains a list of Web page categories, such as education or recreation. The hyperlinks on a Web directory page lead to other pages that contain lists of subcategories that lead to other category lists and Web pages that relate to the category topics. **Web search engines** are Web pages that conduct searches of the Web to find the words or expressions that you enter. The result of such a search is a Web page that contains hyperlinks to Web pages that contain matching text or expressions. These pages can give new users an easy way to find information on the Web. Netscape and Internet Explorer each include a **Search the Internet** button. Clicking this button in either browser opens search engines and Web directories chosen by the companies that wrote the browser software. However, many people prefer to select their own tools for searching the Internet.

Web addresses can be long and hard to remember—even if you are using domain names instead of IP addresses. In Netscape, you use a **bookmark** to save the URL of a specific page so you can return to it. In Internet Explorer, you save the URL as a **favorite** in the Favorites folder. You realize that using the browser to remember important pages will be a terrific asset as you start collecting information for the quintet, so you ask Maggie to explain more about how to return to a Web page.

Using the History List

As you click the hyperlinks to go to new Web pages, the browser stores the locations of each page you visit during a single session in a **history list**. You click the **Back** button and the **Forward** button in both Navigator and Internet Explorer to move through the history list.

When you start your browser, both buttons are inactive (dimmed) because no history list for your new session exists yet. After you follow one or more hyperlinks, the Back button lets you retrace your path through the hyperlinks you have followed. Once you use the Back button, the Forward button becomes active and lets you move forward through the session's history list.

In most Web browsers, you can right-click either the Back or Forward button to display a portion of the history list. You can reload any page on the list by clicking its name in the list. The Back and Forward buttons duplicate the functions of commands on the browser's menu commands. You will learn more about the history list in Sessions 3.2 and 3.3.

Reloading a Web Page

Clicking the **Reload** button in Navigator or the **Refresh** button in Internet Explorer loads the same Web page that appears in the browser window again. The browser stores a copy of every Web page it displays on your computer's hard drive in a **cache** folder, which increases the speed at which the browser can display pages as you navigate through the history list. The cache folder lets the browser load the pages from the client instead of from the remote Web server.

When you click the Reload button or the Refresh button, the browser contacts the Web server to see if the Web page has changed since it was stored in the cache folder. If it has changed, the browser gets the new page from the Web server; otherwise, it loads the cache folder copy. If you want to force the browser to load the page from the Web server, hold down the Shift key as you click the Reload or Refresh button.

Stopping a Web Page Transfer

Sometimes a Web page takes a long time to load. When this occurs, you can click the **Stop** button in Navigator or Internet Explorer to halt the Web page transfer from the server; you can then click the hyperlink again. A second attempt may connect and transfer the page more quickly. You also might want to use the Stop button to abort a transfer when you accidentally click a hyperlink that you do not want to follow.

Returning to a Web Page

You use a Navigator bookmark or Internet Explorer's Favorites feature to store and organize a list of Web pages that you have visited so you can return to them easily without having to remember the URL or search for the page again. Navigator bookmarks and Internet Explorer favorites each work very much like a paper bookmark that you would use in a printed book: They mark the page at which you stopped reading.

You can save as many Navigator bookmarks or Internet Explorer favorites as you want to mark all of your favorite Web pages, so you can return to pages that you frequently use or pages that are important to your research or tasks. You could even bookmark every Web page you visit!

Keeping track of many bookmarks and favorites requires an organizing system. You store bookmarks or favorites in a system folder. Netscape stores bookmarks in one file on your computer, and Internet Explorer stores *each* favorite as a separate file on your computer. Storing each favorite separately, instead of storing all bookmarks together, offers somewhat more flexibility but uses more disk space. You can organize your bookmarks or favorites in many different ways to meet your needs. For example, you might store all of the bookmarks or favorites for Web pages that include information about wind quintets in a folder named "Wind Quintet Information."

Printing **and Saving Web Pages**

As you use your browser to view Web pages, you will find some pages that you want to print or store for future use. Web browsers include both the print and save capabilities. Web browsers allow you to save entire Web pages or just parts of the Web page, such as selections of text or graphics.

Printing a Web Page

The easiest way to print a Web page is to click the **Print** button in Navigator or Internet Explorer. In either case, the current page (or frame) that appears in the Web page area is sent to the printer. If the page contains light colors or many graphics, you might consider changing the printing options so the page prints without the background, or with all black text. You will learn how to change the print settings for Navigator and Internet Explorer in Sessions 3.2 and 3.3, respectively.

Although printing an entire Web page is often useful, there are times when you will want to save all or part of the page to disk, as you will see next.

Saving a Web Page

When you save a Web page to disk, you save only the text portion. If the Web page contains graphics, such as photos, drawings, or icons, they will not be saved with the HTML document. To save a graphic separately, right-click the graphic in the browser window, click Save

Image As or Save Picture As on the shortcut menu, and then save the graphic to the same location to which you saved the Web's HTML document. The graphics file is specified to appear on the HTML document as a hyperlink, so you might have to change the HTML code in the Web page to identify the location of the graphic. Copying the graphics files to the same disk as the HTML document will *usually* work. You will learn more about saving a Web page and its graphics in Sessions 3.2 and 3.3.

Reproducing Web Pages and Copyright Law

Maggie explains that there might be significant restrictions on the way that you can use information or images that you copy from another entity's Web site. The United States and other countries have copyright laws that govern the use of photocopies, audio or video recordings, and other reproductions of authors' original work. A **copyright** is the legal right of the author or other owner of an original work to control the reproduction, distribution, and sale of that work. A copyright comes into existence as soon as the work is placed into a tangible form, such as a printed copy, an electronic file, or a Web page. The copyright exists even if the work does not contain a copyright notice. If you do not know whether material that you find on the Web is copyrighted, the safest course of action is to assume that it is.

You can use limited amounts of copyrighted information in term papers and other reports that you prepare in an academic setting, but you must cite the source. Commercial use of copyrighted material is much more restricted. You should obtain permission from the copyright holder before using anything you copy from a Web page. It can be difficult to determine the owner of a source's copyright if no notice appears on the Web page; however, most Web pages provide a hyperlink to the e-mail address of the person responsible for maintaining the page. That person, often called a **webmaster**, usually can provide information about the copyright status of materials on the page.

Session 3.1 QUICK CHECK

1. True or False: Web browser software runs on a Web server computer.

2. Name two things you can accomplish using HTML tags.

3. Briefly define the term *home page*.

4. Name two examples of hypermedia.

5. A local political candidate is creating a Web site to help in her campaign for office. Describe some of the things she might want to include in her Web site.

6. What is the difference between IP addressing and domain name addressing?

7. Identify and interpret the meaning of each part of the following URL: http://www.savethetrees.org/main.html

8. What is the difference between a Web directory and a Web search engine?

Now that you understand the basic function of a browser and how to find information on the Web, you are ready to start using your browser to find information for the quintet. If you are using Navigator, your instructor will assign Session 3.2; if you are using Internet Explorer, your instructor will assign Session 3.3. The authors recommend, however, that you read both sessions because you might encounter a different browser on a public or employer's computer in the future.

SESSION 3.2

In this session, you will learn how to configure the Netscape Navigator Web browser and use it to display Web pages and follow hyperlinks to other Web pages. You will learn how to copy text and images from Web pages and how to mark pages so you can return to them easily.

Starting **Netscape Navigator**

To be effective in searching the Web for the Sunset Wind Quintet, Maggie is sure that you will want to become familiar with Netscape Navigator, from Netscape Communications Corporation, which is part of a suite of programs called Netscape Communicator. The other programs in the Communicator suite provide e-mail, discussion groups, realtime collaboration, and Web page creation tools. This overview assumes that you have Navigator installed on your computer. You should have your computer turned on so you can see the Windows desktop.

To start Navigator:

1. Click the **Start** button on the taskbar, point to **Programs**, point to **Netscape Communicator**, and then click **Netscape Navigator**. After a moment, Navigator opens.

   TROUBLE? If you cannot find Netscape Communicator on the Programs menu, check to see if a Netscape Navigator shortcut icon appears on the desktop, and then double-click it. If you do not see the shortcut icon, ask your instructor or technical support person for help. The program might be installed in a different folder on the computer you are using.

2. If the program does not fill the screen entirely, click the **Maximize** button on the Navigator program's title bar. Your screen should look like Figure 3-12.

Figure 3-12	NETSCAPE HOME PAGE

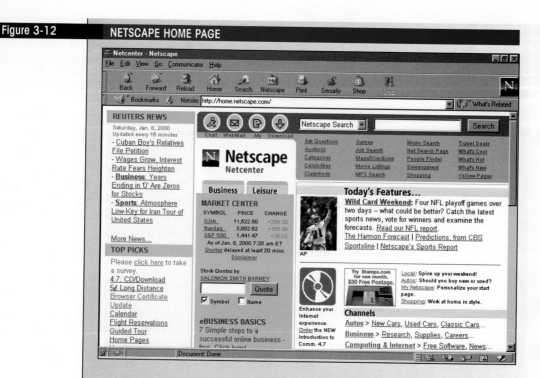

TROUBLE? Figure 3-12 shows the Netscape Netcenter home page, which is the page that Netscape Navigator opens the first time it starts. Your computer might be configured to open to a different Web page, or no page at all.

TROUBLE? If necessary, click View on the menu bar, click Show, and if Personal Toolbar has a check next to it, click to deselect the check so your screen looks like Figure 3-12.

TROUBLE? If a floating component bar, like the one shown in Figure 3-13, appears anywhere in your window, click its Close button to anchor it to the right edge of the status bar.

Figure 3-13	NETSCAPE COMMUNICATOR FLOATING COMPONENT BAR

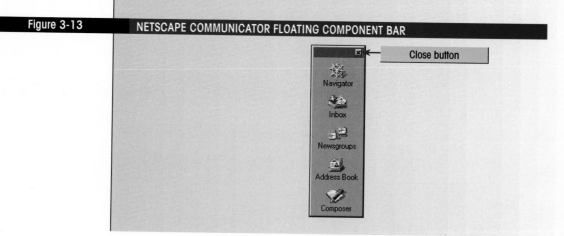

Now that you understand how to start Navigator, you tell Maggie that you are ready to start using it to find information on the Internet. To find information, you need to know how the Navigator toolbars and menu commands work.

Using **the Navigation Toolbar and Menu Commands**

The Navigation toolbar includes 11 buttons that execute frequently used commands for browsing the Web. Figure 3-14 shows the Navigation toolbar buttons and describes their functions. (Depending on which version of Navigator you are using, you might see different toolbar buttons. Use online Help to get more information about buttons not pictured in Figure 3-14.)

Figure 3-14	NAVIGATION TOOLBAR BUTTONS	
BUTTON	**BUTTON NAME**	**DESCRIPTION**
Back	Back	Moves to the last previously visited Web page
Forward	Forward	Moves to the next previously visited Web page
Reload	Reload	Reloads the current page
Home	Home	Loads the program's defined start page
Search	Search	Opens a Web page that has hyperlinks to Web search engines and directories
Netscape	My Netscape	Opens a version of the Netscape's Netcenter page that you can customize
Print	Print	Prints the current Web page
Security	Security	Shows security information about the Web page that is currently displayed
Shop	Shop	Opens the Netscape Shopping directory page
Stop	Stop	Stops the transfer of a new Web page
N	Netscape Home Page (Netcenter)	Opens the Netscape Netcenter page

In addition to the toolbar buttons, the Navigation toolbar contains a toolbar tab that you can click to hide the toolbar so there is more room to display a Web page in the Web page area. You can hide both the Navigation and Location toolbars so that the toolbar tabs fold up and remain visible, or you can hide the toolbars completely by using the options on the View menu, as you will see next.

REFERENCE WINDOW | RW

Hiding or showing a toolbar
- To hide the toolbar, click the toolbar tab for the toolbar that you want to hide. The toolbar tab will appear under any remaining toolbars.
or
- Click View on the menu bar, click Show, and then click the desired toolbar name to hide the toolbar.
- To show a hidden toolbar, click the toolbar tab for the toolbar you want to show.
or
- Click View on the menu bar, click Show, and then click the desired toolbar name to show the toolbar.

To hide the Navigation toolbar and then show it again:

1. Click the **Navigation toolbar** tab, which appears on the left edge of the Navigation toolbar. The toolbar will disappear and its toolbar tab appears under the Location toolbar.

2. Move the pointer to the Navigation toolbar tab below the Location toolbar and notice that the message indicates that you are pointing to the Navigation toolbar.

3. Click the **Navigation toolbar** tab. The Navigation toolbar appears above the Location toolbar.

You can use the toolbar tabs to hide or show the toolbars quickly. However, if you want to hide the toolbars and their tabs, you must use the View menu. The View menu commands are toggles. A **toggle** is like a pushbutton switch on a television set; you press the button once to turn on the television and press it a second time to turn it off.

To hide the Navigation toolbar using the View menu:

1. Click **View** on the menu bar.

2. Click **Show** and then click **Navigation Toolbar** to hide the Navigation toolbar and its toolbar tab. To see the Navigation toolbar again, you repeat the same steps.

   TROUBLE? If the Navigation Toolbar does not have a check mark next to it, then the Navigation toolbar already is hidden. Go to Step 3.

3. Click **View** on the menu bar, click **Show**, and then click **Navigation Toolbar** to show the toolbar again.

Now you are ready to use the Navigation toolbar buttons and the menu commands to browse the Web.

Using the Location Toolbar Elements

Maggie explains that there are five elements in the Location toolbar: the **Location toolbar** tab, the **Location** field, the **Page proxy** icon, the **Bookmarks** button, and the **What's Related** button. Figure 3-15 shows these five elements.

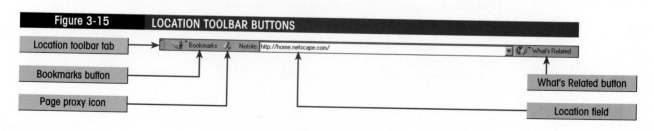

Figure 3-15   LOCATION TOOLBAR BUTTONS

Location toolbar tab

Bookmarks button

Page proxy icon

Bookmarks   Netsite: http://home.netscape.com/   What's Related

What's Related button

Location field

Hiding and Showing the Location Toolbar

You can click the Location toolbar tab or use the View menu commands to hide and show the Location toolbar, just as when you used the Navigation toolbar tab and the View menu commands to hide and show the Navigation toolbar. Clicking the Location toolbar tab hides the toolbar but keeps the tab visible so it folds up under any visible toolbars.

Entering a URL into the Location Field

Maggie tells you to use the **Location field** to enter URLs directly into Netscape Navigator. Marianna gave you the URL for the Pennsylvania Quintet, so you can see its Web page.

REFERENCE WINDOW   **RW**

Entering a URL in the Location field
- Click at the end of the current text in the Location field, and then backspace over the text that you want to delete.
- Type the URL to which you want to go.
- Press the Enter key to load the URL's Web page in the browser window.

To load the Pennsylvania Quintet's Web page:

1. Click in the Location field; if there is text in the Location field, click at the end of the text, and then press the **Backspace** key to delete it.

   TROUBLE? Make sure that you delete all of the text in the Location field so the text you type in Step 2 will be correct.

2. Type **http://www.course.com/newperspectives/internet2/** in the Location field to go to the Student Online Companion page on the Course Technology Web site. In this book, you will go to the Course Technology site and then click hyperlinks to go to individual Web pages.

3. Press the **Enter** key. The Location field's label changes from "Location" to "Go to" and the Student Online Companion Web page loads, as shown in Figure 3-16. When the entire page has loaded, the Location field's label will change back to "Location."

Figure 3-16   STUDENT ONLINE COMPANION WEB PAGE

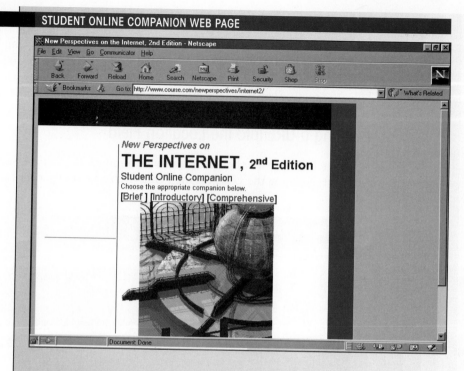

TROUBLE? If a Dial-Up Networking dialog box opens after you press the Enter key, click the Connect button. You must have an Internet connection to complete the steps in this tutorial.

4. Click the link for the book you are using to open the main page, click the **Tutorial 3** link to open the page that contains the links for this tutorial, and then click the **Session 3.2** link in the left frame to see the links in the right frame.

5. Click the **Pennsylvania Quintet** link. The Web page opens, as shown in Figure 3-17.

Figure 3-17   PENNSYLVANIA QUINTET'S WEB PAGE

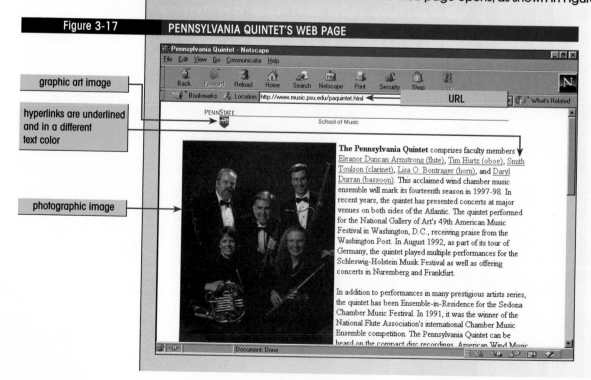

TROUBLE? The Pennsylvania Quintet might change its Web page, so your Web page might look different from the one shown in Figure 3-17. If this Web page is deleted from the server, then you might see an entirely different Web page. However, the steps should work the same.

6. Read the Web page, and then click the **Back** button to return to the Student Online Companion page.

You like the format of the Pennsylvania Quintet's home page, so you want to make sure that you can go back to that page later if you need to review its contents. Maggie explains that you can write down the URL so you can refer to it later, but an easier way is to store the URL in a **bookmark file** to save in the Navigator program for future use.

Creating a Bookmark for a Web Site

You use a **bookmark** to store and organize a list of Web pages that you have visited so you can return to them easily. You use the **Bookmarks** button or the **Page proxy** icon on the Location toolbar in Netscape's bookmarking system. You can use the Bookmarks button to add new bookmarks, to open the Bookmarks menu, or to open the Bookmarks window. Figure 3-18 shows a Bookmarks menu that contains bookmarks that are sorted into categories according to the user's needs.

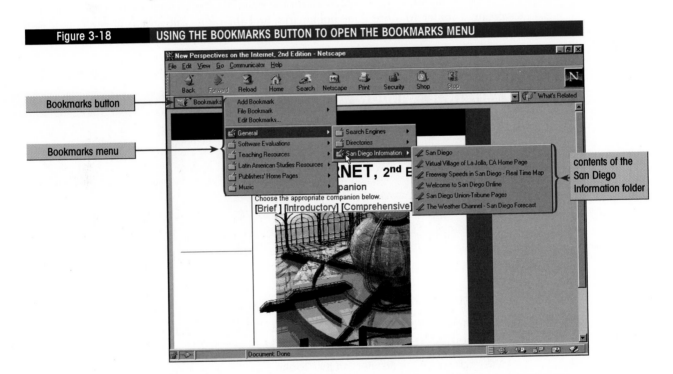

| Figure 3-18 | USING THE BOOKMARKS BUTTON TO OPEN THE BOOKMARKS MENU |

The hierarchical structure of the bookmark file is easy to see in Figure 3-18. The six Web pages shown in the San Diego Information folder provide information about San Diego.

A **Bookmarks window** provides the same information as the cascading Bookmarks menus, but it also includes tools for editing and rearranging the bookmarks. For example, you can use the Bookmarks window menu commands to create new folders, or you can use the drag and drop method to move Web pages to another folder or to move folders to new locations. Figure 3-19 shows the same set of bookmarks in the Bookmarks window, where you can see more details about the user's bookmarks and their organization.

Figure 3-19   EXAMINING BOOKMARKS IN THE BOOKMARKS WINDOW

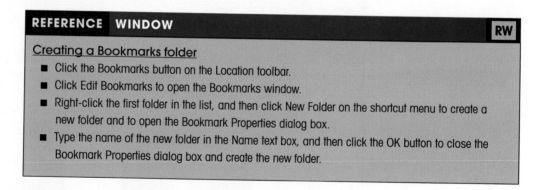

You decide to create a bookmark for the Pennsylvania Quintet Web page. First, you will create a folder to store your bookmarks, and then you will save your bookmark in that folder. You might not work on the same computer again, so you will save a copy of the bookmark file to your Data Disk for future use.

REFERENCE WINDOW   **RW**

Creating a Bookmarks folder
- Click the Bookmarks button on the Location toolbar.
- Click Edit Bookmarks to open the Bookmarks window.
- Right-click the first folder in the list, and then click New Folder on the shortcut menu to create a new folder and to open the Bookmark Properties dialog box.
- Type the name of the new folder in the Name text box, and then click the OK button to close the Bookmark Properties dialog box and create the new folder.

To create a new Bookmarks folder:

1. Click the **Bookmarks** button on the Location toolbar to open the Bookmarks menu, and then click **Edit Bookmarks** to open the Bookmarks window.

2. Right-click the first item in the Bookmarks window; usually, this item is "Main Bookmarks" or "Bookmarks for <name>," but it might have another title on your computer. After you right-click the first item, a shortcut menu opens.

3. Click **New Folder** on the shortcut menu to open the Bookmark Properties dialog box. The text "New Folder" appears selected in the Name text box. To change the new folder's name, you just type the new name.

4. Type **Wind Quintet Information** in the Name text box, and then click the **OK** button to close the Bookmark Properties dialog box and create the new Wind Quintet Information folder in the bookmark file. The new folder should appear under the first item in the Bookmarks window, as shown in Figure 3-20.

| Figure 3-20 | CREATING A BOOKMARK FOLDER |

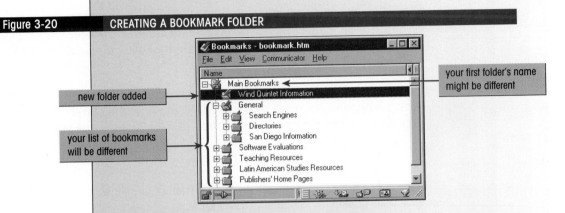

TROUBLE? If your Wind Quintet Information folder appears in a different location, don't worry. Just make sure that the folder appears in the Bookmarks window.

5. Click the **Close** button on the Bookmarks window title bar to close the Bookmarks window.

Now that you have created a folder, you can save your bookmark for the Pennsylvania Quintet's Web page in the new folder. However, first you must return to the Web page that you want to bookmark.

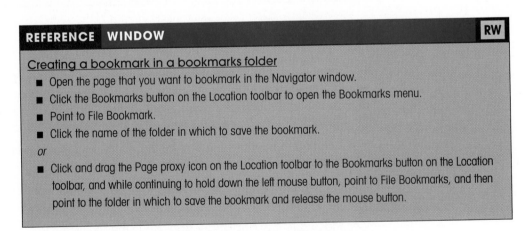

REFERENCE WINDOW   **RW**

Creating a bookmark in a bookmarks folder
- Open the page that you want to bookmark in the Navigator window.
- Click the Bookmarks button on the Location toolbar to open the Bookmarks menu.
- Point to File Bookmark.
- Click the name of the folder in which to save the bookmark.

or
- Click and drag the Page proxy icon on the Location toolbar to the Bookmarks button on the Location toolbar, and while continuing to hold down the left mouse button, point to File Bookmarks, and then point to the folder in which to save the bookmark and release the mouse button.

To save a bookmark for a Web page in a folder:

1. Click the **Forward** button on the Navigation toolbar to return to the Pennsylvania Quintet Web page.

2. Click the **Bookmarks** button on the Location toolbar to open the Bookmarks menu.

3. Point to **File Bookmark**, and then click the **Wind Quintet Information** folder. Now, the bookmark is saved in the correct folder. You can test your bookmark by using the bookmark to visit the site.

4. Click the **Back** button on the Navigation toolbar to go to the previous Web page.

5. Click the **Bookmarks** button on the Location toolbar, point to **Wind Quintet Information**, and then click **Pennsylvania Quintet**. The Pennsylvania Quintet page opens in the browser, which means that you created the bookmark successfully.

   TROUBLE? If the Pennsylvania Quintet page does not open, click Edit Bookmarks on the Bookmarks menu, make sure that you have the correct URL for the page, and then repeat the steps. If you still have trouble, ask your instructor or technical support person for help.

Because you might need to visit the Pennsylvania Quintet page from another client, you can save your bookmark file on your Data Disk.

REFERENCE WINDOW   RW

Saving a bookmark to a floppy disk
- Click the Bookmarks button on the Location toolbar, and then click Edit Bookmarks to open the Bookmarks window.
- Click File on the menu bar, and then click Save As to open the Save bookmarks file dialog box.
- Click the Save in list arrow, and then change to the drive that contains your disk.
- Click the Save button to save the bookmark file and close the dialog box.

To store the revised bookmarks file to your floppy disk:

1. Click the **Bookmarks** button on the Location toolbar, and then click **Edit Bookmarks** to open the Bookmarks window. When you save your bookmarks, you save all of the bookmarks, not just the one that you need: Remember from Session 3.1 that Navigator stores *all* of your bookmarks in a single file.

2. Click **File** on the menu bar of the Bookmarks window, and then click **Save As** to open the Save bookmarks file dialog box.

3. Click the **Save in** list arrow, change to the drive that contains your Data Disk (usually, this is 3½ Floppy (A:)), and then double-click the **Tutorial.03** folder.

4. Make sure that **bookmark** appears in the File name text box, and then click the **Save** button.

   TROUBLE? Your computer might be configured to display file extensions, so you might see bookmark.htm in the File name text box, which is also correct.

   TROUBLE? If bookmark or bookmark.htm does not appear in the File name text box, click in the File name text box, type bookmark.htm, and then click the Save button.

5. Close the Bookmarks window.

When you use another computer, you can open the bookmark file from your Data Disk by starting Navigator, clicking the Bookmarks button on the Location toolbar, clicking Edit Bookmarks, clicking File on the menu bar, and then clicking Open Bookmarks File. Change to the drive that contains your Data Disk, and then open the bookmark.htm file from the disk. Your bookmark file will open in the Bookmarks window, and then you can use it as you practiced.

Hyperlink **Navigation with the Mouse**

Now you know how to use Navigator to find information that will help you with the Sunset Wind Quintet. Maggie tells you that the easiest way to move from one Web page to another is to use the mouse to click hyperlinks that the authors of Web pages embed in their HTML documents. You can also right-click the mouse on the background of a Web page to open a shortcut menu that includes navigation options.

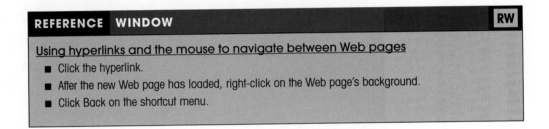

REFERENCE WINDOW   RW

Using hyperlinks and the mouse to navigate between Web pages
■ Click the hyperlink.
■ After the new Web page has loaded, right-click on the Web page's background.
■ Click Back on the shortcut menu.

To follow a hyperlink to a Web page and return using the mouse:

1. Click the **Back** button on the Navigation toolbar to go back to the Student Online Companion page, click the **Lewis Music** link to open that page, and then point to the **Instrument Accessories** hyperlink shown in Figure 3-21 so your pointer changes to 🖑.

Figure 3-21   LEWIS MUSIC HOME PAGE

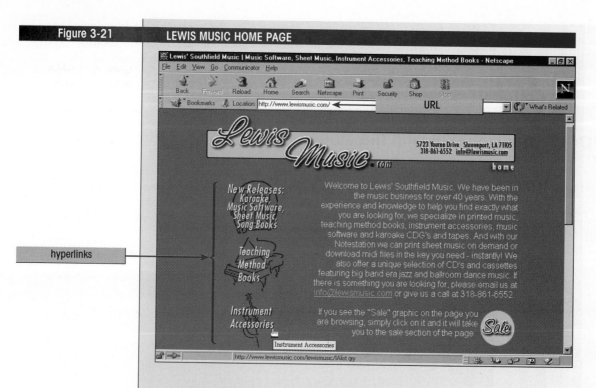

hyperlinks

2. Click the **Instrument Accessories** hyperlink to load the page. Watch the second panel in the status bar. When the shadow disappears, you know that Navigator has loaded the full page.

3. Right-click anywhere in the Web page area to open the shortcut menu, as shown in Figure 3-22.

Figure 3-22   USING THE SHORTCUT MENU TO GO BACK TO THE PREVIOUS PAGE

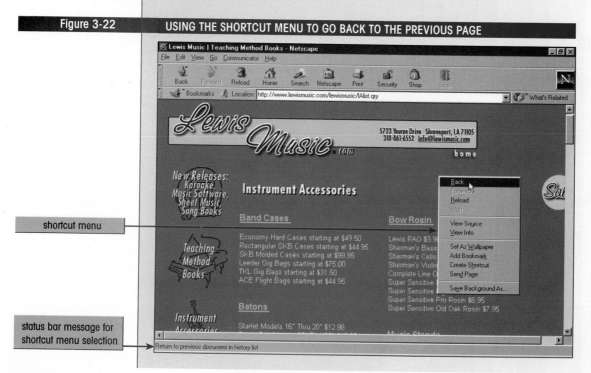

shortcut menu

status bar message for
shortcut menu selection

TROUBLE? If you right-click a hyperlink, your shortcut menu will display a longer list than the one shown in Figure 3-22, and the Back item will be third in the list instead I first. If you don't see the shortcut menu shown in Figure 3-22, click anywhere outside of the shortcut menu to close it, and then repeat Step 3.

TROUBLE? Web pages change frequently, so the Instrument Accessories page you see might look different from the one shown in Figure 3-22, but right-clicking anywhere on the Web page area will still work.

4. Click **Back** on the shortcut menu to go back to the Lewis Music home page.

5. Repeat Step 4 to return to the Student Online Companion page.

You are beginning to get a good sense of how to move from one Web page to another and back again, but Maggie tells you that you have mastered only one technique of many. She explains that the Navigation toolbar and the menu bar offer many tools for accessing and using Web sites.

Using the History List

In Session 3.1 you learned that the Back and Forward buttons let you move to and from previously visited pages. These buttons duplicate the functions of the menu bar's Go command. Clicking Go opens a menu that lets you move back and forward through a portion of the history list and allows you to choose a specific Web page from that list. You also can open a full copy of the history list.

To view the history list for this session:

1. Click **Communicator** on the menu bar, click **Tools**, and then click **History** to open the History window, as shown in Figure 3-23.

Figure 3-23	VIEWING THE HISTORY LIST

entries in your history list will be different

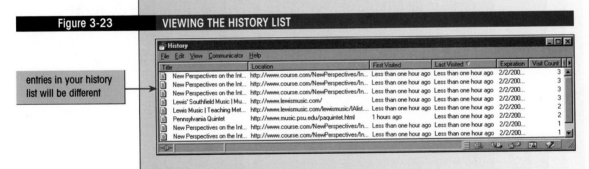

TROUBLE? The History window that appears on your computer might be a different size and contain different entries from the one that appears in Figure 3-23. You can resize the window by clicking and dragging its edges. You can resize the columns in the window by clicking and dragging on the edges of the column headers.

To return to a page, double-click the page in the list. You can change the way that pages are listed by using the commands on the View menu; for example, you can list the pages by title or in the order in which you visited them.

2. Click the **Close** button on the History window title bar to close it.

Reloading a Web Page

You learned in Session 3.1 that clicking the **Reload** button on the Navigator toolbar loads again the Web page that currently appears in the browser window. You can force Navigator to get the page from the Web server by pressing the Shift key when you click the Reload button.

Going Home

The **Home** button displays the home (or start) page for your copy of Navigator. You can go to the Netscape Netcenter page, which is the software's default installation home page, by clicking the **Netscape Home Page** button on the Navigator toolbar. You cannot change the page that loads by clicking the Navigator Home Page button, but you can change the default URL that opens when you click the Home button by using the Preferences dialog box.

REFERENCE   WINDOW   **RW**

Changing the default home page

■ Click Edit on the menu bar, and then click Preferences.

■ Click Navigator in the Category list.

■ In the Navigator starts with section, click an option button to indicate whether you want Navigator to open with a blank page, the last page visited, or a home page that you specify.

■ If you chose to specify a home page, delete the contents of the Location field, and then enter the URL for the home page or use the Browse button to find an HTML document on your computer or LAN that you want to use as your home page.

■ Click the OK button to close the Preferences dialog box.

To modify the Home navigation button settings:

1. Click **Edit** on the menu bar, and then click **Preferences** to open that dialog box.

2. Click **Navigator** in the Category list. See Figure 3-24.

Figure 3-24   CHANGING THE HOME PAGE

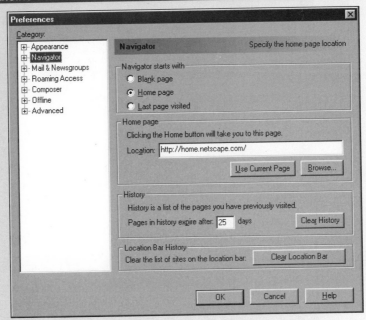

3. To have Navigator open with a **Blank page**, the **Home page** you specify, or the **Last page visited**, click the corresponding option button in the Navigator starts with section of the Preferences dialog box.

   TROUBLE? You might not be able to change these and the following settings if you are using a computer in your school lab or at your office. Some organizations set the home page defaults on all of their computers and lock those settings.

   To specify a home page, select the text in the Location field in the Home page section of the Preferences dialog box shown in Figure 3-24 and enter the URL of the Web page you would like to use. If you loaded the Web page that you would like to be your new home page into Navigator before beginning these steps, you can click the Use Current Page button to place its URL into the Location field. You also can specify an HTML document on your computer or LAN by clicking the Browse button and selecting the disk drive and folder location of that HTML document.

4. Click the **Cancel** button to close the dialog box without making any changes.

Printing a Web Page

The **Print** button on the Navigation toolbar lets you print the current Web frame or page. You can use this button to make a printed copy of most Web pages. (Some Web pages disable the Print command.)

REFERENCE WINDOW   **RW**

Printing the current Web page
- Click the Print button on the Navigation toolbar.
- Use the Print dialog box to choose the printer you want to use, the pages you want to print, and the number of copies you want to make of each page.
- Click the OK button to print the page(s).

To print a Web page:

1. Click in the main (right) frame of the Student Online Companion page to select it.

2. Click the **Print** button on the Navigation toolbar to open the Print dialog box shown in Figure 3-25.

Figure 3-25   **PRINT DIALOG BOX**

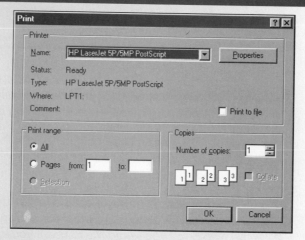

3. Make sure that the printer in the Name text box shows the printer you want to use; if necessary, click the Name list arrow to change the selection.

4. Click the **Pages** option button in the Print range section of the Print dialog box, type **1** in the **from** text box, press the **Tab** key, and then type **1** in the **to** text box to specify that you want to print only the first page.

5. Make sure that the Number of copies text box shows that you want to print one copy.

6. Click the **OK** button to print the Web page and close the Print dialog box.

Changing the Settings for Printing a Web Page

You already have seen how to print Web pages using the basic options available in the Print dialog box. You also learned how to store a bookmark so you can return to a Web page later. Usually, the default settings in the Print dialog box are fine for printing a Web page, but you can use the Page Setup dialog box to change the way a Web page prints. Figure 3-26 shows the Page Setup dialog box, and Figure 3-27 describes its settings.

Figure 3-26   PAGE SETUP OPTIONS FOR PRINTING WEB PAGES

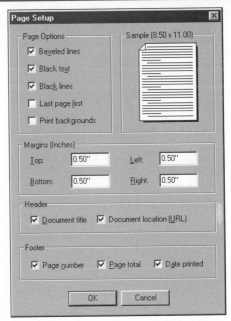

Figure 3-27   PAGE SETUP DIALOG BOX OPTIONS

OPTION	DESCRIPTION	USE
Black Text	Prints all of the text on a Web page as black.	Use when the Web page contains text set in light colors, so it will be legible when printed.
Black Lines	Prints all of the lines on a Web page as black.	Use when the Web page contains light-colored lines, so they will be legible when printed.
Last Page First	Reverses the normal order in which pages are printed.	Some printers eject pages face up. Using this setting will correctly collate the Web page printout.
Print backgrounds	Prints a Web page background, if there is one on the page.	You should leave this option off unless you are using a color printer. Backgrounds can render text and images illegible, and dark colors can waste your printer's toner or ink.
Margins	Use to change the margin of the printed page.	Normally, you should leave the default settings, but you can change the right, left, top, or bottom margins as needed.
Header	Prints the Web page's document title and/or document location (URL).	Selecting these options lets you print the name and location of the page for later reference.
Footer	Prints the Web page's page number, the total number of pages, or the date that the page is printed.	Selecting these options provides a record of the page number, total number of pages, and the date that you printed the page.

When printing long Web pages, another print option that is extremely useful for saving paper is to reduce the font size of the Web pages before you print them. To do this, click Edit on the menu bar, click Preferences, click the Fonts category, and then use the Size list arrow to decrease the size of the font used in the Web page. See Figure 3-28.

Figure 3-28 USING THE PREFERENCES DIALOG BOX TO CHANGE THE WEB PAGE FONT SIZE

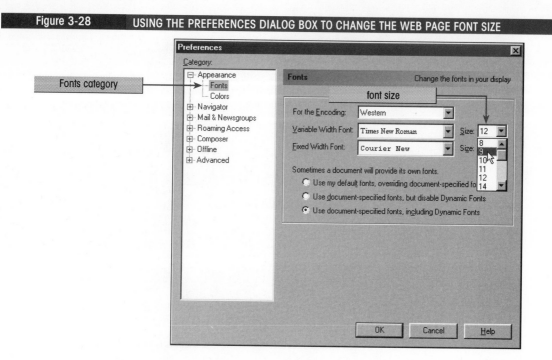

Checking Web Page Security Features

The **Security** button on the Navigation toolbar lets you check some of the security elements of a Web page. This button displays either an open padlock icon or a closed padlock icon. The icon on the Security button will correspond to the icon displayed in the left section of the status bar at the bottom of the Web page to indicate whether the Web page was encrypted during transmission from the Web server. **Encryption** is a way of scrambling and encoding data transmissions that reduces the risk that a person who intercepts the Web page as it travels across the Internet will be able to decode and read the page's contents. Web sites use encrypted transmission to send and receive information, such as credit card numbers, to ensure privacy. You can obtain more information about the details of the encryption used on a Web page by examining the Security Info dialog box that opens when you click the Security button on the Navigation toolbar. Figure 3-29 shows the Security Info dialog box for an encrypted Web page after the user clicked the Security button on the Navigation toolbar.

| Figure 3-29 | SECURITY INFO WINDOW FOR AN ENCRYPTED WEB PAGE |

Netscape

Security Info

Security Info
Passwords
Navigator
Messenger
Java/JavaScript
Certificates
   Yours
   People
   Web Sites
   Signers
Cryptographic
Modules

Encryption

This page **was encrypted**. This means it was difficult for other people to view this page when it was loaded.

You can examine your copy of the certificate for this page and check the identity of the web site. To see the certificate for this web site, click **View Certificate**. For complete details on all the files on this page and their certificates, click **Open Page Info**.

| View Certificate | Open Page Info |

Verification

- Take a look at the page's Certificate.
- Make sure that this is the site you think it is. This page comes from

OK   Cancel   Help

Getting **Help in Netscape Navigator**

The Netscape Communicator suite includes a comprehensive online Help facility for all of the programs in the suite, including Navigator. You open the Help Contents window to use Help.

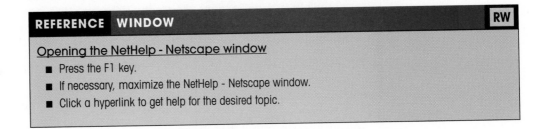

REFERENCE WINDOW   RW

Opening the NetHelp - Netscape window
- Press the F1 key.
- If necessary, maximize the NetHelp - Netscape window.
- Click a hyperlink to get help for the desired topic.

To open the Navigator help window:

1. Press the **F1** key, and then click the **Maximize** button on the NetHelp - Netscape window, which provides help for all the programs in the Netscape Communicator Suite.

2. Click the **Browsing the Web** hyperlink to get help for the Navigator program. Examine the page shown in Figure 3-30, and use the scroll box or scroll down button to move down the page.

Figure 3-30 OPENING THE NETHELP – NETSCAPE WINDOW

Contents icon

Index icon

hyperlinks to Help contents

Back button

Forward button

Print Help topic button

Exit Help button

NetHelp - Netscape

Contents

Index

Click one:

Browsing the Web

Using Email

Creating Web Pages

Newsgroups

Working Offline

Security

Troubleshooting

BROWSING THE WEB

Finding Information on the Web

Viewing a Page

Moving to Another Page

Retracing Your Steps

Retracing Your Steps in Detail: The History List

Viewing a Page's Information

Viewing a Page's Source Code

Searching Within a Page

BROWSING THE WEB

Bookmarking Your Favorite Web Sites

Creating a Bookmark

Creating an Internet Shortcut

Organizing Your Bookmarks

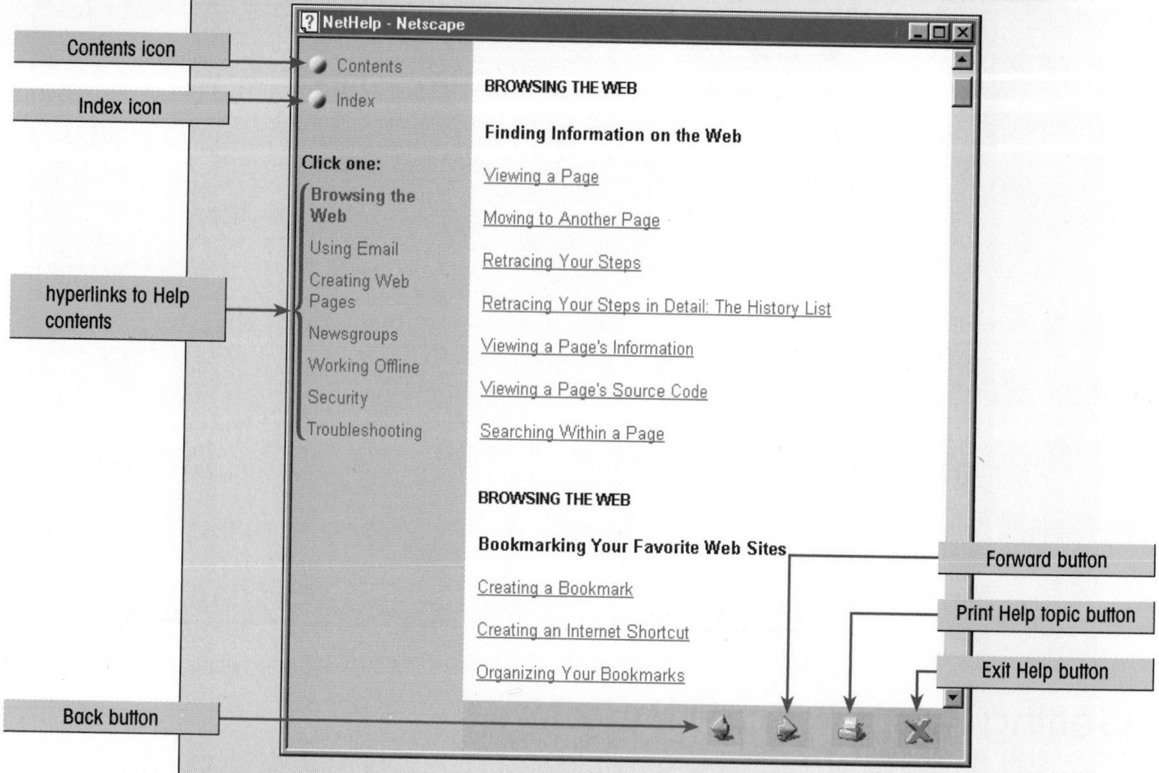

You can click any of the Contents hyperlinks to obtain help on the topics listed. You can also click the Index icon to obtain an alphabetized, searchable list of hyperlinks to specific terms used in the Netscape Help pages, or you can click the Find icon, which opens the standard Windows Find dialog box, and enter search terms.

3. Click the **Close** button to close the NetHelp – Netscape window and return to Navigator.

You are now convinced that you have all of the tools you need to successfully find information on the Web. Marianna probably will be interested in seeing the Pennsylvania Quintet Web page, but you are not sure if she will have Internet access while she's touring. Maggie says that you can save the Web page on disk, so Marianna can open the page locally in her Web browser using the files you saved on that disk.

Using **Navigator to Save a Web Page**

You have learned how to use most of the Navigator tools for loading Web pages and saving bookmarks. Now, Maggie wants you to learn how to save a Web page. Sometimes, you will want to store entire Web pages on disk; at other times, you will only want to store selected portions of Web page text or particular graphics from a Web page.

Saving a Web Page

You like the Pennsylvania Quintet's Web site and want to save the page on disk so you can send it to Marianna. That way, she can review it without having an Internet connection. To save a Web page, you must have the page open in Navigator.

REFERENCE WINDOW RW

Saving a Web page to a floppy disk

- Open the Web page in Navigator.
- Click File on the menu bar, and then click Save As to open the Save As dialog box.
- Click the Save in list arrow, and change to the drive on which to save the Web page.
- Accept the default filename, or change the filename, if you want; however, retain the file extension .htm or .html.
- Click the Save button to save the Web page to the floppy disk.

To save the Web page on your Data Disk:

1. Use your bookmark to return to the Pennsylvania Quintet page.

2. Click **File** on the menu bar, and then click **Save As** to open the Save As dialog box.

3. Click the **Save in** list arrow, click the drive that contains your Data Disk (usually, this is 3½ Floppy (A:)), and then double-click the **Tutorial.03** folder. You will accept the default filename of paquintet.htm.

4. Click the **Save** button. Now the HTML document for the Pennsylvania Quintet's home page is saved on your Data Disk. When you send it to Marianna, she can open her Web browser and then use the Open command on the File menu to open the Web page.

If the Web page contains graphics, such as photos, drawings, or icons, you should note that these items will not be saved with the HTML document. To save the graphics, right-click them in the browser window, click Save Image As, and then save the graphic to the same location as the Web's HTML document. The graphics file is specified to appear on the HTML document as a hyperlink, so you might have to change the HTML code in the Web page to identify its location. Copying the graphics files to the same disk as the HTML document will *usually* work.

Saving Web Page Text to a File

Maggie suggests that you might want to know how to save portions of Web page text to a file, so that you can save only the text from the Web page and use it in other programs. You will use WordPad to receive the text you will copy from a Web page, but any word processor or text editor will work.

Marianna just called to let you know that the quintet will play a concert in Cleveland on a Friday night, and she asks you to identify other opportunities for scheduling local concerts during the following weekend. Often, museums are willing to book small ensembles for weekend afternoon programs, and Marianna has given you the URL for the Cleveland Museum of Art. You will visit the site and then get the museum's address and telephone number so you can contact it about scheduling a concert.

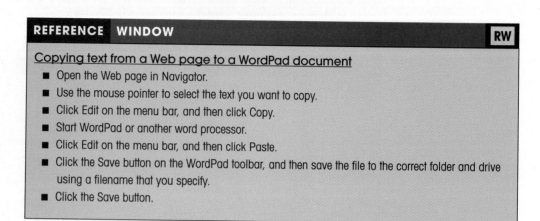

REFERENCE WINDOW   **RW**

<u>Copying text from a Web page to a WordPad document</u>
- Open the Web page in Navigator.
- Use the mouse pointer to select the text you want to copy.
- Click Edit on the menu bar, and then click Copy.
- Start WordPad or another word processor.
- Click Edit on the menu bar, and then click Paste.
- Click the Save button on the WordPad toolbar, and then save the file to the correct folder and drive using a filename that you specify.
- Click the Save button.

To copy text from a Web page and save it to a file:

1. Use the **Back** button to return to the Student Online Companion page, and then click the **Cleveland Museum of Art** link to open that Web page in the browser window.

2. Click the **address** hyperlink in the left frame on the Web page to open the museum information page in the main (right) frame.

3. Click and drag the mouse pointer over the address and telephone number to select it, as shown in Figure 3-31.

Figure 3-31   **SELECTING TEXT ON A WEB PAGE**

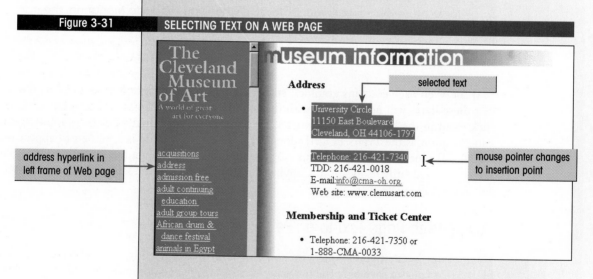

4. Click **Edit** on the menu bar, and then click **Copy** to copy the selected text to the Windows Clipboard.

Now, you can start WordPad and paste the copied text into a new document.

To start and copy the text into WordPad:

1. Click the **Start** button on the taskbar, point to **Programs**, point to **Accessories**, and then click **WordPad** to start the program and open a new document.

2. Click the **Paste** button on the WordPad toolbar to paste the text into the WordPad document, as shown in Figure 3-32.

Figure 3-32	PASTING TEXT FROM A WEB PAGE INTO A WORDPAD DOCUMENT

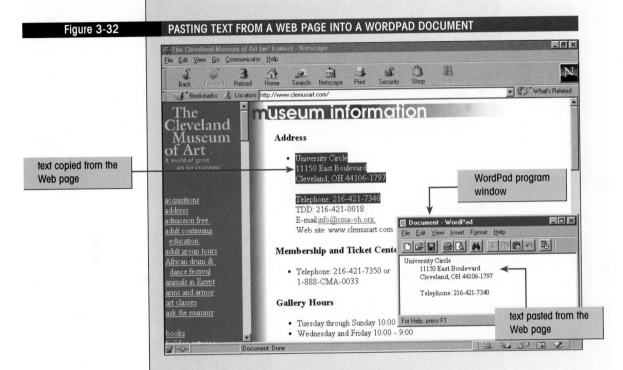

TROUBLE? If the WordPad toolbar does not appear, click View on the menu bar, click Toolbar to turn it on, and then repeat Step 2. Your WordPad program window might be a different size from the one shown in Figure 3-32, which does not affect the steps.

3. Click the **Save** button on the WordPad toolbar to open the Save As dialog box.

4. Click the **Save in** list arrow, change to the drive that contains your Data Disk, and then double-click the **Tutorial.03** folder.

5. Select any text that is in the File name text box, type **CMoA-Address.txt**, and then click the **Save** button to save the file. Now, the address and phone number of the museum is saved in a file on your Data Disk for future reference.

6. Click the **Close** button on the WordPad title bar to close it.

Later, you will contact the museum. As you examine the hyperlinks in the left frame of the Cleveland Museum of Art Web page, you notice a hyperlink titled "how to get here." Clicking the "how to get here" hyperlink loads a page that contains directions and information about transportation to the museum. You find that it includes a hyperlink to a street map of the area surrounding the museum.

Saving a Web Page Graphic to Disk

You decide that the Web page with directions and transportation information might be helpful to Marianna, so you decide to save the map graphic on your disk. You can then send the file to Marianna so she has a resource for getting to the museum.

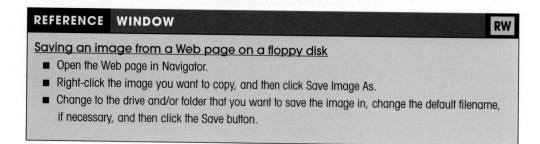

REFERENCE WINDOW   RW

Saving an image from a Web page on a floppy disk
- Open the Web page in Navigator.
- Right-click the image you want to copy, and then click Save Image As.
- Change to the drive and/or folder that you want to save the image in, change the default filename, if necessary, and then click the Save button.

To save the street map image on a floppy disk:

1. Click the **how to get here** hyperlink in the left frame of the Cleveland Museum's home page, and then click the **street map** hyperlink on the Getting around - Directions and Transportation Web page in the main (right) frame. Do not click the hyperlink to the Adobe download version of the map.

2. Right-click the map image to open its shortcut menu, as shown in Figure 3-33.

| Figure 3-33 | SAVING THE MAP IMAGE TO DISK |

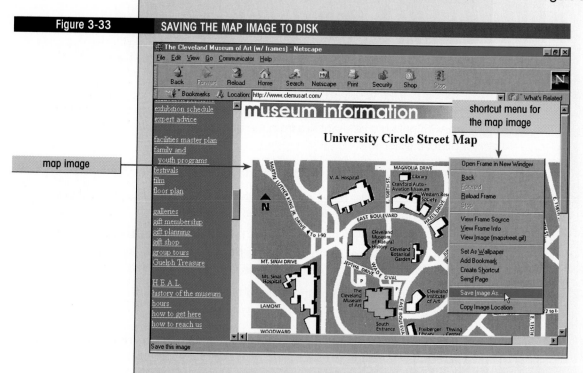

3. Click **Save Image As** on the shortcut menu to open the Save As dialog box.

4. Click the Save in list arrow, change to the drive that contains your Data Disk, and double-click the **Tutorial.03** folder, if necessary. You will accept the default filename, mapstreet, so click the **Save** button. Now the image is saved on your Data Disk, and you can send the file to Marianna. Marianna can use her Web browser to open the image file and print it.

5. Close your Web browser and your dial-up connection, if necessary.

Now you can send a disk to Marianna so she has the Pennsylvania Wind Quintet Web page and a map that shows her how to get to the museum. Marianna is pleased to hear of your progress in using the Web to find information for the quintet.

Session 3.2 QUICK CHECK

1. Describe three ways to load a Web page in the Navigator browser.

2. You can use the _____ in Navigator to visit previously visited sites during your Web session.

3. When would you use the Reload command?

4. What happens when you click the Home button on the Navigation toolbar?

5. Some Web servers _____ Web pages before returning them to the client to prevent unauthorized access.

6. True or False: You can identify an encrypted Web page when viewing it in Navigator.

7. What is a Netscape Navigator bookmark?

If your instructor assigns Session 3.3, continue reading. Otherwise, complete the Review Assignments at the end of this tutorial.

SESSION 3.3

In this session, you will learn how to configure the Microsoft Internet Explorer Web browser and use it to display Web pages. You will learn how to use Internet Explorer to follow hyperlinks from one Web page to another and how to record the URLs of sites to which you would like to return. Also, you will print and save Web pages.

Starting Microsoft Internet Explorer

Microsoft Internet Explorer is Microsoft's Web browser that installs with Windows 95, Windows 98, or Windows 2000. This introduction assumes that you have Internet Explorer installed on your computer. You should have your computer turned on and open to the Windows desktop to begin.

To start Internet Explorer:

1. Click the **Start** button on the taskbar, point to **Programs**, point to **Internet Explorer**, and then click **Internet Explorer**. After a moment, Internet Explorer opens.

TROUBLE? If you cannot find Internet Explorer on the Programs menu, check to see if an Internet Explorer shortcut icon appears on the desktop, and then double-click it. If you do not see the shortcut icon, ask your instructor or technical support person for help. The program might be installed in a different folder on your computer.

2. If the program does not fill the screen entirely, click the **Maximize** button on the Internet Explorer program's title bar. Your screen should look like Figure 3-34.

Figure 3-34	INTERNET EXPLORER MAIN PROGRAM WINDOW

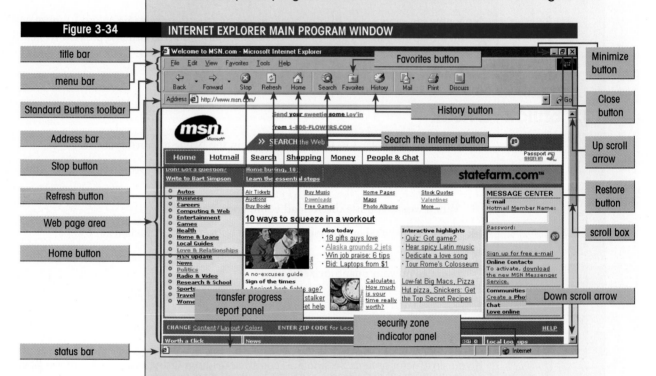

TROUBLE? Figure 3-34 shows the Microsoft Network home page, which is the page that Internet Explorer opens the first time it starts. Your computer might be configured to open to a different Web page or no page at all.

TROUBLE? If you do not see the bars shown in Figure 3-34, click View on the menu bar, point to Toolbars, and then click the name of the bar that you want to turn on.

Internet Explorer includes a Standard Buttons toolbar with 12 buttons. Many of these buttons execute frequently used commands for browsing the Web. Figure 3-35 shows these buttons and describes their functions.

Figure 3-35	STANDARD BUTTONS TOOLBAR BUTTON FUNCTIONS	
BUTTON	**BUTTON NAME**	**DESCRIPTION**
Back	Back	Moves to the last previously visited Web page
Forward	Forward	Moves to the next previously visited Web page
Stop	Stop	Stops the transfer of a new Web page
Refresh	Refresh	Reloads the current page
Home	Home	Loads the program's defined start page
Search	Search	Opens a Search frame in the Internet Explorer window, which displays a Web search engine chosen by Microsoft
Favorites	Favorites	Opens the Favorites frame in the Internet Explorer window, which allows you to return to Web pages that you have saved as favorites
History	History	Opens the History frame in the Internet Explorer window, which allows you to choose from a list of Web pages that you have visited recently
Mail	Mail	Opens the e-mail program specified in the Internet Options settings
Print	Print	Prints the current Web page
Edit	Edit	Opens the current Web page for editing in the default HTML page editor (button varies depending on the default page editor)
Discuss	Discuss	Opens a link to a discussion server (if your computer is connected to one)

Now that you understand how to start Internet Explorer, you tell Maggie that you are ready to start using it to find information on the Internet. To find information, you need to know about the different Internet Explorer functions.

Status Bar

The **status bar** at the bottom of the window includes several panels that give you information about Internet Explorer's operations. The first panel—the **transfer progress report**—presents status messages that show, for example, the URL of a page while it is loading. When a page is completely loaded, this panel displays the text "Done" until you move the mouse over a hyperlink. This panel displays the URL of any hyperlink on the page when you move the mouse pointer over it. This panel also shows a blue **graphical transfer progress indicator** that moves from left to right in the right side of the panel to indicate how much of a Web page has loaded while Internet Explorer is loading it from a Web server. This indicator is especially useful for monitoring progress when you are loading large Web pages.

The third status bar panel displays a locked padlock icon when the browser loads a Web page that has a security certificate. You can double-click on the padlock icon to open a dialog box that contains information about the security certificate for a Web page.

The fourth (rightmost) status bar panel displays the **security zone** to which the page you are viewing has been assigned. As part of its security features, Internet Explorer lets you classify Web pages by the security risk you believe they present. You can open the Internet Security Properties dialog box shown in Figure 3-36 by double-clicking the third status bar panel. This window lets you set four levels of security-enforcing procedures: High, Medium, Medium-Low, and Low. In general, the higher level of security you set for your browser, the slower it will operate. Higher security settings also disable some of the browser features. You can click the Custom Level button to configure the way each security level operates on your computer.

Figure 3-36   INTERNET SECURITY PROPERTIES DIALOG BOX

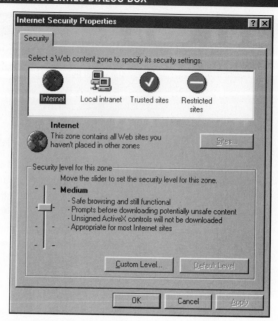

Menu Bar

In addition to the standard Windows commands, the menu bar also provides access to Favorites. The **Favorites** menu command lets you store and organize URLs of sites that you have visited.

Hiding and Showing the Internet Explorer Toolbars

Internet Explorer lets you hide its toolbars to show more of the Web page area. The easiest way to increase the display area for a Web page is to click View (on the menu bar), then click Full Screen.

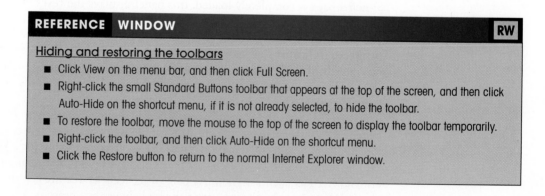

REFERENCE   WINDOW   **RW**

Hiding and restoring the toolbars
- Click View on the menu bar, and then click Full Screen.
- Right-click the small Standard Buttons toolbar that appears at the top of the screen, and then click Auto-Hide on the shortcut menu, if it is not already selected, to hide the toolbar.
- To restore the toolbar, move the mouse to the top of the screen to display the toolbar temporarily.
- Right-click the toolbar, and then click Auto-Hide on the shortcut menu.
- Click the Restore button to return to the normal Internet Explorer window.

To use the Full Screen command and Auto Hide:

1. Click **View** on the menu bar, then click **Full Screen**.

2. Right-click the small Standard Buttons toolbar that appears at the top of the screen to open the shortcut menu, and then click **Auto-Hide** on the shortcut menu if it is not already checked.

3. Move the mouse pointer away from the top of the screen for a moment. Now, you can see more of the Web page area. When the toolbar disappears, return the mouse pointer to the top of the screen to display it again.

4. With the toolbar displayed, right-click the toolbar and then click **Auto-Hide** on the shortcut menu. This removes the check mark from the Auto-Hide entry on the menu and turns the toolbar on again.

5. Click the **Restore** button to return to the normal Internet Explorer window.

You can use the commands on the View menu (and its Toolbars submenu) to **toggle**, or turn on and off, the individual toolbars. Also, you can use the Customize command on the View/Toolbars menu to change the appearance of the toolbars. For example, you can show the Standard Buttons toolbar buttons with or without the text labels that describe each button's function.

Entering a URL in the Address Bar

Maggie tells you that you can use the **Address Bar** to enter URLs directly into Internet Explorer. Marianna gave you the URL for the Pennsylvania Quintet, so you can see its Web page.

REFERENCE   WINDOW   RW

Entering a URL in the Address Bar
- Click at the end of the current text in the Address Bar, and then backspace over the text that you want to delete.
- Type the URL of the location that you want.
- Press the Enter key to load the URL's Web page in the browser window.

To load the Pennsylvania Quintet's Web page:

1. Click in the Address Bar; if there is text in the Address Bar, click at the end of the text, and then press the **Backspace** key to delete it.

   TROUBLE? Make sure that you delete all of the text in the Address Bar so the text you type in Step 2 will be correct.

2. Type **http://www.course.com/newperspectives/internet2/** in the Address Bar to go to the Student Online Companion page on the Course Technology Web site. In this book, you will go to the Course Technology site and then click hyperlinks to go to individual Web pages.

3. Press the **Enter** key. After you press the Enter key, the Student Online Companion Web page loads, as shown in Figure 3-37. When the entire page has loaded, the graphical transfer progress indicator in the status bar will stop moving and the transfer progress report panel will display the text "Done."

Figure 3-37 | STUDENT ONLINE COMPANION WEB PAGE

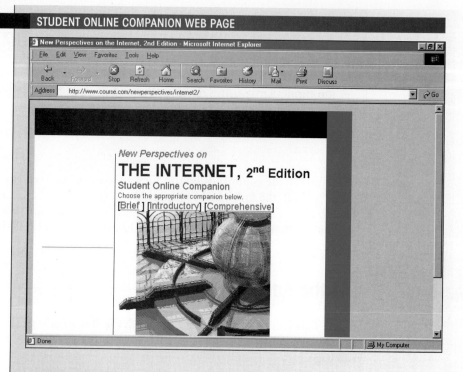

TROUBLE? If a Dial-Up Networking dialog box opens after you press the Enter key, click the Connect button. You must have an Internet connection to complete the steps in this tutorial.

4. Click the link for the book you are using to open the main page, click the **Tutorial 3** link to open the page that contains the links for this tutorial, and then click the **Session 3.3** link in the left frame.

5. Click the link to the **Pennsylvania Quintet** in the right frame. The Web page opens, as shown in Figure 3-38.

Figure 3-38 | PENNSYLVANIA QUINTET'S WEB PAGE

URL

graphic art image

photographic image

hyperlinks are underlined and in a different text color

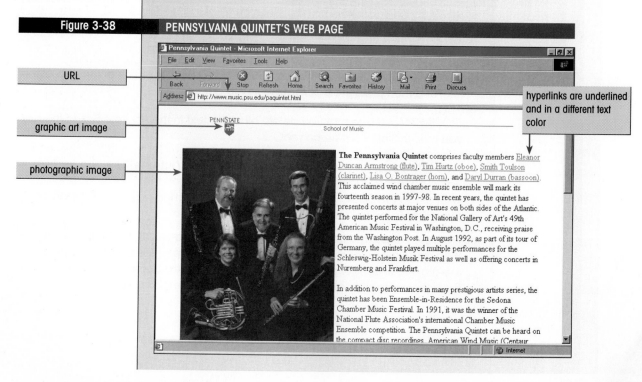

> TROUBLE? The Pennsylvania Quintet might change its Web page, so your Web page might look different from the one shown in Figure 3-38. If this Web page is deleted from the server, you might see an entirely different Web page. However, the steps should work the same.
>
> **6.** Read the Web page, and then click the **Back** button to return to the Student Online Companion page.

You like the format of the Pennsylvania Quintet's home page, so you want to make sure that you can go back to that page later if you need to review its contents. Maggie explains that you can write down the URL so you can refer to it later, but an easier way is to use the Favorites feature to store the URL for future use.

Using the Favorites Feature

Internet Explorer's **Favorites feature** lets you store and organize a list of Web pages that you have visited so you can return to them easily. The **Favorites** button on the Standard Buttons toolbar opens the Favorites frame shown in Figure 3-39. You can use the Favorites frame to open URLs you have stored as Favorites.

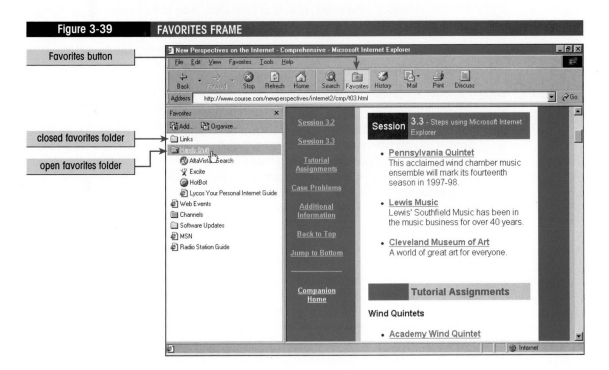

Figure 3-39   FAVORITES FRAME

Figure 3-39 shows the hierarchical structure of the Favorites feature. This user stored four search engine Web pages in a folder named "Handy Stuff." You can organize your favorites in the way that best suits your needs and working style.

You decide to save the Pennsylvania Quintet's Web page as a favorite in a Wind Quintet Information folder.

Creating a new Favorites folder
- Open the Web page in Internet Explorer.
- Click the Favorites button on the Standard Buttons toolbar to open the Favorites frame.
- Click Favorites on the menu bar, and then click Add to Favorites.
- If the Create in window of the Add Favorite dialog box is not displayed, click the Create in button in the Add Favorite dialog box.
- Click the Favorites folder, and then click the New Folder button.
- Type the name of the new folder in the Folder name text box, and then click the OK button.
- Click the OK button in the Add Favorite dialog box.

To create a new Favorites folder:

1. Click the **Forward** button on the Standard Buttons toolbar to return to the Pennsylvania Quintet Web page.

2. Click the **Favorites** button on the Standard Buttons toolbar to open the Favorites frame.

3. Click **Favorites** on the menu bar, and then click **Add to Favorites** to open the Add Favorite dialog box.

4. If the Create in window of the Add Favorite dialog box is not displayed, click the **Create in** button.

5. Click the **Favorites** folder in the Create in window, and then click the **New Folder** button to create a new folder in the Favorites folder.

6. Type **Wind Quintet Information** in the Folder name text box of the Create New Folder dialog box, and then click the **OK** button to close the Create New Folder dialog box. See Figure 3-40. Notice that the page name appears automatically in the Name text box in the Add Favorite dialog box. You can change the page name if you wish by editing the suggested page name.

| Figure 3-40 | CREATING A NEW FAVORITES FOLDER |

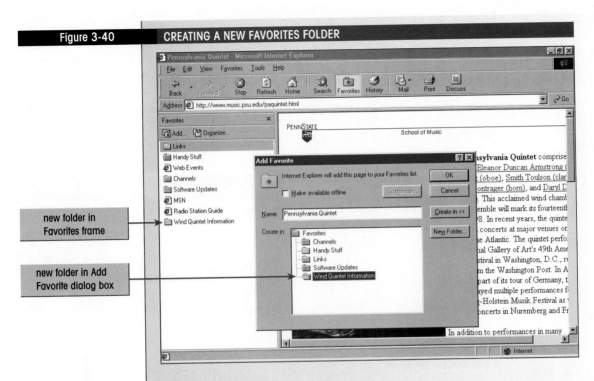

new folder in Favorites frame

new folder in Add Favorite dialog box

7. Click the **OK** button to close the Add Favorite dialog box. Now, the favorite is saved in Internet Explorer. You can test the favorite by opening it from the Favorites frame.

8. Click the **Back** button on the Standard Buttons toolbar to return to the previous page, click the **Wind Quintet Information** folder in the Favorites frame to open it, and then click **Pennsylvania Quintet**. The Pennsylvania Quintet page opens in the browser, which means that you created the favorite correctly.

   TROUBLE? If the Pennsylvania Quintet page does not open, click Favorites on the menu bar, click the Wind Quintet Information folder, right-click the Pennsylvania Quintet favorite, and then click Properties. Click the Internet Shortcut tab and make sure that a URL appears in the Target URL text box. If there is no URL, then click the OK button to close the dialog box, click Favorites on the menu bar, click the Wind Quintet Information folder, right-click the Pennsylvania Quintet folder, and then click Delete. Repeat the steps to recreate the favorite, and then try again. If you still have trouble, ask your instructor or technical support person for help.

As you use the Web to find information about wind quintets and other sites of interest for the group, you might find yourself creating many favorites so you can return to sites of interest. When you start accumulating favorites, it is important to keep them organized, as you will see next.

Organizing Favorites

You explain to Maggie that you have created a new folder for Wind Quintet Information in the Internet Explorer Favorites frame and stored the Pennsylvania Quintet's URL in that folder. Maggie suggests that you might not want to keep all of the wind quintet-related information you gather in one folder. She notes that you are just beginning your work for

Marianna and the quintet and that you might be collecting all types of information for them. Maggie suggests that you might want to put information about the Pennsylvania Quintet in a separate folder named East Coast Ensembles under the Wind Quintet Information folder. As you collect information about other performers, you might add folders for Midwest and West Coast ensembles, too.

Internet Explorer offers an easy way to organize your folders in a hierarchical structure—even after you have stored them. To rearrange URLs or even folders within folders, you use the Organize Favorites command on the Favorites menu.

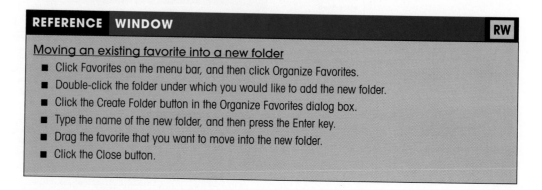

REFERENCE WINDOW   **RW**

<u>Moving an existing favorite into a new folder</u>
- Click Favorites on the menu bar, and then click Organize Favorites.
- Double-click the folder under which you would like to add the new folder.
- Click the Create Folder button in the Organize Favorites dialog box.
- Type the name of the new folder, and then press the Enter key.
- Drag the favorite that you want to move into the new folder.
- Click the Close button.

To move an existing favorite into a new folder:

1. Click **Favorites** on the menu bar, and then click **Organize Favorites**.

2. Double-click the **Wind Quintet Information** folder in the Organize Favorites dialog box.

3. Click the **Create Folder** button in the Organize Favorites dialog box.

4. Type **East Coast Ensembles** to replace the "New Folder" selected text, and then press the **Enter** key to rename the folder.

5. Click and drag the Pennsylvania Quintet favorite to the new East Coast Ensembles folder, and then release the mouse button. Now, the East Coast Ensembles folder contains the favorite, as shown in Figure 3-41.

| Figure 3-41 | REARRANGING FAVORITES IN FOLDERS |

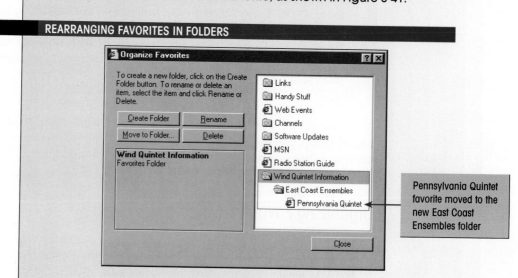

6. Click the **Close** button to close the Organize Favorites dialog box. The Favorites frame is updated automatically to reflect your changes.

7. Click the **Favorites** button on the Standard Buttons toolbar to close the Favorites list.

Hyperlink **Navigation with the Mouse**

Now you know how to use the Internet to find information that will help you with the Sunset Wind Quintet. Maggie tells you that the easiest way to move from one Web page to another is to use the mouse to click hyperlinks that the authors of Web pages embed in their HTML documents. You can also right-click the mouse on the background of a Web page to open a shortcut menu that includes navigation options.

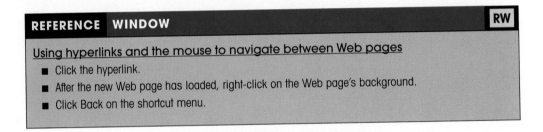

REFERENCE **WINDOW** RW

Using hyperlinks and the mouse to navigate between Web pages
- Click the hyperlink.
- After the new Web page has loaded, right-click on the Web page's background.
- Click Back on the shortcut menu.

To follow a hyperlink to a Web page and return using the mouse:

1. Click the **Back** button on the Standard Buttons toolbar to go back to the Student Online Companion page, click the **Lewis Music** link to open that page, and then point to the **Instrument Accessories** hyperlink shown in Figure 3-42 so your pointer changes to 🖑.

Figure 3-42 | LEWIS MUSIC HOME PAGE

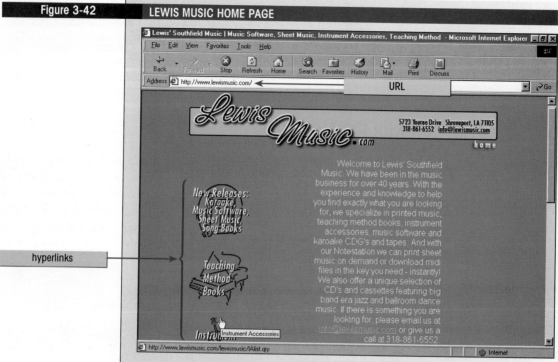

hyperlinks

2. Click the **Instrument Accessories** hyperlink to load the page. Watch the first panel in the status bar—when it displays the text "Done," you know that Internet Explorer has loaded the full page.

3. Right-click anywhere in the Web page area that is not a hyperlink to display the shortcut menu, as shown in Figure 3-43.

Figure 3-43 | USING THE SHORTCUT MENU TO GO BACK TO THE PREVIOUS PAGE

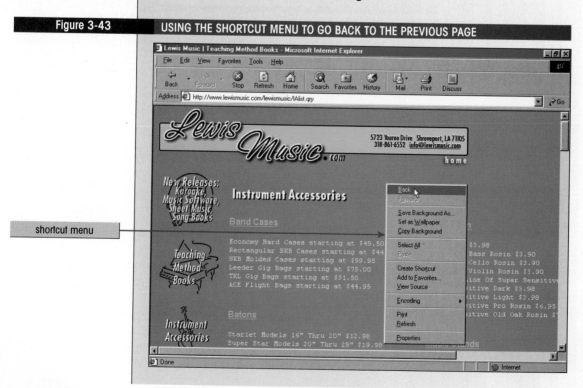

shortcut menu

TROUBLE? If you right-click a hyperlink, your shortcut menu will display a shorter list than the one shown in Figure 3-43, and the Back item will not appear in the menu. If you do not see the shortcut menu shown in Figure 3-43, click anywhere outside of the shortcut menu to close it, and then repeat Step 3.

TROUBLE? Web pages change frequently, so the Instrument Accessories page you see might look different from the one shown in Figure 3-43, but right-clicking anywhere on the Web page area that is not a hyperlink will still work.

4. Click **Back** on the shortcut menu to return to the Lewis Music home page.

5. Repeat Step 4 to return to the Student Online Companion page.

You are beginning to get a good sense of how to move from one Web page to another and back again, but Maggie tells you that you have mastered only one technique of many. She explains that the Standard Buttons toolbar and the menu bar offer many tools for accessing and using Web sites.

Using the History List

In Session 3.1 you learned that the Back and Forward buttons let you move to and from previously visited pages. You also can open a full copy of the history list.

To view the history list for this session:

1. Click the **History** button on the Standard Buttons toolbar. The history list opens in a hierarchical structure in a separate window on the left side of the screen. The history list stores each URL you visited during the past week or during a specified time period. It also maintains the hierarchy of each Web site; that is, pages you visit at a particular Web site are stored in a separate folder for that site. To return to a particular page, click that page's entry in the list. You can see the full URL of any item in the History frame by moving the mouse pointer over the history list item, as shown in Figure 3-44.

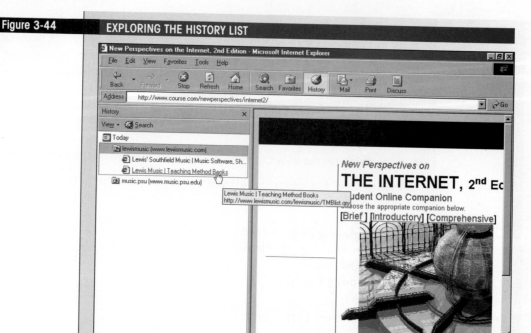

Figure 3-44   EXPLORING THE HISTORY LIST

TROUBLE? Your History frame might be a different size from what appears in Figure 3-44. You can resize the window by clicking and dragging its left edge either right or left to make it narrower or wider.

2. Click the **Close** button on the History frame title bar to close it.

You can right-click any entry in the Internet Explorer history list and copy the URL or delete it from the list. Internet Explorer stores each history entry as a shortcut in a History folder, which is in the Windows folder.

Refreshing a Web Page

The **Refresh** button makes Microsoft Internet Explorer load a new copy of the current Web page that appears in the browser window. Internet Explorer stores a copy of every Web page it displays on your computer's hard drive in a **Temporary Internet Files** folder in the Windows folder. This increases the speed at which Internet Explorer can display pages as you move back and forth through the history list because the browser can load the pages from a local disk drive instead of reloading the page from the remote Web server. When you click the Refresh button, Internet Explorer contacts the Web server to see if the Web page has changed since it was stored in the cache folder. If it has changed, Internet Explorer gets the new page from the Web server; otherwise, it loads the cache folder copy.

Returning to Your Start Page

The **Home** button displays the home (or start) page for your copy of Internet Explorer. You can change the setting for the Home toolbar button, as you will see next.

<u>Changing the Home toolbar button settings</u>
- Click Tools on the menu bar, and then click Internet Options.
- Click the General tab.
- Select whether you want Internet Explorer to open with the current page, its default page, or a blank page by clicking the corresponding button in the Home page section of the Internet Options dialog box.
- If you want to specify a home page, type the URL of that Web page in the Address text box.

To modify your home page:

1. Click **Tools** on the menu bar, and then click **Internet Options** to open the dialog box shown in Figure 3-45.

Figure 3-45	CHANGING THE DEFAULT HOME PAGE

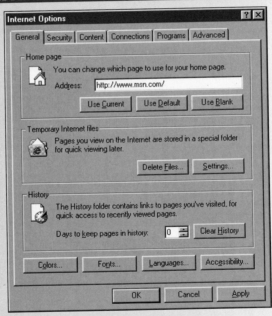

To use the currently loaded Web page as your home page, click the Use Current button. To use the default home page that was installed with your copy of Internet Explorer, click the Use Default button. If you don't want a page to open when you start your browser, click the Use Blank button. If you want to specify a home page other than the current, default, or blank page, type the URL for that page in the Address Bar.

TROUBLE? You might not be able to change these settings if you are using a computer in your school lab or at your office. Some organizations set the home page defaults on all of their computers and then lock those settings.

2. Click the **Cancel** button to close the dialog box without making any changes.

In the next section, you will learn how to print the Web page so you have a permanent record of its contents.

Printing a Web Page

The **Print** button on the Standard Buttons toolbar lets you print the current Web frame or page. You will learn more about saving and printing Web pages later in this session, but you can use the Print command to make a printed copy of most Web pages. (Some Web pages disable the Print command.)

REFERENCE WINDOW   **RW**

Printing the current Web page

- Click the Print button on the Standard Buttons toolbar to print the current Web page with the default print settings.

or

- Click File on the menu bar, and then click Print.
- Use the Print dialog box to choose the printer you want to use, the pages you want to print, and the number of copies you want to make of each page.
- Click the OK button to print the page(s).

To print a Web page:

1. Click in the main (right) frame of the Student Online Companion page to select it.

2. Click **File** on the menu bar, and then click **Print** to open the Print dialog box.

3. Make sure that the printer in the Name text box shows the printer you want to use; if necessary, click the Name list arrow to change the selection.

4. Click the **Pages** option button in the Print range section of the Print dialog box, type **1** in the **from** text box, press the **Tab** key, and then type **1** in the **to** text box to specify that you only want to print the first page.

5. Make sure that the Number of copies text box shows that you want to print one copy.

6. Click the **OK** button to print the Web page and close the Print dialog box.

Changing the Settings for Printing a Web Page

You have seen how to print Web pages using the basic options available in the Print dialog box. Usually, the default settings in the Print dialog box are fine for printing a Web page, but you can use the Page Setup dialog box to change the way a Web page prints. Figure 3-46 shows the Page Setup dialog box, and Figure 3-47 describes its settings.

Figure 3-46	PAGE SETUP DIALOG BOX

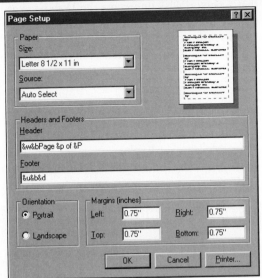

Figure 3-47	PAGE SETUP DIALOG BOX OPTIONS

OPTION	DESCRIPTION	USE
Paper Size	Changes the size of the printed page.	Use the Letter size default unless you are printing to different paper stock, such as Legal or A4.
Paper Source	Changes the printer's paper source.	Use the default AutoSelect Tray unless you want to specify a different tray or manual feed for printing on heavy paper.
Header	Prints the Web page's title, URL, date/time printed, and page numbers at the top of each page.	To obtain details on how to specify exact header printing options, click the Header text box to select it, and then press the F1 key.
Footer	Prints the Web page's title, URL, date/time printed, and page numbers at the bottom of each page.	To obtain details on how to specify exact footer printing options, click the Footer text box to select it, and then press the F1 key.
Orientation	Selects the orientation of the printed output.	Portrait works best for most Web pages, but you can use landscape orientation to print the wide tables of numbers included on some Web pages.
Margins	Changes the margin of the printed page.	Normally, you should leave the default settings, but you can change the right, left, top, or bottom margins as needed.

When printing long Web pages, another print option that is extremely useful for saving paper is to reduce the font size of the Web pages before you print them. To do this, click View on the menu bar, click Text Size, and then click either Smaller or Smallest on the pop-out menu.

Checking **Web Page Security Features**

You can check some of the security elements of a Web page by clicking File on the menu bar, clicking Properties, and then clicking the Certificates button. Internet Explorer will display security information for the page, if it is available, to advise you of the overall security of the page that appears in the browser window.

Encryption is a way of scrambling and encoding data transmissions that reduces the risk that a person who intercepts the Web page as it travels across the Internet will be able to decode and read the page's contents. Web sites use encrypted transmission to send and receive information, such as credit card numbers, to ensure privacy. When Internet Explorer loads an encrypted Web page, a padlock symbol appears in the third pane of the status bar at the bottom of the Internet Explorer window.

Getting Help in Microsoft Internet Explorer

Microsoft Internet Explorer includes a comprehensive online Help facility. You can obtain help by opening the Internet Explorer Help window.

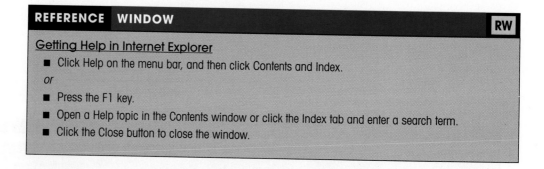

REFERENCE WINDOW   RW

Getting Help in Internet Explorer
- Click Help on the menu bar, and then click Contents and Index.
or
- Press the F1 key.
- Open a Help topic in the Contents window or click the Index tab and enter a search term.
- Click the Close button to close the window.

To open the Internet Explorer Help window:

1. Click **Help** on the menu bar, and then click **Contents and Index** to open the Internet Explorer Help window.

2. If necessary, click the **Maximize** button on the Internet Explorer Help window so it fills the desktop.

3. Click the **Contents** tab in the Contents frame, click **Finding the Web Pages You Want**, and then click **Listing your favorite pages for quick viewing** to open that help topic in the Help window. Notice that the page that opens in the Help frame contains other links to related categories that you can explore. See Figure 3-48.

Figure 3-48	MICROSOFT INTERNET EXPLORER HELP WINDOW

Hide/Show button closes and reopens the Contents frame

Help navigation buttons

click to close Help

Microsoft Internet Explorer Help

Hide   Back   Forward   Options   Web Help

Contents | Index | Search

- [?] Getting started with Internet Explorer
- [?] Taking the Internet Explorer 5 Tour
- Connecting to the Internet
- Finding the Web Pages You Want
  - [?] Finding the information you want
  - [?] Listing your favorite pages for quick viewing
  - [?] Change your home page
  - [?] Sharing bookmarks and favorites
  - [?] Find pages you've recently visited
  - [?] Enter Web information more easily
- Browsing the Web Offline
- Printing and Saving Information
- Sending Information over the Internet Safely
- Protecting Your Computer While You're Online
- Controlling Access to Inappropriate Internet Conte
- Customizing Your Browser
- Accessibility

Listing your favorite pages for quick viewing

When you find Web sites or pages that you like, you can keep track of them, so it's easy to open them in the future.

- Add a Web page to your list of favorite pages. Any time you want to open that page, just click the **Favorites** button on the toolbar, and then click the shortcut in the Favorites list.

  Add a page to your list of favorite pages

- If you have a handful of sites or pages that you visit often, add them to your Links bar.

  Add a page to your Links bar

- If there is one page you visit most, you can make it your home page so that it is displayed every time you start Internet Explorer or click the **Home** button on the toolbar.

  Change your home page

Tip

- If you forget to add Web pages to your Favorites or Links bar, click the **History** button on the toolbar. The History list shows where you've been - today, yesterday, or a few weeks ago. Click a name from the list to display the page.

hyperlinks to detailed Help topics

Contents frame   **Help frame**

4. Click the **Close** button to close the Internet Explorer Help window.

You are now convinced that you have all of the tools you need to successfully find information on the Web. Marianna probably will be interested in seeing the Pennsylvania Quintet Web page, but you are not sure if she will have Internet access while she's touring. Maggie says that you can save the Web page on disk, so Marianna can open the page locally in her Web browser using the files you save on that disk.

Using **Internet Explorer to Save a Web Page**

You have learned how to use most of the Internet Explorer tools for loading Web pages and saving bookmarks. Now, Maggie wants you to learn how to save a Web page. Sometimes, you will want to store entire Web pages on disk; other times, you will only want to store selected portions of Web page text or particular graphics from a Web page.

Saving a Web Page

You like the Pennsylvania Quintet's Web site and want to save the page on disk so you can send it to Marianna. That way, she can review it without having an Internet connection. To save a Web page, you must have the page open in Internet Explorer.

REFERENCE WINDOW   **RW**

Saving a Web page to a floppy disk
- Open the Web page in Internet Explorer.
- Click File on the menu bar, and then click Save As to open the Save Web Page dialog box.
- Click the Save in list arrow, and then change to the drive on which to save the Web page.
- Accept the default filename, or change the filename, if you want; however, retain the file extension .htm or .html.
- Click the Save button to save the Web page on the disk.

To save the Web page on your Data Disk:

1. Use the **Favorites** button to return to the Pennsylvania Quintet page. (You saved the favorite in the East Coast Ensembles folder, which is in the Wind Quintet Information folder.)

2. Click **File** on the menu bar, and then click **Save As** to open the Save Web Page dialog box.

3. Click the **Save in** list arrow, click the drive that contains your Data Disk (usually this is 3½ Floppy (A:)), and then double-click **Tutorial.03** folder. You will accept the default filename of Pennsylvania Quintet.

4. Click the **Save** button. Now the HTML document for the Pennsylvania Quintet's home page is saved on your Data Disk. When you send it to Marianna, she can open her Web browser and then use the Open command on the File menu to open the Web page.

5. Close the Favorites frame.

If the Web page contains graphics, such as photos, drawings, or icons, they will not be saved with the HTML document. To save a graphic, right-click it in the browser window, click Save Picture As, and then save the graphic to the same location as the Web's HTML document. The graphics file is specified to appear on the HTML document as a hyperlink, so you might have to change the HTML code in the Web page to identify its location. Copying the graphics files to the same disk as the HTML document will *usually* work.

Saving Web Page Text to a File

Maggie suggests that you might want to know how to save portions of Web page text to a file, so that you can save only the text from the Web page and use it in other programs. You will use WordPad to receive the text you will copy from a Web page, but any word processor or text editor will work.

Marianna just called to let you know that the quintet will play a concert in Cleveland on a Friday night, and she asks you to identify other opportunities for scheduling local concerts during the following weekend. Often, museums are willing to book small ensembles for weekend afternoon programs, and Marianna has given you the URL for the Cleveland Museum of Art. You will visit the site and then get the museum's address and telephone number so you can contact it about scheduling a concert.

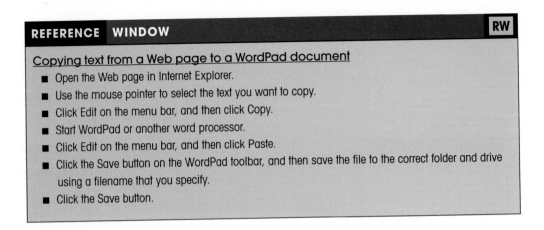

REFERENCE WINDOW **RW**

<u>Copying text from a Web page to a WordPad document</u>
- Open the Web page in Internet Explorer.
- Use the mouse pointer to select the text you want to copy.
- Click Edit on the menu bar, and then click Copy.
- Start WordPad or another word processor.
- Click Edit on the menu bar, and then click Paste.
- Click the Save button on the WordPad toolbar, and then save the file to the correct folder and drive using a filename that you specify.
- Click the Save button.

To copy text from a Web page and save it to a file:

1. Use the **Back** button to return to the Student Online Companion page, and then click the **Cleveland Museum of Art** link to open that Web page in the browser window.

2. Click the **address** hyperlink in the left frame on the Web page to open the museum information page in the main (right) frame.

3. Click and drag the mouse pointer over the address and telephone number to select it, as shown in Figure 3-49.

Figure 3-49	SELECTING TEXT ON A WEB PAGE

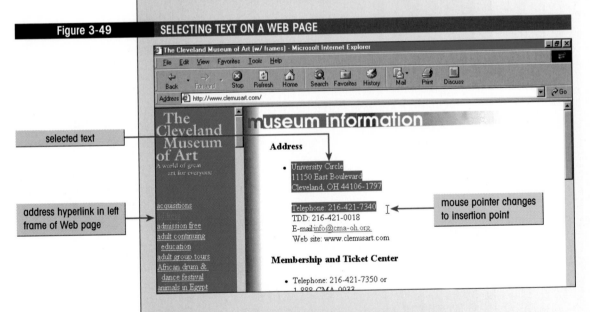

selected text

address hyperlink in left frame of Web page

mouse pointer changes to insertion point

4. Click **Edit** on the menu bar, and then click **Copy** to copy the selected text to the Windows Clipboard.

Now, you can start WordPad and paste the copied text into a new document.

To start and copy the text into WordPad:

1. Click the **Start** button on the taskbar, point to **Programs**, point to **Accessories**, and then click **WordPad** to start the program and open a new document.

2. Click the **Paste** button on the WordPad toolbar to paste the text into the WordPad document, as shown in Figure 3-50.

Figure 3-50   PASTING TEXT FROM A WEB PAGE INTO A WORDPAD DOCUMENT

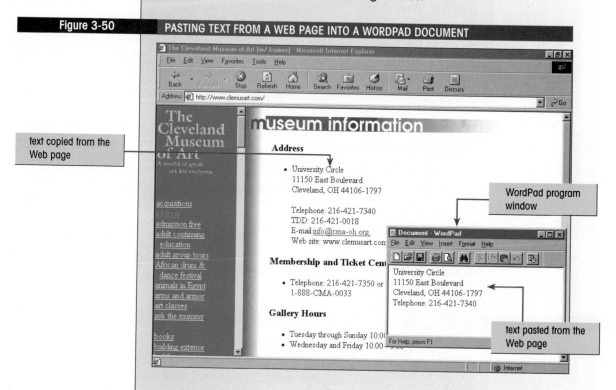

TROUBLE? If the WordPad toolbar does not appear, click View on the menu bar, click Toolbar to turn it on, and then repeat Step 2. Your WordPad program window might be a different size from the one shown in Figure 3-50, which does not affect the steps.

3. Click the **Save** button on the WordPad toolbar to open the Save As dialog box.

4. Click the **Save in** list arrow, change to the drive that contains your Data Disk, and then double-click the **Tutorial.03** folder, if necessary.

5. Select any text that is in the File name text box, type **CMoA-Address.txt**, and then click the **Save** button to save the file. Now, the address and phone number of the museum is saved in a file on your Data Disk for future reference.

TROUBLE? If you also completed the steps in Session 3.2, then a dialog box will open and ask if you want to replace the existing CmoA-Address.txt file on your Data Disk. Click the Yes button to replace it.

6. Click the **Close** button on the WordPad title bar to close it.

Later, you will contact the museum. As you examine the hyperlinks in the left frame of the Cleveland Museum of Art Web page, you notice a hyperlink titled "how to get here." Clicking the "how to get here" hyperlink loads a page that contains directions and information about transportation to the museum. You find that it includes a hyperlink to a street map of the area surrounding the museum.

Saving a Web Page Graphic to Disk

You decide that the Web page with directions and transportation information might be helpful to Marianna, so you decide to save the map graphic on your disk. You can then send the file to Marianna so she has a resource for getting to the museum.

REFERENCE WINDOW **RW**

Saving an image from a Web page on a floppy disk

- Open the Web page in Internet Explorer.
- Right-click the image you want to copy, and then click Save Picture As.
- Change to the drive and/or folder that you want to save the image in, change the default filename, if necessary, and then click the Save button.

To save the street map image on a floppy disk:

1. Click the **how to get here** hyperlink in the left frame of the Cleveland Museum's home page, and then click the **street map** hyperlink on the Getting around - Directions and Transportation Web page in the main (right) frame. Do not click the hyperlink to the Adobe download version of the map.

2. Right-click the map image to open its shortcut menu, as shown in Figure 3-51.

| Figure 3-51 | SAVING THE MAP IMAGE TO DISK |

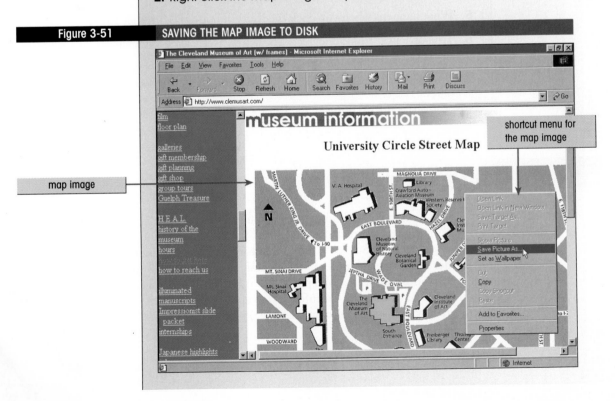

3. Click **Save Picture As** on the shortcut menu to open the Save Picture dialog box.

4. If necessary, click the **Save in** list arrow, change to the drive that contains your Data Disk, and then double-click the **Tutorial.03** folder. You will accept the default filename, mapstreet, so click the **Save** button. Now the image is saved on your Data Disk, and you can send the file to Marianna. Marianna can use her Web browser to open the image file and print it.

TROUBLE? If you also completed the steps in Session 3.2, then a dialog box will open and ask if you want to replace the existing mapstreet.gif file on your Data Disk. Click the Yes button to replace it.

5. Close your Web browser and your dial-up connection, if necessary.

Now, you can send a disk to Marianna so she has the Pennsylvania Quintet Web page and a map to show how to get to the museum. Marianna is pleased to hear of your progress in using the Web to find information for the quintet.

Session 3.3 QUICK CHECK

1. Describe two ways to increase the Web page area in Internet Explorer.

2. You can use the _____ button in Internet Explorer to visit previously visited sites during your Web session.

3. Click the _____ button on the Standard Buttons toolbar to open a search frame that contains a number of different searching options.

4. List the names of two additional Favorites folders you might want to add to the Wind Quintet Information folder as you continue to gather information for the Sunset Wind Quintet.

5. What happens when you click the Refresh button in Internet Explorer?

6. True or False: You can identify encrypted Web pages when viewing them in Internet Explorer.

7. Describe two ways to obtain help on a specific topic in Internet Explorer.

Now you are ready to complete the Review Assignments using the browser of your choice.

REVIEW ASSIGNMENTS

Marianna is pleased with the information you gathered thus far about other wind quintet Web pages and potential recital sites. In fact, she is thinking about hiring someone to create a Web page for the Sunset Wind Quintet. So that she has some background information for her meetings with potential Web designers, Marianna would like you to compile some information about the Web pages that other small musical ensembles have created. Although you have searched for information about wind quintets, a large number of string quartets (two violinists, a violist, and a cellist) play similar venues.

Do the following:

1. Start your Web browser, go to the Student Online Companion (http://www.course.com/newperspectives/internet2), click the link for your book, click the Tutorial 3 link, and then click the Review Assignments link in the left frame.

2. Click the hyperlinks listed under the category headings Wind Quintets, String Quartets, and Other Small Musical Ensembles to explore the Web pages for each entry.

3. Choose three interesting home pages, and print the first page of each. Create a bookmark or favorite for each of these sites, and then answer the following questions for these three sites.

4. Which sites include a photograph of the ensemble? Which photographs are in color and black and white? Which sites show the ensemble members dressed in formal concert dress?

5. Choose your favorite ensemble photograph and save it in the Tutorial.03 folder on your Data Disk.

6. Do any of the sites provide information about the ensemble's CDs? If so, which ones? Is this information on the home page, or did you click a hyperlink to find it?

7. Do any of the sites offer CDs or other products for sale? If so, which ones? Is this information on the home page, or did you click a hyperlink to find it?

8. Write a one-page report that summarizes your findings for Marianna. Include a recommendation regarding what the Sunset Wind Quintet should consider including in its Web site.

9. Close your Web browser and your dial-up connection, if necessary.

CASE PROBLEMS

Case 1. Businesses on the Web Business Web sites range from very simple informational sites to comprehensive sites that offer information about the firm's products or services, history, current employment openings, and financial information. An increasing number of business sites offer products or services for sale using their Web sites. You just started a position on the public relations staff of Value City Central, a large retail chain of television and appliance stores. Your first assignment is to research and report on the types of information that other large firms offer on their Web sites.

Do the following:

1. Start your Web browser, go to the Student Online Companion (http://www.course.com/newperspectives/internet2), click the link for your book, click the Tutorial 3 link, and then click the Case Problems link in the left frame.

2. Use the Case Problem 1 hyperlinks to open the business sites on that page.

3. Choose three of those business sites that you believe would be most relevant to your assignment.

4. Print the home page for each Web site that you have chosen.

5. Select one site that you feel does the best job in each of the following five categories: overall presentation of the corporate image, description of products or services offered, presentation of the firm's history, description of employment opportunities, and presentation of financial statements or other financial information about the company.

6. Prepare a report that includes one paragraph describing why you believe each of the sites you identified in the preceding step did the best job.

7. Close your Web browser, and log off the Internet, if necessary.

Case 2. Browser Wars   Your employer, Bristol Mills, is a medium-sized manufacturer of specialty steel products. The firm has increased its use of computers in all of its office operations and in many of its manufacturing operations. Many of Bristol's computers currently run either Netscape Navigator or Microsoft Internet Explorer; however, the chief financial officer (CFO) has decided the firm can support only one of these products. As the CFO's special assistant, you have been asked to recommend which Web browser the company should choose to support.

Do the following:

1. Start your Web browser, go to the Student Online Companion (http://www.course.com/newperspectives/internet2), click the link for your book, click the Tutorial 3 link, and then click the Case Problems link in the left frame.

2. Use the Case Problem 2 hyperlinks to learn more about these two widely used Web browser software packages.

3. Write a one-page memo to the CFO (your instructor) that outlines the strengths and weaknesses of each product. Recommend one program and support your decision using the information you collected.

4. Prepare a list of features that you would like to see in a new Web browser software package that would overcome important limitations in either Navigator or Internet Explorer. Do you think it would be feasible for a firm to develop and use such a product? Why or why not?

5. Close your Web browser, and log off the Internet, if necessary.

Case 3. Citizens Fidelity Bank   You are a new staff auditor at the Citizens Fidelity Bank. You have had more recent computer training than other audit staff members at Citizens, so Sally DeYoung, the audit manager, asks you to review the bank's policy on Web browser cookie settings. Some of the bank's board members expressed concerns to Sally about the security of the bank's computers. They understand that the bank has PCs on its networks that are connected to the Internet. One of the board members learned about browser cookies and was afraid that an innocent bank employee might connect to a site that would write a dangerous cookie file on the bank's computer network. A browser cookie is a small file that a Web server can write to the disk drive of the computer running a Web browser. Not all Web servers write cookies, but those that do can read the cookie file the next time the Web browser on that computer connects to the Web server. The Web server can then retrieve information about the Web browser's last connection to the server. None of the bank's board members knows very much about computers, but all of them became concerned that a virus-laden cookie could significantly damage the bank's computer system. Sally asks you to help inform the board of directors about cookies and to establish a policy on using them.

Do the following:

1. Start your Web browser, go to the Student Online Companion (http://www.course.com/newperspectives/internet2), click the link for your book, click the Tutorial 3 link, and then click the Case Problems link in the left frame.

2. Use the Case Problem 3 hyperlinks to Cookie Information Resources to learn more about cookie files.

3. Prepare a brief outline of the content on each Web page you visit.

4. List the risks that Citizens Fidelity Bank might face by allowing cookie files to be written to their computers.

5. List the benefits that individual users obtain by allowing Web servers to write cookies to the computers that they are using at the bank to access the Web.

6. Close your Web browser, and log off the Internet, if necessary.

Case 4. Columbus Suburban Area Council   The Columbus Suburban Area Council is a charitable organization devoted to maintaining and improving the general welfare of people living in Columbus suburbs. As the director of the council, you are interested in encouraging donations and other support from area citizens and would like to stay informed of grant opportunities that might benefit the council. You are especially interested in developing an informative and attractive presence on the Web.

Do the following:

1. Start your Web browser, go to the Student Online Companion (http://www.course.com/newperspectives/internet2), click the link for your book, click the Tutorial 3 link, and then click the Case Problems link in the left frame.

2. Follow the Case Problem 4 hyperlinks to charitable organizations to find out more about what other organizations are doing with their Web sites.

3. Select three of the Web sites you visited and, for each, prepare a list of the site's contents. Note whether each site included financial information and whether the site disclosed how much the organization spent on administrative, or nonprogram activities.

4. Identify which site you believe would be a good model for the Council's new Web site. Explain why you think your chosen site would be the best example to follow.

5. Close your Web browser, and log off the Internet, if necessary.

Case 5. Emma's Start Page   Your neighbor, Emma Inkster, was an elementary school teacher for many years. She is now retired and has just purchased her first personal computer. Emma is excited about getting on the Web and exploring its resources. She has asked for your help. After you introduce her to what you have learned in this Tutorial about Web browsers, she is eager to spend more time gathering information on the Web. Although she is retired, Emma has continued to be very active. She is an avid bridge player, enjoys golf, and is one of the neighborhood's best gardeners. Although she is somewhat limited by her schoolteacher's pension, Emma loves travel to foreign countries and especially likes to learn the languages of her destinations. She would like to have a start page for her computer that would include hyperlinks that would help her easily visit and return regularly to Web pages related to her interests. Her nephew knows HTML and can create the page, but Emma would like you to help her design the layout of her start page. You know that Web directory sites are designed to help people find interesting Web sites, so you begin your search with them.

Do the following:

1. Start your Web browser, go to the Student Online Companion (http://www.course.com/newperspectives/internet2), click the link for your book, click the Tutorial 3 link, and then click the Case Problems link in the left frame.

2. Follow the Case Problem 5 hyperlinks to Web directories to learn what kind of organization they use for their hyperlinks.

3. You note that many of the Web directories use a similar organization structure for their hyperlinks and categories; however, you are not sure if that organization structure would be ideal for Emma. You decide to create categories that suit Emma's specific interests. List five general categories around which you would organize Emma's start page. For each of those five general categories, list three subcategories that would help Emma find and return to Web sites she would find interesting.

4. Write a report of 100 words in which you explain why the start page you designed for Emma would be more useful to her than a publicly available Web directory.

5. Close your Web browser, and log off the Internet, if necessary.

LAB ASSIGNMENTS

The Internet:
World Wide
Web

One of the most popular services on the Internet is the World Wide Web. This Lab is a Web simulator that teaches you how to use Web browser software to find information. You can use this Lab whether or not your school provides you with Internet access.

1. Click the Steps button to learn how to use Web browser software. As you proceed through the Steps, answer all of the Quick Check questions that appear. After you complete the Steps, you will see a Quick Check Summary Report. Follow the instructions on the screen to print this report.

2. Click the Explore button on the Welcome screen. Use the Web browser to locate a weather map of the Caribbean Virgin Islands. What is its URL?

3. A SCUBA diver named Wadson Lachouffe has been searching for the fabled treasure of Greybeard the pirate. A link from the Adventure Travel Web site, www.atour.com, leads to Wadson's Web page called "Hidden Treasure." In Explore, locate the Hidden Treasure page and answer the following questions:
   a. What was the name of Greybeard's ship?
   b. What was Greybeard's favorite food?
   c. What does Wadson think happened to Greybeard's ship?

4. In the Steps, you found a graphic of Jupiter from the photo archives of the Jet Propulsion Laboratory. In the Explore section of the Lab, you can also find a graphic of Saturn. Suppose one of your friends wanted a picture of Saturn for an astronomy report. Make a list of the blue, underlined links your friend must click in the correct order to find the Saturn graphic. Assume that your friend will begin at the Web Trainer home page.

5. Enter the URL http://www.atour.com to jump to the Adventure Travel Web site. Write a one-page description of this site. In your paper include a description of the information at the site, the number of pages the site contains, and a diagram of the links it contains.

6. Chris Thomson is a student at UVI and has his own Web pages. In Explore, look at the information Chris has included on his pages. Suppose you could create your own Web page. What would you include? Use word-processing software to design your own Web pages. Make sure you indicate the graphics and links you would use.

QUICK | CHECK ANSWERS

Session 3.1

1. False

2. format text and create hyperlinks

3. The main page of a Web site, the first page that opens when you start your Web browser, or the page that opens the first time you start a particular Web browser

4. Any two: graphics image, sound clip, or video files

5. Candidate's name and party affiliation, list of qualifications, biography, position statements on campaign issues, list of endorsements with hyperlinks to the Web pages of individuals and organizations that support her candidacy, audio or video clips of speeches and interviews, address and telephone number of the campaign office, and other similar information

6. A computer's IP address is a unique identifying number; its domain name is a unique name associated with the IP address on the Internet host computer responsible for that computer's domain.

7. "http://" indicates use of the hypertext transfer protocol, "www.savethetrees.org" is the domain name and suggests a charitable or not-for-profit organization that is probably devoted to forest ecology, and "main.html" is the name of the HTML file on the Web server.

8. A Web directory contains a hierarchical list of Web page categories; each category contains hyperlinks to individual Web pages. A Web search engine is a Web site that accepts words or expressions you enter and finds Web pages that include those words or expressions.

Session 3.2

1. Any three of: type the URL in the Location field, click a hyperlink on a Web page, click the Back button, click the Forward button, click the Bookmarks button and select from the menu, or click Communicator on the menu bar then click Tools and double-click the History listing entry

2. history list

3. when you believe the Web page might have changed since you last visited it

4. Navigator loads the page that is specified in the Home page section of the Preferences dialog box (which you can open from the Edit menu)

5. encrypt

6. True

7. Navigator feature that lets you store and organize a list of Web pages that you have visited

Session 3.3

1. Hide its toolbars or click the Full Screen command on the View menu.

2. History

3. Search

4. Midwest Ensembles, West Coast Ensembles

5. Internet Explorer contacts the Web server to see if the currently loaded Web page has changed since it was stored in its cache folder. If the Web page has changed, it obtains the new page; otherwise, it loads the cache folder copy.

6. True

7. press F1, click Help on the menu bar

New Perspectives on

THE
INTERNET

2nd Edition

Read This Before You Begin

To the Student

Data Disks

To complete the Level II tutorials, Review Assignments, and Case Problems in this book, you need five Data Disks. Your instructor will either provide you with Data Disks or ask you to make your own.

If you are making your own Data Disks, you will need five blank, formatted, high-density disks. You will need to copy onto your disks a set of folders from a file server, a standalone computer, or the Web. Your instructor will tell you which computer, drive letter, and folders contain the files you need. You could also download the files by going to www.course.com, clicking Data Disk Files, and following the instructions on the screen.

The following table shows you which folders go on your disks, so that you will have enough disk space to complete all the tutorials, Review Assignments, and Case Problems:

Data Disk 1

Write this on the disk label:
Data Disk 1: Tutorials 2 and 4

Put these folders on the disk:
Tutorial.02 and Tutorial.04

Data Disk 2

Write this on the disk label:
Data Disk 2: Tutorial 3

Put this folder on the disk:
Tutorial.03

Data Disk 3

Write this on the disk label:
Data Disk 3: Tutorial 6*

Put this folder on the disk:
Tutorial.06

Data Disk 4

Write this on the disk label:
Data Disk 3: Tutorial 6

Put this folder on the disk:
Tutorial.06

Data Disk 5

Write this on the disk label:
Data Disk 3: Tutorial 6

Put this folder on the disk:
Tutorial.06

*Note: In Tutorial 6 you will download several programs and data files to your student data disk. Depending on which Case Problems your instructor assigns, you might need three more Data Disks. If you need additional disks, write "Data Disk 6: Tutorial 6," and "Data Disk 7: Tutorial 6," and "Data Disk 8: Tutorial 6" on the labels, and then create a Tutorial.06 folder on each disk. Also note that over time, the sizes of the files that you download might increase, in which case more disks might be required.

When you begin each tutorial, be sure you are using the correct Data Disk. See the inside back cover of this book for more information on Data Disk files, or ask your instructor or technical support person for assistance.

Course Labs

The tutorials in this book feature two interactive Course Labs to help you understand e-mail and multimedia concepts. There are Lab Assignments at the end of Tutorials 2 and 3 that relate to these Labs.

Windows 95 Installation Instructions

To start a Lab, click the **Start** button on the Windows taskbar, point to **Programs**, point to **Course Labs**, point to **New Perspectives Applications**, and click the name of the Lab you want to use.

Using Your Own Computer

If you are going to work through this book using your own computer, you need:

- **Computer System** Netscape Navigator 4.0 or higher OR Microsoft Internet Explorer 4.0 or higher and Windows 95 or higher must be installed on your computer. This book assumes a complete installation of the Web browser software and its components, and that you have an existing e-mail account and an Internet connection. Because your Web browser may be different from the ones used in the figures or the book, your screens may differ slightly at times.

- **Data Disks** You will not be able to complete the tutorials or exercises in this book using your own computer until you have Data Disks.

- **Course Labs** See your instructor or technical support person to obtain the Course Lab software for use on your own computer.

Visit Our World Wide Web Site

Additional materials designed especially for you are available on the World Wide Web. Go to http://www.course.com.

To the Instructor

The Data files and Course Labs are available on the Instructor's Resource Kit for this title. Follow the instructions in the Help file on the CD-ROM to install the programs to your network or standalone computer. For information on creating Data Disks, see the "To the Student" section above. To complete the tutorials in this book, students must have a Web browser, an e-mail account, and an Internet connection.

You are granted a license to copy the Data Files to any computer or computer network used by students who have purchased this book.

In this tutorial you will:

- Determine whether a research question is specific or exploratory

- Learn how to develop an effective Web search strategy to answer research questions

- Learn about Web search tools and how they work

- Create different kinds of search expressions

- Find information using search engines, directories, and other Web research tools

SEARCHING THE WEB

Using Search Engines and Directories Effectively

CASE

Midland News Business Section

The *Midland News* is a top-rated daily newspaper that serves the Midland metropolitan area. The *News* is especially proud of its business section, which has won a number of awards for business reporting and analysis over the years. Anne Hill is the business editor at the *News* and has recruited an excellent staff of editors, reporters, and columnists, who each specialize in different areas of business. Anne has hired you to fill an intern position as her staff assistant. The writers in the business section offices use computers to write and edit the newspaper. Recently, each writer gained access to the Internet on his or her computer. Anne would like you to work with Dave Burton, who is the paper's international news reporter, and Ranjit Singh, who writes a syndicated column on current economic trends. Dave and Ranjit are busy and do not have time to learn how to use the Internet for the quick, reliable research that they need to create and support their writing.

Anne expects you to begin by doing most of the Web searching for Ranjit and Dave yourself; eventually, she wants you to train them to use the Web. You tell Anne that you are just learning to use the Web yourself, but she explains that this will be your full-time job during your internship and she is counting on you to become skilled in Web searching. Anne also reassures you by telling you that she has been working with the Web quite a bit herself and would be happy to help you with questions you might have as you find your way around the Web.

SESSION 4.1

In this session, you will learn about two types of search questions, how to create search expressions, and how to use Web search engines and directories. Also, you will use other Web resources to find answers to your questions or information related to topics in which you are interested.

Types of Search Questions

Anne is present at your first meeting with Dave and Ranjit. Dave asks about what kinds of Web information can help him do his job better. You reply that Dave's Internet connection provides him with information about every country in the world and on most major businesses and industries. No matter what type of story he is writing, you probably can find relevant facts that he can use. Dave mentions that his stories always can use more facts. Anne agrees and says that one of the most frequent editor comments on reporters' stories is to "get the facts."

Ranjit says that his columns do not rely as much on current events and facts—they are longer, more thought-provoking pieces about broad economic and business issues. Quick access to facts is not nearly as important to him as it is to a business news reporter like Dave. Ranjit hopes that the Web can provide him with new ideas that he could explore in his columns. So, instead of fast answers to specific questions, Ranjit explains that he wants to use the Web as a resource for interesting concepts and ideas. He knows that the Web is a good way to find unusual and interesting views on the economy and general business practices. Ranjit is always looking for new angles on old ideas, so he is optimistic that you can find many useful Web resources for him.

Both writers were happy to have an eager assistant "working the Web" for them. Anne explained to you that each writer will need a different kind of help because of their different writing goals. Dave will need quick answers to specific questions. For example, he might need to know the population of Bolivia and perhaps some related information about demographic trends. Ranjit will need to find Web sites that contain, for example, collected research papers that discuss the causes of the Great Depression.

You can use the Web to obtain answers to both of these question types—specific and exploratory—but each question type requires a different search strategy. A **specific question** is a question that you can phrase easily and one for which you will recognize the answer when you find it. In other words, you will know when to end your search. The search process for a specific question is one of narrowing the field down to the answer you seek. An **exploratory question** is an open-ended question that can be harder to phrase; it also is difficult to determine when you find a good answer. The search process for an exploratory question requires you to fan out in a number of directions to find relevant information. You can use the Web to find answers to both kinds of questions, but each requires a different search strategy.

Specific questions require you to start with broad categories of information and gradually narrow the search until you find the answer to your question. Figure 4-1 shows this process of sequential, increasingly focused questions.

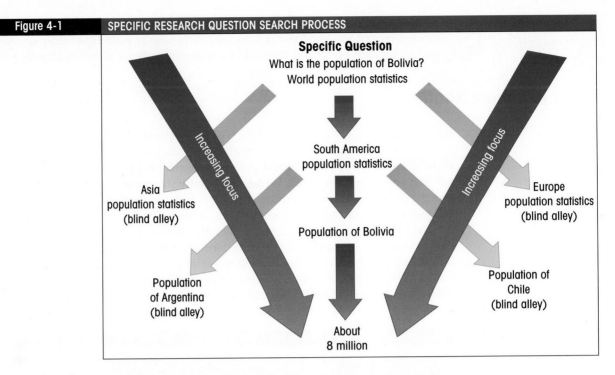

Figure 4-1 SPECIFIC RESEARCH QUESTION SEARCH PROCESS

As you narrow your search, you might find that you are heading in the wrong direction, or down a blind alley. In that case, you need to move back up the funnel shown in Figure 4-1 and try another path.

Exploratory questions start with general questions that lead to other, less-general questions. The answers to the questions at each level should lead you to more information about the topic in which you are interested. This information then leads you to more questions. Figure 4-2 shows how this questioning process leads to a broadening scope as you gather information pertinent to the exploratory question.

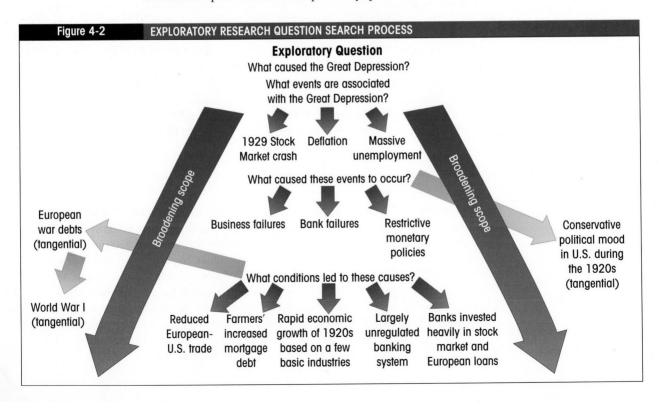

Figure 4-2 EXPLORATORY RESEARCH QUESTION SEARCH PROCESS

As your search expands, you might find yourself collecting tangential information that is somewhat related to your topic but does not help answer your exploratory question. The boundary between useful and tangential information is often difficult to identify precisely.

Web Search Strategy

Now that you understand the different types of questions that Ranjit and Dave will ask as you begin to work for them, Anne suggests that you learn something about searching the Web. You tell her that you know the Web is a collection of interconnected HTML documents and that you know how to use Web browser software to navigate the hyperlinks that connect these documents. Anne explains that the search tools available on the Web are an integral part of these linked HTML documents, or Web pages.

To search the Web effectively, you should first decide whether your question is specific or exploratory. Second, you should carefully formulate and state your question. The third step is to select the appropriate tool or tools to use in your search. After obtaining your results from a Web search tool, you might need to re-define or refine your question and select a different search tool to see if you get a different result. Figure 4-3 shows the search process.

Figure 4-3	WEB SEARCH PROCESS
1. Is the question specific or exploratory?	
2. Formulate and state the question.	
3. Select the appropriate Web search tool.	
4. Evaluate the search results.	
5. Repeat the previous steps until you find the answer.	

You can repeat this process as many times as necessary until you obtain the specific answer or the range of information regarding your exploratory topic that you find satisfactory. Sometimes, you might find that the nature of your original question is different than you had originally thought. You also might find that you need to reformulate, or more clearly state, your question. As you restate your question, you should try to think of synonyms for each word. Unfortunately, many words in the English language have multiple meanings. If you use a word in your search that is common and has many meanings, you will be buried in irrelevant information or be led down many blind alleys. Identifying unique phrases that relate to your topic or question is a helpful way to avoid some of these problems.

Web Search Tools

To implement any Web search strategy, you will use one or more Web search tools. The four broad categories of Web search tools include search engines, directories, meta-search engines, and other Web resources. The Additional Information section of the Student Online Companion Web page for Tutorial 4 includes hyperlinks to many of these Web search tools. In this section, you will learn the basics of using each type of search tool. Remember that searching the Web is a challenging task for any of these tools. No one knows how many pages exist on the Web, but current estimates suggest over 800 million pages. Each of these pages might have thousands of words, images, or downloadable files. Unlike any library, the content of the Web is not indexed in any standardized way. Fortunately, the tools you have to search the Web are powerful.

Using Search Engines

A Web **search engine** is a special kind of Web page that finds other Web pages that match a word or phrase you enter into it. The word or phrase you enter, called a **search expression** or a **query**, might include instructions that tell the search engine how to search. A search engine does not examine every Web page to find a match; it only searches its *own* database of Web pages and Web page information. Therefore, if you enter the same search expression into different search engines, you will get different results. Most search engines report the number of hits they find. A **hit** is a Web page that is indexed in the search engine's database and contains text that matches your search expression. All search engines provide a series of **results pages**, which are Web pages that contain hyperlinks to the Web pages that contain text that matches your search expression.

Each search engine uses a Web robot to build its database. A **Web robot**, also called a **bot** or a **spider**, is a program that automatically searches the Web to find new Web sites and update information about old Web sites that already are in the database. One of a Web robot's more important tasks is to delete information in the database when a Web site no longer exists. The main advantage of using an automated searching tool is that it can examine far more Web sites than an army of people ever could.

Many search engines allow Web page creators to submit the URLs of their pages to search engine databases. Most search engine operators screen such Web page submissions to prevent a Web page creator from submitting a large number of duplicate or similar Web pages.

The business firms and other organizations that operate search engines often sell advertising space on the search engine Web page and on the results pages to sponsors. They use the advertising revenue to generate profit after covering the costs of maintaining the computer hardware and software required to search the Web and create and search the database. The only price you pay for access to these excellent tools is that you will see advertising banners on many of the pages; otherwise, your usage is free.

You just received an e-mail message from Dave with your first research assignment. He wants to mention the amount of average rainfall in Belize to make a point in a story that he is writing. First, you must determine what tasks to perform. You can use the five steps shown in Figure 4-3 as follows:

1. Decide that the question "What is the average annual rainfall in Belize?" is a specific question, not an exploratory question.

2. Next, formulate and state the question. You identify key search terms in the question that you can use in your search expression: *Belize*, *rainfall*, and *annual*. You decide to use these terms because they should each appear on any Web page that includes the answer to Dave's question. None of these terms are articles, prepositions, or other common words. None of the words have multiple meanings. The term *Belize* should be especially useful in narrowing the search to relevant Web pages.

3. Since the question is very specific but could require a search of many categories in a directory, you decide that a search engine might return the answer more efficiently than a search of directories.

4. When you obtain the results, you will examine them and decide whether they provide an acceptable answer to your question.

5. If the results do not answer the question, you may reconsider whether the question is specific or exploratory and conduct a second search using a different tool, question, or search expression.

To find the average annual rainfall in Belize:

1. Start your Web browser, go to the **Student Online Companion** Web page (http://www.course.com/newperspectives/internet2), click the hyperlink for your book, click the **Tutorial 4** hyperlink, and then click the **Session 4.1** hyperlink.

2. Click the **AltaVista** link to open the AltaVista search engine page.

3. Type **Belize annual rainfall** in the AltaVista search text box, as shown in Figure 4-4.

| Figure 4-4 | TYPING THE SEARCH EXPRESSION INTO THE ALTAVISTA SEARCH ENGINE |

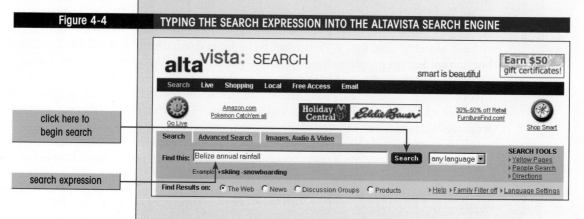

click here to begin search

search expression

4. Click the AltaVista **Search** button (see Figure 4-4) to run the search. The search results appear on a new page—there are over 100,000 Web pages that match your search criteria!

5. Scroll down the results page and examine your search results. Click some of the links until you find a page that provides the average annual rainfall for Belize. Click the **Back** button on your Web browser to return to the results page after going to each hyperlink. You should find that Belize has several climate zones and that the annual rainfall ranges from 50 to 170 inches, or 130 to 430 centimeters.

Dave expected you to find one rainfall amount that would be representative for the entire country, which is not the case. Web searches often disclose information that helps you adjust the assumptions you made when you formulated the original research question. Remember that the Web changes constantly and information is updated continuously, so you might find different information. Dave wants you to check another source to confirm your results, so you decide to search for the same information in another search engine.

To conduct the same search using another search engine:

1. Use your browser's **Back** button to return to the Student Online Companion page, and then click the **HotBot** search engine link to open the HotBot search engine page.

2. Type **Belize annual rainfall** in the Search Smarter text box, as shown in Figure 4-5.

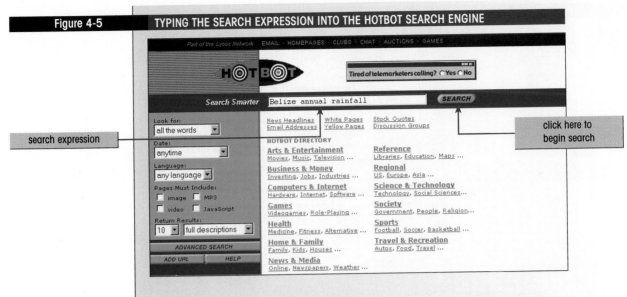

Figure 4-5 **TYPING THE SEARCH EXPRESSION INTO THE HOTBOT SEARCH ENGINE**

search expression

click here to begin search

3. Click the HotBot **SEARCH** button to run the search. The search results appear on a new page, and this time, your search returns about 200 hits.

4. Scroll down the results page and examine your search results, and then click some of the links until you find a page that provides the average annual rainfall for Belize. Click the **Back** button on your Web browser to return to the results page after going to each hyperlink. Once again, you should find that Belize has several climate zones and that the annual rainfall ranges from 50 to 170 inches, or 130 to 430 centimeters.

HotBot returned substantially fewer Web pages than the AltaVista search engine for two reasons: First, each search engine includes different Web pages in its database; second, the HotBot search engine, by default, only returns hits for pages that include *all* of the words you enter in a search expression. The AltaVista search engine's default is to return hits for pages that include *any* of the words. You found the same information after running both searches, so you can give Dave an answer with the second confirmation he requested.

As you can see, different search engine databases store different collections of information about the pages that exist on the Web at any given time. Many search engine robots do not search all of the Web pages at a particular site. Further, each search engine database indexes the information it has collected from the Web differently. Some search engine robots only collect information from a Web page's title, description, keywords, or HTML tags; others only read a certain amount of the HTML code in each Web page. Figure 4-6 shows the HTML code from a Web page that contains information about electronic commerce.

Figure 4-6   **META TAGS FOR A WEB PAGE**

```
<HEAD>

<TITLE>
Current Developments in Electronic Commerce
</TITLE>

<META NAME ="description" CONTENT="Current
news and reports about electronic commerce
developments.">

<META NAME ="keywords" CONTENT ="electronic
commerce, electronic data interchange,
value added reseller, EDI, VAR, secure
socket layer, business on the internet">

</HEAD>
```

The description and keywords tags are examples of HTML META tags. A **META tag** is HTML code that a Web page creator places in the page header for the specific purpose of informing Web robots about the content of the page. META tags do not cause any text to appear on the page when a Web browser loads it; rather, they exist solely for the use of search engine robots.

The information contained in META tags can become a key part of a search engine's database. For example, the keywords META tag shown in Figure 4-6 includes the phrase "electronic data interchange." These keywords could be a very important phrase in a search engine's database because the three individual words *electronic*, *data*, and *interchange*, are common terms that often are used in search expressions that have nothing to do with electronic commerce. The word *data* is so common that many search engines might be programmed to ignore it. A search engine that includes the full phrase "electronic data interchange" in its database will greatly increase the chances that a user interested in that topic will find this particular page.

If the terms you use in your search expression are not in the part of the Web page that a search engine stores in its database, the search engine will not return a hit for that page. Some search engines store the entire content of every Web page they place in their databases. This practice is called **full text indexing**. All search engines, even those that are full text indexed search engines, omit common words such as *and*, *the*, *it*, and *by* from their databases. Many search engine operators include information about their search engines, robots, and databases on their Web sites. You will learn more about several of the major search engines in Session 4.2.

Using Directories and Hybrid Search Engine Directories

Search engines provide a powerful tool for executing keyword searches of the Web. However, because most search engine URL databases are built by computers running programs that perform the search automatically, they can miss important classification details that you would notice instantly. For example, if a search engine's robot found a Web page with the title "Test Data: Do Not Use," it would probably include content from the page in the search engine database. If you were to read such a warning in a Web page title, *you* would know not to include the page's contents. However, keep in mind that with over 800 million Web pages on the Web, the volume of data that a search engine robot obtains as it travels the Web precludes screening by people.

Web directories use a completely different approach from search engines to build useful indexes of information on the Web. A **Web directory** is a listing of hyperlinks to Web pages that is organized into hierarchical categories. The difference between a search engine and a Web directory is that *people* select the Web pages to include in a Web directory. These people, who are knowledgeable experts in one or more subject areas and skilled in various classification techniques, review candidate Web pages for inclusion in the directory. When the experts decide that a Web page is worth listing in the directory, they determine the appropriate category in which to store the hyperlink to that page. Many directories allow a Web page to be indexed in several different categories. The main weakness of a directory is that you must know which category is likely to yield the information you desire. If you begin searching in the wrong category, you might follow many hyperlinks before you realize that the information you seek is not in that category. Some directories overcome this limitation by including hyperlinks in category levels that link to lower levels in other categories.

One of the oldest and most respected directories on the Web is **Yahoo!**. Two Stanford doctoral students, David Filo and Jerry Yang, who wanted a way to keep track of interesting sites they found on the Internet, started Yahoo! in 1994. Since 1994, Yahoo! has grown to become one of the most widely used resources on the Web. Yahoo! currently lists hundreds of thousands of Web pages in its categories—a sizable collection, but only a small portion of the hundreds of millions of pages on the Web. Although Yahoo! does use some automated programs for checking and classifying its entries, it relies on human experts to do most of the selection and classification work. You can open the Yahoo! directory by clicking the Yahoo! link on the Session 4.1 Student Online Companion page. The Yahoo! home page appears in Figure 4-7.

Figure 4-7   **YAHOO! WEB DIRECTORY**

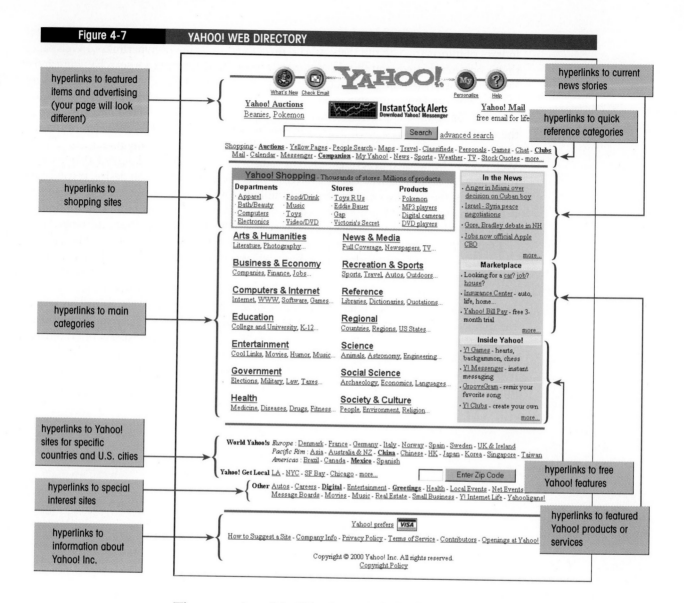

The top section of the Yahoo! page includes featured items and advertising. The featured items change regularly and usually highlight timely topics that the Yahoo! editors believe will interest many of the site's visitors.

The search tool that appears below the advertising banner is a search engine within the Yahoo! directory. You can enter search terms into this tool, and Yahoo! will search its listings to find a match. This combination of search engine and directory, called a **hybrid search engine directory**, can provide a powerful and effective tool for searching the Web. Using a hybrid search engine directory can help you identify which category in the directory is likely to contain the information you need. After you enter a category, the search engine is useful for narrowing a search even further; you can enter a search expression and limit the search to that category.

The next section of the Yahoo! page includes quick reference categories, which are commonly used categories that might otherwise be hard to find because they would be buried several layers under a main category heading. Also, users might find it difficult to guess which main categories might include these items. For example, "weather" might be classified under the main category headings "News and Media" or "Science." The quick reference section makes often-sought information categories easier to find.

The Yahoo! Shopping section includes hyperlinks to sites that offer goods and services for sale on the Web. Some of these sites are operated by Yahoo!, which rents the space to businesses. Others are independent sites operated by major companies that have paid Yahoo! for this hyperlink space on the Yahoo! page.

The main categories section of the Yahoo! page is the primary tool for searching the directory's listings. Under each of the 14 main categories, Yahoo! lists several subcategories. These are not the only subcategories; they are just a sample of those that are the largest or most used. You can click a main category hyperlink to see all of the subcategories under that category.

The right side of the page includes three sections. The first includes hyperlinks to current news stories. The second includes hyperlinks to featured Yahoo! products or services. The third includes links to free Yahoo! features designed to encourage you to return to the site frequently.

The lower section of the Yahoo! main page includes hyperlinks to Yahoo! directories for other countries and large U.S. cities. The lower section also has a collection of hyperlinks to other parts of the directory that contain specialized categories of hyperlinks, such as the Yahooligans! site, which is a version of Yahoo! designed for children. The very bottom of the page includes links to Yahoo! Inc., the company that operates the site.

Just as you are becoming familiar with the layout of the Yahoo! directory, Dave calls you. He is up against a deadline and needs some information from Intel Corporation's financial statements for a story he is writing. Not all firms publish financial statements on the Internet, but Dave wants you to see what you can find. You tell Dave that you will call him back as quickly as possible. Following your guidelines for searching on the Web, you:

1. Decide that the question is specific: Where can I find the Intel Corporation's Web site?

2. Identify a key search term—Intel—in the question that you will use in your search expression.

3. Use a Web directory to find the answer, so you can search in the business directory instead of searching the entire Web.

4. Examine the results and decide whether a second search using a different category, question, or search expression is necessary.

To find Intel Corporation's financial statements on the Web:

1. Use your browser's **Back** button to return to the Student Online Companion page, and then click the Yahoo! link to open the **Yahoo!** page.

   You consider the main categories on the Yahoo! page and determine that you could probably find your information in either the Business & Economy category or the Computers & Internet category because you know that Intel manufactures computer chips. You decide to look in the Business & Economy category first. You make a note that if this search does not work, you will try the Computers & Internet category next.

2. Click the **Business & Economy** category hyperlink, which opens the page shown in Figure 4-8. The page shown in Figure 4-8 includes hyperlinks to lower levels in the hierarchy and to other points in the hierarchies of other categories. The hyperlinks to lower-levels in this hierarchy include numbers in parentheses that indicate the number of Web pages included in each lower-level category. The hyperlinks that include the "@" symbol are links to other points in the hierarchies of other categories. New categories and categories that include new Web pages are indicated by a "NEW!" icon.

3. Click the **Companies** subcategory hyperlink (see Figure 4-8) to open the Companies page.

| Figure 4-8 | YAHOO! BUSINESS AND ECONOMY CATEGORIES PAGE |

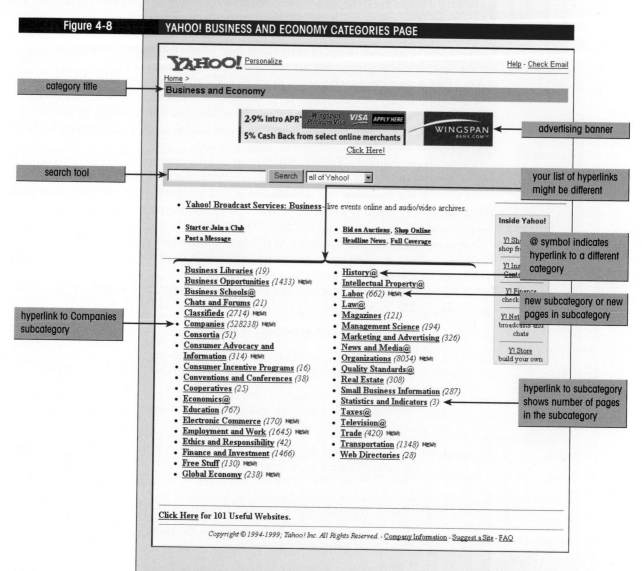

4. Type **Intel** in the search text box, and then click the down arrow in the next text box to select **just this category**, as shown in Figure 4-9. Click the **Search** button.

The results page partially shown in Figure 4-10 opens and lists the hits.

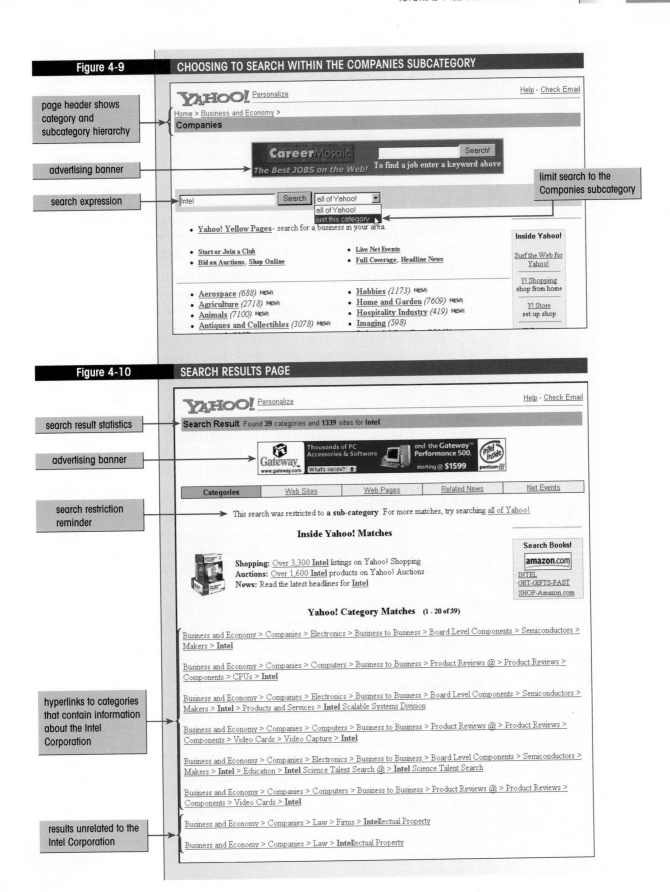

Figure 4-9   CHOOSING TO SEARCH WITHIN THE COMPANIES SUBCATEGORY

page header shows category and subcategory hierarchy

advertising banner

search expression

limit search to the Companies subcategory

Figure 4-10   SEARCH RESULTS PAGE

search result statistics

advertising banner

search restriction reminder

hyperlinks to categories that contain information about the Intel Corporation

results unrelated to the Intel Corporation

The results shown in Figure 4-10 include 39 category hits and 1,339 Web page hits for Intel. As you can see, the first category on the results page is for Intel Corporation. Using the search tool lets you complete your search faster; following the hierarchy down from the Companies subcategory page through Electronics, Semiconductors, and Makers to find Intel would have been many more steps. Many of the categories and sites that this search identifies are completely unrelated—the letters "intel" appear as part of category names, such as Artificial Intelligence and Intelligent Agents. The results page reminds you that the search was restricted to a subcategory. The results page also gives you hyperlinks to Web Sites, Web Pages, Related News, and Internet activities (the Net Events hyperlink) about Intel. If you were researching an exploratory question instead of Dave's specific question, you might want to use these results pages to expand your information-gathering range.

5. Click the **Business and Economy > Companies > Electronics > Business to Business > Board Level Components > Semiconductors > Makers > Intel** hyperlink to open the Intel subcategory page, and then scroll down that page and click the **Financials** hyperlink. The Web page that opens should include a list of recent Annual Reports and financial information for Intel. Click the hyperlink for the latest Annual Report that is available on the Financials subcategory page to open the related Web page at the Intel Corporation.

You have found the location for Intel Corporation's latest financial statements, so you can call Dave back with the information and help him beat his deadline. Now that you have seen how to use a search engine and a hybrid search engine directory, you are ready to use an even more powerful combination of Web research tools: the meta-search engine.

Using Meta-Search Engines

A **meta-search engine** is a tool that combines the power of multiple search engines. Some meta-search tools also include directories. The idea behind meta-search tools is simple. Each search engine on the Web has different strengths and weaknesses because each search engine:

- Uses a different Web robot to gather information about Web pages.
- Stores a different amount of Web page text in its database.
- Selects different Web pages to index.
- Has different storage resources.
- Interprets search expressions somewhat differently.

You saw how these differences cause different search engines to return vastly different results for the same search expression. To perform a complete search for a particular question, you might need to use several individual search engines. Using a meta-search engine lets you search several engines at the same time, so you need not conduct the same search many times. A meta-search engine accepts your search expression and transmits it to several search engines, such as the AltaVista and HotBot search tools you used earlier in this session. These search engines run the search expression against their databases of Web page information and return results to the meta-search engine. The meta-search engine reports consolidated results from all of the search engines it queried. Meta-search engines use the same kinds of programs to run their queries, but they do not have their own databases of Web information.

You want to learn how to use meta-search engines so you can access information faster. You decide to test a meta-search engine using Dave's Belize rainfall question. **Dogpile** is one of the more comprehensive meta-search engines available; it forwards your queries to a number of major search engines and directories, including About.com, AltaVista, Google, GoTo.com, InfoSeek, LookSmart, Lycos, Yahoo!, and several others. The list of search engines and directories might be different when you use this tool because newer and better search tools become available and old favorites disappear over time. Dogpile reports results from each search engine or directory separately and does not eliminate duplicate hits. The list of hyperlinks returned by each search engine remains in the order that the search engine reports them to Dogpile. Like most regular search engines, Dogpile now includes a directory feature that it calls the Web Catalog.

REFERENCE WINDOW   **RW**

Using the Dogpile meta-search engine
- Formulate your search question.
- Open the Dogpile home page in your Web browser.
- Enter the search terms into the Dogpile search text box.
- Evaluate the results and decide whether to revise the question or your choice of search tools.

To use the Dogpile meta-search engine:

1. Click the **Back** button on your Web browser until you return to the Student Online Companion page for Session 4.1, and then click the **Dogpile** link to open the Dogpile meta-search engine page.

2. Type **Belize annual rainfall** in the Dogpile search text box, as shown in Figure 4-11.

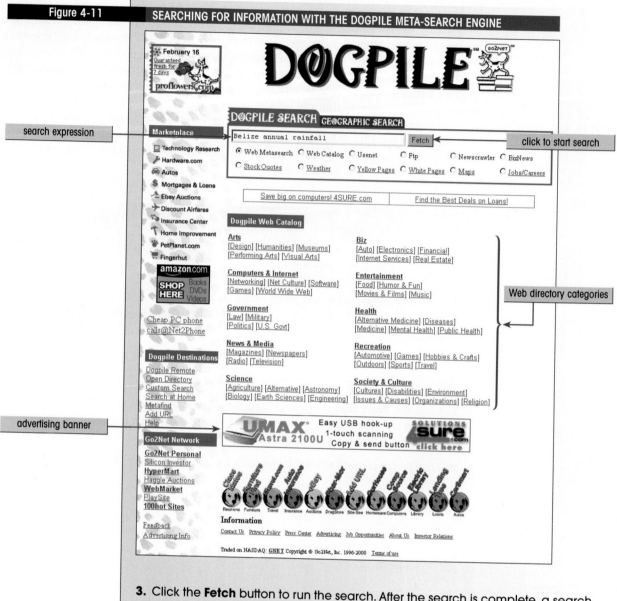

Figure 4-11   SEARCHING FOR INFORMATION WITH THE DOGPILE META-SEARCH ENGINE

3. Click the **Fetch** button to run the search. After the search is complete, a search results page opens and shows the hits for each search engine.

4. Examine your search results.

As you scroll through the search results pages, you can see that there is a wide variation in the number and quality of the results provided by each search engine and directory. You might see many hits, but no hyperlinks. You also might notice a number of duplicate hits; however, most of the Web pages returned by one search tool are not returned by any other. You can click the Next Set of Search Engines button at the bottom of the results page to see the hits returned by other search engines.

Using Other Web Resources

A variety of other resources are available for searching the Web that do not fit exactly into the three preceding categories. These search resources are similar to bibliographies, but instead of listing books or journal articles, they contain lists of hyperlinks to Web pages. Just as some bibliographies are annotated, many of these resources include summaries or reviews of Web pages.

These other resources can be very useful when you want to obtain a broad overview or a basic understanding of a complex subject area. A search for such resources that uses a search engine or directory is likely to turn up a narrow list of references that are too detailed and that assume a great deal of prior knowledge. For example, using a search engine or directory to find information about quantum physics will probably give you many references to technical papers and Web pages devoted to current research issues in quantum physics. However, your search probably will yield very few Web pages that provide an introduction to the topic. A Web bibliography page can offer hyperlinks to information regarding a particular subject that is presented at various levels. Many of these resources include annotations and reviews of the sites they list. This information can help you identify Web pages that fit your level of interest.

Some of the names used to identify these Web bibliographies include **resource lists**, **guides**, **clearinghouses**, and **virtual libraries**. Many of these bibliographies are general references, such as the Librarian's Index to the Internet, the Free Internet Encyclopedia, the Scout Report Signpost, and the Argus Clearinghouse. Others are more focused, such as the Martindale Reference Desk, which emphasizes science-related links. You can visit any of these Web sites by clicking their links on the Tutorial 4 page of the Student Online Companion. The hyperlinks for these resources appear in the Additional Information section of the page under the Other Search Tools and Resources heading.

Ranjit stops by your office and asks for your help. He is planning to write a series of columns on the business and economic effects of current trends in biotechnology. The potential effects of genetic engineering research particularly intrigue him, but he admits that he does not know much about any of these topics. Ranjit wants you to find some Web sites that he could explore to learn more about biotechnology trends in general and genetic engineering research in particular. He mentions that it would be nice, but not essential, to find some recent news summaries about biotechnology and business. You decide to use the Argus Clearinghouse site as a resource to work on the exploratory question that Ranjit has given you. The **Argus Clearinghouse** reviews and provides hyperlinks to subject guides. You determine that Ranjit's request is an exploratory search. You know that biotechnology is a branch of the biological sciences, so you identify three category terms: *biotechnology*, *genetic engineering*, and *biology* to use as your search categories.

REFERENCE WINDOW   **RW**

Using the Argus Clearinghouse Web site
- Identify categories and search terms that might lead you to the desired information resources.
- Open the Argus home page in your Web browser.
- Explore the Argus categories that are related to the categories and search terms you identified.
- Follow the category hyperlinks to subcategories and Web pages.
- Evaluate the results and decide whether to revise your categories or choice of Web resources.

To use Argus to conduct an exploratory search:

1. Return to the Student Online Companion page for Session 4.1, and then click the **Argus Clearinghouse** link to open that page.

2. As you scan the main categories on the Argus Clearinghouse home page, you do not see any of your search categories listed; however, you know that biology is a science, so click the **Science & Mathematics** hyperlink.

3. Click the **biology** link that appears on the Science & Mathematics subcategory page. You see two of your search terms in the keywords list on the biology page and decide to follow both of them.

4. Click the **biotechnology** keyword hyperlink to open the Web page shown in Figure 4-12.

| Figure 4-12 | BIOTECHNOLOGY SUBCATEGORY IN ARGUS CLEARINGHOUSE |

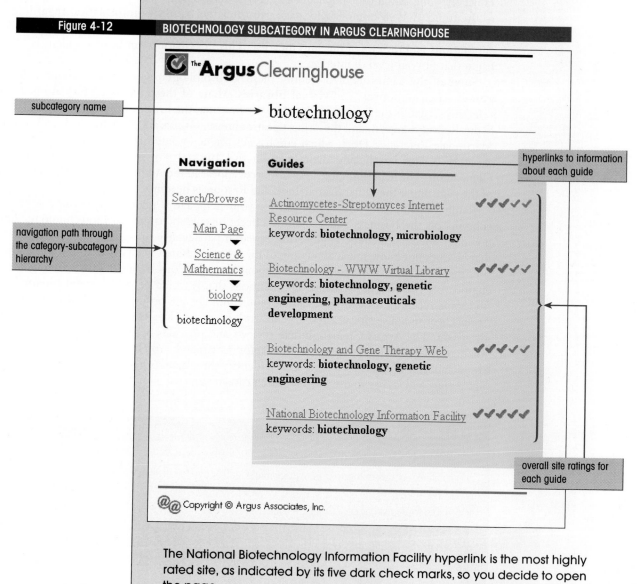

The National Biotechnology Information Facility hyperlink is the most highly rated site, as indicated by its five dark check marks, so you decide to open the page.

5. Click the **National Biotechnology Information Facility** hyperlink to open the Guide Information page for the site shown in Figure 4-13. The Guide Information page includes a hyperlink to the Web site, indexing keywords, information about the author of the site, and detailed ratings on several dimensions. You can follow this site to gather specific information for Ranjit or give him the site's URL and let him explore the site. You might want to gather the URLs of this and other sites that you find and send them all to Ranjit in one e-mail message. You have explored the biotechnology subcategory; next, you will explore the genetic engineering subcategory.

Figure 4-13	INFORMATION ABOUT THE BIOTECH GUIDE WEB SITE

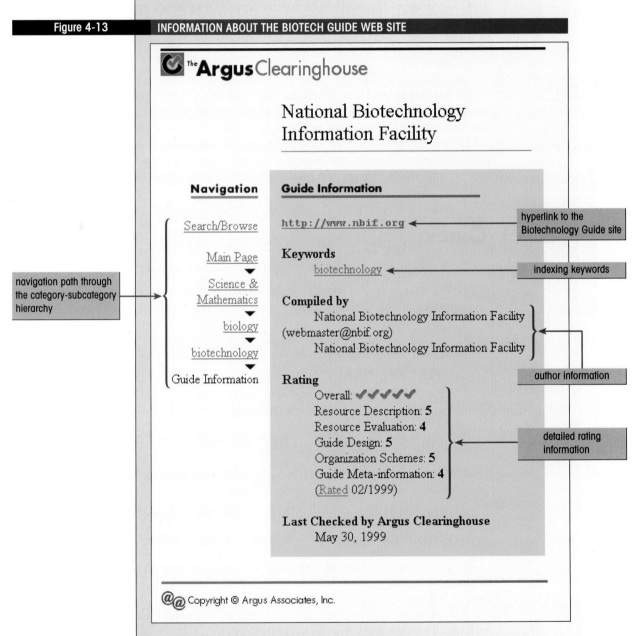

6. Click the **biology** hyperlink that appears in the Navigation path on the left side of the Web page to return to the list of biology keywords.

7. Click the **genetic engineering** hyperlink to open the Argus list of Guides to that topic. The genetic engineering Guide lists three entries. One of these entries is the WWW Virtual Library Biotechnology page that also appeared on the biotechnology Guide page shown in Figure 4-12.

8. Click the **Biotechnology and Gene Therapy Web** hyperlink to explore the resources at that site. Remember that Ranjit does not expect you to understand the contents of the Web pages you find; he just wants you to identify resources to help him learn more about trends in this area of scientific research.

9. Examine your search results and determine whether you have gathered sufficient useful information to respond to Ranjit's request.

10. Close your browser, and log off the Internet, if necessary.

You have completed your search for Web sites that might help Ranjit. Many of these sites contain hyperlinks to other useful sites that Ranjit might want to explore. You can deliver information from these pages to Ranjit by printing copies of the Web pages, sending the URLs by e-mail, or saving the Web pages and attaching them to an e-mail message. Because your answer to Ranjit's question involves so many pages at different sites, your best approach would be to send an e-mail message with a list of relevant URLs.

Session 4.1 QUICK CHECK

1. What are the key characteristics of an exploratory search question?

2. What steps do you take to use the Web to find the answer to a specific type question?

3. What is a Web robot, and how does it work?

4. True or False: Web search engine operators use advertising revenue to cover their expenses and earn a profit.

5. True or False: Search engines consider all words in their database; words such as *and* or *the* are included in their databases.

6. What is one advantage and one disadvantage of using a Web directory instead of a Web search engine to locate information?

7. How does a hybrid search engine-directory overcome the disadvantages of using either a search engine or a directory alone?

8. How does a meta-search engine process the search expression you enter into it?

9. What are the key features offered by Web bibliographies?

In this session, you learned how to identify the two basic types of search questions and formulate a search process for each type. You also used Web search engines, directories, meta-search engines, and other information-finding resources on the Web. In the next session, you will use these Web search tools to conduct more complex searches so you can filter out irrelevant hits and narrow your search more quickly.

SESSION 4.2

Although you can find the answers to many research questions on the Web with a simple search using one of the tools described in Session 4.1, some questions are more complex. In this session, you will learn how to use the advanced features of Web search engines, directories, and other Web resources to answer complex questions. Many of these Web search tools use Boolean logic and other filtering mechanisms to select and sort search results; however, many of these search tools implement these mechanisms differently. After learning the basics of Boolean logic and filtering techniques, you will use those techniques in a variety of Web search tools.

Boolean Logic and Filtering Techniques

The most important factor in getting good results from a search engine, a meta-search engine, or a search tool within a hybrid search engine-directory is to select carefully the search terms you use. When the object of your search is straightforward, you can choose one or two words that will work well. More complex search questions require more complex queries, which you can use along with Boolean logic, search expression operators, or filtering techniques, to broaden or narrow your search expression. In the next three sections, you will learn how to use each of these techniques.

Boolean Operators

When you enter a single word into a Web search tool, it searches for matches to that word. When you enter a search expression into a Web search tool that includes more than one word, the search tool makes assumptions about the words that you enter. You learned in Session 4.1 that the AltaVista search engine assumes that you want to match any of the keywords in your search expression, and HotBot assumes that you want to match all of the keywords. These different assumptions can make dramatic differences in the number and quality of hits returned. Many search engine operators, realizing that users might want to match all of the keywords on one search and any of the keywords on a different search, have designed their search engines to offer these options. The most common way of implementing these options is to offer Boolean operators as part of their search engines.

George Boole was a nineteenth century British mathematician who developed a branch of mathematics and logic that bears his name, **Boolean algebra**. In Boole's algebra, all values are reduced to one of two values. In most practical applications of Boole's work, these two values are *true* and *false*. Although Boole did his work many years before practical electrically powered computers became commonplace, his algebra was useful to computer engineers and programmers. At the very lowest level of analysis, all computing is a manipulation of a single computer circuit's on and off states.

Some parts of Boolean algebra are also useful in search expressions. **Boolean operators**, also called **logical operators**, are a key part of Boolean algebra. **Boolean operators** specify the logical relationship between the elements they join, just as the plus sign arithmetic operator specifies the mathematical relationship between the two elements it joins. Three basic Boolean operators—AND, OR, and NOT—are recognized by most search engines. You can use these operators in many search engines by simply including them with search terms. For example, the search expression "exports AND France" returns hits for pages that contain both words, the expression "exports OR France" returns hits for pages that contain either word, and "exports NOT France" returns hits for pages that contain the word *export* but not the word *France*. Some search engines use "AND NOT" to indicate the Boolean NOT operator.

Figure 4-14 shows several ways to use Boolean operators in more complex search expressions that contain the words *exports*, *France*, and *Japan*. The figure shows the matches that a search engine will return if it interprets the Boolean operators correctly. Figure 4-14 also describes information-gathering tasks in which you might use these expressions.

Figure 4-14	USING BOOLEAN OPERATORS IN SEARCH EXPRESSIONS	
SEARCH EXPRESSION	**SEARCH RETURNS PAGES THAT INCLUDE**	**USE TO FIND INFORMATION ABOUT**
exports AND France AND Japan	All of the three search terms.	Exports from France to Japan or from Japan to France.
exports OR France OR Japan	Any of the three search terms.	Exports from anywhere, including France and Japan, and all kinds of information about France and Japan.
exports NOT France NOT Japan	Exports, but not if the page also includes the terms *France* or *Japan*.	Exports to and from any countries other than France or Japan.
exports AND France NOT Japan	Exports and France, but not Japan.	Exports to and from France to anywhere else, except exports shipped to Japan.

Other Search Expression Operators

When you join three or more search terms with Boolean operators, it is easy to become confused by the expression's complexity. To reduce the confusion, you can use precedence operators, a tool you probably learned in basic algebra, along with the Boolean operators. A **precedence operator**, also called an **inclusion operator** or a **grouping operator**, clarifies the grouping within a complex expression and is usually indicated by the parentheses symbols. Some search engines use double quotation marks to indicate precedence grouping; however, other search engines use double quotation marks to indicate search terms that must be matched exactly as they appear (that is, search for the exact search phrase) within the double quotation marks. Figure 4-15 shows several ways to use precedence operators with Boolean operators in search expressions.

Figure 4-15	USING BOOLEAN AND PRECEDENCE OPERATORS IN SEARCH EXPRESSIONS	
SEARCH EXPRESSION	**SEARCH RETURNS PAGES THAT INCLUDE**	**USE TO FIND INFORMATION ABOUT**
exports AND (France OR Japan)	Exports and either France or Japan.	Exports from or to either France or Japan.
exports OR (France AND Japan)	Exports or both France and Japan.	Exports from anywhere, including France and Japan, and all kinds of other information about France and Japan.
exports AND (France NOT Japan)	Exports and France, but not if the page also includes Japan.	Exports to and from France, except those going to or from Japan.

Some search engines recognize variants of the Boolean operators, such as "must include" and "must exclude" operators. For example, a search engine that uses the plus sign to indicate "must include" and the minus sign to indicate "must exclude" would respond to the expression "exports + France - Japan" with hits that included anything about exports and France, but only if those pages did not include anything about Japan.

Another useful search expression tool is the location operator. A **location operator**, or **proximity operator**, lets you search for terms that appear close to each other in the text of a Web page. The most common location operator offered in Web search engines is the

NEAR operator. If you are interested in French exports, you might want to find only Web pages in which the terms *exports* and *France* are close to each other. Unfortunately, each search engine that implements this operator uses its own definition of how close "NEAR" is. One search engine might define NEAR to mean "within 10 words," whereas another search engine might define NEAR to mean "within 20 words." To use the NEAR operator effectively, you must read the search engine's help file carefully.

Wildcard Characters and Search Filters

Most search engines support some use of a wildcard character in their search expressions. A **wildcard character** allows you to omit part of the search term or terms. Many search engines recognize the asterisk (*) as the wildcard character. For example, the search expression "export*" would return pages containing the terms *exports, exporter, exporters,* and *exporting* in many search engines.

Many search engines allow you to restrict your search by using search filters. A **search filter** eliminates Web pages from a search. The filter criteria can include such Web page attributes as language, date, domain, host, or page component (URL, hyperlink, image tag, or title tag). For example, many search engines provide a way to search for the term *exports* in Web page titles and ignore pages in which the term appears in other parts of the page.

Advanced Searches

Most search engines implement many of the operators and techniques you have learned about, but search engine syntax varies. Some search engines provide separate advanced search pages for these techniques; others allow you to use advanced techniques such as Boolean operators on their simple search pages. Next, you will learn how to conduct complex searches using the advanced search features of several different search engines.

Advanced Search in AltaVista

Ranjit is working on a series of columns about the role that trade agreements play in limiting the flow of agricultural commodities between countries. This week's column concerns the German economy. He wants you to find some Web page references for him that might provide useful background information for his column. Ranjit is especially interested in learning more about the German perspective on trade issues, but he cannot read German.

You recognize this as an exploratory question and decide to use the advanced query capabilities of the AltaVista search engine to conduct a complex search for Web pages that Ranjit might use for his research. You want to provide Ranjit with a reasonable number of hyperlinks to Web pages, but you do not want to inundate him with thousands of URLs, so you decide to use Boolean and precedence operators to create a search expression that will focus on useful sites. To create a useful search expression, you must identify search terms that might lead you to appropriate Web pages. Some terms you might use are *Germany, trade, treaty,* and *agriculture.* You decide to use Boolean and precedence operators to combine your search terms. You also decide to use the wildcard character to allow the search to find plural and extended forms of the terms *treaty* (such as *treaties*) and *agriculture* (such as *agricultures, agricultural,* and *agriculturally*). Ranjit's primary interest is in trade issues, so you decide to rank the hits returned by *trade.*

REFERENCE WINDOW

Conducting a complex search using AltaVista
- Open the AltaVista search engine in your Web browser.
- Select the Advanced Search option.
- Choose a language filter.
- Devise and enter a suitable search expression.
- Click the Search button.
- Evaluate the results and revise your search expression as necessary.

To perform an advanced search using AltaVista:

1. If necessary, start your Web browser, go to the **Student Online Companion** (http://www.course.com/newperspectives/internet2), click the link for your book, click the **Tutorial 4** link, and then click the **Session 4.2** link.

2. Click the **AltaVista** link to open that page.

3. Click the **Advanced Search** hyperlink on the AltaVista page. Ranjit only reads English, so you need to filter the language.

4. Click the list arrow that says "any language," and then click **English**.

5. Click in the **Boolean query** text box, and then type **Germany AND (trade OR treat*) AND agricult***.

6. Click the **Search** button to start the search. The search settings and results appear in Figure 4-16.

The search returns about 100,000 hits, so you need to refine your search expression. You examine some of the descriptions provided for the first search results listed and find that many of them include information about fertilizer treatments. You decide that narrowing the search to exclude those sites would make the search results more useful to Ranjit.

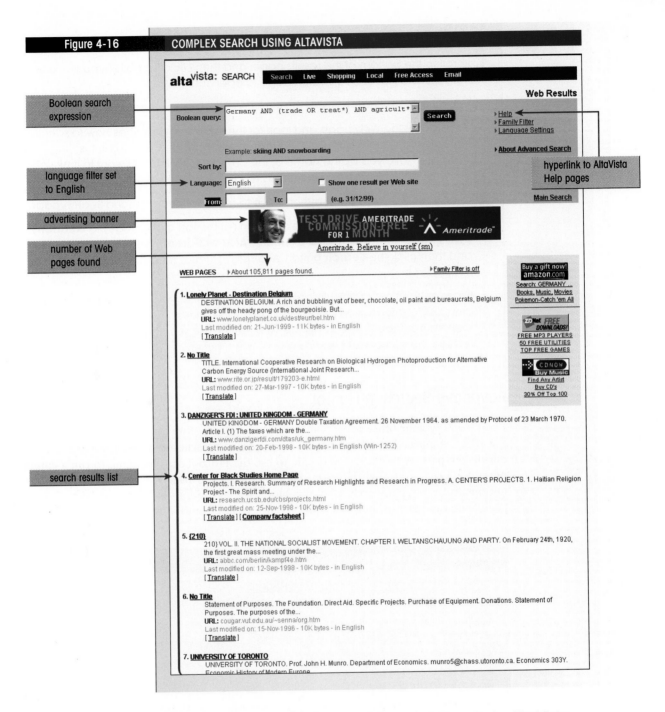

| Figure 4-16 | COMPLEX SEARCH USING ALTAVISTA |

Getting Help and Refining an Advanced Search in AltaVista

Each search engine follows different rules and offers different features. To obtain help for a particular search engine, examine its home page and look for a hyperlink to help pages for that search engine. The AltaVista Advanced Search page includes a hyperlink titled "Help." You decide to exclude the word *treatment* from your Boolean search expression and, to obtain a narrower search that focuses better on the German viewpoint, you decide to restrict the domain to German Web sites.

To obtain help and refine an advanced search in AltaVista:

1. Scroll to the bottom of the results page, and then click the **Help** hyperlink on the AltaVista Advanced Search page to open that page.

2. Click the **Main Search** link at the left side of the Introduction page.

3. Scroll down the Web page and look for the table that describes how to specify keywords in searches. You will find that, in AltaVista, the domain filter is "domain:" followed by the name of the domain to which you want to limit your search. Ranjit tells you that the domain name for Germany is "de."

4. Click your browser's **Back** button twice to return to the Advanced Search page.

5. Change your Boolean search expression (at the top of the page) to **Germany AND (trade OR treat*) AND agricult* AND NOT treatment AND domain:de**, and then click the **Search** button. AltaVista returns a much smaller number of hits this time.

6. Examine your search results and determine whether you have gathered sufficient useful information to respond to Ranjit's request. There are many sites to explore. You could give Ranjit this list or define the search expression further to reduce the number of hits.

Advanced Search in HotBot

Dave stops by your office to tell you he is working on a story for tomorrow's edition about the effect of unusual weather patterns and recent rainstorms on Southeast Asian rice crops during the past six months. You decide to use the HotBot search engine to run a complex query for Dave. Although HotBot offers a SuperSearch page with a wide array of search options (to use SuperSearch, click the More Search Options button on the HotBot main page), you can perform Boolean and filtered searches from HotBot's main search page.

REFERENCE WINDOW	RW

Conducting a complex search using HotBot

- Open the HotBot search engine page in your Web browser.
- Open the HotBot Advanced Search page.
- Set the Look For field to allow Boolean operators.
- Choose a date and geographic region filters.
- Devise and enter a suitable search expression.
- Click the SEARCH button.
- Evaluate the results and revise your search expression as necessary.

To perform a complex search using HotBot:

1. Use your browser's **Back** button to return to the Student Online Companion page for Session 4.2, and then click the **HotBot** link to open that page.

2. Click the **ADVANCED SEARCH** button to open the HotBot SuperSearch page that appears in Figure 4-17.

Figure 4-17 | ADVANCED SEARCH FEATURES OF THE HOTBOT MAIN SEARCH ENGINE PAGE

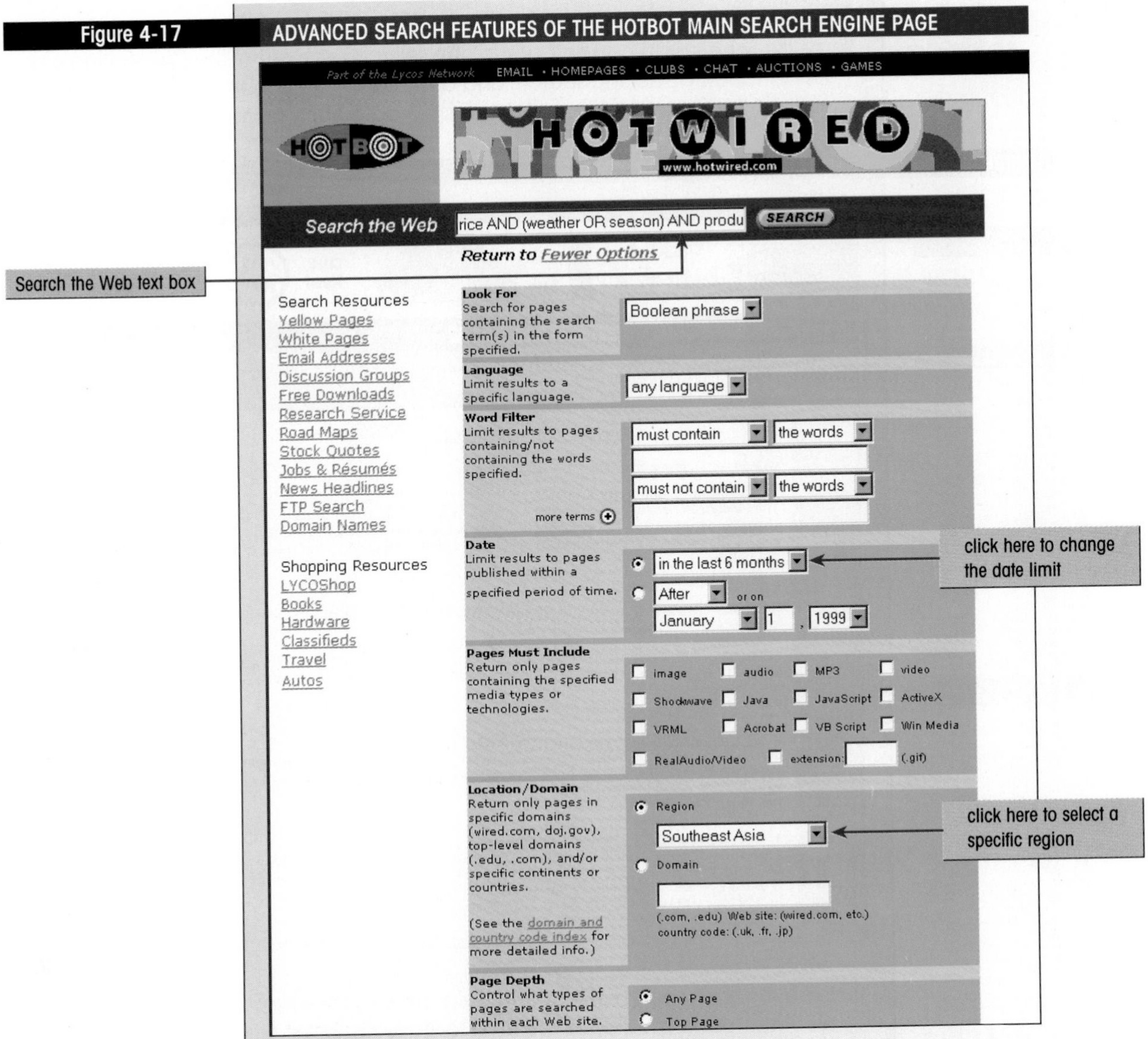

Search the Web text box

3. Click the **Look For** list arrow on the HotBot page (see Figure 4-17), and choose **Boolean phrase**.

4. Click the **Date** list arrow and change the Date limit from *anytime* to **in the last 6 months** (see Figure 4-17).

5. Click the **Location/Domain** list arrow and change the Region from *anywhere* to **Southeast Asia** (see Figure 4-17).

To create a useful search expression, you must identify search terms that might lead you to appropriate Web pages. Some terms you might use are *rice*, *weather*, and *production*. Dave told you that Southeast Asia has a rainy season, so the term *season* might appear instead of *weather* on Web pages that contain information that Dave could use. You decide to use Boolean and precedence operators to combine your search terms. HotBot does not recognize wildcard characters, but it does allow you to set precedence operators.

6. Click in the Search the Web text box (see Figure 4-17), and then type **rice AND (weather OR season) AND production**.

7. Click the **SEARCH** button to start the search. Figure 4-18 shows the search results page, where you can see part of the search expression, the filter settings, information about the search, and a partial list of hyperlinks to related Web pages. The description also includes the date each page was last updated.

Figure 4-18	HOTBOT SEARCH RESULTS PAGE

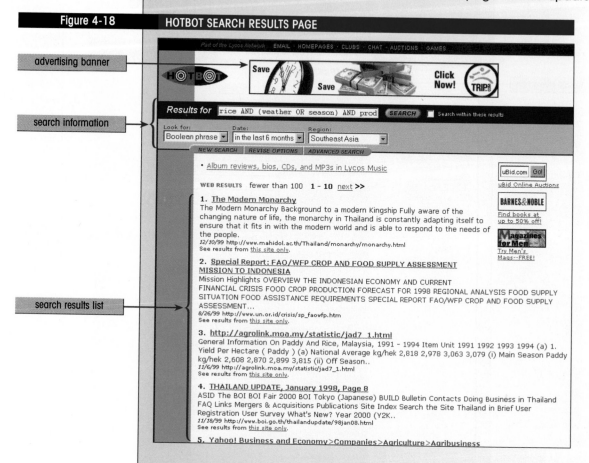

8. Examine your search results and determine whether you have gathered sufficient useful information to respond to Dave's request. Since the search returned a small number of links that contained information relevant to Dave's query, you can conclude your work by forwarding the URLs to Dave.

Complex Search in Excite

Dave calls and has a quick request for your research help. He is working on a story about Finland and remembers that he met a professor who taught graduate business students there. He does not remember the professor's name or the name of the university at which the professor teaches. Dave is confident that he would recognize the university's name if he saw it again. He would like to interview the professor for his story. Dave asks if you can find some Finnish university names on the Web. After evaluating Dave's request, you decide to use the Excite search engine for this task. To create a useful search expression, you must identify search terms that might lead you to appropriate Web pages. Some terms you might use include *Finland*, *university*, and *business*. You consider that a university with a graduate business program might have an academic unit, "school," so you add that to your search expression as an alternative to "university." Hopeful that someone might have placed a list of universities on the Web, you decide to include *list* as a search term, too. The Excite search engine permits Boolean operators in its main page, so you decide to use that page for your query.

REFERENCE   WINDOW   RW

<u>Conducting a complex search using Excite</u>
- Open the Excite search engine page in your Web browser.
- Devise and enter a suitable search expression.
- Click the Search button.
- Evaluate the results and revise your search expression as necessary.

To perform an advanced search using Excite:

1. Use your browser's **Back** button to return to the Student Online Companion page for Session 4.2, and then click the **Excite** link to open that page.

2. Click in the Search for text box at the top of the page, and then type **finland AND list AND (university OR school) AND business**.

3. Click the **Search** button to start the search. Figure 4-19 shows the results page after scrolling it down to the first hit. Note that Excite provides a rating for each hyperlink that it returns. It also provides a hyperlink to a page that automatically performs a search using terms that Excite extracts from the Web page shown in the hyperlink reference.

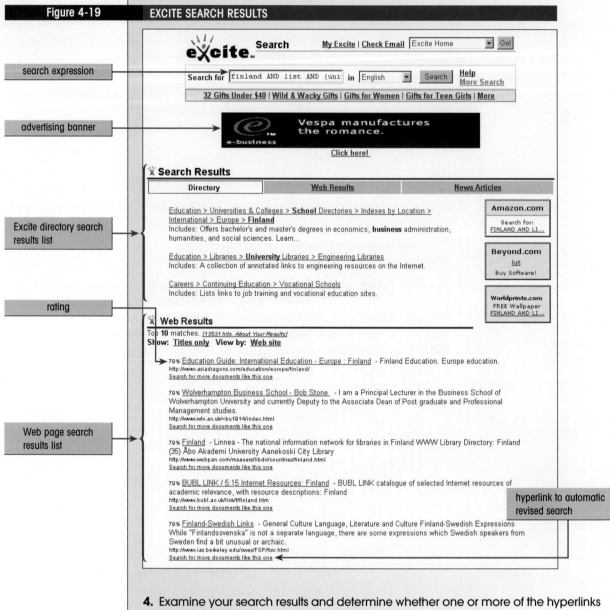

Figure 4-19   EXCITE SEARCH RESULTS

search expression

advertising banner

Excite directory search results list

rating

Web page search results list

hyperlink to automatic revised search

4. Examine your search results and determine whether one or more of the hyperlinks in the search results leads you to a list of Finnish universities that you can give to Dave.

Complex Search in Northern Light

Ranjit is working on a series about fast-food franchises in various developing countries around the world. He would like to feature this industry's experience in Indonesia in his next column and asks you for help. He mentions that he would like to use industry publications in addition to Web sites for his research on this column. You know that the Northern Light search engine indexes not only the Web, but also a collection of periodicals. Therefore, you decide to run this search for Ranjit on the Northern Light search engine. To create a useful search expression, you must identify search terms that might lead you to appropriate Web pages. Some terms you might use include *fast*, *food*, *franchise*, and *Indonesia*. You decide that you are not interested in Web pages that have the individual terms *fast* and *food* as much as you are interested in Web pages that contain the phrase "fast food." The Northern Light search engine does not support full Boolean logic, so you decide to enter a simple expression and use Northern Light's folders feature to filter your results.

REFERENCE WINDOW   **RW**

Conducting a complex search using Northern Light
- Open the Northern Light search engine page in your browser.
- Devise and enter a suitable search expression.
- Click the Search button.
- Evaluate the results and revise your search expression as necessary.

To perform a complex search using Northern Light:

1. Use your browser's **Back** button to return to the Student Online Companion page for Session 4.2, and then click the **Northern Light** link to open that page.

2. Click in the Search for text box, and then type **"fast food" franchise Indonesia**. Make sure that you type the quotation marks, so you find the phrase "fast food," instead of the individual terms.

3. Click the **Search** button to start the search. Figure 4-20 shows the search results page; these hyperlinks look promising.

Figure 4-20	NORTHERN LIGHT SEARCH RESULTS PAGE

advertising banner

search expression

indicates a non-Web search result

search results collected into folders of related hyperlinks

Web search result

Simple Search | Power | Business | Investext | Stock Quotes | Search News   Special Editions™

www.landsend.com
click here to shop

Buy books at
BARNES & NOBLE

1,059 items for:
"fast food" franchise Indonesia   Search   Tips | Save Alert
Edit this search

Narrow Your Search with Custom Search Folders™

Your search returned 1,859 items which we have organized into the following Custom Search Folders:

📁 Search Current News
📁 Special Collection documents
📁 Franchises
📁 Energy & Utilities industry
📁 Commercial sites
📁 ICON (full reports)
📁 Investext (full reports)
📁 MarkIntel Market Research (full reports)
📁 Company information
📁 Indonesian Commercial Newsletter (magazine)
📁 World Sources Online (newswire)
📁 MarkIntel Market Research (single pages) (report)
📁 Investext (single pages) (report)
📁 all others...

US Patent 5,924,090

Home
Help Center
Accounts
About
Alerts
Portfolio

ONE DOT SHOPPING!
StoreRunner

COMPAQ
OpenVMS AlphaServer Solutions

📄 **Documents that best match your search**

1. *Special Collection* INDONESIA HAS THE POTENTIAL TO DEVELOP THE FRANCHISE BUSINESS
   94% - Articles & General info: With a rapidly growing middle , Indonesia is proving a fertile ground the franchising business. At present there are 20 local franchise brands, the most successful... 09/11/95
   Indonesian Commercial Newsletter (magazine): Available at Northern Light
   92%: AMIDST THE BLOOMING FRANSCHISE BUSINESS, CFC CONTINUES TO GROW
   📁 More results from this publication

2. *Special Collection* U.S. franchises strive to rebound from prolonged Indonesia economic woes
   59% - Articles & General info: Twenty percent of McDonald's 100 restaurants in Indonesia have closed in the last year; KFC has 60 of 71 stores still open; and Wendy's... 11/09/98
   Advertising Age International Supplement (magazine): Available at Northern Light
   📁 More results from this publication

3. *Special Collection* Lotteria Hopes to Take Bite Into Indonesian Fast-Food Market
   59% - Articles & General info: Lotteria, the leading fast-food chain affiliated with the Lotte Group, will likely move into Indonesia under a franchise contract with a local company. Sources... 07/23/97
   COMLINE Business News (newswire): Available at Northern Light

4. *Special Collection* INDONESIAN RESTAURANTS
   55% - Industry overviews: Report of IBIS 04/01/98
   MarkIntel Market Research (full reports): Available at Northern Light
   46%: Indonesia - Travel & Tourism Services
   📁 More results from this publication

5. *Special Collection* Smoke on the water
   53% - Articles & General info: Slow-smoked barbecue is moving into international markets. Red Hot & Blue opened its first international franchise Jun 10, 1996, in Amsterdam in partnership with a... 08/10/96
   Restaurant Business (magazine): Available at Northern Light
   53%: Trouble in paradise
   📁 More results from this publication

6. Wendy's Homepage - Old Fashioned Hamburgers
   52% - Articles & General info: In January 1995, Sierad Produce initiated the next phase in the group's expansion programmed when it entered the fast foods industry with the acquisition... 12/29/97
   Personal page: http://engine2.dnet.net.id/wendys/inindo/ii_isi.html

7. Indonesia: Agri-Food Export Market Assessment Report
   48% - Articles & General info: Publication Date: February 1997. INDONESIA. AGRI-FOOD EXPORT MARKET ASSESSMENT REPORT. FEBRUARY 1997. TABLE OF CONTENTS. EXECUTIVE SUMMARY. Indonesia, with a population of 200 million... 07/28/99
   Canadian site: http://atn-riae.agr.ca/public/htmldocs/e1378.htm
   📁 More results from this site

4. In the list of Custom Search Folders links at the left side of the page, click the **Food products & services** link. Examine your search results and determine whether you have gathered enough information about the fast-food industry in Indonesia for Dave.

5. Close your Web browser, and your dial-up connection, if necessary.

Northern Light provides hyperlinks to Web pages and to its own collection of several thousand journals, books, and other print resources. It provides a hyperlink to Web pages it finds and provides a summary of the print resources in its collection. For a fee, you can purchase the right to download and print an item from its collection. However, you can often find the original source in your school or company library if you do not want to purchase the item from Northern Light. Downloading the item would be a nice convenience if you used this search engine frequently.

The first five hyperlinks that appear in the results shown in Figure 4-20 begin with the words "Special Collection" to indicate that they are from Northern Light's own collection. The other hyperlinks are to Web pages.

Another unique feature of Northern Light is that it collects search results into folders, as shown in Figure 4-20. These folders are organized collections of related hyperlinks found in the search. Clicking one of these folders—for example "Commercial sites"—will narrow your results page to include only those hits that fit the category of commercial sites. Your search provides Dave with the information he needs and he congratulates you on a job well done.

Future of Web Search Tools

A number of different companies and organizations are working on ways to make searching the Web easier for the increasing number of people who use the Web. One company, **About.com**, hires people with expertise in specific subject areas to create and manage their Web directory entries in those areas. Although Yahoo! uses subject matter experts this way, About.com takes the idea one step further and identifies their experts. Each of the About.com experts, called Guides, hosts a page with hyperlinks to related Web pages, moderates discussion areas, and provides an online newsletter. This creates a community of interested persons from around the world that can participate in maintaining the Web directory.

Other search tools, such as **Google**, apply advanced technology to the task of Web searches. The Google search engine uses a database of URLs that has been weighted by how each page is linked to other pages. The underlying method is complex, but the general idea is that pages most often linked to other pages are given greater weight than pages with fewer links. This tends to push frequently accessed Web pages to the top of the search results list. Search tools such as **Ask Jeeves** offer a natural language interface. You can type in a search expression just as you would ask a person a question. For example, you might enter, "How far is it to the moon?" The Ask Jeeves search engine takes the question and, using a database that combines URLs and information about sentence structure, identifies Web sites that might offer the answer to that question. The operation of such natural language interfaces is far from perfect, but they provide an easy-to-use alternative for persons who have not learned to create Boolean search expressions or use other advanced search techniques.

Session 4.2 QUICK CHECK

1. The three basic Boolean operators are _____, _____, and _____.
2. Write a search expression using Boolean and precedence operators that returns Web pages that contain information about wild mustang horses in Wyoming but not information about the Ford Mustang automobile.
3. True or False: The NEAR location operator always returns phrases that contain all keywords within 10 words of each other in a search expression.
4. True or False: In most search engines, the wildcard character is a * symbol.
5. Name three kinds of filters you can include in a HotBot search run from its main search page.
6. Name one distinguishing feature of an Excite results page.
7. Name one distinguishing feature of the Northern Light search engine.

Dave and Ranjit are pleased with the information that you collected for them. They are anxious to start using search engines, directories, meta-search engines, and other Web resources to help them write their stories. Anne is so impressed with your work that she wants you to conduct some short classes to demonstrate the use of Web search tools to all staff members.

REVIEW ASSIGNMENTS

Dave and Ranjit are keeping you busy at the *Midland News*. Your internship will be over soon, so you would like to leave Anne and the *News* with hyperlinks to some resources that the international business news section can use after you leave.

Do the following:

1. Start your Web browser, go to the Student Online Companion (http://www.course.com/newperspectives/internet2), click the link for your book, click the Tutorial 4 link, and then click the Tutorial Assignments link. The Tutorial Assignments page contains links to search engines, directories, and meta-search engines.
2. Choose at least one search tool from each category and conduct a search using the keywords "international" and "business."
3. Extend or narrow your search using each tool until you find ten Web sites that you believe are comprehensive guides or directories that Anne, Dave, and Ranjit should include in their bookmark or favorites lists to help them get information about international business stories.
4. For each Web site, record the URL and write a paragraph that explains why you believe the site would be useful to an international business news writer. Identify each site as a guide, directory, or other resource.
5. When you are finished, close your Web browser and your dial-up connection, if necessary.

CASE PROBLEMS

Case 1. Key Consulting Group   You are a manager at Key Consulting Group, a firm of geological and engineering consultants who specialize in earthquake-damage assessment. When an earthquake strikes, Key Group sends a team of geologists and structural engineers to the quake's site to examine the damage in buildings and determine what kinds of reconstruction will be needed. In some cases, the buildings must be demolished. An earthquake can occur without warning in many parts of the world, so Key Group needs quick access to information about local conditions in various parts of the world, including the temperature, rainfall, money exchange rates, demographics, and local customs. It is early July when you receive a call that an earthquake has just occurred in Northern Chile. You decide to use the Web to obtain information about local mid-winter conditions there.
Do the following:

1. Start your Web browser, go to the Student Online Companion (http://www.course.com/newperspectives/internet2), click the link for your book, click the Tutorial 4 link, and then click the Case Problems link. The Case Problems section contains links to search engines, directories, and meta-search engines.
2. Use one of the search tools to conduct searches for information on local conditions in Northern Chile in July.
3. Prepare a short report that includes the daily temperature range, average rainfall, the current exchange rate for U.S. dollars to Chilean pesos, and any information you can obtain about the characteristics of the local population.
4. When you are finished, close your Web browser and your dial-up connection, if necessary.

Case 2. Lightning Electrical Generators, Inc.   You work as a marketing manager for Lightning Electrical Generators, Inc., a firm that has built generators for over 50 years. The generator business is not as profitable as it once was, and John Delaney, the firm's president, has asked you to investigate new markets for the company. One market that John would like to consider is the uninterruptible power supply (UPS) business. A UPS supplies continuing power to a single computer or to an entire computer system if the regular source of power to the computer fails. Most UPSs provide power only long enough to allow an orderly shutdown of the computer. John would like you to study the market for UPSs in the United States. He would like to know which firms currently make and sell these products, and he would like some idea of what the power ratings and prices are of individual units.

Do the following:

1. Start your Web browser, go to the Student Online Companion (http://www.course.com/newperspectives/internet2), click the link for your book, click the Tutorial 4 link, and then click the Case Problems link. The Case Problems section contains links to search engines, directories, and meta-search engines.
2. Use one of the search tools to conduct searches for information about UPSs for John. You should design your searches to find the manufacturers' names and information about the products that they offer.
3. Prepare a short report that includes the information you have gathered, including the manufacturer's name, model number, product features, and suggested price for at least five UPSs.
4. When you are finished, close your Web browser and your dial-up connection, if necessary.

Case 3. Dunwoody Cams, Inc.   Gunther Dunwoody is the founder of Dunwoody Cams, Inc., a manufacturer of automobile parts. Buyers for the major auto companies frequently visit Dunwoody's factory Web page to obtain quotes on parts. Gunther would like you to find Web pages that contain information about the history of the automobile so he can place hyperlinks to those pages on the Dunwoody Web page, so the site is more interesting to use. He is especially interested in having links to Web sites that have photographs of old autos.

Do the following:

1. Start your Web browser, go to the Student Online Companion (http://www.course.com/newperspectives/internet2), click the link for your book, click the Tutorial 4 link, and then click the Case Problems link. The Case Problems section contains links to search engines, directories, and meta-search engines.
2. Use one of the search tools to find Web sites that contain historical information about automobiles and automobile manufacturing.
3. Prepare a list of at least five URLs that Gunther might want to include on the Dunwoody Web page. Be sure that at least one of the URLs is for a Web site that includes photographs of old automobiles.
4. When you are finished, close your Web browser and your dial-up connection, if necessary.

Case 4. Glenwood Employment Agency   You work as a staff assistant at the Glenwood Employment Agency. Eric Steinberg, the agency's owner, wants you to find Web resources for finding open positions in your geographic area. Eric would like this information to gauge whether his own efforts are keeping pace with the competition. He would like to monitor a few good pages but does not want to conduct exhaustive searches of the Web every week.

Do the following:

1. Start your Web browser, go to the Student Online Companion (http://www.course.com/newperspectives/internet2), click the link for your book, click the Tutorial 4 link, and then click the Case Problems link. The Case Problems section contains links to search engines, directories, and meta-search engines.
2. Use one of the search tools to find Web sites that contain information about job openings in your geographic area. You can use search expressions that include Boolean and precedence operators to limit your searches.
3. Prepare a list of at least five URLs of pages that you believe would be good candidates for Eric's monitoring program.
4. For each URL that you find, write a paragraph that explains why you selected it and then identify any particular strengths or weaknesses of the Web site based on Eric's intended use.
5. When you are finished, close your Web browser and your dial-up connection, if necessary.

Case 5. Lynda's Fine Foods Lynda Reuss has operated a small store that sells specialty foods, such as pickles and mustard, and related gift items for many years. Lynda is thinking about selling her products on the Web because they are small, relatively expensive, and easy to ship. She believes that people who buy her products might appreciate the convenience of ordering via the Web. Lynda would like to find some specialty food store sites on the Web so she can determine what the competition might be and to obtain some ideas that she might use when she creates her own Web site.

Do the following:

1. Start your Web browser, go to the Student Online Companion (http://www.course.com/newperspectives/internet2), click the link for your book, click the Tutorial 4 link, and then click the Case Problems link. The Case Problems section contains links to search engines, directories, and meta-search engines.

2. Use one of the search engine tools to find Web sites that offer gift items such as pickles or mustard. You can use search expressions that include Boolean and precedence operators to limit your searches.

3. Repeat your search using one of the Web directory tools.

4. Compare the results you obtained using a search engine and using a Web directory. Explain in a memorandum of about 100 words which search tool was more effective for this type of search.

5. When you are finished, close your Web browser and your dial-up connection, if necessary.

QUICK | CHECK ANSWERS

Session 4.1

1. open-ended, hard to phrase, difficult to determine when you have found a good answer
2. Start with broad categories of information and ask increasingly narrow questions, trying to avoid blind alleys.
3. a program that automatically searches the Web to find new Web sites and update information about old Web sites that already are in a search engine's database of URLs
4. True
5. False
6. Advantage: Experts have selected, examined, and classified the entries in a Web directory. Disadvantage: You must know which category to search to find information.
7. The power of the search engine operates on the expert-selected and classified entries in the directory.
8. It forwards the expression to a number of other search engines, and then presents and organizes the search results it receives from them.
9. They offer lists of hyperlinks to other Web pages, frequently including summaries or reviews of the Web sites, organized by subject.

Session 4.2

1. AND, OR, NOT
2. One possibility is: (mustang OR horse) AND Wyoming NOT (Ford OR automobile OR auto OR car)
3. False
4. True
5. time period, language, pages that include a specific type of media
6. It provides a hyperlink to an automatic revised search for each search result and then rates each search result.
7. It includes non-Web search results from its special collection and organizes search results into folders of related hyperlinks.

In this tutorial you will:

- Find current news and weather information on the Web

- Obtain maps and city guides

- Find graphics, sounds, and video resources

- Use online library resources

- Use and evaluate other research resources

INFORMATION RESOURCES ON THE WEB

Finding, Evaluating, and Using Web Information Resources

CASE

Cosby Communications

You just started a new position as the executive assistant to the president of Cosby Communications, Marti Cosby. Cosby Communications is a growing public relations firm that handles publicity and media relations for a large number of medium-sized firms, non-profit organizations, and political candidates. Marti explains that the public relations business is fast moving—clients and their needs often change and current events often determine what promotional strategy will work best for a particular client.

Your main job is to help Cosby Communications' staff members stay current on news items that might affect their clients. Marti expects you to use your basic understanding of Web searching techniques to help the firm identify and track important information about the firm's clients and the environments within which they operate. Your other duties will include updating executives on local conditions at travel destinations and working with the firm's Web site design team to develop an effective Web presence for the firm.

In addition to working with Marti and the executive team, you will work closely with Franco Devries, the firm's webmaster, and Susan Zhu, the firm's research director. Franco is new at Cosby Communications and has created a project team to design and build the firm's first Web site. Susan has worked at Cosby Communications for six years in a variety of research jobs. The research department undertakes background investigations related to issues that arise in the firm's dealings with its clients. For example, whenever Marti starts working on a proposal for a potential client in an industry that is new for the firm, she asks Susan to provide some background information on current and future trends in that industry. Susan is looking forward to having you work with her as part of the Cosby Communications research team.

SESSION 5.1

In this session, you will search for current news, weather, and travel information. You will find individual and business listings in directories. Finally, you will find multimedia resources and learn about some common Web multimedia formats.

Current Information

You have learned how to use search engines, directories, and other resources to find information on the Web. As you begin your new job, Marti explains that many of your assignments will be to find recent news and information about clients, potential clients, client industries in general, and changes in the environment within which clients and potential clients operate.

To help you find current news and information, many search engines and directories include a hyperlink to a "What's new" page. The Yahoo! directory, for example, includes hyperlinks titled "News," "Sports," and "Weather" at the top of its home page. The Excite search engine's main page includes a collection of hyperlinks to current events, as shown in Figure 5-1.

| Figure 5-1 | EXCITE'S MAIN SEARCH PAGE |

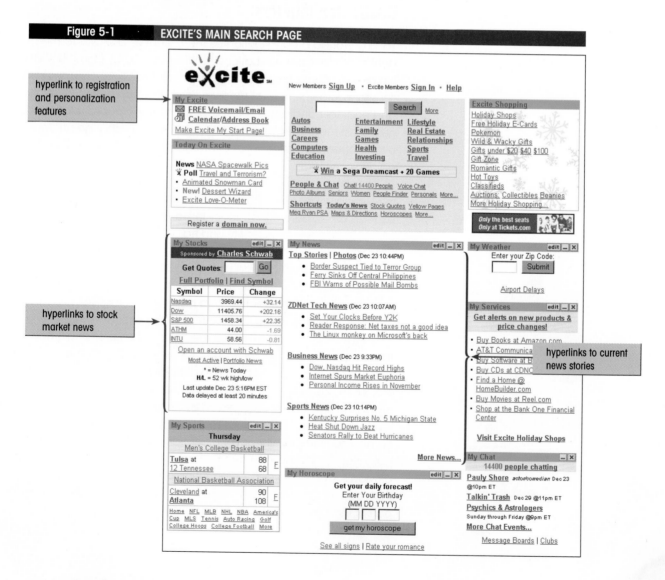

You can see Excite's stock market and current news hyperlinks in Figure 5-1. The page also includes hyperlinks for sports news, weather, and even horoscopes. If you are willing to register with Excite, you can follow the My Excite hyperlink to personalize the page. This personalization feature lets you specify the kind of information that appears on this page when you log on.

Many search engines, including HotBot and AltaVista, allow you to choose a date range when you enter a search expression. HotBot provides two ways to do this. On its main page, you can specify one of a range of time options, such as "in the last week" or "in the last 3 months," to limit your search to sites that were last modified within your selected time period. HotBot's SuperSearch page includes the same range of time options. To open the HotBot SuperSearch page shown in Figure 5-2, click the ADVANCED SEARCH button that appears on the HotBot search engine's main page.

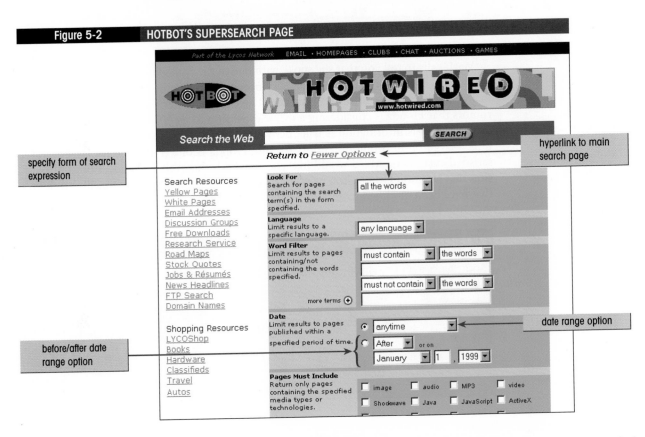

Figure 5-2 **HOTBOT'S SUPERSEARCH PAGE**

Alternatively, you can limit a SuperSearch page search to include only sites last modified before or after a specific date by using the date controls that appear below the range of time options. HotBot, even on its SuperSearch page, does not provide a way to search for sites *within* a specific date range. For example, you could not limit a HotBot search to sites modified between April 24, 2000, and November 11, 2000. The AltaVista search engine does not have the pre-set range of time options that HotBot offers, but it does allow you to set an exact date range on its advanced search page. Figure 5-3 shows the AltaVista advanced search page with an exact date range set.

Figure 5-3	DATE RANGE SETTINGS IN AN ALTAVISTA ADVANCED SEARCH

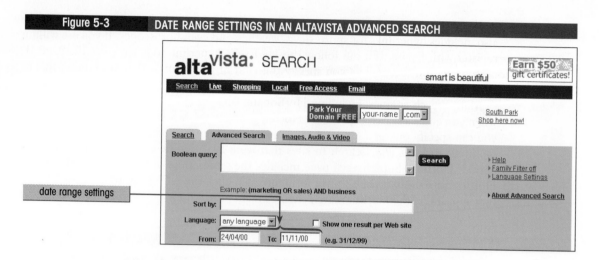

date range settings

Marti calls to tell you that she spoke with one of the firm's clients about future expansion plans. This client manufactures and distributes industrial paint-spraying equipment and is a major supplier to several auto companies. The client told her that his salespersons reported rumors that Honda is considering a major expansion to its North American manufacturing facilities. If this information is true, he would like Cosby Communications to begin planning a large tie-in promotion effort because Honda is one of the client's largest and most satisfied customers. Marti would like you to search the Web and collect the URLs of any sites that mention Honda. You need the most recent information, so you will search for sites that have been modified within the last three months.

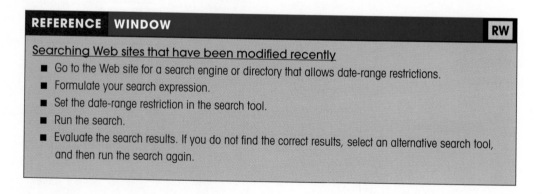

REFERENCE WINDOW   RW

Searching Web sites that have been modified recently
- Go to the Web site for a search engine or directory that allows date-range restrictions.
- Formulate your search expression.
- Set the date-range restriction in the search tool.
- Run the search.
- Evaluate the search results. If you do not find the correct results, select an alternative search tool, and then run the search again.

Consider the search tools available. Your search term—Honda—is a brand name, so it is likely that directory builders will collect many useful sites that include that term in their databases. Yahoo! is a directory that includes a date-range restriction option, so you decide to use it for your first search. If you do not find what you are looking for with one search tool, you can try your search again using different tools until you are satisfied with your results.

To find specific Web pages based on last modified dates:

1. Start your Web browser, and then go to the Student Online Companion page by entering the URL **http://www.course.com/newperspectives/internet2** in the appropriate location in your Web browser. Click the hyperlink for your book, click the **Tutorial 5** link, and then click the **Session 5.1** link. Click the **Yahoo!** hyperlink and wait while the browser loads the Yahoo! home page.

2. Click the **advanced search** hyperlink to the right of the Search button to open the Yahoo! Search Options page.

3. Type **Honda** in the search text box.

4. Click the **Find only new listings added during the past** list arrow, click **3 months** (see Figure 5-4), and then click the **Search** button to start the search.

Figure 5-4	SEARCHING THE YAHOO! DIRECTORY USING DATE CRITERIA

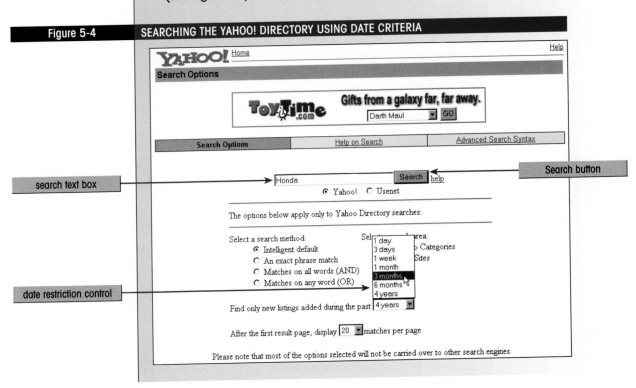

Your search should return approximately 50 hits for Honda motorcycle products and Honda automobile dealers. However, after examining the results, you decide that you did not find what Marti needs. Marti suggests that you try your search again using HotBot because HotBot has more date controls than Yahoo!.

To search for last modified dates using HotBot:

1. Use your browser's **Back** button or the history list to return to the Student Online Companion page for Session 5.1, and then click the **HotBot** hyperlink and wait for the HotBot home page to load in your Web browser.

2. Type **Honda AND (auto OR automobile) AND (manufacture OR manufacturing)** in the Search Smarter text box to search for URLs of Web pages that relate to Honda's auto manufacturing operations.

3. Click the **Look for** list arrow, and then click **Boolean phrase**.

4. Click the **Date** list arrow, and then click **in the last 3 months** to search for URLs that have been modified in the last three months.

5. Click the **SEARCH** button to start the search. Your search returned many more pages than Yahoo!—over 1,000 more—based on the specified criteria. You are certain that Marti can find the information she is looking for from your list of URLs.

You can send the URLs to Marti in an e-mail message, or you can tell her how to obtain the same search results. For now, you decide to cut and paste the URLs that look promising and then send them to her in an e-mail message.

Getting the News

Marti stops by to see you the day after you send her the URLs she requested. She is pleased with many of the recently modified Web pages you found. Now, she asks you to find any recent news stories about Honda that might not appear as part of a recently modified Web page.

Finding current news stories on the Web is an easy task. Almost every search engine and directory includes a list of current news hyperlinks to broadcast networks, wire services, and newspapers. All of the major U.S. broadcasters, including ABC, CBS, CNN, Fox, MSNBC (the Microsoft-NBC joint venture), and National Public Radio (NPR) have Web sites that carry news features. Broadcasters in other countries, such as the BBC, also provide news reports on their Web pages. The Reuters Web page includes current news stories in addition to the news services that it sells. Major newspapers, such as *The New York Times*, *The Washington Post*, and the *London Times*, have Web sites that include current news and many other features from their print editions. Many of these broadcast news, wire service, and newspaper Web sites include search features that allow you to search the site for specific news stories. However, there are not many search tools available on the Web to search multiple news sources at the same time. You begin to think about the time it will take to do a comprehensive search of just the major news sites for Marti and you begin to worry.

Marti tells you that the **Internet Public Library** site includes hyperlinks to hundreds of international and domestic newspapers. Figure 5-5 shows a portion of the Internet Public Library Web site.

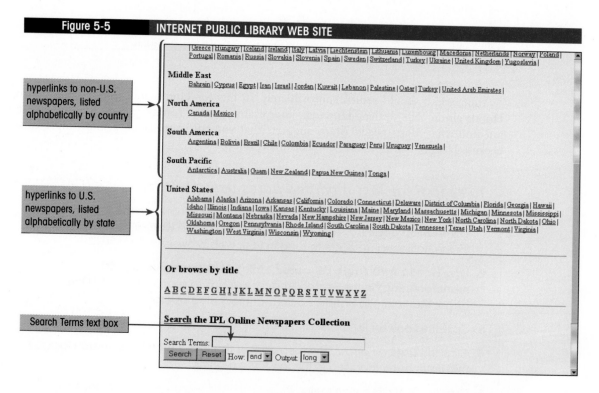

Figure 5-5   **INTERNET PUBLIC LIBRARY WEB SITE**

hyperlinks to non-U.S. newspapers, listed alphabetically by country

hyperlinks to U.S. newspapers, listed alphabetically by state

Search Terms text box

As you can see in Figure 5-5, this site has a search field, but it searches only the title and the main entry for each newspaper and does not search the newspaper sites' contents. Therefore, you could use it to identify all of the newspapers that were in New Jersey or all of the newspapers that had the word *Tribune* in their titles, but you could not use it to find news stories that include the word *Honda*.

Fortunately, at least two Web sites provide you with the ability to search the content of current news stories in multiple publications—these Web sites are Excite's NewsTracker and VPOP Technologies' NewsHub. **NewsTracker** searches the contents of over 300 newspapers, magazines, and wire services. **NewsHub** updates its news database with information from several major wire services every 15 minutes. Therefore, NewsTracker offers a broad range of coverage and NewsHub offers timely coverage of news events. To obtain both breadth and currency of coverage, you might want to run the same query using both search tools.

REFERENCE WINDOW   **RW**

<u>Searching current news stories</u>

- Determine whether you need the currency of NewsHub, the broad coverage of NewsTracker, or both.
- Open the NewsHub or the NewsTracker Web site in your Web browser.
- Enter your search expression into the search text box.
- Run the search and evaluate your results.

You would like search coverage that is both current and broad, so you decide to use both the NewsHub and the NewsTracker search tools.

To find recent news stories on the Web that mention Honda:

1. Return to the Student Online Companion Web page for Session 5.1, and then click the **NewsHub** hyperlink and wait while your Web browser loads the NewsHub page.

2. Type **Honda** in the search text box (you might need to scroll down the page to see the search text box), and then click the **Go!** button. Examine the hits returned by the search and note the URLs of any that might interest Marti. You probably will find fewer than 100 hits, with even fewer of those hits related to Honda's expansion plans. Your search results might be different because the business world—and news reported about the business world—changes daily. You do not see many relevant hits, so you decide to try the NewsTracker search tool.

3. Return to the Student Online Companion Web page for Session 5.1, and then click the **NewsTracker** hyperlink to load that page in your Web browser.

4. Type **Honda** in the search text box (you might need to scroll down the page to see the search text box), and then click the **Go!** button to start your search. Figure 5-6 shows a portion of the search results page. Examine the hits returned by the search and see if any of the listed pages relate to Honda's expansion plans.

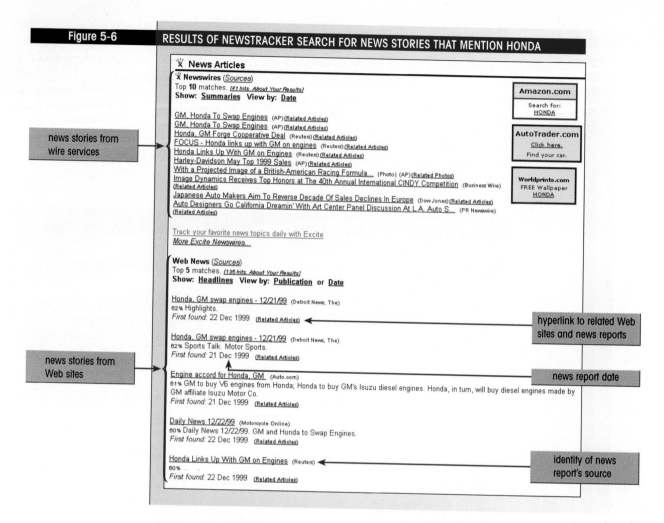

Figure 5-6   RESULTS OF NEWSTRACKER SEARCH FOR NEWS STORIES THAT MENTION HONDA

The search results page returned by the NewsTracker tool provides some useful information. The search results are sorted into stories that NewsTracker gathered from wire services (Newswires) and those it gathered from Web sites that publish current news (Web News). Each news report entry includes a hyperlink to the Web site that contains the story, the news report's source, a brief summary, the date that NewsTracker's spider first found the item on the Web, and a hyperlink to a list of related news stories. After you have identified a useful item on the search results page, the Related Articles hyperlink for that item provides a useful way to narrow your search.

Now, you have accumulated a respectable list of URLs about Honda's expansion plans for Marti. You have gained experience in searching for current topics by examining Web pages that have been modified recently and by using two tools that search the Web specifically for news reports.

Weather Reports

Marti will travel to Nashville later in the week to meet with several of the firm's clients in the country music business. Marti already has made her travel plans, and she is interested in the weather forecast for the area. You decide to check two sources for the information because you know that meteorology is not an exact science—forecasts from different sources can differ.

REFERENCE WINDOW   **RW**

<u>Obtaining a weather forecast</u>
- Open the weather information Web site you would like to use in a Web browser.
- Locate the weather report for the city or area in which you are interested.
- Repeat the steps to find other weather information in different Web sites.

To obtain weather forecasts for the Nashville area:

1. Return to the Student Online Companion Web page for Session 5.1, and then click the **The Weather Channel** hyperlink and wait while your Web browser loads the Weather Channel page.

2. Type **Nashville** in the Any City or US Zip text box, and then click the **go!** button.

3. A page appears showing a number of hyperlinks to U.S. cities named "Nashville." You are interested in weather in Nashville, Tennessee, so click that hyperlink to open a page similar to the one shown in Figure 5-7. The Weather Channel page for Nashville includes a report of current conditions and a five-day forecast for the Nashville area. The images at the bottom of Figure 5-7 are hyperlinks to a detailed local area forecast, Doppler radar images, and regional satellite photographs. The left side of the page includes links to special reports and other Weather Channel features.

Figure 5-7   WEATHER CHANNEL NASHVILLE LOCAL FORECAST PAGE

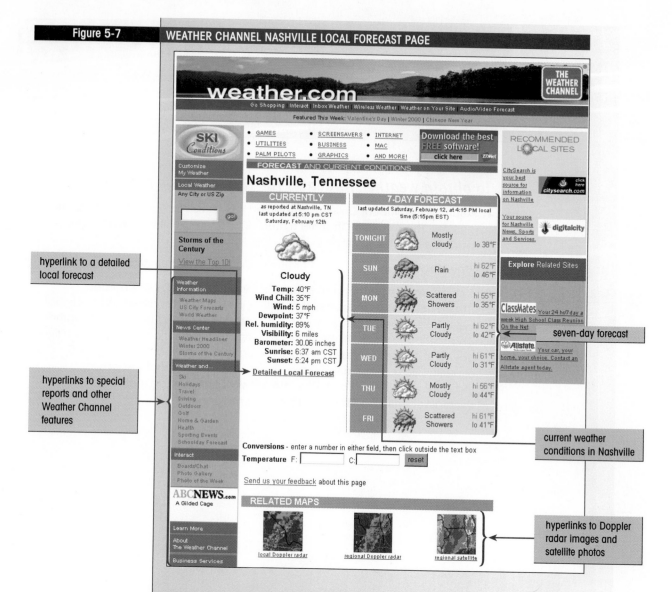

hyperlink to a detailed local forecast

hyperlinks to special reports and other Weather Channel features

seven-day forecast

current weather conditions in Nashville

hyperlinks to Doppler radar images and satellite photos

4. Click your browser's **Print** button to print the forecast for Marti. Now, use a different weather source to search for weather conditions in Nashville.

5. Return to the Student Online Companion page for Session 5.1, and then click the **AccuWeather** hyperlink and wait for your Web browser to load the page. The AccuWeather page that opens includes hyperlinks to a variety of weather information, including local forecasts for U.S. cities.

6. Type **Nashville, TN** in the Choose your U.S. location text box, and then click the **Get My Page!** button to open the AccuWeather local forecast page for Nashville. This page includes a five-day forecast and hyperlinks to Current Conditions, a longer range forecast, an hourly forecast, a local radar image, satellite photos, and a variety of weather maps.

7. Click your browser's **Print** button to print the forecast for Marti.

Usually, weather-forecasting sites will report slightly different (and sometimes totally different) forecasts for the same time period in the same area. Many people who obtain weather forecasts from the Web regularly check two or three sites and compare the forecasts. If you are planning a trip, you might want to check the traveler's forecasts offered by both the Weather Channel *and* the AccuWeather sites. The Weather Channel traveler's forecasts include estimates of what the next day's weather-related flight delays will be at domestic and international airports.

Obtaining Maps and City Guides

Marti is excited about her trip to Nashville because this will be her first visit, and she is a country music fan who grew up listening to broadcasts of the Grand Ole Opry on the radio. Marti would like to include a stop at Ryman Auditorium, the home of the Grand Ole Opry, while she is in Nashville. You offer to find a map of Nashville on the Web that shows the location of Ryman Auditorium. Marti gives you the address, 116 Fifth Avenue North, and you are ready to go to work. You tell Marti that you also will look for some information about restaurants and other things to do in Nashville.

REFERENCE WINDOW | RW

Finding a local area map on the Web
- Open the map page in your Web browser.
- Enter the location of the map you need to find.
- Zoom the map scale in or out to suit your requirements.
- Include any reference points you would like to appear on the map.
- Print or download the finished map.

To obtain a map of the Nashville area near Ryman Auditorium:

1. Return to the Student Online Companion Web page for Session 5.1, and then click the **MapQuest** hyperlink and wait while your Web browser loads the Web page.

2. Click the **Online Maps** hyperlink, and then wait for the next page to open, where you can specify the address of the desired map location.

3. Type the address of Ryman Auditorium, **116 Fifth Avenue North**, in the Address/Intersection text box under the Map Search heading.

4. Press the **Tab** key, and then type **Nashville** in the City text box.

5. Press the **Tab** key, type **TN** in the State/Province text box, and then click the **Get Map** button. Figure 5-8 shows the map for Ryman Auditorium.

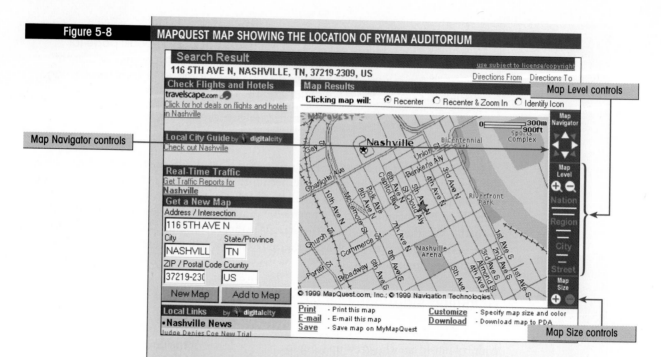

Figure 5-8   MAPQUEST MAP SHOWING THE LOCATION OF RYMAN AUDITORIUM

The map provided identifies the location you requested with a red star, on Fifth Avenue North, just above the intersection with U.S. Route 70. You can adjust the map scale using the controls on the right side of the map. It is often useful to have a street-level version of a map to show detail and a lower-scale version of a map to show more of the surrounding area. You can use the Map Navigator controls to move the map within the window in any of the eight geographic directions, the Map Level controls to zoom in or out, and the Map Size controls to make the map appear larger or smaller in your browser window. MapQuest provides icons that let you e-mail, print, or save the map on the MapQuest server. (You must register as a MapQuest member to use the save option.) Before you print or download information from a Web page, it is always a good idea to check the site for copyright and use restrictions.

6. Click the **Copyright Notice/Terms of Use** hyperlink at the bottom of the page (this link does not appear in the screen shown in Figure 5-8) and review the terms under which you can use printed or e-mailed maps obtained from this server.

You have obtained a map or a reference to a Web page that contains a map that will meet Marti's needs on the Nashville trip. You also would like to find some information about Ryman Auditorium and other things to do in Nashville. The Web offers a number of city guides; hyperlinks to some of these sites appear in the Additional Information section of the Student Online Companion page for Tutorial 5.

REFERENCE WINDOW   RW

Obtaining travel destination information
- Go to a city guide Web site in your Web browser.
- Search the site for your destination city, region, or country.
- Explore the hyperlinks provided by the site for your destination.

To obtain information about Nashville and the Ryman Auditorium:

1. Return to the Student Online Companion Web page for Session 5.1, and then click the **CitySearch** hyperlink and wait while your Web browser loads the Web page.

2. Select **Nashville** from the Complete City Guides drop-down list. The CitySearch page for Nashville should open (if it does not open, click the **go!** button).

3. Type **Ryman Auditorium** in the I'm Looking For text box, and then click the **go!** button.

4. Click the **Ryman Auditorium** hyperlink that appears on the search results page to open the Web page shown in Figure 5-9.

Figure 5-9	CITYSEARCH WEB PAGE

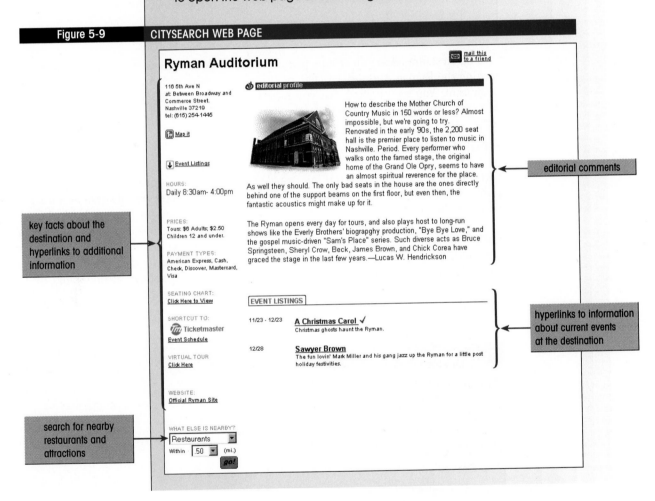

Figure 5-9 shows hyperlinks and other useful information that Marti can use for her trip. The key facts presented include the auditorium's telephone number, hours of operation, and tour prices. The page includes hyperlinks to a map of the local area—provided by the MapQuest server—and a seating diagram for the venue. The editorial comments provide a short history of the building and its role in the development of country music. Below the editorial comments is a list of information about upcoming events scheduled at the auditorium with hyperlinks that you can follow for more information. The hyperlinks at the top of the page link to information about restaurants, nightclubs, bars, theaters, and movies in the area. You know that Marti will want to visit some restaurants while she is there, so you decide to use the hyperlinks to find a list of nearby restaurants.

5. Click the **WHAT ELSE IS NEARBY?** list arrow, click **Restaurants**, and then click the **go!** button.

The Restaurants search results page lists over a dozen places that Marti can visit after touring the Ryman Auditorium. The page includes a map with numbered markers for each restaurant. You are satisfied that you have found more than enough information to make Marti's Nashville trip memorable and successful.

Finding Businesses

Over the next few years, Marti is interested in developing reciprocal relationships with local public relations firms in Nashville. She would like to make some initial contacts during this trip and asks you to search the Web to find a list of public relations firms in Nashville.

There are a number of search engines on the Web that specialize in finding people and businesses. Many of these search engines include information in their databases about people and businesses. The sites that store only information about businesses are often called **yellow pages** sites. One of these search engines is the **BigYellow** site operated by Bell Atlantic, which has listings for over 17 million businesses. You decide to use BigYellow to create the public relations list for Marti.

REFERENCE WINDOW   **RW**

Finding business listings on the Web
- Navigate to a page that provides business listings or a business listing search engine in your Web browser.
- Enter information about the nature and geographic location of the business that you want to find.
- Run the search.
- Examine and evaluate the results to determine whether you should revise your search or try another search engine.

To find Nashville public relations firms on the Web:

1. Return to the Student Online Companion Web page for Session 5.1, and then click the **BigYellow** hyperlink and wait while your Web browser loads the Web page.

2. Type **Public Relations** in the Category text box.

3. Press the **Tab** key twice, and then type **Nashville** in the City text box.

4. Click the **State** list arrow, and then click **TN**. See Figure 5-10.

Figure 5-10	BIGYELLOW WEB PAGE

hyperlinks to other BigYellow services

BigYellow search engine controls

5. Click the **Find It** button to begin the search. Evaluate your search results and report them to Marti.

Your search should find approximately 75 business listings from the BigYellow Public Relations Counselors category, with 15 firms listed per page. The listings include the name, address, telephone number, and a hyperlink to a map server entry for each firm. BigYellow also provides a hyperlink to listed firms' Web sites. It is possible that none of the public relations firms listed in the results pages that you obtain have Web sites and, therefore, your results pages might not include any hyperlinks. Now, you are ready to prepare a report for Marti that contains the firms' information so she can investigate potential reciprocal relationships.

Finding People and Related Privacy Concerns

Many Web sites let you search for individuals' names, addresses, and telephone numbers. These sites often are called **white pages** sites. One comprehensive site that includes search tools for finding information about businesses and individuals is **Switchboard**. Switchboard collects information from published telephone directories and other publicly available information and indexes it by last name.

Many people expressed concerns about privacy violations when this type of information became easily accessible on the Web. In some cases, Web sites made unpublished and unlisted telephone numbers available for public use. Some sites grouped individual listings by category, including categories such as religious or political affiliations. In response to these privacy concerns, most white pages sites offer individuals ways to remove their listings. For example, Switchboard will accept a list removal request sent via its Web page, e-mail, or a letter. You might want to determine whether white pages sites have a correct listing for you and whether you want your listing to appear in a white pages site.

REFERENCE WINDOW   RW

<u>Searching for your white pages listing</u>
- Open a white pages Web site in your Web browser.
- Enter your name and part of your address.
- Run the search, and then examine the search results.
- Consider repeating the search with various combinations of partial address information or variants of the correct spelling of your name.

To search for your listing on the Switchboard white pages site:

1. Return to the Student Online Companion Web page for Session 5.1, and then click the **Switchboard** hyperlink and wait while your Web browser loads the Web page.

2. Click the **Find a Person** hyperlink to open the Find a Person Web page.

3. Click in the **Last Name** text box, and then type your last name.

4. Press the **Tab** key to move to the City text box, and then type the name of the city in which you live.

5. Press the **Tab** key to move to the State text box, and then type the two-letter U.S. Postal Service abbreviation for the state in which you live.

6. Click the **Search** button. Your name might appear in the first results page. If it does not appear, click the **Next Matches** hyperlink to go to the next page.

    TROUBLE? If your telephone number is listed in another person's name, use that person's name to find your listing.

    TROUBLE? If you do not find your listing, click the Modify Search hyperlink, add more information to the search text boxes, and then run the search again. If you still cannot find your listing, try searching for a friend's listing or for your parents' listing.

You might need to run the search several times using different information to find your listing. If you do not want Switchboard to list your name and information, click the Policies hyperlink at the bottom of the page and then click the Deleting Listings hyperlink. Follow the instructions on the page that appears to have your listing removed from the Switchboard directory.

The Student Online Companion page for Tutorial 5 contains hyperlinks to other white pages Web sites in the Additional Information section under the heading "Find People, Businesses, and Other Organizations." You can search those sites for your listing and follow similar steps to remove or change it, if you want.

Multimedia Resources

Franco has been working on a number of Web page designs for the firm, and now that Marti is in Nashville, he stops by your office to talk about these projects. He would like you to undertake a long-term assignment for him by paying close attention to the multimedia elements of the Web pages you view as you undertake searches for other staff members. He asks you to note any particularly effective uses of Web page design elements and forward any relevant URLs to him. So that you will understand how these elements work and be better able to gather this information for him, Franco has decided to give you a tour of multimedia elements in Web pages. The first issue he wants to discuss with you is how copyright law governs the use of these elements.

Copyright Issues

Franco explains that when you use your Web browser to see a graphic image, listen to a sound, or view a video clip, your Web browser downloads the multimedia element from the Web server and stores it in a temporary file on your computer's hard drive. This process creates a new, intermediate level of ownership that did not exist before the emergence of the Web. For example, when you go to an art gallery and view a picture, you do not take possession of the picture in any way; in fact, if you went around touching all of the pictures in the gallery, someone would ask you to leave. When you visit an online art gallery, however, your Web browser takes temporary possession of a copy of the file containing the image. As you have learned in earlier tutorials, it is easy to make a permanent copy of Web page images—even though your copy might violate the image owner's rights.

Making a photocopy of a picture that appears in a book can be a copyright violation. Because computer files are even easier to copy than a picture in a book, the potential for Web copyright violations is much greater. Some Web site owners disclaim liability by storing only hyperlinks to other Web pages that contain copyright-violating multimedia elements; whether this is an effective shield against liability is not clear.

In most cases, scanning a copy of a popular cartoon from a newspaper or magazine and placing it on a Web page is a violation of the owner's copyright. Some cartoonists regularly search the Web, looking for unauthorized copies of their work. They threaten or take legal action when they find Web sites that appear to violate their copyrights.

Some uses of multimedia elements do not present a copyright violation. For example, some sites provide graphics files that are in the **public domain**, which means that you are free to copy the files without requesting permission from the source. Even though you can freely use public domain information, you should check the site carefully for requirements about if and how you acknowledge the source of the material when it is used. Acknowledging a source can be especially important when you use public domain material in papers, reports, or other school projects. Failure to cite the source of public domain material that you use can be a serious violation of your school's academic honesty policy.

Other sites offer some files free as samples and offer other files for sale. The free files often carry a restriction against selling or redistributing them, even though you can use them without cost on your Web page. You must carefully examine any site from which you download multimedia files to determine what usage limitations apply. If you cannot find a clear statement of copyright terms or a statement that the files are in the public domain, you should not use them on your Web page or anywhere else.

Images and Graphics

The Student Online Companion page for Session 5.1 contains many hyperlinks to Web pages that offer photographs and images. Some of these sites encourage downloading of at least some of the files.

Most images on the Web are in one of two file formats, GIF and JPEG. **GIF**, an acronym for **Graphics Interchange Format**, is an older format that does a very good job of compressing small- or medium-sized files. Most GIF files you find on the Web will have a .gif extension. This file format can store only up to 256 different colors. The GIF format is widely used on the Internet for images that have only a few distinct colors, such as line drawings, cartoons, simple icons, and screen objects. Some of the more interesting screen objects on the Web are animated GIF files. An **animated GIF file** combines several images into a single GIF file. When a Web browser that recognizes the animated GIF file type loads an animated GIF file, it cycles through the images in the file and gives the appearance of cartoon-like animation. The size and color-depth limitations of the GIF file format prevent animated GIFs from delivering high-quality video, however. **JPEG**, an acronym for **Joint Photographic Experts Group**, is a newer file format that stores many more colors than the GIF format—over 16 million more, in fact—and more colors yields a higher-quality image. The JPEG format is particularly useful for photographs and continuous-tone art; that is, images that do not have sharp edges. Most JPEG files that you find on the Web usually have a .jpg file extension.

Both of these formats offer file compression, which is important on the Web. Uncompressed graphics files containing images of significant size or complexity are too large to transmit efficiently. JPEG file compression is "lossy." Any **lossy compression** procedure erases some elements of the graphic so that when it is displayed, it will not resemble the original image. The greater the level of compression, the more graphic detail is lost.

There are many other file formats in use for graphic images on the Web—including Windows bitmap file format (.bmp), Tagged Image File Format (or TIFF) format (.tif), PC Paintbrush format (.pcx), and the new Portable Network Graphics (or PNG) format (.png)—but most images you encounter will be in either the JPEG or GIF formats. The Windows bitmap, TIFF, and PC Paintbrush formats are all noncompressed graphics formats. Web page designers usually avoid these formats because a Web browser takes too long to download them. The PNG format is a new format that the World Wide Web consortium has approved as a standard. Although its promoters hope that it will become the prevailing Web standard, it is not yet widely used.

One of the best Web resources for the fine arts is the **WebMuseum** site, which occasionally features special exhibitions. The WebMuseum's mainstay is its Famous Paintings collection, which includes images of artwork from around the world. Franco wants you to see the museum's portrait of Vincent van Gogh so you can gain experience using and searching for graphics files at a museum Web site.

REFERENCE WINDOW   **RW**

Viewing an image in an online museum

- Open the online museum Web page in your Web browser.
- Follow the directory's hyperlinks or use the site's search engine to find the artist or work in which you are interested.
- Art works are often presented as small images called thumbnails that you can click to open a larger version of the image.

To view Vincent van Gogh's self-portraits at the WebMuseum site:

1. Return to the Student Online Companion Web page for Session 5.1, and then click the **WebMuseum** hyperlink and wait while your Web browser loads the Web page.

2. Scroll down the WebMuseum main page to the General Exhibitions section, and then click the **Famous Paintings** collections hyperlink.

3. Click the **Artist Index** hyperlink.

4. Scroll down the list of artists to find the **Gogh, Vincent van** hyperlink, and then click it.

5. Click the **Self-Portraits** hyperlink to open the page shown in Figure 5-11.

| Figure 5-11 | WEBMUSEUM WEB PAGE |

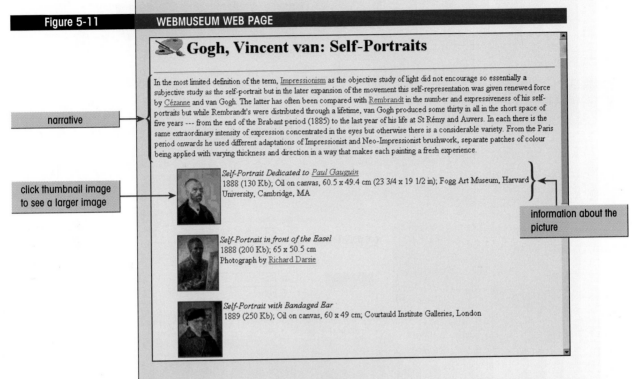

narrative

click thumbnail image
to see a larger image

information about the
picture

This page, devoted to van Gogh's self-portraits, includes a narrative about these works; the title, date created, file size, media, size of the original; and information about the work's owner (if it is a public institution). You can click any of the small (or thumbnail) images to view a larger version of the image.

6. Close your Web browser, and close your dial-up connection, if necessary.

Finding image files on the Web can be difficult because the robots that gather information for search engines do not read graphics files to identify their attributes. A search engine, therefore, cannot find all images that contain a particular shade of green, for example. Search engines rely on HTML image tags that Web page builders include in their HTML documents that contain terms that describe the image. One Web site that can help you find clip-art images is the **Clip Art Searcher**, shown in Figure 5-12. The Student Online Companion page for Tutorial 5 contains a link to the Clip Art Searcher Web site in the Additional Information section under the heading "Photographs and Images."

Figure 5-12   CLIP ART SEARCHER WEB PAGE

WebPlaces | Clip Art Searcher

Advertising Information for this web site [Menu]

advertising banner

ArtToday. CLICK HERE AND GET 40,000 IMAGES FREE!

ArtToday - over 1.4 million images - easy-to-use search engine.

hyperlinks to customized search controls on this page

Clip Art Searcher: search forms optimized to find graphics files.

Anzwers	**HotBot**	**Lycos**	**Filez**	**1-Click**
images and sounds	clip art, icons, & more	3 ways to search	searches FTP sites	Yahoo and Euroseek

Clip Art Review: Backgrounds | Bullets | Animations | Lines, Bars | Photos | Sounds | AudioPlaces.com

FANWEAR.com
Teamwear and gifts for sports fans.

SportsPlaces.com
The Best Sports Links on the Net

ANZWERS

Search the Web for: all the words

SEARCH

Where to Search:

○ The World
○ edu

(Domain, e.g. **edu** or **com** or **uk**)

customized ANZWERS search controls

Tip: yes, *include* the file extension (.gif, .jpg) with your keyword
Examples: *house.gif bulldog.jpg cymbal.au bell.wav*

HotBot

Search HotBot for exact phrase

SEARCH

Search for:
clip art
icons
background images
animations

Return 25 results with full descriptions

Results must not contain the words

customized HotBot search controls

Tip: yes, *include* the file extension (.gif, .jpg) with your keyword
Examples: *house.gif bulldog.jpg cymbal.au bell.wav*

customized Lycos search controls

Lycos

Lycos Image Gallery: Go Get It

Pictures on the Web: Go Get It

Three ways to search   FTP Files: Pictures   Go Get It

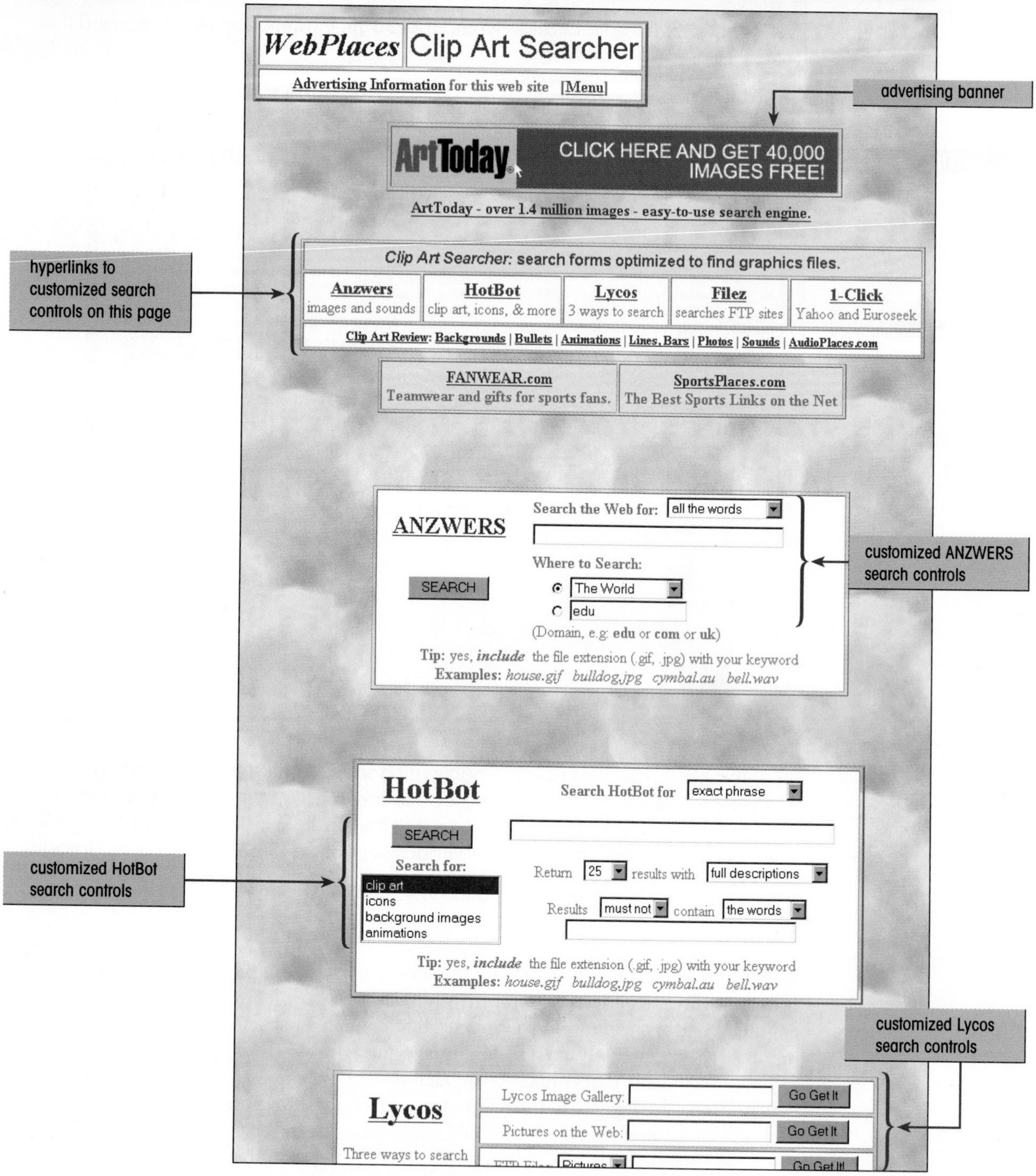

The Clip Art Searcher Web page is not a search engine, but it includes customized search controls for six search engines and directories. These search controls are optimized for each search engine or directory to help you locate the specific types of graphics files you want to find.

Sounds, Music, and Video Clips

The animated GIF format has only a limited ability to present moving graphics and cannot store audio information along with the video animation. Many Web site designers include sound or video clips to enhance the information on their pages. Unlike graphics files, sound and video files appear on the Web in many different formats and often require that you add software extensions to your Web browser. These software extensions, or **plug-ins**, are usually available as free downloads. The firms that offer media players as free downloads earn their profits by selling encoding software to developers who want to include audio and video files in that format on their Web sites. Each firm that creates a format has an incentive to promote its use, so no clear standards for using audio or video files on the Web have emerged. Another difficulty that you might encounter when playing audio files is that your computer must be equipped with a sound card and either a speaker or earphones. The computers in your school's lab or in your employer's offices might not have a sound card installed; if that's the case, you will not be able to listen to sounds.

One widely used audio file format is the **Wave** format, which was jointly developed by Microsoft and IBM. **Wave (WAV)** files digitize audio waveform information at a user-specified sampling rate and play on any Windows computer that supports sound. WAV files that are recorded at a high sampling rate (the higher the sampling rate, the higher the sound quality) can be very large. A WAV file that stores one minute of CD-quality sound can be over 1 megabyte in size. The size of WAV files limits their use on the Web to situations that require only short, lower-quality audio information. You can recognize a WAV file on the Web by its .wav file extension.

Another commonly used Web file format is the MIDI format. The **MIDI (Musical Instrument Digital Interface)** format is a standard adopted by the music industry for controlling devices that create and read musical information. The MIDI format does not digitize the sound waveform. Instead, it digitally records information about each element of the sound, including its pitch, length, and volume. Most keyboard synthesizers use MIDI so that music recorded on one synthesizer can be played on other synthesizers or on computers that have a MIDI interface. It is much easier to edit music recorded in the MIDI format than it is to edit music recorded in the WAV format because you can manipulate the individual characteristics of the sound with a great deal of precision. MIDI files are much smaller than WAV files and are, therefore, often used on the Web. Usually, MIDI files have either a .midi or .mid file extension.

Other audio formats used on the Web are less common than WAV and MIDI formats. Since the Web originated largely on computers running the UNIX operating system, that system's audio file format still appears on the Web. Both Navigator and Internet Explorer can read this format, which is known as the AU format because its file extension is normally .au. These files are approximately the same size as WAV files that store the same information.

A new technique for transferring both sound and video files on the Web is called streaming transmission. In a **streaming transmission**, the Web server sends the first part of the file to the Web browser, which begins playing the file. While the browser is playing the file, the server is sending the next segment of the file. Streaming transmission allows you to access very large audio or video files in much less time than the download-then-play procedure requires because you start playing the file before you finish downloading. RealNetworks, Inc. has pioneered this technology and developed the RealAudio format for audio files and the RealVideo format for video files. To play these files, which you can recognize by their .ra or .ram file extensions, you must download and install one of the Real file players from the firm's Web site. The RealNetworks formats are compressed to increase further the efficiency with which they can be transferred over the Internet. For example, you can compress a 1-megabyte WAV file into a 30-kilobyte RealAudio file.

Video files are also available in older formats on the Web. Windows computers are able to play Microsoft's **AVI (Audio Video Interleaved)** format files and, with the proper software downloaded and installed, also can play Apple's **QuickTime** format files. One minute of video and sound recorded in either of these formats results in a file that is about 6 megabytes, which is a very large file to transmit over slower types of Internet connections. Because of the larger file sizes, development of better ways to transmit video files over the Internet continues. The International Standards Organization's **Moving Picture Experts Group (MPEG)** has created a series of standards for compressed file formats. As in JPEG graphic files, this compression technique deletes information from the file and can deteriorate quality. Another compressed video file format that is appearing on the Web is the **Vivo** format. Both MPEG and Vivo format files require you to download and install plug-ins that enable your Web browser to play the files.

Session 5.1   QUICK CHECK

1. The Reuters News Wire Service sells information to newspapers, broadcasters, and other firms. Why do you think they would provide some of this information on their Web page for free public access?

2. Compare the news-story indexing and retrieval capabilities of NewsHub and NewsTracker.

3. Explain why you might want to consult two or three Web resources for weather information before leaving on an out-of-town trip.

4. List two advantages of using a Web map server instead of a paper map or atlas.

5. Describe three types of information that you might obtain from a City Guide Web page.

6. True or False: An image on a Web page that does not carry a copyright notice is in the public domain.

7. Most images on the Web are in one of two compressed file formats. The _____ format is a good choice for storing cartoon animations, and the _____ format is a good choice for storing photographs.

8. Explain what problems you might encounter if you conduct a search for multimedia files using a Web search engine.

9. List two of the individual attributes of a sound that are stored separately in a MIDI file.

10. Name and briefly describe the key advantage of the streaming transmission file transfer technique.

Now that you know more about where to find Web resources, you need to learn how to evaluate the information that you gather on the Web. In Session 5.2, Franco will tell you how to assess the quality of the information resources you find on the Web.

SESSION 5.2

In this session, you will learn how to evaluate the quality of Web research resources based on a site's author, content, and appearance. You will then learn how to use library research resources to find information about a specific topic. You also will learn more about the future of electronic publishing.

Evaluating the Quality of Web Research Resources

In your morning meeting with Susan, you reviewed some of the research department's standards and practices for information that the firm collects using the Internet. One of the most important issues in doing Web research is determining the quality of the information provided on individual sites. Because the Web has made publishing so easy and inexpensive, it allows virtually anyone to create a Web page on almost any subject. Research published in scientific or literary journals is subjected to peer review. Books and research monographs are often reviewed by peers or edited by experts in the appropriate subject area. Information on the Web is seldom subjected to this review and editing process that has become a standard practice in print publishing.

When searching the Web for entertainment, general information, news, or weather information, you are not likely to encounter a site that someone has intentionally created to misinform you. Further, the potential damage you might experience as a result of getting a bad weather report or false news is typically not that great. When you are searching the Web for an answer to a serious research question, however, the risks are greater on both counts.

You can reduce your risks by carefully evaluating the quality of any Web resource on which you plan to rely to supply you with information related to an important judgment or decision. To develop an opinion about the quality of the resource, you can evaluate three major components of any Web page. These three components are the Web page's authorship, content, and appearance.

Author Identity and Objectivity

The first thing you should try to do when evaluating a Web research resource is to determine who authored the page. If you cannot easily find authorship information on the Web site, you should question the site's credibility. A Web site that does not identify its author has no credibility as a research resource. Any Web page that presents empirical research results, logical arguments, theories, or other information that purports to be the result of a research process should identify *and* present background information and credentials about the author. This information should be sufficient to establish the author's professional qualifications. You also should check secondary sources for corroborating information. For example, if the author of a Web page indicates that he or she is a member of a university faculty, you can find the university's Web site and see if the author is listed as a faculty member. The Web site should provide author contact information, such as a street, e-mail address, or telephone number, so you can contact the author or consult information directories to verify the addresses or telephone numbers.

It can be difficult to determine who owns a specific Web server or provides the space for the Web page. You can make a rough assessment, however, by examining the domain identifier in the URL. If the site claims affiliation with an educational or research institution, then the domain should be .edu for educational institution. A not-for-profit organization would most likely have the .org domain, and a government unit or agency would have the .gov domain.

You also should consider whether the qualifications presented by the author pertain to the material that appears on the Web site. For example, the author of a Web site concerned with gene-splicing technology might list a Ph.D. degree as a credential. If the author's

Ph.D. is in history or sociology, it would not support the credibility of the gene-splicing technology Web site. If you cannot determine the specific areas of the author's educational background, you can look for other examples of the author's work on the Web. By searching for the author's name and terms related to the subject area, you should be able to find other sites that include the author's work. The fact that a Web site author has written extensively on a subject may add some evidence—though not necessarily conclusive—that the author has expertise in the field.

In addition to identifying the author's identity and qualifications, the author information should include details about the author's affiliations—either as an employee, owner, or consultant—with organizations that might have an interest in the research results or other information included in the Web site. Information about the author's affiliations will help you determine the level of independence and objectivity that the author can bring to bear on the research questions or topics. For example, research results supporting the contention that cigarette smoke is not harmful that are presented in a site authored by a researcher with excellent scientific credentials might be less compelling if you learn that the researcher was the chief scientist at a major tobacco company. By reading the page content carefully, you might be able to identify any bias in the results that is not justified by the evidence presented.

Content

Content is a criterion that is much more difficult to judge than the author's identity and objectivity; after all, you were searching for Web sites so you could learn more about your search topic, which implies that you probably are not an expert in that content area. However, you can look for some things in the Web site's presentation to help determine the quality of information. If the Web page has a clearly stated publication date, you can determine the timeliness of the content. You can read the content critically and evaluate whether the included topics are relevant to the research question at hand. Possibly, you can determine whether important topics or considerations were omitted. You also might be able to assess the depth of treatment the author gives to the subject.

Form and Appearance

The Web does contain pages full of outright lies and misinformation that are nicely laid out, include tasteful graphics, and have grammatically correct and properly spelled text. However, many pages that contain low-quality or incorrect information are poorly designed and not well-edited. For example, a Web page devoted to an analysis of Shakespeare's plays that contains spelling errors indicates a low-quality resource. Loud colors, graphics that serve no purpose, and flashing text are all Web page design elements that often suggest a low-quality resource.

Having explained how these principles of assessing Web page quality are applied to the research team's work at Cosby Communications, Susan asks you to evaluate a Web page. One of the firm's prospective new clients is a lobbying group that is concerned about global warming. Susan has been gathering a list of URLs from which she plans to take information to include in a briefing report for Marti and the two sales executives who will be making the presentation to the prospective client. Susan would like you to evaluate the quality of a URL titled "Environmental Health Update" that is on her list.

To evaluate the quality of the environmental health update Web page:

1. Start your Web browser, if necessary, and then go to the Student Online Companion page by entering the URL **http://www.course.com/newperspectives/internet2** in the appropriate location in your Web browser. Click the hyperlink for your book, click the **Tutorial 5** link, and then click the **Session 5.2** link. Click the **PSR Program Update** link and wait while the browser loads the Web page that appears in Figure 5-13. Examine the content of the Web page; read the text, examine the titles and headings, and consider the page's appearance.

Figure 5-13	PSR PROGRAM UPDATE WEB PAGE

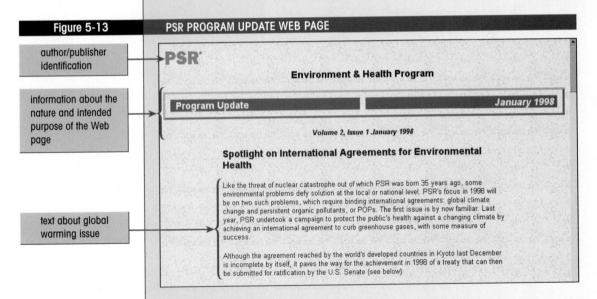

author/publisher identification

information about the nature and intended purpose of the Web page

text about global warming issue

You can see in Figure 5-13 that the author or publisher of the page is identified only as "PSR" and the page has a simple, clear design. The .org domain in the URL tells you that the publisher is a not-for-profit organization. You note that the grammar and spelling are correct, and that the content—although it clearly reflects a strong specific viewpoint on the issue—is not inflammatory or overly argumentative. As you read more of the page, you see that this style of layout and content is consistent in passages related to global warming and other issues discussed on the page. You note that the text cites such authorities as the U.S. National Oceanic and Atmospheric Administration and the *New England Journal of Medicine*. The reputable references and the consistent style of the page suggest that this might be a good-quality site.

2. Use your browser's scroll bar to scroll to the bottom of the page, which looks like Figure 5-14.

Figure 5-14	IDENTIFYING INFORMATION IN THE PSR PROGRAM UPDATE WEB PAGE

contact information for the national organization

contact information for this program

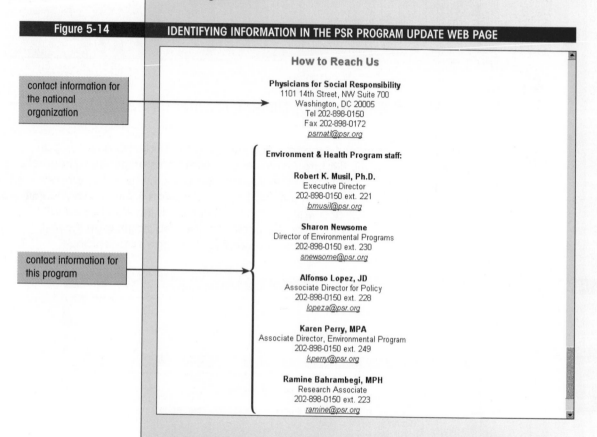

How to Reach Us

Physicians for Social Responsibility
1101 14th Street, NW Suite 700
Washington, DC 20005
Tel 202-898-0150
Fax 202-898-0172
psrnatl@psr.org

Environment & Health Program staff:

Robert K. Musil, Ph.D.
Executive Director
202-898-0150 ext. 221
bmusil@psr.org

Sharon Newsome
Director of Environmental Programs
202-898-0150 ext. 230
snewsome@psr.org

Alfonso Lopez, JD
Associate Director for Policy
202-898-0150 ext. 228
lopeza@psr.org

Karen Perry, MPA
Associate Director, Environmental Program
202-898-0150 ext. 249
kperry@psr.org

Ramine Bahrambegi, MPH
Research Associate
202-898-0150 ext. 223
ramine@psr.org

Now you can see that "PSR" is an acronym for the Physicians for Social Responsibility organization. Further, you can see that the organization's address, telephone number, and e-mail address are listed along with contact information for key individuals in the PSR's Environment and Health Program. To find more information about PSR, you might want to visit the organization's home page. The Web page shown in Figure 5-14 does not include a home page hyperlink, but you can guess that it might be the first part of the URL for this page.

3. Click in your browser's Location field or Address Bar, and then delete all of the text to the right of the .org/ domain name portion of the URL. Press the **Enter** key to load the Web page shown in Figure 5-15 with the shortened URL.

Figure 5-15 | PSR HOME PAGE

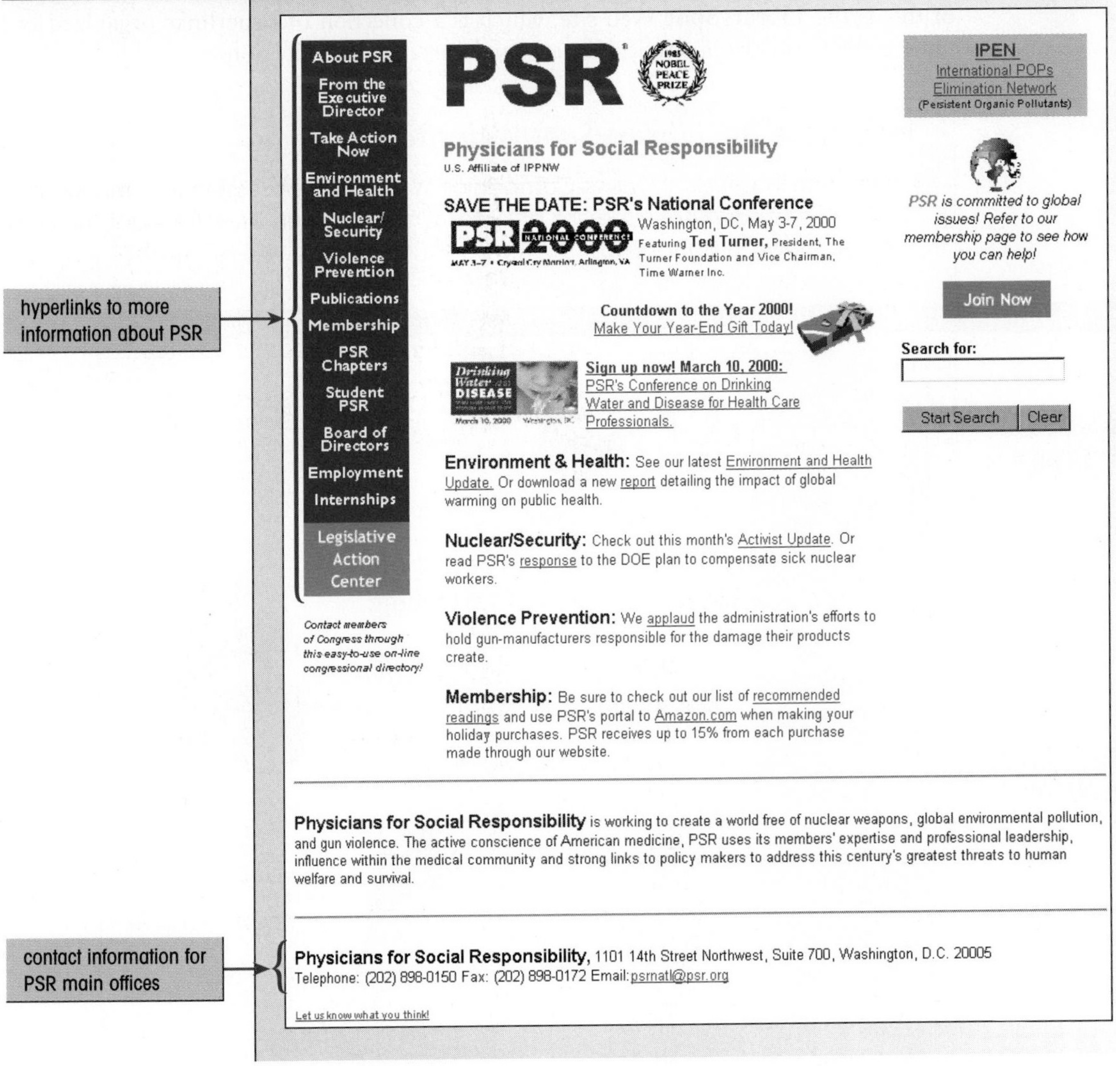

hyperlinks to more information about PSR

contact information for PSR main offices

The Web page shown in Figure 5-15 is, in fact, the U.S. National PSR Office home page that includes hyperlinks to information about the organization, its goals, activities, directors, and membership. This information will allow you to make a worthwhile evaluation of the site and help you to determine how you can use its contents as you prepare your report for Marti and the Cosby Communications sales team.

Library Resources

Susan is very happy with your evaluation of the environmental health update Web page and needs you to do more work for the research department. You ask Susan about the future of traditional libraries, given that so much information is available on the Web. She admits that she might be biased, having worked in a library for several years, but says that libraries will likely be around for a long time. In fact, the Web has made existing libraries more accessible to more people. As traditional libraries and online collections of works that have serious research value begin to recognize each other as complementary rather than as competing, library users should see many new and interesting research resources. One example of this is the **LibrarySpot** Web site, which is a collection of hyperlinks organized in the same general way that a physical library might arrange its collections.

To explore the LibrarySpot Web site:

1. Return to the Student Online Companion Web page for Session 5.2, and then click the **LibrarySpot** hyperlink and wait while your Web browser loads the Web page shown in Figure 5-16.

| Figure 5-16 | LIBRARYSPOT WEB SITE |

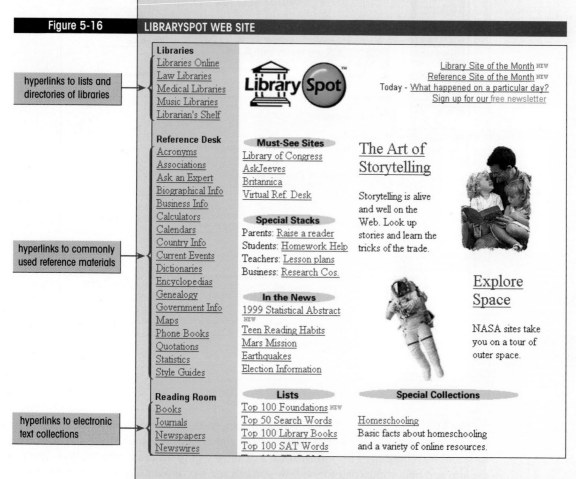

hyperlinks to lists and directories of libraries

hyperlinks to commonly used reference materials

hyperlinks to electronic text collections

Figure 5-16 shows that the LibrarySpot includes many of the same things you would expect to find in a public or school library. This library is, however, open 24 hours a day and seven days a week. The LibrarySpot site lets you access reference materials, electronic texts, and other library Web sites from one central Web page.

2. Close your Web browser, and close your dial-up connection if necessary.

The Student Online Companion page for Tutorial 5 contains many other hyperlinks to useful library and library-related Web sites in the Additional Information section under the "Library Resources" heading. Feel free to explore the libraries of the Web the next time you need to complete a research assignment for school or your job.

Many libraries have made their collection catalogs available on the Web. The St. Joseph County Public Library's List of Public Libraries with Gopher/WWW Servers includes a list of over 500 libraries with online catalogs and other information. The Student Online Companion for Tutorial 5 contains hyperlinks to these library Web sites in the Additional Information section under the "Library Resources" heading.

Figure 5-17 shows the U.S. Library of Congress Web site, which includes links to a huge array of research resources, ranging from the Thomas legislative information site to the Library of Congress archives.

Figure 5-17	U.S. LIBRARY OF CONGRESS WEB SITE

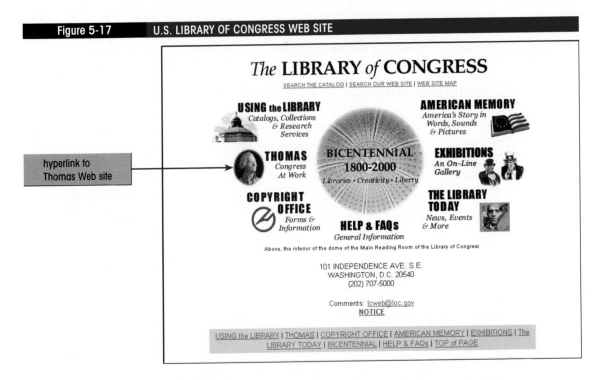

The **Thomas** Web site provides you with search access to the full text of bills that are before Congress, the *Congressional Record*, and Congressional Committee Reports. The Using the Library and American Memory hyperlinks lead you to archived photographs, sound and video recordings, maps, and collections of everything from seventeenth-century dance instruction manuals to baseball cards. The Exhibitions hyperlink leads you to information about and graphic images of historical documents, such as the Declaration of Independence and the Gettysburg Address.

Text on the Web

In addition to library catalogs and indexes to other information, the Web contains a number of text resources, including dictionaries, thesauri, encyclopedias, glossaries, and other reference works. Many people find reference works easier to use when they have a computerized search interface. For example, when you open a dictionary to find the definition of a specific word, the structure of the bound book actually interferes with your ability to find the answer you seek. A computer interface allows you to enter a search term—in this case, the word to be defined—and saves you the trouble of scanning several pages of text to find the correct entry.

Of course, publishers sell dictionaries and encyclopedias on CDs, but there are many alternatives on the Web. These alternatives range in quality from very low to very high. Many of the very best resources offered on the Web require you to pay a subscription fee. The free reference works on the Web are worth investigating, however; they are good enough to provide acceptable service for many users. In addition to dictionaries and encyclopedias, the Web includes grammar checkers, thesauri, rhyming dictionaries, and language-translation pages. The Student Online Companion page for Tutorial 5 includes a collection of hyperlinks to these resources in the Additional Information section.

The Web also offers a number of full text copies of works that are no longer protected by copyright. Two of the most popular Web sites for full text storage are the **Project Gutenberg** and **Project Bartleby** Web sites. These volunteer efforts have collected the contributions of many people throughout the world who have spent enormous amounts of time entering or converting printed text into electronic form. The Student Online Companion page for Tutorial 5 includes hyperlinks to these and several other Web sites that offer electronic texts in the Additional Information section.

Citing Web Research Resources

As you search the Web for research resources, you should collect information about the sites so you can include a proper reference to your sources in any research report you write based on your work. As you collect information, you should record the URL and name of any Web site that you use, either in a word-processor document, as a Navigator bookmark, or as an Internet Explorer favorite. Citation formats are very well defined for print publications, but formats for electronic resources are still emerging. For academic research, the two most widely followed standards for print citations are those of the **American Psychological Association** (**APA**) and the **Modern Language Association** (**MLA**). Various parties have proposed a number of additions to these two styles, but without reaching a consensus.

One of the problems that both standards face is the difficulty of typesetting long URLs in print documents. No clear standards that specify where or how to break long URLs at the end of a print line have emerged. Another typesetting problem is how to distinguish between punctuation that is included in the URL and punctuation that is part of the sentence in which the URL appears. One solution used by some publishers is to enclose the URL with chevron symbols (< >); however, this solution is not generally accepted. The Additional Information section of the Student Online Companion page for Tutorial 5 includes hyperlinks to several citation style and formatting resources on the Web. You can check these Web pages periodically for updates to these changing standards. You also can request specific guidance from your instructor, if your research report is for a course requirement, or from the editor of the publication to which you plan to submit your work.

Any method of citing Web pages faces one serious, yet-unsolved problem—moving and disappearing URLs. The Web is a dynamic medium that changes constantly. The citation systems that academics and librarians use for published books and journals work well because the printed page has a physical existence. A Web page exists only in an HTML document on a Web server computer. If that file's name or location changes, or the Web server is disconnected from the Internet, the page is no longer accessible. Perhaps future innovations in Internet addressing technologies will solve this problem.

Future of Electronic Publishing

Marti returned from her trip to Nashville and you are meeting with her, Susan, and Franco to discuss your experiences thus far working for Cosby Communications. As you talk about what you have learned and how you have shared your learning with members of the firm, the conversation turns to the future of the public relations business.

One of the key changes that the Internet and the Web have brought to the world is that information can now be disseminated more rapidly than ever in very large quantities with a very low required investment. The impact of this change is that firms in the public relations business—firms that spend great amounts of time and money trying to present their clients through the major media in the best possible light—might be facing a significantly changed business environment. The ease of publishing electronically on the Web might help reduce the concentration of media control that has been occurring over the past two or three decades as newspapers merged with each other and, along with radio and television stations, were purchased by large media interests.

To be successful in publishing in the print media—such as a monthly magazine—a publisher must have a large subscription market. The fixed costs of composing and creating the magazine are spread over enough units so that the publisher can earn a profit. The costs of publishing a Web page are very low compared to printing magazines or newspapers. Therefore, the subscription market required for a Web publication to be successful can be very small or even nonexistent. If a Web-based magazine, or an **e-zine**, can attract advertisers, it can be financially successful with no subscribers and a small number of readers. As a result, e-zines are appearing on the Web in increasing numbers. An e-zine does not require a large readership to be successful, so these electronic publications can focus on very specialized, narrow interests. E-zines have become very popular places for publishing new fiction and poetry, for example. The Additional Information section of the Student Online Companion page for Tutorial 5 includes hyperlinks to several e-zine Web sites that you might want to explore.

Session 5.2 QUICK CHECK

1. Explain why it is important to determine a Web page author's identity and credentials when you plan to use the page's information as a research resource.

2. What information about Web page authors can help you assess their objectivity with respect to the contents of their Web pages?

3. True or False: Domain names in URLs can help you assess the quality of Web pages.

4. How can you assess the quality of a Web page that deals with a subject area in which you are not very knowledgeable?

5. Briefly describe two ways that libraries use the Web.

6. True or False: The U.S. Library of Congress Web site includes hyperlinks to the full text of all U.S. Federal Court decisions.

7. What are the advantages of using online reference works such as dictionaries or encyclopedias instead of print editions?

When you need to use the Web to find information for your classes or your job, remember to return to the Additional Information section of the Student Online Companion page for Tutorial 5 for a comprehensive list of Web resources.

REVIEW ASSIGNMENTS

Marti is preparing a proposal for a potential new client, Toddle Inn, which owns and operates a chain of day-care centers in several Midwestern states from its headquarters in Minneapolis, Minnesota. The directors are interested in undertaking a national expansion program that will require outside financing and an effective public relations program that integrates with their strategic marketing plans. Marti thinks that this would be a good chance for Cosby Communications to present a proposal that integrates a Web site into a public relations program. She has asked you and Franco to join her on the trip to Minneapolis to make the presentation and would like you to help her plan the trip and prepare the proposal.

Do the following:

1. Start your Web browser, go to the Student Online Companion (http://www.course.com/newperspectives/internet2), click the link for your book, click the Tutorial 5 link, and then click the Review Assignments link in the left frame.

2. Use the NewsHub and Excite NewsTracker news search engines to find at least three current (within the past three months) news reports about the child-care industry. Write a memo to Marti that summarizes the major issues identified in these reports.

3. Obtain weather forecasts for the Minneapolis area from the Weather Channel and CNN Weather. Print the five-day forecasts from each site.

4. The potential client's headquarters offices are located near the corner of Ninth Street and Lasalle Avenue in downtown Minneapolis. Print two maps from the MapQuest site: one street-level map and one higher-level map that shows the surrounding area in Minneapolis.

5. Use the TheTrip.com Business Traveler's Guide site to locate information about restaurants and entertainment in the Minneapolis area. Prepare a report that lists three restaurants and one entertainment location. Include an explanation of why you feel each of your choices would be appropriate for entertaining a business client.

6. Marti has collected the URLs of a few Web sites that Franco might want to consider as he designs a rough outline of the promotional Web site for the prospective client. She would like you to conduct an evaluation of the Child Care Parent/Provider Information Network Web site. Prepare an evaluation of that site that considers the author's or publisher's identity and objectivity, and the site's content, form, and appearance.

7. One of the things that any public relations campaign must consider is the impact of pending legislation. Marti asks you to see if there are any bills pending in the U.S. Congress that will affect the child-care industry. Use the link on the Student Online Companion to open the Thomas legislative information Web site, and then type "child care" in the By Word/Phrase text box. Read one of the bills listed and prepare a one-paragraph summary for Marti of the bill's likely effects on the child-care industry.

8. When you are finished, close your Web browser and your dial-up connection, if necessary.

CASE PROBLEMS

Case 1. **Portland Concrete Mixers, Inc.**   You are a sales representative for Portland Concrete Mixers, Inc., a company that makes replacement parts for concrete mixing equipment. This equipment is mounted on trucks that deliver ready-mixed concrete to buildings and other job sites. You have been transferred to the Seattle area and would like to plan your first sales trip there. Because you plan to drive to Seattle, you need information about the best route as well as a map of Seattle. You hope to generate some new customers on this trip and, therefore, need to identify sales-lead prospects in the Seattle area. Companies that manufacture ready-mixed concrete are good prospects for you.

Do the following:

1. Start your Web browser, go to the Student Online Companion (http://www.course.com/newperspectives/internet2), click the link for your book, click the Tutorial 5 link, and then click the Case Problems link in the left frame.

2. Click the MapQuest hyperlink to open the MapQuest map server Web page.

3. Click the Driving Directions hyperlink to obtain driving directions. Your starting address is Portland, OR, and your destination address is Seattle, WA. Type these city and state names in the appropriate boxes.

4. Click the City-to-City Route Type option button, and then click the Calculate Directions button. Print the new Web page that opens.

5. Click the first map at the top of the Web page.

6. Click the Region link in the Map Level settings area to the right of the map to obtain a more detailed route from Portland to Seattle, and then print it.

7. To obtain a map of Seattle, click the Recenter & Zoom In option button above the map image, and then click Seattle on the map. You can click the plus and minus sign icons in the Map Level settings area to adjust the map to the level of detail you desire.

8. To identify sales leads in Seattle, return to the Student Online Companion and then click the Yellow-Page.Net hyperlink. Type concrete in the Search For box, Seattle in the City box, and WA in the State box. Click the Find It! button.

9. The results page includes a hyperlink to Concrete – Ready Mixed. Click that link to search for information about companies engaged in the ready-mixed concrete business in Seattle.

10. When you are finished, close your Web browser and your dial-up connection, if necessary.

Case 2. Ragtime Tonight   You are the owner of a popular nightclub, Ragtime Tonight, near the convention center. Although you have a good local following with the nightclub's program of stand-up comedy and ragtime piano music, many of your patrons are visitors to the city who stay in hotels near the convention center. You realize that an increasing number of these travelers are making airline, hotel, and car-rental reservations using the Web, and you would like to create a Web site that reaches them. As you are designing the site, you decide that you would like to add some ragtime audio clips that play when the site is opened using a Web browser. You have heard that single musical instruments, particularly pianos, sound realistic when synthesized in the MIDI format and you would, therefore, like to find some ragtime pieces in that format. Of course, you are willing to locate the composer and performer of any MIDI file you use and obtain the necessary permissions before adding the sound clip to your Web page.

Do the following:

1. Start your Web browser, go to the Student Online Companion (http://www.course.com/newperspectives/internet2), click the link for your book, click the Tutorial 5 link, and then click the Case Problems link in the left frame.

2. Click the Audio Searcher hyperlink to open that Web page.

3. Use one of the search panels to search for MIDI ragtime sound files. (*Hint*: Read the page's directions for searching tips.)

4. Follow several of the hyperlinks on the results page and evaluate the files offered. Write a short report summarizing your experience. In your report, describe what copyright restrictions are described on the Web site that offers the file or files that you would like to use.

5. When you are finished, close your Web browser and your dial-up connection, if necessary.

Case 3. International Professional Standards   You are conducting research on the standards of professional regulatory bodies throughout the world. Currently, you are studying the accounting profession in Mexico. You have located what appears to be a useful resource—a Web page on the Institute of Mexican Public Accountants site. The text of the Web page is in Spanish, and you would like to get a rough translation so you can determine whether it pertains to your work. As a researcher of international issues, you have access to a translation service, but it is expensive and you would prefer to use it for translating documents that you know have value rather than for screening research resources.

Do the following:

1. Start your Web browser, go to the Student Online Companion (http://www.course.com/newperspectives/internet2), click the link for your book, click the Tutorial 5 link, and then click the Case Problems link in the left frame.

2. To see the Web page that you would like to translate, click the Institute of Mexican Public Accountants hyperlink on the Student Online Companion Web page.

3. Click and drag the mouse over all of the text on the Web page to select it.

4. Press Ctrl + C to copy the Web page text to the Windows Clipboard.

5. Click the Back button on your Web browser to return to the Student Online Companion Web page.

6. Click the AltaVista Translation Service hyperlink to open its Web page.

7. Select Spanish to English in the Translate from field.

8. Click in the translate input area, and press Ctrl + V to paste the text from the Windows Clipboard.

9. Click the Translate button.

10. Review the translated page, and prepare a short evaluation of how well the translation software worked on this text.

11. When you are finished, close your Web browser and your dial-up connection, if necessary.

Case 4. Arnaud for Senate Campaign   You work for the campaign team of Jessica Arnaud, who is running for a seat in the state senate. One issue that promises to play a prominent role in the upcoming election campaign is her opponent's position on privatization of the state prison system. It is important for Jessica to establish a clear position on the issue early in the campaign, and she has asked you to prepare a briefing document for her to consider. Jessica tells you that she has no particular preference on the issue and that she wants you to obtain a balanced set of arguments for each side. Once the campaign takes a position, however, she will need to defend it. Therefore, Jessica wants to have an idea of the quality of the information you gather. You decide to do part of your research on the Web.

Do the following:

1. Start your Web browser, go to the Student Online Companion (http://www.course.com/newperspectives/internet2), click the link for your book, click the Tutorial 5 link, and then click the Case Problems link in the left frame.

2. Click the AltaVista hyperlink to open that search engine.

3. Type the words "privatization prisons" (without the quotation marks) in the search text box, and then click the Search button.

4. Examine your list of search results for authoritative sites that include positions on the issue. You might need to follow a number of results page hyperlinks to find suitable Web pages. In general, you should avoid current news items that appear in the results list.

5. Find one Web page that states a clear position in favor of privatization and another that states a clear position against privatization. Print a copy of each.

6. For each page, prepare a three-paragraph report that evaluates the quality of the page on each of the three criteria: author identity and objectivity, content, and form and appearance.

7. When you are finished, close your Web browser and your dial-up connection, if necessary.

Case 5. Dalton Precision Castings   You are the office manager for Dalton Precision Castings, a company that makes metal parts for packaging machinery and sells them throughout the world. Two of Dalton's major customers, one from Portugal and one from Italy, are arriving next week for a briefing on new technologies and products. Tom Dalton, the company's president, has asked you to help make these visitors feel welcome. He would like to have a local artist create replicas of the Portuguese and Italian flags as gifts for the visitors. He would like you to find images of the flags from which the artist can create the replicas. You decide to do your research on the Web.

Do the following:

1. Start your Web browser, go to the Student Online Companion (http://www.course.com/newperspectives/internet2), click the link for your book, click the Tutorial 5 link, and then click the Case Problems link in the left frame.

2. Click the Clip Art Searcher hyperlink to open that Web site.

3. Type the word "flag" (without the quotation marks) in the search text box for the first search engine that appears on the Clip Art Searcher page.

4. Examine your list of search results for sites that might include images of the Portuguese or Italian flags. You might need to follow a number of results page hyperlinks to find suitable Web pages.

5. If you do not find any suitable pages, repeat your search in the Clip Art Searcher search controls for the other search engines on its Web page.

6. When you find a Web page or pages that offer suitable images, examine the Web site to determine what copyright or other restrictions exist regarding your use of the images.

7. Prepare a one-paragraph report for each flag that describes the source you plan to use. Include the URL of the site where you found the flag image and a summary of the restrictions on Dalton's use of that image. If the Web site does not include any description of restrictions, refer to the text and state your opinion regarding what restrictions might exist on Dalton's use of the image.

8. When you are finished, close your Web browser and your dial-up connection, if necessary.

QUICK CHECK ANSWERS

Session 5.1

1. to increase recognition of their brand name among all news information consumers and to provide a sample of their services to potential customers.
2. NewsTracker offers broader coverage; NewsHub offers more timely coverage.
3. Different meteorologists often predict different weather conditions for the same location; gathering several forecasts provides a range of likely weather conditions.
4. You can change the map's scale, and you can select which reference points to include on the map.
5. any three of: recommendations and reviews of restaurants, entertainment, sports, shopping, landmarks, and other visitor information
6. False
7. animated GIF, JPEG
8. Multimedia files are not indexed in search engines by their features (e.g., color, size, shape, length, subject, author).
9. any two of: pitch, length, and volume
10. The Web browser starts playing the file before it finishes downloading the entire file, which increases the perceived speed of transmission for large files.

Session 5.2

1. Author identity and credentials help establish the credibility of Web page content.
2. their employment or other professional affiliations
3. True
4. timeliness, inclusion of relevant topics, depth of treatment
5. by adding online resources to their collections and by making their collections accessible to remote users and other libraries
6. False
7. available 24 hours a day, seven days a week; can be easier and faster to search

In this tutorial you will:

- Learn what FTP is and how it works

- Access an FTP server and download a program

- Learn how to compress and upload data

- Learn the difference between freeware and shareware

- Locate and download freeware and shareware programs

- Use a Web browser to find and download data

- Identify several important sources of both programs and data

- Decompress a downloaded file

- Check your disk for computer viruses

FTP

AND DOWNLOADING PROGRAMS AND DATA

Obtaining Software Tools and Data for Your Work

CASE

DigiComm Wireless Communication

DigiComm Wireless Communication is a rapidly growing company that produces and installs digital wireless communications products and technologies worldwide. It creates, assembles, and distributes communications systems for a wide range of markets and applications. Founded in 1989, DigiComm employs over 5,000 people in 16 offices around the world.

Among its major products is the UniTrack system, which is one of the world's leading two-way mobile satellite tracking systems. The UniTrack system keeps tabs on commercial trucks and provides continuous position information so supervisors at the truck fleet headquarters know the precise location of each truck in the fleet at all times. Another of DigiComm's enormously successful products is its digital wireless telephone, the D-phone. The D-phone (for digital phone) provides communications services using a special encoding scheme that makes conversations impervious to eavesdropping and reduces background noise and static.

Nancy Moore, DigiComm's director of international sales and installations, has asked you to help her equip all of the members of her communications ground-station installation team with software they need. Besides the usual productivity software packages, such as e-mail and spreadsheet software, you are responsible for providing each team member with a specially configured notebook computer and unique programs and data that are not usually available. In particular, you will ensure that each person's computer has the latest version of a software compression/decompression program, a Web browser, an Internet file transfer program, a special document reader and decoder, and an antivirus program. The team will require access to data and statistics files maintained on the Web at various sites. You will make sure that they either know where the data is located or already have the data loaded on their notebook computers.

SESSION 6.1

In this session, you will learn what FTP is and how to use it to search a site and download a program. Then, you will learn how to upload information from your computer to another computer that is connected to the Internet.

What Is FTP and Why Do You Need It?

FTP, or **file transfer protocol**, is one of several services built into and supported by the Internet suite of protocols. It is the program for transferring files from one computer that is connected to the Internet to another computer that is connected to the Internet. When a file is transferred over the Internet, whether you are viewing it with a Web browser or not, FTP is responsible for sending the file between computers. Examples of files that you can send include spreadsheets, pictures, movies, sounds, programs, or documents. For example, if you want to send your résumé to a company, you can use FTP to upload the file to the company's computer. To **upload** a file means to send it from your computer to another computer. To **download** a file means to receive on your computer one or more files from another computer. Downloading is more common because people usually receive more files than they send to other computers. Whether files are uploaded or downloaded, FTP is the program that accomplishes the transfer. FTP can run from a Web browser, with an FTP client program, or through a command-line interface. A **command-line interface** is one in which you enter a command and press the Enter key; the receiving computer then acts on the command you sent. This process continues until you have typed enough single-line commands to complete a task. An **FTP client** program is a Windows program that resides on your PC and transfers files between your computer and another computer connected to the Internet. Like any Windows client program, an FTP client program has a menu bar and, usually, one or more toolbars. Figure 6-1 shows a popular FTP client program, WS_FTP LE from Ipswitch, Inc., that is communicating with a remote computer.

Figure 6-1	FTP CLIENT PROGRAM

contents of user's system (local)

contents of FTP site (remote)

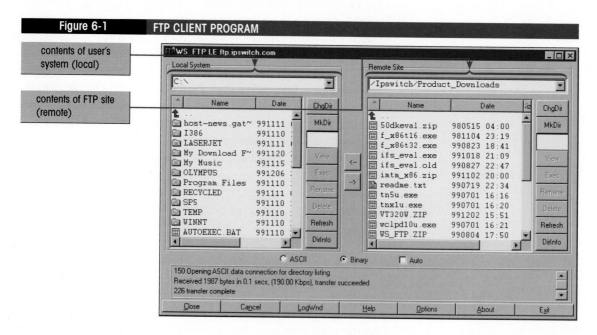

FTP programs that you execute using a command-line interface do not require Windows, but they are trickier to understand because you have to know a few commands to transfer files: commands such as *get*, *put*, *cd*, and others. Figure 6-2 shows an FTP session using a Telnet command-line FTP interface.

Figure 6-2	FTP COMMAND-LINE INTERFACE USING TELNET

```
Telnet - teetot.acusd.edu
Connect  Edit  Terminal  Help
/home/debit> ftp
ftp> open pwa.acusd.edu
Connected to pwa.
220 pwa.acusd.edu FTP server (SunOS 5.6) ready.
Name (pwa.acusd.edu:debit): debit
331 Password required for debit.
Password:
230 User debit logged in.
ftp> ls
200 PORT command successful.
150 ASCII data connection for /bin/ls (192.55.87.19,36871) (0 bytes).
BAS3EBrief
BAS4
Mail
bin
public_html
226 ASCII Transfer complete.
42 bytes received in 0.018 seconds (2.23 Kbytes/s)
ftp>
```

Like other Internet protocols, FTP follows the standard client/server model. The client FTP program resides on your computer. When you want to download or upload a file, you connect to a remote computer and request that the FTP server either receive files from you or transfer files from the remote computer to yours. An **FTP server** program receives file transfer requests from your FTP client program and then acts on those commands. The FTP program manages the details of transferring files between your computer and the FTP server. FTP is operating-system neutral. For example, your PC might use FTP on a Windows 2000 system while it is communicating with a large minicomputer running the FTP server on a UNIX operating system. It makes no difference that the operating systems are different on each computer; FTP seamlessly transfers files between them. If you know how to use a Web browser, then you already know how to use FTP. Web browsers support FTP and provide a simple and familiar interface for you to locate and download files. In this tutorial, you will learn how to transfer files using a standalone FTP program and a Web browser.

Accessing an FTP Server

To transfer files between your PC and another computer, you must first connect to the remote computer, which you can do by logging on to it directly or from your Web browser. (The Netscape Navigator and Internet Explorer Web browsers both recognize the FTP protocol.) In order to use a remote computer, you must identify yourself (or log on) by supplying your user name and a password. Some computer systems provide public access to their computers, which means anyone can connect to the FTP site. When you connect to a publicly accessible site, you are restricted to particular files and directories on the public computer. Other systems allow restricted access to their computers. To access these computers, you must have an account on the computer.

Anonymous FTP

Logging on to one of the many publicly accessible, remote computers is known as an **anonymous login** because you type the user name **anonymous** as your user name. You do not need a password to access public computers. However, it is both customary and polite to enter your full e-mail address when you are prompted for your password. That way, the organization hosting your access can identify which groups are accessing the public areas of their computer. When you transfer files—either by downloading or uploading—using an anonymous connection, you are participating in an **anonymous FTP session**. Figure 6-3 shows an example of an anonymous login.

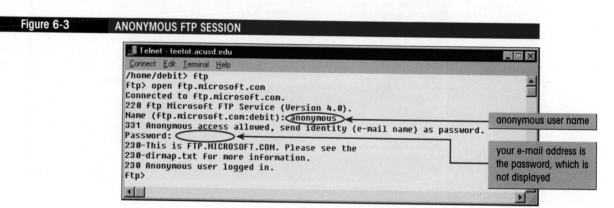

Figure 6-3 ANONYMOUS FTP SESSION

There are many anonymous FTP computers connected to the Internet. You can use these anonymous FTP computers to download many valuable and interesting files. Usually, you will use anonymous FTP to transfer files from another computer to your PC. Very infrequently, if ever, will you use full-privilege FTP. You rarely will need to subscribe to an FTP computer where you are given full access because most FTP computers allow anonymous logins. However, anonymous FTP computer sites impose limits on what you can do. Most publicly accessible computers prevent you from uploading files or provide only one publicly accessible directory to which you can upload files. Usually, anonymous FTP computers limit your access to selected directories and files on their systems. Anyone who logs on anonymously cannot open and view all the directories and files on the system. You can store uploaded files in a special directory accessible to all anonymous users called *pub* (short for *public*), if it exists. Other directories on the computer might not be accessible. You can determine which directories you can access by experimenting. If you attempt to open other directories or examine files in other directories that are not accessible, you will receive an error or warning message indicating that you do not have access to a particular area. It is unlikely that the "security police" will cite you for a violation, but you should obey all rules and regulations regarding anonymous access. Remember that you are using another person's or organization's computer at no cost to download files for your use.

You can connect to an anonymous FTP site using a Web browser, such as Navigator or Internet Explorer. When you connect to an FTP site using a Web browser, the browser automatically supplies the user name *anonymous* and an appropriate password to access the computer. Figure 6-4 shows the Navigator browser with a connection to the FTP address for the Microsoft FTP site. Web browsers automatically understand how to handle FTP communications: simply type **ftp://**, instead of **http://**, and the site's full URL to indicate that you want to use the FTP protocol and access an FTP site.

Figure 6-4 | ANONYMOUS FTP USING A WEB BROWSER

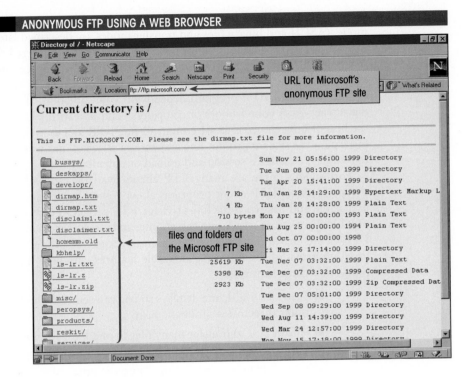

Full-Privilege FTP

Logging on to a computer on which you have an account (with a user name and password) and using it to send and receive files is called **named FTP** or **full-privilege FTP**. Even though you might have an account on a particular machine, such as your school's computer, you are probably limited to reading and writing files from and to a particular selection of directories. When you log on to a computer with your user name and password, the system automatically directs you to a particular directory on that computer. Usually, you have full read and write access rights within that directory. Having named FTP access is convenient when you want to send a file to your company branch office or your account on the school's computer from another computer connected to the Internet. Anyone who is developing Web pages will enjoy the convenience of full-privilege FTP. You can develop Web pages on your PC using any of several full-featured Web page design programs, such as Microsoft's FrontPage, Macromedia's Dreamweaver, or Adobe's Page Mill. When your Web pages are complete, you can upload them to your own directory on the Internet available through your Internet service provider (ISP) or your school. That Web space can be altered only if you use the correct user name and corresponding password. Of course, anyone can read your Web pages, but no one can change them without full-privilege FTP access. When you have an account on a computer that is connected to the Internet, you can typically store larger files for longer periods than you could on an anonymous FTP computer.

FTP Software

You learned that there are two general classes of FTP programs available: Windows-based (GUI) and command-line FTP clients. GUI FTP client programs are commonly used on Windows PCs. Command-line FTP programs are used on nongraphical interfaces, such as UNIX computer systems. You can use either an FTP client program or your Web browser to access FTP sites. If you use a graphical FTP client, be aware that the FTP client programs have two distinct advantages over Web browsers. First, FTP client programs usually transfer files faster than a Web browser. Second, when you use a Web browser to transfer files, it automatically determines if a file is ASCII or binary and then transfers the file in that mode. (ASCII and binary files and transfer modes are described later in this session.) If the browser makes a bad determination, it can corrupt the transferred files. FTP clients do not make this file type determination, so *you* are able to determine a file's type and set it properly with an FTP client program.

The choice of FTP program depends on your situation. If you are traveling and have dial-up access to your school's or company's computer with a UNIX operating system, then the best or only choice is to use command-line FTP. You then start an FTP program by typing **ftp** on the system prompt line and enter a series of one-word commands, one at a time, to establish your FTP session and upload or download files.

Fortunately, there are many FTP clients available, and all of them provide basic file transfer service. FTP client programs allow you to log on anonymously or log on with a user name and password for full-privilege FTP service. There are dozens, if not hundreds, of FTP clients from which you can choose, and most of them are either free or inexpensive. FTP clients provide many features that vary from one product to another. An FTP client program provides the following desirable features, although no single FTP program supports *all* of these features:

- Provides multipane displays so you can see both the local and remote computer directories simultaneously.
- Allows you to transfer many files in one FTP session.
- Permits drag and drop file transfer so you can drag a file from one pane (the remote computer) and drop it into the other pane (the local computer).
- Simplifies deleting directories and files on remote and local computers.
- Displays a familiar and comfortable Windows Explorer style appearance for both the local and remote computers.
- Allows you to set up scheduled file transfers for future times so selected files can be transmitted automatically at a designated future date and time.
- Gracefully recovers from interrupted file transfers by continuing from the point where the transfer was interrupted.
- Automatically reconnects to sites that disconnect you when your connection exceeds the maximum connect time.

Many GUI FTP clients are easy to use because they have menus, toolbars, and help files to simplify the process of connecting and transferring files. However, an FTP client has one major advantage over a Web browser when transferring files: Whereas Web browsers and FTP clients both allow you to download files from the Internet, you can use only an FTP client program to upload a file using a full-privilege FTP connection. So, if you are traveling and want to send a file from a branch office back to your account in another city, then you must use an FTP client, and not a Web browser, to transfer the file. On the other hand, you will be downloading files most of the time using anonymous FTP, so a Web browser is all you need to download files from a remote computer to your PC. Figure 6-5 shows an FTP client program before it logs on to a remote computer.

Figure 6-5	LOGGING ON TO A REMOTE COMPUTER WITH AN FTP CLIENT

Figure 6-5 illustrates the login screen for the WS_FTP LE FTP client. (The Student Online Companion page for Session 6.1 contains a link to this and other Web sites that you can use to download FTP clients.) The user enters the remote computer's Internet address in the Host Name/Address text box, a user name in the User ID text box, and a password in the Password text box. This information establishes a full-privilege FTP connection. You can establish an anonymous FTP connection by entering the computer's Internet address, the user ID *anonymous* in the User ID text box, and your full e-mail address in the Password text box. If you click the Anonymous check box, the software will automatically enter *anonymous* in the User ID text box. In either case—full-privilege or anonymous—you click the OK button to transmit the login information to the remote computer and start the FTP session. Other FTP clients use a similar process to start the FTP session.

Locating Files and Exploring Directories

Because you are familiar with one or more Web browsers and know how hyperlinks work, you will have no difficulty navigating an FTP site in search of files. Using FTP is especially easy when you use a Web browser to log on to an FTP site anonymously. When you need to upload files to a site requiring full-privilege FTP access rights, then you will want to use an FTP client. FTP clients are simple to master.

FTP Hyperlinks

When you visit an FTP site, your first goal should be to become familiar with its organization. FTP sites are organized hierarchically. A **hierarchical structure** is organized like an upside-down tree. When you access an FTP site, you are at the site's **root directory**, or the **home directory** or **top-level directory**. Beneath the root directory are several "branches" corresponding to other directories that contain files and other directories, as shown in Figure 6-6. Most sites prevent you from moving to a directory that is above the FTP root directory, which is restricted for anonymous FTP users. When you visit a root directory for the first time, a brief message indicates which file contains important information about the site. To search an FTP site for files you want to download, you need to understand how to interpret FTP screens and how to navigate directory hyperlinks to other directories.

Figure 6-6   FTP SITE'S HIERARCHICAL STRUCTURE

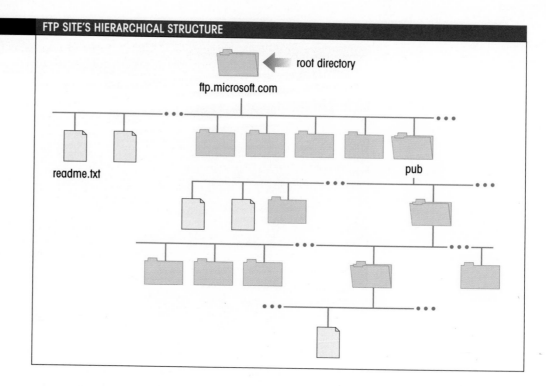

Regardless of what software you use to access an FTP site, the FTP site will look about the same and include two types of hyperlinks. A directory hyperlink will take you to another level in the hierarchical structure—to a page with more links. The other type of hyperlink represents a file. Clicking this hyperlink will either open the file so you can view it or will begin downloading the file to your computer. FTP client software displays different icons to distinguish between the two types of hyperlinks.

Of course, the two types of hyperlinks behave differently when you click them. If you are using a Web browser as your FTP program, clicking a file hyperlink might open the file or download the file to your computer after you respond to a dialog box requesting permission to download. Clicking a directory hyperlink opens the directory and reveals the directories and files within it—at the next level down the hierarchy. Whether you use a browser, FTP client, or command-line FTP program, the FTP server provides a special return link that takes you up one level in the directory hierarchy, when you are not at the root directory. In some browsers and FTP client programs, the return link is a special icon that is a right angle arrow that points up. Usually, this link contains the text "Up to higher level directory" and appears at the top of a page.

Because Nancy has asked you to supply a standard inventory of Internet programs, you want to visit an FTP site using a Web browser to see exactly what the DigiComm staff will see. Besides, you know that Nancy expects you to aid the DigiComm training staff when they instruct the installation teams. Therefore, you want to view several FTP sites and try to predict if the installation team members might encounter problems as they use the Internet software you will provide on their computers.

To open an FTP site using any Web browser:

1. Start your Web browser, and then go to the Student Online Companion page by entering the URL **http://www.course.com/newperspectives/internet2** in the appropriate location in your Web browser. Click the hyperlink for your book, click the **Tutorial 6** link, and then click the **Session 6.1** link. Click the **Microsoft FTP** link

and wait while the browser loads the page. Microsoft's FTP server displays the directories and files in its root directory, as shown in Figure 6-7, which accesses the site using Internet Explorer. Your screen might be different because the site's contents change regularly.

| Figure 6-7 | MICROSOFT'S FTP SITE ROOT DIRECTORY IN INTERNET EXPLORER |

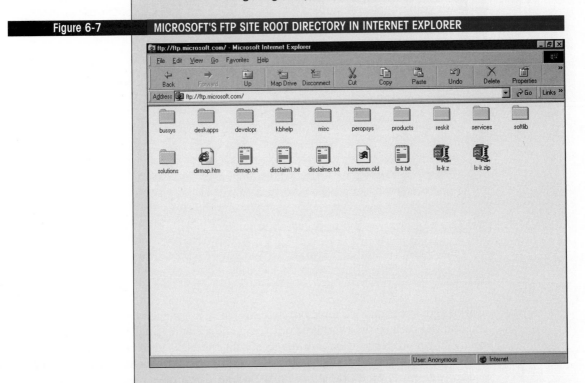

If you are using Netscape Navigator, notice that directories are labeled as such next to the hyperlink (see Figure 6-8). Both Netscape Navigator and Internet Explorer show folder icons for directories and page icons for files.

| Figure 6-8 | MICROSOFT'S FTP SITE ROOT DIRECTORY IN NAVIGATOR |

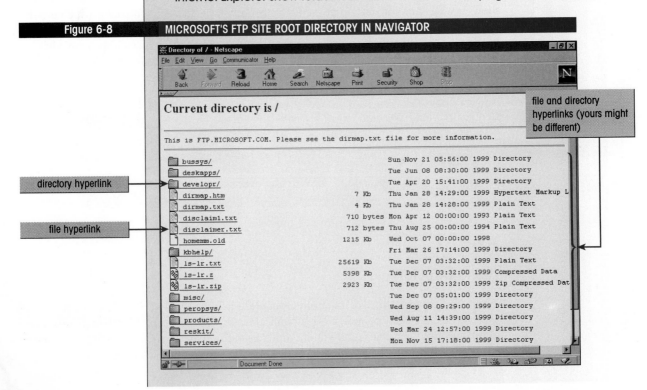

2. Locate and then click the **deskapps/** directory link to move down one level in the directory hierarchy. (If you are using Internet Explorer, then double-click the **deskapps** folder.) The new page that opens lists a set of directories with familiar names, such as access, excel, and word. Notice at the top of the page is an "Up to higher level directory" link that leads back to the root directory where you started. The hyperlink might be an icon or a text hyperlink, depending on your browser.

3. If you are using Netscape Navigator, click the **Up to higher level directory** link to return to the previous page. If you are using Internet Explorer, click your browser's **Back** button. You can always use your browser's Back button to return to the previous Web page.

4. Click the **dirmap.txt** file hyperlink (or double-click the dirmap.txt page icon) to open the page that lists files and directories available on the entire Microsoft FTP site. Sometimes, you might find site information in the readme.txt or about.txt files. You might encounter other names, but they all serve the same function—that is, to provide an overview of the site's structure and file locations.

5. Use your browser's **Print** button to print the site map so you can use it as a reference while you are visiting the site.

6. Close your Web browser, and your dial-up connection, if necessary.

If you get lost in an FTP directory structure, there is a simple way to determine your location and get back to the root directory. (Remember the inverted-tree analogy: "up" a tree means moving toward the root of the tree from one of its branches, or directories, in this analogy.) Look at the URL in your browser's address field, which lists all the directories that lead to your current location. As you move deeper down the directory hierarchy, a forward slash (/) separates the individual directory names. To move back toward the root directory, click at the end of the URL and press the Backspace key to delete the rightmost (or current) directory name. Then press the Enter key to move up to the previous directory. Figure 6-9 shows a URL that indicates that the user currently is in the /unix directory, which is a directory in the /ie directory, which is a directory in the /deskapps directory, which is a directory in the root ftp.microsoft.com directory. To return to the /ie directory, you can delete the "/unix/" directory from the URL and then press the Enter key. Using the URL to move back toward the root is the same as clicking the Up to higher level directory link.

Figure 6-9	USING THE URL TO MOVE TO THE ROOT DIRECTORY

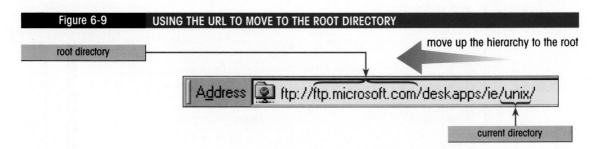

Public Directory

Some FTP servers allow users anonymous FTP access to only one directory and any files or other directories it contains. By custom, that directory is named *pub* (for *public*). Besides permitting download access by anonymous users, the site's manager might allow users to upload files. Frequently, public directories provide a temporary location for users to upload and share data or programs that they think others might find useful. One problem with sites permitting users upload privileges is that the site's manager (or webmaster) must monitor the files uploaded to a public directory on a regular basis. In addition to worrying about harmful programs that might be hidden in uploaded programs, the site manager must find and delete any copyrighted programs that were uploaded to the site illegally for public use. For example, uploading a program such as Microsoft Word to a public directory is a clear copyright violation because Microsoft's license agreement prohibits you from sharing your program with other users. Many FTP sites have specific policies that force you to acknowledge, before you upload files, that you are the owner of the material or that its transfer to the FTP site will not violate any copyright or intellectual property restrictions. There are many legitimate uses for public directories, such as sharing data or results that you have accumulated with others. Just be sure that someone else does not hold the copyright to the data or results you are sharing.

Most sites have extensive rules about acceptable use of both the anonymous FTP in general and any public directories in particular. Be sure to read the site's "readme" files to learn any rules about acceptable use when you enter an FTP site.

Downloading Files

Frequently, you use FTP to download free programs, data files, and software patches (programs that correct known problems in a particular application) from many different sites. Many software vendors use the Internet to distribute and sell new software releases. When you want the latest version of a particular program, you can browse the vendor's Web site, submit your address and credit card information, and then download a program. Software is delivered directly to your computer, and you avoid having to go to a store to purchase the software in person. You can download software and data using a command-line FTP program, a Windows FTP client program, or your Web browser. To download files using a command-line FTP program, you must first log on to an FTP site using a Telnet session. A **Telnet session** occurs when you establish a connection on the Internet with another computer and log on to it with a user name and password. Telnet is one of the several protocols that the Internet supports. Once you are connected, you can navigate the directories and locate files and programs you want to download.

Using either an FTP client or a Web browser makes locating and downloading files much simpler. To download a file using a command-line FTP program, you must understand and use commands such as *cd* and *mget*. With an FTP client or a Web browser, you click the mouse to download files.

REFERENCE WINDOW   **RW**

__Downloading a file using an FTP client program__
- Log on to the remote computer by supplying its Internet address, your user name or *anonymous*, and your password.
- Navigate to the file you want to download by clicking directory links or file icons until you locate the file.
- Click the filename on the remote computer to select it.
- Select binary transmission mode.
- Execute the command that sends the file from the FTP site to your computer.
- End the FTP session by disconnecting from the remote host site.

Why do you need to know about the transmission mode mentioned above? The next section describes the two FTP transmission modes.

File Transfer Modes

Many files, including Web pages and e-mail messages, consist of ASCII or plain text. **ASCII text** contains symbols typed from the keyboard and does not include any nonprintable, binary codes. Besides ASCII, many files, such as pictures, movies, sound clips, and graphics, are **binary**. Any file created by a word-processing program or a file containing character formatting, such as bold or italicized text, is binary. FTP can handle both ASCII and binary files easily. You select which of the two **file transfer modes**—ASCII or binary—that you want to use before transferring the file. Choose **ASCII mode** to transfer plain-text files; choose **binary mode** for transferring everything else. People usually read plain-text files, whereas computer programs, such as Word or Excel, read binary files. Though it is important to distinguish between the two types of files, they are related. ASCII characters or codes are actually a subset of the larger binary code set. That is, all ASCII characters are also binary characters. The opposite is not true; not all binary representations or codes are ASCII characters. People cannot read many binary codes—only programs can make sense of them. If you open a file and it contains gibberish—a bunch of codes—then you have chosen the wrong transfer mode. Simply execute the FTP operation again using the correct transfer mode.

If you download a program, be sure to select binary mode. Programs contain binary data that will be destroyed if you transfer it as ASCII text. You should transfer ASCII files in ASCII mode. Figure 6-10 shows an FTP client with the binary mode option selected.

| Figure 6-10 | FTP SESSION USING BINARY FILE TRANSFER MODE |

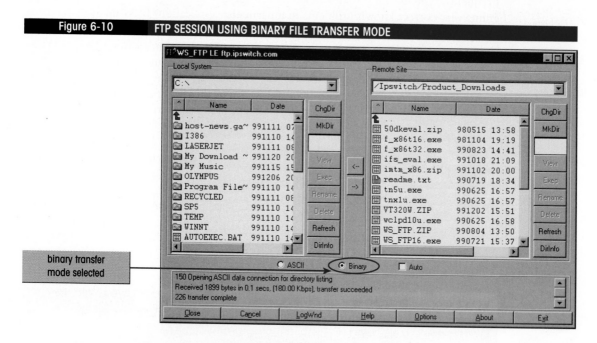

binary transfer mode selected

File Types and Extensions

The decision to transfer a file using binary or ASCII mode is largely determined by noting a file's type—much like Windows programs do. Programs such as Excel, Word, or Internet Explorer determine a file's type by its file extension. A **file extension**, or simply an **extension**, is the last three characters following the period in the filename. You can download files with a file extension of .txt in ASCII mode. For other file types, you should use binary FTP mode. It is helpful to understand the relationship between a file's extension and programs that manipulate that file type. That way, you can determine a file's general use before you download it.

File extensions are added automatically by the program that created the file based on a widely agreed-upon convention for associating files with programs. Filenames without periods (called "dots") do not have file extensions. Your PC operating system (Windows, for example) keeps track of most file extension associations and maintains a list of file extensions and programs that can open files with those extensions. Each computer that you use maintains different information about the file types stored on that computer. You can use Windows Explorer to learn about the file associations for your computer.

To view Windows file extension associations:

1. Click the **Start** button on the taskbar, point to **Programs**, and then click **Windows Explorer** to start the program.

2. Click **View** on the menu bar, and then click **Folder Options** (or **Options**) to open that dialog box.

3. Click the **File Types** tab to see your computer's file types and the programs it uses to open those files. This list is known as the **registered file types**. Figure 6-11 shows the registered file types for one user's computer; your list will probably be different. The file types are registered each time you install a new software program, so your list of registered file types depends on what programs are installed on your computer.

| Figure 6-11 | VIEWING YOUR COMPUTER'S REGISTERED FILE TYPES |

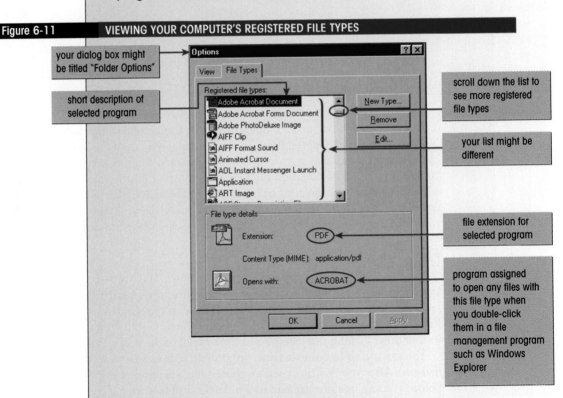

4. Click the **Cancel** button to close the dialog box without making any changes.

5. Close Windows Explorer by clicking its **Close** button.

Figure 6-12 shows several filenames with common file extensions, transfer modes, and programs that open them. Don't worry about remembering all of the different file extensions. You will encounter only a small number of the listed extensions repeatedly. Most often, you will see files on the Internet with extensions of .doc, .exe, .html, .txt, or .zip. At first, the .doc extension might confuse you because on most computers any file with the .doc extension indicates a Microsoft Word document. This is not the case on the Internet. Some Internet files with the .doc extension are plain-text files, where the .doc extension is short for "documentation."

Figure 6-12	COMMON INTERNET FILE EXTENSIONS, TRANSFER MODES, AND ASSOCIATED PROGRAMS		
FILENAME AND EXTENSION	**EXTENSION**	**TRANSFER MODE**	**TYPE OF FILE**
Picture.bmp	.bmp	Binary	Microsoft Paint
Readme.doc	.doc	ASCII	Plain-text document
Spinner.exe	.exe	Binary	Program
Image.gif	.gif	Binary	Image
Index.html	.html	ASCII	Web page
Employee.mdb	.mdb	Binary	Access database
Help.pdf	.pdf	Binary	Acrobat portable document
Marketing.ppt	.ppt	Binary	PowerPoint slides
Sample.txt	.txt	ASCII	Notepad text file
Profit.xls	.xls	Binary	Excel worksheet
File.zip	.zip	Binary	Compressed file

Sometimes, you will need to translate the file format of downloaded files into another form before you can read and use them. To translate files, you use a **file utility program**, which is a computer program that transforms the downloaded file into a form that is usable on your computer. The most common file type that you find on the Internet is a **compressed file**, which is a file that has been saved in a special format that makes its file size smaller to conserve space and shorten download time. There are many file utility programs that you can use to read compressed files. These file utility programs are described next.

Decompressing Files

Internet files of all types are frequently stored in compressed form. Compressed files use less space when stored, and they take less time to transmit from one computer to another. For example, a 1,200-kilobyte file might compress to 400 kilobytes. Imagine the time savings of downloading the compressed file instead of the original 1,200-kilobyte file.

You can use a **file compression** program to reduce nearly any file to a fraction of its original size. After you download a compressed file, you must restore the file to its original form before you can open or execute it. The process of restoring a compressed file to its original form is called **file decompression**, or **file expansion**. FTP recognizes most compressed files by their extensions; the most common extension is .zip, which is why some people refer to compressed files as **zip files** or **zipped files**. Phil Katz invented the zip format, and his file compression and decompression programs, PKZIP and PKUNZIP—where the "PK" program name prefixes are the inventor's initials—are widely used today. In the last few years, many other compression programs that imitate the original PKZIP and offer new features have flooded the market. (You will learn how to use compression programs later in this tutorial.) But before you install that new software program you just downloaded or you use a decompressed spreadsheet, you must first check it for viruses.

Checking Files for Viruses

For anyone using the Internet, computer viruses pose a real and potentially costly threat. Computer viruses made their debut shortly after 1985 and have evolved from a nuisance to a hazard for your computer. Computer **viruses** are programs that "infect" your computer and cause harm to your disk or programs. People create viruses by coding programs that attach themselves invisibly to other programs on your computer. Some viruses simply display an annoying or silly message on your screen and then go away, whereas others can cause real harm by reformatting your hard drive or changing all of your file extensions. You have to know how to detect and eradicate virus programs if you plan to download anything—including data, programs, or e-mail attachments from either reputable or questionable sources—from the Internet.

Virus detection software regularly scans the files on your disk looking for any infected files. It recognizes infected files by a signature that known viruses carry. A **virus signature** is a sequence (string) of characters that is always present in a particular virus program. A virus detection program can scan a single file, folder, or your entire hard drive looking for infected files. When the virus detection software spots a virus signature, it warns you. You can either erase the file containing the virus or ask the virus detection program to remove the virus. **Virus cleaning software** physically removes the virus from files, rendering the infected program "healthy" again.

Uploading Files

Periodically, you might want to upload one or more of your files to another host computer, either to share it with the world or to provide a private copy to an individual. This process of uploading a file is the reverse of downloading one. First, you should check the file(s) for viruses. If your file is large, or if you want to combine several files into one file, then you should compress the file(s) before uploading them to save time in transit and space on the destination computer. With full-privilege access to another computer, you can send the file to a particular folder on another machine. Without full-privilege access, you are restricted to uploading a file to a publicly accessible directory on a remote host.

The job of uploading files falls to either an FTP client program or a command-line FTP program. Though they do a good job downloading files, Web browsers are awkward, at best, when it comes to uploading files. You could also upload files by sending them as e-mail attachments. That can work, but if you send a large file, the recipient might not be able to receive it because many e-mail systems will not transfer files over one or two megabytes, and sometimes a single attachment can easily exceed that limit. If you can choose between using an FTP client program or a command-line FTP program, select the FTP client program because it is intuitive and much easier to use. If you must use a command-line FTP program, then you will need to learn commands to transfer files and navigate FTP folders. You will use both types of programs in this tutorial.

REFERENCE WINDOW   **RW**

Uploading a file using an FTP client program

- Log on to the remote computer by supplying its Internet address, your user name or *anonymous*, and your password (or your full e-mail address if using anonymous FTP).
- Navigate to the folder into which you want to upload the file.
- Click the filename of the local PC file on your computer to upload.
- Select the appropriate transmission mode.
- Click the button or execute the command that sends the file from your PC to the remote computer.
- End the FTP session by logging off and disconnecting from the remote host site.

Compressing and Uploading Files

You can compress files that you upload to another computer to save time and file space. To compress files, you need a compression program. You can download compression programs from the Internet—many programs are free or ask you to send the developer a small licensing fee. Fortunately, nearly all compression programs available on the Internet allow you to try them before you make a purchase decision. In addition to PC compression programs, larger UNIX-based machines provide a built-in compression program that you can run by typing the *compress* command at the UNIX prompt. You can choose to compress files on your PC and then upload them, or you can upload them to a UNIX machine and compress them there. The Additional Information section of the Student Online Companion contains links to FTP client program Web sites so you can learn about and download these programs.

You can upload a file with anonymous FTP or full-privilege FTP. With anonymous FTP, most sites to which you are uploading files restrict where you can place files. Sometimes, a site also restricts maximum file sizes and how long the uploaded files can stay on the site. You might already be familiar with FTP as a means of submitting homework assignments to your instructors. Students and other users frequently use anonymous FTP to upload group projects to university or other publicly accessible sites so each member of the group can access the project files. Most files must be placed in the *public* (or *pub*) directory, and they often have a maximum life span of a few days or weeks. The site's manager determines how long files can remain in the public directory. Usually, the file-deletion schedule and other policy statements are stored in the readme or readme.txt file in the public directory. If you find a file by that name or one like that, be sure to read it carefully.

Freeware, Shareware, and Limited Use Software

Internet surfers are often pleasantly surprised to discover that many Internet programs are available for downloading at little or no cost. The Internet provides a perfect incubator for programmers who want to test their software in the "real world" or who simply want to demonstrate their programming prowess by providing limited editions of their work for free. When you freely share software, the developer makes the software available for free and requests that any users provide the developer with usage feedback. Later, a new, better version of the software becomes available at little or no cost. Anyone who has used the software and likes it is usually willing to pay a small amount to upgrade to the latest version. Software that is available to anyone for no cost and with no restrictions attached to its user is called **freeware**. Anyone who uses freeware does so with the implicit or explicit knowledge that the software might contain errors, called **bugs**, that could cause the program to halt or misbehave or even to do some real damage to the user's computer. The main risk associated with using freeware is that it is sometimes not well-tested and as a result, it might contain a lot of bugs. The software's developer is rarely liable for any damage that the freeware program might cause. On the other hand, a lot of good-quality commercial software started as freeware. Before you use freeware, it is best to read reviews about it to see what kinds of successes and problems its users report. Use a Web search engine to locate newsgroups, discussion groups, or magazine reviews before you download, install, and use the software. Of course, always use a good virus program to scan and clean any viruses from all downloaded software.

Shareware is similar to freeware, but it is not entirely free and usually is available only for a short evaluation period. After that evaluation period expires—usually either a specified number of days or a given number of uses of the software—it stops functioning. Shareware users are expected to stop using the shareware after an initial trial period and uninstall it from their computers. Otherwise, anyone who likes the program and wants to continue using it can purchase a license. There are three popular ways to turn shareware users into paying customers. The first way is to build a counter into the program that keeps track of the number of times you have used a program. After you have reached a usage limit, then the software is disabled. The second way is by inserting an internal date checker as a time-expiration technique that causes the shareware to stop working after a specific time period has elapsed, such as 30 days, from the time that you installed the shareware program. Lastly, many shareware developers use a "nag" screen that appears each time you start the program to encourage users who do not purchase a license to stop using the shareware, although the program might continue to work. The screen usually displays a message with the developer's name and Web address and asks you to abide by the licensing agreement and submit payment for the shareware version of the product. You usually click an OK button to move past the nag screen to use the program.

Shareware is usually slightly more reliable than freeware because the shareware developer is sometimes willing to accept responsibility for the operation of the program. Usually, shareware developers have an established way for users to report any bugs and receive free or low-cost software upgrades and bug fixes.

Clever developers with good software products sometimes distribute restricted versions of their software for free. A restricted version of a shareware program is called a **limited edition** (or **LE**), and it provides most of the functionality of the full version that is for sale. However, LE software omits one or more useful features of the complete version. You might download an LE version and use it for free. If you really like the LE, then you are likely to want the full version of the same software. Both the e-mail program Eudora Light and the FTP client program WS_FTP LE are examples of free, limited edition programs. WS_FTP LE is the limited edition of the product called WS_FTP. The limited edition performs all the standard FTP tasks but omits some of the advanced features that make the full product especially attractive. Because the complete versions of limited edition software are inexpensive, most users of the limited edition are happy to purchase the upgraded, comprehensive version so they can use its additional capabilities.

Session 6.1 QUICK CHECK

1. True or False: Only an FTP client program is capable of downloading files from the Internet.

2. You can connect to a remote FTP server by logging on to it first. If you do not have an account on the FTP server, you can log on as a guest, which is called _____ FTP.

3. To transfer an Excel workbook to another computer using FTP, you must make sure the transfer mode is set to _____ before you transfer the file so the file will transfer correctly.

4. The overall structure in which directories and folders are organized is like an upside-down tree called a(n) _____ structure.

5. Suppose you want to go to an FTP server whose domain name is ftp.goodsoftware.com so you can download a file. What is the complete URL that you would enter in your Web browser's address field to go to that FTP site?

6. After you download software, it is always advisable to check it for a(n) _____ to make sure that your use of the program will not damage your computer.

7. Special programs that greatly reduce a file's size and its transmission time on the Internet are called _____ programs.

8. True or False: All software that you can download from the Internet and use is free.

In Session 6.2, you will start using your knowledge of FTP to download the files that the members of Nancy's team need to have on their notebook computers.

SESSION 6.2

In this session, you will learn how to use an FTP client program and a Web browser to download programs from the Internet. You will visit several sites containing links to several freeware, shareware, and limited edition programs. Also, you will download some useful utility programs.

Locating Software Download Sites

Nancy wants you to locate software tools and information from the Internet and install it on the computers used by the ground-station installation team. She gave you a list of productivity aids and useful software tools to locate and download. Your first objective is to make sure that the software is reliable. Cost is not a high-priority issue, although it is always nice to save money when you can. Perhaps equally important is how various software tools stack up against each other, so you hope to find some sort of ratings system that will guide you in making good decisions about which of several software product alternatives to choose. So far, your software list includes a Web browser, an FTP client program, a program to read special documents in a portable document format, a compression/decompression program, an e-mail client, and an antivirus program. You are sure to locate other useful programs as you conduct your research.

A good way to locate software on the Internet is to use one or more Internet search engines. If you are searching for FTP client programs, you can look for reviews or comparisons of the software by users or vendors. For example, several popular PC magazines feature articles comparing Internet utility programs where they often designate one or more programs in a class as the "best of the class" or a "best buy." Of course, the criteria they use to judge which program is best might be different from your criteria. However, it never hurts to review the ratings when you can. You decide to use a search engine to find information about FTP client programs.

To use a search engine to locate software on the Internet:

1. Start your Web browser, and then go to the Student Online Companion page by entering the URL **http://www.course.com/newperspectives/internet2** in the appropriate location in your Web browser. Click the hyperlink for your book, click the **Tutorial 6** link, and then click the **Session 6.2** link. Click the **HotBot** link and wait while the browser loads the HotBot home page.

2. Type **FTP client** in the Search Smarter text box, and then click the **SEARCH** button to start the search. Figure 6-13 shows the search results, which located several matches. (Your search list might look different.)

| Figure 6-13 | SEARCHING FOR FTP CLIENTS WITH HOTBOT |

3. Click the first few links on the results page to learn more about FTP clients.

When you explore some of the links returned by HotBot, you will find that some are relevant and others are not. PC magazines frequently review software using their specially designed software testing laboratories, conduct product comparisons, and report the results. They should not have a vested interest in the outcome, but always view the results with a critical eye to identify any biases.

You can also try searching for software download sites using the search phrase "software download." The search engine will return a list of sites that contain links to software that you can download from the Web. In the next session, you will visit several of the best download sites as you conduct your research.

Visiting and Using Popular Download Sites

Several Web sites provide links to freeware and shareware programs; some of these same sites also allow you to download programs directly. Continuing with Nancy's request for you to use the Internet to identify, locate, and download mission critical software, you decide to visit some Web sites that specialize in freeware and shareware. In addition, you will also browse through Microsoft's Web site and a few other vendors' sites. You begin by examining a well-known site, **DOWNLOAD.COM**, which contains many freeware and shareware programs in many different categories.

To browse the DOWNLOAD.COM Web site:

1. Return to the Student Online Companion Web page for Session 6.2, and then click the **DOWNLOAD.COM** hyperlink and wait while your Web browser loads the Web page.

2. Type **ftp client** in the Search text box, as shown in Figure 6-14. Notice that you could select a category in which to search, such as Games, Home & Personal, or Internet. Each category contains subcategories so you can narrow your search.

| Figure 6-14 | SEARCHING FOR FTP CLIENTS IN DOWNLOAD.COM |

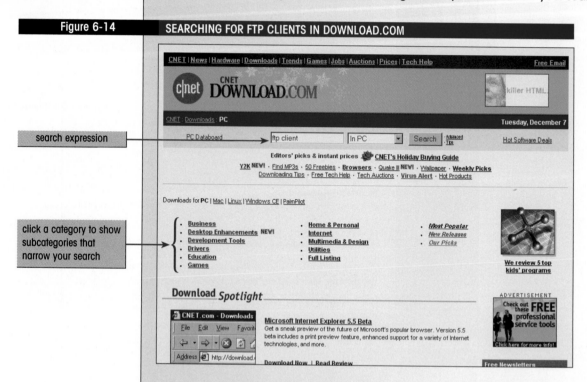

search expression

click a category to show subcategories that narrow your search

3. Click the **Search** button to search for FTP client programs. Figure 6-15 shows the search results and the different FTP clients that are available for download from DOWNLOAD.COM. (Your list might be different.)

| Figure 6-15 | FTP CLIENTS FOUND IN DOWNLOAD.COM |

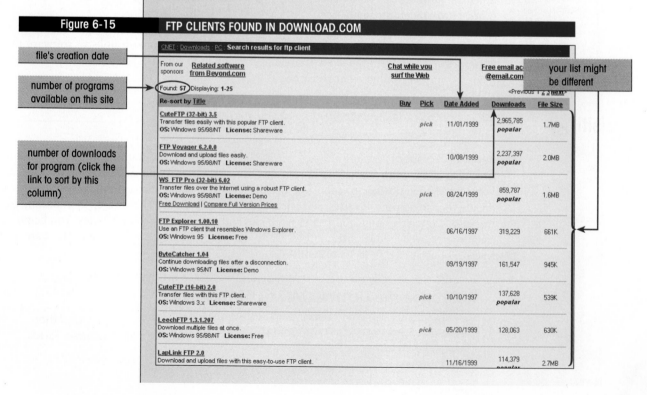

file's creation date

number of programs available on this site

number of downloads for program (click the link to sort by this column)

Figure 6-15 shows that the search returns the date when the files were uploaded to the site and the current number of times each file has been downloaded from DOWNLOAD.COM's site. Sometimes, the download count is a good resource for discovering popular and useful programs because popular programs usually have larger download counts.

4. Return to the DOWNLOAD.COM home page by clicking your browser's **Back** button.

CNET also owns SHAREWARE.COM, which provides search capabilities for freeware, shareware, and limited edition software. CNET indicates that the two sites complement each other. DOWNLOAD.COM provides more details about software and advanced search techniques, so that site might provide the best value.

You might need to narrow your search, in which case you can use DOWNLOAD.COM's categories list. Next, you will explore the Internet category to see if you can find any additional Internet utility programs that might be useful for the ground-station installation team.

To browse for Internet software on DOWNLOAD.COM:

1. Click the **Internet** link in the Categories list on the DOWNLOAD.COM home page. The Internet category Web page shown in Figure 6-16 opens and displays a list of Internet software by subcategory. Clicking any of the subcategory links opens a new page that lists related software.

Figure 6-16 INTERNET SOFTWARE LISTED BY SUBCATEGORIES

links to Internet software subcategories

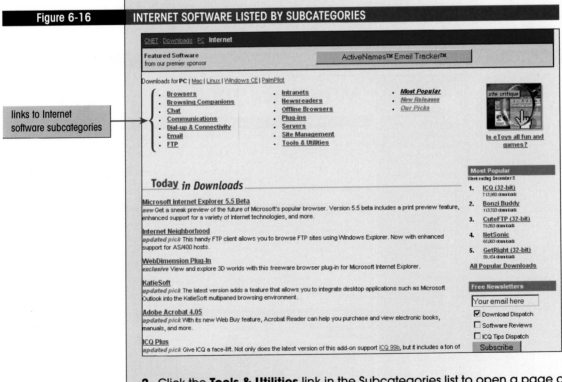

2. Click the **Tools & Utilities** link in the Subcategories list to open a page of Internet software tools and utility programs. (You may need to scroll down to find this link.) See if you can find any programs that the ground-station installation team can use, and then explore the links to those sites, but do not download any programs yet.

3. Click your browser's **Back** button twice to return to the DOWNLOAD.COM home page.

TUCOWS (The Ultimate Collection Of Winsock Software) is another popular site that provides quick access to free, inexpensive, and full-cost software. TUCOWS lists its software products by type. You decide to search the TUCOWS site to see if you can find software that would help the installation team.

To browse the TUCOWS Web site:

1. Return to the Student Online Companion Web page for Session 6.2, and then click the **TUCOWS** hyperlink and wait while your Web browser loads the Web page. TUCOWS is a busy site with worldwide servers, so the first thing you need to do is click the link for the server closest to you.

2. Click the continent or country link corresponding closest to your location. For example, U.S. students should click the **United States** link to open a list of states.

3. Click the link that corresponds to your region or state to open the Welcome to TUCOWS page. Notice that you can search for software for different operating systems: Windows 95/98, Windows NT, Windows 2000, Windows 3.x, Linux, or Macintosh. You will search for Windows 2000 software because that is what the installation team will use.

   TROUBLE? You might see more than one link for your state or region. You can click any entry to open the TUCOWS main page. If you cannot open a link, try another state or region until you succeed.

4. Click the **Windows 2000** link to open the TUCOWS main download page shown in Figure 6-17. Similar to DOWNLOAD.COM, there is a category for Internet tools. You decide to explore it to see if there are any interesting programs that the installation team can use.

Figure 6-17	TUCOWS SOFTWARE CATEGORIES

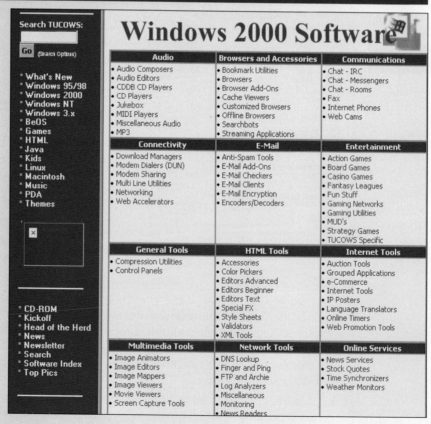

5. Click the **Internet Tools** link in the Internet Tools category. A page opens listing various Internet programs. Examine the page by scrolling up and down the list. Each file contains a description, cost, file size, and other important information that you can use to determine which programs might be valuable for the team. Notice that the tools are arranged in alphabetical order by program name.

You realize that most members of the DigiComm team are equipped with at least one Microsoft Office program, and you want to see if there are any enhancements or updates to the Internet Explorer program. You decide to visit the Microsoft site and investigate its free software offerings.

To locate Microsoft Internet Explorer files on Microsoft's Web site:

1. Return to the Student Online Companion Web page for Session 6.2, and then click the **Microsoft Web site** hyperlink and wait while your Web browser loads the Web page shown in Figure 6-18.

| Figure 6-18 | MICROSOFT.COM DOWNLOAD CENTER WEB PAGE |

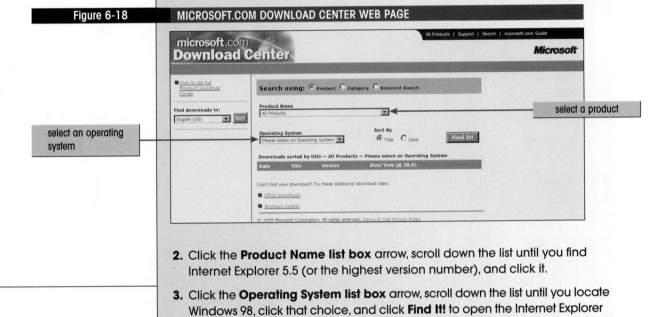

2. Click the **Product Name list box** arrow, scroll down the list until you find Internet Explorer 5.5 (or the highest version number), and click it.

3. Click the **Operating System list box** arrow, scroll down the list until you locate Windows 98, click that choice, and click **Find It!** to open the Internet Explorer Download page. You can download Internet Explorer for free. See if you can find anything else that might help the team, but do not download any programs yet.

Nancy just told you about another software download site that is maintained by a magazine-publishing company, ZDNet. The magazine publisher runs a software-testing laboratory, where it tests some of the freeware and shareware programs it reviews. ZDNet publishes ratings based on tests and evaluations of users who e-mail their impressions to the publisher. You decide to check the site to see if you can locate antivirus programs for the installation team.

To search the ZDNet Software Library Web site for antivirus software:

1. Return to the Student Online Companion Web page for Session 6.2, and then click the **ZDNet Software Library** hyperlink and wait while your Web browser loads the Web page.

2. Locate the search text box near the top of the page, type **antivirus** in the text box, and then click the **GO** button to search for antivirus programs. Your search results are arranged in alphabetical order by program name, as shown in Figure 6-19. Your results might be different from those shown in Figure 6-19, but you should find many antivirus programs in the list.

Figure 6-19	ZDNET ANTIVIRUS PROGRAM SEARCH RESULTS

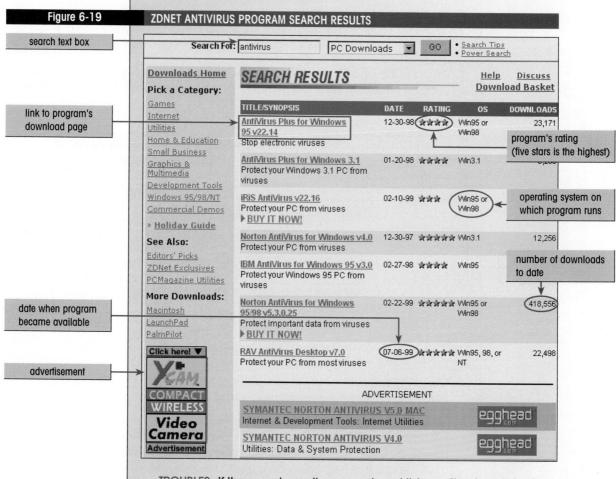

TROUBLE? If the search results pages do not list any files, type "virus" or "antivirus" (without the quotation marks) in the search text box shown in Figure 6-19, and then click the GO button again. You might need to search several times using different search expressions to find the antivirus software.

3. Click the hyperlink for the program named **Norton AntiVirus 2000 (Windows NT/2000)** to open the page shown in Figure 6-20, which supplies more information about the program, including a detailed description and its compressed file size. You can use this page to download the program by clicking the Download Now button. You can also click the Add to Basket button to place the program in your virtual shopping cart so you can continue selecting programs to download at one time.

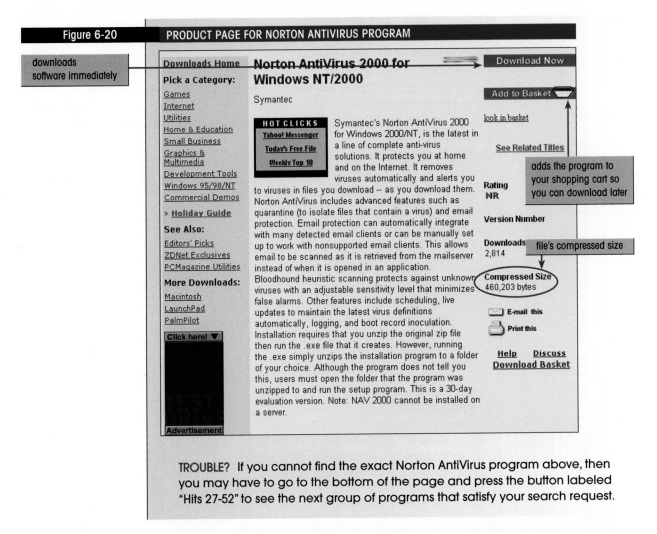

Figure 6-20   PRODUCT PAGE FOR NORTON ANTIVIRUS PROGRAM

TROUBLE? If you cannot find the exact Norton AntiVirus program above, then you may have to go to the bottom of the page and press the button labeled "Hits 27-52" to see the next group of programs that satisfy your search request.

You are satisfied that you have several good software download sites from which to locate software tools for DigiComm's installation team. Now, you are ready to locate and download selected software. You decided to use a Web browser to download your software, including an FTP client program for future use.

Downloading Programs

You want to locate and download five programs for the DigiComm team members so they can perform various tasks on the Internet quickly and smoothly. The team requires the following programs:

- FTP client program
- Program to read portable document format (PDF) files
- File compression/decompression program
- E-mail client program
- Antivirus program

After you download the programs, you will test them to make sure that they work correctly and will satisfy the team's requirements. (*Note*: Do not install the downloaded programs unless your instructor directs you to.)

Downloading an FTP Client

One of the most important software tools that you want to provide the DigiComm team is an FTP client program that is user-friendly and contains many features. You conducted your research on FTP client programs by visiting sites that review software searching and reviewed articles about FTP programs. From your studies, you conclude that the WS_FTP Limited Edition FTP client is the best choice for the team, so you will download it next.

To download a limited edition FTP client program:

1. Return to the Student Online Companion Web page for Session 6.2, and then click the **Ipswitch, Inc.** hyperlink and wait while your Web browser loads the Web page. The Ipswitch home page opens.

2. Locate and click the **Download Evaluations** link on the navigation bar that appears near the top of the page to open the Download Evaluations page.

3. Scroll down the page and locate WS_FTP LE 5.06.

   TROUBLE? The WS_FTP version available when you read this may be a newer version than the WS_FTP LE 5.06 described in this text. Ipswitch is continually improving its product. Therefore, if you do not see the exact version number mentioned in this step, locate WS_FTP LE with a higher number such as 6.1 or 7.02. A higher number normally indicates a newer version.

4. Click the **WS_FTP LE 5.06** option button or the one corresponding to the latest version.

5. Type your first name, last name, e-mail address, and telephone area code in the appropriate text boxes in the left panel of the Download Evaluations page. Use the drop-down list arrows to select your country, and select **Individual** as your user type. (You should be aware that as a student, you will use the Individual option. However, if you were acting as a representative of DigiComm, you would use the Business option.) Figure 6-21 shows a completed registration form.

| Figure 6-21 | IPSWITCH DOWNLOAD EVALUATIONS PAGE WITH COMPLETED REGISTRATION |

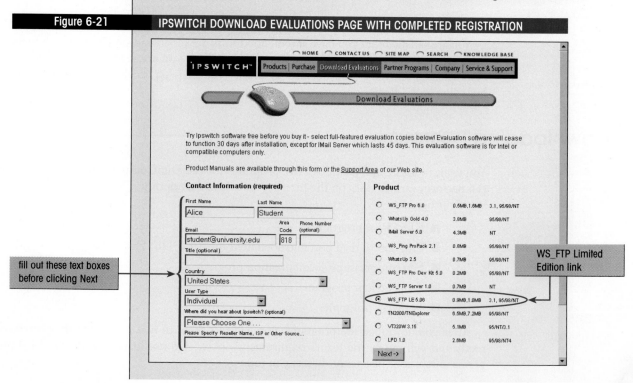

6. Click the **Next** button to submit your registration form and start the download process. A page opens displaying mirror sites from which you can choose.

TROUBLE? If you receive a message that the Web is busy and that you should try again later, you can bookmark or create a favorite for the Web page, read the remainder of the steps in this series, and then try re-submitting your registration.

TROUBLE? After registering with the site, you might receive e-mail messages from Ipswitch to inform you of forthcoming products and new versions of existing products. If you do not want to receive these e-mail messages, you can reply to a message that you receive with the word *DELETE* in the Subject line of your reply.

7. Click a link corresponding to the download site that is closest to your current location (see Figure 6-22). Click **Win95/98/NT** if you have Windows 95 or higher, or click **Win3x** if your operating system is Windows 3.1. If you are using Internet Explorer, then a dialog box opens and asks you to click an option button to either run this program from its current location or save it to disk. If this happens, click the option button to save the file to disk, and then click the **OK** button to open the Save As dialog box.

| Figure 6-22 | DOWNLOAD LOCATIONS IN THE UNITED STATES |

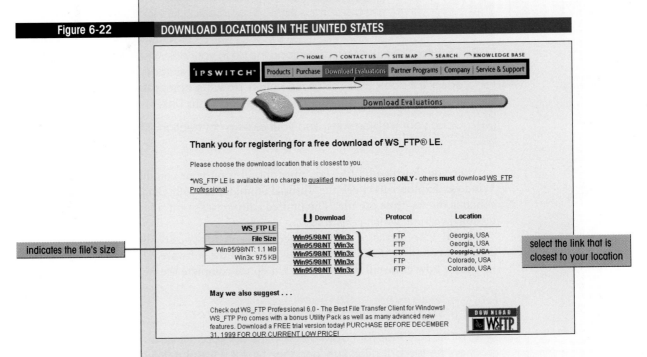

indicates the file's size

select the link that is closest to your location

8. Make sure your Data Disk is in the appropriate drive, click the **Save in** list arrow, click **3½ Floppy (A:)** (or whichever drive contains your Data Disk), and then double-click the **Tutorial.06** folder to open it. You will accept the default file-name of ws_ftple.exe (see Figure 6-23).

Figure 6-23

DOWNLOADING THE FILE AND SAVING IT ON YOUR DATA DISK

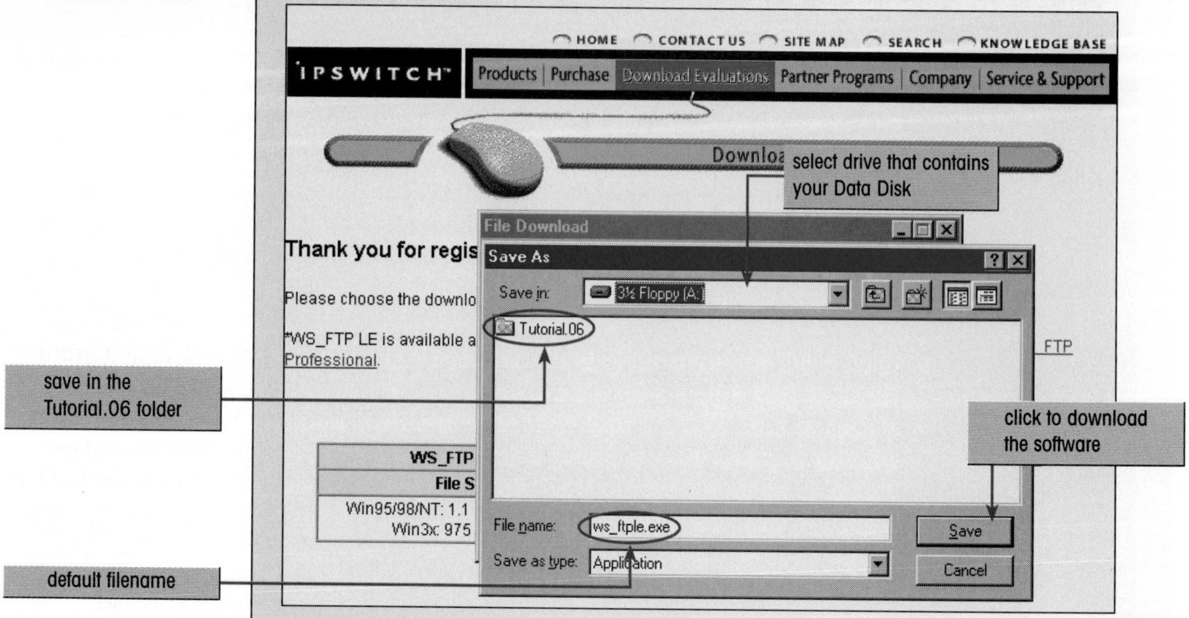

9. Click the **Save** button to download the file to your disk. When the file is completely transferred, a Download Complete or Download successful dialog box might open; if it does, click the **Close** button. Now, the compressed file that contains the FTP client program files is saved on your Data Disk.

10. Close your Web browser, and your dial-up connection, if necessary.

After you download a file, you must install it on your computer to use it. You can use Windows Explorer to check the Tutorial.06 folder on your Data Disk to make sure that it contains the ws_ftple.exe file. The limited edition lacks only a few features of the full, professional version, which is *not* free.

Note: If your instructor or lab manager tells you that you are allowed to install and use the program, complete the next set of steps to install the software. Otherwise, read the steps so you know how to install the software, but do *not* complete the steps at the computer.

To install WS_FTP LE on your computer:

1. Make sure that your Data Disk is in the appropriate drive, click the **Start** button on the taskbar, click **Run**, and then type **A:\Tutorial.06\ws_ftple.exe** in the Open text box in the Run dialog box. If your Data Disk is not in drive A, then substitute your drive letter in the Open text box.

2. Click the **OK** button to start the installation process. A Welcome screen displays.

   TROUBLE? The installation steps that you encounter might be different from the ones in the following steps. If your on-screen instructions are different, answer the questions in each dialog box, and click the appropriate option buttons and check boxes to continue, or seek your instructor's help.

3. On the Welcome screen, click the **Next** button to continue. The Question dialog box opens.

4. Click the **Yes** button to answer the question "Are you a student, faculty member, or staff member of an educational institution...." The Software License Agreement dialog box opens.

5. Read the End User License Agreement, and click the **Yes** button to indicate that you accept the terms of the agreement. (If you click the No button, then the installation process stops.) A WS_FTP LE Installation dialog box opens with a default destination directory.

6. Click the **Next** button to accept the default directory in which the program files will be stored. (The default directory is C:\Program Files\WS_FTP.) The Select Program Folder dialog box opens.

7. Click the **Next** button to accept the suggested name, WS_FTP LE, for the Program Manager group name. (The Program Manager group name is the name of the folder whose name appears in the Start menu Programs list.)

8. Click the **Finish** button to complete the installation process.

After you are finished installing the program, you may want to read the "Readme" file to learn how to use the program, or you can use the program's Help files for program instructions.

Downloading Acrobat Reader

The DigiComm Company provides many of its user and training manuals in a special form called Portable Document Format. **Portable Document Format (PDF)**, developed by Adobe Corporation, provides a convenient, self-contained package for delivering and displaying documents containing text, graphics, charts, and other objects. PDF files and ZIP files are both special formats for storing files, but they are not related. PDF files simply provide a universal and convenient way to represent documents, whereas ZIP files condense files so they occupy much less space. Compressed files cannot be viewed until you decompress them.

When you download a PDF file, you do not need to use the same program as the file's creator to display and print the document; you use the **Adobe Acrobat Reader** program to display, zoom, browse, and print PDF documents. For example, if you download a PDF file that was created in Microsoft Word, then you can use Adobe Acrobat Reader to access the files, even if you don't have Word installed on your computer. Most Web browsers contain the Acrobat Reader program so you can use your Web browser to read PDF documents without downloading them first, or you can download the Acrobat Reader program separately to read files that you already downloaded.

Many Web documents are available in PDF format, so you are sure that the Acrobat Reader will be a valuable addition to the DigiComm team's software tools. Acrobat Reader is a relatively small program, and it is free and simple to install. You will use DOWNLOAD.COM's site to search for and download the Acrobat Reader.

Note: You cannot download the Acrobat Reader program to your Data Disk because its file size (approximately 4 megabytes) exceeds your Data Disk's storage capacity. Your instructor might ask you to download the program to your hard drive or to simply read the following steps without actually downloading the file.

To download the Acrobat Reader from DOWNLOAD.COM:

1. Return to the Student Online Companion Web page for Session 6.2, and then click the **DOWNLOAD.COM** hyperlink and wait while your Web browser loads the Web page.

2. Type **Acrobat Reader** in the Search text box on the DOWNLOAD.COM home page, and then click the **Search** button. Your search results page should look similar to Figure 6-24.

Figure 6-24   ACROBAT READER SEARCH RESULTS USING DOWNLOAD.COM

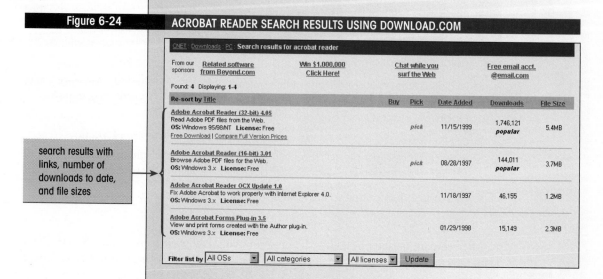

search results with links, number of downloads to date, and file sizes

Notice that the right column of the search results page shows the number of downloads that have occurred to date—a larger number generally indicates that the software is popular and reliable, whereas a smaller number indicates that the software might be unstable or relatively new.

3. Click the **Adobe Acrobat Reader (32-bit) 4.05** link (or the version for the latest version of Windows) to open the program's description page where you download the software (see Figure 6-25).

Figure 6-25   ADOBE ACROBAT READER DOWNLOAD PAGE

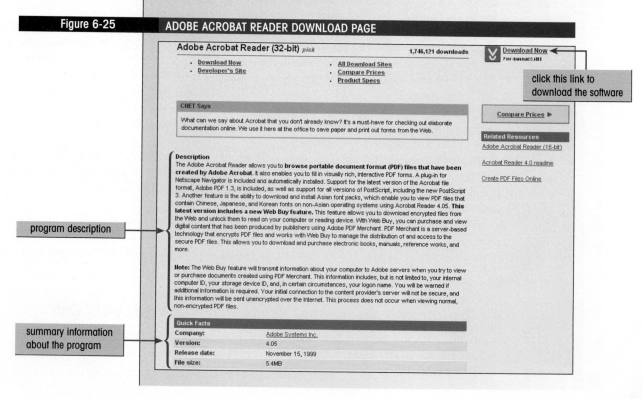

program description

summary information about the program

TROUBLE? Software vendors update and improve their programs regularly, so your Acrobat Reader program version number might be different. If the version number is larger than the one shown in Figure 6-25, then download that program because it will be more current.

4. Read the program summary and requirements, and then click the **Download Now** link to open the Download page. You have a choice of locations from which you can download the software; these sites are identified with links below the "All download sites" heading near the middle of the page. Each download location has a reliability rating, with three dots indicating the most reliable location.

5. After a short delay, a File Download dialog box opens automatically. Depending on your browser, the dialog box might open with one of two options: to run this program from its current location or to save this program to disk. If this dialog box opens, click the **Save this program to disk** option button and then click the **OK** button. If this dialog box does not open, then your browser will automatically choose to save the file to disk.

TROUBLE? Ask your instructor or technical support person to see if you can download the file to your hard drive. If you cannot download the file, or if you are unsure about downloading the file, then click the Cancel button now and read the rest of the steps without completing them at the computer.

6. In the Save As dialog box, click the **Save in** list arrow, click the drive and folder in which to save the file, and then click the **Save** button to start downloading the file. Figure 6-26 shows the dialog box that Internet Explorer displays while it downloads the file. (Navigator displays a different dialog box.)

Figure 6-26	FILE DOWNLOAD DIALOG BOX

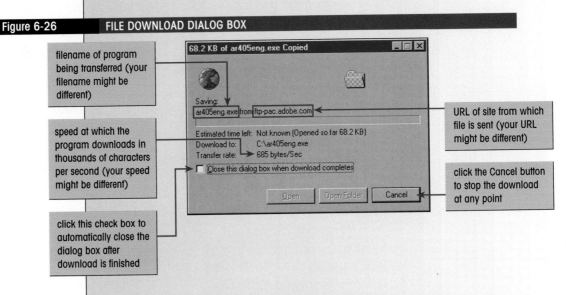

filename of program being transferred (your filename might be different)

speed at which the program downloads in thousands of characters per second (your speed might be different)

click this check box to automatically close the dialog box after download is finished

URL of site from which file is sent (your URL might be different)

click the Cancel button to stop the download at any point

7. If you are using Internet Explorer, when the file is completely transferred, a Download Complete dialog box may open. If so, then click the **Close** button to continue.

Now the downloaded Acrobat Reader file is saved on your hard drive. You can install the program by double-clicking its filename in Windows Explorer and then following the steps.

After installing the Acrobat Reader program, you can delete the downloaded executable file from your computer.

Downloading with an FTP Client

Nancy also wants you to train DigiComm staff members to download files using a Web browser and an FTP client, so you decide to use the WS_FTP Limited Edition FTP client program, which you already downloaded, to download the next program on Nancy's list.

Many file compression programs available on the Internet are reliable and easy to use. One popular program is **WinZip**, which is available for free during your evaluation. WinZip has been downloaded over 5 million times and has received a number of awards from computing magazines and other sources.

Note: In the following steps, you will use the WS_FTP Limited Edition FTP client program to download the WinZip program. If you do not have an FTP client or cannot install one on your school's computer, then read the steps without completing them at the computer.

In the first set of steps, you will establish the FTP server address and user login information that you will save in a list of profiles that operates much like an e-mail program's address book. When you want to return to an FTP site, you can select the saved FTP profile information and click the OK button to connect.

To establish and save an FTP session profile:

1. Click the **Start** button on the taskbar, point to **Programs**, point to **WS_FTP LE**, and then click **WS_FTP LE** to start the WS_FTP program. The Session Properties dialog box opens.

   TROUBLE? If you do not see WS_FTP LE on the Programs menu, then make sure that you downloaded and installed the WS_FTP Limited Edition program. Ask your instructor or technical support person for help, if necessary.

2. Click the **New** button in the Session Properties dialog box to create a new user profile.

3. Type **WinZip** in the Profile Name text box (the name serves only as a way to identify this profile), and then press the **Tab** key to move to the Host Name/Address text box.

4. Type **ftp.winzip.com** in the Host Name/Address text box.

5. Click the **Anonymous** check box to place a check mark in it—this simplifies data entry because the system automatically places "anonymous" in the User ID text box and places "wsftple@" in the Password text box.

6. Press the **Tab** key to move to the Password text box.

7. Type your full e-mail address in the Password text box. Figure 6-27 shows the Session Properties to establish an anonymous FTP session with the site ftp.winzip.com.

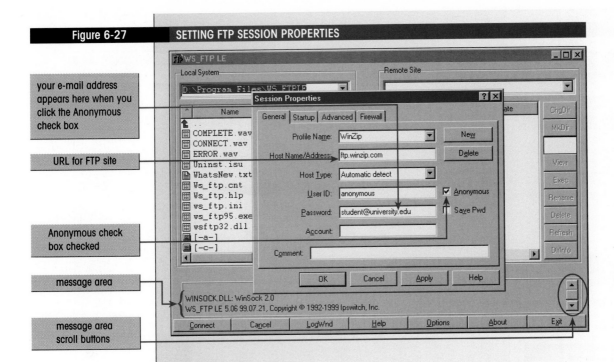

Figure 6-27 — SETTING FTP SESSION PROPERTIES

your e-mail address appears here when you click the Anonymous check box

URL for FTP site

Anonymous check box checked

message area

message area scroll buttons

8. Click the **Apply** button to save the WinZip session properties. (Clicking the Apply button will not start the FTP process; it only saves the session properties.)

Now you can easily visit the WinZip FTP site the next time by clicking the Profile Name list arrow in the Session Properties dialog box and then clicking WinZip. With the URL and user information entered, you are ready to log on to the FTP site anonymously and download the WinZip program.

Note: If you cannot use an FTP client program, then read the following steps without actually completing them at the computer.

To log on anonymously and download a file:

1. Click the **OK** button to log on to the WinZip FTP site anonymously. The main WS_FTP LE window opens. Several messages scroll in the message area at the bottom of the WS_FTP window. You can use the up and down arrows to scroll the message area to review all messages passed between your client and the FTP server.

2. If necessary, click the **Maximize** button to maximize the program window.

3. Click the **ChgDir** button in the left panel to open the Input dialog box.

4. Make sure that your Data Disk is in the appropriate drive, type **A:\Tutorial.06** in the text box (see Figure 6-28), and then click the **OK** button. The left panel changes and displays the files in the Tutorial.06 folder on your Data Disk. The left panel represents your PC, and the right panel represents the FTP site. By changing the left panel to your Data Disk, any files you download will be saved on that drive.

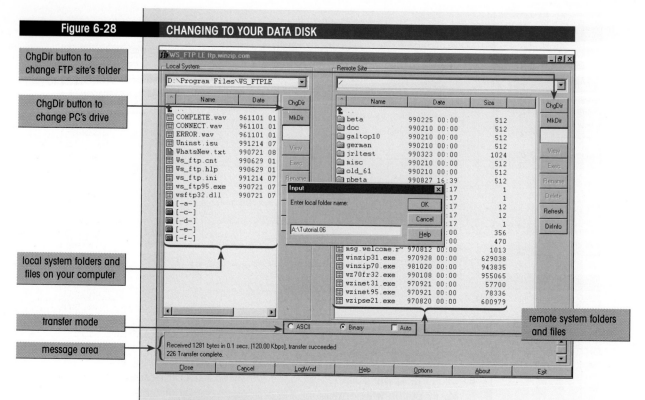

Figure 6-28　　**CHANGING TO YOUR DATA DISK**

ChgDir button to change FTP site's folder

ChgDir button to change PC's drive

local system folders and files on your computer

transfer mode

message area

remote system folders and files

TROUBLE? If you cannot establish a connection with the WinZip FTP server, then click the Close button on the button bar. Click the Connect button on the button bar to open the Session Properties dialog box, click the Profile Name list arrow, and then click WinZip. Make sure you entered ftp.winzip.com in the Host Name/Address text box. Click the OK button to connect, and then follow the steps.

TROUBLE? If you tried more than once to connect to the WinZip site without success, the site might be busy. When the number of anonymous logins exceeds a large number, the WinZip site rejects all subsequent anonymous FTP sessions. Try again later, or just read the steps so you understand how to use an FTP client to download files.

The file you want to download appears in the right panel in the remote system's listing of folders and files.

5. If necessary, click the **Binary** transfer mode option button to ensure that the program file is transferred correctly.

6. Examine the right panel, which contains the remote site's listing of files and folders. Locate and then click the **winzip70.exe** filename to select it.

7. Click the **left** pointing arrow located in the median strip between the left and right panels. Clicking this arrow begins the transfer process to download the selected file in the right pane to the selected folder in the left pane. A Transfer Status dialog box opens and displays download progress information, including a standard rain gauge and percent indicators (see Figure 6-29). When the Transfer Status dialog box closes, the file transfer is complete and the winzip70.exe program is saved on your Data Disk.

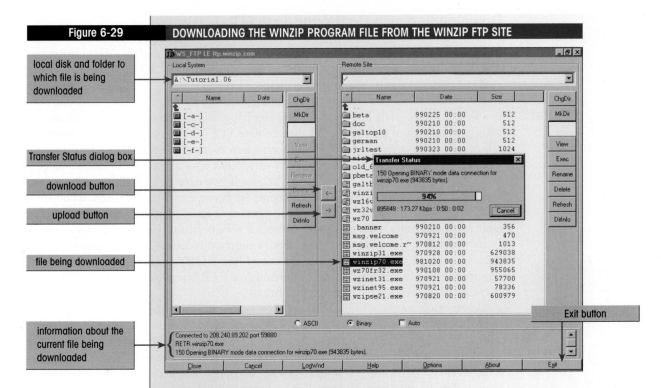

| Figure 6-29 | DOWNLOADING THE WINZIP PROGRAM FILE FROM THE WINZIP FTP SITE |

TROUBLE? WS_FTP might place a file called WS_FTP.LOG on your disk in addition to the file you download. The log file merely indicates the status of the download operation. You can safely delete the WS_FTP.LOG file from your disk. (Do not, of course, delete the winzip70.exe program file from your disk.)

8. Click the **Exit** button on the button bar to log off the WinZip FTP site and close the WS_FTP program.

The time it takes to transfer the program file varies with the type of connection you have and your modem's speed. If you are on a local area network (LAN) with a T1 Internet connection, then the transfer time is a few seconds. If you are using a modem and a dial-up network connection, then the transfer time could take several minutes. Another factor in the download time is the amount of traffic at the FTP site. Several simultaneous users (more than 4,000 for example) can directly affect the download process. If you encounter problems while downloading a file, then stop the process by clicking the Cancel button and try again later.

You've accomplished a lot this session. Now that you have the WinZip software on your computer, you can evaluate it for use by the team members. The version you downloaded is called an evaluation version, which means that you can use it to evaluate the software at no charge. Each time you load the software, though, it displays an opening screen reminding you that you are using an evaluation copy that is not yet registered. Typically, opening screens such as WinZip's evaluation reminder require you to acknowledge the screen by clicking a button. If you continue using the software or need the full-capacity version, you will have to pay a small licensing fee to the developer. If you are allowed to install the WinZip program, open Windows Explorer, change to the Tutorial.06 folder on your Data Disk, double-click the winzip70.exe file, and then follow the on-screen instructions. (Ask your instructor or technical support person first before installing the program.)

Downloading with Command-Line FTP

In this tutorial, you have downloaded files using a Web browser and an FTP client program. The third option of transferring files is to use **command-line FTP**, where you execute a series of one-line commands to connect to an FTP site, navigate to a folder at the FTP site, and download a file. You type commands at the command prompt instead of clicking buttons in a Windows program. For example, you might log on to your school's host computer using your user name and password, and then initiate an FTP session from your computer to a remote site on the Internet. You should know how to execute a few simple FTP commands so that you can use command-line FTP if you do not have access to a Windows-based program. Command-line FTP is especially helpful if you have dial-up access to your school's computer and cannot run an FTP client from your home computer. Similarly, if you are traveling and want to transfer files between your notebook computer and your school's or employer's computer, then you usually must use command-line FTP to transfer the files.

By definition, the ground-station installation team is mobile, so it is important for the team members to know how to use command-line FTP. You realize that Nancy does not require the DigiComm staff to use command-line FTP, but you can teach them how to use it in case they need it while traveling on business.

When using command-line FTP, you first start your command-line FTP program either by invoking the Windows 2000 built-in version or by logging on to a UNIX computer that has command-line FTP and then executing that version. You then execute a series of commands. The first command you execute is to connect to a remote server. Next, you locate the folder containing the file you want to download using a simple command to open successive folders. Finally, you issue the one-line command that downloads the file from the remote host to your computer or the local UNIX computer on which you have an account and a connection. Most of the files that the DigiComm staff will transfer from and to DigiComm's main computer run the UNIX operating system, which has FTP available, and DigiComm staff members can log on to that computer with their own accounts. Then, they can transfer files using command-line FTP when necessary.

In order to use command-line FTP, you must either have a command-line FTP program installed on your PC (most Windows systems come equipped with command-line FTP) or you must have access to a host computer that has a command-line FTP program. In the following steps, you will use the Windows built-in FTP program to access a remote host. As you are working, it is important to remember that if you use FTP on a UNIX computer, all commands are case-sensitive; that is, typing "FTP" is not the same as typing its lowercase equivalent, "ftp." Figure 6-30 shows some common FTP command-line program commands that FTP client programs issue automatically.

Figure 6-30	COMMON FTP COMMANDS

COMMAND	DESCRIPTION
binary	Sets the transfer mode to binary
cd directory	Changes the remote directory to *directory*
close	Disconnects from the current remote computer
get filename	Downloads *filename* from the remote computer
help	Obtains help on various FTP topics
lcd directory	Changes the current local directory to *directory*
ls or dir	Displays the current folder's filenames and directory names
open remote	Connects to a remote FTP server on *remote*
put filename	Uploads *filename* to a remote computer
quit	Exits the FTP program and logs off a remote server

REFERENCE   WINDOW   **RW**

Downloading a file using command-line FTP

- Start your FTP program and then type open <*ftp-address*> where *ftp-address* is the address of the remote FTP server.
- Log in using "anonymous" as the user name and your e-mail address as the password.
- Navigate to the program you want to download. Type the *cd* and *dir* commands at the command prompt to change directories and list directory contents, respectively.
- Set the transfer mode to binary by typing the binary command at the command prompt, and then press the Enter key.
- Download the file by typing the *get* command at the command prompt with the filename you want to download, and then press the Enter key.
- When the download is complete, disconnect from the remote site by typing the *quit* command, and then press the Enter key.

Three members of the DigiComm installation team prefer to use a different compression program from the one that you downloaded—they are using another popular program named PKZIP developed by PKWARE. You could use the FTP command-line program on your company's computer to download the PKZIP file, but you prefer to use your Windows built-in FTP program, which is found in the Windows directory on your PC's hard drive. The first steps show you how to connect to a remote FTP server.

To connect to a remote FTP server using the Windows FTP program:

1. Click the **Start** button on the taskbar, click **Run**, type **ftp** in the Open text box in the Run dialog box, and then click the **OK** button. The Windows-supplied command-line FTP program opens and executes.

TROUBLE? If your Windows installation is located on another hard drive, then type that drive letter in place of "C" in the command. If your Windows installation is located in a folder with another name, then type that folder name in place of "Windows" in the command. (Alternatively, you can click Start, point to Find, click Files or Folders, and then type FTP in the "Named" text box to search for the FTP program on your computer. The file is called FTP.exe.) If the FTP window does not open after clicking the OK button, ask your instructor or technical support person for help.

2. Type **open ftp.pkware.com** at the ftp> prompt, and then press the **Enter** key to execute the FTP command that establishes a connection to the remote server.

   TROUBLE? If you get an error message that says "ftp.pkware.com Unknown host." then you need to make a dial-up networking connection to your server before typing the open command. Ask your instructor or technical support person for help.

   TROUBLE? If nothing happens after you press the Enter key, the remote FTP site might be shut down for routine maintenance, or too many users might be attempting to access the site at once. If you cannot connect, try again later.

3. When the FTP session establishes a connection with the remote FTP site, the remote site responds with a request for you to log on. Type **anonymous** at the User prompt, and then press the **Enter** key to send your user name to the site. When the remote site displays a Password prompt, type your full e-mail address (nothing displays in the password line as you type, so do not be concerned), and then press the **Enter** key. When the remote site accepts your user name and password, the system prompt, ftp>, reappears (see Figure 6-31).

| Figure 6-31 | COMMAND-LINE FTP CONNECTED TO A REMOTE FTP SERVER |

```
C:\WINNT\System32\ftp.exe
ftp> open ftp.pkware.com
Connected to ftp.pkware.com.
220 ProFTPD 1.2.0pre8 Server (ftp.pkware.com) [207.250.4.5]
User (ftp.pkware.com:(none)): anonymous
331 Anonymous login ok, send your complete e-mail address as password.
Password:
230-
You are user 43 out of 125 possible connections.
230 Anonymous access granted, restrictions apply.
ftp>
```

Now that you have established a connection between your command-line FTP program and the remote server, you can search for the file you want to download. First, you will list the files at the remote site's root directory. Then, you can determine where the file you need is located. If it is in the root directory, check the spelling of the filename, set the transfer mode to binary, and then send the command to begin sending the file to your PC.

Note: If you cannot use your computer to download the PKZIP program file, then read the following steps without completing them at the computer.

To locate and download a file using a command-line FTP program:

1. Type **dir** at the ftp> prompt, and then press the **Enter** key to display the file listing for the root directory. The file you need is named PK270WSP.EXE.

2. Type **binary**, and then press the **Enter** key to set the transmission mode to binary (the site will respond with the message "Type set to I."). Always specify binary transmission mode when you send programs or data because only Web pages and e-mail attachments can be sent using ASCII transmission mode.

   TROUBLE? The program that you will download is over 750K. If your Data Disk does not have enough free space available, then use a new disk for these steps. Create a Tutorial.06 folder on the new disk, and write "Data Disk 2: Tutorial 6" on the disk's label.

3. Make sure that your Data Disk is in the appropriate drive, and then type **lcd A:\Tutorial.06** and press the **Enter** key. The site responds to let you know that the local directory is now A:\Tutorial.06, which means that all down-loaded files will be saved in the Tutorial.06 folder on your Data Disk.

4. Type **get PK270WSP.EXE** (make sure to type the space between the word **get** and the filename and type all capital letters for the file name) at the command prompt, and then press the **Enter** key. Immediately, the site starts downloading the file to your Data Disk. When the file transfer is complete, a message indicates the total number of characters transferred and the transfer rate (see Figure 6-32). Both the time and transfer rate will vary with your Internet connection speed and current Internet traffic.

| Figure 6-32 | DOWNLOADING THE PKZIP PROGRAM |

```
C:\WINNT\System32\ftp.exe
-rw-r--r--    1 1004     pkware      93755 Nov  1 22:46 pkzf15.exe
-rw-r--r--    1 1004     pkware       9596 Nov  1 22:46 pkzgetst.zip
-rw-r--r--    1 1004     pkware     189365 Nov  1 22:46 probdesc.zip
drwxr-xr-x    3 1004     pkware        512 Nov  1 22:46 pub
-rw-r--r--    1 1004     pkware      72463 Nov  1 22:46 qdpni101.zip
-rw-r--r--    1 1004     pkware       8052 Nov  1 22:46 renz10a.zip
-rw-r--r--    1 1004     pkware       4756 Nov  1 22:46 rurpkup.zip
-rw-r--r--    1 1004     pkware       5219 Nov  1 22:46 rurpkzp.zip
-rw-r--r--    1 1004     pkware     205819 Nov  1 22:46 sd-500.exe
drwx--x--x    3 1004     pkware        512 Nov  1 22:45 share
d--x--x--x    2 1004     pkware        512 Nov  1 22:45 usr
-rw-r--r--    1 1004     pkware      59489 Nov  1 22:46 vlmup2.zip
-rw-r--r--    1 1004     pkware      99911 Nov  1 22:46 zzap66a.zip
226 Transfer complete.
3988 bytes received in 0.26 seconds (15.28 Kbytes/sec)
ftp> binary
200 Type set to I.
ftp> lcd A:\Tutorial.06
Local directory now A:\Tutorial.06
ftp> get PK270WSP.EXE
200 PORT command successful.
150 Opening BINARY mode data connection for PK270WSP.EXE (1067555 bytes).
226 Transfer complete.
1067555 bytes received in 244.79 seconds (4.36 Kbytes/sec)
ftp>
```

5. Type **quit** and then press the **Enter** key at the command prompt to disconnect from the remote site, and close the FTP command-line session. If you are using a dial-up connection, close it now. (Your instructor will inform you of how to close a dial-up connection, if necessary. However, if you are using your school's computer lab, it is likely that you are not using a dial-up connection.)

Nancy is pleased with the programs that you found for the ground-station installation team. After testing the programs to make sure that they will serve the team's needs and fulfilling any licensing agreements, you can install them on the team's computers.

Session 6.2 QUICK CHECK

1. List an advantage of using a download site such as TUCOWS.com or DOWNLOAD.COM when you want to download a variety of programs.

2. What is the name of the special document format for storing documents on the Web so users can print them without needing the document's native program?

3. Describe several factors that could cause a download to progress slowly.

4. What is the general name for a program that reduces the size of one or more files and can save multiple files using a single filename?

5. What is a file extension, and what purpose does it serve? That is, are file extensions simply randomly assigned, three-character names, or do they have a purpose?

6. List two advantages of using an FTP client over a Web browser for transferring files between two computers connected to the Internet.

You successfully downloaded many programs from the Internet. You also can download specific data from a Web site, as you will see in Session 6.3.

SESSION 6.3

In this session, you will use an FTP client program and a Web browser to download data from the Internet. You will discover several sites containing interesting data, including numeric data and documents that can help you prepare research papers and worksheets.

The Internet is a rich source for documents and data of all varieties. Internet data and documents come from sources that range from questionable and risky to highly respectable and reliable. Always be aware of the source before you download data or programs. In this session, you download data files (documents) and raw data, such as census information.

Internet Cookies

Some FTP and Web sites you visit collect and record cookies, or information about your preferences based on your selections while visiting the site and your computer's resources. A **cookie** is a small text file that your browser exchanges with the Web site or FTP server and then subsequently saves on your computer. Cookies contain information that makes your Web-browsing experience simpler and more personalized. For example, a cookie file stored by a retail merchant site might contain your shirt and shoe size (after you reveal that information on a previous exchange, of course), or an online bookstore might store your book preferences in a cookie. When you revisit the bookstore, the site will inform you of new books available by the same author as one whose book you purchased previously.

Sometimes, cookies are intrusive and are created without your consent. Whether you allow cookies to accumulate on your PC is up to you; you can set your Web browser to warn you when a site is attempting to create a cookie file, or you can block storing cookie files altogether. Because cookie files can be useful, you might want your browser to warn you when a site attempts to create them, so you can decide on a case-by-case basis whether to allow cookies from an individual site. Everyone who uses the Internet should know that sites on the Internet might collect information about you, and most of the time this information is used to make access to particular sites more convenient. If you are concerned about cookies, there are several freeware and shareware cookie-manager programs that you can download and install to control their use. (You can find these cookie-manager programs by searching for "cookie manager" in any search engine.)

Instead of using a cookie manager, you can implement limited cookie management directly within your Web browser. For example, in Internet Explorer, click Tools on the menu bar, and then click Internet Options to open that dialog box. Then, click the Security tab, click the Custom Level button, and scroll down the list until you see the Cookies entry. Finally, click one of three option buttons under each of the two security entries to enforce (or not to enforce) cookie security. You can choose to disable, enable, or prompt for cookies that are to be stored on your computer. You can choose any of these options for session cookies, which are not stored on your computer. Navigator offers the same general options. You can click Edit on the menu bar, and then click Preferences, and select the Advanced tree branch. You can select options to accept all cookies or disable cookies. By checking the Warn me before accepting a cookie check box, you can choose whether or not to block cookies on an individual basis.

Tracing an Internet Route

Sometimes, you might experience delays when you download programs and data files. Frequently, when you download programs, you can choose to download programs and data from several mirror sites in different physical locations. You might think that the physical difference between you and an Internet site is unimportant, but it is. If you are in the United States and you are given the option to download a file from either Europe or Canada, chances are that Canada will be your best choice. As you know, the Internet is a complex network of interconnected computers. The distance between your PC and a remote server is measured in hops. A **hop** is a connection between two computers. If a file travels through 15 computers before arriving at your PC, then it has gone through 14 hops (the number of computers in the path minus one). Minimizing the number of hops traveled by a file between your PC and the site reduces your total download time.

You can list the computers that lie between your PC and a remote server and compute the hops with a program built into Windows called **tracert** (for *trace route*). You can use the tracert program to make an informed choice between alternative download sites. Tracert will show you up to 30 hops and indicate the response time, the site name, and the IP address of each hop along the route. (If you do not have tracert installed on your computer, use a Web search engine to search for "**ping**," or **Packet Internet Groper**, which is a program that tests to see if a computer is connected to the Internet. You can find several freeware and shareware ping programs that accomplish the same thing as tracert.) For example, in your work for the ground-station installation team, you might be offered the choice of downloading software from one of two locations, so you want to make sure that you are able to see if there is an appreciable difference in the number of hops.

To compute and display hops between your PC and an Internet site:

1. Click the **Start** button on the taskbar, click **Run**, type **command** in the Open text box, and then click the **OK** button to open the MS-DOS Prompt window.

2. Type **tracert www.uaf.edu** at the prompt, and then press the **Enter** key to list the hops between your PC and the server at the University of Alaska, Fairbanks. Tracert produces a list of each computer's IP address on the path between your PC and the target machine. When it is completed, the message "Trace complete." appears at the bottom of site trace list. Figure 6-33 shows all but the first few hops in the trace from the user's PC to the server in Fairbanks. (Your trace will be different.)

| Figure 6-33 | TRACING THE ROUTE FROM A PC TO A SERVER IN ALASKA |

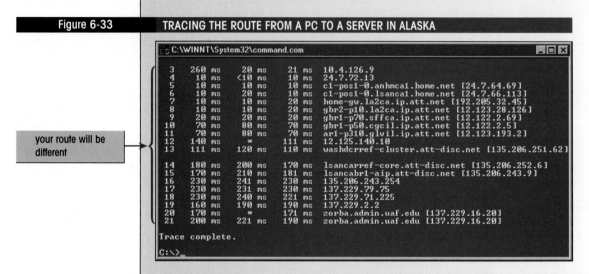

TROUBLE? If you receive an error message that says "Unable to resolve target system name www.auf.edu," then you need to make a dial-up connection to your server prior to issuing the tracert command. Ask your instructor or technical support person for help, and then repeat the steps.

TROUBLE? If the tracert program stops or pauses for a long time, press Ctrl + C to abort the tracert program and to re-display the DOS command prompt. Repeat Step 2 to try tracing the route again. If you still have problems, ask your instructor or technical support person for help. Delays are a common occurrence on the Internet, and you should not be concerned. They are part of the congestion that occurs when millions of people use the same infrastructure.

3. To close the MS-DOS program window, type **exit** and then press the **Enter** key.

When you are downloading very large program files, you can use the tracert program any time—even while your browser is running—to find the path with the fewest hops, because that path might reduce your download time significantly. To trace a route while your browser is running, write down the URL to the target site, click the Start button on the taskbar, click Run, and then type *tracert* followed by the URL of the target site. Finally, click the OK button to trace the route. However, once the trace is complete, the tracert window closes immediately, so look quickly!

Downloading Census Bureau Data

Nancy stopped by your office late yesterday afternoon and asked you to locate some U.S. Census Bureau software that might be useful for the DigiComm team. You will use a browser to locate the Web site, find the file Nancy wants, and download it. The file that

Nancy wants is special purpose software to extract information from Census bureau data files Nancy already has on CD-ROM. Nancy would like you to download the software and save it for later use.

To download a census file from the U.S. Census Bureau:

1. If necessary, start your Web browser, and then go to the Student Online Companion page by entering the URL **http://www.course.com/newperspectives/internet2** in the appropriate location in your Web browser. Click the hyperlink for your book, click the **Tutorial 6** link, and then click the **Session 6.3** link. Click the **U.S. Census Bureau** link and wait while the browser loads the page shown in Figure 6-34.

| Figure 6-34 | U.S. CENSUS BUREAU HOME PAGE |

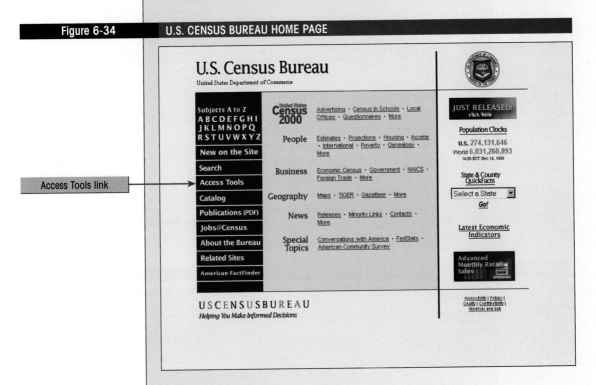

Access Tools link

2. Click the **Access Tools** link to open that page. You will use this page to locate the file that Nancy requested.

3. Scroll down to the "Downloadable Software" section of the page and click the **Extract Software** link shown in Figure 6-35.

Figure 6-35   **DATA ACCESS TOOLS PAGE**

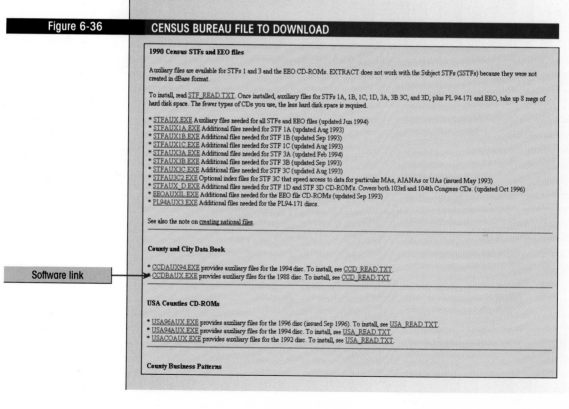

Extract Software link

The American FactFinder - This is our NEW Interactive database engine for...the 1997 Economic Census...the American Community
Survey...the 1990 Census...Census 2000 Dress Rehearsal ... and Census 2000.

Interactive Internet Tools

○ Censtats - Applications available include: Census Tract Street Locator, County Business Patterns, Zip Business Patterns,
Annual Survey of Manufactures, International Trade Data, and more.
○ Map Stats - An easy way to view profiles of states and counties.
○ TIGER | TIGER Map Service Info | Maps - Topologically Integrated Geographic Encoding and Referencing system.
○ US Gazetteer - Place name, and ZIP code search engine.
○ 1990 Decennial Census Lookup - Create your own extract files from the 1990 summaries.
○ Data Extraction System (DES) Create custom data extracts from Current Population Survey, 1990 Census Public Use
Microdata, and more.
○ Ferret Data - Extraction and review tool [in collaboration with the Bureau of Labor Statistics and other statistical agencies].
○ MABLE/GeoCorr - Geographic Correspondence Engine [mirrored at Columbia University and University of Missouri].

Downloadable Software

○ CD-ROM Software Correction/Update - Software, user notes, data file revisions and more for those who have purchased
CD-ROM products from our Customer Services office.
○ Extract Software - General purpose data display and extraction tool that works with Census Bureau CD-ROMs recorded in
dBASE format - (for: IBM-PC's and compatibles with CD-ROM player)
○ VPLX Software - Variance Estimation for Complex Samples (for IBM-PC's and compatibles and UNIX [Sun/Solaris])
○ IMPS software - The Integrated Microcomputer Processing System (IMPS) software performs the major tasks of census and
survey processing.

Direct File Access

○ **Browse Public Directories and Files** (HTTP or FTP).
○ **Census OUTGOING File Directory** (HTTP or FTP) - Pickup files from Census Employees.
○ **Census INCOMING File Directory** (HTTP or FTP) - Files sent to Census Bureau Employees (invisible to non-
employees).
○ Public file send utility

Access Tools at Other Sites

○ Government Information Sharing Project [Oregon State University].
○ Integrated Public Use Microdata Series - iPUMS [University of Minnesota].

4. Use the scroll bar to scroll the display until you see the County and City Data
Book entry shown in Figure 6-36.

Figure 6-36   **CENSUS BUREAU FILE TO DOWNLOAD**

1990 Census STFs and EEO files

Auxiliary files are available for STFs 1 and 3 and the EEO CD-ROMs. EXTRACT does not work with the Subject STFs (SSTFs) because they were not
created in dBase format.

To install, read STF_READ.TXT. Once installed, auxiliary files for STFs 1A, 1B, 1C, 1D, 3A, 3B 3C, and 3D, plus PL 94-171 and EEO, take up 8 megs of
hard disk space. The fewer types of CDs you use, the less hard disk space is required.

* STFAUX.EXE Auxiliary files needed for all STFs and EEO files (updated Jun 1994)
* STFAUX1A.EXE Additional files needed for STF 1A (updated Aug 1993)
* STFAUX1B.EXE Additional files needed for STF 1B (updated Sep 1993)
* STFAUX1C.EXE Additional files needed for STF 1C (updated Aug 1993)
* STFAUX3A.EXE Additional files needed for STF 3A (updated Feb 1994)
* STFAUX3B.EXE Additional files needed for STF 3B (updated Sep 1993)
* STFAUX3C.EXE Additional files needed for STF 3C (updated Aug 1993)
* STFAU3C2.EXE Optional index files for STF 3C that speed access to data for particular MAs, AIANAs or UAs (issued May 1993)
* STFAUX_D.EXE Additional files needed for STF 1D and STF 3D CD-ROM's. Covers both 103rd and 104th Congress CDs. (updated Oct 1996)
* EEOAUXIL.EXE Additional files needed for the EEO file CD-ROMs (updated Sep 1993)
* PL94AUX3.EXE Additional files needed for the PL94-171 discs.

See also the note on creating national files.

_____

County and City Data Book

* CCDAUX94.EXE provides auxiliary files for the 1994 disc. To install, see CCD_READ.TXT.
Software link → CCDBAUX.EXE provides auxiliary files for the 1988 disc. To install, see CCD_READ.TXT.

_____

USA Counties CD-ROMs

* USA96AUX.EXE provides auxiliary files for the 1996 disc (issued Sep 1996). To install, see USA_READ.TXT.
* USA94AUX.EXE provides auxiliary files for the 1994 disc. To install, see USA_READ.TXT.
* USACOAUX.EXE provides auxiliary files for the 1992 disc. To install, see USA_READ.TXT.

_____

County Business Patterns

5. Click the **CCDBAUX.EXE** link to display the File Download dialog box. Depending on your browser and its security settings, a dialog box might open and ask if you want to run the file or save it. Make sure that the save option button is selected, and then click the **OK** button to continue. The Save As dialog box opens if you are using Internet Explorer.

6. Insert a new Data Disk in your floppy drive and create a folder called Tutorial.06. Click the **Save in** list arrow, change to the drive that contains your Data Disk, double-click the **Tutorial.06** folder to open it, and then click the **Save** button to download the file and save it on your Data Disk. If you are using Internet Explorer and a Download Complete box opens, click the **Close** button to close the dialog box. If you are using Navigator, you will know that the download is complete when the progress dialog box closes.

Now the data file is saved on your Data Disk. Nancy is pleased you found exactly what she wanted. Later, you might want to explore other Census Bureau pages.

Downloading a Graphic File

One of the data files Nancy wants you to download shows the launch of one of DigiComm's communication satellites into space. Launched in 1997, the DC-JP4 satellite is one of the key links in the communication infrastructure that connects DigiComm headquarters to its other divisions. Nancy wants a copy of the photograph that was taken as the shuttle and its satellite cargo lifted off of the Kennedy Space Center launch pad. You have located the photograph, which appears on the Internet at the Kennedy Space Center site.

To download a graphic image to your PC:

1. Return to the Student Online Companion Web page for Session 6.3, click the **Kennedy Space Center** link, and wait while your Web browser loads the Web page. Nancy knows the catalog number for the photograph, so you can enter and search for its number directly, instead of searching the entire site.

2. Type **KSC-97EC-0962** in the Search the Web text box (see Figure 6-37), and then press the **Enter** key to start the search. The search results page opens with several links highlighted. Nancy gave you the complete index number for the photograph so you know which link to click.

Figure 6-37   KENNEDY SPACE CENTER HOME PAGE WITH SEARCH CRITERIA IN PLACE

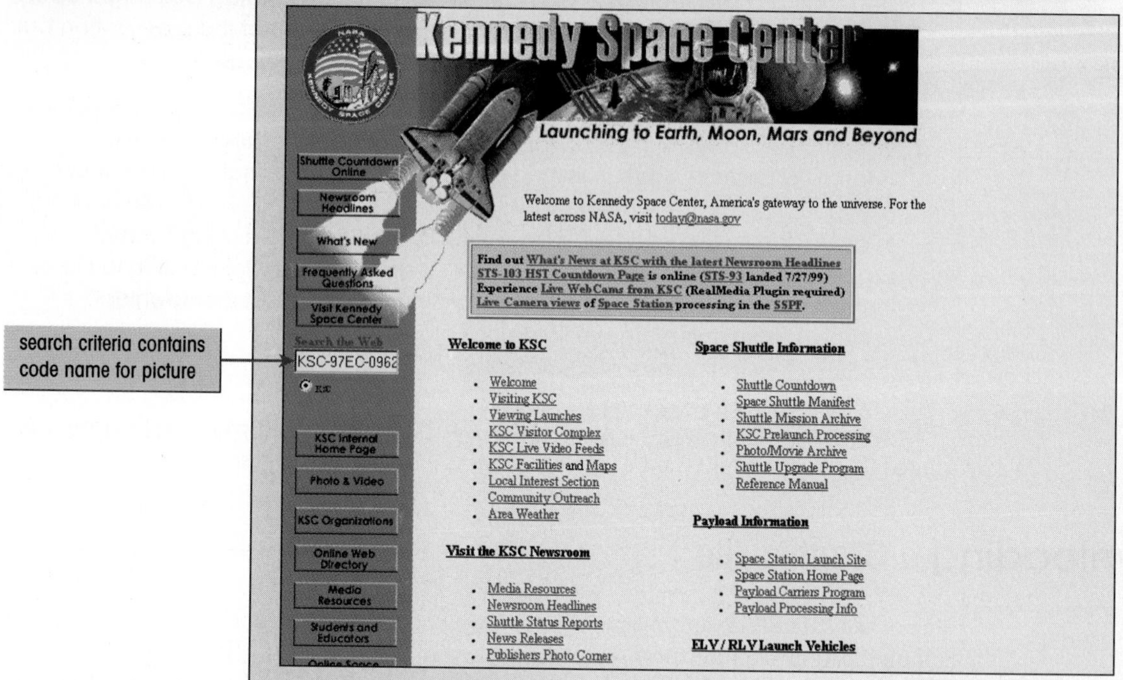

3. Click the **STS-94 KSC-97EC-0962 – STS-94 Columbia's Launch from Pad 39-A** link to open a page with a small picture (or thumbnail) of the launch.

4. If necessary, scroll down the page until you see the links near the bottom of the page, and then click the **KSC-97EC-0962 Medium (JPEG format, 1024x768 pixels x 256 colors, approx 250 Kbytes)** link to open the image of the shuttle launch.

5. Right-click the picture, and then click **Save Picture As** (if you are using Internet Explorer) or click **Save Image As** (if you are using Navigator) on the shortcut menu. The Save Picture dialog box opens in Internet Explorer, or the Save As dialog box opens in Navigator.

6. Make sure that your Data Disk is in the appropriate drive, click the **Save in** list arrow, change to the drive that contains your Data Disk, and then double-click the **Tutorial.06** folder to open it.

7. Double-click in the File name text box, type **launch97** to replace the default filename for the image, and then click the **Save** button to save the file on your Data Disk.

8. Close your Web browser, and then close your dial-up connection, if necessary.

You successfully navigated your browser to the NASA-operated Kennedy Space Center and downloaded a graphic from that site that Nancy can use in future promotional materials. Now, you are ready to meet with Nancy to see if she wants you to locate and download any other software or data files.

Session 6.3 QUICK CHECK

1. Some FTP and Web servers store information about your visit to their site on your computer. This information is called a(n) _____.

2. True or False: Your Web browser can permit or block sites from storing information about you on your computer.

3. The term _____ is used to measure distance on the Internet and is expressed as the number of computers a message travels through minus one.

4. You can run a program built into Windows called _____ to trace the path between your PC and another computer connected to the Internet.

5. True or False: You can download only programs from the Internet.

Nancy is pleased with the material that you found on the Internet. Now, you are ready to install and configure the material on the installation team members' computers.

REVIEW ASSIGNMENTS

DigiComm purchased 25 notebook computers for members of the installation team and its supervisory staff. More than six months have passed since you first started investigating FTP programs and using FTP to download programs and data. You used your personal notebook computer to test the programs, and Nancy has been pleased with your work. You have installed the WS_FTP Limited Edition FTP program and have used it to transfer files on the Internet. In addition, you have downloaded and installed two compression programs—WinZip and PKZIP. Both programs work flawlessly, and you are ready to install a standard set of programs on the DigiComm team members' computers. Nancy notices that your suite of programs includes both Navigator and Internet Explorer and their associated e-mail programs. However, seven members of the installation team like to use Eudora Light, an e-mail program from Qualcomm, at work and at home. Nancy has asked you to locate Eudora Light and download it; you will install it later. You will use an FTP client program to download Eudora Light to your PC. Your research reveals that Eudora Light is a free version that you can use without restriction. If it turns out that other members of the installation team like the program, then you can approach Nancy about purchasing 25 licenses to the more powerful, commercial version, Eudora Pro. The file size of the Eudora Light program is nearly five megabytes. You decide to read the user's manual before you download the file to see if you can expect any problems with other programs that you might install on the team members' computers. Fortunately, you can download, and then review and print, a user manual for Eudora Light in PDF. First, you will download the manual so you can review its requirements. Then you will download the program.

Do the following:

1. Place your Data Disk in the appropriate drive.

2. Start the WS_FTP Limited Edition FTP client program on your computer. (*Note*: The Review Assignments are written for the WS_FTP Limited Edition FTP client program. However, you can use any FTP client to complete the steps by using equivalent steps in your FTP client.)

3. Create a new session profile named Eudora. The host name or address is ftp.qualcomm.com. You will log on using an anonymous login and your full e-mail address as the password.

4. Connect and log on to the Qualcomm FTP server. (*Hint*: You might need to make a dial-up connection before connecting to the Qualcomm server.)

5. Change the remote directory to /eudora/eudoralight/windows/english.

6. Change the local PC directory to the Tutorial.06 folder on your Data Disk.

7. Select the file named eul3man1.pdf on the remote server, and then download that file to the Tutorial.06 folder on your Data Disk. This file contains the Eudora Light user's manual in PDF format.

8. After the download is complete, disconnect from the remote server, close your FTP client, and then close your dial-up connection, if necessary.

9. If necessary, install the Adobe Acrobat Reader program saved in the Tutorial.06 folder on your Data Disk. (*Note*: Check with your instructor or technical support person before installing any program on your computer's hard drive.)

10. Open Windows Explorer, open the Tutorial.06 folder on your Data Disk, and then double-click the eul3man1.pdf file that you just downloaded. Acrobat Reader will open the Eudora user's manual on your screen.

Explore ▶ 11. Locate the pages that describe "Using a Signature" found somewhere in the first 30 pages. (*Hint*: In Acrobat Reader, click Edit and then click Find to search for the three-word term. You'll find an entry in the Contents first, so you'll need to use Find again to locate the text.) The description of signature files may span more than one page. Print up to two pages describing signature files. (*Hint*: Use the Acrobat Reader's Help system to learn more about using the Reader program to read Eudora's program documentation.)

CASE PROBLEMS

Case 1. County Assessor's Office   Herb Merrell is the County Assessor for Lancaster County in eastern Nebraska. He has access to the county assessor's property records for the past 12 years. The county assessor's property office has a large database of information stored on an FTP server that the public can access for a small fee. Realtors and real-estate appraisers are the primary users of this information. However, many other businesses are taking advantage of the handy, online access to Lancaster County real-estate information. Herb has received complaints from customers in the southern part of the county about long delays in accessing the system. You are Herb's chief architect of the information system that supports the entire county assessor's online real-estate information system. Herb wants you to investigate the system's processing delays. You realize that because the Lancaster system is on the Internet, some delays are caused by Internet traffic and, therefore, are unresolvable. Herb wants you to see if the problem is with one of the computer systems that is connected to the main computer that stores the county assessor's files.

You decide to begin your research by installing an Internet ping program to test the Internet connections for delays. First, you will need to research and find programs that can identify processing problems, and then you will download the program.

Do the following:

1. Start your Web browser, and then go to the Student Online Companion page by entering the URL http://www.course.com/newperspectives/internet2 in the appropriate location in your Web browser. Click the hyperlink for your book, click the Tutorial 6 link, and then click the Case Problems link. Click the Excite link and wait while the browser loads the page.

2. Search for information about ping programs using the search phrase "packet Internet groper". Follow some of the hits, and then print at least one page of a definition you think is plausible.

3. Return to the Student Online Companion page, and then click the TUCOWS link to open that page. Use the links to connect to a server in a region or state that is the closest to your location.

4. Click the Windows 95/98 link (look in the left panel).

5. Scroll the display until you see the Network Tools section. Click the FTP and Archie link.

6. Scroll the display until you locate the CuteFTP program entry (the programs are listed in alphabetical order by name), click the link next to Home Page, which takes you to the publisher's home page. Finally, print the CuteFTP home page using your browser. (As an optional exercise, you can download the program, save it in the Tutorial.06 folder on your Data Disk, and install it if you want. Be aware that the program is 1.2 megabytes, though.)

7. Close your Web browser and your dial-up connection, if necessary.

8. Write a short report paraphrasing the description of CuteFTP found on the TUCOWS site.

Case 2. Internet Adventures   Internet Adventures is a one-person consulting company providing a variety of consulting services to small- and medium-sized companies. Jessica Leonard, owner of Internet Adventures, charges an hourly rate to help companies find and download information on the Internet. She is working for a large CPA firm that wants her to create bookmarks and favorites to Web sites that are of interest to tax preparers. Some members of the tax-preparation team use Internet Explorer, and others use Navigator. When team members find interesting Web sites, they use their browser to create either a Navigator bookmark or an Internet Explorer favorite to the location. The team members don't always have time to bookmark the site in the other browser, so they end up losing some of the URLs to important sites. Jessica remembers reading a review about several shareware products that might be able to maintain a library of common bookmarks that Internet Explorer and Navigator can share.

Do the following:

1. Start your Web browser, and then go to the Student Online Companion page by entering the URL http://www.course.com/newperspectives/internet2 in the appropriate location in your Web browser. Click the hyperlink for your book, click the Tutorial 6 link, and then click the Case Problems link. Click the TUCOWS link under Case Problem 2 and wait while the browser loads the page. Use the links to connect to a server in a region or state that is the closest to your location.

2. Click the Windows 95/98 link to open the page of Windows Internet programs.

3. Locate the Browsers and Accessories category, and then click the Bookmark Utilities link.

4. On the Bookmark Utilities page, scroll the list and locate Bookmark Converter. If you cannot find that bookmark program in the list, then scroll down the list looking for a bookmark program whose description indicates it can convert bookmarks between Internet Explorer and Navigator.

5. Download the Bookmark Converter program and save it on the Tutorial.06 folder on your Data Disk.

6. Close your Web browser and your dial-up connection, if necessary.

Case 3. *Baseline High School Computer Laboratory*   Marco Lozario is director of computing at Baseline High School. He and his staff of three people ensure that the school's computer lab of 45 Windows-based computers function properly. Last week, a virus infected every computer in the lab, and Marco had to close the lab to prevent the virus from spreading to students' disks and other computers. Each lab computer has McAfee Virus Scan software installed, but the installed version does not recognize and cannot eradicate the new virus pattern. Help Marco download the latest virus data file from McAfee. (Insert a new, empty Data Disk into the floppy drive and create a folder called Tutorial.06 on it.)

Do the following:

1. Start your FTP client program.

2. Create a new session profile using the profile name McAfee and the host address ftp.mcafee.com. You will connect as an anonymous user and use your full e-mail address as your password.

3. Connect to McAfee's FTP site.

4. Change the remote computer's directory to /pub/antivirus/datfiles/3.x so that you can see the antivirus data files on the remote system's list of files.

5. Change your PC's directory to the Tutorial.06 folder on your Data Disk.

6. Select the file whose name begins with dat and ends with the file extension zip. (There may be several files, but you are interested only in the compressed antivirus file.) Download the file and save it in the Tutorial.06 folder on your Data Disk.

7. After the data file transfers successfully to your disk, log off the McAfee site and close the FTP client program.

Explore   8. The WS_FTP Limited Edition FTP client program creates a log file showing the date and time you downloaded the software. If you used WS_FTP Limited Edition, then locate the log file (it is called Ws_ftp.log) and open it with Word or WordPad.

9. Print the log file to show that you downloaded the antivirus data file. Be sure to add your name and any other identifying information your instructor requests to the document before you print it.

Case 4. *Internet Marketing Pros*   Eddie Ponzi owns Internet Marketing Pros, an Internet marketing and advertising agency. It helps businesses create a Web presence to attract customers. The U.S. Census Bureau maintains records about retail sales and inventory information at its Web and FTP sites. Eddie wants to download some historic sales information from 1996 so he can compare it to the data for the current year. Use a command-line FTP program to download a retail sales worksheet in Lotus 1-2-3 format and an accompanying FAQ (frequently asked questions) file to print for your instructor.

Do the following:

1. Click the Start button on the taskbar, click Run, type ftp in the Open text box of the Run dialog box, and then click the OK button to start the Windows-supplied FTP program.

2. Click the FTP window maximize button to enlarge the window. (It might not maximize to fill your entire screen, however.)

3. To the right of the "ftp>" prompt, type *open ftp.census.gov*, and press the Enter key to execute the command, which opens the U.S. Census Bureau ftp site.

4. Type anonymous, and press the Enter key at the User prompt.

5. Type your full e-mail address as your password, and then press the Enter key.

6. Type *cd pub/svsd/retlmon/download*, and then press the Enter key to change the remote directory.

7. Place your Data Disk in the appropriate disk drive.

8. Type lcd A:\Tutorial.06, and press the Enter key to change your local computer's current directory to the Tutorial.06 folder on your Data Disk.

9. Type binary, and then press the Enter key to establish binary transfer mode.

10. Type get 95reldte.txt, and press the Enter key to download a file to the Tutorial.06 folder on your Data Disk.

11. Type get area96.wk1 (the last character in the second name is the digit one), and then press the Enter key to download the file and save it in the Tutorial.06 folder on your Data Disk.

12. Type quit and press Enter to log off of the Census Bureau FTP server. If necessary, close your dial-up connection.

13. Open the 95reldte.txt file that you downloaded in WordPad or any other word processor, and then type your name at the top of page. Save your changes.

14. Print the page and then close WordPad.

Case 5. Seaworthy Engineering   Seaworthy Engineering is an engineering consulting group based in San Antonio, Texas. Judy Seaworthy, the company's chief technical officer, oversees the consultants' computer needs. Among her many duties, she is responsible for outfitting each consultant with the latest microcomputer hardware and software. Because the consultants spend up to 75 percent of their time in the field with engineering clients, the consultants must carry their office with them. Computers are their most important asset, because their computers contain all the software needed to service their clients, produce reports to send back to the home office, and schedule the least expensive travel between client locations. Each computer has both Internet Explorer and Netscape Navigator Web browsers. Recently, Judy has read several good reviews of a relatively new Web browser called Opera. She wants you to find out more information about Opera and print a few pages of product information and ratings, if available, so she can investigate it further. Help Judy find out more about Opera.

Do the following:

1. Start your Web browser, and then go to the Student Online Companion page by entering the URL http://www.course.com/newperspectives/internet2 in the appropriate location in your Web browser. Click the hyperlink for your book, click the Tutorial 6 link, and then click the Case Problems link. Click the DOWNLOAD.COM link and wait while the browser loads the page.

2. In the DOWNLOAD.COM search text box type Opera and click the Search button to begin a site search.

3. When the CNET search-results page opens, sort the results in descending order by the number of downloads. The most popular download in the results will be listed at the top.

4. Locate the latest version of Opera (the 32-bit version).

5. Click the Opera link to display more information about the software on the CNET site.

6. Print the CNET Opera description page.

7. Locate the link to Opera's developer on the CNET description page. Click the link to open the Developer's (Opera Software) home page.

8. Print the first page of Opera Software's home page.

9. Locate on Opera Software's home page a link to more information about the Opera browser. The link may be labeled "read more about Opera" or "more information about Opera."

10. Click the information link to display more details about Opera software.

11. Print the first page of the detailed Opera browser description.

12. Click your browser's Back button to return to Opera's home page.

13. See if you can determine the name of Opera Software's Chief Executive Officer. Write down his or her name somewhere (labeled) on the page that you printed in step 11. Be sure to write your name and any other required identification on all pages you turn in to your instructor.

14. Close your browser.

QUICK | CHECK ANSWERS

Session 6.1

1. False
2. anonymous
3. binary
4. hierarchical
5. ftp://ftp.goodsoftware.com
6. virus
7. compression
8. False

Session 6.2

1. Visiting a "download supermarket" provides you with many more choices. You can select from dozens of compression programs, for example.

2. Portable Document Format, or PDF

3. lots of Internet traffic on the site, several people downloading the same program as you, and delays along the Internet at one or more hosts

4. compression program

5. A file extension can be associated with a program that opens the file. For example, a secondary name of .xls means that the file is an Excel workbook.

6. File transfers are faster with an FTP client; with a browser, you cannot upload files to a site requiring a password and user name—an account. Only anonymous FTP is handled by a browser.

Session 6.3

1. cookie
2. True
3. hop
4. tracert
5. False

New Perspectives on

THE INTERNET

2ⁿᵈ Edition

Read This Before You Begin

To the Student

Data Disks

To complete the Level III tutorials, Review Assignments, and Case Problems in this book, you need six Data Disks. Your instructor will either provide you with Data Disks or ask you to make your own.

If you are making your own Data Disks, you will need six blank, formatted, high-density disks. You will need to copy onto your disks a set of folders from a file server, a standalone computer, or the Web. Your instructor will tell you which computer, drive letter, and folders contain the files you need. You could also download the files by going to www.course.com, clicking Data Disk Files, and following the instructions on the screen.

The following table shows you which folders go on your disks, so that you will have enough disk space to complete all the tutorials, Review Assignments, and Case Problems:

Data Disk 1

Write this on the disk label:
Data Disk 1: Tutorials 2 and 4

Put these folders on the disk:
Tutorial.02 and Tutorial.04

Data Disk 2:

Write this on the disk label:
Data Disk 2: Tutorial 3

Put these folders on the disk:
Tutorial.03

Data Disk 3:

Write this on the disk label:
Data Disk 3: Tutorial 6*

Put these folders on the disk:
Tutorial.06

Data Disk 4:

Write this on the disk label:
Data Disk 4: Tutorial 6

Put these folders on the disk:
Tutorial.06

Data Disk 5:

Write this on the disk label:
Data Disk 5: Tutorial 6

Put these folders on the disk:
Tutorial.06

Data Disk 6:

Write this on the disk label:
Data Disk 6: Tutorials 7 and 9

Put these folders on the disk:
Tutorial.07 and Tutorial.09

Note: In Tutorial 6 you will download several programs and data files to your student data disk. Depending on which Case Problems your instructor assigns, you might need three more Data Disks. If you need additional disks, write "Data Disk 6: Tutorial 6," and "Data Disk 7: Tutorial 6," and "Data Disk 8: Tutorial 6" on the labels, and then create a Tutorial.06 folder on each disk. Also note that over time, the sizes of the files that you download might increase, in which case more disks might be required.

When you begin each tutorial, be sure you are using the correct Data Disk. See the inside back cover of this book for more information on Data Disk files, or ask your instructor or technical support person for assistance.

Course Labs

The tutorials in this book feature two interactive Course Labs to help you understand e-mail and multimedia concepts. There are Lab Assignments at the end of Tutorials 2 and 3 that relate to these Labs.

Windows 95 Installation Instructions

To start a Lab, click the **Start** button on the Windows taskbar, point to **Programs**, point to **Course Labs**, point to **New Perspectives Applications**, and click the name of the Lab you want to use.

Using Your Own Computer

If you are going to work through this book using your own computer, you need:

Computer System Netscape Navigator 4.0 or higher OR Microsoft Internet Explorer 4.0 or higher and Windows 95 or higher must be installed on your computer. This book assumes a complete installation of the Web browser software and its components, and that you have an existing e-mail account and an Internet connection. Because your Web browser may be different from the ones used in the figures or the book, your screens may differ slightly at times.

Data Disks You will not be able to complete the tutorials or exercises in this book using your own computer until you have Data Disks.

Course Labs See your instructor or technical support person to obtain the Course Lab software for use on your own computer.

Visit Our World Wide Web Site

Additional materials designed especially for you are available on the World Wide Web. Go to http://www.course.com.

To the Instructor

The Data files and Course Labs are available on the Instructor's Resource Kit for this title. Follow the instructions in the Help file on the CD-ROM to install the programs to your network or standalone computer. For information on creating Data Disks, see the "To the Student" section above. To complete the tutorials in this book, students must have a Web browser, an e-mail account, and an Internet connection.

You are granted a license to copy the Data Files to any computer or computer network used by students who have purchased this book.

OBJECTIVES

In this tutorial you will:

- Learn about different types of mailing lists

- Join and leave a mailing list

- Post messages to a mailing list

- Locate mailing lists

- Retrieve and read a mailing list's archived files

- Attach a file to an e-mail message

- Detach a file from an e-mail message

- Use an Internet search service to locate an e-mail address

ADVANCED E-MAIL TOPICS

Using Mailing Lists, Attaching Files, and Finding E-Mail Addresses

CASE

Lincoln Art Glass Company

Lincoln Art Glass Company (LAG) is a small art glass company located in Lincoln, Nebraska. From its combined showroom and studio, LAG sells stained glass, glass supplies, and books to the public. LAG also produces beveled glass that it sells to both wholesale and retail customers, although almost all of its beveled glass sales are to wholesale customers throughout the United States. In addition to beveled glass, LAG sells glass-beveling machinery to wholesale customers. Mike DeMaine, LAG's owner, has heard some members of the Lincoln Chamber of Commerce mention how effective the Internet is as a marketing and information tool. For example, several members said that the Internet provides a means for customers and potential customers to contact their businesses, learn about their product lines, and even receive helpful tips about various topics. Mike wants you to investigate how he could use the Internet to reach customers.

One potential lead is for Mike to use mailing lists as a way to reach interested customers. You also think that Mike can attach the company's catalog, pictures of equipment, and other documents to e-mail messages and send them to interested customers. Mike might want to contact other glass-supply businesses to form a consortium, so you need to find a way to identify other suppliers by e-mail. You will use mailing lists and e-mail address search engines to help Mike. When you have completed this research, you will be able to make several recommendations about how to use the Internet resources as well as serve as the company's Internet liaison.

What Are Mailing Lists?

Besides providing information on the Web, the Internet stores information on a wide variety of topics that you can access using e-mail. A popular way of sharing information is to join, or **subscribe** to, a mailing list. A **mailing list** is a list of names and e-mail addresses for a group of people who share a common interest in a subject or topic and exchange information by subscribing to the list. You send your information and opinions to a mailing list through e-mail by **posting** (or sending) a message to the list. When you post a message to a mailing list, the **list server** automatically forwards your message to *everyone* on the mailing list. The list server automatically manages users' requests to join or leave a list and receives and reroutes mail messages posted to the list. The list server program usually runs on larger computers running the UNIX operating system.

You can think of an Internet mailing list just like a mailing list that you might receive in printed form. When you subscribe to a printed newsletter, the newsletter's manager automatically sends you new documents as they become available. Postings to mailing lists work in much the same way: They arrive at the list server, which then automatically sends the new messages to every e-mail address on the list. In other words, mailing lists are named collections of e-mail addresses that can receive mail from other members of the same mailing list. The list server and its list of e-mail addresses together provide a simple and convenient way of sending a single message to many people to create a large electronic distribution list. These distribution lists are not like the personal e-mail groups that you created in Tutorial 2, in which you grouped related individuals in your e-mail program's address book for convenience. Mailing lists and the groups they represent (sometimes known as **discussion groups**) do not require you to enter any individual addresses into your e-mail program's address book. On the contrary, each person who wants to join a mailing list is responsible for subscribing to the list. Figure 7-1 illustrates how a single message that is sent to a mailing list is forwarded to every list member.

| Figure 7-1 | INFORMATION FLOW IN A MAILING LIST |

"Hey list members, where is the ..."

Robert

Mailing-list server

Phil

Alice

Boris

Adolpho

Barbara

Mailing lists exist for many topics. For example, users of Microsoft Office products can join any of several mailing lists devoted to Word, Excel, Access, PowerPoint, Internet Explorer, and Outlook Express. Mailing lists also exist for hobby topics, such as woodcarving, tennis, or aviation. You can even find college courses conducted through mailing lists. Students enroll in the course by joining the mailing list, and then the instructor delivers "lectures" by sending documents, reading assignments, and quizzes to students on the mailing list.

You also can find examples of **commercial mailing lists**, in which advertisers send recipients promotional materials for specific products or categories of products. For example, a commercial mailing list might send a list of shareware programs, their ratings, and the URLs where you can locate and download the shareware programs to the list's members.

Moderated and Unmoderated Lists

Sometimes one person, known as the **list moderator**, moderates a mailing list to ensure that the list always receives and sends appropriate and relevant information to its members. When a list moderator is responsible for discarding any messages that are inappropriate for or irrelevant to the list's members, the list is known as a **moderated list**. If a moderated list receives many postings, managing it can require a lot of time. When an individual does not moderate the list and postings are sent to list members automatically, the list is an **unmoderated list**. Because of the nature of unmoderated lists, you might receive irrelevant or inappropriate messages. However, when you subscribe to a moderated list, the moderator serves as a censor because he or she passes judgment on which messages to send to the list's members. Most mailing lists are unmoderated because of the time it takes to read and evaluate the content of the many messages posted each day to a mailing list by its members.

Mailing Lists and Usenet

Usenet is an information network to which people can post and read messages and opinions. **Usenet newsgroups** group postings by topic. Although newsgroups seem similar to mailing lists, there are three important differences. First, you need to know how to use your e-mail program to participate in a mailing list, whereas you must use a news reader program to access a newsgroup. The second difference is the way you retrieve information. Any information sent to a mailing list is delivered automatically to every e-mail address on the list; however, in a newsgroup, *you* must retrieve the information. The third difference is that when you send a message to a newsgroup, *anyone* with Internet access and a news reader can read it. A message sent to a mailing list has limited circulation in that only the list's members can read it.

Warnings About Lists

Whereas mailing lists can be essential tools for receiving current and useful information in one or more topic areas, you should be aware of some of their potential problems. Depending on the mailing list's activity, you might receive many messages every day. If you subscribe to many mailing lists, then you might find that the mail volume is more than you can read; it is not uncommon to receive hundreds of messages within a couple of days of joining a particularly active list. L-Soft International, Inc., a mailing-list software producer, reports that one of the largest LISTSERV mailing lists has over 275,000 members on a single list. Another LISTSERV customer's list delivers over 18 million messages per day!

Another potential problem is one that new list members encounter: that is, repeating questions that have been posed on the mailing list several times before. If you are new to a list, you should monitor the list's content for a while before sending messages to it, so you do not comment on topics that other subscribers already have discussed. The best advice is to "listen" first on any list you join. When you are confident that your messages won't repeat recent information, then you can share your ideas with list members. Another resource containing answers is the frequently asked questions (FAQ) list, which contains answers to common questions that users ask. If the list has a FAQ, look there first before sending a question to list members.

Subscribing to a Mailing List

When you find a mailing list whose members share your interests, then you need to join the list so you can exchange ideas and information with the list's members. You join, or subscribe to, a mailing list by sending an e-mail message to the list server with a request to join the list's membership. If you are subscribing to a moderated list, then the list's moderator must accept you as a member; if you are subscribing to an unmoderated list, your acceptance is automatic as long as you have formatted the e-mail request properly.

Mailing-list programs manage two types of e-mail: messages and commands. **Messages** are simply e-mail messages that express ideas or ask questions that each member of the mailing list receives. **Commands** request the mail server to take a prescribed action. Commands are e-mail messages with a special form and content that are intercepted by the mailing-list program and acted upon immediately; commands are not forwarded to other list members. To subscribe to and withdraw from a mailing list, you must send the appropriate command to the mailing list program. Figure 7-2 illustrates how a command flows to the mailing-list server; other list members do not receive copies of the command message.

| Figure 7-2 | COMMAND FLOW IN A MAILING LIST |

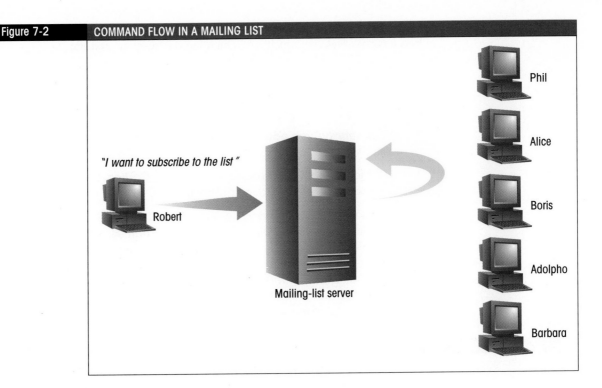

The programs that run mailing lists, such as LISTSERV, ListProc, Mailbase, or Majordomo, send messages from the originator to every list member. The only difference between mailing-list programs lies in the *commands* they recognize. Fortunately, most mailing-list programs process the same commands, so that once you learn a few commands for one list, you have learned the basic command set for several programs.

The mailing-list server receives many requests every hour. Because of the large volume of messages and requests that a mailing list must process, the clerical functions are automated. Mailing-list servers respond to requests in preprogrammed ways. Subscribing to a list is one of those requests to which a mailing-list program responds automatically.

You want to learn more about mailing lists by joining one or more lists so that you can report back to Mike. After a few weeks, you will be ready to make a preliminary report about the effectiveness of a mailing list. Mike suggests that you join a mailing list that discusses computer viruses because viruses are a potential concern for any mailing list or newsgroup. Mike has given you the list's name and address. First, you will send a subscribe command to the mailing list. Later, you might join other lists and actively engage in discussions with other list members.

REFERENCE   WINDOW   **RW**

Subscribing to a mailing list
- Use your e-mail program to create a new message.
- Enter the mailing list's administrative e-mail address in the To text box.
- Leave the Cc, Bcc, and Subject lines blank.
- Type *subscribe listname yourname* on one line in the message area as your subscription request.
- Disable your signature file.
- Send the message.

Mike tells you about the valert-l mailing list that is administered by a group with the e-mail address *listserv@lehigh.edu*, which is a Lehigh University-sponsored site.

To subscribe to the valert-l mailing list:

1. Start your e-mail program, and create a new message.

2. Type **listserv@lehigh.edu** in the To text box. This is the e-mail address of the mailing-list server, or the administrator.

3. Leave the remaining message header fields—Cc, Bcc, and Subject—blank. Move the insertion point to the message area.

4. Type the following command on one line: **SUBSCRIBE VALERT-L** *yourname*, and replace *yourname* with your first and last names, separated by a space. (The mail server will ignore the case for your name and all commands.) Your message should look like Figure 7-3, which shows a subscription request using the Outlook Express e-mail program. Be sure to disable your signature so that the message body contains only the Subscribe command. Otherwise, sending your signature along with the Subscribe command will cause an error.

Figure 7-3   SENDING A SUBSCRIPTION REQUEST TO A MAILING LIST

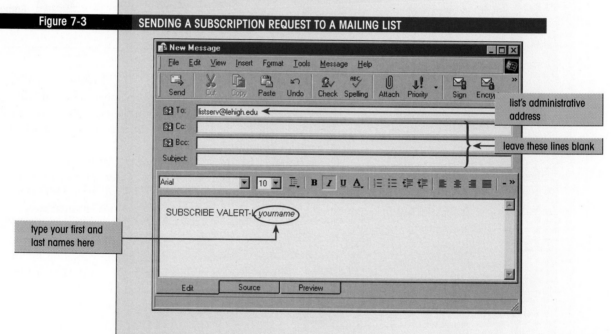

list's administrative address

leave these lines blank

type your first and last names here

5. Send the message.

TROUBLE? If your e-mail program warns you that the Subject line is blank, click the OK button to continue.

When you subscribe to a mailing list, you provide your first and last names, but not your e-mail address, because the mailing-list server identifies your e-mail address in the From line of your message. When you type your first and last names in the message area of your subscribe message, the mail server posts it in the membership rolls along with your e-mail address so that other list members can identify you using your name and e-mail address. (You will learn how to list members' names later in this tutorial.)

Usually, your subscription request reaches the mailing-list server quickly, but the time it takes to confirm your addition to the list can vary from several minutes to several hours, depending on the mailing list's popularity. However, if you do not receive a confirmation within 24 to 36 hours, you should resend the subscription request.

If you submit an incorrect subscription request, the mailing-list server returns it without processing. If this occurs, make sure that you spelled the word *subscribe* correctly, that you typed your first and last names, and that you did not include a signature file. If you type additional information in a subscribe message, the mailing-list server will interpret it as another command set that it cannot process.

Sometimes, the mailing-list server will send you a confirmation message that you must return so it can confirm your e-mail address. You usually will need to reply in this context for high-volume lists so the mailing-list server can maintain the mailing list's member information. If the mailing-list server does not receive your reply message within a particular time period (usually 48 hours), then the server automatically cancels your request.

Mailing lists are either closed or open. A **closed list** is one in which membership is *not* automatic. The **list administrator**, who is a person assigned to oversee one or more mailing lists, can either reject or accept your request. The list administrator might reject your membership request if the list has too many members or if your e-mail address indicates that you are not part of the group's specified community. For example, if you try to subscribe to a list devoted to accounting professors, then your subscription might be rejected if you do not have the edu domain in your e-mail address. However, most lists are **open lists** that automatically accept all subscription requests.

Once the mailing-list server has accepted and processed your subscription request, you will receive a welcome message to confirm your membership in the list. The welcome message contains valuable information about how to leave the mailing list, special features of the list, and other list details, so you should file it in a safe place. Keeping the subscription welcome message also is a good way to remember which lists you have joined.

To retrieve the welcome message from the list:

1. Retrieve your new mail messages from your mail server. You should receive the welcome message shown in Figure 7-4 from the valert-l mailing list. (Figure 7-4 shows the message in Outlook Express.) Read the message. The message confirms your desire to join the list and provides information about the site's future password implementation program.

| Figure 7-4 | MEMBERSHIP CONFIRMATION WELCOME MESSAGE |

Subject line displays the subscribe command you submitted

TROUBLE? If you do not receive the confirmation message, wait a few minutes and then retrieve your e-mail messages again. Depending on Internet traffic, it might take several minutes for the list server to respond.

Posting **Messages**

People interact with mailing lists by posting messages. Posting a message means to send an e-mail message to a mailing list. The mailing-list server receives the message, sends it to the list administrator for approval, if necessary, and then forwards the message to every e-mail address in the membership list. However, before you post a message to a mailing list, you should "lurk before you leap." **Lurking** is the activity of silently observing the postings others make to the list and reading the FAQ file to learn about the list's nature and purpose, so messages that you post are consistent with other list members' interests.

When you send a message to a mailing list, you send it to the list address; when you send a command (such as *subscribe*) to a mailing list, you send it to the administrative address. The list address, or the list name, is the name of the list, such as valert-l@lehigh.edu. The administrative address is the e-mail address to which you send commands, such as the address that you use to subscribe to a list (for example, listserv@lehigh.edu). If you inadvertently send a message with a command to leave the list to the list address instead of to the administrative address, everyone on the mailing list sees your mistake—except for the mailing-list server—and your name will not be removed from the list.

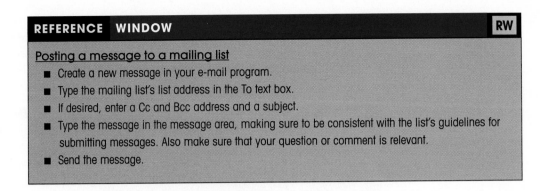

Figure 7-5 shows a sample message that you might post to the valert-l mailing list, formatted in Netscape Messenger.

| Figure 7-5 | POSTING A MESSAGE TO A MAILING LIST |

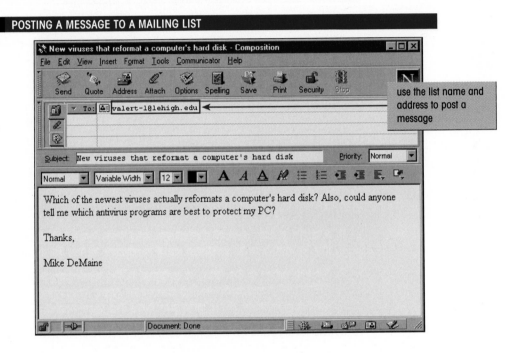

Reading a Mailing List's Archived Files

Many mailing-list servers file every message received by the list in an **archive**, although the list server might delete the messages periodically to recover disk space. When you join a new mailing list, you might want to review past messages to find messages of interest. To access the archive, you can send a request for the messages from a particular time frame to the mailing-list server, or you can use special functions to search the archive for relevant messages and then ask the server to send them to you. The first method is simpler; however, using the search functions might make it easier for you to find the messages you need.

Whichever method you use, you must retrieve a list of available archive filenames and data. You then request the list server to send you one or more of the named files. You send the **index** command to the mailing list's administrative address to find out which archive files are available from the list. For example, to receive a list of files available for the valert-l list, you would send the command *index valert-l* to the list's administrative address. The list server will process the command and send you an e-mail message that contains the archive filename information. You then can select which files you would like to receive and send a **get** command to the list's administrative address. After the list server processes your document-retrieval commands, it returns the requested file(s) to you by e-mail.

REFERENCE   WINDOW   **RW**

Retrieving an archive filename list
- Create a new message in your e-mail program.
- Type the list's administrative address in the To text box. Leave the Cc, Bcc, and Subject lines blank.
- Type the *index* command followed by the list's name in the message area. Do not include a signature file in your message.
- Send the message.

Mike wants to learn more about the glass industry outside of Lincoln, so he asks you to subscribe to a list that announces new mailing lists when they become available in order to see if you can find lists related to the glass industry or lists with related interests. First, you will join the list, and then you will search the list's archives and download at least one archive file and read it. The list, called NEW-LIST, is housed at listserv@hypatia.cs.wisc.edu, which is maintained by the Computer Science department of the University of Wisconsin, Madison. Subscribing to NEW-LIST is a two-step process: First, you must send a subscription request, and then you must return the mailing list server's confirmation message. After you complete the subscription process, you can send a request to retrieve an archive.

To subscribe to the NEW-LIST mailing list:

1. Create a new e-mail message, and then type **listserv@hypatia.cs.wisc.edu** in the To text box to address your message to the list administrator.

2. Do not enter a Cc, Bcc, or subject in the message header. Type **SUBSCRIBE NEW-LIST** *yourname* in the message area, replacing *yourname* with your first and last names. (You also can type the command in lowercase.)

3. Disable your signature file so it is not sent with the message.

4. Send the message.

5. Wait a few minutes, and then retrieve your new messages. You should receive an e-mail request from the list server for you to reply to the address to confirm your intent to join the list. Read this message carefully, and then continue with Step 6.

6. Use your e-mail program's **Reply** button to reply to the message.

7. Delete everything in the message area, and then type **OK**.

8. Send the message. Within a short time, the mailing-list server responds with a "welcome" message. When you receive the welcome message, it will tell you that you have been added to the list. Now you can request an archive file.

Now that you are a full member of the NEW-LIST mailing list, you can send a request to the mailing-list server for a list of past e-mail messages that it has saved in its monthly archives. You will send an *index* command to the list server to get this information.

To get a list of archive filenames:

1. Create a new message in your e-mail program.

2. Type **listserv@hypatia.cs.wisc.edu** in the To text box. Leave all other header lines blank, and move to the message area.

3. Type the message **index NEW-LIST** in the message area. Make sure nothing else appears in the message area. If necessary, disable your signature file so your signature doesn't automatically appear in the message.

4. Send the message.

5. Wait a few minutes, and then retrieve your new e-mail messages. The list server sends you a list of archive filenames in one message and an "Output of your job" in a second message. Open the first message, which usually has the subject line "NEW-LIST FILELIST." Discard the Output of your job message. The list of archive files may be short if the list is new or if it has moved. Figure 7-6 shows the archive list in an Outlook Express message.

| Figure 7-6 | **LIST OF AVAILABLE ARCHIVE FILES** |

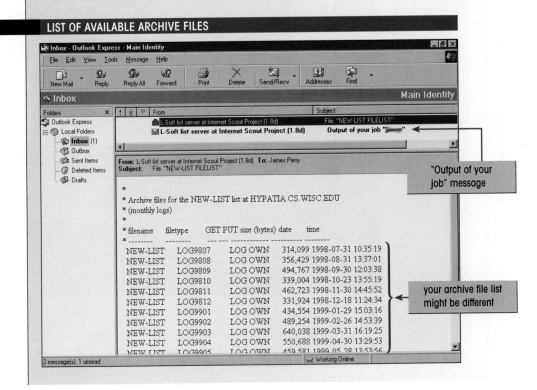

You observe that the NEW-LIST administrator keeps monthly archives of all the e-mail messages sent to the list. You will retrieve the messages sent to the list during December 1999. The filename corresponding to that month's archive is LOG9912. You might need to scroll down the message returned in response to your index command to locate the filename. To retrieve the file, you use the *get* command followed by the filename.

To retrieve an archive file:

1. Create a new message in your e-mail program.

2. Type **listserv@hypatia.cs.wisc.edu** in the To text box, and leave all other header lines blank.

3. Type **get NEW-LIST LOG9912** in the message area, disable your signature file (if necessary), and then send the message. (Be sure to type a space after *get* and after *NEW-LIST* so the server handles your command to retrieve the file correctly.)

4. After a few minutes, retrieve your new e-mail messages. You will receive an e-mail message that contains the text of all messages sent to the list during December 1999. To see if you can find any new lists that discuss topics that might be of interest to Mike, you can read the postings. When you are finished, close the e-mail message.

Identifying Other List Members

Usually, when you join a mailing list, you can receive a directory that lists the names and e-mail addresses of other list members. The administrator who controls the list, known as the **list owner**, has the option of making the mailing list members' information available when you use the **review** command. To obtain a listing of members' names and e-mail addresses, you send the command *review listname* to the list's administrative address, where *listname* is the name of the list. The server will send you a list with users' names in one column and their corresponding e-mail addresses, which normally are sorted in alphabetical order by domain name, in the second column. If you want to review members' listings by name, you can send the *review listname by name* command, which sorts the list by name instead of by e-mail address.

REFERENCE WINDOW   **RW**

__Retrieving member information from a mailing list__

- Create a new message in your e-mail program, and type the list's administrative address in the To text box of a new message. Leave the Cc, Bcc, and Subject lines blank.
- Type the *review <listname>* command in the message area, and substitute the list's actual name for *<listname>*. Do not include a signature file in your message.
- Send the message.

You are interested in getting the names of other people on the valert-l mailing list because you are likely to find members who share your concerns about viruses. Next, you will retrieve the member information.

To receive members' names and e-mail addresses from the valert-l list:

1. Create a new message in your e-mail program, and then type **listserv@lehigh.edu** in the To text box. This address is the list's administrative address.

2. In the message area, type the single-line message **review valert-l**.

3. Make sure you disable your signature file.

4. Send the message.

5. Wait a few minutes and then retrieve your new e-mail messages.

The mailing-list server will send you a list of e-mail users. If you scroll to the end of the list of current subscribers, you will find the total number of members, such as "Total number of subscribers: 9845 (9456 shown here)," which means that the list has over 9,000 members. The difference between the two numbers in the total, if any, is the number of members' names that are concealed.

Concealing Your Information from a Mailing List

You can conceal your name and e-mail address from a list when you do not want that information revealed to other list members. By default, your name and e-mail address are available and can be listed by any list member who executes the *review* command. Naturally, a list's administrator always can review all members' names and e-mail addresses, regardless of whether list members have their individual names and e-mail addresses concealed.

REFERENCE WINDOW   **RW**

Concealing your name on a mailing list
- Create a new e-mail message, and type the list's administrative address in the To text box. Leave the Cc, Bcc, and Subject lines blank.
- Type the *set <listname conceal>* command (or *set <listname conceal> yes*) in the message area, and substitute the list's name for *<listname>*. Do not include a signature file in your message.
- Send the message.

Mike wants you to maintain a low profile on any mailing lists that you join, so you ask him to show you how to conceal your name and e-mail address when you use LISTSERV software.

To conceal your name on the valert-l list:

1. Create a new message in your e-mail program, and then type **listserv@lehigh.edu** in the To text box. This address is the list's administrative address.

2. In the message area, type the single-line message **set valert-l conceal**

3. Be sure to disable your signature file.

4. Send the message.

5. Wait a few minutes, and then retrieve your new e-mail messages. You should receive a message from the server to indicate that your command was executed successfully.

If you decide that you want your name to appear again on a LISTSERV list, follow the same steps but substitute *noconceal* in place of *conceal* in the *set* command.

ListProc mailing-list server software has slightly different commands to hide and reveal list-member information. You issue the command *set listname conceal yes* to hide your information and issue the command *set listname conceal no* to reveal your information.

Leaving a Mailing List

When you remove your name from a mailing list—**drop** the mailing list or **unsubscribe** from the mailing list—you will stop receiving messages. Usually, the command to leave a mailing list is *unsubscribe* (or *signoff*) followed by the list's name. As with all administrative requests, you send your unsubscribe message to the list's administrative address.

You have observed the messages with interest on both the valert-l and NEW-LIST mailing lists and decide to concentrate on other work for Mike. Later, you might search for other lists, especially those related to art glass marketing and retailing. For now, however, you decide to leave these lists to reduce the number of e-mail messages that you receive each day.

REFERENCE   WINDOW   **RW**

Leaving a mailing list
- Create a new message in your e-mail program.
- Type the list's administrative address in the To text box. Leave the Cc, Bcc, and Subject lines blank.
- If you have more than one e-mail account, make sure you are logged on to the same e-mail account that you used when you joined the list originally. If you are unsure, check the welcome message you received when you joined the list.
- Check the welcome message to confirm what the command to leave the list should be. It usually is *unsubscribe* or *signoff*.
- Type the *unsubscribe* or *signoff* command, followed by the list's name in the message area. Disable your signature file, if necessary. Do not include your e-mail address in the command.
- Send the message.

First, you will unsubscribe from the valert-l list. Then, you will follow the same steps to unsubscribe from the NEW-LIST mailing list.

To unsubscribe from a mailing list:

1. Create a new message in your e-mail program, and then type **listserv@lehigh.edu** in the To text box. This address is the list's administrative address.

2. In the message area, type the single-line message **unsubscribe valert-l**

3. If necessary, disable your signature file and send the message.

   Now, send a message to unsubscribe from the NEW-LIST mailing list. The command to remove your name from this list is *signoff*, instead of unsubscribe.

4. Create a new message in your e-mail program, and then type **listserv@hypatia.cs.wisc.edu** in the To text box. This address is the list's administrative address.

5. In the message area, type the single-line message **signoff NEW-LIST**

6. If necessary, disable your signature file and send the message.

7. Wait a few minutes, and then retrieve your new e-mail messages. You should receive messages from both mailing lists to confirm your removal.

   TROUBLE? If a mailing list returns an error message, then you were not removed from the list. Check your unsubscribe message carefully and make sure you used the correct command to leave the list (*unsubscribe* or *signoff*), that you spelled the command and list name correctly, and that you did not include your name or signature file in the message. Correct any problems, and then resend the corrected message to remove your information from the list.

   TROUBLE? If the list is experiencing high traffic, it might take several minutes to return your confirmation message. If you do not receive an error message or a confirmation message, recheck your mail later.

   TROUBLE? If you continue to receive e-mail messages from the list, then send the unsubscribe command again.

8. Exit your e-mail program.

As soon as you receive confirmation messages from the list servers, you should stop receiving messages from the lists.

Locating Other Mailing Lists

The Internet houses thousands of mailing lists on many different topics—the difficulty is locating them. You can begin your search for lists on your own campus. Frequently, colleges and universities sponsor several mailing lists. To discover which lists are locally housed, send an e-mail message to your college's administrative address (it usually begins with *listserv* or *listproc*, followed by the host name). In the message body, type the **lists** command and then send the message. The mailing-list server will return an e-mail message containing a list of locally hosted mailing lists.

Finding lists outside of your school requires some searching. The Web contains several "lists of lists" sites that you use to search for interesting lists. Once you find these lists, you can look for lists that are related to art glass—lists that would suit Mike DeMaine's needs—so you can subscribe to them.

Searching for mailing lists is easier if you use a Web browser to go to sites that include master lists of mailing lists. There are several places to start your search. One list is called **Liszt**, which contains a searchable list of mailing lists. You will visit the Liszt site next.

To locate a list of mailing lists:

1. Start your Web browser, and then go to the Student Online Companion page by entering the URL **http://www.course.com/newperspectives/internet2** in the appropriate location in your Web browser. Click the **Comprehensive** book link, click the **Tutorial 7** link, and then click the **Session 7.1** link. Click the **Liszt** link, and wait while the browser loads the page (see Figure 7-7).

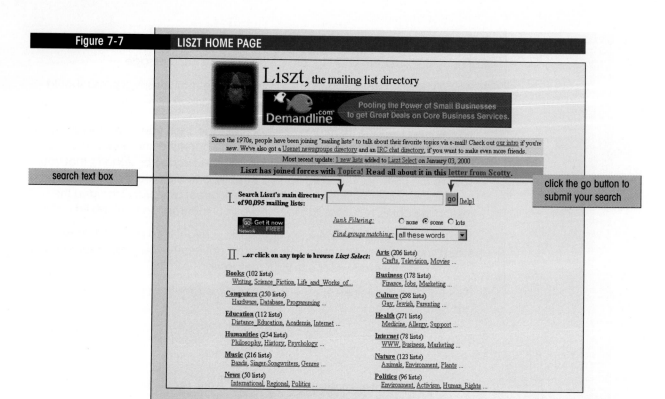

| Figure 7-7 | LISZT HOME PAGE |

search text box

click the go button to submit your search

2. Type **art glass** in the search text box, and then click the **go** button. Liszt returns a list of mailing lists that match your search criteria. Figure 7-8 shows an example, but keep in mind that Web pages and mailing lists change; your search might find fewer or more lists. Notice that the lists that match your search appear with a green background. You can click these links to get more information about the list. If you don't find what you are looking for, you can click one of the links at the top of the page to go to related categories, or search again from the results page.

Figure 7-8	LISZT HIT LIST OF ART GLASS MAILING LISTS

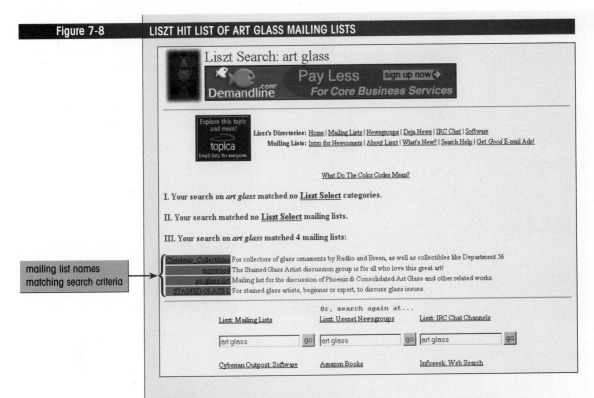

mailing list names
matching search criteria

3. Click one of the returned links, shown in green, to view information about the list. (You might see different lists from what is shown in Figure 7-8.) The page that opens should provide you with the list's name, where it is stored, and instructions for subscribing to and unsubscribing from the list. See if you can find some interesting lists for Mike, but for now, do not subscribe to any of them.

Just as with search engines, different mailing-list sites store information about different lists. Sometimes, you might find more or better lists by searching different sites. You will search for art and glass information using the PAML site next.

To locate other master mailing lists:

1. Use your browser's **Back** button to return to the Student Online Companion page for Session 7.1, and then click the **PAML** link to open the site (see Figure 7-9). Scroll to the bottom of the Web page and click the **Index** link. The PAML — Lists by Subject and Name page opens.

Figure 7-9	PAML'S MAILING LIST SITE

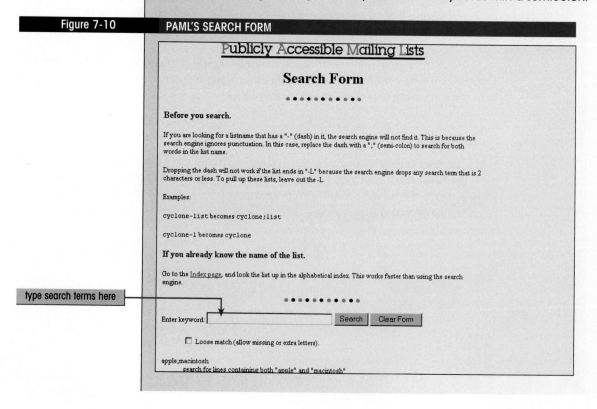

Welcome to the Internet's premier Mailing List Directory! We're better because we actively keep our mailing list entries up to date. We might not be the biggest, but we personally guarantee that our listings are the most accurate.

Publicly Accessible Mailing Lists

howswhen.com   Em

Send

Want to see your banner here?

Names

0 A B C D E F G H I J K L M N O P Q R S T U V W X Y Z

Subjects

Search hyperlink

0 a b c d e f g h i j k l m n o p q r s t u v w x y z

[Intro | Answers | Index | Search | Submit]

topica   All your lists.   All in one place.   Free.
EMAIL LISTS MADE EASY   click!

Please visit our sponsor!

Built Sat Dec 25 15:43:56 CST 1999   © 1999 Stephanie and Peter da Silva

2. Click the **Search** hyperlink located near the bottom of the page. The PAML Search Form opens, as shown in Figure 7-10. Read the instructions on the Search Form to discover how it is used. You need to search for entries that contain the words *art* and *glass*, so you will separate these keywords with a semicolon.

Figure 7-10	PAML'S SEARCH FORM

Publicly Accessible Mailing Lists

Search Form

• • • • • • • • • • •

Before you search.

If you are looking for a listname that has a "-" (dash) in it, the search engine will not find it. This is because the search engine ignores punctuation. In this case, replace the dash with a ";" (semi-colon) to search for both words in the list name.

Dropping the dash will not work if the list ends in "-L" because the search engine drops any search term that is 2 characters or less. To pull up these lists, leave out the -L.

Examples:

cyclone-list becomes cyclone;list

cyclone-l becomes cyclone

If you already know the name of the list.

Go to the Index page, and look the list up in the alphabetical index. This works faster than using the search engine.

• • • • • • • • • • •

type search terms here

Enter keyword: [   ]   Search   Clear Form

☐ Loose match (allow missing or extra letters).

apple;macintosh
       search for lines containing both "apple" and "macintosh"

3. Type **art;glass** in the Enter keyword text box, and then click the **Search** button. The results page opens and shows your search results. You can scroll down through the list and click any list links that might interest Mike. If you do not find any matches, you can refine your search expression or try searching another list.

4. Close your Web browser, and your dial-up connection, if necessary.

The Additional Information section of the Student Online Companion for Tutorial 7 contains links to other sites that you can use to search for information about mailing lists.

Session 7.1 **QUICK** | **CHECK**

1. True or False: To join a mailing list, you must send your information to the mailing list's server.

2. True or False: The primary difference between a moderated mailing list and an unmoderated mailing list is that a moderated list's contents are monitored by an individual or group of individuals.

3. What kinds of messages would you send to a list address? How do these messages differ from ones that you might send to the administrative address?

4. Monitoring a mailing list's messages for a sufficient time before posting your first message is called _____.

5. To add your name to a mailing list named EXERCISE-L, send the _____ command to the list's administrative address.

6. To receive a list of members' names and e-mail addresses for a specific list, use the _____ command.

7. The two commands that you can use to remove your name from a list are _____ and _____.

Now, you can report to Mike about your experiences subscribing to and using mailing lists. Mike will be pleased with your progress. You have a lot to tell him, including how to subscribe to interesting mailing lists, how to send messages to the mailing list, and how to leave a mailing list. You are sure Mike will want to subscribe to one or more art glass mailing lists to keep up with the latest industry information.

SESSION 7.2

In this session you will learn how to attach files to and detach files from an e-mail message. You will encode and decode files and learn about two popular mail-encoding techniques: MIME and uuencode.

What Are Encoded Files?

In Tutorial 1, you learned that when the Internet was being developed, e-mail was the main traffic flowing between computers. Initially, the interconnection of the computers and their networks enabled scientists and military personnel to exchange messages. Because e-mail messages flowed across and between many different computer types, Internet users quickly encountered problems interpreting characters and messages from different machines. Computer manufacturers used diverse schemes to represent digital information. The **American National Standards Institute (ANSI)** was formed to develop a standard character representation so all computers can represent data in the same way.

This standard survives today and is called the **American Standard Code for Information Interchange**, or **ASCII** (pronounced "ask-ey"). ASCII has a unique representation for every character you can type on a keyboard and send in a message. Codes represent every uppercase and lowercase letter in the English alphabet, the digits 1 through 9, and special characters such as %, #, $, and so on. Because ASCII represents each character as a series of seven bits (*bit* is short for binary digit and can have the value of either zero or one), there are not enough unique characters to represent graphics information as well. This limitation was not a problem until the Internet changed to allow the transmittal of graphics, sound, and other non-ASCII information through e-mail.

All e-mail software can send messages only as ASCII text; an e-mail program cannot send non-ASCII information, such as pictures, audio clips, or video segments. However, you learned in Tutorial 2 that you can attach different types of files to your e-mail messages. When you attach a file to your e-mail message, the binary data are transformed into ASCII data, in a process called **encoding** the data. Once the data are encoded to a "safe" ASCII form, they can be sent over e-mail. The only limitation of encoding occurs on the receiver's side—the receiver's e-mail program must be able to decode the message. **Decoding** a message simply means to transform ASCII data back into its original binary form (such as a picture, sound, or movie, for example).

Attaching a File to an E-Mail Message

To convert your non-ASCII data (or binary data) into ASCII data that any e-mail program can read, you must encode the binary data. There are several programs that encode binary data. Binary data that people send daily through e-mail messages include spreadsheets, word-processor documents, database files, sound files, digital photographs, and programs. One of the earliest encoding programs, used initially on larger computers, is **uuencode** (pronounced "you-you-encode"). Before PCs had mail-client programs running on them, uuencode converted binary files into ASCII data. The ASCII files were then simply included in a message's body and sent to another user. When the addressee received the message, he or she extracted the encoded message and reversed the encoding procedure to produce the original binary data. At that point, the binary data could be loaded into the program that could manipulate the data. The companion program that decodes uuencode files, which is still used on larger computers and PCs, is called **uudecode**.

Today, binary data are handled differently. Instead of transforming binary data into ASCII and then sending them as a message, binary data are attached to an e-mail message. When data are attached to an e-mail message, they are encoded but reside outside the normal e-mail message body—as an attachment to the message. E-mail programs encode data in one of a few popular formats and automatically attach that data to a message. When the message arrives at the recipient's mailbox, the attachment automatically is downloaded, decoded, and removed from the message. Once the attachment is removed, the addressee can use the binary data immediately, without needing to decode the data.

Be aware that some ISPs limit the size of e-mail attachments. For example, Yahoo! Mail allows subscribers to keep up to 3 MB (approximately 3,000,000 characters) in their mail boxes. Other ISPs might impose per message limits. Also consider the receiver when sending attachments. Large attachments can take a long time for the recipient to download on a slow modem connection. A 3MB attachment can take several minutes to download and might be inconvenient for the recipient.

Besides uuencode and uudecode, there are two other popular programs used by e-mail programs: **Multipurpose Internet Mail Extensions (MIME)** and **BinHex**. MIME is the general standard for PCs, and BinHex is the Macintosh standard. If you use ISPs such as America Online, WorldNet, or the Microsoft Network, then you are using a MIME-compliant e-mail program. A **MIME-compliant program** is an e-mail program that provides MIME encoding when you attach files to your e-mail messages.

It is important for Mike DeMaine to be able to attach pictures and voice recordings to his e-mail messages. He wants to send beveled and art glass pictures to current and potential customers. He has asked you to experiment with sending graphics in e-mail messages. To help you, Mike has given you a photograph of one of the beveled glass windows he produced for a customer. You have already scanned the picture into the computer and saved it in a file named bevel.jpg. You are now ready to experiment with sending graphics and messages on the Internet. You will send the picture to yourself to simulate sending and receiving a message with an attached picture file.

Note: The steps that follow are written so they will work with most e-mail programs. If you have trouble attaching and detaching your files, refer to Session 2.2 if you are using Netscape Messenger or Session 2.3 if you are using Microsoft Outlook Express, and then review the instructions for attaching and detaching files. If you still have problems, consult online Help for your e-mail program or ask your instructor or technical support person for help.

REFERENCE WINDOW   **RW**

Attaching a file to an e-mail message
- Create a new message in your e-mail program.
- If you are using Messenger, click the Attach button on the Message toolbar, and then click File. Double-click the filename to attach.
  or
- If you are using Outlook Express, click the Attach button on the toolbar, and then double-click the filename to attach.

To attach a file to an e-mail message:

1. Create a new message in your e-mail program, and then type your complete e-mail address in the To text box.

2. Click in the Subject text box, and then type **Test message with attached picture**.

3. Move to the message area, and then type **Enclosed is a picture of a typical beveled glass panel that we produce. It is a fine example of the high-quality beveled glass panels produced by our artisans.**

4. Press the **Enter** key twice to insert a blank line.

5. Type your first and last names, separated by a space. Now, you can attach the picture to your e-mail message.

6. Make sure your Data Disk is in the appropriate drive. If you are using Messenger, go to Step 7. If you are using Outlook Express, go to Step 8.

7. If you are using Messenger, click the **Attach** button on the Message toolbar, and then click **File** to open the Enter file to attach dialog box. Click the **Look in** list arrow and click **3½ Floppy (A:)** (or whichever drive contains your Data Disk), double-click the **Tutorial.07** folder, and then double-click the **bevel.jpg** file. The Enter file to attach dialog box closes and the Attach Files & Documents tab in the message header lists the image file (see Figure 7-11). Now you are ready to send your message. Go to Step 9.

Figure 7-11   **SENDING AN ATTACHMENT IN MESSENGER**

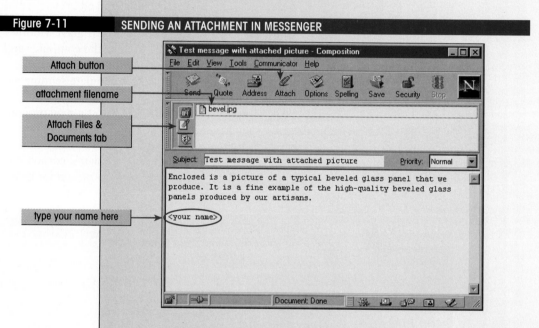

8. If you are using Outlook Express, click the **Attach** button on the toolbar to open the Insert Attachment dialog box, click the **Look in** list arrow and select **3½ Floppy (A:)** (or whichever drive contains your Data Disk), double-click the **Tutorial.07** folder, and then double-click the **bevel.jpg** file. The Insert Attachment dialog box closes, and the attachment appears as an icon below the message subject (see Figure 7-12). You are now ready to send your message. Go to Step 9.

Figure 7-12	SENDING AN ATTACHMENT IN OUTLOOK EXPRESS

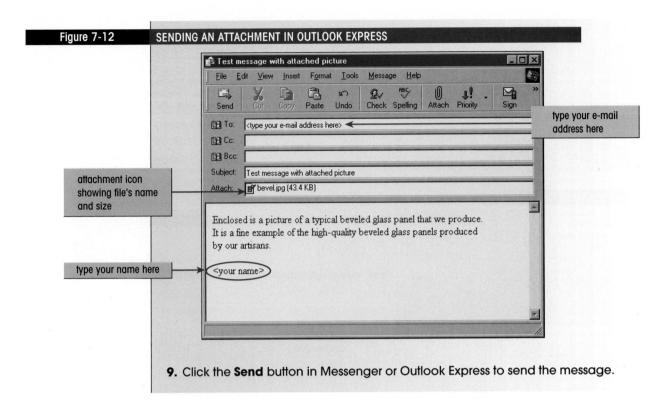

attachment icon showing file's name and size

type your e-mail address here

type your name here

9. Click the **Send** button in Messenger or Outlook Express to send the message.

Now you can check for new messages and see if your experiment was successful.

Detaching a File from an E-Mail Message

When you detach a file from an e-mail message, you specify a location in which to save the file, and then either accept the original filename or assign a new one. Some mail programs let you preview attached files in a special window; other programs show the file in the program window that created it if you have that program on your PC. If you decide to delete a message containing an attachment, the attachment usually is deleted along with the message. (With most e-mail clients, you can set an option that determines whether an attachment is deleted when you delete the message.)

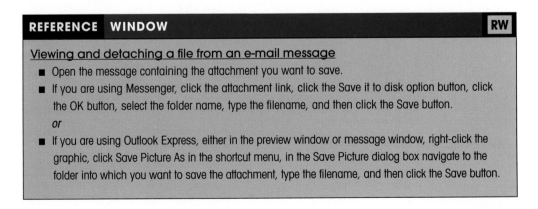

REFERENCE   WINDOW   **RW**

Viewing and detaching a file from an e-mail message
- Open the message containing the attachment you want to save.
- If you are using Messenger, click the attachment link, click the Save it to disk option button, click the OK button, select the folder name, type the filename, and then click the Save button.
  or
- If you are using Outlook Express, either in the preview window or message window, right-click the graphic, click Save Picture As in the shortcut menu, in the Save Picture dialog box navigate to the folder into which you want to save the attachment, type the filename, and then click the Save button.

To view an e-mail attachment on screen and then save it:

1. Use your e-mail program to retrieve your new messages, and then go to the Inbox, if necessary.

2. Make sure that you received your message, which has the subject "Test message with attached picture," and then open the message. Depending on your e-mail program and its settings, the bevel.jpg file will display either as an icon or as a picture. Figure 7-13 shows the message in Messenger; Figure 7-14 shows the message in Outlook Express.

Figure 7-13	REVIEWING AN ATTACHED FILE IN MESSENGER

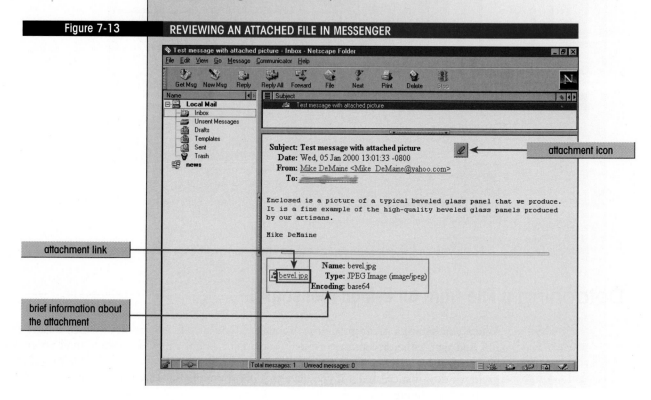

attachment icon

attachment link

brief information about the attachment

Figure 7-14	REVIEWING AN ATTACHED FILE IN OUTLOOK EXPRESS

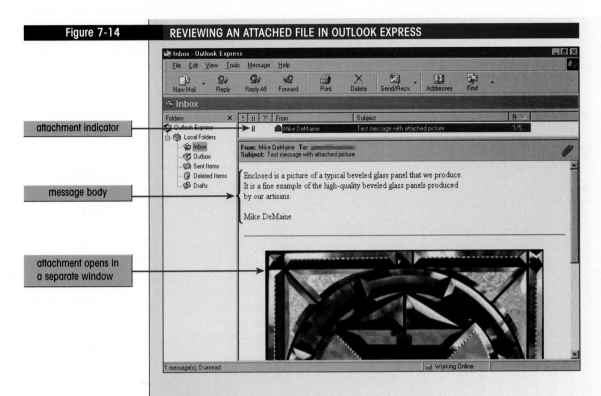

attachment indicator

message body

attachment opens in
a separate window

If you are using Messenger, go to Step 3. If you are using Outlook Express, go to Step 5.

3. If you are using Messenger, click the attachment link (see Figure 7-13) to open a dialog box. Click the **Save it to disk** option button. Click the **OK** button. The Save As dialog box opens. Click the **Save in** list arrow, change to the drive that contains your Data Disk, and then double-click the **Tutorial.07** folder to open it. Change the filename in the File name text box to **bevel2.jpg**, and then click the **Save** button to save the attached file.

4. If you are using Outlook Express, right-click the graphic (the glass panel picture) in the lower portion of the window and then click **Save Picture As** in the shortcut menu. The Save Picture dialog box opens. Click the **Save in** list arrow, change to the drive that contains your Data Disk, and then double-click the **Tutorial.07** folder to open it. Change the filename in the File name text box to **bevel2.jpg**, and then click the **Save** button to save the attached file.

5. Close your e-mail program.

Now, you have a copy of the original file (bevel.jpg) and the file that you received over e-mail (bevel2.jpg) on your Data Disk. You are certain that Mike will be pleased with the results.

Session 7.2 QUICK CHECK

1. True or False: You can insert a Word document or an Excel spreadsheet directly into an e-mail message to send it to another user.

2. What do programs such as MIME and uuencode do? What is their purpose?

3. List some examples of the types of objects that must be encoded before being sent with e-mail.

4. Uuencode converts binary data into a readable form of "safe" data called _____.

5. The encoding standard commonly used for Macintosh computers is _____.

6. The encoding standard commonly used for PCs is _____.

Mike is happy to hear that your test of sending graphics files was successful. The real test, however, will be when you begin sending files to people with e-mail addresses on other servers. Mike wants you to find some information about businesses in certain areas. He then asks you to find an individual's e-mail address. In Mike's opinion, knowing how to locate individuals and businesses using Internet services will be critical in locating new sales leads, distributors, and equipment.

SESSION 7.3

In this session you will learn how to find business e-mail addresses. You will use several Web sites that specialize in searching for people and places.

Using Internet Directory Services

In Tutorial 5, you learned how to use the Internet to search for news, weather, business, and personal information, such as your street address and phone number. You also can use the Web's white pages and yellow pages sites to search for a person's e-mail address. However, searching for an e-mail address is not always a straightforward process. Although there are many searchable e-mail address directories and sites, the Internet is a highly volatile environment. People change e-mail addresses frequently and sometimes disappear from the Internet altogether. To make matters worse, there is no central, comprehensive repository of names and Internet e-mail addresses. Before you search the Web, remember that placing a phone call to the person you want to contact through e-mail might be the best way to find that person's e-mail address.

To look up a friend or acquaintance, you use a white pages directory service. You can search for e-mail addresses or phone numbers by supplying a minimal amount of information, such as the person's first and last names. A yellow pages directory service provides the same e-mail lookup capability, but it searches business directories instead of personal ones.

Whether you use the white pages or yellow pages, you may find many names or businesses in your search results. There are several ways to look for someone's e-mail address. For instance, if you want to locate Fred Gallagher, submit a search request with *F Gallagher*, *Fred Gallagher*, or *Frederick Gallagher* because his information might be listed in any (or all) of those ways. Also, if you don't find someone, try using initials or a last name only. Of course, many more names result when you supply less information, and fewer names result when you supply more information, such as the e-mail domain name or the state in which the person lives. Don't be surprised if a search turns up a list of hundreds of people or businesses. The Internet is a huge entity, and there are millions of e-mail addresses listed in thousands of directories all over the world.

Mike asks you to use a yellow pages directory service to search for art glass supply houses. You are eager to try searching for people and start by using the Yahoo! People Search directory service. You might be able to uncover some good business contacts and their e-mail addresses.

Searching with Yahoo! People Search

Yahoo! People Search is one of the Internet's many white pages directory services. You can use Yahoo! People Search to search for individuals or businesses listed on the Internet. Directory search engines work in the same way as other Internet search resources—first, you enter a few keywords, and then you send your keywords to the server, which in turn returns a hit list. Mike asked you to search for glass shops in the Los Angeles area because he will travel there in the spring for a conference. You can use Yahoo! People Search to search for businesses in the Los Angeles area.

To use the Yahoo! People Search directory:

1. If necessary, start your Web browser, and then go to the Student Online Companion page by entering the URL **http://www.course.com/newperspectives/internet2** in the appropriate location in your Web browser. Click the **Comprehensive** book link, click the **Tutorial 7** link, and then click the **Session 7.3** link. Click the **Yahoo! People Search** link and wait while the browser loads the page. The Yahoo! People Search home page opens.

2. Click the **Yellow Pages** link under the Yahoo! Resources heading in the left panel to open the Yellow Pages page shown in Figure 7-15.

| Figure 7-15 | YAHOO! YELLOW PAGES OPENING PAGE |

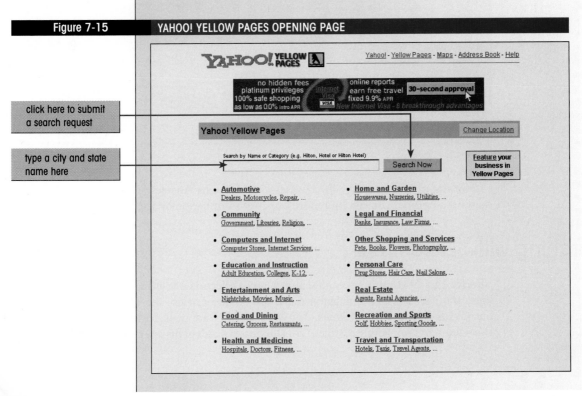

3. Click the **Change Location** link located near the top of the page. The Search in a City page opens.

4. Type **Los Angeles CA** in the City, State Zip text box, and then click the **Continue** button.

5. Type **art glass** in the search text box, and then click the **Search Now** button. The Yahoo! Yellow Pages Results page lists businesses in the Los Angeles area that specialize in art glass (see Figure 7-16). (Your search results might be different because listings change over time.) Notice that you can extend your search to outside the Los Angeles area by clicking the Beyond Los Angeles link. When you click this link, you will open another results page that orders relevant businesses by name and by the number of miles outside of the Los Angeles area. Each of the business names listed in blue is a hyperlink. You can click one or more of the hyperlinks to go to a page displaying the address of the business and a map showing where the business is located.

| Figure 7-16 | LOS ANGELES ART GLASS BUSINESSES LOCATED BY YAHOO! PEOPLE SEARCH |

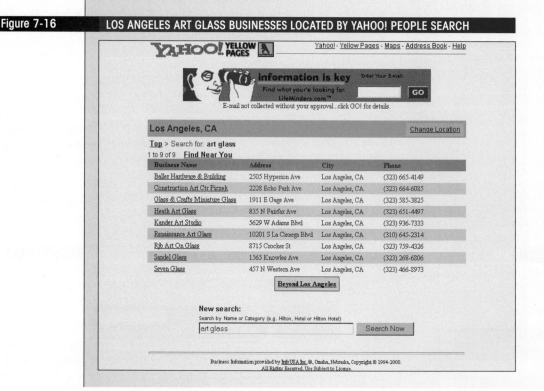

You found many listings for businesses in the Los Angeles area for Mike. As with any search, sometimes you can find more or better information by selecting a second search tool.

Searching with SEARCH.COM

SEARCH.COM can access and search a large collection of e-mail addresses, white pages listings, and yellow pages listings on the Internet. You can use the Yellow Pages to find many businesses in the United States. You want to find art glass businesses that are located in Portland, Oregon, because Mike is considering expanding his marketing efforts into that area.

To use the SEARCH.COM search service:

1. Return to the Student Online Companion Web page for Session 7.3, and then click the **SEARCH.COM** hyperlink and wait while your Web browser loads the SEARCH.COM home page.

2. Click the **Yellow Pages** link. The Snap! Yellow Pages page opens. You can search the entire database using the text boxes, or use the individual listings at the bottom of the page to search a specific database.

3. Type **art glass** in the search word(s) text box, press the **Tab** key to move to the city text box and type **Portland**, and then press the **Tab** key to go to the state text box and type **OR**. Click the **by type** option button (see Figure 7-17).

Figure 7-17	USING SEARCH.COM TO FIND ART GLASS BUSINESSES IN PORTLAND, OREGON

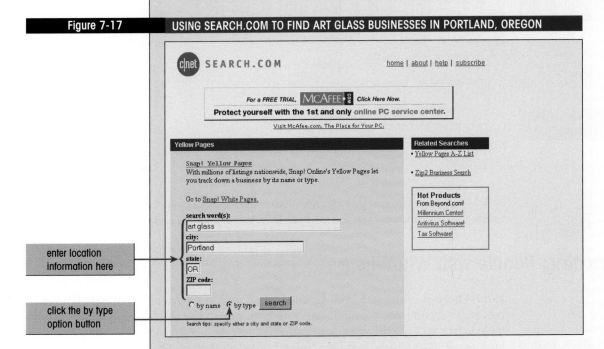

enter location information here

click the by type option button

4. Click the **search** button to submit the search. The Snap:Yellow Pages:Results page opens. Click the **Glass-Stained & Leaded** link near the top of the page to open pages listing businesses related to stained and leaded glass. Figure 7-18 shows the search results page that opens and lists several businesses that fit the search criteria. (Your search results might be different.) Although the business names are not hyperlinks, you can print the search results page to get a list and use the Map It hyperlink to see a map that shows each business location. Then, you can zoom in the map image to see a detailed map or zoom out the image to see a satellite view of the state. The Drive It hyperlink gives you detailed driving directions to the store from any starting location you specify.

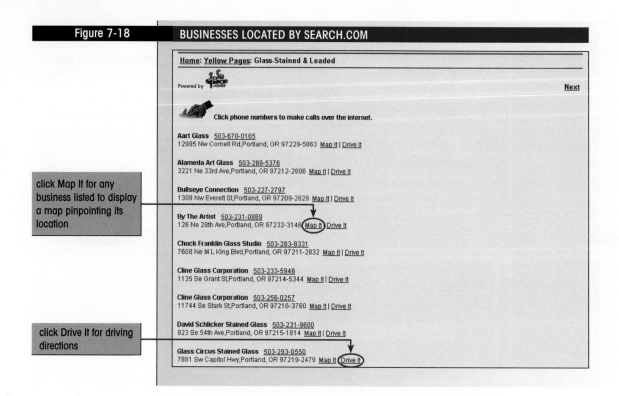

Figure 7-18   BUSINESSES LOCATED BY SEARCH.COM

click Map It for any business listed to display a map pinpointing its location

click Drive It for driving directions

You can tell Mike that you can now locate businesses in a specific area as well as maps to locate those businesses. You are now ready to locate people's e-mail addresses.

Locating People with WhoWhere

WhoWhere provides free Web-based communication applications that enable people and businesses to find and communicate with each other. The company's available directories include free access to lists of e-mail addresses, telephone listings, personal home pages, and business Web pages. Remember, however, that sometimes the best way to get an e-mail address is to ask, because it is difficult to find the correct address.

Mike just returned from a meeting of glass dealers where he met Lynn Mason, who is willing to manage his northwestern marketing efforts. Mike has misplaced her e-mail address and asks you to find it for him—Lynn travels extensively, and e-mail is the best way to reach her.

To use "WhoWhere" to find an e-mail address:

1. Return to the Student Online Companion Web page for Session 7.3, click the **WhoWhere** hyperlink, and wait while your Web browser loads the page.

2. In the First Name text box type **Lynn**, press the **Tab** key to move to the Last Name text box, and then type **Mason** (see Figure 7-19).

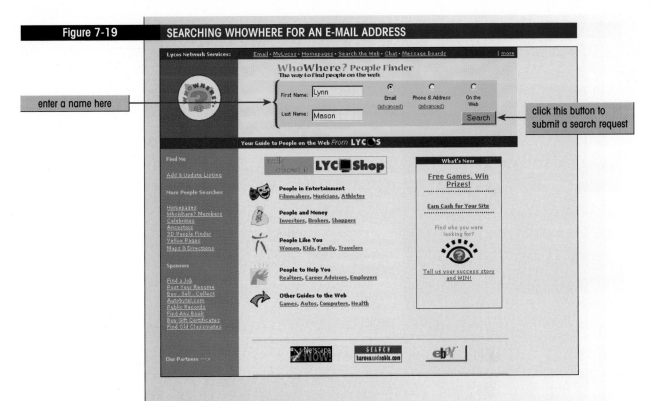

Figure 7-19   SEARCHING WHOWHERE FOR AN E-MAIL ADDRESS

3. Click the **Search** button to search for the e-mail address. Figure 7-20 shows the search results page that opens and lists several people with that name. (Remember that your search results might be different.) Mike told you that Lynn was based in Salem, OR, so you scan the list to see if anyone lists Salem as an address. If you don't find what you are looking for, then you can run the search using another white pages listing. However, Mike tells you not to worry about the address and says that he will see if a colleague in Portland has it.

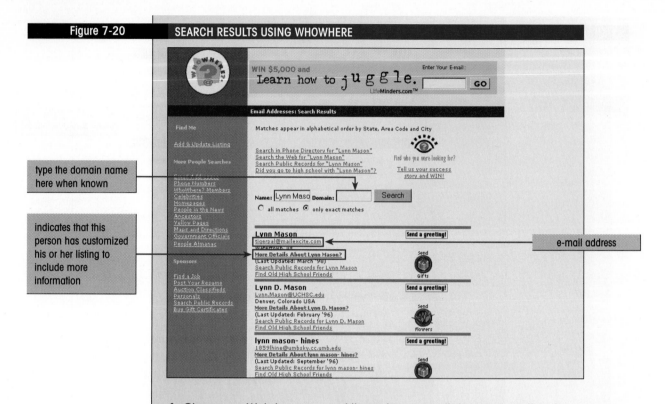

Figure 7-20   SEARCH RESULTS USING WHOWHERE

type the domain name here when known

indicates that this person has customized his or her listing to include more information

e-mail address

4. Close your Web browser, and then close your dial-up connection, if necessary.

The Additional Information section of the Student Online Companion contains links to other white and yellow pages search directories that you can use to find listings for individuals and businesses.

Session 7.3 QUICK CHECK

1. Why would you use an Internet white pages directory service?

2. What is a yellow pages directory service?

3. Is there a way to determine the location of a business once you find it with Yahoo! People Search, SEARCH.COM, or WhoWhere?

4. Most search services are free. How does the search service earn a profit?

5. Suppose you use WhoWhere to locate Earl Butz (U.S. Secretary of Agriculture under President Richard Nixon), which returns over 100 hits. What ways can you suggest to refine your search?

6. Suppose you want to find Al Frankston's e-mail address using one of the directory services. Briefly explain how you might vary the name to broaden your search.

Now that you know more about where to find information about the art glass business, you are ready to prepare your final report for Mike.

REVIEW ASSIGNMENTS

After careful study and research, you understand mailing lists, how to create attachments and detach them from e-mail messages, and how to use search services to locate businesses and e-mail addresses. You are ready to prepare a summary for Mike of what you have discovered and include in it your opinion about using the Internet to establish two art glass mailing lists. One list will be for art glass businesses and art glass professionals. The other list will provide a forum for hobbyists to ask and answer questions. You will send Mike a brief report as an attachment to an e-mail message.

Do the following:

1. Start any word processor (such as WordPad or Microsoft Word).

2. Place your Data Disk in the correct drive. Use the Open command on the File menu to open the Open dialog box. Click the Look in list arrow and select 3½ Floppy (A:) (or whichever drive contains your Data Disk), double-click the Tutorial.07 folder, and then double-click the memo.doc file to open it.

3. Replace the text <current date> with today's date.

4. Replace the text <your name> with your first and last names.

5. Write a new paragraph following the last paragraph. Using the Tab key or your word processor's table feature, create two columns. In the left column, type the names of three Web sites that Mike could visit to locate e-mail addresses of people and businesses. In the right column next to each name, type each site's full URL.

6. Write a concluding paragraph of at least three complete sentences summarizing the advantages of using a LISTSERV or ListProc product rather than using a conventional e-mail distribution list in which you type each recipient's name or in which you use an e-mail group with its associated names. One sentence should list the commands to join and leave a mailing list. Give a complete example of each command on two separate lines using your name and the list name GlassList-L.

7. Save the file as demaine.doc in the Tutorial.07 folder on your Data Disk.

8. Close your word processor.

9. Start your e-mail program, and create a new message.

10. Type your instructor's e-mail address in the To text box, and your e-mail address in the Cc text box.

11. Type "Attached is my brief report" as the subject.

12. Type "I am attaching my report about mailing lists, attached files, and search engines to this message. The filename is demaine.doc. Please call or e-mail me if you have any questions." Add a blank line, and then type your first and last names.

13. Attach the memo you just saved on your Data Disk (demaine.doc) to the e-mail message, and then send the message.

14. Wait a few minutes, and then retrieve your new messages. When you receive your Cc message, save the demaine.doc file as demaine1.doc in the Tutorial.07 folder on your Data Disk. Print the message, and then delete it.

15. Close your e-mail program.

CASE PROBLEMS

Case 1. Big Island Coffee Company Big Island Coffee Company (BICC) grows and ships coffee beans to many of the Hawaiian Islands and parts of the continental United States. Manoa Kileahu, BICC's owner, wants to establish a mailing list to answer questions about coffee-roasting techniques and coffee processing in general. First, Manoa wants you to find mailing lists that might be relevant to a coffee bean supplier's marketing efforts. Manoa is interested in "plugging into" any existing Internet marketing groups. You will send a message to a mailing list to retrieve the names of known mailing lists.

Do the following:

1. Start your e-mail program, and create a new message.

2. Type the address listserv@listserv.net in the To text box, and leave the other message header lines blank.

3. In the message area, type "list global marketing". Your request will return a list of all known lists with the word *marketing* in their titles or names.

4. Send the message. The mailing-list server will return candidate mailing-list names from a large number of known mailing lists.

5. When you receive an answer from the mailing-list server, scan the list of mailing lists and note which ones related to marketing look interesting.

6. Save the message as mailing.txt in the Tutorial.07 folder on your Data Disk.

7. Close your e-mail program and open any word processor, such as WordPad, Notepad, or Microsoft Word.

8. Open the document mailing.txt file that you saved. Delete everything from the document except for the first 15 list entries so that the entire listing will fit on one page.

9. Move to the top of the document, and then press the Enter key twice to create two blank lines.

10. Type your first and last names on the first line in the document.

11. Save the new document as mailing2.txt on your Data Disk.

12. Print the list, and then close your word processor.

Case 2. Join a Mailing List Based on a friend's recommendation, you decide to join a mailing list. First, you will locate one that looks interesting to you. You will then lurk for a while and listen to the messages. Follow these instructions to locate and then join a mailing list of your choice.

Do the following:

1. Start your Web browser, go to the Student Online Companion (http://www.course.com/newperspectives/internet2), click the Comprehensive book link, click the Tutorial 7 link, and then click the Case Problems link in the left frame.

2. Click the L-Soft link and wait while the L-Soft International organization's Web page opens. (L-Soft produces and licenses the LISTSERV mailing-list software.) The official catalog of LISTSERV lists page opens.

3. Scroll down the page until you see the heading "List information," and then click the View lists with 10,000 subscribers or more hyperlink. A page opens that lists hundreds of mailing lists. Each list is a hyperlink.

Explore 4. Scroll the list of mailing lists and locate one that interests you. Click the blue link of a list you want to join. A new page opens revealing information about the list. Scroll down so you can see a line describing how you subscribe to the list. The line will read, in part: "To subscribe, send mail to…" Make a note of the list's name and the administrative address.

5. Start your e-mail program, and create a new message.

6. Compose the message to subscribe to the list, and then send the message.

7. If the list server has any specific instructions, follow its requests.

8. When the list server sends you a welcome message, forward it to your instructor.

9. Read the messages on the list for a few days. After you have read several messages, unsubscribe from the list.

10. When you receive the confirmation of your removal from the list, forward it to your instructor.

11. Close your e-mail program.

Case 3. Milk Specialists Milk Specialists is a small dairy farm located in the Midwest. Milk Specialists sells its entire supply of milk to a local dairy. Lars Svelten, the dairy's manager, has asked you to help him send advertising materials to clients using e-mail. Lars already has an ISP and has sent a few e-mail messages to friends and the local dairy several times, but he is having trouble including his logo—a graphic of a cow—in his messages. You will send an e-mail message to your instructor as a test. Then, you will show Lars how to send his own e-mail messages to other dairies in the region.

Do the following:

1. Start your e-mail program, and create a new message.

2. Type your instructor's e-mail address in the To text box, and then type your e-mail address in the Cc text box.

3. Type "Lars Svelten dairy cows are happy cows" as the message subject.

4. Make sure your Data Disk is in drive A: (or whichever drive contains your Data Disk). Attach the file named bovine.bmp, which is saved in the Tutorial.07 folder on your Data Disk, to your message.

5. Type "The Svelten dairy produces all Grade-A milk. Our modern chillers maintain milk at a constant, cool, and safe temperature. You can trust Svelten milk!" in the message area.

6. Press the Enter key twice, and then type your name to sign the message.

7. Send the message.

Explore 8. When you receive your Cc message, print it and then save the graphic as bovine2.bmp in the Tutorial.07 folder on your Data Disk. Start the Paint program by clicking the Start button on the taskbar, pointing to Accessories, and then clicking Paint. Open the bovine2.bmp file, and then print it.

9. Delete the message.

10. Close your e-mail program.

Case 4. People Finder Services People Finder Services is an Internet search service that locates address and e-mail information for clients seeking to reestablish contact with distant relatives and long-lost friends. People Finder is popular because it is much less expensive than hiring a private investigator, although an investigator might have a higher success rate. Ethyl Laskowski, the office manager, has hired you to work weekends and perform Internet searches. Before she puts you to work, she asks you to demonstrate your Internet searching skills by finding information about individuals.

Do the following:

1. Start your Web browser, go to the Student Online Companion (http://www.course.com/newperspectives/internet2), click the Comprehensive book link, click the Tutorial 7 link, and then click the Case Problems link in the left frame.

2. Click the Internet Oracle link to open the Internet Oracle home page.

Explore 3. Use the Yahoo! People Search yellow pages search to locate your hometown mayor's office address, phone number, fax number, and e-mail address.

Explore 4. Find a map that shows the street location of the mayor's office. Save the map image in the Tutorial.07 folder on your Data Disk. Create a new e-mail message, type your instructor's e-mail address in the To text box, type your e-mail address in the Cc text box, and then attach the map that you saved to the message. Send the message.

5. Check for new messages. When you receive the message that you sent in Step 4, detach it from the message and save it with the filename newmap (use the default file extension) in the Tutorial.07 folder on your Data Disk, and then delete the message.

6. Locate the e-mail addresses of the U.S. Senators from the state where you attend school.

7. Use an Internet search service to find the street address of George Bush. All you know is that the George Bush you are looking for lives in Texas. Print the first page of responses to your search request.

8. Close your Web browser, and close your dial-up connection, if necessary.

Case 5. Court Reporting Specialists Court Reporting Specialists is a local group of court reporters who are interested in increasing discussion and communication among court reporters and interested parties. Ginny Rodriguez, one of the group's most active members, has heard that mailing lists are a convenient way for people sharing a common interest to interact in a virtual, unintimidating environment. She is very interested in creating and administering the court reporting discussion group. She would like to create a virtual meeting room where interested people could ask specific questions, receive answers from veteran court reporters, learn about the latest court reporting software, and exchange ideas. Her first good choice is to enlist your help in locating information about mailing list software. Ginny's supervisor in the County Reporter's office has promised Ginny seed money to purchase an "adequate and inexpensive" mailing list package. Your task is to locate the major mailing list software packages, determine the cost of each one, and provide a summary about the capabilities of each package.

Do the following:

1. Start your Web browser, go to the Student Online Companion (http://www.course.com/newperspectives/internet2), click the Comprehensive book link, click the Tutorial 7 link, and then click the Case Problems link in the left frame.

2. Begin your research by clicking the LISTSERV link. When the L-Soft (LISTSERV owners) home page opens, look around the page and click on links that look like they will lead you to pricing information or a complete description of the package's capabilities.

3. Print the page that describes different price plans.

4. Print any pages that describe the software's capabilities.

5. Repeat Steps 2 through 4 for ListProc, Majordomo, and Petidomo. Each link is listed in the Online Companion in the Case Problems (Case Problem 5) section.

6. When you complete your research, you should have at least two printed pages on each of the four mailing list programs. Turn in your results to your instructor.

7. Close your browser.

QUICK | CHECK ANSWERS

Session 7.1

1. True
2. True
3. You can send questions about the list's main topics or you can answer another list member's questions by sending a message to the list address. You send only *commands* to a list's administrative address.
4. lurking
5. subscribe EXERCISE-L *yourname*
6. review
7. unsubscribe, signoff

Session 7.2

1. False
2. MIME and uuencode change a binary file into an ASCII file so that the file can be attached to an e-mail message.
3. spreadsheets, pictures, word-processed documents, voice recordings, and movies
4. ASCII
5. BinHex
6. MIME

Session 7.3

1. to find information about an individual
2. A yellow pages directory service lists information about businesses and provides maps to their locations.
3. Click the appropriate map button when provided.
4. by allowing advertising on the service
5. Narrow the search by entering as much additional information about the person as possible. For example, knowing the state or city where the person lives helps to focus the search.
6. Try searching for *Albert Frankston* or *A Frankston*, and so on.

In this tutorial you will:

- Learn about and use Internet chat facilities

- Explore virtual worlds that offer entertainment and learning opportunities

- Use the Web to find useful information in Usenet newsgroups

- Reply to and post original articles to Usenet newsgroups

ADVANCED COMMUNICATION TOOLS

Using Chat, Virtual Worlds, and Newsgroups

CASE

MFact Marketing Research

MFact Marketing Research helps clients gather and evaluate information about the marketability of products and services they currently offer or that are in development. Founded by Isaac Shores 10 years ago, MFact has grown rapidly. The firm's many satisfied customers include manufacturers of household goods, food products, consumer electronics products, and software. Recently, MFact has started working with clients in the retail merchandising business. Isaac hopes to obtain more service-industry clients, such as law firms, real-estate brokers, and investment advisors. You started working at MFact last year and are impressed with the wide variety of clients that the firm serves.

Marketing researchers use many different approaches to gather their data. Many of MFact's projects have used mail or telephone surveys of potential product buyers. In other research projects, MFact gathers a small number of potential product users and asks them to discuss product features with a trained moderator. These discussion sessions, called focus groups, can be expensive and difficult to arrange because all participants must meet at the same place and time. To obtain a good cross-section of the market for a particular product or service, MFact must conduct focus groups in many different cities. You also have noticed that the sales team at MFact needs to learn many details about a product, market, or industry when they are presenting to new clients. Selling opportunities often arise on short notice; therefore, MFact account executives need to obtain this information quickly.

During a conversation one morning, Isaac mentions that he is concerned about two issues: the cost of conducting focus groups and the need to gather in-depth information quickly about potential new clients and their products. Isaac tells you he has discussed these issues with Denise Allen, who has held various positions in the computer software industry. Denise told Isaac that he might want to use the Internet to lower the cost of gathering market research data. She had mentioned a number of possibilities that use advanced communication tools on the Internet. Denise will serve as a consultant to MFact to help identify ways in which the Internet's advanced communication tools might reduce costs and increase the quality of the marketing research services that MFact offers its clients. Isaac has assigned you to work with Denise to explore the potential that these tools might offer.

SESSION 8.1

In this session you will learn how to communicate "live" with individuals or groups of people using the chat facilities that exist on the Internet and the Web. You also will learn about virtual worlds that people have created on the Internet.

What Is Chat?

In Tutorials 2 and 7, you learned how to use Internet e-mail to communicate with one or more people. You also learned how to use mailing lists to communicate with a group of people. When you use e-mail, however, you must send your message and then wait for a response (or responses). E-mail does not permit realtime conversations, such as those you might conduct using the telephone.

During your first meeting with Denise, she suggests that chat technology might offer a way to conduct focus groups without requiring participants to meet in a specific location. Denise explains that **chat** is a general term for realtime communication on the Internet or the Web. Originally, the term *chat* described the act of users exchanging typed messages. Today, however, chats can include the exchange of pictures, animations, sounds, and other multimedia files.

A **private chat** occurs between two individuals. Often, the two individuals participating in a private chat meet while chatting among others in a group chat area, or **public chat**. Chats can be continuous, with participants entering and leaving ongoing discussions, or they can be planned to occur at a specific time and last for a specific length of time. Some chats are open to discussions of any topic, whereas others are focused on a specific topic or category of participants. Some chats feature participation by a celebrity or an authority on the chat topic. These chats give worldwide users an opportunity to join discussions with people they would never have the chance to meet otherwise. Most chat implementations allow users to save a transcript of the chat session for future reference, which can be especially valuable for chats that focus on highly technical or detailed topics.

Denise notes that chat session transcripts would provide documentation similar to that provided by the video and audio recordings that MFact makes of its in-person focus group sessions. Denise explains that you can join public chat sites and simply read the messages sent by other members; you do not need to send messages to the group. This practice of reading messages and not contributing to the discussion is called **lurking**.

In recent years, the Web has offered expanded chat facilities that offer a richer interactive experience than the simple text interchanges that occurred on the original Internet chat servers. For example, Web chat sites enable users to send graphic images that are displayed for all chat participants to see. Web chat sites that use the browser client software interface to create combined text and graphic environments for chat participants are called **chat rooms**.

Chatting requires participants to type quickly, even in the enhanced graphical environment of the Web. Therefore, chat participants often omit capitalization and do not worry about proper spelling and grammar. Chat participants use the same emoticons (or smileys) that e-mail users find helpful to display humor and emotions in their messages. In addition, chat participants use some of the acronyms shown in Figure 8-1 for common expressions. Although the acronyms in Figure 8-1 appear as all capital letters, remember that most chat participants type everything—including these acronyms—in lowercase letters because typing in all capital letters usually is interpreted as shouting.

Figure 8-1	COMMONLY USED CHAT ACRONYMS

ACRONYM	MEANING
AFK	Away from keyboard
ATM	At the moment
BBL	Be back later
BRB	Be right back
BTW	By the way
C U L8R	See you later
C Ya	See you
EG	Evil grin
IMHO	In my humble opinion
IRL	In real life (contrasted with one's online existence)
JK	Just kidding
LOL	Laughing out loud
NP	No problem
OIC	Oh, I see
ROTFL	Rolling on the floor laughing
RTFM	Read the fine manual (usually a suggestion to read a program's documentation)
TTFN	Ta-ta (goodbye) for now
WB	Welcome back

Some chat systems use one server site as a repository for the messages typed by persons at many different locations. Other chat systems use a series of connected servers that pass messages from user to user so quickly that the messages appear to be stored in one place.

Internet Relay Chat

The early networks that became the Internet included many computers that used the UNIX operating system. Many of these UNIX computers included a program called **Talk** that allowed users to exchange short text messages. In 1988, Jarkko Oikarinen wrote a communications program that extended the capabilities of the Talk program for his employer, the University of Oulu in Finland. He called his multiuser program **Internet Relay Chat (IRC)**.

By 1991, IRC was running on over 100 servers throughout the world. IRC became popular among scientists and academicians for conducting informal discussions of experiments and theories with colleagues at other universities and research institutes.

Commercial use of IRC soon followed, with firms using it for virtual meetings with clients and employees at worldwide branch offices. Using IRC in business saves travel costs and is less expensive than long-distance conference calling. Businesses that sell computer software have used IRC to provide customer support and to host user group meetings. News-gathering organizations have used IRC to enhance live coverage of breaking news events. For example, many news reports from the 1991 Gulf War were based on information that came from the war area through IRC and the Internet. By the mid-1990s, there were hundreds of IRC servers connecting thousands of IRC clients.

How IRC Works

IRC uses a client-server network model: IRC servers are connected through the Internet to form an IRC network. Individual chat participants use IRC clients that connect to the servers in the network. There are many different IRC networks that operate independently of each other. The original network was **EFNet**, which is still in operation today as one of the largest IRC networks. Other major IRC networks include **IRCNet**, **Undernet**, **DALnet**, and **NewNet**. Although the servers in each of these individual IRC networks are connected to each other as part of the Internet, IRC traffic is segregated by network. For example, a person using an EFNet client can chat only with another person who also is using an EFNet client—even though the message packets might travel through DALnet and IRCNet servers that are part of the Internet. Figure 8-2 shows this simultaneous interconnection and segregation of IRC network traffic.

Figure 8-2	INDEPENDENT IRC NETWORKS ON THE INTERNET

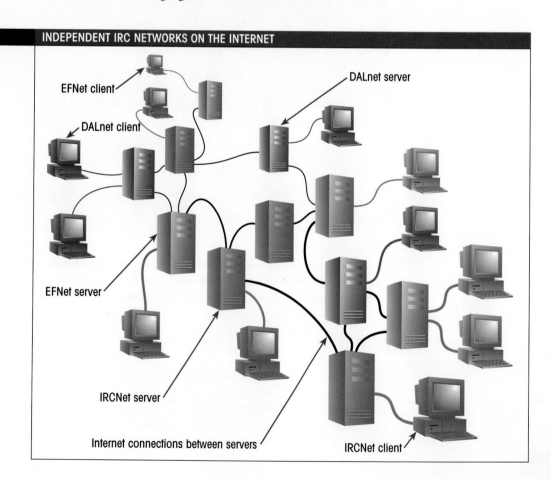

EFNet client

DALnet server

DALnet client

EFNet server

IRCNet server

Internet connections between servers

IRCNet client

Chat participants usually run special IRC client software on their computers, although some IRC networks allow clients to connect to their servers using Telnet. IRC client programs often include features such as scripts for commonly used chat commands that can make using IRC easier.

IRC networks organize the chats that they carry by topic. Each topic area is called a **channel**, and participants who connect to an IRC network join specific channels in which they conduct their chats. Most IRC networks allow participants to join and participate in several chats simultaneously using *one* connection. Users who have joined a channel receive all messages sent to that channel. Each channel has a name, or a **channel heading**, that indicates the chat's topic using the pound sign (#). For example, a channel in which participants discuss current political issues might have a channel heading of #politics. Most IRC networks maintain lists of their channels, but these lists are never current because chat participants can create new channels at any time. When the last participant leaves, the channel is closed.

When a participant creates a new channel, he or she becomes responsible for managing the channel and is called the **channel operator**, **channel op**, or **IRCop**. The channel operator has rights that other participants who join the channel later do not have. For example, a channel operator can change the channel's topic and heading at any time. The channel operator determines which users may participate in the channel and can change whether the channel is public or private. IRC networks give these powers to channel operators so that each channel can operate smoothly and stay focused on a specific topic. Channel operators can expel users from a channel temporarily or ban them permanently. The high degree of authority that channel operators are granted conveys a responsibility, as well. IRC networks expect channel operators to assist participants who experience problems accessing or using their channels.

IRC participants select nicknames when they log on to an IRC server. The nickname must be unique and cannot be in use anywhere else on that IRC network. A channel operator's nickname is preceded by an "at" symbol (@). IRC servers run automated programs, called **IRC robots** or **bots**, that perform routine services on the IRC system. For example, a bot might announce a new channel participant's entry or respond to participants' help requests. Other bots perform more sophisticated functions, such as detecting banned participants who try to rejoin a channel. Some bots can even detect behavior that violates channel rules (such as profane language or excessive repetition of the same phrase to jam the channel) and automatically expel the offending participant.

Using IRC

Most people connect to an IRC server by using IRC client software on their computer. Many IRC programs are inexpensive shareware programs that you can download from Web pages. Hyperlinks to some of those Web pages appear in the Additional Information section of the Student Online Companion for this tutorial. The computers at your school might already have an IRC client program installed; ask your instructor or technical support person for more information. No matter which IRC client program you use, you will find the commands that appear in Figure 8-3 to be helpful.

Figure 8-3	COMMONLY USED IRC COMMANDS
COMMAND	**EFFECT**
/away	Tells other channel participants that you have left your computer temporarily.
/help	Presents a list of commands for which the IRC server maintains a Help file.
/ignore *nickname*	Suppresses the display of messages from the user with *nickname*.
/invite *nickname #channelname*	Sends a message to the user with *nickname* asking him or her to join you on the *channelname* channel.
/join *#channelname*	Adds you to the *channelname* channel; if such a channel does not exist, this command creates one.
/leave *#channelname*	Removes you from the *channelname* channel.
/msg *nickname*	Sends a private message to the user with *nickname*.
/names *#channelname*	Displays a list of participants in the *channelname* channel.
/nick *newname*	Changes your nickname to *newname*.
/quit	Closes your connection to the IRC server.
/who *#channelname*	Displays the e-mail addresses of participants in the *channelname* channel.

Internet Chat

In addition to IRC, there are other programs that use the Internet for chat communication links but do not connect to IRC servers. These Internet chat client programs require that each person in the chat have a copy of the program and be connected to the Internet. ICQ (pronounced "I seek you") is one of the most popular Internet chat clients available. The software was created by a small Israeli company, Mirabilis, in 1996. America Online (AOL) purchased the software in 1998 and has continued to offer it as freeware.

To find ICQ client software on the Web:

1. Start your Web browser, and then go to the Student Online Companion page by entering the URL **http://www.course.com/newperspectives/internet2** in the appropriate location in your Web browser. Click the hyperlink for your book, click the **Tutorial 8** link, and then click the **Session 8.1** link.

2. Click the **CNET** link to open the CNET home page. CNET includes information about a number of different Internet chat client programs and offers downloads for many of them.

3. Click in the search box that appears near the top of the CNET home page, type **icq** (in lowercase letters), and then click the **Search** button.

4. Among the hyperlinks that appear on the search results page should be one titled **ICQ resource center**. Click that hyperlink to open the page shown in Figure 8-4.

Figure 8-4   ICQ RESOURCE CENTER

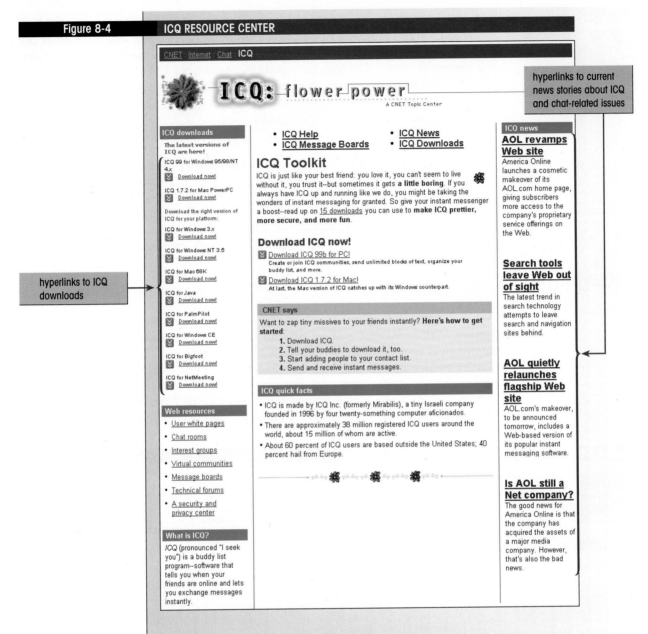

5. You can follow the links that appear on CNET's ICQ information page to learn more about the ICQ chat client program. Do not download any of the software unless you are using your own computer or your instructor or lab supervisor gives you permission to download and install software. When you have finished examining this page and its links, use your browser's Back button to move back through your history list until you return to the Student Online Companion page.

6. Click the **ICQ** hyperlink on the Student Online Companion page to open the official AOL information page for the software. You can explore the hyperlinks on the page that opens to find out more about ICQ. When you have finished browsing this site, use your browser's Back button to return to the Student Online Companion page.

7. AOL also offers a chat software program called AOL Instant Messenger (AIM). It was created originally by AOL to allow its members to chat with each other, but now AOL has made AIM available to anyone for use on the Web. You can learn more about the AIM Web chat client by clicking the AIM hyperlink on the Student Online Companion page and browsing the hyperlinks on the page that opens. When you have finished, use your browser's Back button to return to the Student Online Companion page.

Denise explains that IRC and Internet chat both continue to be popular with many users. AOL's "Instant Messaging" has also grown in popularity. However, as more people have access to Web browsers, a new kind of chat has emerged. Web sites that offer chat sessions do not need the IRC network, special IRC client software, Internet chat client software, or the AOL Instant Messenger software to function. You agree with Denise that Web chat might be a good alternative to IRC for many of MFact's intended uses.

Web-Based Chat

Web-based chat sites offer the same capabilities as text-based IRC chat networks and more. Further, Web-based chat is often easier to use. The Web's graphical user interface (GUI) environment provides helpful visual cues to the user that text-based IRC does not offer, even for participants using IRC client software. In addition to making chats more accessible to users, Web chat sites allow participants to include multimedia elements and hyperlinks in their messages. These multimedia elements can include pictures, audio clips, and video clips. Figure 8-5 shows a Web chat session in progress that includes multimedia elements.

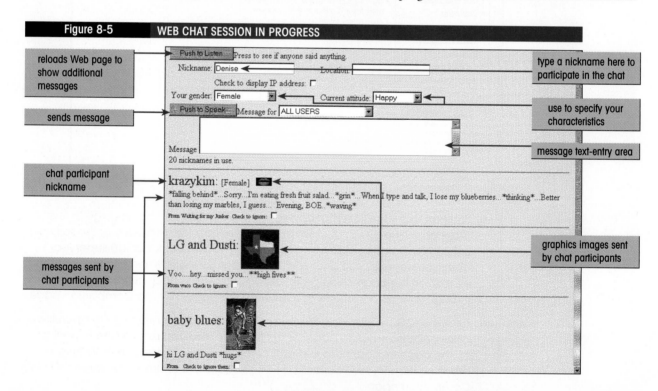

Figure 8-5   WEB CHAT SESSION IN PROGRESS

Figure 8-5 shows messages from three of the 20 participants in the chat. These three participants have chosen graphic images that they believe represent them in some way. This chat page also permits users to identify their genders and describe their attitudes by selecting text from the drop-down list boxes at the top of the page. You also can use these controls to specify a nickname, identify your location, and reload the Web page to see messages posted after you first open the page in your browser. The large message text-entry area lets you type a message, and the controls immediately above the text-entry area let you choose to send your message to all or specific chat participants. Note that the participants indicate actions or feelings by enclosing the text that describes them in asterisks (such as *grin*), which is a common practice on most Web chat sites.

MFact often conducts focus groups that discuss the package design of a new or improved product. You tell Denise that you can see how MFact might use Web chat's multimedia facilities to send pictures of the new package design to focus group participants in a chat session. Denise explains that she has worked with many businesses that send pictures of products and design drawings during private Web chat sessions with customers.

How Web Chat Works

Denise explains that a Web chat page loads into your Web browser just as any other Web page does. The page is constructed and reconstructed continually by Web chat server software in response to the messages that the site accepts from chat participants. The chat server software re-creates the page every time it accepts a message.

The operation of a Web chat server differs from that of an IRC network. A Web browser loads the chat site page from a Web server when you connect to it and then waits for your next command. When you connect to an IRC channel, you obtain a continuous flow of messages from the participants on that channel. If you leave your computer for a minute or two, you will find that your last message has scrolled off the screen of your IRC or Telnet client. To follow a Web chat, you must reload the Web chat page periodically from the Web server that is hosting the chat. You can reload the Web chat page by clicking your browser's Reload or Refresh button. (If you see a message asking if you want to repost from data, click the No button.) Many Web chat sites include reload buttons on the Web page itself; some Web chat sites automatically reload the page for you periodically.

Web chat servers accept messages and instructions from participants' Web browsers and convert those messages and instructions to HTML. The Web chat server then uses this HTML code to update the chat page and save it to a publicly accessible area on the Web chat server computer. Web chat site administrators can write instructions for accomplishing these tasks in one of several scripting languages or the Java programming language.

Using Web Chat

Denise suggests that you join a Web chat site to see how it works. There are many Web sites that offer chats, but most sites require you to register before you use their Web chat facilities. Some sites ask you to identify yourself on a registration page before admitting you to the Web chat pages. You should consider carefully whether to provide detailed personal information when you register because most current laws do not require a Web site administrator to maintain the confidentiality of your information. If one Web chat site requires information that you do not want to disclose, simply look for another site with a less intrusive registration page. One Web chat site that has a simple log-in procedure is the Lycos chat site.

REFERENCE WINDOW   **RW**

Entering a Lycos chat
- Open the Lycos chat page in your Web browser.
- Select a chat category.
- Register your user name and password.
- Select the Java Light page presentation option.
- Observe the conversation and send messages to other participants, if desired.

To enter a Lycos Web chat:

1. Click the **Lycos chat** hyperlink on the Session 8.1 Student Online Companion page and wait while your Web browser loads the Web page shown in Figure 8-6. The Web page you see will show different Upcoming Special Events from what appears in Figure 8-6.

Figure 8-6	LYCOS CHAT WEB PAGE

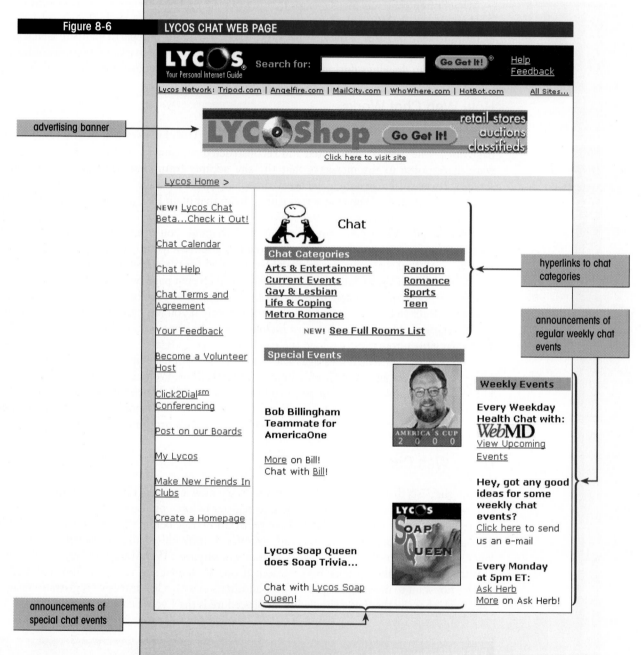

advertising banner

hyperlinks to chat categories

announcements of regular weekly chat events

announcements of special chat events

2. Click the **Random** category hyperlink to open the Lycos Random page. This page includes hyperlinks to a number of chats. Choose one of the categories, and then click its hyperlink. The Lycos registration page will open since you are a new user of this chat site.

3. Click the **Create a new account** hyperlink.

4. On the page that opens, type the name you would like to use in the User Name text box. Lycos does not permit duplicate names in its registry, so you should choose a name that includes numbers or is otherwise unusual.

5. Type your first name and last name in the text boxes with those titles, type a password in the Password text box, and then type your e-mail address in the Email Address text box.

6. Click the **Submit Profile** button to open the Lycos chat welcome page.

   TROUBLE? If Lycos sends a message that you have selected an existing user name, repeat Steps 4 through 6 using a different user name until you find one that is unique.

7. If necessary, click the **Remember my Username and Password for next time** check box to clear the check mark, if you are using a computer in your school's lab or any other computer to which another person has access.

8. Click the **Java Light** option button in the Please select a chat client section.

9. Click the **Enter Now** button. In a few moments, the Lycos Random Chat window opens, as shown in Figure 8-7. If the chat room has many users, you might have to wait several minutes to enter the chat.

Figure 8-7	PARTICIPATING IN A LYCOS RANDOM CHAT SESSION

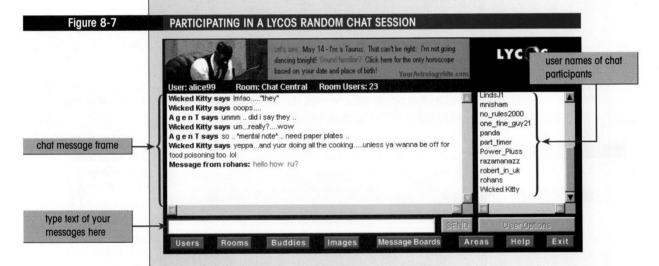

A list of the chat participants appears in the right frame of the Chat window. To participate in the chat, type the text of your message in the text box underneath the chat message frame and then click the Send button. In a few moments, you will see your message appear at the top of the chat message frame. Remember that most chats are not censored, so the text that you read might be offensive to you. If you find a chat room to be offensive, try clicking the Rooms button and follow one of the links to another chat room until you find one that you prefer.

10. When you have chatted enough to experience a Web chat server, click the **Exit** button to return to the main Lycos Chat page.

Denise explains that in a public Web chat site, such as the Lycos page, you cannot limit the participants to the people in which you are interested. However, you begin to understand the potential for effective discussion that a Web chat server might offer. You plan to meet with Isaac to describe how you believe that Web chat might be a useful tool for conducting focus groups and strategy meetings with clients.

Finding Web Chat Sites

The Web has thousands of sites that sponsor chats on topics that range from current movies to investing in the stock market. Many Web chat sites run separate chats for specific age groups. You are convinced that Web chat might be a good way to conduct focus groups with participants who cannot meet because of physical distance limitations, but you are also intrigued by the potential of Web chats as a resource for obtaining a sense of new trends in consumer preferences. Many of MFact's clients need to stay aware of changes in their customers' needs and tastes. These clients look to MFact as their marketing research expert for help in this area. You believe that visiting Web chats on topics related to client concerns might be a good way to get an informal sense of how consumer preferences might be changing.

You suspect that one way to find Web chat sites devoted to a particular topic would be to use a Web search engine and include the word *chat* in the search expression. When you discuss this idea with Denise, she explains that although search engine queries can often identify useful chat sites, there are several directories that provide organized lists of chat site hyperlinks. One of these directories is LookSmart. Isaac told you about a potential new client that is in the fitness and exercise equipment business. You decide to try the LookSmart directory as you search for information about current trends in this business.

To use the LookSmart directory to identify fitness Web chat sites:

1. Return to the Student Online Companion Web page for Session 8.1, and then click the **LookSmart Web Directory** hyperlink and wait while your Web browser loads the Web page.

2. Find the **Connecting** section of the Web page, and then click the **Chat** hyperlink . At this point, your screen should resemble Figure 8-8. (Your list of links might differ from those shown.)

Figure 8-8	USING THE LOOKSMART WEB DIRECTORY TO FIND WEB CHATS ON FITNESS TOPICS

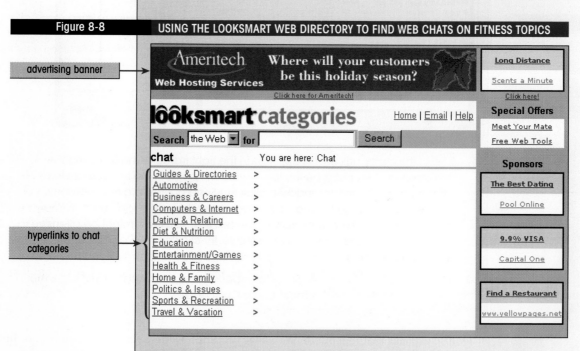

3. Click the **Health & Fitness** hyperlink in the Chat by Subject list to open a page of hyperlinks that lead to Web chat sites on related topics.

The descriptions for each hyperlink tell you more about the nature of the chat to which it leads. Some of the links you see should describe Web chats scheduled to occur in the near future with fitness and health experts. You can follow some of the links and read more about the chat sites or even participate in one or two of the chats, if you wish.

You can find other directories of Web chat sites by subject. Most Web directories offer some kind of chat site list. However, chat site lists sorted by subject often include hyperlinks to general information Web pages for IRC networks along with actual Web chat sites, which can make such lists difficult to use. You will use a Yahoo! chat site list next.

To use lists of Web chat sites:

1. Return to the Student Online Companion Web page for Session 8.1, and then click the **Yahoo! Chat by Subject** hyperlink and wait while your Web browser loads the Web page.

2. Follow some of the category and chat list links on the page. You will find many Web pages that are not chat sites. These Web pages either provide descriptions of IRC channels or require you to download and install software before you can use the site's Web chat pages. However, some of the links do lead to Web chat sites that use HTML pages or Java programs and thus do not require you to download and install additional software.

3. Click the **Back** button on your Web browser to return to the Student Online Companion, and then click the **Yahoo! Web Chat** hyperlink and wait while your browser loads the page. Examine the list of Web chat clients and notice that it is not listed by subject. To find chats on subjects in which you are interested, you must follow the links and evaluate each chat site.

You are somewhat disappointed to find that Web chat sites devoted to specific topics are not easy to locate. After discussing this with Denise, you realize that MFact will likely use Web chat as a tool to conduct focus groups and virtual meetings with clients and research staff in remote locations. Thus, the lack of easy-to-use subject listings of Web chat sites will not impair MFact's ability to use Web chat as a tool for cutting costs and providing better service to clients.

Virtual **Worlds**

Computer games date back to the early days of computing research. Computer scientists amused themselves by creating puzzles and other games that would run on their computers. One of these games, Adventure, became very popular and was widely duplicated, improved, and expanded. In the basic adventure game, the player's goal is to find hidden treasure. The player travels through virtual time and space, gathering clues and tools that will aid in the quest. As adventure games became more sophisticated, the virtual time and space through which the player traveled became more complex. The game programs started including characters that could interact with the game player. Many computer games sold today still use variations of this adventure theme.

MUDs, MOOs, and Similar Programs

The creation of the interconnected networks that eventually became the Internet allowed game players to interact with each other across time and space using their computers. Players at multiple sites on the network could participate in the same games and, in some cases, could replace the preprogrammed characters in the games. Other adventure-theme games pitted multiple participants against each other in a race to acquire the game's treasure. In 1979, an Essex University student named Roy Trubshaw wrote a multiuser adventure game program that ran on the university's experimental packet-switched network. He called his program **multiuser dungeon** (**MUD**). The university network was connected to the U.S. ARPANET and, later, to the JANET academic network in Great Britain.

The original MUD program became very popular on these networks during the 1980s. Because many of the players were computer scientists and programmers, some of them worked to improve and modify the program. Most of these MUDs were virtual worlds with fixed rules and features. Each program had dragons to slay, lanterns to carry, inscriptions to decipher, and gold to find. By 1990, new forms of the program were being created that allowed participants to modify the game's structure as they played it. Some of these programs used object-oriented programming techniques, which make programming easier by allowing the reuse of program modules. These programs were called **MUD, object oriented**, or **MOOs**.

The creative and building nature of these programs led to a decreased emphasis on the battles and quests for treasure that had characterized the early MUDs. MOOs that were highly oriented toward creative tasks and programming objectives were called **multiuser shared hallucinations**, or **MUSHs**. In these user-extensible programming environments, many players spend most of their time creating new virtual spaces, objects, and puzzles for other participants to enjoy.

Using a Text-Based Virtual World

A number of text-based MUDs and MOOs remain in operation after many years. Some of these virtual worlds have created very formal hierarchies of user authority with titles such as domain master and wizard. At many of these sites, you must apply for permission to build objects. Many of these text-based virtual worlds let you use a common command set to interact with their objects and other participants. A list of some basic MUD/MOO commands is shown in Figure 8-9.

Figure 8-9	SOME BASIC MUD/MOO COMMANDS
COMMAND	**ACTION**
: *action*	Tells other participants that you are engaging in *action*.
@examine *object*	Provides detailed information about the *object*, including its name, owner's name, description, contents, and a list of actions you can perform on it.
@look *object*	Provides a description of the *object* you specify; if you omit *object*, the command provides a description of the room or other virtual space that you currently occupy.
@quit	Exits the virtual world.
@who	Lists the names of current participants.
help *topicname*	Provides help on the *topicname* topic; if you omit *topicname*, the command provides a general Help listing.
north, south, east, west, up, down, out	Takes your character to other areas in your current virtual space or moves you to another. Most systems allow you to execute any of these commands by typing its first letter.
say *expression*	Informs other participants that you have spoken the words in *expression*; the double-quote character (") also issues this command.

You type these commands at the screen prompt after you enter a text-based virtual world. When participants use the *say* command to communicate with each other, the activity in a virtual world resembles that of an IRC channel. Virtual worlds, however, offer objects with which you can interact. Even if there are no other participants in a virtual world room when

you enter it, you still can interact with the objects that exist in that room. One popular text-based virtual world is ChibaMOO, which is based on William Gibson's science-fiction novel, *Neuromancer*.

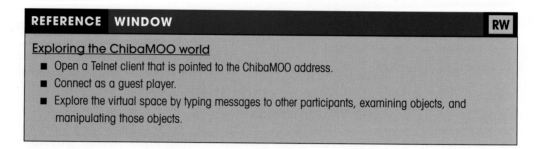

REFERENCE   WINDOW   **RW**

Exploring the ChibaMOO world
- Open a Telnet client that is pointed to the ChibaMOO address.
- Connect as a guest player.
- Explore the virtual space by typing messages to other participants, examining objects, and manipulating those objects.

To explore ChibaMOO:

1. Return to the Student Online Companion Web page for Session 8.1, and then click the **ChibaMOO** hyperlink. Your Web browser launches a Telnet client and, after a few moments, your screen resembles Figure 8-10.

Figure 8-10	CHIBAMOO WELCOME SCREEN

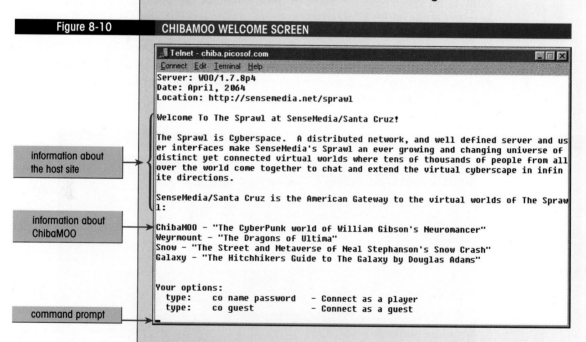

2. Type **co guest**, and then press the **Enter** key to connect to the ChibaMOO system as a guest user. The screen informs you that you are in the Visitor's Center and encourages you to explore the ChibaMOO world. Try some of the commands listed in Figure 8-9. The objects in the Visitor's Center change from time to time, but there usually are a few objects with which a new guest player can interact. You can move to other areas of the ChibaMOO world using the movement commands.

TROUBLE? You might not be able to see your typed commands until you press the Enter key. If you find that you typed a command incorrectly, retype it and then press the Enter key again.

> **3.** When you have finished exploring the ChibaMOO world, type **@quit** and then press the **Enter** key. Disconnect and close your Telnet window. If you are asked if you want to save, click **No**.

You are intrigued by the possibilities of using virtual worlds such as the ChibaMOO site for some types of marketing research studies, but you are concerned that the text-based interface might be difficult for some participants to use. Denise explains that newer virtual spaces have been created on the Web that offer more sophisticated interfaces.

GUI Virtual Worlds

A GUI extends the potential of virtual worlds because participants can interact with each other almost as they would in real life. The GUI allows each participant to assume a virtual physical existence and appearance. Such an artificial persona is called an **avatar**. A participant's avatar can be any kind of graphic that the participant would like to use as his or her online representation. Usually, avatars resemble comic-book characters, but other forms are possible. Some firms will, for a fee, create an avatar based on a photo that you provide.

Many of the virtual worlds that incorporate GUIs require that you install special client software on your computer. Some of these programs are standalone programs; your Web browser can run others. However, there are a few Web sites that offer GUI virtual worlds implemented in the Java programming language. Most current Web browsers are Java-enabled and can access these sites without requiring additional software. One of these Java-based virtual worlds is U&I Interactive's VisitMe site. This firm charges a monthly fee if you create a room at the site, but you can visit a demonstration version of the site and try many of its features for free. Figure 8-11 shows a room at the VisitMe site with three avatars present.

| Figure 8-11 | VISITME VIRTUAL-REALITY DEMONSTRATION SITE |

You have gathered a great deal of information about how MFact might be able to incorporate chat facilities and virtual world simulations into its business activities.

Session 8.1 QUICK CHECK

1. Entering a chat and reading the messages posted by other participants without joining the discussion is called _____.

2. True or False: A data packet from an IRC client on one network might travel through another IRC network server.

3. True or False: The owners of the IRC network appoint IRC channel operators.

4. Name one advantage and one disadvantage of using Web chat instead of IRC.

5. To see the most current messages on a Web chat site, you often must _____ the Web page.

6. The original virtual worlds on computer networks were multiplayer versions of _____-type games.

7. True or False: You can use FTP client software to connect to a text-based MUD or MOO virtual world on the Internet.

8. Virtual worlds on the Web that provide a GUI often allow participants to assume an on-screen persona, or a(n) _____.

Before you finish your search activities and prepare your report to Isaac, Denise suggests that you also consider the potential of another Internet-based tool, Usenet newsgroups.

SESSION 8.2

In this session you will learn how to search Usenet newsgroups to gather information and find answers to specific questions. You also will learn how to post newsgroup articles and reply to existing newsgroup articles.

Usenet Newsgroups

Denise tells you that the **Usenet News Service**, or **Usenet**, was founded in 1979 at Duke University as a way of collecting information and storing that information by topic category. The original Usenet News Service was devoted to transmitting computing news and facilitating discussions among employees of university computing facilities on topics such as operating systems and programming languages.

The topic categories on Usenet originally were called **newsgroups** or **forums**. Many people still use these terms when they refer to Usenet categories, but another term, **Internet discussion groups**, is also becoming popular. Most of these newsgroups are available to the general public; however, some newsgroups are limited to users at a specific site or to those affiliated with a particular organization. Each site that participates in Usenet has the option of selecting which newsgroups it will carry. Therefore, not all newsgroups—even the public ones—are available on every computer system that is connected to Usenet.

Usenet Is Not a Mailing List

Usenet was one of the first large, distributed information databases in the world. A **distributed database** is stored in multiple physical locations, with portions of the database replicated in different locations. The multiple physical locations do not, however, each store a complete copy of the database. Usenet is probably the largest decentralized information utility in the world

today. There are over 50,000 newsgroups in existence, and messages that total hundreds of megabytes are added to Usenet newsgroups each day. In practice, people use the terms *Usenet*, *Usenet News*, and *newsgroups* interchangeably when referring to this large distributed database.

Newsgroups are similar to mailing lists in that they accept messages from users and make them generally available to other users. However, newsgroups do not use the e-mail list technique of forwarding copies of submitted messages to subscribers. Instead, a newsgroup stores messages on an electronic bulletin board as **articles** or **postings** that are sorted by topic. Users who are interested in learning about a particular topic can connect to the bulletin board and read the posted newsgroup articles. Therefore, newsgroups are more suitable for discussions of broad topics that might interest a large audience because they do not require a server to send a separate e-mail message to each potential reader. Each person reads the same copy of the posted article on the newsgroup bulletin board. This subtle difference between how newsgroups and mailing lists operate was critical in the early days of Usenet because bandwidth and computing power were limited, expensive resources.

When users read Usenet articles to which they would like to respond, they can reply to that article. If a Usenet article is particularly interesting to many newsgroup readers, it might generate hundreds of responses within a day or two. These responses, in turn, might generate even more responses on the same issue. Most newsgroups have discussions occurring on many different issues simultaneously. A series of postings on a particular issue is called a **thread**. Participants in newsgroups use various types of newsreader software to organize postings by thread within each discussion group.

Some newsgroups have a moderator who reviews all postings before they appear in the newsgroup. These moderated lists tend to focus on technical or specialized topics. Moderators provide a valuable service to Usenet by reducing the number of off-topic postings and messages sent by persons who do not have the necessary qualifications to make a contribution to advanced-level or highly technical discussions.

Usenet Structure

Usenet is a network of computers called **news servers**. This network operates without any central control authority. When a user sends a posting to a particular Usenet newsgroup, it is routed to the news server computer site that has agreed to maintain that newsgroup. The news server stores all of the articles for that newsgroup. News servers share their public newsgroups with each other. Periodically—daily, hourly, or even more frequently—news servers connect to other news servers and compare a list of the articles that each currently is storing. Each newsgroup article has a unique identifying number that makes this comparison possible. After this comparison, each news server obtains copies of the articles it does not have. This store-and-forward process is called obtaining a **newsfeed**. Large news servers often maintain a continuous newsfeed connection to other large news servers to maintain the currency of their newsgroup article inventory.

Each news server site employs a **news administrator**, who specifies which other news servers will be newsfeed providers and newsfeed recipients. The news administrator also chooses which newsgroups to carry. Because newsgroups are so large, computer file storage space can be a constraint. Computer sites that operate news servers include most Internet service providers (ISPs), universities, large businesses, government units, and other large organizations. In response to the large volume of newsgroup postings, most news servers regularly delete articles after a short period of time. The news administrator is responsible for setting the deletion schedule.

The transmission of newsgroup traffic between news servers originally occurred over leased telephone lines dedicated to that task. Now, however, most newsfeeds occur over the Internet. Newsfeeds use the **Network News Transfer Protocol** (**NNTP**), which is part of the TCP/IP protocol suite that is used by all computers connected to the Internet. News servers' universal use of this standard protocol makes it possible for Usenet to function without a central controlling authority.

Newsgroup Hierarchies

Newsgroups are organized into topical hierarchies in which each newsgroup has a unique name that shows its position and classification in the hierarchy. Top-level hierarchies are shown as the first part of a newsgroup's name and then the subcategories follow; these two names are separated from the top-level hierarchy name and each other by periods. For example, one newsgroup that includes discussions of organic chemistry issues is named *sci.chem.organic*. This newsgroup's name shows that it is classified in the top-level category *science* (sci), the science subcategory *chemistry* (chem), and the chemistry subcategory *organic*. The original Usenet News Service included the eight main top-level categories—including one miscellaneous category for alternative topics—that appear in Figure 8-12.

Figure 8-12	ORIGINAL USENET NEWS SERVICE TOP-LEVEL CATEGORIES

CATEGORY	INCLUDES TOPICS RELATED TO
comp	Computers
rec	Recreation and entertainment
sci	Science
soc	Social issues and socializing
news	Operation and administration of Usenet
talk	Conversations, debates, and arguments
misc	Miscellaneous topics that do not fall within other categories
alt	Alternative and controversial topics

As Usenet grew, the hierarchy of categories that served the original participants—employees of university computing departments—were no longer sufficient to classify the wide range of topics that were being discussed in the newsgroups. Usenet developed a procedure for proposing and voting on the creation of new newsgroups for all categories except the alternative category, which allows users to create new categories at will. Any person can initiate Usenet's official procedure for adding new newsgroups or categories. All new categories must conform to the existing Usenet hierarchical structure. A portion of the hierarchy under business (biz) appears in Figure 8-13.

Figure 8-13	PORTION OF THE HIERARCHICAL STRUCTURE OF THE BIZ CATEGORY

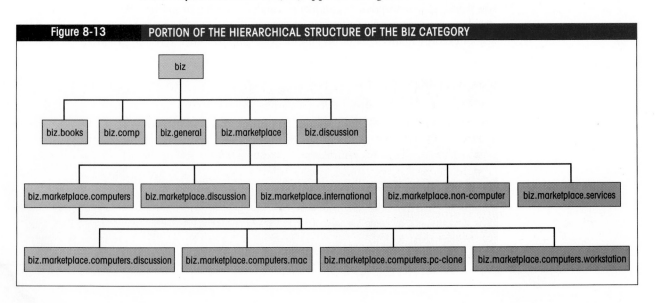

Business (biz) is one of the top-level categories that was added to the original eight categories to accommodate the growing interest of Usenet participants in business matters. The second-level categories include newsgroups devoted to, for example, books about business (biz.books) and about using computers in business (biz.comp). The biz.marketplace category, which includes discussions of how to use newsgroups to conduct business, includes subcategories for newsgroups devoted to buying and selling computers and computer parts through newsgroups (biz.marketplace.computers), conducting international business through newsgroups (biz.marketplace.international), and so on. The biz.marketplace.computers subcategory is further divided into separate subcategories for newsgroups about doing business for specific computer parts, such as the Macintosh (biz.marketplace.computers.mac) or Windows-Intel and similar computers (biz.marketplace.computers.pc-clone).

You tell Denise that newsgroups look as if they might offer a great deal of useful information that MFact could use, but you are concerned about searching through something the size of Usenet. You explain that the hierarchical approach to classifying information makes sense for smaller databases, but for something this large, even the categories might not help. Denise tells you that your fears are well founded and that several businesses have developed tools for searching newsgroups effectively. Two of these firms allow users to read and search newsgroups from their Web sites.

Web Access to Newsgroups

Denise explains that when the Usenet News Service began operating in 1979, the only way to read or post to newsgroups was to run newsreader software on your computer. **Newsreaders** were programs designed for the sole purpose of communicating with news server computers. More recently, e-mail client programs began to include newsreader features. (You will learn how to use two e-mail clients to read and post to newsgroups later in this session.) The most recent improvement in Usenet accessibility has been the emergence of Web sites that archive newsgroup articles. These Web sites offer search engines that make finding articles on specific topics much easier than was previously possible.

Liszt Newsgroups Directory

Originally, the Liszt Web Directory was devoted to archiving and indexing Internet mailing lists. The Liszt Web Directory has added IRC channels and Usenet newsgroups to its databases. You can browse the hierarchical structure of Usenet or use Liszt's search engine to find specific articles on topics in which you are interested. As you recall from your last conversation with Isaac, MFact was working on a proposal to conduct research for a chain of specialty retail-clothing stores. You decide to see what kind of information exists in Usenet about the fashion industry that MFact's account representatives might find useful as they prepare their research proposal.

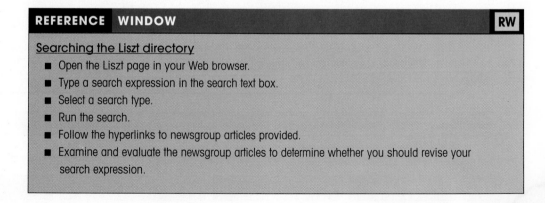

REFERENCE   WINDOW   **RW**

<u>Searching the Liszt directory</u>
- Open the Liszt page in your Web browser.
- Type a search expression in the search text box.
- Select a search type.
- Run the search.
- Follow the hyperlinks to newsgroup articles provided.
- Examine and evaluate the newsgroup articles to determine whether you should revise your search expression.

To search the Liszt Directory for fashion industry information:

1. Start your Web browser, and then go to the Student Online Companion page by entering the URL **http://www.course.com/newperspectives/internet2** in the appropriate location in your Web browser. Click the hyperlink for your book, click the **Tutorial 8** link, and then click the **Session 8.2** link. Click the **Liszt Newsgroups Directory** link and wait while the browser loads the page shown in Figure 8-14.

| Figure 8-14 | LISZT'S USENET NEWSGROUPS DIRECTORY PAGE |

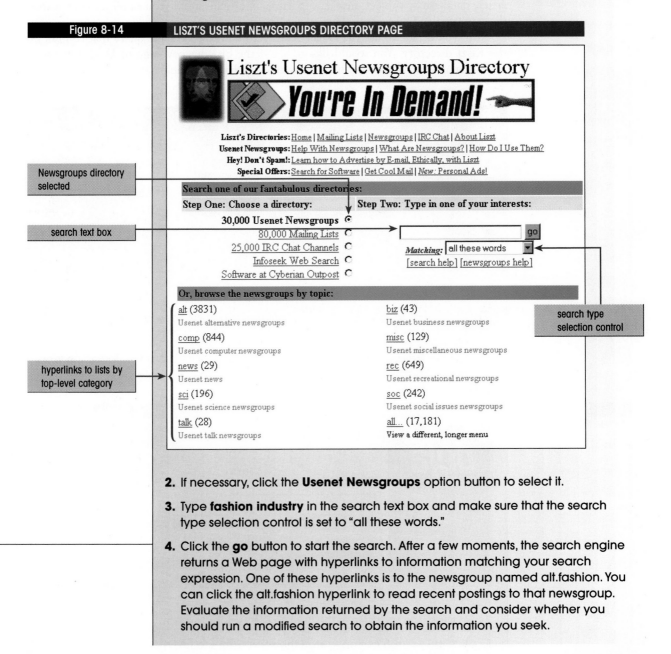

Newsgroups directory selected

search text box

hyperlinks to lists by top-level category

search type selection control

2. If necessary, click the **Usenet Newsgroups** option button to select it.

3. Type **fashion industry** in the search text box and make sure that the search type selection control is set to "all these words."

4. Click the **go** button to start the search. After a few moments, the search engine returns a Web page with hyperlinks to information matching your search expression. One of these hyperlinks is to the newsgroup named alt.fashion. You can click the alt.fashion hyperlink to read recent postings to that newsgroup. Evaluate the information returned by the search and consider whether you should run a modified search to obtain the information you seek.

Denise tells you that there are other directories that store and index newsgroup articles besides the Liszt site. One Web site that can be very helpful is the Deja.com directory of Usenet newsgroups.

Deja.com Directory

The **Deja.com** directory is an advertiser-supported Web site that offers many useful tools for accessing Usenet newsgroups. One of the drawbacks of using newsgroup articles for serious research is that most news servers delete articles fairly frequently—often within days, and almost always within several weeks. Deja.com does not delete newsgroup articles. It has stored over 100 million newsgroup articles dating from 1995 in its database and plans to continue adding older articles going all the way back to Usenet's origin in 1979. More important is that the Deja.com site has a search engine that allows you to query its newsgroup article database by subject, newsgroup name, or article author. You can limit your search by these criteria and by posting date.

Next, you decide to use the Deja.com directory to run the same query that you ran using the Liszt directory. You would like to see if the broader coverage of Deja.com provides additional information about the fashion industry that might help MFact prepare its proposal.

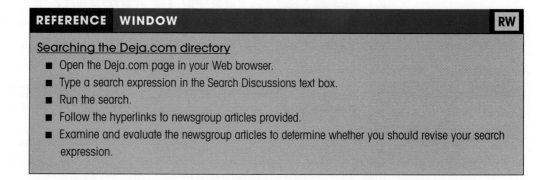

REFERENCE WINDOW   RW

Searching the Deja.com directory

- Open the Deja.com page in your Web browser.
- Type a search expression in the Search Discussions text box.
- Run the search.
- Follow the hyperlinks to newsgroup articles provided.
- Examine and evaluate the newsgroup articles to determine whether you should revise your search expression.

To search Deja.com for fashion-industry information:

1. Return to the Student Online Companion Web page for Session 8.2, and then click the **Deja.com** hyperlink and wait while your Web browser loads the Web page shown in Figure 8-15. (Your page might look different.)

Figure 8-15   DEJA.COM NEWSGROUPS ARCHIVE WEB SITE

2. Type **fashion industry** in the Search Discussions text box.

3. Click the **Search** button to start the search. After a few moments, the search engine returns a Web page with hyperlinks to information matching your search expression.

4. You notice that Deja News returns a list of individual news articles in addition to the newsgroup names that the Liszt directory returned. You can click the article hyperlinks to read individual newsgroup postings related to the fashion industry. To obtain a more complete list of discussion groups on topics related to the fashion industry, click the **View All** hyperlink that appears above the list of Discussion Forums found. Evaluate the information returned by the search and consider whether you will need to run a modified search to obtain the information you seek.

5. When you have finished reading the newsgroup postings, return to the Student Online Companion page for Session 8.2.

After reviewing the information provided by the two different searches, you conclude that the Liszt directory and the Deja News site each offer a different view of the current fashion scene. You found information in both searches that might be helpful to MFact as it prepares the client proposal.

Using Newsreaders

After learning how to find newsgroup articles and reading a few of them, you become interested in finding out how to post articles of your own to newsgroups that you find interesting. Denise explains that you must use some type of newsreader software to reply to articles or to post original messages. The Deja News Web site includes a built-in newsreader facility that you can use if you register with the site. Also, both Netscape and Microsoft include newsreader software in their Web browser suites.

Note: If you are using Netscape Navigator as your Web browser, complete the steps under the "Netscape Messenger Newsreader" heading. If you are using Microsoft Internet Explorer as your browser, complete the steps under the "Microsoft Outlook Express Newsreader" heading.

Netscape Messenger Newsreader

The **Netscape Messenger newsreader** software is included with the Netscape Communicator software suite. There are several ways to start Messenger, but the easiest way to start it is from the Navigator browser window.

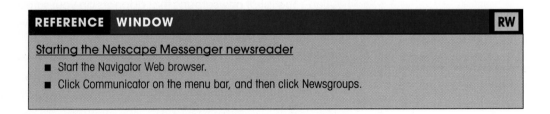

REFERENCE WINDOW   **RW**

Starting the Netscape Messenger newsreader
- Start the Navigator Web browser.
- Click Communicator on the menu bar, and then click Newsgroups.

To start the Messenger newsreader:

1. Click **Communicator** on the menu bar, and then click **Newsgroups**. The Netscape Message Center window opens, as shown in Figure 8-16.

Figure 8-16 NETSCAPE MESSAGE CENTER WINDOW

news folder icon

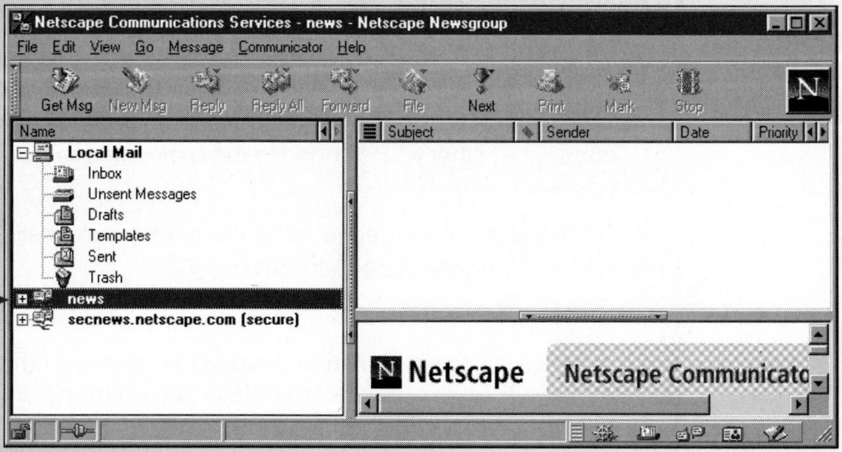

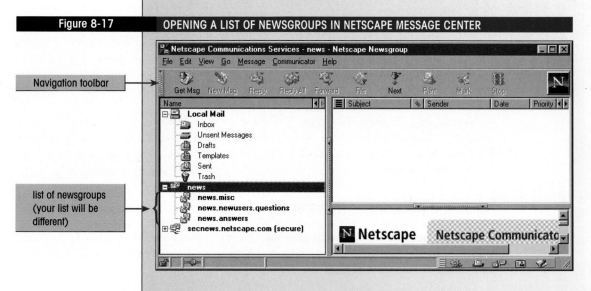

2. Double-click the **news folder icon** to open a list of newsgroups for your computer, as shown in Figure 8-17.

Figure 8-17 OPENING A LIST OF NEWSGROUPS IN NETSCAPE MESSAGE CENTER

Navigation toolbar

list of newsgroups (your list will be different)

TROUBLE? The list of newsgroups that appears on your screen will be different from the list that appears in Figure 8-17, depending on which newsgroups other computer users have selected.

TROUBLE? If you haven't selected any newsgroups on your computer, then you won't see a plus box in front of the news folder (see Figure 8-16). If this happens, read the material that follows without completing the steps at the computer.

TROUBLE? If your computer displays an error message stating that "No NNTP server is configured," ask your instructor or technical support person to add the name of your host's news server to the Netscape installation on that computer.

You can use the Netscape Message Center window to read, reply to, and create your own newsgroup articles. The news.misc newsgroup provides a place where new users can send test messages and otherwise become familiar with the operation of newsreader software.

REFERENCE   WINDOW   RW

Reading and sending articles using Messenger

- Start Navigator.
- Click Communicator on the menu bar, and then click Newsgroups.
- In the left frame of the Netscape Message Center window, double-click the icon of the newsgroup that you would like to open.
- Click messages in the newsgroups pane to read them, or click the New Msg button on the Navigation toolbar button to send a message to the selected newsgroup.

To read and send articles using Messenger:

1. Double-click the **news.misc** icon in the left frame of the Netscape Message Center window. If a Download Headers dialog box appears, click the option button to Download __ Headers, enter **50** in the text box, then click the **Download** button. The top pane of the window displays message headings and the bottom pane of the window displays the contents of the selected message, as shown in Figure 8-18.

Figure 8-18	READING MESSAGES IN MESSENGER

selected message header

selected newsgroup

message text appears in bottom pane

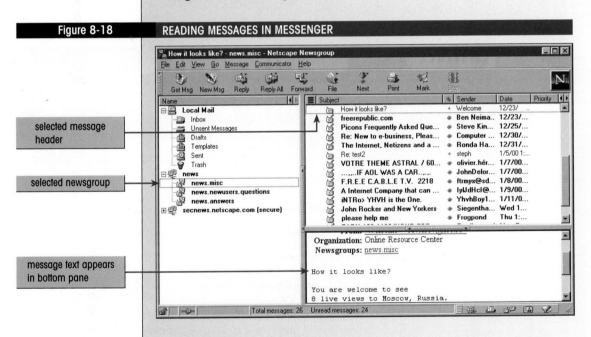

TROUBLE? The messages that appear in the list on your screen will be different from those that appear in Figure 8-18.

To read a message, click the message header in the top pane of the newsreader window. The bottom pane will display the text of the message.

2. To reply to a message, click the message header in the top pane of the newsreader window of the message to which you would like to reply.

3. Click the **Reply** button on the Navigation toolbar to post your reply to the newsgroup. You can click the **Reply All** button to send your reply to the sender and the newsgroup.

4. To post your own original message to the newsgroup, click the **New Msg** button on the Navigation toolbar.

5. When you have finished experimenting with reading, replying to, and sending messages to newsgroups, click **File** on the menu bar, and then click **Close** to close Messenger.

6. Close your Web browser and your dial-up connection, if necessary.

Because the Netscape newsreader uses the Netscape Messenger e-mail software for sending and replying to messages, you can apply the skills you learned in Tutorial 2 to working with newsgroups. You also already know how to save and print newsgroup articles because you performed these tasks for e-mail messages.

Microsoft Outlook Express Newsreader

The **Microsoft Outlook Express newsreader** is included as part of the Outlook Express e-mail software, which is part of the Microsoft Internet Explorer Web browser. There are several ways to start Outlook Express, but because you are already familiar with the Internet Explorer Web browser, it will be easy for you to start the Outlook Express newsreader from within Internet Explorer.

REFERENCE   WINDOW

<u>Starting the Microsoft Outlook Express newsreader</u>
- Open the Internet Explorer Web browser.
- Click the Mail button on the Standard Buttons toolbar.
- Click Read News on the drop-down menu that appears below the Mail button.

To start the Microsoft Outlook Express newsreader:

1. Click the **Mail** button on the Standard Buttons toolbar.

2. Click **Read News** on the drop-down menu that appears below the Mail button.

TROUBLE? If an Internet Connection Wizard dialog box opens, type your name as you want it to appear in the newsgroup, click the Next button, and then follow the remaining steps. Your instructor will provide you with your news server's name (the news server name at most, but not all, organizations is "news").

TROUBLE? If a Browse for Folder dialog box opens, accept the default folder and continue.

3. Click the **plus box** for the News icon in the left pane of the Outlook Express News window to expand the list of newsgroups so that your screen looks like Figure 8-19.

| Figure 8-19 | OUTLOOK EXPRESS NEWSREADER |

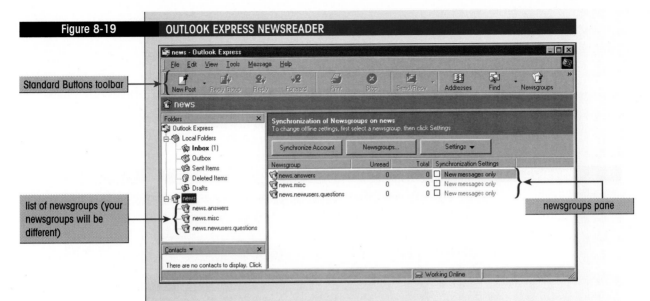

Standard Buttons toolbar

list of newsgroups (your newsgroups will be different)

newsgroups pane

TROUBLE? The list of newsgroups on your screen will be different from the list shown in Figure 8-19. Newsgroups that previous users of the computer on which you are working have used will appear in the list. If you or previous users of the computer have not read newsgroups, a dialog box will open and ask if you would like to view a list of available newsgroups. If this occurs, click the Yes button. Outlook Express will open its Newsgroups dialog box and download a list of newsgroups, which can take several minutes. When the list has finished loading, scroll down the list and click the news.misc newsgroup. Click the Subscribe button, and then click the OK button to close the Newsgroups dialog box.

TROUBLE? If your computer displays an error message stating that "No NNTP server is configured," ask your instructor or technical support person to add the name of your host's news server to the Outlook Express installation on that computer.

You can use the newsreader in the Outlook Express e-mail program to read, reply to, and create your own newsgroup articles. The news.misc newsgroup provides a place where new users can send test messages and otherwise become familiar with the operation of newsreader software.

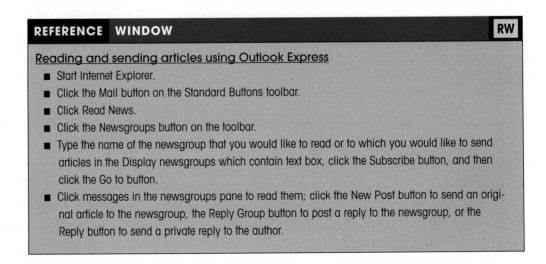

REFERENCE   WINDOW   **RW**

Reading and sending articles using Outlook Express
- Start Internet Explorer.
- Click the Mail button on the Standard Buttons toolbar.
- Click Read News.
- Click the Newsgroups button on the toolbar.
- Type the name of the newsgroup that you would like to read or to which you would like to send articles in the Display newsgroups which contain text box, click the Subscribe button, and then click the Go to button.
- Click messages in the newsgroups pane to read them; click the New Post button to send an original article to the newsgroup, the Reply Group button to post a reply to the newsgroup, or the Reply button to send a private reply to the author.

To read and send articles using Outlook Express:

1. Click the **Newsgroups** button on the toolbar.

2. Type **news.misc** in the Display newsgroups which contain text box, then click the **news.misc** icon that appears in the window. Click the **Subscribe** button, and then click the **Go to** button. The newsgroups pane of the window displays message headings and the message text pane displays the contents of the selected message, as shown in Figure 8-20.

| Figure 8-20 | READING A NEWSGROUP ARTICLE IN OUTLOOK EXPRESS |

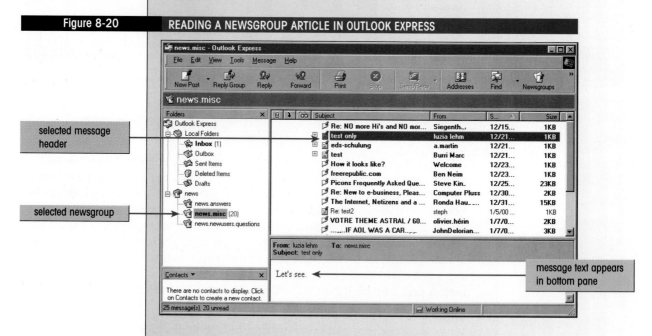

TROUBLE? The messages that appear in the list on your screen will be different from those that appear in Figure 8-20.

To read a message, click the message header in the newsgroups pane of the Outlook Express window. The message text pane will display the contents of the message.

3. To reply to a message, click the message header in the newsgroups pane of the message to which you would like to reply.

4. Click the **New Post** button on the toolbar to send an original article to the newsgroup, click the **Reply Group** button to post a reply to the newsgroup, or click the **Reply** button to send a private reply to the author.

5. When you have finished experimenting with reading, replying to, and sending messages to newsgroups, click **File** on the menu bar, and then click **Exit** to close Outlook Express.

6. Close your Internet Explorer and your dial-up connection, if necessary.

Because the Outlook Express newsreader is a part of the Outlook Express e-mail software, you can apply the skills you learned in Tutorial 2 to sending and replying to newsgroup articles. You also already know how to save and print newsgroup articles because you performed these tasks for e-mail messages.

You are convinced that Usenet newsgroups can offer MFact an excellent vehicle for obtaining current information about the business environments in which their clients operate. You also believe that newsgroups will give MFact a way to obtain detailed information about rapidly changing opinion among consumers that will interest MFact's market research staff and MFact's clients. You can see how MFact can use newsgroups and, particularly private newsgroups, to hold discussions among MFact employees, and between MFact and its clients, when scheduling online chat sessions or conference telephone calls is inconvenient.

Session 8.2 QUICK CHECK

1. True or False: The original function of the Usenet News Service was to transmit news reports for newspapers and network broadcasting companies.

2. Messages posted to a newsgroup are called _____.

3. A series of messages posted to a newsgroup that discuss the same subject is collectively called a(n) _____.

4. Most newsgroups allow anyone to post a message to the newsgroup. Some newsgroups, however, have a(n) _____ who reviews messages and only posts those messages that are relevant to the newsgroup's topic and/or from credible senders.

5. True or False: The news server computers in the Usenet network send newsfeeds to each other using a part of the Internet's TCP/IP protocol suite called the Network News Transfer Protocol (NNTP).

6. A friend tells you about some messages she read on the rec.autos.makers.honda newsgroup. What do you think is the focus of that newsgroup?

7. True or False: Most news servers in the Usenet network keep newsgroup messages for one year before deleting them.

8. _____ is a Web site that provides a search engine for finding newsgroups and newsgroup messages on specific topics.

9. To create a message or to reply to another user's message and post it to a newsgroup, you must use a(n) _____ program.

Isaac is impressed with the information you gathered about Usenet newsgroups. Now you are ready to continue your work by preparing a report of your findings so Isaac can evaluate the usefulness of the Internet's advanced communication tools for conducting MFact focus groups.

REVIEW ASSIGNMENTS

You met with Isaac and briefed him on what you learned about the Internet's advanced communication tools. Isaac is pleased with the work you have done and is interested in learning more about each tool. He realizes that chat, virtual worlds, and newsgroups each offer MFact an opportunity to conduct advanced communications within the firm and with worldwide clients, but Isaac wonders whether the participation in these public forums is truly global. To assess the breadth of participation in chat, virtual worlds, and newsgroups, Isaac asks you to undertake a research project that will provide some measure of breadth of participation.

Do the following:

1. Start your Web browser, go to the Student Online Companion (http://www.course.com/newperspectives/internet2), click the link for your book, click the Tutorial 8 link, and then click the Review Assignments link in the left frame.

2. Click the Lycos Chat hyperlink, log in, and open a chat that you find interesting.

3. Join the chat session and ask participants where they are physically located. Write down the name of the country or, if in the United States, the name of the state in which three participants are located.

4. After you have collected some location names, exit the chat.

5. Load your newsreader software from your browser.

6. Open the news.misc newsgroup.

7. Examine 10 or 20 of the postings to see if you can determine the country of the messages' origin and write down any origins that you can identify.

8. When you have finished, close your newsreader and Web browser, and then close your dial-up connection, if necessary.

9. Prepare a short summary of your findings.

CASE PROBLEMS

Case 1. Rockin' Tees   Laura Jensen is president of Rockin' Tees, a small manufacturer of printed T-shirts that specializes in creating designs using images of famous rock bands. Rockin' Tees either must purchase the rights to use band names and likenesses or must agree to pay negotiated per-shirt royalties to the bands. It is, therefore, important for Rockin' Tees to estimate the demand for their T-shirt designs before they negotiate with the bands' agents and agree to payment terms.

Do the following:

1. Start your Web browser, go to the Student Online Companion (http://www.course.com/newperspectives/internet2), click the link for your book, click the Tutorial 8 link, and then click the Case Problems link in the left frame.

2. Click the Yahoo! Music Chat link.

3. Explore the hyperlinks on the Yahoo! Web page and examine some of the Web sites to which they lead. Remember that you are collecting information for Laura, so keep focused on her research question.

4. When you have finished, close your Web browser and your dial-up connection, if necessary.

5. Write a short memo that explains how Laura might use surveys of Web chat activity on some of the chat sites you found to estimate the popularity of a particular band.

Case 2. Southern State University   Del Valerio is a professor of foreign languages at Southern State University (SSU). SSU has been facing budget cuts the past few years, and Del is concerned that the quality of foreign language instruction might be suffering at SSU. He is looking for inexpensive ways to improve students' exposure to written and spoken foreign languages. New audio and video tapes for the language lab have become very expensive, and additional reading materials written in foreign languages have just been cut from the library's budget for next year. Del asks you to use the Internet to find new language resources.

Do the following:

1. Start your Web browser, go to the Student Online Companion (http://www.course.com/newperspectives/internet2), click the link for your book, click the Tutorial 8 link, and then click the Case Problems link in the left frame.

2. Click the Lingua MOO link, and then examine the contents and links on that Web site.

3. Prepare a one-page report describing the kinds of things that a MOO-based virtual world site might offer the SSU foreign languages program. Be sure to address Del's budget concerns in your report.

4. When you have finished, close your Web browser and your dial-up connection, if necessary.

Case 3. West Park Employment Agency   Elaine Tagliaferri is the owner of the West Park Employment Agency. Elaine is always looking for new sources of employment leads and regularly scans the local and regional newspaper help-wanted ads. Unfortunately, most jobs that become available are never advertised. To identify these potential opportunities, Elaine also tries to stay aware of new businesses openings and larger firms that are moving operations to the area. Elaine asks you to help her find new job sources.

Do the following:

1. Start your Web browser, go to the Student Online Companion (http://www.course.com/newperspectives/internet2), click the link for your book, click the Tutorial 8 link, and then click the Case Problems link in the left frame.

2. Click the Deja News Browse Page link.

3. Assume that the West Park Employment Agency is located in your city or town. Browse through the newsgroup postings indexed at the Deja News Web site and identify three messages that provide leads that you would recommend to Elaine.

4. For one of the messages you identify, write a short reply to the posting's author or to the newsgroup. Do not send the message, but include it with copies of the three messages in a short report to your instructor.

5. When you have finished, close your Web browser and your dial-up connection, if necessary.

Case 4. Triangle Research   Dan Rivetti is the director of Triangle Research, a small laboratory that tests metal parts and assemblies using physical and computer models. Usually, Dan knows enough about the general design of the parts and assemblies that he can develop the testing procedures. Sometimes, however, he would like to conduct background research and contact experts in the field before designing his testing procedures. Dan has heard that Usenet newsgroups might offer the information and the opportunity to post inquiries that he desires, but he has also heard that some newsgroups are more reliable than others. Dan asks you to help him evaluate the quality of some newsgroups.

Do the following:

1. Start your Web browser, go to the Student Online Companion (http://www.course.com/newperspectives/internet2), click the link for your book, click the Tutorial 8 link, and then click the Case Problems link in the left frame.

2. Click the Liszt Science Newsgroups link.

3. Examine and follow some of the links on the Liszt Science Hierarchy Web page. You will notice that some of the links are identified as "Moderated."

4. Select a topic area that has at least one moderated and one unmoderated newsgroup.

5. Examine a sample of messages from each type of newsgroup devoted to the same topic.

6. Prepare a short report describing the differences you found between the postings in the moderated and unmoderated newsgroups. Include an explanation of which type of newsgroup would best serve Dan's needs.

7. When you have finished, close your Web browser and your dial-up connection, if necessary.

Case 5. Mt. Adams Family Counseling Center   Paige Beckett is a family therapist at the Mt. Adams Family Counseling Center. Paige works with parents and teenagers who are having serious problems communicating with each other. Often, her clients are having so many difficulties that they have trouble even being in the same room. She has become interested in the potential for virtual reality simulations as part of her therapies. Paige is thinking about putting each family member in a separate room with a computer and having them meet online in a virtual setting. She asks you to explore the VisitMe site to determine whether that site might provide settings for her virtual reality therapies.

Do the following:

1. Start your Web browser, go to the Student Online Companion (http://www.course.com/newperspectives/internet2), click the link for your book, click the Tutorial 8 link, and then click the Case Problems link in the left frame.

2. Click the VisitMe link.

3. Enter the Demo portion of the site and create an avatar.

4. Click the Guide button to open the Guide Window with its list of rooms.

5. Click a room to move your avatar to that location. Explore the room and write one paragraph describing the room and why you believe it would be a good or bad choice for Paige's purposes. In your evaluation, consider whether the room has enough space for several avatars to interact and whether the room is set up for group activities. Also consider whether the furnishings in the room would help or hinder discussions about family problems.

6. Use the Guide button to visit at least two other rooms. Write a similar paragraph for each room.

7. When you have finished, close your Web browser and your dial-up connection, if necessary.

QUICK CHECK ANSWERS

Session 8.1

1. lurking
2. True
3. False
4. Advantages: Do not need Telnet or IRC client software, messages can include multimedia elements and hyperlinks, GUI can be easier to use. Disadvantages: Must reload page to obtain new messages.
5. reload or refresh
6. adventure
7. False
8. avatar

Session 8.2

1. False
2. articles or postings
3. thread
4. moderator
5. True
6. The newsgroup's focus is probably on the features and styling of automobiles made by Honda.
7. False
8. Liszt or Deja.com
9. newsreader

ADVANCED
WEB TOPICS

Browser Extensions and
Internet Security

OBJECTIVES

In this tutorial you will:

- Learn how to enhance your Web browser's capabilities with browser extensions

- Discover where to locate popular browser extensions for Netscape Navigator and Microsoft Internet Explorer

- Find Web locations where you can test your browser's extensions

- Investigate Internet security and learn about secrecy, integrity, necessity, and privacy

- Identify several ways to defend against security risks

- Learn about copyright and intellectual property rights on the Internet

LABS

Multimedia

Remes Video Productions

Remes Video Productions (RVP) is a seven-person, full-service video-production facility that specializes in producing training and safety videos. RVP also consults on smaller jobs, such as producing wedding and family-reunion videos and taping other nonbusiness events. Located in Van Buren, Arkansas, RVP's business has grown steadily since Mark Remes, the company's CEO, founded it in 1993. Mark has acquired video cameras and sophisticated editing equipment to create professional-quality video productions.

Mark wants to expand his business outside the limited Van Buren market and increase his sales by 25 percent next year. One way to increase video-production sales is to increase RVP's market visibility. He has used print advertising successfully in the past, but now he needs to reach a larger audience. He is particularly interested in using the Internet to market RVP to Arkansas and the surrounding states.

Mark has hired you as a consultant, and your first job is to create a plan for a future Web presence with appealing Web pages, graphics, video clips, and sound. At first, Mark only wants you to help him understand the current capabilities of Web browsers to deliver rich and diverse Web content to potential customers. Mark has heard that Web browsers can handle graphics, sound, movies, and interactive graphics. He wants you to install the browser software enhancements that will run these exciting and dynamic forms of content. Mark wants you to show him examples of Web sites that provide various forms of rich content so he can decide which of them might be effective and attractive for RVP's Web pages. Of course, if RVP's Web pages will require any special software for viewers' Web browsers, Mark wants you to make it simple for RVP customers to download the required Web browser enhancements.

After you advise Mark about Web content enhancements, he wants to create a site that customers can use to request the company's services and pay a required 20 percent down payment using a credit card. Mark is concerned about security and wants you to update him about the possible threats unique to conducting business using the Internet.

SESSION 9.1

In this session you will learn about, find, and use browser extensions. You will learn about the browser languages Java, JavaScript, and ActiveX, which make plug-ins work in your browser. You will visit a few of the download sites that feature browser plug-ins and other browser accessories. Finally, you will visit a Web site that tests your installed browser accessories.

Browser Extensions

When the Web was being developed, Web browsers displayed only text and graphics. Very quickly, people actively browsing the Web expressed a desire for more Web page features, such as sound and animation. However, these features were then, and still are, beyond the capabilities of the HTML model that provides the accepted language for Web pages. Because of HTML limitations, companies developed their own software that enhanced the capabilities of Web browsers. These enhancements, called **plug-ins**, **helper applications**, **browser extensions**, or **helper apps**, allow your browser to do things it was not originally designed to do. Frequently, the plug-ins and helper applications are offered free of charge from different Web software developers whose sites require them to enhance the site's contents. **Browser extension players** deliver content to an end user. For example, browser extensions might deliver and play audio clips or display on-screen movies.

What Are Plug-ins and Helpers?

Plug-ins differ slightly from helper applications in the way they run. Whereas both plug-ins and helper applications enhance browsers and extend their capabilities, helper applications are independent programs that are stored on your computer and are activated automatically when needed. Plug-ins, on the other hand, do their work *inside* the browser and do not activate a standalone program that is stored on your computer. Many plug-ins began as helper applications; in fact, several helper applications have been reissued as plug-ins because they provide seamless activation from inside your browser. Another difference between plug-ins and helper apps is that unlike helper apps, plug-ins cannot execute by themselves. Plug-ins do not exist as independent programs; they can start only from within a browser. Helper apps, on the other hand, are useful in their own right. For example, spreadsheet programs can function as helper applications when a browser calls them to display a spreadsheet. When your browser encounters a MIDI sound file, for instance, the browser will start a MIDI player helper application on your computer to play it. Because your computer probably has a number of helper applications already installed, this tutorial concentrates on plug-ins, which are not always installed on your computer but are useful for displaying a variety of input and storage formats that you will encounter on the Web.

When you install a Web browser, usually many popular plug-ins are installed with it. When you encounter a Web page that requires a plug-in you do not have, you will see a message that a particular plug-in is required to view the element you have clicked. If you do not have the required plug-in, you can download or purchase it. The majority of plug-ins—and all of the plug-ins featured in this tutorial—are free.

You might wonder why most plug-ins are free. The companies and individuals offering free browser plug-ins often charge money for the plug-in content-development programs or for their server programs designed to *deliver* multimedia content. Plug-in **content-development programs** are the programs that are required to *create* content using that technology so that Web browsers have a file they can view, listen to, or play. For example, RealAudio offers a free plug-in named RealPlayer, which plays streaming audio files over the Internet. (Remember from Tutorial 5 that streaming is a technology that delivers a continuous flow of information from the server to your browser and allows you to play the information—audio, video, etc.—*before* the entire file has been downloaded to your browser.) Streaming can reduce the time required to play a file from several minutes to several seconds. RealPlayer works with most Web browsers. Besides RealPlayer, RealAudio offers a low-cost and more capable plug-in named RealPlayer Plus, which has more features and richer audio-playing capabilities. RealAudio also licenses server software that companies can install on their Web servers. The server-side software helps to deliver the streaming information. This arrangement works well because the Web browsing public can download and install free or inexpensive plug-ins that enhance their Web experiences, and companies can provide attractive and rich content on their Web sites that will attract new customers.

How Do Plug-ins Operate?

Each time you start your browser, it checks your computer to see which plug-ins you have installed. As you move from one Web site to another, your browser will encounter links that refer to files whose file extensions are *not* .htm or .html, which are the universal extensions for Web pages. Instead, your browser might encounter .zip or .mov files, for example. If your browser cannot interpret the filename you click, then it usually will prompt you to save the file on your computer. If you do have a plug-in that can interpret a file or link you click, then the plug-in will execute the appropriate action. For instance, if you click a link with the extension .mov (for a QuickTime movie file), the QuickTime plug-in starts, downloads the file, and plays a movie within the Web page—all automatically.

How Do You Know When You Need a Plug-in?

When you are viewing Web pages, you might encounter pages that indicate you need a particular browser plug-in to view or listen to the current page's content. If you do not have the required plug-in to play or listen to the content, nothing happens; you see only what your Web browser can display, without hearing a sound or seeing a video. For example, Figure 9-1 shows a Web page that displays animation and three-dimensional views of a scene. The user's browser is missing a required plug-in, so a small cube in a large frame appears instead of the scene that a plug-in would display. When you see icons or empty frames, similar to the ones that appear in Figure 9-1, you know that you are missing a plug-in.

| Figure 9-1 | WEB PAGE REQUIRING A PLUG-IN THAT IS NOT CURRENTLY INSTALLED |

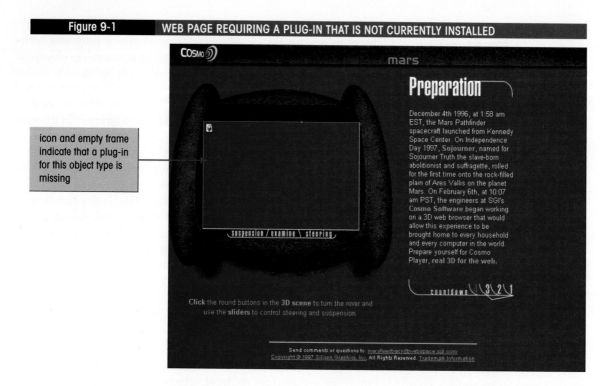

icon and empty frame indicate that a plug-in for this object type is missing

When you click the object shown in Figure 9-1, Figure 9-2 shows the dialog box that opens and provides information about the missing plug-in and where to obtain it. When you view pages that require plug-ins that your browser does not have, you miss some of the richness of the page supplied by the plug-in.

| Figure 9-2 | SAMPLE DIALOG BOX THAT OPENS WHEN A PLUG-IN IS MISSING |

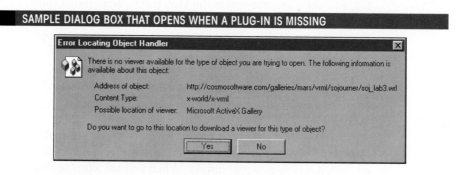

Locating Missing Plug-ins

When you encounter a file that your browser cannot execute, it will not be able to perform the operation required by the file, such as playing audio files or displaying animation. In some cases, your browser might automatically prompt you with an alert dialog box and then describe the location of where to acquire the required plug-in. When this occurs, the browser might open a site containing the missing plug-in; usually, this is the plug-in developer's site. Most Web pages that store files which require a plug-in contain a link to the site where you can download the required plug-in. For example, Figure 9-3 shows a Web page that requires the Shockwave plug-in. When you click the Shockwave icon, your browser will open the Shockwave developer's Web site so you can download the Shockwave plug-in. The Shockwave plug-in plays movies, animations, interactive games, slide-shows, streaming audio, and background music that are required by this Web page.

Figure 9-3 | WEB PAGE THAT REQUIRES THE SHOCKWAVE PLUG-IN

click to download the Shockwave plug-in

notice to users that this page requires the Shockwave plug-in

snowmobile game requires Shockwave to animate players

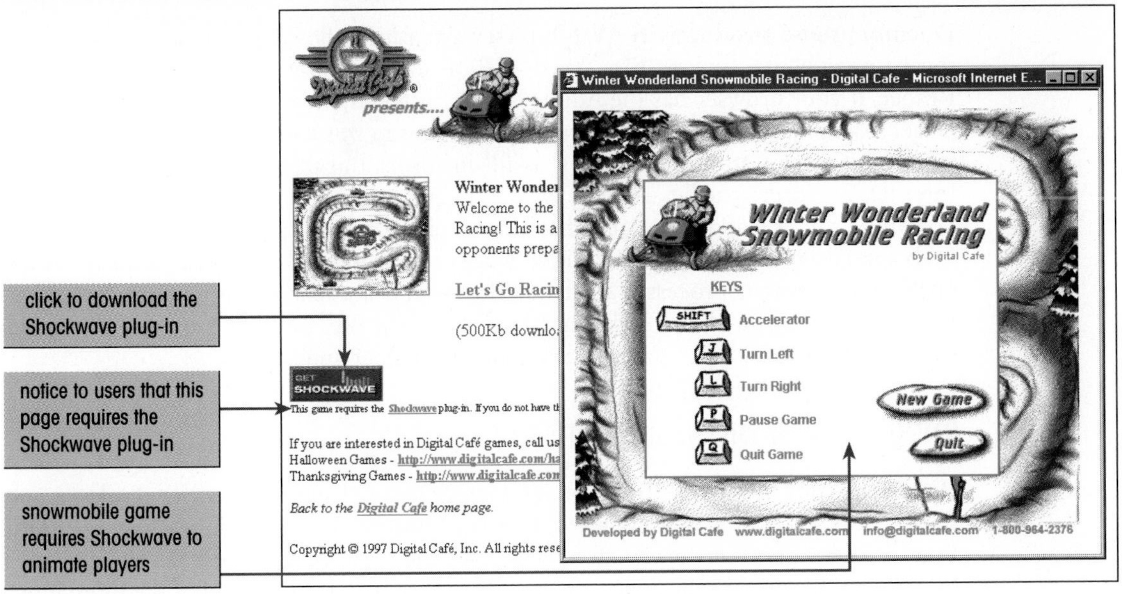

When you upgrade your browser to a newer version, you sometimes lose many or all of its plug-ins and helper applications, so you have to reinstall your browser extensions. However, when you upgrade to a new browser version, it might automatically install plug-ins that you previously had to install yourself. For example, recent versions of Netscape Navigator include LiveAudio, Live3D, and Live Video plug-ins. As plug-ins become popular and essential for Web browsing, most browsers will install them automatically.

Browser Extension Categories

Mark is interested in examining many Web extension types to locate the right mix to build an exciting and refreshing set of Web pages for RVP. You want to investigate each of the extension categories and see how other Web sites use them to design effective Web presences. Because there are many browser extensions available today, it is helpful to discuss them by groups or categories. There are no formal groupings for extensions, but you will find most people agree that browser extensions fall into one or more of the categories, although not every Web extension fits neatly into one category. The general categories of Web browser extensions are:

- Document and productivity
- Image viewer
- Multimedia
- Sound player
- Video player
- VRML and 3-D

Each of these categories is described next.

Document and Productivity Browser Extensions

Document and productivity Web browser extensions allow you to use a browser to read special documents, such as files saved in PDF format and viewed by the Adobe Acrobat Reader. If your browser has the Adobe Reader installed, it can display and print PDF files. Other examples of plug-ins and helper applications in this category are worksheet manipulation and display programs as well as fill-in forms and display programs. For example, Internet Explorer usually uses Excel as a helper application to display worksheet files. Formula One, a standalone spreadsheet program, provides an alternative way to handle Web spreadsheets, which are identified with a special secondary name. Jetform has developed a plug-in that processes electronic forms and automates business processes on the Internet. When you click a link that is a PowerPoint file, Internet Explorer automatically starts the PowerPoint program, which is another helper application.

Image Viewer Browser Extensions

Web extensions that fall into the **image viewer** category let the browser display graphics, such as interactive road maps or alternative file formats and viewers for GIF and JPEG files. Fractal Viewer lets you view Web fractal image file formats. AutoDesk developed a plug-in to display line drawings in the proprietary Drawing Web format. One of the more interesting plug-ins from IPIX lets you view a special scene from all angles by panning an image left, right, up, or down to see an image from the sky, ground, or to turn it in a circle. Automobile dealers use the IPIX format to display an unrestricted spherical view of an automobile's interior.

Multimedia Browser Extensions

Multimedia, perhaps the largest category, contains Web extensions that appeal to most of the senses. Shockwave, a popular multimedia player produced by Macromedia, provides animation and entertainment on the Web. You can use Shockwave to play interactive games, view animated interfaces, listen to streaming CD-quality audio music and speech, and view instructional presentations. Shockwave was one of the first plug-ins available for Web browsers, and it has a large and loyal audience.

Sound Player Browser Extensions

Sound player extensions, such as Crescendo, RealPlayer, and Beatnik, let your Web browser play sounds. Many extensions, including Crescendo and Beatnik, play CD-quality streaming audio. RealPlayer is widely distributed and plays audio over a variety of slow to fast connections ranging from 28.8K modems to faster cable modems.

Video Player Browser Extensions

Video players deliver movies to the Internet. When you click a movie link, the movie downloads and begins playing in its own window. QuickTime, which makes video, sound, music, 3-D, and virtual reality come alive on both Macintosh and PCs, was one of the first movie players developed. Other successful movie players include ClearFusion, RealPlayer, and VDOLive. Some of these browser extensions download a complete movie before playing it, whereas others use streaming technology to play a movie before it is completely downloaded. Several video players can play either live downloads or on-demand files, such as movie files. Playing movies delivered on a modem connection, however, can be a painfully slow process.

VRML and 3-D Browser Extensions

Virtual Reality Modeling Language or **VRML** (pronounced "ver-muhl") is an Internet programming language which creates three-dimensional environments that can mimic known worlds or define fictional ones. With VRML, you can navigate and interact with a three-dimensional scene. The three-dimensional space can appear almost like real space. VRML plug-ins permit your Web browser to interact with and move through a scene by opening doors, rotating the view to show the landscape behind you, and then moving ahead. VRML modelers can create fictional planet environments complete with red skies and harmful vegetation, or modelers can create a realistic three-dimensional tour of the human brain for medical students. Special VRML browsers work alongside your browser, which reads only HTML documents and not VRML files, to wander through a VRML-enabled site. Your Web browser automatically detects a VRML-enabled site and starts the VRML browser extensions required to produce the VRML content. More than display screens, VRML browsers and VRML extensions are three-dimensional generating engines containing navigation controls that allow you to explore a three-dimensional landscape and investigate its objects. A popular VRML plug-in is Cosmo Player, produced by Silicon Graphics, which is a company whose three-dimensional graphics-modeling program served as the basis of version 1.0 of the VRML specification.

Finding **Browser Extensions**

Browser extensions reside in many places on the Internet—each browser extension developer stores its plug-in or helper app on its own site. Some Web sites are browser extension supermarkets that include convenient collections of links to extensions grouped by type or by the functions they perform. Some of the plug-in supermarkets also have ranked extensions in descending order by the number of times people have downloaded each one, which acts as a type of popularity ranking. Some browser extension download sites also provide a reliability ranking. All such sites include download links to each product. The Student Online Companion for Tutorial 9 contains links to several plug-in supermarket sites in the Session 9.1 and Additional Information sections.

Because you want to show Mark the variety of plug-ins and helper applications available, you decide to locate and examine some of the plug-in download sites. You are especially interested in the audio, video, and multimedia plug-ins and their reliability ratings. You decide to start your browser extension research by visiting BROWSERS.COM, which lists available browser plug-ins.

To search for plug-ins on the BROWSERS.COM site:

1. Start your Web browser, and then go to the Student Online Companion page by entering the URL **http://www.course.com/newperspectives/internet2** in the appropriate location in your Web browser. Click the hyperlink for your book, click the **Tutorial 9** link, and then click the **Session 9.1** link. Click the **BROWSERS.COM** link and wait while the browser loads the page.

2. Scroll down the page until you see the Plug-ins and add-ons section shown in Figure 9-4. Click the **More plug-ins** link (see Figure 9-4). The Plug-ins page opens and lists plug-ins in descending order by the date when the software was added to the list. (Your page might look different because the downloadable plug-ins and their statistics change over time.)

Figure 9-4

BROWSERS.COM HOME PAGE

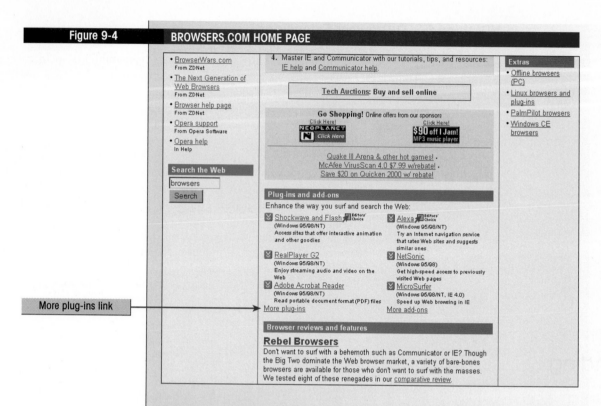

More plug-ins link

3. Click the **Downloads** link above the list to sort the list by decreasing download count (see Figure 9-5).

Figure 9-5

PLUG-INS LISTED IN DESCENDING ORDER BY DOWNLOADS

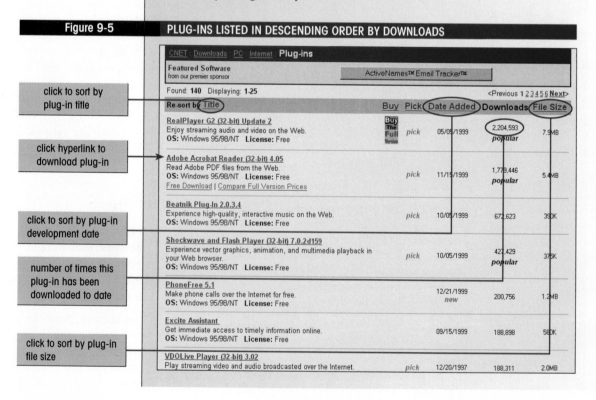

click to sort by plug-in title

click hyperlink to download plug-in

click to sort by plug-in development date

number of times this plug-in has been downloaded to date

click to sort by plug-in file size

4. Scroll down the page and note the number of times that the plug-ins have been downloaded. The Downloads and Date Added columns indicate each plug-in's popularity and release date, respectively. If you click the Title link at the top-left of the plug-in listing, the list will display alphabetically by title. Similarly, clicking the Date Added link will order the plug-ins based on their development dates. Clicking the Downloads link organizes the list into descending order by the number of times the plug-in has been downloaded. Clicking the File Size link sorts the list into ascending order by program size. At the top of the page, you will see the Search text box, which lets you search the entire site for a specific category or product. If you scroll to the bottom of the page, you will see a Filter list by text box pair, which allows you to select an operating system or software class (Demo, Freeware, or Shareware) and display software filtered by those criteria.

One of the advantages of the BROWSERS.COM Web site is that you can display the plug-ins list in different orders. If you want to see the most popular plug-ins, then sort the plug-ins by download count. If you want to locate a plug-in by name, then sort the list in alphabetical order.

Of course, you can search for plug-ins and information about them by using an Internet search engine. Using a search term such as *plug-ins* or *plug-in* will yield many sources of plug-ins. You will find it a much simpler task to review and download browser plug-ins and other extensions if you use a site that specializes in them. Another good source for browser extensions grouped in a convenient place is TUCOWS, as you learned in Tutorial 6. TUCOWS includes a large collection of plug-ins grouped by the functions they perform.

To search for plug-ins on the TUCOWS site:

1. Use your browser's **Back** button to return to the Student Online Companion Web page for Session 9.1, and then click the **TUCOWS** hyperlink and wait while your Web browser loads the Web page.

2. Click the link corresponding to the continent or region closest to you. If you are in the United States, for example, then click the **United States** link.

3. If a list of other regions or states displays, then select a site closest to you. For example, if you selected United States in Step 2, then click any link to a state closest to you.

4. Click the **Windows 2000** link to open a page with a list of Windows 2000 programs grouped by various categories. See Figure 9-6.

Figure 9-6

Browsers and Accessories category

Browser Add-Ons link

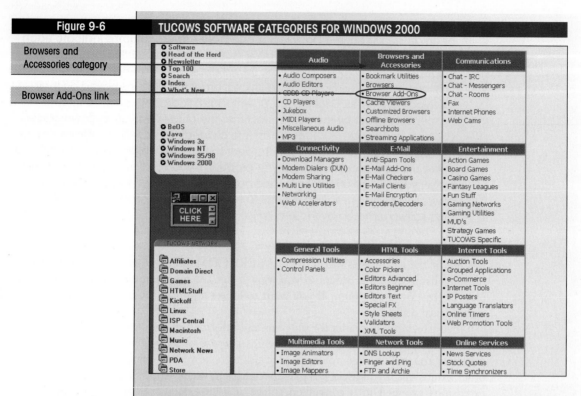

TUCOWS SOFTWARE CATEGORIES FOR WINDOWS 2000

5. Click the **Browser Add-Ons** link in the Browsers and Accessories category. A page opens and lists browser plug-ins alphabetically by title. See Figure 9-7. TUCOWS lists each plug-in's version number, revision date, filename and file size, license, description, and other helpful information.

Figure 9-7

plug-in name and download link

link to developer's home page

TUCOWS rating (5 cows is the best rating)

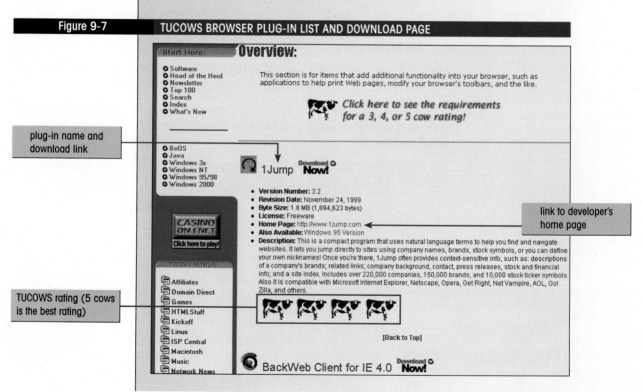

TUCOWS BROWSER PLUG-IN LIST AND DOWNLOAD PAGE

6. Scroll down the page and notice all of the different plug-ins that you can download from TUCOWS. You would click the plug-in's name to start the download process, but you will not download anything now.

The BrowserWatch Web site organizes its available plug-ins by function, such as multimedia, graphics, sound, document, productivity, and VRML/3-D. The Full List category includes all of the plug-ins available from the entire site. For example, if you want a plug-in that plays sounds in a particular way, then you can narrow your search quickly by clicking the Sound category. To make sure you are familiar with this categorization of plug-ins, you decide to view the site and look at plug-ins in the multimedia category because multimedia plug-ins will be an integral part of the RVP Web site.

To view multimedia plug-ins on the BrowserWatch site:

1. Return to the Student Online Companion Web page for Session 9.1, and then click the **BrowserWatch** hyperlink and wait while your Web browser loads the BrowserWatch home page. On the left side of the page is the Plug-in Plaza! link, which leads to the plug-ins page.

2. Click the **Plug-in Plaza!** link to open the Plug-in Plaza page shown in Figure 9-8. The plug-ins are listed by category.

Figure 9-8	BROWSERWATCH PLUG-IN PLAZA PAGE

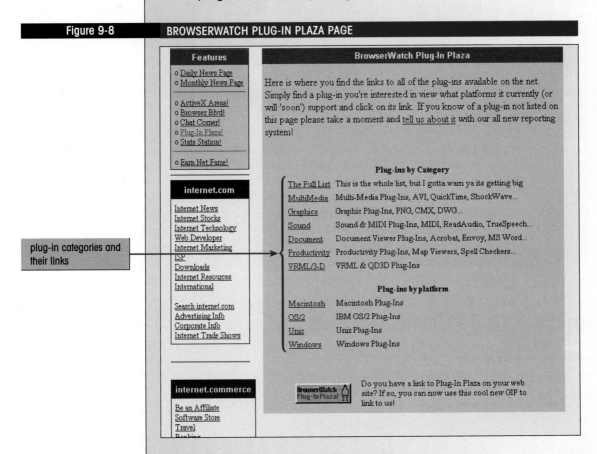

plug-in categories and their links

3. Click the **MultiMedia** link to open the page with a list of multimedia plug-ins arranged in alphabetical order.

4. Scroll down the page and examine the plug-in listings. Figure 9-9 shows an example of several multimedia plug-ins. Notice that the listing for each plug-in includes the name, developer, URL to download the link, and a link to a page that contains a sample file that the plug-in can play.

Figure 9-9	BROWSERWATCH MULTIMEDIA PLUG-INS

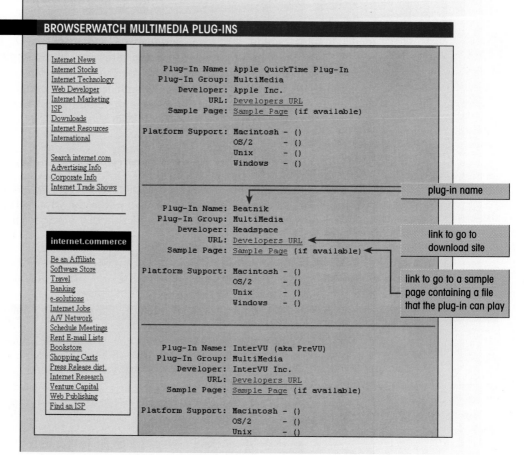

The BrowserWatch site is handy because you can narrow your examination of plug-ins quickly by clicking a plug-in category. Or, if you know the first few characters of the plug-in's name, you can click the Full List link and scroll down to the desired plug-in.

You are satisfied that you can locate Web browser extensions using the three download sites you visited. Now, you are ready to download some plug-ins. The next section shows you how to locate and download plug-ins using your Web browser.

Downloading **Document and Image Viewer Plug-ins**

Document viewer browser extensions help your browser to display and arrange a document that is stored on the Web. If you have installed the Microsoft Office suite, then you already have a helper application available to display documents stored on the Web. For example, when you click a file with the .xls extension on a Web page displayed by Internet Explorer, the browser opens Microsoft Excel so you can open the document directly. Internet Explorer gives you the option of downloading the file or opening the file from its current location. If you choose to open the file, then the browser automatically starts the Excel program and opens the file. Another plug-in with which you are familiar is Acrobat Reader, which will open documents with .pdf extensions.

Image viewer plug-ins display graphics images of various formats. There are several different image formats on the Web; no single format is dominant, so you will need more than one graphic viewer on your computer. You can wait to download each graphic viewer until you encounter Web sites that indicate you need it to enjoy the site.

The Session 9.1 page of the Student Online Companion for Tutorial 9 contains links that you can use to download several plug-ins, as well as links to download supermarkets, so you can explore other plug-ins that you might need as you use the Web.

When you download a plug-in, you will need to install it by following the instructions provided on the developer's Web site. To install a plug-in, double-click the downloaded file and then follow the on-screen instructions. *Note:* If you are using a university computer system, you should check with your instructor or lab supervisor before you download or install any software on your computer's hard drive. Frequently, your school's download policy prohibits you from installing software without approval from your instructor or lab manager. If you are downloading software to your own computer, then you can decide to download and install it. However, you should know that some plug-ins are unreliable and can cause damage. This textbook does *not* require you to install plug-in software to understand how to use it.

Other Important Browser Extensions

One of the projects that Mark envisions is producing a Web site with a complete audio and visual experience for potential RVP customers. Because RVP is a video-production company, Mark wants its Web site to reflect the same high-quality presentations reflected in his video productions. Mark is particularly interested in evaluating the latest plug-ins that will help his customers see and hear his message: High-quality video productions at a reasonable cost. You conduct your research by visiting several plug-in sites, reading the user comments, and noticing the number of downloads for each plug-in. Mark read that Shockwave is a well-respected standard for multimedia plug-ins. You find there are several contenders for high-quality and popular sound plug-ins. Among the most popular are Beatnik, Crescendo, RealPlayer, and QuickTime. Finally, in the VRML arena you notice that there are several good VRML players. One that is consistently mentioned is Cosmo Player. You can visit the Web sites for these plug-ins using the links on the Session 9.1 page of the Student Online Companion for Tutorial 9.

Shockwave

Macromedia's Shockwave is a browser plug-in that provides animated interfaces, interactive advertisements, interactive demonstrations, and streaming CD-quality audio. Some instructors use Shockwave to deliver audio instruction and interact with students. Shockwave is a very popular extension; according to Macromedia, people download the software at the rate of nearly 200,000 copies per day. Because Shockwave uses streaming technology, you do not have to wait for an entire audio file to download before playing it—the animation or sound plays almost immediately. Figure 9-10 shows an example of a Shockwave-enhanced game. Shockwave provides animation and sound for this Broderbund-produced game.

Figure 9-10   SHOCKWAVE-ENHANCED WEB GAME

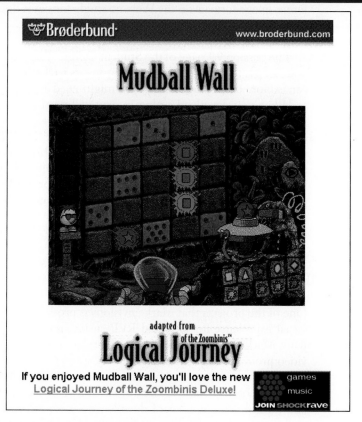

Beatnik, Crescendo, and RealPlayer

Beatnik, Crescendo, and RealPlayer are all examples of Web audio players that play audio files of various formats. Beatnik and Crescendo deliver high-quality interactive music and sound on the Web, whereas RealPlayer brings to the Web the ability to deliver MIDI music in very small file sizes. In addition, Beatnik can embed copyright information in the delivered audio files by using an encrypted character string that is hidden within the music file. The embedded information is similar to a watermark on a sheet of paper.

Besides supporting its native Rich Music Format (RMF) files, Beatnik supports the commonly used Web audio formats of MIDI, WAV, and AIFF. RealPlayer, once known as RealAudio, plays streaming audio and video on the Web, though the music is less than CD quality. RealPlayer provides a feature called **buffered play**, in which music is downloaded and queued for play when the transfer/play rate exceeds your modem's speed.

QuickTime

Apple Computer's QuickTime technology plays video, sound, and music for both Macintosh and Windows platforms, almost immediately after clicking the link containing the sound or video files. QuickTime is the plug-in of choice to play stored digital media. The QuickTime proprietary format allows developers to store video frames and audio tracks and also to store a complete description of the media composition. One key advantage of the QuickTime movie format is that it is computer-platform neutral: that is, it works equally well on Windows, Macintosh, or UNIX systems. Another advantage is that the QuickTime format is a widely accepted format. The International Standards Organization (ISO) has adopted Apple's QuickTime file format as the starting point for the development of an improved and unified digital media storage format for the MPEG-4 specification. (You learned in Tutorial 5 that MPEG stands for Moving Picture Experts Group, an important governing body that discusses and sets standards for Web digital movie formats.) Figure 9-11 shows examples of available QuickTime movies; you can click the Movie link on the Session 9.1 page of the Student Online Companion to visit this site. (You must install a movie viewer plug-in to see the movies; check with your instructor or lab manager before downloading and installing any plug-ins on a school computer.)

| Figure 9-11 | QUICKTIME MOVIES |

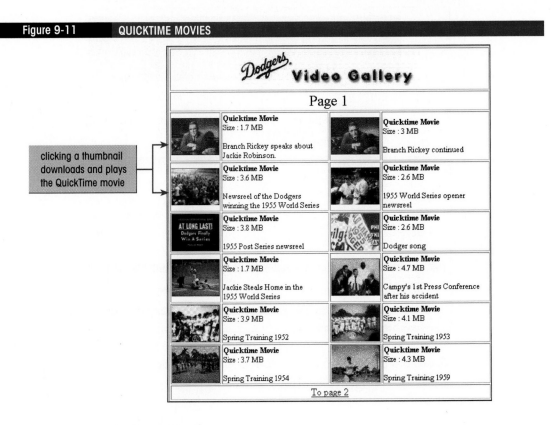

Cosmo Player

Cosmo Player is a VRML player from Silicon Graphics that lets you experience three-dimensional Web worlds without having special three-dimensional graphics acceleration hardware installed on your computer. Sometimes, VRML sites are set up so game players can wander through fictional three-dimensional worlds and interact with objects they encounter. Another class of applications that take advantage of a VRML player's capabilities are product and location tours. A university can produce a virtual campus tour, allowing the observer to turn any direction and walk around and through buildings. An automobile manufacturer can provide a virtual driving experience for the viewer. Another popular VRML player is Microsoft VRML, which is available from the Microsoft Web site.

Mark asks you to find some Web sites that explain more about VRML technology. Mark is unsure about investing time and money in creating virtual-reality worlds right now, but he does want to study the issue. You decide to use a search engine to find sites that explain browsing with VRML plug-ins and creating virtual-reality sites.

To locate and read more about VRML on the Web:

1. Return to the Student Online Companion Web page for Session 9.1, and then click the **VRML Repository** hyperlink and wait while your Web browser loads the Web page shown in Figure 9-12.

Figure 9-12	THE VRML REPOSITORY WEB PAGE

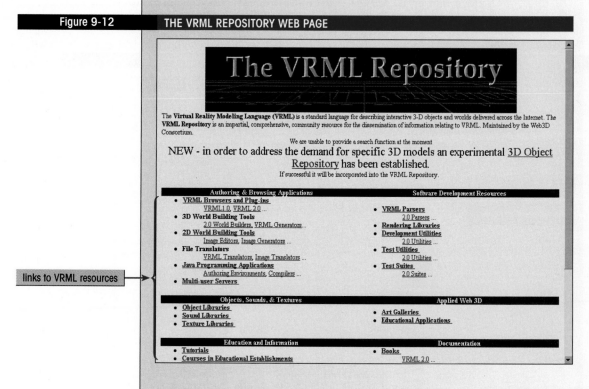

links to VRML resources

2. Explore the links on The VRML Repository Web page to find out more about virtual-reality applications.

Mark is impressed with the opportunities offered by virtual-reality sites. He wants to study virtual-reality and VRML plug-ins more before making a decision about whether to use the technology.

Installing **and Testing Browser Extensions**

Once you locate browser extensions and download them to your computer, the next step is to install them. Of course, if you are using a computer in your school's computer laboratory, you should not install any plug-ins without first checking with your instructor and the lab supervisor. Generally, you should *not* install plug-ins on any computer except your own. Here, you learn how to install and test plug-ins, but you should not install the plug-ins on a lab computer without proper authorization. Testing to see which plug-ins are installed is always permissible because this activity will not alter the software on the computer you are using. If you cannot install a browser extension, read the material without completing the steps at the computer so you will know about the installation process.

Installing a Browser Extension

The method you use to install a browser extension depends in part on which browser you are using. For example, if you are using Navigator, then you typically install a downloaded extension by double-clicking the extension's filename in Windows Explorer. The same is true for Internet Explorer. However, if you are using Internet Explorer and download an extension from Microsoft's Web site, then the download and installation processes occur automatically, so you do not need to do anything other than download the file. For example, when you download Microsoft's VRML extension using Internet Explorer, the Microsoft Web site recognizes that you are using Internet Explorer and downloads and installs the VRML extension for you. No matter which browser you are using, double-check that the Web extension you are downloading will work with your browser. If there is only one download link available, then the extension usually will work with most popular browsers.

Mark is impressed with sites that you have demonstrated that use Shockwave. He wants to consider using the Shockwave plug-in on the RVP Web site, so he asks you to download and install it. Having a Shockwave-enhanced site will add punch to the site and attract the type of viewers that typify RVP's clients. There are two sets of steps that follow to install Shockwave. If you are using Internet Explorer, follow the first set of steps. If you are using Netscape Navigator, follow the second (longer) set of steps.

To install Shockwave in Internet Explorer:

1. Return to the Student Online Companion Web page for Session 9.1, and then click the **Macromedia** hyperlink and wait while your Web browser loads the Macromedia Shockwave Download Center page.

2. Click the **Shockwave Player** link in the Web Players section.

3. Click the **Autoinstall Now** link. A Security dialog box opens. The installation might be quick or it might take several minutes, depending on the speed of your Internet connection. In either case, animated icons will appear to indicate the installation was successful. If you have a sound card installed, you also will hear digital sound.

4. Click the **Yes** button in the Security dialog box to continue.

   TROUBLE? If an Internet Redirection dialog box opens, click the Yes button to continue.

5. Click the **Next** button.

6. Register your copy of the plug-in by filling in your name and e-mail address in the text boxes. Click the **Next** button to continue.

7. Click the **Finish** button. "Your Free Shockwave player is installed" displays.

8. Click the **Next** button to complete the installation.

9. Close the "Welcome to Shockwave" page that displays.

Follow the next steps to install Shockwave using Navigator.

To install Shockwave in Navigator:

1. Return to the Student Online Companion Web page for Session 9.1, and then click the **Macromedia** hyperlink and wait while your Web browser loads the Macromedia Shockwave Download Center page.

2. Click the **Shockwave Player** link in the Web Players section.

3. Click the **Download Now** (or **Click to Download**) link in the Step 1 panel. The Save As dialog box opens.

4. Click the **Save in** list arrow, click the drive for your Data Disk, and then double-click the **Tutorial.09** folder to open it.

5. Click the **Save** button to download the software to your Data Disk. When the download is complete, close Navigator.

6. Click the **Start** button on the Windows taskbar, click **Run**, and then click the **Browse** button. The Browse dialog box opens.

7. In the Look in text box, type the disk drive name containing your Data Disk, double-click **Tutorial.09** to open it, click the file **shockwaveinstaller.exe**, and then click the **Open** button. Click the **OK** button in the Run dialog box to start the installation process. The first of several Shockwave installation screens opens.

8. Click the **Next** button to go to the next step in the installation.

9. Select your Netscape browser from the list of Web browsers installed on your computer, and then click the **Install** button.

10. Click the **Continue** button. The Macromedia Web Player Download Center Web page opens.

11. Close Netscape Navigator, and then restart it to complete the installation process.

Now that you have downloaded and installed the Shockwave plug-in on your Web browser, you need to test it to make sure that it is working correctly. The next section shows you some Web sites where you can put Shockwave to work.

Testing Browser Extensions

Usually, your newly installed plug-in is transparent until you visit a Web page that requires it. If you have the required plug-in, it begins performing whatever task it is programmed to perform. Audio plug-ins, for instance, often will begin playing music when you go to the audio plug-in developer's site. Movie plug-ins play when you double-click an icon representing a movie. If you do not have a required plug-in installed, it is not immediately obvious that you are missing it until you visit a site that requires it. Some Web sites let you test your browser to see which plug-ins are installed on your computer. Next, you will visit a Web site where you can test your Shockwave plug-in.

To test your Shockwave browser plug-in:

1. Return to the Student Online Companion Web page for Session 9.1, and then click the **Shockwave test** hyperlink and wait while your Web browser loads the test page shown in Figure 9-13.

Figure 9-13 | SHOCKWAVE TEST PAGE

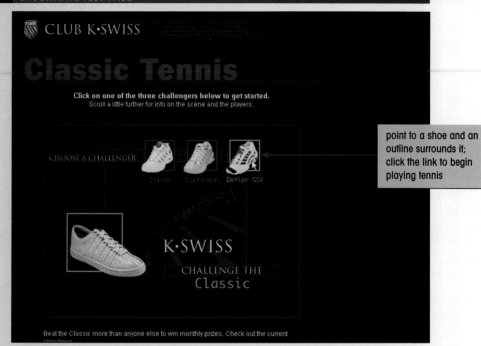

point to a shoe and an outline surrounds it; click the link to begin playing tennis

The test page is an interesting example of using Shockwave to catch people's attention and gain their interest. The site advertises athletic shoes, and it does so in an interesting way by offering games and sound. You can play a table-tennis game by clicking on any of the pictured athletic shoes. A Shockwave-enabled game starts if your browser has the Shockwave plug-in installed.

2. Click one of the athletic shoes pictured to start a table-tennis game.

3. Click the **Ready? click to serve** icon to start the game (see Figure 9-14) and be ready to return the ball. Unlike tennis or table tennis, the ball can bounce off the sides of the table and still remain in play. Position your shoe "paddle" so that the ball will hit your shoe before it hits the end of the court on your side. Try a front-net smash. If you have a sound card installed, you will hear the ball hit the paddles and swoosh across the court.

Figure 9-14	TESTING SHOCKWAVE WITH A TABLE-TENNIS GAME

CLUB K·SWISS

Classic Tennis

Click on one of the three challengers below to get started.
Scroll a little further for info on the scene and the players.

your score displays here

opponent's score displays here

ball

opponent's paddle (it misses shots randomly)

your paddle, which your mouse controls

click here to see scores of the top players

K·SWISS
TENNIS

06   00
Classic   Player

Beat the Classic more than anyone else to win monthly prizes. Check out the current standings.

4. Continue clicking **Ready? click to serve** as needed to serve and continue playing the game. You can click the **standings** link to view other users' scores.

5. When you are finished, close your browser, and if necessary, close your dial-up connection.

Another fun site to try out your Shockwave plug-in is Macromedia ShockRave, which contains cartoons, games, music, and talk, all of which use your Shockwave plug-in. You can visit this site by clicking ShockRave in Session 9.1 of the Student Online Companion.

You can test your browser for the presence of other plug-ins by going to another site that contains several plug-in tests. Click the Plug-in test site link in Session 9.1 of the Student Online Companion. That page includes plug-in tests for MPEG movies, sound plug-ins, and text tests. Click one or more of the test buttons next to the plug-in test you want to perform.

Mark was pleased to hear of your progress in understanding and using different file formats on the Web. Based on your information, Mark is ready to begin designing the RVP Web site. He's especially excited about the possibility of using one or more animation, sound, and movie files to capture interest. He wants to place a short movie segment on the RVP Web site to show potential customers an example of RVP's work.

Session 9.1 Quick Check

1. What is the main difference between browser plug-ins and helper applications?

2. True or False: Most Web pages requiring a particular plug-in also contain a link to the site where you can download the plug-in.

3. What does the acronym "VRML" stand for?

4. What is the primary advantage of using streaming audio files on the Web?

5. What is a content-development program?

6. List the names of three Web browser sound-player plug-ins.

7. How do plug-in creators earn a profit when they give away their plug-in players? For example, how does Macromedia make any money if it gives away the Shockwave player?

Mark's vision of the RVP Web site is to allow customers to book and pre-pay their productions using the RVP Web site. For this reason, he asks you to learn more about the security of the Internet, which is a concern of any Web site that customers can use to conduct commerce.

SESSION 9.2

In this session you will learn about Internet security topics, including secrecy, privacy, integrity, necessity, and fraud. Once you understand the potential threats on the Internet, you will learn some good defenses to protect against them. Finally, you will learn about copyright and intellectual property issues related to the Internet.

Security Overview

Mark is excited about producing a Web presence with the sophisticated Web tools that you discovered and demonstrated in Session 9.1. He envisions that the next major phase in the evolution of his Web site will be to allow consumers to interact with his site, instead of relying on it only as a source of information about the company. Mark has noticed an increasing number of newspaper and trade magazine reports about various companies that allow customers to order goods and services over the Web. He would like RVP to provide this capacity, as well, by allowing customers to review a list of RVP services and indicate ones they would like to purchase. Mark is concerned about whether customers can rely on the RVP site to conduct secure transactions. For example, how can RVP protect a customer's credit card number when it is entered on a Web page? Until RVP can ensure secure transactions, customers will be reluctant to submit their credit card numbers or other personal information.

Security is broadly defined as the protection of assets from unauthorized access, use, alteration, or destruction. There are two types of security: physical security and logical security. The security provided by Fort Knox is almost entirely physical security. **Physical security** includes tangible protection devices, such as alarms, fireproof doors, security fences, safes or vaults, and bombproof buildings. Protection of assets using non-physical protections is called **logical security**. Protection of computer assets—both data and procedures to deal with the data—is an example of logical security, which also is broadly called **computer security**. Any act or object that threatens computer assets is known as a **threat**.

Countermeasure is the general name for a procedure, either physical or logical, that recognizes, reduces, or eliminates a threat. Countermeasures vary depending on the importance of the asset at risk. Countermeasures can recognize and manage threats or they can eliminate them. Other threats that are deemed low-risk and are unlikely to occur can be ignored when the cost to protect against the threat is more than the value of the protected asset. For example, a tornado is a low-risk threat to computer networks located in Southern California, but it is a high-risk threat for networks located in Kansas. It would make sense to protect a computer network in Kansas, where there is a lot of tornado activity, but not to protect one in Los Angeles, where tornadoes are unlikely to strike. The risk management model shown in Figure 9-15 illustrates four actions that you could take, depending on the impact (cost) and the probability of the physical threat. In this model, a tornado in Kansas would be in the quadrant for high probability and high impact, whereas a tornado in Los Angeles would be in the quadrant for low impact and low probability.

Figure 9-15	RISK MANAGEMENT MODEL

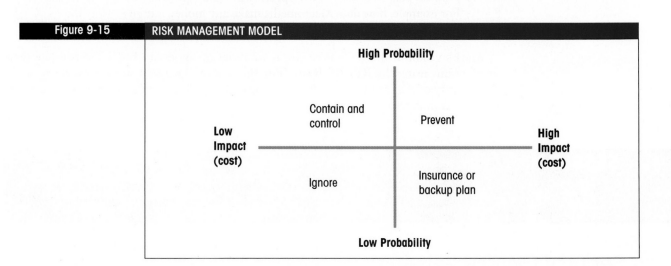

The same sort of risk management model applies to protecting Internet assets from non-physical threats, such as impostors, eavesdroppers, and thieves. To implement a good security scheme, you identify the risk, determine how you will protect the affected asset, and calculate how much you can spend to protect the asset. Your primary focus in risk management protection is not on the protection costs or value of assets; instead, your concern is on the central issues to identify the threats and to determine ways to protect the assets from those threats.

Computer Security Classification

Computer security experts generally agree that you can classify computer security into three categories. The names of these categories sometimes vary, but the widely accepted ones are secrecy, integrity, and necessity. **Secrecy** prevents unauthorized data disclosure and ensures the authenticity of the data's source; **integrity** prevents unauthorized data modification; and **necessity** prevents data delays or denials. Secrecy and threats to secrecy are the best known of the computer security categories. Every month, newspapers report accounts of illegal break-ins to governmental computers or unauthorized uses of stolen credit card numbers to order goods and services. Integrity threats tend to be reported less frequently and thus might be less familiar to the public. An integrity violation occurs when a message's or property's shipping address is changed from the intended receiver to another individual's address, thereby stealing the message or property. Instances of necessity violations occur frequently. For example, if you send an important e-mail message to a shipper and ask to cancel an order—and someone prevents the shipper from receiving it—then the message is never delivered and the shipment is sent.

Delaying a message can have huge consequences, as well. For example, if you send an e-mail message to your stockbroker and ask him to buy 10,000 shares of company X at 10:00 A.M., and he does not receive the message until 3:00 P.M. when the stock's price increases 15 percent, the delay costs you an additional price on the stock.

Copyright and Intellectual Property

Copyright and safeguarding intellectual property rights are also security issues, although they are protected with different countermeasures. **Copyright** is the protection of expression—someone's or some entity's intellectual property—and it typically covers items such as literary and musical works; pantomimes and choreographic works; pictorial, graphic, and sculptural works; motion pictures and other audio-visual works; sound recordings; and architectural works. (**Intellectual property** is the ownership of ideas and control over the tangible or virtual representation of those ideas.) Like violating computer security, breaching a copyright causes damage. However, unlike computer security breaches, the damages as a result of copyright violation are narrow and have a smaller impact on an organization or individual. The U.S. Copyright Act of 1976 protects items, such as those in any of the preceding categories, for a fixed period. For items published before 1978, the copyright expires 75 years from the item's publication date. For items published after January 1, 1978, the copyright expires 50 years beyond the life of the author for an individual holder or 75 years after the date of the publication for employers of the author. In other words, unless you have received permission to reproduce the item protected by copyright, you violate the Copyright Act if you illegally reproduce an item in any form before its copyright expires.

On the Internet, there are thousands of examples of copyright violations. You can go to any search engine, type the search term *copyright*, and locate hundreds of Web sites that discuss copyright. Several of these Web sites document explicit and famous cases of copyright violations.

Mark wants to know more about copyright protection on the Web. He is unsure about what is covered, and he wants to ensure that any video clips he places on the RVP Web site are properly covered by copyright protection. You tell him about an informative site called the Copyright Clearance Center, Inc. and decide that's a good place to start researching copyright issues.

To open the Copyright Clearance Center Web page:

1. Start your Web browser, and then go to the Student Online Companion page by entering the URL **http://www.course.com/newperspectives/internet2** in the appropriate location in your Web browser. Click the hyperlink for your book, click the **Tutorial 9** link, and then click the **Session 9.2** link. Click the **Copyright Clearance Center, Inc.** link and wait while the browser loads the page shown in Figure 9-16.

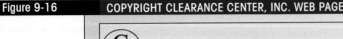

Figure 9-16   COPYRIGHT CLEARANCE CENTER, INC. WEB PAGE

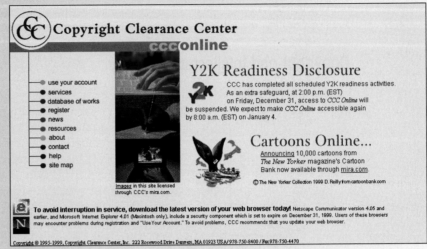

2. Click the **resources** link to view a page of links to copyright information on the Web. Notice that you can link to copyright decisions handed down by U.S. and foreign courts, as well as general information such as classroom copyright guidelines. You are certain that this site can provide Mark with sufficient information on copyright protection for RVP.

Now, you have some basic information about Internet security and know where to find some guidelines. You will learn about security threats that might affect the RVP Web site next.

Security Threats

You can examine security threats by category. Secrecy and privacy threats are the best-known types, but integrity and necessity (also called delay or denial threats) are equally destructive.

Secrecy and Privacy Threats

Many Web site visitors eagerly embrace doing business on the Web. The possibility of someone stealing your credit card number in a Web transaction is perhaps the most visible of the secrecy threats, but it represents only one of many. Intelligence gathering or industrial espionage can cause financial damage. For example, a **sniffer program** monitors and analyzes network traffic. Used illegally, a sniffer program also can capture data being transmitted on a network including login information, passwords, and other personal information. **Authentication** is verifying that the source or sender is identified correctly. Anyone on the Internet can pretend to be someone else, which poses a security risk. For example, if you receive a software update from Microsoft and install the update, how do you ensure that the sender is indeed Microsoft and not someone interested in gaining access to your computer? A few years ago, you could log on to the Internet and have a chat session with Russian President Boris Yeltsen. For a one-hour period, users from around the world could send questions to Mr. Yeltsen. From the 4,000 questions received, Yeltsen responded to fewer than two dozen questions. Was it Yeltsen who actually responded to questions, or was it someone else? That's authentication's role in security.

Usually, cookies are used for harmless reasons, but they can pose a security threat. A **cookie** is a small text file that is sent by a Web server to your computer. A cookie stores information that the Web server can read when you visit it again. Cookies normally store information about your interests and your **click stream**, which are the links you clicked while visiting the site. Creating and saving cookies in this way is harmless. However, cookies can store login, password, and credit card information, which allows illicit Web sites to store and use information about you without your knowledge by reading a cookie file stored on your computer.

Mark wants you to learn more about cookies so RVP can protect its Web customers from unauthorized access by outside sources.

To learn more about cookies:

1. Return to the Student Online Companion Web page for Session 9.2, and then click the **Cookie Central** hyperlink and wait while your Web browser loads the Cookie Central Web page shown in Figure 9-17.

TROUBLE? If you are using Internet Explorer and a Security Warning dialog box appears, then your Internet Explorer browser is missing an ActiveX control. You can choose Yes to load the ActiveX control or No. Choosing No does not greatly affect your Cookie Central viewing experience.

Figure 9-17	COOKIE CENTRAL WEB PAGE

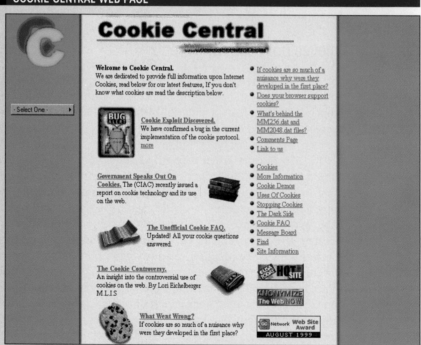

2. Follow several of the links and learn more about cookies. Notice that this page contains information about cookie security, frequently asked cookie questions, and how to stop Web servers from writing cookies on your computer.

Mark is pleased with the cookie resources that you found. Still, he is concerned about other types of threats, so you continue your Web research.

Integrity Threats

An integrity threat, also known as active wiretapping, exists when an unauthorized party can alter a message stream of information. Unprotected banking transactions, such as deposits transmitted over a network, are subject to integrity violations. For example, a person could monitor a bank transmission sent over a network to alter a deposit transaction's amount by increasing its real value. By tampering with an electronic shipping address, someone could divert equipment purchased using the Internet to an address other than the intended recipient's. Unlike secrecy or inactive wiretapping, where the viewer simply sees illicit information, integrity threats can change the actions a person or corporation takes because the transmission was altered.

Delay/Denial Threats

The goal of a delay/denial attack is to disrupt normal computer processing or, possibly, to deny processing entirely. A program exhibiting this behavior slows down processing to an intolerably slow speed. For example, if the processing speed of a single ATM machine transaction slows down from one to two seconds to 30 minutes, then users will abandon ATM machines entirely. Delaying processing can render a service unusable or unattractive; for example, a newspaper that reports three-day-old news is worth little when you need current information. Denial attacks remove a service altogether or delete information from a transmission or file. One documented denial attack caused selected PCs that have Quicken (an accounting program) installed to divert money to a different bank account—the denial attack, in this case, denied money from its rightful owners.

Intellectual Property Threats

Intellectual property threats are a large problem due to the Internet and the relative ease with which one can use existing material without the owner's permission. Actual monetary damage resulting from a copyright violation is more difficult to measure than damage from secrecy, integrity, or necessity violations, but the harm can be just as great. The Internet presents a particularly easy and tempting target for at least two reasons. First, it is very simple to reproduce an exact copy of anything you find on the Internet, whether or not it is subject to copyright restrictions. Second, many people are simply naïve or unaware of copyright restrictions that protect intellectual property. Examples of both unwitting and willful copyright infringements are evident on the Internet and occur on a daily basis. Although copyright laws were enacted before the creation of the Internet, the Internet itself has complicated the enforcement of copyrights by publishers. Recognizing the unauthorized reprinting of written text is relatively easy; perceiving when a photograph has been borrowed, cropped, and illegally used on a Web page is a more difficult task. Most experts agree that copyright infringements on the Web occur because of ignorance of what cannot be copied. Most people do not maliciously copy a protected work and post it on the Web. The most misunderstood part of the U.S. copyright law is that a work is protected when it is created—the work does not require a copyright notice, such as *Copyright © 2001 So and So Company*, to be protected.

Threat Delivery Mechanisms

There are many ways to breach security and threaten a system's integrity. Over the last decade, the most visible computer attacks have come from software. A **hacker**—usually a computer programmer who writes programs that damage computers—uses Trojan horses, viruses, and worms to attack computers and the programs they run.

A **Trojan horse** is a (usually small) program hidden inside another program. Taking its name from the legendary battle in which the city of Troy received a gift of a large wooden horse, Trojan horse programs are not what they appear to be. They claim to be legitimate programs that accomplish some task when, in fact, they do harm. They are unleashed when the program in which they are hidden is executed. Trojan horse programs range from prank programs that display a message and then disappear to destructive programs that reformat hard drives or delete program and data files. A Trojan horse does not replicate itself, nor does it affect other files or programs.

You learned in Tutorial 6 that a computer virus is a computer program that harms your computer and attaches itself to legitimate programs. Besides being destructive, a virus infects other programs in the computer system. Because a virus cannot exist alone, it must attach itself to a host program. When a program containing a virus is run, the virus has another opportunity to replicate itself. The term *virus* has come to mean any program that attempts to disguise its true function. Although all viruses are Trojan horses (because they hide within other legitimate programs), not all Trojan horse programs are viruses because Trojan horses cannot infect other programs. Like Trojan horses, viruses range from mildly annoying to extremely destructive.

An organization named **CERT (Computer Emergency Response Team)** has teams around the world to recognize and respond to computer attacks. The CERT Coordination Center is responsible for studying Internet security and responding to security incidents reported to it. CERT publishes various security alerts and develops plans for individual computer sites to improve their security. RVP wants to allow its customers to conduct transactions using the Internet, so it is important for you to have access to the CERT site in case a security threat occurs.

To visit the CERT Web site:

1. Return to the Student Online Companion Web page for Session 9.2, and then click the **CERT Center** hyperlink and wait while your Web browser loads the Web page.

2. Scroll down the page to view the headings and links on the CERT home page. See Figure 9-18. Notice that you can get information about improving security, use the FTP site to retrieve data from the archives, or learn more about the CERT information. Explore some of these links for Mark to find out what information is available on the site.

Figure 9-18   CERT COORDINATION CENTER WEB PAGE

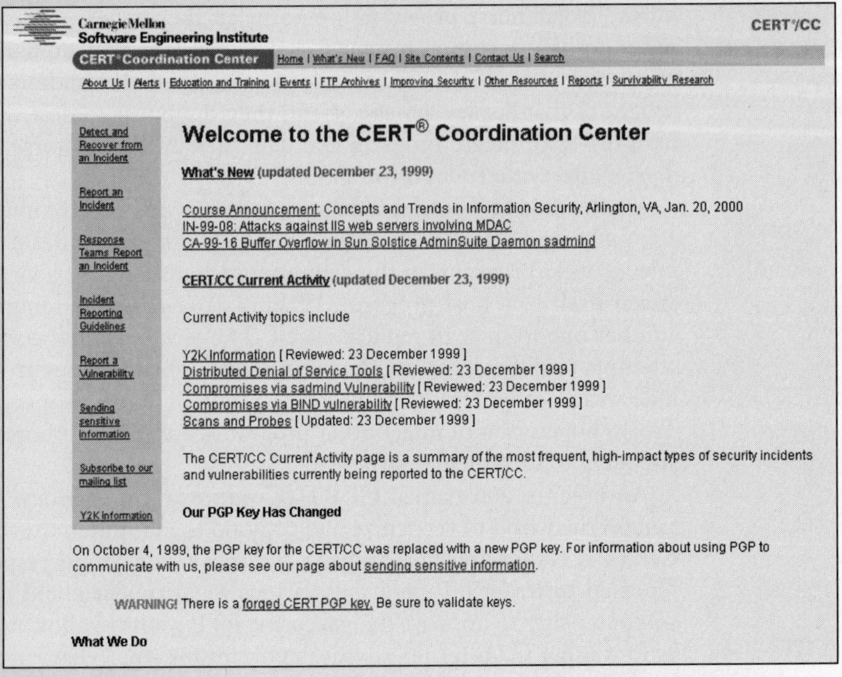

How does a computer virus spread from a single "infected" source? You might download a file from a Web site that contains a virus. When you access the file, you deploy the virus, which might attach itself to other files on your hard drive without your knowledge. Meanwhile, you might attach an infected file to an e-mail message, which transfers the virus to another user's computer. A virus's reproduction cycle is fast: Once the program is installed on a computer, it silently infects other programs. Those programs, in turn, can infect other people's systems when they are copied and installed there. Without virus detection software, a long time can pass before you see and detect the virus.

Now that you are aware of the different types of computer threats, Mark asks you to investigate ways to prevent them.

Security Countermeasures

Security countermeasures are procedures, programs, and hardware that detect and prevent computer security threats. No single countermeasure is effective against all security attacks, but selected countermeasures can provide excellent protection from selected security threats. Countermeasures should, when used together, protect against various secrecy, integrity, and necessity threats. The security countermeasures necessary for Internet transactions should ensure that the transaction or message being sent:

■ Cannot be read by anyone except the intended recipient.

■ Is tamperproof, ensuring that no one was able to modify its contents or delete it entirely.

■ Is authored by the person who claims to be the sender.

Mark is concerned about the security of all transactions on his Web site—especially those involving confidential customer information, such as credit card numbers, names, and addresses. He wants to assure his customers that there will be no security breach of personal information during a transaction. In addition, he wants to enact countermeasures to prevent impostors from ordering services from the RVP Web site. Finally, he wants to ensure that no customer's request for services is delayed or denied.

Identification and Authentication

User identification is the process of identifying yourself to the computer. Most computer systems implement user identification with user names and passwords. Similarly, most Web sites require you to establish a user ID and password before you can order goods or services. When you revisit the Web site, you can log in with your name and password combination and then proceed to purchase and ship goods to your office or home. Clearly, you can create almost any user name and password you like. The issue is not the user name/password combination (your login information) you choose and whether it matches your real name. Rather, the protection is that only *you* know the particular user name and password character strings. As long as these facts are not compromised, the Web or other computer system assumes that the person who enters the login information is, in fact, the identified user. The efficacy of the identification system is tied to the strength of the password. A hacker cannot guess a long and/or complicated password. Creating a strong password involves using uncommon strings of letters not found in a dictionary, including numbers and special characters; using uppercase and lowercase letters; and creating a long password. Hackers can run programs that create and enter passwords from a dictionary or a list of commonly used passwords to break into a system. Called a **brute force attack**, such a program tries character combinations until the system accepts one. Some systems will send a warning to the computer's operator when someone attempts to log in to a system an excessive number of times without succeeding. An intruder who successfully guesses your user name and password is **masquerading** as you.

User authentication is the process of associating a person and his identification with a very high level of assurance. In other words, authentication techniques give a high level of confidence that *you* are correctly identified when *you* log in. Authentication techniques include using biometrics, such as a retina scan or fingerprint scan, or asking a series of questions to which only the authentic user could know the correct answers, such as entering a password code or your mother's maiden name.

The system accepting your user name and password when you first create them must save your login information securely. Otherwise, an attacker could locate the system file containing user name and password combinations and obtain login information for all users. Most systems store passwords (and sometimes user names) in a special, encrypted form. **Encrypted** data are the unreadable, scrambled letters created by an encryption program. (Encryption programs are described later in this session.)

Users connected to the Internet from networked PCs, such as computers in a university computer lab, usually do not have to log in with a user name and password. Starting a Web browser almost never requires you to enter a user name and password. All e-mail client programs require you to log on to the mail system with a user name and password. However, it is possible, but not recommended, to send mail under an assumed name with a fictitious return address.

How can you authenticate an e-mail message's name and address? One way to authenticate users is to use digital certificates, which combine identification and authentication. A **digital certificate** is an encrypted and password-protected file that contains sufficient information to authenticate and prove a sender's identity. Usually, a digital certificate contains the following information:

- The certificate holder's name, address, and e-mail address.
- A special key that "unlocks" the digital certificate, thereby verifying the certificate's authenticity.

- The certificate's expiration date or validity period.
- A trusted third party, called a **certificate authority** (**CA**), which verifies the person's identity and issues the digital certificate.

A digital certificate is an electronic equivalent of an identification card. By looking at a person's driver's license, you can verify a person's identity by confirming the stated height, weight, and eye color printed on the license. Netscape Messenger, Outlook Express, and Eudora all provide the technology to send and receive digital certificates with e-mail messages, so a recipient can verify your identity. Although there are many personal digital certificates used by individuals, Web servers currently account for the largest percentage of digital certificates. Server-side digital certificates provide you with assurance that the Web site that *looks* like Microsoft.com really *is* Microsoft's site. Navigator and Internet Explorer both automatically receive and process digital certificates from Web sites. Figure 9-19 shows how a server receives and processes a digital certificate.

Figure 9-19	SENDING AND PROCESSING A DIGITAL CERTIFICATE

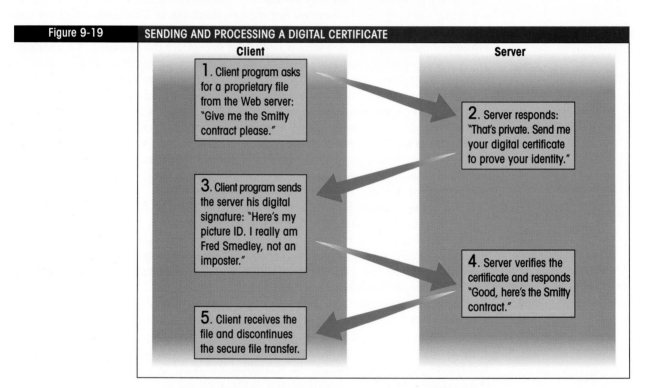

The first and largest commercial certifying authority is VeriSign, Inc. Mark asks you to visit the VeriSign Web site to explore it for information related to secure Web transactions.

To open the VeriSign Web site:

1. Return to the Student Online Companion Web page for Session 9.2, and then click the **VeriSign** hyperlink and wait while your Web browser loads the page shown in Figure 9-20.

Figure 9-20   **VERISIGN WEB PAGE**

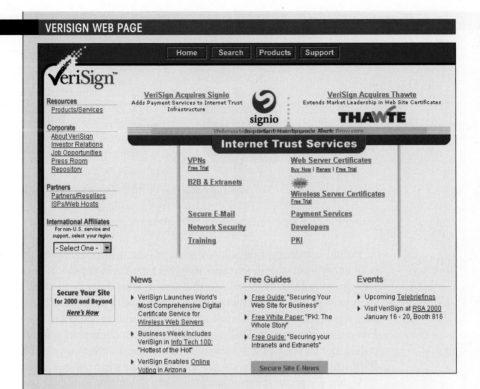

2. Explore the VeriSign Web site for information that is relevant to RVP's security needs.

Secrecy and Privacy

Security measures involve both people procedures and computer processes. For privacy, Mark is interested in computer processes to protect information automatically, but he knows that there must be some administrative procedures for people to follow—one of the most important procedures people can follow is authentication.

Mark understands that sending information on the Internet is subject to alteration, being copied, or being read by an unauthorized individual who is monitoring messages. Protecting business transactions is necessary before you can set up a Web business site. The solution to protecting messages from prying eyes and to safeguarding its contents from tampering is to use encryption. Encryption is coding information using a mathematical-based program and a secret key to produce a string of characters that is unreadable. To read the encrypted information, you need a key or password to convert the meaningless characters back into a readable form. The process of reversing encrypted text is called **decryption**. In order to decrypt text, you need a key to "unlock" the text. Without the key, the program alone cannot reveal the encrypted message's content. Encrypted information is called **cipher text**, whereas unencrypted information is called **plain text**.

There are two types of encryption used today: symmetric encryption (private-key) and asymmetric encryption (public-key). **Symmetric encryption** uses a single key that is known by the sender and receiver. This method works well in a highly controlled environment in which the sender can safely pass the secret key to the receiver via a human courier or other procedure. Symmetric encryption breaks down when it is used in an uncontrolled environment in which you cannot ensure that the key has been sent to the receiver safely. In addition, exchanging secret keys with people to whom you want to send encrypted messages is nearly impossible. Figure 9-21 shows how a symmetric-encryption system works.

Figure 9-21   SYMMETRIC (PRIVATE-KEY) ENCRYPTION

Public-key encryption solves the secret-key distribution problem. **Public-key encryption** is an encryption system that uses two different keys—a *public key* known to everyone and a *private* or *secret key* known only to the person who owns both keys. With a public-key system, each person has a private key that is secret and a public key that is shared with other users. Messages encrypted with a private key must be decrypted with the public key, and vice versa. For example, when an RVP customer sends an encrypted transaction, he or she uses RVP's public key to encrypt the message—that's the only key anyone outside of RVP knows. The RVP site then uses its private key to decrypt the message and process the transaction.

Using a similar scheme, you can verify that the sender is genuine. To send your electronic signature, you encrypt your message with your own, personal *private* key. The receiver verifies that the message is from you by decrypting the message with the public key you distribute or post on your Web site. If the message decrypts correctly, then the message's recipient can be confident the sender is authentic. In other words, if you try to pretend to be Ralph Nader and send a message to Mark Remes, Mark will try to decrypt the message with Ralph Nader's public key, but the message will consist of random characters after decryption. That is the signal that the pretender who sent you the message is *not* Ralph Nader. Figure 9-22 shows how a public-key encryption system works.

Figure 9-22   ASYMMETRIC (PUBLIC-KEY) ENCRYPTION

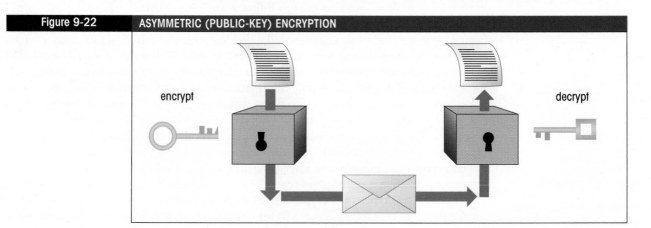

Encryption is considered weak or strong based on its algorithm and the length of the encryption key. An **algorithm** is a formula or set of steps to solve a particular problem. Years of research have yielded several secure algorithms with no inherent security weaknesses. The key(s) used to encrypt a message are equally important to the strength of the encryption method. Keys can be any set of characters that are used to encode the text. Longer keys provide significantly stronger protection than shorter keys. Experts estimate that it would take about 30 hours of computation time to decrypt a 40-bit (or six-character) key. On the other hand, a key that is 56 bits long (about eight characters) would take an estimated 228 *years* to discover through analysis of encrypted text. Further, 128-bit keys would take about 1,024 years to untangle. These calculations are all based on the number of possible keys that must be tried to "break" an encrypted message to read the plain-text message. Keys that are 128 bits long are called **strong keys**. Navigator and Internet Explorer make use of both symmetric- and asymmetric-encryption methods employing 128-bit keys.

Protecting Web Commerce Transactions

In certain circumstances, you want information you enter to be protected so someone else cannot see it. For example, when a customer purchases services from RVP, he or she will need to enter a credit card number and additional identification information. The customer will expect that this information is available to RVP employees only. How will RVP protect transactions between customers and the Web site? The RVP Web site will use a special facility called Secure Sockets Layer to handle the transactions. After the customer leaves the transaction site, this special security mechanism will turn off. **Secure Sockets Layer (SSL)** is a widely used security protocol that travels as a separate layer or "secure channel" on top of the TCP/IP Internet protocol. SSL provides a security handshake when your browser and the Web page to which you are connected want to conduct a secure communication. Most Web sites automatically switch to a secure state before asking you for sensitive information. Even if you haven't selected a public- and private-key set, SSL automatically handles the details of obtaining a temporary pair for you. The result is that the client browser and server automatically arrange to encrypt information flowing between them; in this case, your Web browser will display a security icon (which is usually a closed padlock) on the status bar to let you know that you are using a secure site. Figure 9-23 shows the Navigator padlock, and Figure 9-24 shows the Internet Explorer padlock. When you finish your transactions and go to another Web page, the browser and Web server return to a nonsecure state, which is indicated by an open padlock.

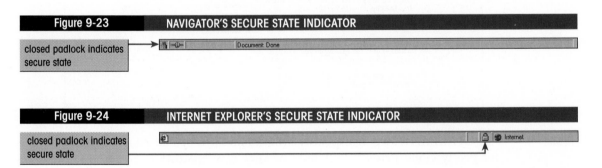

| Figure 9-23 | NAVIGATOR'S SECURE STATE INDICATOR |

closed padlock indicates secure state

Document: Done

| Figure 9-24 | INTERNET EXPLORER'S SECURE STATE INDICATOR |

closed padlock indicates secure state

Internet

SSL uses both symmetric and asymmetric encryption and keys to ensure privacy. SSL creates a public-key pair so that it can safely transmit data using a *symmetric* key. The symmetric key is encrypted using public-key encryption and sent to your browser. Using the symmetric key protects the remainder of the information transfer between your browser and the Web site. Symmetric encryption is faster than asymmetric encryption—that's why the remainder of the session's messages are encrypted with the symmetric key. When the session ends, these temporary keys, or **session keys**, are discarded—session keys exist only during a single, active session between the browser and server.

Protecting E-Mail

Encryption is used to protect e-mail and to authenticate the sender. Encryption protects a message's contents from inadvertent or malicious exposure, much like an envelope shields a letter's contents before it is opened. Two Internet protocols—S/MIME and PGP/MIME—are vying for acceptance as the encryption standard for e-mail. The main difference between these protocols is in the cryptographic programs they use. S/MIME is an e-mail security protocol introduced in 1995 by RSA Data Security. S/MIME uses a "digital envelope" approach, whereby the digital signature and a symmetric key are encrypted with a public key. Most other encryption, including the message, is encrypted with a symmetric key. The symmetric key is encrypted with the digital signature to protect it when it is sent to the receiver. Figure 9-25 shows RSA's home page and some links that you can use to find out more about encryption. You can open the RSA site by clicking the RSA link on the Session 9.2 page of the Student Online Companion.

Figure 9-25   **RSA DATA SECURITY'S HOME PAGE**

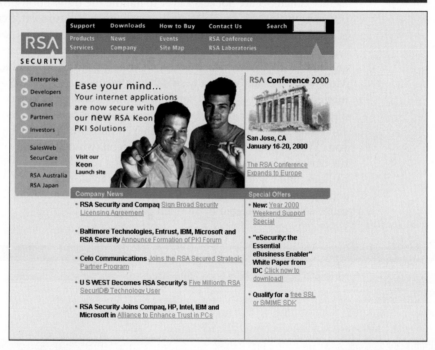

PGP/MIME is an e-mail security protocol invented by Phil Zimmermann. **PGP** stands for **Pretty Good Privacy**. PGP uses the same basic approach to create a protective envelope; the technical details aren't important for this discussion. Network Associates, Inc., a company formed with several others, including McAfee, Network General, PGP, and Helix, has PGP software. You can visit the Network Associates Web page by clicking the PGP link on the Session 9.2 page of the Student Online Companion. Figure 9-26 shows the Network Associates home page. You can click the links to learn more about how to purchase PGP or download free trial versions.

Figure 9-26	NETWORK ASSOCIATES, INC. HOME PAGE

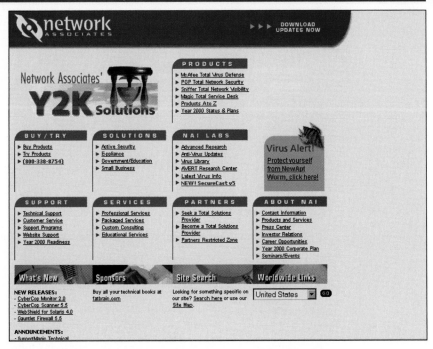

The Massachusetts Institute of Technology (MIT) distributes PGP *free* for noncommercial use in cooperation with Phil Zimmermann and with RSA Data Security, Inc., which licenses patents to the public-key encryption technology on which PGP relies. If you are interested in learning more about PGP and downloading a free version, click the Free PGP link on the Session 9.2 page of the Student Online Companion. Many software vendors, including Netscape Communications, Microsoft, and Lotus Development, support S/MIME in their products. Other vendors, such as Qualcomm, support PGP.

Integrity

Protecting an e-mail message by encrypting it is analogous to sealing a letter in an envelope—if the envelope's seal is broken when you receive it, you can suspect that someone intercepted, and possibly altered, the letter's contents. Sealing an envelope preserves the letter's integrity. To maintain the integrity of an e-mail message, you send the message through a **message digest function program** (or a **hash code function program**) to produce a number called a **message authentication code**, or **MAC**. This scheme works because it is almost impossible for a message and any other altered version of it to have an identical MAC. Figure 9-27 shows how the message digest function produces the MAC "AC2345HJ" for the text message "preserve this message." After it receives the MAC, the e-mail program sends the message and matching MAC together (or you can encrypt both pieces to preserve secrecy) to the recipient. The recipient's e-mail program recomputes the message's MAC and compares the computed MAC to the received MAC. If they match, then the message is unaltered. If they do not match, then the message has been altered and cannot be trusted.

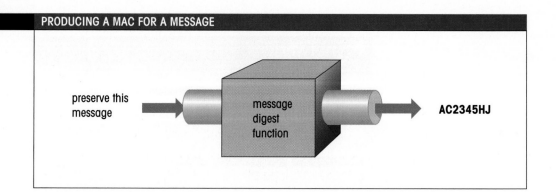

Figure 9-27   PRODUCING A MAC FOR A MESSAGE

There are many ways to encode a message to produce a value. But to be useful, the message digest function must exhibit these characteristics:

- It must be impossible or costly to reverse the MAC and produce the original message.
- The MAC should be random to prevent creating the original message from the MAC.
- The MAC must be unique to the message so there is an extremely small chance that two messages could ever produce the same MAC.

The Additional Information section of the Student Online Companion for Tutorial 9 includes additional links that you can explore to read more about various security topics and preserving message integrity.

Necessity

A necessity attack can slow down processing, completely remove an item, or deny its use. Although you cannot do much to protect the Web servers you browse from being attacked, you can protect your own browser program and your PC. One of the most dangerous entry points for delay and resource denial threats come from programs that travel with applications to your browser and execute on your PC. These programs are Java, JavaScript, and ActiveX components, all of which run programs on your PC. When you visit Web sites with active content—information that changes because of behind-the-scenes programs driving them—then you run a risk of loading a Trojan horse that can slow down your computer, reformat your hard drive, or perform other destruction.

For example, a destructive **Java applet**, which is a small program written in the Java programming language, could execute and consume all your computer's resources. Similarly, a **JavaScript program** can pose an additional problem because its programs can execute directly without being compiled (translated into special codes) before running on your computer. A cleverly written JavaScript program could examine your PC's programs and e-mail a file from your computer back to the Web server. **ActiveX components** are Microsoft's technology for writing small applications that perform some action in Web pages—these components have full access to your PC's file system. For example, a hidden ActiveX component in a Web page could scan your hard drive for PCX and JPEG files and print them on any network printer. Similarly, a renegade ActiveX program could reformat your hard drive.

Although most Java, JavaScript, and ActiveX components are beneficial, you can protect your computer from these delay/denial attacks. Perhaps the simplest strategy is to disallow Web programs from running them. Next, you will disable your Web browser from running Java and JavaScript programs. If you are using Navigator, complete the first set of steps. If you are using Internet Explorer, skip to the next set of steps.

To strengthen security in Navigator:

1. Click **Edit** on the menu bar, and then click **Preferences** to open the Preferences dialog box.

2. Click **Advanced** in the Category panel to display the advanced settings in the right panel of the Preferences dialog box.

3. If necessary, click the **Enable Java** check box to clear it.

4. If necessary, click the **Enable JavaScript** check box to clear it.

5. Disabling cookies is an added security precaution, so click the **Disable cookies** option button. Your Preferences dialog box should look like Figure 9-28.

| Figure 9-28 | NAVIGATOR PREFERENCES DIALOG BOX |

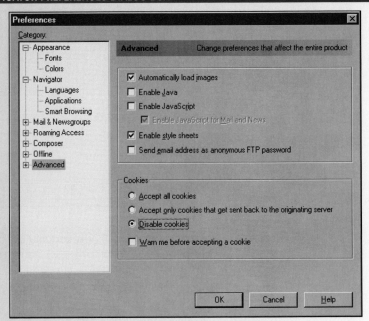

6. Click the **OK** button to save your security settings.

Internet Explorer also has security safeguards you can set.

To strengthen security in Internet Explorer:

1. Click **Tools** on the menu bar, and then click **Internet Options**. The Internet Options dialog box opens.

2. Click the **Security** tab to display security settings.

3. If directed to do so by your instructor, select a different zone by clicking the appropriate icon in the top panel. Internet is the default zone.

4. Move the slider to the top position (High appears in the right panel) to provide the highest level of security (see Figure 9-29). If you are an advanced user and want to customize your security settings, then you can click the **Custom Level** button and set many individual options for allowing ActiveX, Java, and JavaScript commands to execute on your PC.

Figure 9-29	INTERNET EXPLORER OPTIONS DIALOG BOX

5. Click the **OK** button to save your new security settings.

You can apply other defensive strategies to minimize your exposure to security threats, such as:

- Whenever possible, avoid filling out Web page registration forms unless you are sure that you are sending material to a trusted and secure site. Pay attention to what information is required. For example, if you are only requesting a product catalog, the form should not ask you to enter a credit card number.

- If you publish your own Web pages, omit your résumé and other sensitive information from the site.

- Disable cookies in your Web browser so that various sites cannot record and process your click stream.

- Purchase and use a good virus detection program. Whenever possible, purchase virus detection programs that also keep tabs on your Web activities, including download operations.

- Download software from known and trustworthy sources. If you are not familiar with a source, search for information about that source and try to determine its credibility before downloading anything.

Now, you are prepared to ensure the safe transaction of customer information over the Web.

Session 9.2   QUICK | CHECK

1. Three widely accepted categories of computer security are _____, _____, and _____.

2. What is the name for the protection of expression?

3. True or False: A Web cookie is always harmful.

4. What type of threat prevents a message from arriving in a timely fashion?

5. Protecting a message so that no one except the intended recipient can read it is an example of preserving integrity, necessity, or secrecy?

6. Another term for a public-key system is a(n) _____-key system.

7. Who invented the PGP (Pretty Good Privacy) protocol?

8. Web pages can transmit programs as well as data when you load them. What are the names of some of these programming languages that create the programs that run on your computer?

Mark is impressed with the information you found about security threats and protection measures. He will find these resources to be valuable as he collects his thoughts about the RVP site.

REVIEW ASSIGNMENTS

Mark still would like you to investigate computer virus protection to ensure that RVP doesn't unwittingly transmit viruses to customers. And, he wants to "jazz up" his browser so it can handle movies, animations, and sound. Help Mark by locating security information and plug-in information for Navigator and Internet Explorer. Mark asks you to print material about the plug-ins that you find so he can approve them. He also wants printed security information.

Do the following:

1. Start your Web browser, go to the Student Online Companion (http://www.course.com/newperspectives/internet2), click the link for your book, click the Tutorial 9 link, and then click the Tutorial Assignments link in the left frame. Click the Yahoo! link to open that Web site.

2. Click the Computers & Internet category to find information about both Internet security and browser plug-ins.

3. Click Security and Encryption to zoom in on security links.

4. Click the PGP – Pretty Good Privacy link to examine more information about the PGP protection system.

5. Scroll the page and try to locate and click the MIT distribution site for PGP. (The document describes how to obtain a freeware version of PGP.) If you cannot find that exact link, then locate any other link that looks interesting and click it. Either MIT's PGP home page (if you found the MIT link) or another page will open. In either case, your next task is to print the page.

6. If you are using Internet Explorer, follow these steps to print the page:
   a. Click File on the menu bar, and then click Page Setup. The Page Setup dialog box opens.
   b. In the Header text box, type your name followed by a space and then the characters &u (type the ampersand followed by the letter *u*). The string &u displays the Web page's URL on output.
   c. Click the OK button to close the Page Setup dialog box.
   d. To print the security Web page you found, click File on the menu bar and then click Print. You need to print only one page, so click the Pages option button and then type 1 in the from text box and type 1 in the to text box. Click the OK button to print the single page.

7. If you are using Navigator, follow these steps to print the page:
   a. Click File on the menu bar, and then click Edit Page. The Web page opens in Composer.
   b. Click at the top of the page, and then type your name. Press the Enter key twice to insert two blank lines.
   c. To print the security Web page you found, click File on the menu bar and then click Print. You only need print one page, so click the Pages option button and then type 1 in the from text box and type 1 in the to text box. Click the OK button to print the single page.
   d. Click File on the menu bar, and then click Close to close Composer.
   e. Click the No button when asked if you want to save the changed page.

8. Return to the Yahoo! home page, click the Computers & Internet category, and then click the World Wide Web@ link.

9. Click the Browsers@ link, and then click Plug-Ins.

10. Click Sound and Video. When the list of links opens, click any link that looks interesting to you and print the page using Step 6 or 7.

11. Close your browser and close your dial-up connection, if necessary.

CASE PROBLEMS

Case 1. Rowing Marvels Rowing Marvels (RM) manufactures racing shells, including singles, quads, and eights (eight-seat shells), used by rowing crews throughout Europe and the United States. Made from very thin polymers and resins, racing shells are expensive and delicate. Hannah Friedmann, owner and CEO of RM, wants to expand its marketing efforts with a Web site. She wants to advertise and sell shells ranging upwards to $18,000. In addition, she wants to sell accessories, including videos, rowing machines, unisuits, graphite blades ("oars"), and riggers. Hannah wants to have an enhanced site employing virtual reality, motion, and sound. Of course, she is concerned with providing a secure site so her customers can interact with her Web site confidently. Hannah wants you to locate Navigator and Internet Explorer plug-ins that will enhance customers' experiences. Also, she would like you to locate competitors' Web pages and examine what they have done.

Do the following:

1. Start your Web browser, go to the Student Online Companion (http://www.course.com/newperspectives/internet2), click the link for your book, click the Tutorial 9 link, and then click the Case Problems link in the left frame. Click the Netscape link to open the Web page.

2. Locate and click the Download link. A download page opens complete with links to the latest version of the browser, newsletters, and plug-ins.

3. Click the Browser Plug-ins link. The Browser Plug-ins page opens and lists plug-ins by category.

4. See if you can locate a link that leads to sound and video plug-in information. When you find the page of sound and movie plug-ins, print a single page. Use the steps provided in the Tutorial Assignments to add your name to the page header.

5. Next, locate information about Microsoft's commerce server. Return to the Student Online Companion, and then click the Microsoft link to open Microsoft's home page.

6. Click the Back Office link located near the top of the page.

7. Click Exchange Server on the right side of the page. A page devoted to Microsoft Exchange Server opens.

8. Print the first page of the Exchange Server Web page. Add your name to the page header.

9. Use a search engine to find Web pages for racing shells. When you find a site about rowing, racing shells, or related material, print the first page.

10. Now that you have visited the Netscape Plug-ins Web page, do you know how many plug-ins are featured at the Netscape site? See if you can determine that number.

11. Close your browser and your dial-up connection, if necessary.

Case 2. Pet Pleasin' Groomers Pet Pleasin' Groomers, a small pet grooming service located in Redding, California, provides grooming services to dogs of all sizes. Though grooming pets provides most of her income, the owner, Eloise Truce, wants to expand her client base by advertising on the Internet. Eloise would like to hire someone to build a Web site that is simple and attractive. In addition to advertising the services she and her groomers provide, she wants to collect information from Web browsers about their pets, what pet services would best suit them, and information about the owners such as their names and addresses. Later, she can use the collected pet owner information to send out brochures to those browsers from the surrounding community. Later, she will set up a full-fledged online store selling and shipping pet supplies to anyone in the world. Eloise is most concerned about security. In particular, she wants to provide her Internet-browsing customers with assurance that she will protect their privacy and security. Eloise has asked you to investigate the privacy policies of several prominent online stores and report back to her.

Do the following:

1. Start your Web browser, go to the Student Online Companion (http://www.course.com/newperspectives/internet2), click the link for your book, click the Tutorial 9 link, and then click the Case Problems link in the left frame. Click the BBBOnline hyperlink to open that page.

2. Examine the Web site assurance criteria presented on this site.

3. Click your browser's Back button to return to the Student Online Companion page, and then click the Amazon.com hyperlink.

4. Locate the link to Amazon.com's privacy policy. What does the policy say about revealing your name and address to other companies?

5. Click your browser's Back button to return to the Student Online Companion page, and then click the Cisco Systems hyperlink.

6. Locate the link to Cisco Systems' privacy policy. (Many organizations place their privacy statements near the bottom of their home page.)

7. Write a two-page (double-spaced) summary of your findings. In one paragraph, compare how the Amazon and Cisco privacy statements are similar (or not). Be sure to recommend a specific minimum set of sentences for Eloise's privacy policy that she can place on her Web site.

8. Close your browser and your dial-up connection, if necessary.

Case 3. Apartment Referrals, Inc. Apartment Referrals, Inc. is a student-run service that matches university students with available apartments in the community. The database of apartments is growing, and former tenants submit some of the apartments and their amenities for inclusion in the database. The business is highly competitive, and the main source of communication between the referral service and students is by e-mail. Besides a database of available apartments, the referral service provides free e-mail accounts to students living in apartments listed in the database. As one of the members of the student advisory board, you are concerned that the e-mail system that tenants use to submit names and available apartments might not be secure. You want to ensure that anything submitted over the e-mail system is protected and private. You decide to use the Web to research secure e-mail and see what is available.

Do the following:

1. Start your Web browser, go to the Student Online Companion (http://www.course.com/newperspectives/internet2), click the link for your book, click the Tutorial 9 link, and then click the Case Problems link in the left frame. Click the HotBot link to open that page.

2. Search for information about public-key encryption. (*Hint:* Avoid commercial papers and sales sites.)

3. Click one of the links in the returned list of links. Print the first three pages (or less) of the Web sites you visit that contain useful information.

4. Write a two-page paper about public-key encryption using at least three Web sites in your list of references.

5. Return to the Student Online Companion, and then click the AltaVista link to open the AltaVista search engine.

6. Search for information about secure e-mail.

7. Locate three appropriate links that describe e-mail security schemes and print the first two pages of each of the three Web sites.

8. Write a two-page paper about e-mail security using the information that you found.

9. Close your browser and your dial-up connection, if necessary.

Case 4. Venture Capital Experts Group Alex Fermi provides startup money for promising, fledgling Internet businesses. VCEG also operates an incubator office complex in San Jose, California, where small groups of their funded businesses can maintain small offices complete with phone systems, office equipment, and limited staff support. VCEG has had trouble lately with hacker attacks on their site. Three times in the last six months, attackers have successfully penetrated their system and placed electronic graffiti on the VCEG home page and several of its other pages. In addition, they believe that someone has copied their corporate logo and other copyrighted material and posted it on another site masquerading as VCEG. Because Alex and his group are busy with their venture capital business, they have hired you to look into the security measures they could take to prevent the break-ins they are experiencing. Also, they would like to see if there is a way to protect Web graphics and other VCEG corporate property by somehow secretly stamping it with an imperceptible mark clearly identifying the rightful owner. They want you also to learn about digital certificates, because they suspect that a small fraction of their e-mail has come not from trusted clients but from imposters. You go to the Internet to launch your research.

Do the following:

1. Start your Web browser, go to the Student Online Companion (http://www.course.com/newperspectives/internet2), click the link for your book, click the Tutorial 9 link, and then click the Case Problems link in the left frame. Click the Thawte link to open that page, which compares the cost of different providers' digital certificates.

2. Note the cost of three personal certificates.

3. Click the Enterprise Solutions button to examine what certificates are available for companies.

4. Locate and click the Web server's button that reveals which Web servers they support. When the Web page opens, print it.

5. Click your browser's Back button three times to return to the Student Online Companion and then click the VeriSign link. When VeriSign's home page opens, click the Products button to reveal their full line of security products.

6. Locate and click the link for Individual Digital Certificates for E-Mail. Print one page that describes the VeriSign Digital ID.

7. Click your browser's Back button a sufficient number of times to return to the Student Online Companion. Click the WebArmor link.

8. Once the WebArmor home page opens, locate the link describing the benefits of using WebArmor. Print the first page of the WebArmor key benefits description.

9. Close your browser and your dial-up connection, if necessary.

Case 5. Personal Research about Cookies You are writing a research paper on the Internet and the use of cookies. While you are not yet ready to open your own Web site and collect information, you want to know more about cookies that other sites store on your computer. Exactly what are cookies and how are they used are two questions you hope to answer after completing your search.

Do the following:

1. Start your Web browser, go to the Student Online Companion (http://www.course.com/newperspectives/internet2), click the link for your book, click the Tutorial 9 link, and then click the Case Problems link in the left frame.

2. Click the Cookie Central FAQ link to reveal the Cookie Central list of frequently asked questions.

3. Locate a link that describes how a cookie actually works. Click that link. When the page opens, print the first page. Click your browser's Back button to return to the Cookie Central FAQ page.

4. Look in the Introduction section and click a link that leads to a discussion of where the term *cookie* came from. Print that page.

5. Click your browser's Back button twice to return to the Student Online Companion.

6. Click the Cookie Pal link to open that home page. Click various links and discover exactly what the Cookie Pal product does. Print a list of Cookie Pal's features.

7. Close your browser and your dial-up connection, if necessary.

LAB ASSIGNMENTS

Multimedia brings together text, graphics, sound, animation, video, and photo images. In this Lab, you will learn how to apply multimedia and then have the chance to see what it might be like to design some aspects of multimedia projects. See the Read This Before You Begin page for information on installing and starting the Lab.

1. Click the Steps button to learn about multimedia development. As you proceed through the Steps, answer the Quick Check questions. After you complete the Steps, you will see a Quick Check Report. Follow the instructions on the screen to print this report.

2. In Explore, browse through the STS-79 Multimedia Mission Log. How many videos are included in the Multimedia Mission Log? The image on the Mission Profile page is a vector drawing. What happens when you enlarge it?

3. Listen to the sound track on Day 3. Is this a WAV file or a MIDI file? Why do you think so? Is this a synthesized sound or a digitized sound? Listen to the sound track on page 8. Can you tell if this is a WAV file or a MIDI file?

4. Suppose you were hired as a multimedia designer for a multimedia series targeting fourth- and fifth-grade students. Describe the changes you would make to the Multimedia Mission Log so it would be suitable for these students. Also, include a sketch showing a screen from your revised design.

5. When you view the Mission Log on your computer, do you see palette flash? Why or why not? If you see palette flash, list the images that flash.

6. Multimedia can be effectively applied to projects such as encyclopedias, atlases, and animated storybooks; to computer-based training for foreign languages, first aid, or software applications; for games and sports simulations; for business presentations; for personal albums, scrapbooks, and baby books; for product catalogs and Web pages.

7. Suppose you were hired to create one of these projects. Write a one-paragraph description of the project you would be creating. Describe some of the multimedia elements you would include. For each of the elements, indicate its source and whether you would need to obtain permission for its use. Finally, sketch a screen or two showing your completed project.

QUICK CHECK ANSWERS

Session 9.1

1. Plug-ins operate within the browser; helper applications are separate programs that execute when you click a link requiring them.

2. True

3. Virtual Reality Modeling Language

4. You do not have to wait until the entire file downloads to start playing the file.

5. programs that are required to create Web pages containing files that demand special browser helper applications or plug-ins

6. Beatnik, Crescendo, and RealPlayer

7. Plug-in creators make money from licensing their Web page plug-in development software. Developers license the software to create Web pages that deliver content to users who browse the Web.

Session 9.2

1. secrecy, integrity, necessity

2. copyright

3. False

4. necessity

5. secrecy

6. asymmetric

7. Phil Zimmermann

8. ActiveX, JavaScript, and Java

OBJECTIVES

In this tutorial you will:

- Learn about portals and how to customize them

- Create and customize a Web calendar

- Create and customize a Web address book

- Visit Web sites that carry on electronic commerce

- Discuss the likely future direction of electronic commerce

PERSONALIZED
INFORMATION DELIVERY AND ELECTRONIC COMMERCE

Portals and Electronic Commerce

CASE

Software Solution Providers, Inc.

Software Solution Providers, Inc. (SSP) is a privately held computer software company located in Plano, Texas. Steven French founded the computer consulting services company in 1985 with only four employees. Since then, he has hired 48 additional employees and broadened the company's focus to include a variety of system design, development, and testing projects. Most of SSP's staff members are computer scientists, information systems analysts, and software engineers who design software systems for city and state governments. SSP's software contracts include large systems, such as the Plano Investigative and Crime Information System (PICIS), which is an extensive database that holds crime reports, information about ongoing investigations, and automotive license information. The system is accessible from police cars and displays information from the PICIS database on notebook computers mounted on the dashboard. Over half of SSP's contracts are smaller jobs involving only two to four software engineers and spanning three to six months' time.

SSP discovers contracts on which to bid by consulting periodicals that list hundreds of government projects seeking contractors, such as the *Commerce Business Daily*, a U.S. Department of Commerce publication, and the local commerce newspaper, *The Daily Transcript*. Currently, Melinda Olson, vice president of research, reads these publications and notes any jobs for which SSP would be an appropriate contractor. When Melinda locates an appropriate project, she quickly assembles a team to write a proposal to do the work identified in the project description. Usually, the team must write and submit the 30-page proposal within a few days. Then, they plan a series of milestone meetings as they research a project and after they are the successful bidder. One of the milestone meetings is creating a workflow structure, which includes the people assigned to various parts of the project. Work teams keep track of each project's contact persons, their mobile and office phones, and the best times to contact them.

Because of the number of appointments that the SSP staff must handle—appointments to meet with clients and related business functions—each staff member must carefully schedule client meetings so they do not conflict with group meetings. So far, each person has kept his or her appointments and contact information in his or her Personal Digital Assistant (PDA), such as a PalmPilot. That arrangement does not allow other staff members on the same project to coordinate their schedules. What they all need is a group-public way to post their respective appointments so that other team members can check the group schedule before committing to individual appointments. Steven wants you to learn more about Web technologies that might help his company schedule appointments and store client contact information so that company team members can access the client information. He wants you to help the company become more efficient in scheduling its appointments and gain a competitive advantage. Helping Melinda with this research will speed the work.

SESSION 10.1

In this session you will learn about Web portals and visit a few popular portal sites. You will customize a portal to deliver just the information that interests you. Then, you will create your own Yahoo! Calendar and enter your appointments and important engagements into it. Finally, you will open your private Yahoo! address book.

Web Portals

Web portals represent a way to supply clients with current, customized information. A **Web portal** (or simply a **portal**) is a "cyber door" on the Web that you can enter to customize its contents. Portals are starting points for Web surfers—they usually include general interest information and can help you find just about anything on the Web. Portals are not aimed at a particular target audience, which is part of their attraction—you can customize a portal for your needs. Examples of portals include Excite, Amazon.com, Yahoo!, Netscape's Netcenter, and Microsoft's Start sites. Web portals share common characteristics, including free e-mail; links to search engines and to categories of information; membership services; news, sports, and business headlines and articles; personalized space with the user's selections displayed; discussion groups; links to chat rooms; links to virtual shopping malls; and calendars, address books, and Web directories.

When you visit your customized portal site, your requested information is ready and waiting for you to use. Portals are a key strategy in electronic commerce. Large and small enterprises that conduct business over the Web have found that the simple "build it and they will come" strategy isn't sufficient to attract and keep customers.

The term used by advertisers and webmasters for the number of people (or "eyes") who visit a site or see an advertisement is **eyeballs**. An eyeball measure is important because sites with a high eyeball count can attract more advertisers and charge higher advertising fees than a site with a smaller eyeball count. A chief goal of portals and channel providers is to maximize their eyeball counts. Another way of measuring portal and Web page popularity is a page view. A **page view** measures the number of unique visitors to a Web page; in other words, it measures only the number of people who visit the site, and not the number of total visitors, which includes people who visit it more than once. A page view count is a good measure of a site's popularity. Portals usually have page view counts higher than those for other Web pages. The quality of a portal has a tremendous effect on *keeping* people coming back to a site.

Steven wants you to show him examples of portal sites. Melinda suggests that you start with Excite, which is a familiar and popular portal.

To examine the Excite portal site:

1. Start your Web browser, and then go to the Student Online Companion page by entering the URL **http://www.course.com/newperspectives/internet2** in the appropriate location in your Web browser. Click the hyperlink for your book, click the **Tutorial 10** link, and then click the **Session 10.1** link. Click the **Excite** link and wait while the browser loads the page shown in Figure 10-1. The **Create your Start Page!** link at the top of the page allows you to customize this Web page in many ways.

Figure 10-1	EXCITE PORTAL SITE

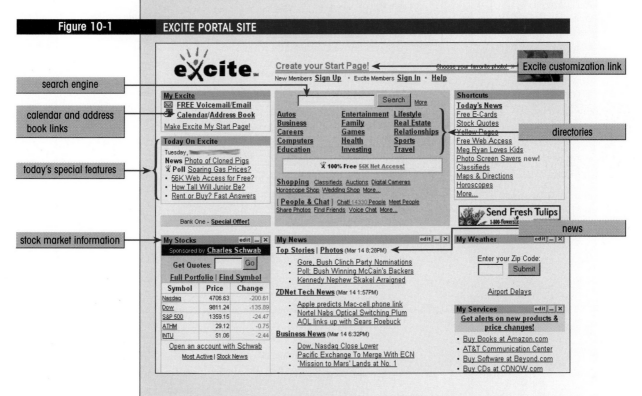

2. Click the **Create your Start Page!** link to display the Excite Sign Up page shown in Figure 10-2. (Your page might look different.) In order to personalize a portal page, most sites ask you for information that helps them identify how you customized your Web page. Frequently, at least part of the identification data is saved as a cookie on your computer. If you scroll to the bottom of the page, you will notice a link to Excite's privacy policy. Excite permits multiple accounts on a single computer if more than one user completes and submits the registration information.

Figure 10-2   **EXCITE SIGN UP PAGE**

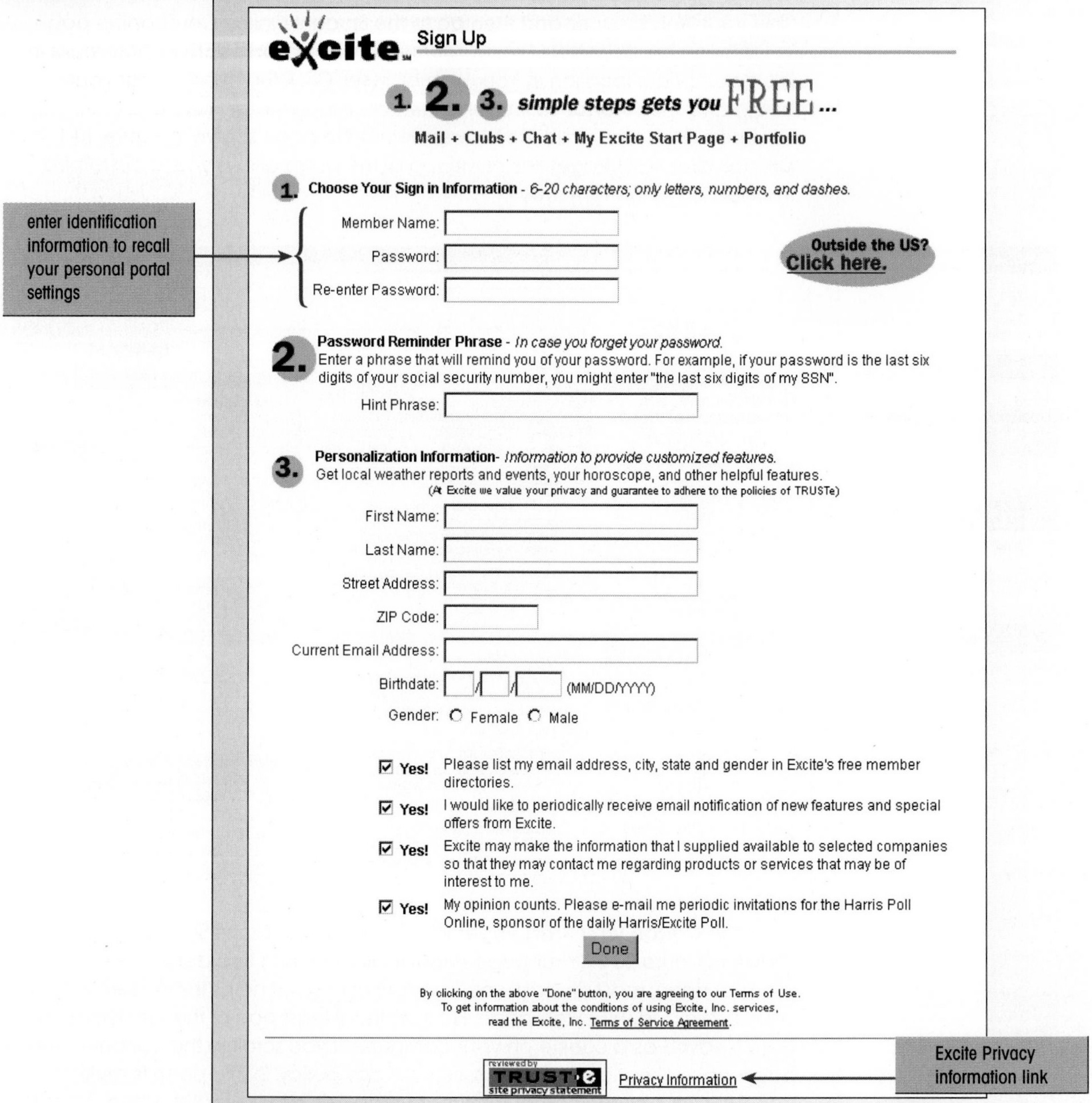

eXcite℠ Sign Up

1. **2.** 3. *simple steps gets you* FREE...

Mail + Clubs + Chat + My Excite Start Page + Portfolio

1. **Choose Your Sign in Information** - *6-20 characters; only letters, numbers, and dashes.*

Member Name:

Password:

Re-enter Password:

Outside the US?
Click here.

enter identification information to recall your personal portal settings

2. **Password Reminder Phrase** - *In case you forget your password.*
Enter a phrase that will remind you of your password. For example, if your password is the last six digits of your social security number, you might enter "the last six digits of my SSN".

Hint Phrase:

3. **Personalization Information**- *Information to provide customized features.*
Get local weather reports and events, your horoscope, and other helpful features.
(At Excite we value your privacy and guarantee to adhere to the policies of TRUSTe)

First Name:

Last Name:

Street Address:

ZIP Code:

Current Email Address:

Birthdate: /   /   (MM/DD/YYYY)

Gender: ○ Female ○ Male

☑ **Yes!** Please list my email address, city, state and gender in Excite's free member directories.

☑ **Yes!** I would like to periodically receive email notification of new features and special offers from Excite.

☑ **Yes!** Excite may make the information that I supplied available to selected companies so that they may contact me regarding products or services that may be of interest to me.

☑ **Yes!** My opinion counts. Please e-mail me periodic invitations for the Harris Poll Online, sponsor of the daily Harris/Excite Poll.

Done

By clicking on the above "Done" button, you are agreeing to our Terms of Use.
To get information about the conditions of using Excite, Inc. services,
read the Excite, Inc. Terms of Service Agreement.

reviewed by
TRUSTe
site privacy statement   Privacy Information

Excite Privacy information link

3. Click your browser's **Back** button until you return to the Student Online Companion page for Session 10.1.

Next, you want to look at the Snap.com portal site. You have heard a lot of good things about that site and others, and your research would be incomplete if you did not investigate Snap.

To examine the Snap.com portal site:

1. Click the **Snap** link to open the Snap home page.

2. Click the **My Snap** tab located at the top of the page. The Snap:Welcome to my.snap.com page opens, as shown in Figure 10-3. You can indicate how you want to customize your Snap portal page.

Figure 10-3	SNAP:WELCOME TO MY.SNAP.COM PAGE

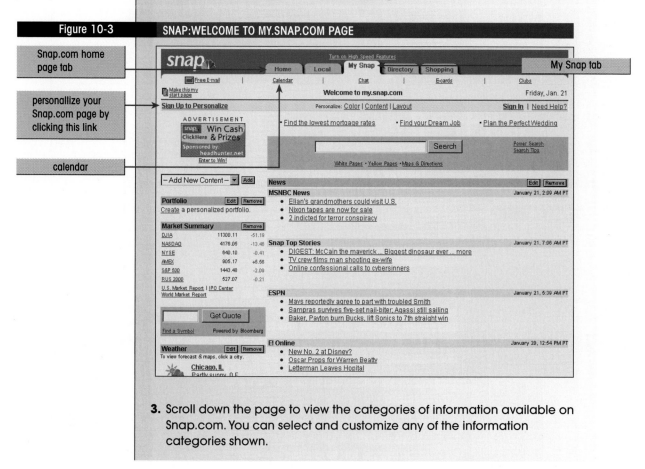

Snap.com home page tab

personallize your Snap.com page by clicking this link

calendar

My Snap tab

3. Scroll down the page to view the categories of information available on Snap.com. You can select and customize any of the information categories shown.

Next, you want to look at the Lycos and the AltaVista portal sites.

To view the Lycos portal site and then the AltaVista portal site:

1. Return to the Student Online Companion page for Session 10.1, and then click the **Lycos** link to open the Lycos home page shown in Figure 10-4.

Figure 10-4	LYCOS PORTAL SITE

LYC S, Your Personal Internet Guide   Internet Access · Check Email · My Lycos

search for text box

Shop&Win Romantic   Baby, we've got it all!   You Could Win an IBM
       Gifts!   click to shop   ThinkPad

personalize your
start page

Search for [   ] Go Get It!®

Advanced Search | Parental Controls | RichMedia Search

Tools Chat Clubs Boards Email **Instant Messenger** HomePages Guides Games Kids Travel more...
Find FTP Stocks News MP3 Lycos 50 Yellow Pages People Maps Shop Gifts Auctions Banking Books

What do Snowboards and Steaks have in common? You could win them here!

News Edit   Customize this page   Boston, MA
                                  Sign up | Log In to My Lycos   Partly Cloudy, 3°F
• Clinton: More Money For   Change to your city
  Science, Tech
                                  Arts & Entertainment   **Recreation**
news   Music, Celebrities, Movies...   Food, Outdoors, Humor...
• Elian's Grandmas Meet
  Atty. Gen. Reno   **Autos**   **Reference**
• Sundance Film Festival   Parts, Repair, Buying...   Education, Maps, Databases...
  Preview
       More Lycos News...   **Business & Careers**   **Regional**
                                  Jobs, Investing, Real Estate   US, Europe, Asia...
Shopping
                                  Computers & Internet   **Science & Technology**   directories
• Valentine's gifts at   Software, Internet, Hardware   Biology, Astronomy, Earth...
  barnesandnoble.com!
                                  Games   **Shopping**
shopping links   • Vacation Getaways a low   Card, Computer, Arcade...   Toys, Electronics, Classifieds...
                   as $50
                                  Health   **Society & Culture**
• Apply for Fixed APR Lycos   Diseases, Women, Medicine...   Relationships, People, Women...
  MasterCard
       More Shopping...

2. Scroll down the page and examine its contents. Links at the bottom lead to Lycos job descriptions and help and provide an opportunity to send Lycos feedback. Locate and click the **Affiliate Program** link. The Lycos Affiliate Program Welcome Page opens, describing how members earn money whenever anyone clicks your link leading to Lycos.

3. Click your browser's **Back** button twice to return to the Student Online Companion.

4. Click the **AltaVista** portal link to open the AltaVista home page. AltaVista is a well-known search engine that many users customize as a portal. You can use the Home Pages link to customize AltaVista (see Figure 10-5).

Figure 10-5   ALTAVISTA PORTAL SITE

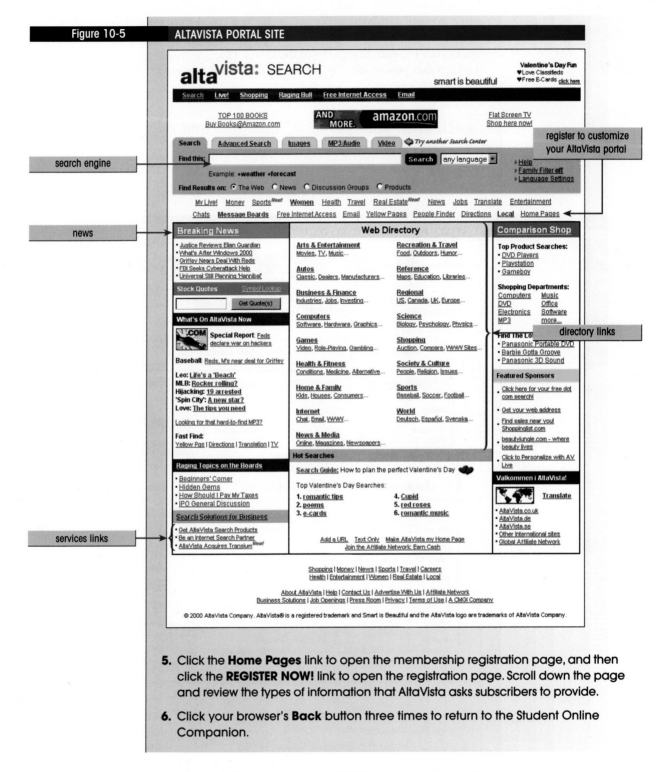

5. Click the **Home Pages** link to open the membership registration page, and then click the **REGISTER NOW!** link to open the registration page. Scroll down the page and review the types of information that AltaVista asks subscribers to provide.

6. Click your browser's **Back** button three times to return to the Student Online Companion.

Next, you will customize a portal Web page to understand the process.

Customizing a Portal

Yahoo! is a busy site that receives a large number of hits each day and thus is a prime location for advertising. Over the years, Yahoo! has grown from a directory-only service to a true portal. Yahoo! offers all of the services and features of a typical portal site. What makes Yahoo!

especially appealing, like other portals, is that you can design a portal page tailored to your interests. You can use the My Yahoo! feature to save your preferences and deliver current information to your PC each time you visit the Yahoo! site.

Steven wants you to use My Yahoo! to customize a page that he can use to see how a portal works.

To establish your personal Yahoo! ID and password:

1. Return to the Student Online Companion Web page for Session 10.1, if necessary, and then click the **Yahoo!** hyperlink and wait while your Web browser loads the Web page shown in Figure 10-6.

Figure 10-6	YAHOO! SITE BEFORE CUSTOMIZATION

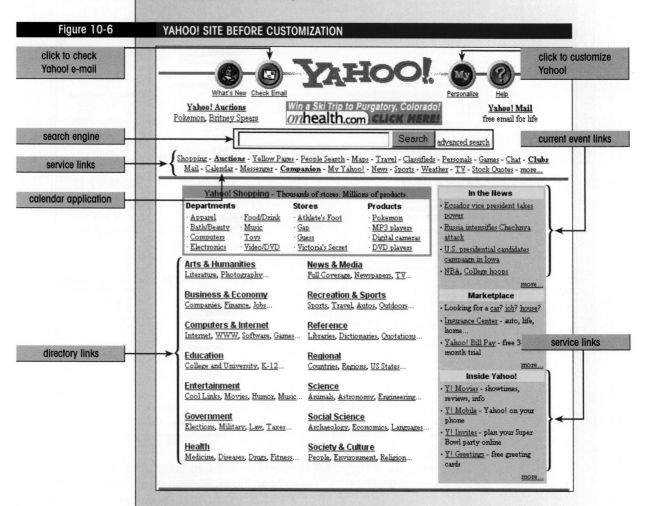

2. Click the **Personalize** button at the top of the Yahoo! home page (see Figure 10-6) to open the Welcome to My Yahoo! page. You must enter and submit a Yahoo! ID and a password, which the Yahoo! server stores as a cookie on your PC, to visit this site. (If you use a different computer the next time you visit Yahoo!, you can ask Yahoo! to find your information on its server.)

TROUBLE? If you already have a Yahoo! ID, enter your Yahoo! ID and your Yahoo! password in the appropriate text boxes, click the Sign in button, and then skip the remaining steps.

3. Click the **Get Your Own My Yahoo!** link in the frame at the left side of the page to open the Welcome to Yahoo! page shown in Figure 10-7.

| Figure 10-7 | CREATING YOUR YAHOO! ID AND PASSWORD |

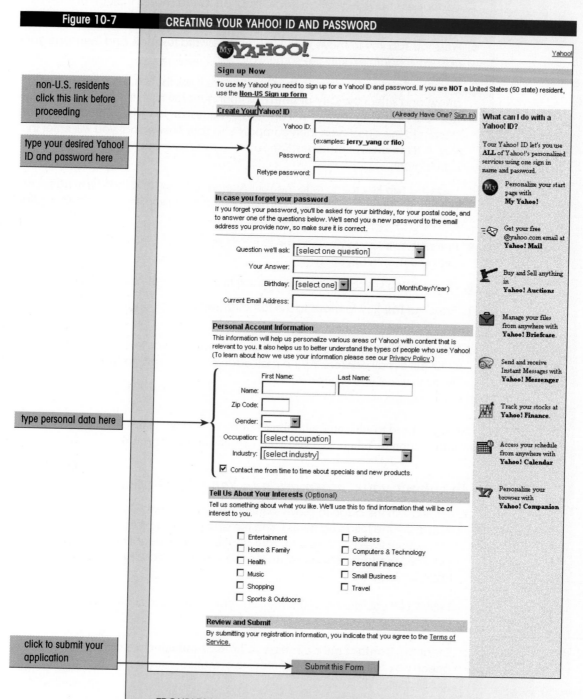

non-U.S. residents click this link before proceeding

type your desired Yahoo! ID and password here

type personal data here

click to submit your application

TROUBLE? If you are *not* a U.S. resident, then click the Non-US Sign up form link at the top of the page and enter your information in that form.

4. Click in the **Yahoo ID** text box, and then type a user ID to identify you. There are several examples below the Yahoo ID text box on the form. You can use numbers, letters, and the underscore character in your user ID; however, you cannot use any spaces.

5. Press the **Tab** key to move to the Password text box. Type a password that you can remember easily in the Password text box. For security reasons, asterisks appear as you type your password. Your password should include at least six characters (letters and/or numbers) to provide good security.

6. Press the **Tab** key to move to the Retype password text box, and then type your password again exactly the same way as the first time.

7. Press the **Tab** key to move to the Question we'll ask list box, click the list box arrow, and select the **City of birth?** as your question from the list box. If you forget your password, Yahoo! will ask you this question to verify your identity. Your answer to this question is then compared to Your Answer that you will enter in Step 8. If the answer matches, Yahoo! will e-mail your password to you so you can log on.

8. Press the **Tab** key to move to the Your Answer text box, and then type name of the city where you were born. Remember the exact spelling and capitalization in case you need to recover your password.

9. Press the **Tab** key to move to the Birthday list box, click the list box arrow, and click the month of your birth.

10. Press the **Tab** key to move to the next text box and type the day (1–31) of your birth.

11. Press the **Tab** key to move to the last birthday text box and type the four-digit year of your birth.

12. Press the **Tab** key to move to the Current Email Address text box, and then type your full e-mail address. Your e-mail address is used only to send your password to you if you request it.

Now, you need to add some additional information about yourself. Then, you can submit your information to Yahoo! and visit your new customized portal site.

To submit your information to Yahoo! and create your page:

1. Scroll down the page to move to the Personal Account Information section, and then enter the following items using the appropriate text or list boxes: your name, your five-digit Zip code, your gender, your occupation (select **college/graduate student** from the list), and your industry (select **other**, the last entry in the list).

   TROUBLE? If you are not a U.S. resident, enter the appropriate information in the Country and Primary Language text boxes.

2. Clear the **Contact me from time to time about specials and new products** check box so that you will not receive any unsolicited e-mail from Yahoo! or its affiliates.

3. In the third section of the form, click at least one check box that indicates your interests. (Click as many check boxes as you want.)

4. Click the **Submit this Form** button to submit your responses. Yahoo! records your responses and displays a summary of your account ID information and e-mail address, as shown in Figure 10-8.

| Figure 10-8 | YAHOO! ID SUCCESSFUL COMPLETION NOTICE |

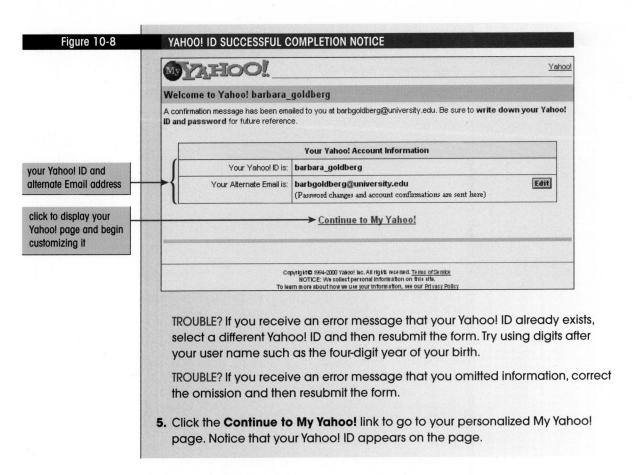

your Yahoo! ID and alternate Email address

click to display your Yahoo! page and begin customizing it

TROUBLE? If you receive an error message that your Yahoo! ID already exists, select a different Yahoo! ID and then resubmit the form. Try using digits after your user name such as the four-digit year of your birth.

TROUBLE? If you receive an error message that you omitted information, correct the omission and then resubmit the form.

5. Click the **Continue to My Yahoo!** link to go to your personalized My Yahoo! page. Notice that your Yahoo! ID appears on the page.

The information that you entered is saved as a cookie file on your PC and on the Yahoo! server. If you established a Yahoo! ID on your own computer, then you do not need to worry about someone else using your Yahoo! ID. If you created your account on a public computer, then the next person who uses a Web browser to visit the Yahoo! Web site will see your Yahoo! customized Web page by default. To avoid this problem, always sign out of your Yahoo! account before visiting other Web sites.

To sign out of your Yahoo! account:

1. With the My Yahoo! page displayed, click the **Sign Out** link at the top of the page (see Figure 10-9). When you sign out, Yahoo! displays a screen similar to the one shown in Figure 10-10.

| Figure 10-9 | SIGNING OUT OF MY YAHOO! |

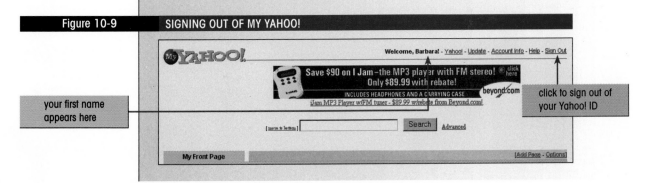

your first name appears here

click to sign out of your Yahoo! ID

Figure 10-10	YAHOO! INDICATION THAT SIGN OUT WAS SUCCESSFUL

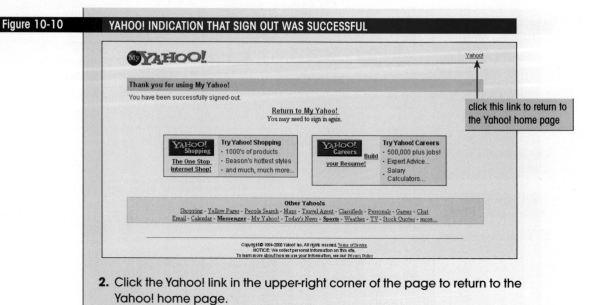

2. Click the Yahoo! link in the upper-right corner of the page to return to the Yahoo! home page.

Next, you will sign in to your Yahoo! account so you can demonstrate to Steven how he can customize a portal site.

To sign in to your personal Yahoo! account:

1. Return to the Student Online Companion Web page for Session 10.1, and then click the **My Yahoo!** hyperlink and wait while your Web browser loads the Web page.

2. Type your Yahoo! ID in the Yahoo! ID text box, press the **Tab** key to move to the Yahoo! Password text box, and then type your password. Figure 10-11 shows an example of user barbara_goldberg signing in with her user name and password. Notice that the password displays asterisks instead of the actual password for security reasons.

Figure 10-11	SIGNING IN TO A YAHOO! ACCOUNT

highlighted tab indicating the current open page, My Front Page

click here to customize the content of your Front Page

click here to customize the design and layout of your Front Page

type your Yahoo! ID here

type your password here

click here to sign in

Welcome to My Yahoo! - Yahoo! - Help - Sign In

My Front Page   My Other Page   [A...

Personalize ▶ Content Layout

Message Center

You are not currently signed in

Get Your Own My Yahoo!

Already have a Yahoo ID?

Yahoo! ID: bara_goldberg

Yahoo! Password: ••••••••••

☐ Remember my ID & Password

Sign in

Need help signing in?

Portfolios   🗗 Edit X
▽ **Indices**
* DJIA   11251.71   -99.59
* NASDAQ   4235.40   +45.89
* S&P 500   1441.36   -4.21

Lead Photo - Jan 22 11:05am

Cuban Grandmothers Meet Reno Asking Elian's Return
Mariela Quintana (L) and Raquel Rodriguez (R), the grandmothers of Elian Gonzalez, arrive at John F. Kennedy International Airport in New York on Friday. Elian's grandmothers will meet with U.S. Attorney General Janet Reno on Saturday to press their emotional appeal for the six-year-old shipwreck survivor to be returned to his Cuban homeland. (Peter Morgan/Reuters)

My Front Page Headlines - Jan 22 11:05am   🗗 Edit X
Customize your My Yahoo Headlines to see only the news of interest to you.

Top Stories from Reuters   Jan 22 10:55am
* Cuban Grandmothers Meet Reno Asking Elian's Return
* Candidates Canvass Iowa in Final Dash to Caucuses
* Ecuador's Congress Approves Noboa As New President

World from Reuters   Jan 22 10:52am
* Ecuador's Congress Approves Noboa As New President
* Trimble Says IRA Has 9 Days to Begin Disarmament
* North Korea Threatens to Resume Missile Tests

Top Sports Stories from AP   Jan 22 9:58am

3. If you are on a public computer, then make sure to clear the **Remember my ID & Password** check box, if it is not already clear, so that your identification and password are not saved on the local computer. (Yahoo! stores that valuable information for you on their site.)

4. Click the **Sign in** button below the Yahoo! Password text box to open your Front Page. Once you sign in, your Front Page opens. The My Front Page tab is highlighted, indicating the name of your open Web page. You can add other pages by clicking the Add Page link. If you choose to do that, a tab placed to the right of your Front Page tab represents each page.

Now that you have signed in, you can customize your Yahoo! page in many ways. First, you can customize the general layout of your page by selecting particular modules that you want to see. Second, you can select specific content for each module that you choose. Next, you will customize the general layout of your page.

To personalize your Yahoo! Front Page:

1. Click the **Content** button (see Figure 10-11) to open a Personalize Page Content page. Several categories are listed beneath the Choose Your Content heading. You can select the contents of your Front Page by checking or clearing the contents check boxes. Checked items are included on your Front Page, and unchecked ones are not. You can change the arrangement of the left and right sides of your display by clicking the Change Layout button.

2. Clear all check boxes in every My Yahoo! Category.

3. In the My Yahoo! Essentials list, check the **Headlines, Weather,** and **Stock Portfolios** check boxes.

4. Check the **Best Fares** check box in the Travel category.

5. Click the **Change Layout** button. (A Change Layout button is located at both the top and bottom of the page.) The Personalize Page Layout page opens. Next, you will arrange the content you selected on your Front Page.

6. Click **Best Fares** in the Left Side list box.

7. Click the **up arrow** twice to move Best Fares to the top of the list.

8. Click **Stock Portfolios** and then click the **down arrow** once to move Stock Portfolios to the bottom of the list. When you have completed these steps, your screen should look like Figure 10-12.

Figure 10-12	CUSTOMIZING YOUR FRONT PAGE LAYOUT

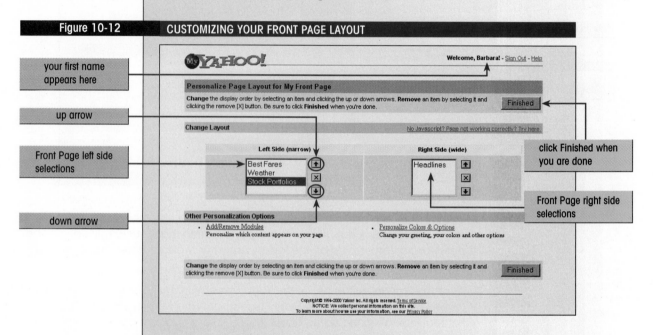

9. Click the **Finished** button to submit your Front Page layout choices. Your newly customized Front Page opens. Notice that the left side displays best airline fares, the weather for your city, and some stock prices. Yahoo! knows which city's temperature to display based on the Zip code that you entered when you obtained your account. The right side contains news (see Figure 10-13).

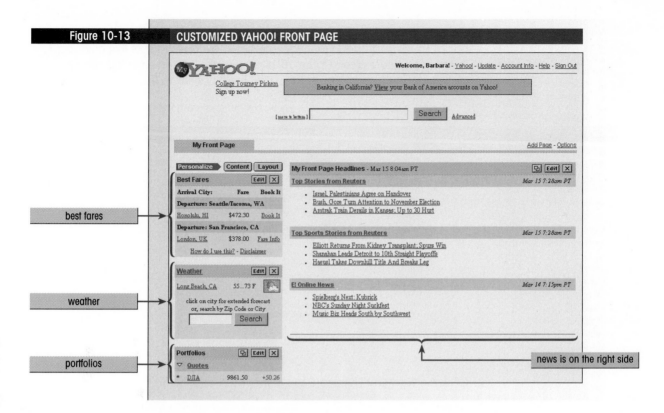

Figure 10-13   **CUSTOMIZED YAHOO! FRONT PAGE**

You can personalize other pages by clicking the Add Page link at the top of your Front Page and then following a similar procedure.

Once you have established the general layout of a page, such as your Front Page, you can fine-tune the contents of each section of a page. You have kept your Front Page simple, but there is still room for further refinement. Steven travels extensively, so you will modify the Weather section of your Front Page to display weather for five cities.

To modify the Weather section of your Front Page:

1. Scroll down your Front Page so you can see Weather displayed on the left side, and then click the **Edit** button in the Weather title bar. The Edit your Weather Module page opens.

2. Scroll to the bottom of the page, and then click the **Delete all cities** link to clear all cities from your weather display.

3. Locate and click the **U.S. Eastern** link under the North America heading of the Available Sections list. The Choose your Weather Cities page opens.

4. Click **U.S. Eastern: Boston, MA** from the Available Cities list. (Cities are arranged alphabetically by country name, then by section of the country, and then by state.) Click the **Add** button to place Boston in the Your Choices column. Click the **Finished** button to return to the Edit your Weather Module.

5. Repeat Steps 3 and 4 to add the following cities to your list: **Paris** (Europe, France), **London Heathrow Airport** (Europe, UK and Ireland), **Tokyo** (Asia, Japan), and **Sydney** (South Pacific, Australia and New Zealand).

6. Click the **Finished** button at the bottom of the Edit your Weather Module page. Your customized Front Page opens showing the list of five cities and their temperatures (see Figure 10-14). If you are interested in learning more about a particular city's weather, click the city's link in the Weather section of your Front Page.

| Figure 10-14 | WEATHER DISPLAY FOR SELECTED CITIES |

7. Click the **Sign Out** link at the top of the My Yahoo! page.

8. Close your browser, and your dial-up connection, if necessary.

You can customize other Web pages, such as Excite and Lycos in much the same way you created a customized Yahoo! portal site. You might want to make My Yahoo! or another Web portal site your home page that opens when you start your browser. (Review Tutorial 3 to recall how to make a Web page your starting page.)

Now Steven can use the customized Yahoo! site by logging in with your Yahoo! ID and password. An added benefit of a Yahoo! account is that you can create an e-mail address tied to that Yahoo! ID automatically. Just click the Check Email button on the Yahoo! home page and follow the simple e-mail sign-up procedure.

Steven is impressed with his new portal site. He's anxious to learn about setting up a calendar and address book on the Web.

Creating and Using a Web Calendar

Melinda wants the teams that work on various contracts to be able to enter their appointments and see when the group has scheduled meetings. While all team members pack PalmPilots to keep the critical data, they cannot share their scheduled appointments very easily. Electronic mail helps, but sometimes the groups need to glance at a globally accessible team calendar to keep up to date with appointments. Melinda has read that several portal sites, including Yahoo!, have free calendar services available. She wants you to investigate calendar features, try a test run of the calendar on the Flagstaff project group, and determine if the Web calendars can synchronize their data with PalmPilots.

Logging into the Yahoo! Calendar

You remember seeing a link to a calendar the last time you visited Yahoo! (see Figure 10-6), so you begin your research of Web calendars with that portal.

To log onto the Yahoo! Calendar:

1. Start your Web browser, and then go to the Student Online Companion page by entering the URL **http://www.course.com/newperspectives/internet2** in the appropriate location in your Web browser. Click the hyperlink for your book, click the **Tutorial 10** link, and then click the **Session 10.1** link. Click the **Yahoo! Calendar** link and wait while the browser loads the Yahoo! home page. Alternatively, you can open the Yahoo! home page and click the **Calendar** link located near the top of the Yahoo! home page in the list of links below the Search text box. Either way, the Yahoo! Calendar page opens and displays Welcome Guest at the top of the page and a calendar page for the current day.

TROUBLE? If the Yahoo! Calendar page displays "Welcome" followed by a user name, then someone who was using the Yahoo! pages previously forgot to sign out. If so, click the Sign Out link near the top of the page. On the subsequent Yahoo! page that opens, click the Yahoo! link near the top, right side of the page. Then click the Calendar link as directed in Step 1.

2. Type your Yahoo! ID and password in the text boxes and then click the **Sign in** button to open your personal Yahoo! Calendar. The welcome message at the top displays "Welcome" followed by your Yahoo! ID (see Figure 10-15).

Figure 10-15 **PERSONAL YAHOO! CALENDAR**

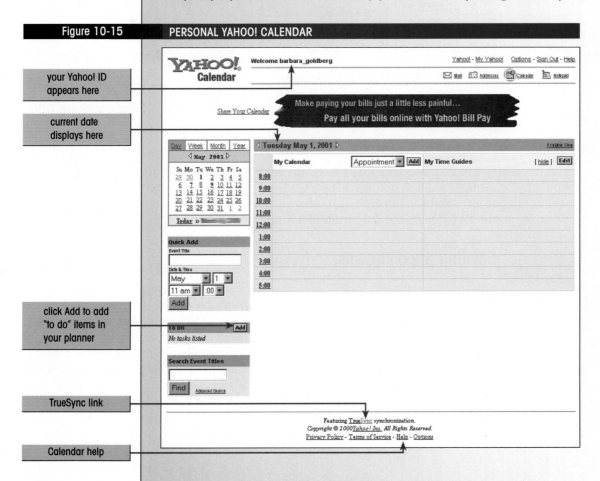

- your Yahoo! ID appears here
- current date displays here
- click Add to add "to do" items in your planner
- TrueSync link
- Calendar help

3. Scroll to the bottom of the Yahoo! Calendar page and click the **TrueSync** link. The Yahoo! Calendar page opens (see Figure 10-16). You can learn here how to synchronize and upload your team member's schedules from their PalmPilot devices.

| Figure 10-16 | YAHOO! CALENDAR SYNCHRONIZATION PAGE |

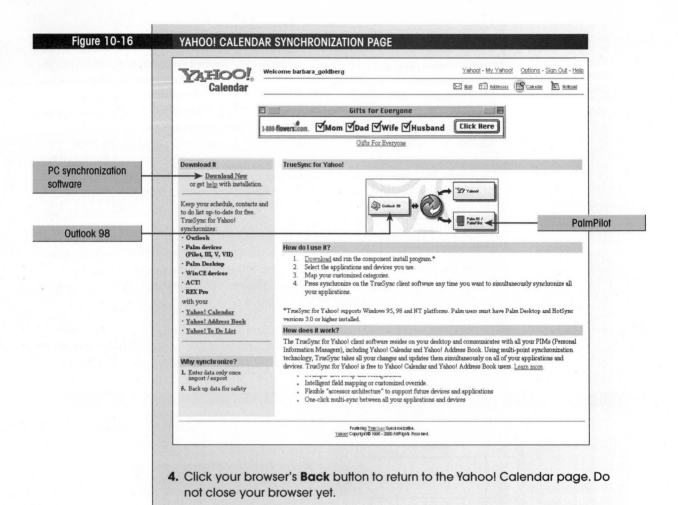

4. Click your browser's **Back** button to return to the Yahoo! Calendar page. Do not close your browser yet.

Yahoo! Calendar appears to be the answer—or one of them, at least—to keeping your teams' schedules coordinated on a Web-accessible calendar system. You are also encouraged to learn that you can download software to provide interaction between your PalmPilot and the Web calendar. You push ahead in your research.

Entering Appointments

Entering appointments such as a project design review are important to your group and the company. You decide to see how easy that is. A memo arrived today reminding you about your meeting on May 1, 2001, with Design Team 26 to review their plans. Although the entry is on your personal calendar, you want everyone to be able to see the details about your appointment—the title, description, and its time—so you will create a **public** entry. (Later, you will make your personal calendar visible to the public.) Yahoo! Calendar also lets you set an event to **Show as Busy**, which indicates you have an event scheduled that day, but the details are private. By default, all calendar events you enter are **private**, and no one except you knows you have an appointment that is marked private.

Entering a Single Appointment

Melinda has asked you to begin adding calendar events to your own calendar to help you evaluate the product. The first event you will add, a one-time design review meeting, is on May 1, 2001. Titled "Design review, Team 26," the meeting should last less than three hours. You will create your first Yahoo! Calendar entry next.

To enter a single, public appointment:

1. Click the **Year** link located to the left of today's empty appointment list.

2. Click **2001** (you may have to use the scroll arrows to the right and left of the current year to advance to the 2001 year link).

3. Click the **Month** link and then select **May**, if it is not already displayed.

4. Click the **Day** link to open the day's calendar for May 1, 2001.

5. The design review meeting is scheduled for 11:00 AM. Click the **11:00** link in the calendar to open up a page in which you can enter the appointment details.

6. In the Title text box type **Design review, Team 26** and ensure that the Type list box displays Appointment.

7. Click the **Public** option button so that anyone can see the appointment once you publish your calendar (see Figure 10-17).

| Figure 10-17 | RECORDING AN APPOINTMENT |

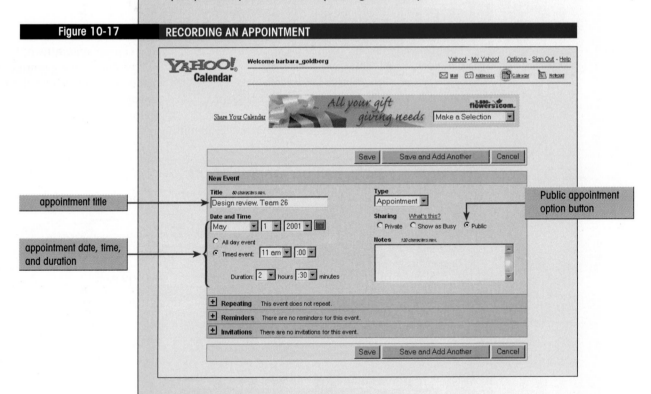

8. Click the Duration **hours** list box and select **2**, and click the Duration **minutes** list box and select **:30** to indicate that the meeting is scheduled to last 2 hours and 30 minutes.

9. Click the **Save** button to save the new appointment. (You can click the Save button at either the top or bottom of the page.) The new appointment appears in the calendar for May 1, 2001 (see Figure 10-18).

Figure 10-18	A NEW, PUBLIC APPOINTMENT

Yahoo! Calendar is easy to use and very convenient. You can create an appointment that others in your group (and anyone else) can see. On May 9, 2001, you have an appointment with your dentist. Because this is a private appointment and you do not want anyone else to know about it, you will create a private appointment. The dental appointment is 10:00 AM and lasts 45 minutes (you hope). Follow these steps to create a private appointment. The procedure is almost the same as setting up a public appointment.

To enter a single, private appointment:

1. With your Yahoo! Calendar still open, click the **Year** link and click **2001**, if necessary.

2. If necessary, click the **Month** link and click **May** to display the calendar in Month view.

3. Click the **Add** link next to the 9th, which corresponds to May 9.

4. In the Title text box type **Dental checkup** and ensure that the Type list box displays Appointment.

5. Click the **Private** option button, if necessary, in the Sharing category. Nobody needs to know about this appointment.

6. Click the **Timed event** list arrow and select **10 am**.

7. Click the Duration **hours** list box and select **0**, and click the Duration **minutes** list box and select **:45** to indicate that the appointment should last 45 minutes.

8. Click the **Save** button to save the new appointment. The new appointment appears in your calendar (see Figure 10-19).

Figure 10-19   MAY'S TWO APPOINTMENTS

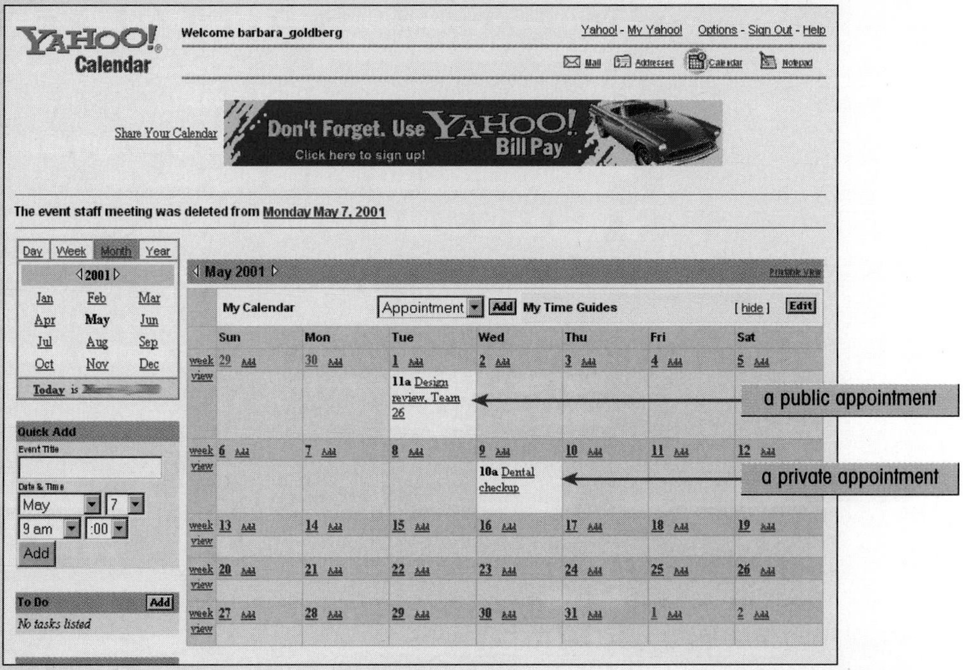

You decide to try entering recurring appointments. One time when you were experimenting with Yahoo! Calendar, you clicked Help and learned a great deal about recurring appointments. (Yahoo! Calendar has very good help. Simply click the Help link at the bottom of any calendar page—see Figure 10-15.) Recurring events can appear in your calendar daily, weekly, on a certain day every week, every two weeks, every month, and every year. You also control how long the recurring event occurs. Birthday reminders are an example of an annually recurring event that Yahoo! Calendar can record.

Entering a Recurring Appointment

Your group has a staff meeting every Monday morning from 9:00 AM until 10:00 AM to discuss the current week's plans. They plan to have this meeting for three months beginning in May, 2001. You set out to pencil in that appointment. You want your colleagues to know you are busy during that time each week, but they do not need to know the details about the meeting. Thus, you designate the meeting as "Show as Busy."

To enter a recurring, limited-duration appointment:

1. If necessary, log back into Yahoo! Calendar with your Yahoo! ID.

2. Click the **Year** link to display your calendar in year view and select **2001**, if necessary. Click the **Month** link and select **May**, if necessary. Click the **Day** link and select **7**, the first Monday in the month.

3. Click the **9:00** link to open that time slot.

4. Click the **Title** text box and type **staff meeting**, and click the **Type** list box and type **m**. Event names are arranged alphabetically in the Type list. When you type the first few letters of the listed event types, the list scrolls to the event type automatically. The type Meeting appears in the Type list box. The default duration of 1 hour is fine.

5. In the Sharing category, click **Show as Busy**.

6. Click the **+** button, called Edit Details, to the left of "Repeating" to specify more details about the meeting.

7. Click the **Repeat on the** option button.

8. Click the list arrow on the first list box to the right of the "Repeat on the" option button and click **First** from the drop-down list.

9. Click the list arrow on the day list box and click **Mon** from the drop-down list.

10. If necessary, click **month** in the third list box to the right of the "Repeat on the" option button.

11. Next, limit the duration of the repeating event by clicking the **Until** option button. Then, click **July** in the month list box and click **31** in the day list box. Your completed recurring event information should look like Figure 10-20.

| Figure 10-20 | CREATING A RECURRING CALENDAR EVENT |

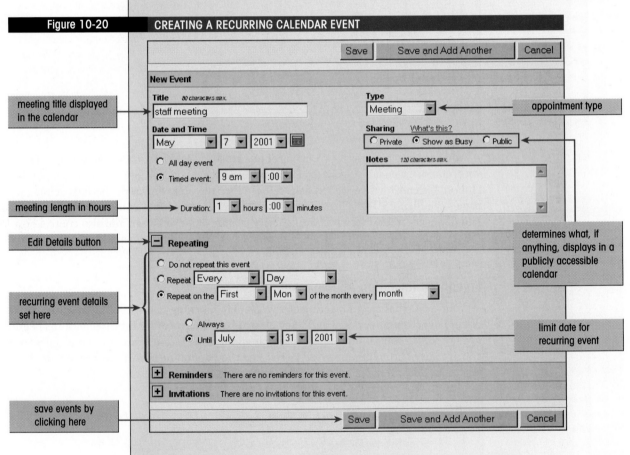

12. Click the **Save** button to post your recurring event to your calendar.

Scroll through your calendar to verify that the staff meeting occurs the first Monday of May, June, and July of 2001. Select the Month view and then click, in turn, June, July, and August. Notice that the first Monday of August has no staff meeting scheduled. Because you are viewing your own calendar, all three of May's appointments appear. You have complete control over your own calendar. You can see public, "Show as Busy," and private calendar entries that you make.

Next, you are going to make your calendar visible to anyone who cares to view it. That procedure is called **publishing** (or **sharing**) a calendar.

Publishing a Calendar

You can use a **published calendar** to make it easier for others in your organization to schedule meetings that affect several people. When you create a calendar event, designate it "public" if you want others to be able to see the appointment when you publish your calendar. Otherwise, your personal calendar events are invisible to others. Because you want others to view your calendar, you decide to publish it.

To publish your calendar:

1. If necessary, log back into the Yahoo! Calendar with your Yahoo! ID.

2. Scroll to the bottom of your calendar page and click the **Options** link located next to the Help link. A page opens displaying Yahoo! Calendar options.

3. Click the **Calendar Sharing** link. A page opens displaying several calendar-sharing options.

4. Click the **Allow anyone to view my calendar** option button in the Active Sharing section. Doing so opens any public appointments to the public. (If you wanted to share your calendar with a select group, then you could choose the "Allow only people on this list to view my calendar" option; see Figure 10-21).

Figure 10-21	SETTING CALENDAR SHARING OPTIONS

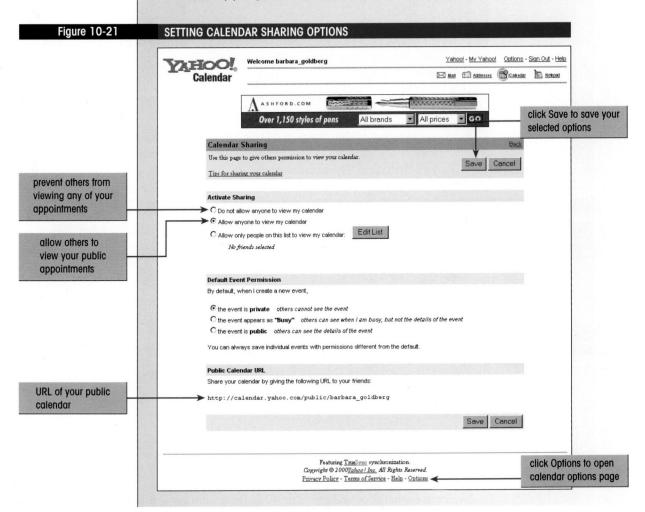

5. Write down the URL displayed at the bottom of the page. That is the link you will place on a company or group Web page to allow others to access your public calendar. Notice that Barbara Goldberg's URL is http://calendar.yahoo.com/public/barbara_goldberg. The Yahoo! ID is placed on the end of the URL that points to Yahoo! public calendars.

6. Click the **Save** button to confirm your changes.

7. On the Confirmation page that opens, click the **Activate Sharing** button.

8. Click the **Calendar Home** link on the Options title bar to return to your calendar.

9. Click the **Sign Out** link in the upper-right corner of the calendar page to log out of your Yahoo! account. Leave your browser open.

How do you view a public calendar? You can navigate to anyone's posted Yahoo! Calendar URL and view their public appointments. To try it out, you decide to go to Barbara Goldberg's calendar, whose URL is posted on the Student Online Companion.

To view the public events of someone's private Yahoo! Calendar:

1. Go to the Student Online Companion page by entering the URL **http://www.course.com/newperspectives/internet2** in the appropriate location in your Web browser. Click the hyperlink for your book, click the **Tutorial 10** link, and then click the **Session 10.1** link.

2. Click the **Barbara Goldberg's Public Calendar** link and wait while the browser loads her calendar.

3. Navigate to the month of May 2001 using the **Year** and **Month** links. Display the calendar in Month view to see Barbara's public appointments in May. Figure 10-22 shows Barbara's public appointments.

Figure 10-22	BARBARA GOLDBERG'S PUBLIC CALENDAR

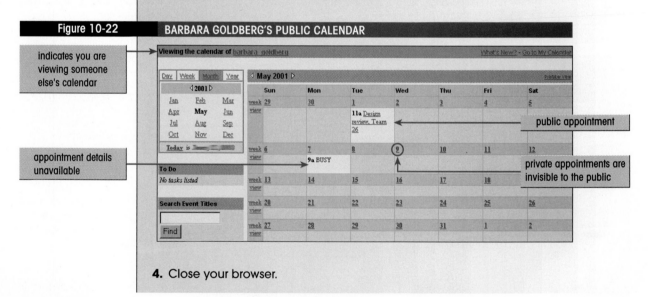

indicates you are viewing someone else's calendar

appointment details unavailable

public appointment

private appointments are invisible to the public

4. Close your browser.

Notice in Barbara's calendar that the May 1 appointment exhibits a complete description, and you can click on the link and view details of that public appointment. Also notice that the May 7th appointment displays only "BUSY." That is, in effect, a semi-private appointment. The details of that appointment are not available. Finally, notice that nothing appears in May 9th, the day when Barbara scheduled her dental appointment. That appointment was designated "Private" to hide it from public view.

Deleting Appointments

Yahoo! Calendar lets you delete appointments easily. You can delete a single appointment, one of several recurring appointments, all appointments of a series of recurring appointments, or even clear the entire calendar.

Deleting One Appointment in a Recurring Set

One of the people who was to present important project information at next Monday's first staff meeting is sick. Rather than trying to find a substitute presenter, Melinda asks you to simply cancel that single meeting. Remembering that the meeting is scheduled for the first Monday of the next three months, you want to be careful not to delete all the meetings. Only the calendar's owner—the one who made the original appointment—can delete any calendar entries. Next you will cancel a single meeting in the recurring set.

To delete an appointment from your Yahoo! Calendar:

1. Launch your browser and go to the Student Online Companion page by entering the URL **http://www.course.com/newperspectives/internet2** in the appropriate location in your Web browser. Click the hyperlink for your book, click the **Tutorial 10** link, and then click the **Session 10.1** link.

2. Click the **Yahoo! Calendar** link and wait while the browser loads the Yahoo! Calendar page.

3. Log into Yahoo by typing your Yahoo! ID and password in the text boxes and clicking the **Sign in** button. Your personal calendar opens.

4. Navigate to the date May 7, 2001, by using the Year and Month links and click the **Month** link to display your calendar in Month view. Your appointments for May appear.

5. Click the **staff meeting** link displayed for May 7, 2001. A page opens displaying editable details of that appointment.

6. Click the **this date only** option button in the Apply changes to row so that you delete only *this particular* date, not all recurring dates.

7. Click the **Delete** button to delete the entry. May's appointments reappear, but the May 7th staff meeting is gone.

When you delete an appointment, you cannot undo the deletion, so be very careful. Double check that you are not deleting *all* appointments whenever an appointment recurs periodically.

Deleting a One-Time Appointment

To delete a one-time appointment—one that does not recur—follow the same steps as above except that you do not need to click the *this date only* option button. In other words, click the appointment to open an appointment details page and click the Delete button.

Clearing the Entire Calendar

When you decide to clear out your entire calendar and start over, you can do so almost too easily. Melinda doesn't want you to do this, but she does want to make sure Yahoo! Calendar provides that function. She asks you to look into it. You decide that you can recreate the three appointments and that it would be instructive to make sure you can clear all your appointments. Do the following to clear out *all* appointments in your Yahoo! Calendar. (Yahoo! calls the operation *resetting* your calendar.) **Warning**: If you really do keep appointments in your Yahoo! Calendar and you have entered several that you want to keep, then *do not* do the steps in this section. There is no way to undo the calendar clearing action.

To clear all appointments from your Yahoo! Calendar:

1. With your personal calendar still available in your browser, click the **Options** link located at the bottom of every Yahoo! Calendar page. The Options page opens (see Figure 10-23).

| Figure 10-23 | YAHOO! CALENDAR OPTIONS PAGE |

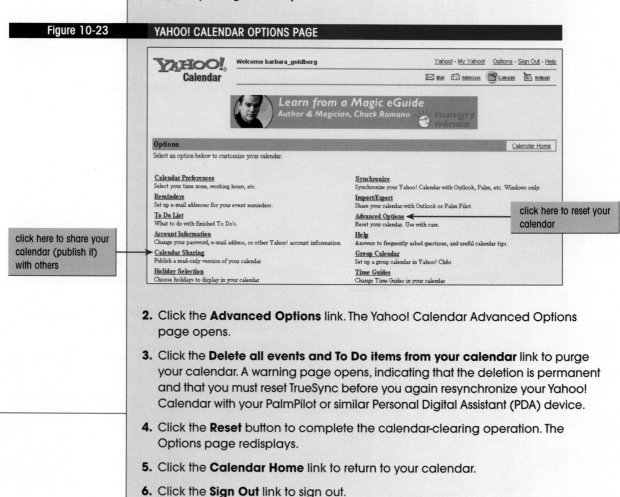

2. Click the **Advanced Options** link. The Yahoo! Calendar Advanced Options page opens.

3. Click the **Delete all events and To Do items from your calendar** link to purge your calendar. A warning page opens, indicating that the deletion is permanent and that you must reset TrueSync before you again resynchronize your Yahoo! Calendar with your PalmPilot or similar Personal Digital Assistant (PDA) device.

4. Click the **Reset** button to complete the calendar-clearing operation. The Options page redisplays.

5. Click the **Calendar Home** link to return to your calendar.

6. Click the **Sign Out** link to sign out.

7. Close your browser.

Printing a Calendar

Though the purpose of a Yahoo! Calendar is primarily online viewing through a browser from anywhere at any time, you can also print a copy of a schedule for a day, a week, a month, or a year. (A year view doesn't show your appointments and is useless for that purpose.) Simply display the calendar in whichever view you want to print (day, week, etc.) and then click the Printable View link in the upper-right corner of the calendar. The view opens in a Web page more suitable for printing. Then, you simply use your browser's Print command in the File menu to print the calendar. When you have finished printing the calendar item, click the Calendar Home link on the right side of the calendar to return to the normal calendar view.

Creating and Using a Web Address Book

Melinda wants you to learn how to store customer contact information in a Web address book so that staff members can access critical telephone numbers and addresses from any location that has a Web browser. Having a Web-based address book relieves employees from remembering to carry their PDAs everywhere they travel. It also serves as a safe backup location for valuable information in case their hand-held organizers should fail. Storing valuable information in two locations makes a lot of sense and provides an electronic insurance policy against loss. You set off to investigate Yahoo! address books.

Entering Address Information

Yahoo!, like other popular portals, provides a convenient way to store name, address, and phone number data—contact information—on the globally accessible Web site. The process of creating and maintaining addresses on the Yahoo! site costs you nothing, and it is sometimes more convenient than always carrying an electronic organizer everywhere you go. You want to store several staff members' addresses on the Yahoo! site, and you are eager to see for yourself if the software is easy to use.

To add contacts to a Yahoo! Address Book:

1. Launch your browser and go to the Student Online Companion page by entering the URL **http://www.course.com/newperspectives/internet2** in the appropriate location in your Web browser. Click the hyperlink for your book, click the **Tutorial 10** link, and then click the **Session 10.1** link.

2. Click the **Yahoo! Calendar** link to open up the Yahoo! Calendar page.

3. Log into your Yahoo! account: type your Yahoo! ID in the Yahoo! ID text box, type your password in the Password text box, and click the **Sign in** button. Your private calendar showing today's appointments opens.

    TROUBLE? If you are using Internet Explorer and an AutoComplete dialog box pops up asking you if you want it to remember your password, click **No** if you are on a public computer that anyone can access. It is not a good idea to store your password on public computers (it is saved in a cookie). If you are on your own, private computer that only you use, then you can click **Yes** to store the password and save some steps the next time.

    If you logged in correctly, the top of the page should display a personal welcome message ("Welcome barbara_goldberg," for example). Notice that there are links to Mail, Addresses, Calendar, and Notepad to the right of the message, at the top right of the page.

4. Click the **Addresses** link. The Yahoo! Address Book page opens (see Figure 10-24).

Figure 10-24	YAHOO! ADDRESS BOOK PAGE

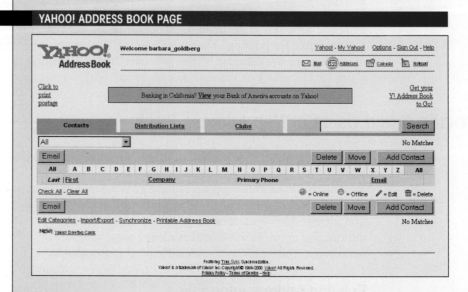

5. Click the **Contacts** tab, if necessary, to prepare to add a new address book entry.

6. Click the list box arrow below the Contact tab and click the **Professional** entry to designate the type of entry you are about to enter—information about a client.

7. Click the **Add Contact** button. The Yahoo! Address Book – Add Contact page opens. Enter the following three names, addresses, and telephone numbers. Click the **Work** Primary Phone option button for each address entry. After you enter each person's information, click the **Save** button to store the information. Then click the **Add Contact** button to add the next person. Figure 10-25 shows the Yahoo! Address Book Add Contact page after entering Lin Choong's contact information but before clicking the Save button. After you have added the third contact's information and saved it, your completed address book shows the names you have added (see Figure 10-26).

First	Last	Email	Company	Work Phone
David	**Golkin**	**dgolkin@cavco.com**	**Cavco Industries Inc.**	**(602) 555-6141**
James	**Garcia**	**jgarcia@roanoke.com**	**Roanoke Electric Steel Corp.**	**(703) 555-1909**
Lin	**Choong**	**choong@lilly.com**	**Lilly Industries Inc.**	**(317) 555-6762**

Figure 10-25	YAHOO! ADDRESS BOOK ADD CONTACT PAGE

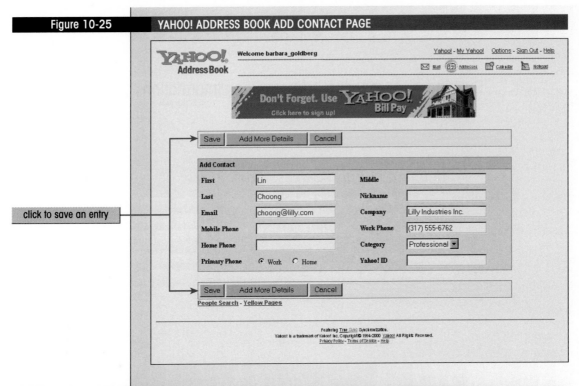

click to save an entry

Figure 10-26	COMPLETED YAHOO! ADDRESS BOOK

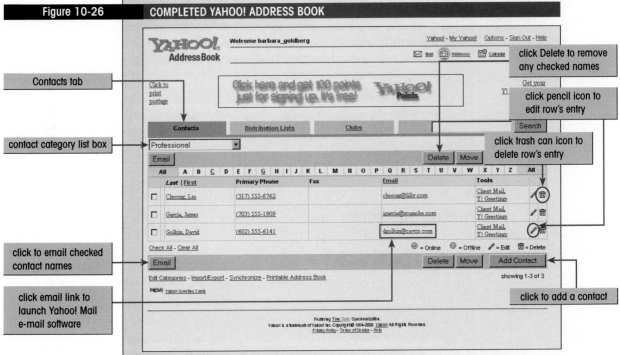

Contacts tab

contact category list box

click to email checked contact names

click email link to launch Yahoo! Mail e-mail software

8. Click the **choong@lilly.com** link in the Email column. The Yahoo! Mail e-mail program opens, and Lin Choong's e-mail address appears in the To: field. How convenient.

TROUBLE? If a dialog box opens indicating that you do not have a Yahoo! Mail account, then you can choose to obtain one and repeat this series of steps or ignore the remainder of them.

9. Click the Yahoo! Mail window's close button to close the window. Keep your browser open with your Yahoo! Address Book displayed.

Deleting and Updating Address Book Information

Deleting and updating the Yahoo! Address Book is straightforward. You realize that James Garcia's contact information should be removed because James is no longer your client.

To delete a Yahoo! Address Book entry:

1. With the Yahoo! Address Book displayed, click the **trash can** icon on the right end of the row that corresponds to James Garcia to delete that address book entry. The Yahoo! Address Book Confirm Delete page opens.

2. Click the **Delete** button to confirm that you do want to delete the address book entry. Once you delete an entry, it cannot be recovered. If you delete the wrong address book entry, you must add it as a new entry.

David Golkin has a new e-mail address. You want to update his entry in your address book.

To update a Yahoo! Address Book entry:

1. With the Yahoo! Address Book displayed, click the **pencil** icon on the right end of the row that corresponds to David Golkin to update that address book entry. The Yahoo! Address Book Edit Contact page opens. It resembles the Yahoo! Address Book Add Contact page, except there are a lot more text boxes into which you can add detailed contact information.

2. Click in the **email** text box, type the new e-mail address **DavidGolkin@cavco.com**, and click the **Save** button to update your address book entry.

3. Leave your browser open.

Printing an Address Book

Sometimes it is handy to print your address book. You may want to share a paper copy of it with co-workers or simply have a backup copy for emergencies. Printing a Yahoo! Address Book is uncomplicated. Do the following to print your two-entry address book.

To print a Yahoo! Address Book:

1. With the Yahoo! Address Book open, click the **Printable Address Book** link below your list of addresses.

2. Click the **Summary Layout** option button for brevity's sake.

3. Click the **Clear All** link to clear all checked entries in the Customize Layout Options panel and place a checkmark next to these fields: **First Name**, **Work**, **Last Name**, and **Email**. Your screen should resemble Figure 10-27.

Figure 10-27	SELECTING YAHOO! ADDRESS BOOK FIELDS TO PRINT

click to clear all checked fields

click to preview a printable copy of your address book

4. Click the **Display for Printing** button to preview the printed address book.

5. Click your browser's **Print** command in the **File** menu and then click **OK** to print your short address book.

6. Click your browser's **Back** button to return to your Yahoo! Address Book.

7. Click the **Sign Out** link near the top, right of the Yahoo! Address Book page to sign out.

8. Close your browser.

Session 10.1 QUICK CHECK

1. What measure can Web advertisers use to determine whether their advertisements will be widely viewed?

2. Usually, portal sites require you to establish a(n) _____ and a(n) _____ before customizing a portal.

3. True or False: You can customize every Web page to display only the information you need.

4. True or False: By marking an appointment in your Yahoo! Calendar as "Public," you ensure that the public can view that entry in your private calendar. Explain.

5. Explain briefly one advantage of using a Web-based calendar compared to a Personal Digital Assistant or similar electronic organizer.

SESSION 10.2

In this session you will learn about electronic commerce and visit several sites that use electronic commerce effectively to conduct business. You also will explore some of the concerns that consumers have when using electronic commerce sites.

What Is Electronic Commerce?

Steve has heard many people in his industry talk about how electronic commerce is becoming the growth market of the future. He would like you to find out more about electronic commerce and how SSP might use it.

You begin your research by talking with a number of businesspersons that you know. You find that everyone you ask seems to have a different idea of what electronic commerce is. In one of your business courses, you remember learning that **commerce** occurs when two parties engage in a business transaction. A **transaction** occurs when two parties exchange two or more items of economic value. For example, when you go to a convenience store and buy batteries, you are exchanging cash for the batteries. You give up the economic value of the cash in exchange for the value of the batteries. The owners of the convenience store also are engaging in a transaction: They give up the economic value of the batteries in exchange for the value of the cash.

As you talk with more businesspersons, it becomes clear that **electronic commerce** is commerce that parties conduct over various kinds of networks instead of in person. Most people do not include telephone and mail-order purchases and sales in their definition of electronic commerce. Instead, they reserve the use of the term to describe businesses that are using interconnected networks, including the Internet, to complete business transactions.

History of Electronic Commerce

Although the Internet and the Web have made electronic commerce possible for many businesses and individuals, electronic commerce has existed for many years. For decades, banks have been using **electronic funds transfers** (**EFTs**, also called **wire transfers**), which are electronic transmissions of account exchange information over private networks. Businesses also have engaged in a form of electronic commerce known as electronic data interchange for many years. **Electronic data interchange** (**EDI**) occurs when one business transmits computer-readable data in a standard format to another business. The standard formats used in EDI have been designed to contain the same information that businesses would include in standard paper forms, such as invoices, purchase orders, and shipping documents.

For EDI to work, both parties to the transaction must have compatible computer systems, must have some kind of communications link to connect them, and must agree to follow the same set of EDI standards. When two businesses meet these three criteria, they are called **trading partners**. Figure 10-28 compares the paper flow that occurs in a traditional sale purchase transaction with the electronic information flow that occurs when two businesses use EDI.

| Figure 10-28 | COMPARISON OF TRADITIONAL AND EDI IMPLEMENTATIONS OF SALE-PURCHASE TRANSACTIONS |

Traditional Sale-Purchase Transaction

buyer — purchase order → seller
buyer ← invoice — seller

EDI Sale-Purchase Transaction

buyer — purchase order data — seller
buyer — invoice data — seller

EDI replaces the paper purchase order and invoice with electronic messages. When it was originally introduced, EDI required trading partners to purchase expensive computers and maintain communication links between them. The initial cost of early EDI installations was prohibitive for use by smaller businesses. However, as large businesses realized cost savings from EDI, they began requiring all of their suppliers to use it. Installing EDI systems presented great difficulties for many smaller firms that wanted to sell products to larger firms but could not afford to implement EDI. As the cost of computers decreased and the availability of communications links (including the Internet) increased, more smaller firms were able to participate as EDI trading partners.

The transaction shown in Figure 10-28 is not complete—it does not show the buyer's payment for the goods received. To consummate the traditional transaction, the buyer sends a check to the seller in payment for the goods received. Early EDI implementations used electronic transfer for the transaction information but still handled payments by mailing checks. As EDI became more common, trading partners wanted to handle the payments electronically, too. When EDI includes payment information, it is called **financial EDI**.

Although banks use EFTs to transfer funds for their own accounts and for large customer transactions that require immediate settlement, EFTs are too expensive to use for large volumes of ordinary business transactions. Banks settle most of their customers' business transactions through **automated clearinghouses** (**ACHs**), which are systems created by banks or groups of banks to electronically clear their accounts with each other. Many individuals have their employers make ACH deposits of their paychecks or use ACH withdrawals to make their monthly car payments.

As the number of businesses using EDI has grown, the demand for efficient networking and payment systems has increased. Businesses called **value-added networks** (**VANs**) were created to meet the demands imposed by EDI. A VAN accepts EDI transmissions in a variety of formats, converts the formats as needed, ensures that the EDI transmissions are received and acknowledged, and can forward the financial transaction instructions to the trading partners' banks or ACHs. A VAN is a neutral third party that can offer assurances and dispute-resolution services to both EDI trading partners.

Future of Electronic Commerce

The Internet has allowed far more businesses, organizations, and individuals to become interconnected by their computers than the pioneers of EDI and EFT ever could have imagined. The Web has given the Internet an easy-to-use interface. The combination of the Web's interface and the Internet's extension of computer networking have opened new opportunities for electronic commerce. Businesses that in the past sold retail goods to consumers through catalogs using mail or telephone orders can now use the Internet to make shopping more convenient. Other retailers, such as booksellers, can use large-volume buying power to provide Internet shoppers with low prices and a wide variety of products. Information providers, such as newspapers, magazines, and newsletters, find that the Internet offers new ways to sell existing products and platforms on which to deliver entirely new products. Software manufacturers see that the Internet is an excellent vehicle for distributing new products, delivering upgrades to existing products, and providing low-cost support to users. The immediacy of the medium offers businesses such as stockbrokerages an attractive way to accept orders from investors. In the following sections, you will learn how some firms have used the Internet and the Web to engage in electronic commerce and how others plan to use it in the near future.

Catalog Retailing

A number of businesses that have traditionally sold goods through catalogs using mail and telephone orders have established electronic commerce sites on the Web. This is a natural transition because these businesses already have functioning product-delivery systems and know how to anticipate their customers' needs to stock the right merchandise. Lands' End sells over $1 billion of clothing, luggage, domestics, and related products each year through its catalogs. Since 1995, Lands' End also has advertised and sold its products through its Web site. Lands' End has a number of competitors that also have established Web presences for conducting retail electronic commerce. One of those competitors is L.L.Bean, a firm that has used catalogs to sell clothing and outdoor gear for many years.

As part of your research for SSP, Melinda asks you to visit these two sites and compare their electronic commerce approaches.

To compare the Lands' End and L.L.Bean Web sites:

1. Start your Web browser, and then go to the Student Online Companion page by entering the URL **http://www.course.com/newperspectives/internet2** in the appropriate location in your Web browser. Click the hyperlink for your book, click the **Tutorial 10** link, and then click the **Session 10.2** link. Click the **Lands' End** link and wait while the browser loads the page.

2. Examine the Lands' End home page shown in Figure 10-29.

Figure 10-29 | **LANDS' END ELECTRONIC COMMERCE SITE**

hyperlinks to various services

allows customer to order from printed catalog

hyperlinks to other features

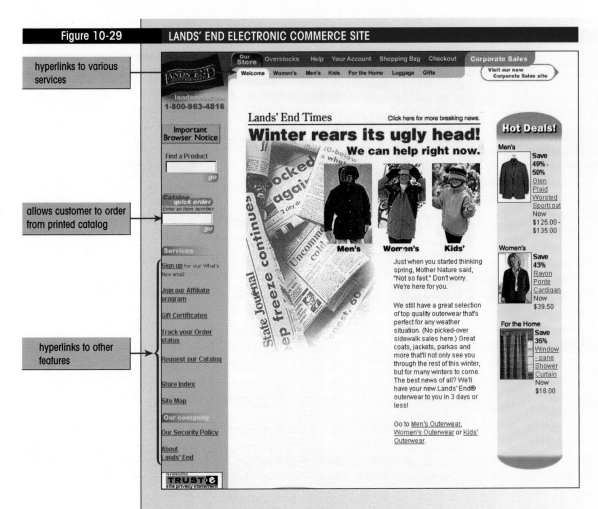

The Lands' End home page is an example of effective Web page design for electronic commerce. The banner across the top of the page includes hyperlinks to the main commercial functions of the site. For example, the Men's hyperlink leads to the men's store. The Overstocks hyperlink leads to a list of reduced-price items. The left side of the page includes hyperlinks to information and other site features. The Help link provides live help, called *Lands' End Live*, for those who are having difficulty locating merchandise. You can choose between live phone help or using live chat in which Lands' End employees answer your questions in a chat-room setting. Other useful features of this page include the Catalog quick order, which lets customers easily order items they have found in the printed catalog, and Store Index, which displays a hierarchical list of links to all the Lands' End departments.

3. After exploring the Lands' End site, use your browser's **Back** button to return to the Student Online Companion page for Session 10.2.

4. Click the **L.L.Bean** hyperlink to open the page shown in Figure 10-30.

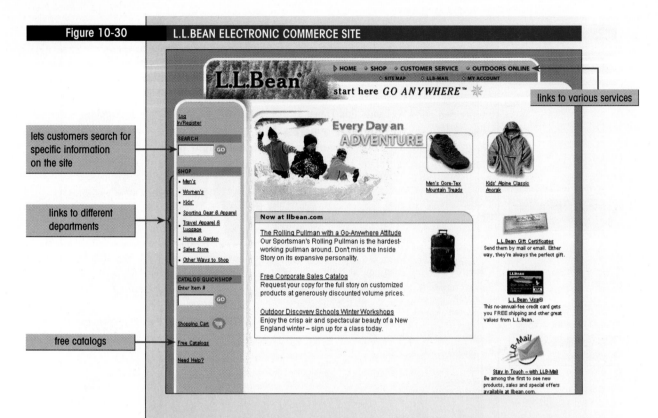

Figure 10-30   L.L.BEAN ELECTRONIC COMMERCE SITE

lets customers search for specific information on the site

links to different departments

free catalogs

links to various services

The L.L.Bean home page is another example of how a catalog retailer can create an effective Web page design for an electronic commerce site. The page gives customers hyperlinks that they can use to conduct business—the Free Catalogs hyperlink, for example—and obtain more information about L.L.Bean and the Web site. The page prominently features a hyperlink to a page that explains to potential customers how the firm provides security for online orders. The page also includes a Search text box to help site visitors find specific information on the site. Just as the Lands' End site offers free information that is not directly related to its products, the L.L.Bean site includes an OUTDOORS ONLINE hyperlink leading to Outdoor Sports and Park Search hyperlinks. The Park Search hyperlink leads to information about hundreds of National and State Parks, Forests, and Wildlife Refuges; including several thousand photographs.

As you examine these two Web sites, you note design features, hyperlinks, and layout ideas that might be useful for SSP's future electronic commerce Web site. You decide that both Lands' End and L.L.Bean carefully considered their customers' needs, desires, and concerns when they created their Web sites. You note that these will be important considerations for Melinda as SSP establishes an electronic commerce presence on the Web.

Book and Music Retailing

Although catalog retailers such as Lands' End and L.L.Bean have developed successful electronic commerce Web sites for their customers, they have expanded an existing business model. To convert their catalog retail businesses into Web-based businesses, they only had to replace their printed catalogs and their telephone order-takers with properly designed Web pages. These firms still carry the same inventory and order that inventory the same way they always have. In other words, their basic business models did not change.

In contrast, the retail booksellers' business has seen significant transformation over the past 20 years. During this time, the once-predominant small neighborhood bookshop has been replaced by ever-larger book superstores throughout the United States. In 1995, Amazon.com opened its online doors for business with a goal of outselling even the largest book superstores. It has accomplished that goal and is currently selling over 2 million books annually.

One of the main reasons that larger bookstores have been more successful than smaller ones is that they can offer a wider selection. Many bookstore customers want to buy a particular book when they go shopping, whereas other customers know that they want to buy a book with some specific characteristic. For example, a customer might be looking for a book on a particular topic or by a particular author. A larger bookstore has a higher likelihood of having the title or author that a customer wishes to purchase.

Amazon.com set out to create a Web site that would allow customers to search through a very large database of books by topic, title, and author. The firm capitalized on the Web's ability to provide multiple hyperlinks. For example, when a customer searches for a specific title, the results page provides links to other books by that book's author, books on the same or similar topics, and even a list of books that other customers bought when they purchased that title. Figure 10-31 shows the Amazon.com home page.

Figure 10-31   AMAZON.COM ELECTRONIC COMMERCE SITE

Amazon.com uses the Web to provide the same services that customers once obtained from the knowledgeable clerk in a neighborhood bookshop, while offering a greater selection than the largest physical book superstore could offer. Other characteristics of books helped make book-selling electronic commerce a good idea. For example, books are readily identifiable products and have a high value-to-weight ratio. These characteristics helped make electronic commerce in retail book sales successful because a customer does not need to examine a book physically to determine its desirability and books can be shipped cost-effectively.

Of course, Amazon.com's success did not escape the notice of large booksellers that built successful book-superstore chains. Barnes & Noble followed the marketing model of Amazon.com and now has a highly successful competing Web site, which is shown in Figure 10-32.

Figure 10-32   **BARNES & NOBLE ELECTRONIC COMMERCE SITE**

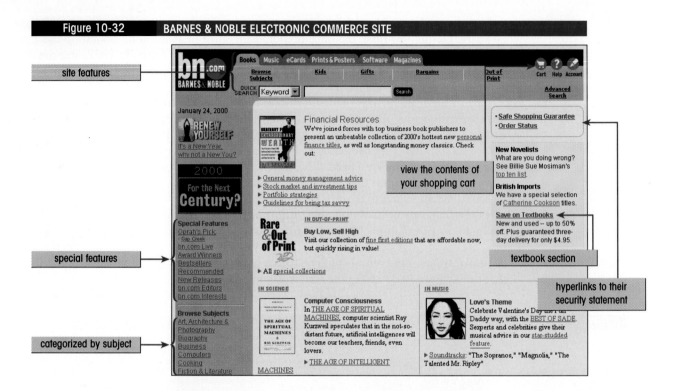

The characteristics of book sales—customers that have specific titles or characteristics in mind, easily identifiable product, high value-to-weight ratio—are also characteristics of music CD sales. Firms such as CDnow have created successful Web sites that sell music CDs. Interestingly, Amazon.com has recently added a new product to its line—music CDs. The main CDnow Web page appears in Figure 10-33.

Figure 10-33   **CDNOW ELECTRONIC COMMERCE SITE**

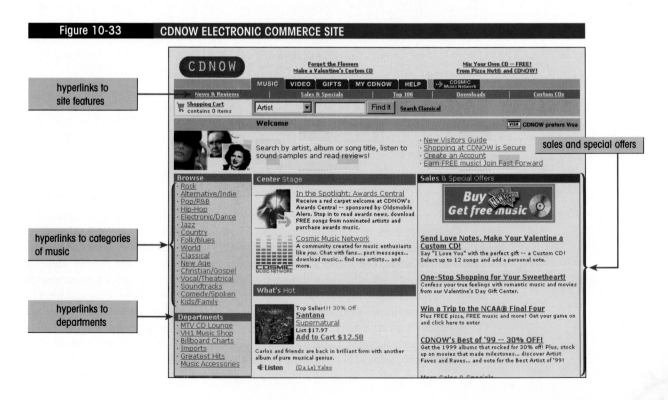

You decide to examine these three sites to identify useful features that Melinda might want to incorporate in the SSP Web site design.

To explore the book and music Web sites discussed in this section:

1. Return to the Student Online Companion Web page for Session 10.2, and then click the **Amazon.com** hyperlink and wait while your Web browser loads the Web page.

2. Examine the Amazon.com home page.

   You can explore the Amazon.com site by using the hyperlinks that appear on the home page, by typing terms in the keyword search field, or by selecting a subject to browse from the main subject categories listing. As you navigate the site, look for features that add value to the customer's use of the Web page. For example, Amazon.com posts reviews and numeric ratings for many titles that have been submitted by persons who have read those books.

3. After exploring the Amazon.com site, use your browser's **Back** button to return to the Student Online Companion page for this session.

4. Click the **Barnes & Noble** hyperlink to open its Web page.

   Take a few minutes to explore the Barnes & Noble site. Compare the features it offers to those on the Amazon.com Web site. For some books, the Barnes & Noble site provides sample chapters that you can read before purchasing an item.

5. After exploring the Barnes & Noble site, use your browser's **Back** button to return to the Student Online Companion page for this session.

6. Click the **CDnow** hyperlink to open its CD music sales Web page.

   You can examine and compare this Web site's features with the bookseller sites. Although selling music is similar to selling books, you will find some interesting differences. For example, the CDnow site offers sample sound clips for many of its CDs that you can download and play if you have the appropriate software installed on your computer.

Although each of these three sites has created a different shopping experience for customers, they all have tried to incorporate elements of personalized service. The Amazon.com reader book reviews, the Barnes & Noble sample chapters, and the CDnow preview sound clips are all ways in which these merchants have tried to make their Web stores uniquely valuable to customers.

Cost-Reduction Features

Although the Web sites you have examined thus far are retail sales sites, there are many electronic commerce sites driven by other aspects of firms' business models. One reason that firms engage in electronic commerce is to control costs. For example, software manufacturers incur significant costs to provide after-sale support for their products' users. Many software firms have used Web sites to provide this support instead of hiring more telephone support engineers. Informational Web sites can provide users with answers to frequently asked questions (FAQs) about the software and can provide downloadable updates and software patches.

One example of a firm that uses the Web to reduce its costs and provide its customers with better service is the Federal Express Corporation, commonly known as FedEx. The express-shipping business is very labor and information intensive. Every customer call for information about rates, shipping services, and shipment tracking costs FedEx money. Of course, FedEx wants its customers to be happy, so it wants to provide the best service possible at the lowest cost. The FedEx Web site is an integral part of the firm's cost-control strategy.

To examine the cost-control features of the FedEx Web site:

1. Return to the Student Online Companion Web page for Session 10.2, and then click the **FedEx** hyperlink and wait while your Web browser loads the Web page shown in Figure 10-34.

Figure 10-34	COST-CONTROL FEATURES ON THE FEDEX SITE

hyperlinks to FedEx cost-reduction features

track your packages online

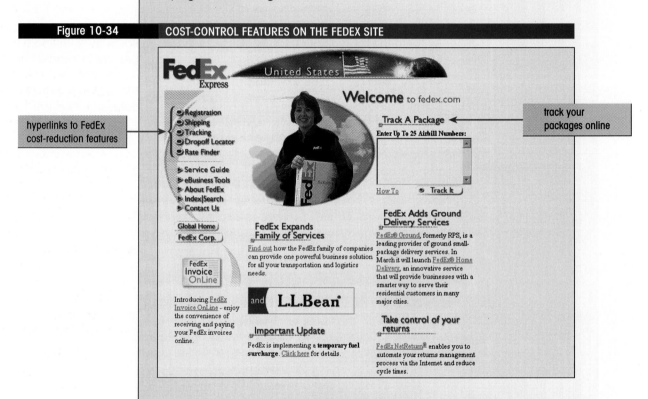

The FedEx Web page includes hyperlinks to various services offered by the firm. The four hyperlinks that offer cost-control opportunities are the Shipping, Tracking, Dropoff Locator, and Rate Finder hyperlinks. Each of these links allows a FedEx customer to perform a function using the Web page that formerly required a telephone call. For example, you can use the Dropoff Locator page to find a convenient location.

2. Click the **Dropoff Locator** hyperlink.

3. Type your Zip code in the **Zip** text box, and then click the **Search Dropoff Locations** button to obtain a list of FedEx dropoff locations near you.

   TROUBLE? If FedEx does not have any package drop off locations in the Zip code you entered, the page will contain a statement to that effect. Click your browser's Back button, and then repeat step 3 and enter a different Zip code.

4. After you examine the list of locations and view any maps or directions you find interesting, use your browser's **Back** button to return to the page shown in Figure 10-34.

5. Explore the other FedEx cost-control features by following the other three cost-control hyperlinks.

Now, you have examined a Web site that includes a number of cost-saving features. You note that Melinda might consider incorporating these kinds of features in the SSP Web site to help reduce the costs of running the business while maintaining a high level of customer satisfaction.

News, Information, and Advertising

The news media have changed over the course of this century as technology has changed. At the start of the 1900s, improvements in printing presses and distribution methods made newspapers much more widely available. Newspapers changed their editorial and advertising policies to serve their new audiences better by including many more members of low and moderate socioeconomic groups. Broadcast radio, television, and cable television were technological innovations that increased the competition for audience and advertising dollars.

All three traditional media outlets—print, radio, and television—provide their audiences with news and other information. They obtain their revenues by charging a subscription fee, accepting paid advertisements, or by some combination of both. Your local newspaper most likely sells subscriptions and single copies on newsstands, but it also obtains significant revenue from its advertisers. In many cities, you can find weekly newspapers that are distributed free; these newspapers are completely supported by advertising. Similarly, advertising supported broadcast radio and television for many years. The advent of cable television introduced viewer subscription payments to the electronic media.

The online world offers all three payment schemes: advertising supported, subscription supported, and various combinations of the two. Many of the news sites on the Web are completely free to visitors; they display advertising banners to generate revenues sufficient to offset their costs and earn a profit. Other sites, particularly those that offer highly specialized news information, such as earnings forecasts or stock purchase recommendations, require you to pay a subscription fee and obtain a password for access. An increasingly common revenue model for Web sites is a combination of some free information, sometimes accompanied by advertising, with a more extensive set of information available on a subscription or pay-per-item basis. Two news Web sites that offer this combination are the BusinessWeek Online and The Wall Street Journal Interactive Edition sites that you will explore next.

To explore the BusinessWeek Online and The Wall Street Journal Interactive Edition sites:

1. Return to the Student Online Companion Web page for Session 10.2, and then click the **BusinessWeek Online** hyperlink and wait while your Web browser loads the Web page.

2. Examine the BusinessWeek Online home page.

   The BusinessWeek site offers an interesting mix of options. Some of the news items are available to all visitors; others require that you register or are accessible only to subscribers of the print edition of *Business Week*. The site offers Web-only subscriptions to persons who want access to the full online content but are not interested in receiving the print edition. The site also offers a separate subscription or pay-per-article access to its archived issues.

3. When you have completed your review of the BusinessWeek Online site, use your browser's **Back** button to return to the Student Online Companion page, and then click the **Wall Street Journal Interactive Edition** hyperlink to open its Web page. Click the **Go to U.S. View** link.

   The Wall Street Journal site provides free access to a more limited set of information. Notably, the classified job ads and the annual report service are both included in the free information set. Because advertisers pay to have the widest possible distribution of these features, it is in the site's best interest to offer them to all visitors. Subscribers to the print edition must pay to access the rest of the site, although their fee is lower than the subscription charge for persons who do not subscribe to the print edition.

4. Click the **Careers** hyperlink, located under the Other WSJ.com sites heading, to open the Careers Information page, and then click the **JOB SEEK** hyperlink to open the **Job Seek** search engine page shown in Figure 10-35. (Your page might differ.)

| Figure 10-35 | THE WALL STREET JOURNAL INTERACTIVE EDITION JOB SEARCH ENGINE PAGE |

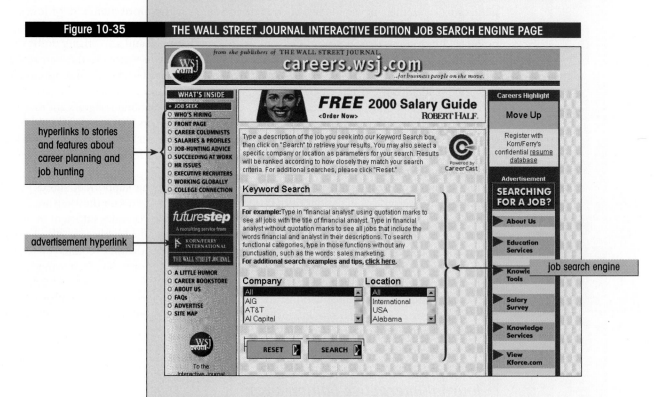

The Job Seek search engine allows visitors to select ads for positions by company, industry, job function, and location. This can be a much more efficient way to search the ads than scanning them in the print edition. It also exposes the ads to potential applicants who are not subscribers, which should allow the Journal to charge higher rates for the ads.

Although many members of the Internet community feel that information on the Web should be freely available to the browsing public, an increasing number of firms are offering valuable information and charging for it. One compromise solution, as you have seen in the BusinessWeek and The Wall Street Journal sites, is to offer a combination of free and subscription-charge information on the same Web site.

Online Auctions

One of the more interesting and innovative implementations of electronic commerce is the creation of Web sites that conduct online auctions. Although some of these sites offer merchandise that is the inventory of the Web site owner, most of these sites auction the property of others much as an auctioneer would at a public auction.

Each site establishes its own bidding rules; however, most auctions remain open for a few days or a week. Some sites provide automated agents that bidders can instruct to place bids as needed to win the auction, subject to a maximum limit set by the bidder. Because bidders face a significant risk of buying a misrepresented product in a sight-unseen online auction, some auction sites offer mediation/escrow services that hold the buyer's payment until he or she is satisfied that the item matches the seller's description. The advantages of conducting online auctions include a large pool of potential bidders, 24-hour access, and the ability to auction hundreds of similar items simultaneously.

Two very different implementations of the online auction idea appear on the Haggle Online site and the Onsale Auction Supersite. Haggle Online auctions items for individuals and small businesses. Buyers and sellers assume most of the risks of transacting business over the Internet and must negotiate their own payment and shipment procedures. Haggle provides an auction history so that participants can examine bidding on similar items in the past. The site also maintains a list of comments from prior participants about each other. Most of the comments refer to previous sellers of merchandise. The Onsale Auction site, in contrast, predominantly offers items from its own inventory. It accepts credit card payment and arranges shipping for many items.

To explore the Haggle Online and Onsale Auction sites:

1. Return to the Student Online Companion Web page for Session 10.2, and then click the **Haggle Online** hyperlink and wait while your Web browser loads the Web page.

   Most items auctioned on the Haggle Online site are computers, computer parts, and software. Other items such as cameras, musical instruments, and jewelry sometimes appear on this site. Note that most sellers are individuals or small businesses. Many auctions at this site, once closed, require negotiations between buyer and seller to establish terms of payment, shipment, and acceptance of the auctioned item.

2. When you have completed your review of the Haggle Online site, use your browser's **Back** button to return to the Student Online Companion page.

3. Click the **Onsale Auction** hyperlink to open its Web page.

   The Onsale site is organized by product category and includes separate pages for computer products, sports and fitness equipment, and home and office items. These pages include items offered by Onsale or firms with which it regularly contracts as a consignment sales agent.

These two sites promote online auctions in similar ways. Haggle Online and Onsale Auction emphasize the practical side of this electronic commerce variant. Online auctions differ significantly from in-person auctions, but they still present the same hazards to unwary bidders. As many an auction attendee can attest, it is easy to become caught up in the excitement of the bidding and pay more than you intended; this risk exists in online auctions, too. Online auctions should be good for both sellers and buyers because they expose the items on the auction block to a larger group of potential bidders. As the number of participants in a market increases, the market becomes more efficient and should make prices more accurate.

Consumer Concerns

Participants in electronic commerce have two major concerns. Their first concern is for transaction security. Buyers in an electronic marketplace often do not know who is operating a Web site from which they would like to make a purchase. They also desire assurance that the payments they make for goods purchased via the Internet are secure.

Buyers' second major concern is that their privacy not be violated in the course of conducting electronic commerce. Web sites can gather a great deal of information about their customers, even before customers purchase anything from the site. The Web electronic commerce community has made efforts toward ensuring both transaction security and buyer privacy, but these efforts are not yet complete. Many potential consumers are reluctant to make purchases over the Internet because of continuing concerns about these two issues. Several assurance providers have begun operations in recent years. An **assurance provider** is a third party that, for a fee paid by the electronic commerce Web site, will certify that the site meets some criteria for conducting business in a secure and privacy-preserving manner.

Transaction Security and Privacy

Potential customers worry about a number of issues when they consider dealing with a Web-based business. They wonder whether the firm is a real company that will deliver the merchandise ordered or, if the merchandise is defective, will replace it or refund the purchase price within a reasonable period. Potential customers of any business worry about the same issues; however, the virtual nature of a Web electronic commerce site increases these concerns. In addition, potential customers are concerned about the security of their credit card numbers as those numbers travel over the Internet.

As you learned in Session 9.2, many Web sites use the SSL security protocol to encrypt information flowing between a Web server and a Web client. Many Web sites used in electronic commerce use the SSL protocol to protect sensitive information as it travels over the Internet. A consortium of firms, including Visa International and MasterCard International, have begun work on the **Secure Electronic Transaction** (**SET**) protocol. SET is a more complex and considerably more secure protocol than the SSL protocol.

Although trials of the SET protocol are underway, the costs of implementing it and the lack of consumer demand for it have prevented many sites from adopting the protocol. Most experts predict that SET eventually will become the standard for Web electronic commerce security, however.

Many potential customers of Web-based businesses are concerned about their privacy. Web sites can collect a great deal of information about customers' preferences—even before they place an order. By recording a user's click stream, the Web server can gather knowledge about that visitor. Some Web sites even use click-stream information to display different ad banners to different visitors.

No general standards currently exist for maintaining confidentiality regarding such information, much less general identifying information about Web site visitors and customers. Many business Web sites include statements of privacy policy directed at concerned customers, but no laws exist requiring such statements or policies.

Assurance Providers

To fill the need for some kind of assurances over Web site transaction security and privacy policies, several assurance providers have started offering various kinds of certifications. Web sites can purchase these certifications and display the logo or seal of the assurance provider on the Web site for potential customers to examine. Most of these logos are hyperlinks to the assurance provider's site, at which customers can find out more about the nature of the specific assurances given by that provider. Currently, there are five major assurance providers: the Better Business Bureau (BBB), TRUSTe, the International Computer Security Association (ICSA), VeriSign, and WebTrust.

The Better Business Bureau's BBBOnLine certification program grants a Web site the right to use its logo after it has joined the BBB; been in business for at least one year; compiled a satisfactory complaint-handling record; and agreed to follow BBB member guidelines for truthful advertising, prompt response to customer complaints, and binding arbitration of customer disputes. The BBB conducts a site visit during which it verifies the street address, telephone number, and existence of the business.

The TRUSTe program focuses on privacy issues. To earn the right to display the TRUSTe logo, a Web site must explain and summarize its information-gathering policies in a disclosure statement on the site. The site must adhere to its stated policies and several other guidelines concerning the privacy of communications. TRUSTe enforces its program by various methods, including surprise audits that it and two accounting firms conduct.

The ICSA is an independent association that has developed a series of computer security certifications. The goal of ICSA Web certification is to reduce Web site risks and liability for the site and its customers. ICSA conducts an initial on-site evaluation using its certification field guide and uses subsequent remote testing and random spot-checking of site availability, information-protection measures, and data-integrity provisions.

VeriSign provides a range of services to electronic commerce Web sites, including certification of secure server status and EDI certifications. It is also a partner with the American Institute of Certified Public Accountants (AICPA) in the WebTrust program. The WebTrust program is a comprehensive assurance that requires reviews by a licensed CPA (or Chartered Accountant in Canada) before the site is approved. The review includes examination of Web site performance disclosures, such as delivery times and handling of customer complaints. The site is granted a WebTrust logo only after it satisfies a number of criteria relating to business practices, transaction integrity, and information protection. The WebTrust program requires recertification every 90 days.

Session 10.2 QUICK CHECK

1. Briefly define the term *electronic data interchange* (EDI).

2. Why would a firm use a value-added network instead of the Internet for electronic commerce?

3. Name three business activities that a software manufacturer might conduct from its Web site.

4. Explain why a firm might include information that is not related to its products on a Web site designed to sell merchandise.

5. Why are music CDs and videotapes good candidates for electronic commerce?

6. Describe three risks that you would face as a successful bidder in an online auction.

7. Name two concerns that potential customers often have about making a purchase from a Web site.

8. Briefly describe the role that assurance providers play in the conduct of electronic commerce.

REVIEW ASSIGNMENTS

Steven liked using your my Yahoo! portal page, and now he would like for you to help him personalize a portal site of his own. He wants to include directories, news, and business information that could be helpful in obtaining critical business information about the software industry in general and software contracting in particular. Then Steven wants you to create customized portals for three of SSP's key sales people so they can stay on top of current industry trends.

Do the following:

1. Start your Web browser, go to the Student Online Companion (http://www.course.com/newperspectives/internet2), click the link for your book, click the Tutorial 10 link, and then click the Review Assignments link in the left frame. Click the Excite custom portal link to open that page.

2. Click the Sign Up link. Use the registration page to create an appropriate member name and a password for Steven.

3. Type a member name and password, and then enter the password again.

4. Type a password reminder phrase.

5. Type your first name, last name, street address, Zip code, e-mail address, and birth date in the appropriate text boxes. Complete any other information requested by the registration form.

6. Click the Done button, and then click the Go to My Excite Start Page now link.

7. On the Content tab, use the Select Content section to indicate topics that would interest Steven, a business professional who travels frequently.

8. Click the Layout link to display the Layout tab and customize the layout of the page as desired. (Click OK if a dialog box pops up asking if you want to save your changes.)

9. Click Done when finished selecting content and layout choices.

10. After the personalized page opens, change the My Weather information to include the weather forecasts for the following five cities: Anchorage, Alaska; Austin, Texas; Boston, Massachusetts; Lincoln, Nebraska; and San Diego, California. Click the Save button to submit your changes.

11. In the My News section, add Technology News, and delete Sports News and Oddly Enough News. Click the Finished button to submit your changes.

12. Add a "My birthday" reminder to the page so that Excite tells you the number of days until your birthday. (*Hint:* You might need to change the page's content to do this.) Set the Start Reminding Me text box to *Now* so that the reminder will be permanent, no matter how far away your birthday is. Submit your changes.

13. Print the first page of your personalized Excite page.

14. Sign out of your Excite page to restore the default Excite page.

15. Close your Web browser, and your dial-up connection, if necessary.

CASE PROBLEMS

Case 1. Direct Electronics Darren Issal owns Direct Electronics, which sells car alarms directly to automobile dealerships. Direct's salespersons spend most of their week in the field meeting with car dealership parts department supervisors, and Darren wants the salespersons to keep all their appointments in their own, private, Web-based calendars. Darren has asked you to train his sales manager, Shirley Laskowitz, and three of her assistants. Once they learn how to create Web calendars, then Shirley will create Web calendars for each of her salespersons. You want to investigate Excite.com to see what calendaring tools that Web site supplies.

Do the following:

1. Start your Web browser, go to the Student Online Companion (http://www.course.com/newperspectives/internet2), click the link for your book, click the Tutorial 10 link, and then click the Case Problems link in the left frame. Click the Case Problem 1 Excite Calendar hyperlink to open that page.

2. You will need an Excite Member Name and Password to complete this exercise. If you do not have one, then click the Sign me up! hyperlink under the New User panel. Type a Member Name that you choose. (Append your four-digit birth year to your first and last names. That should provide an available member name.) Then type a password and fill in the text boxes in the Password Reminder Phrase and Personalization Information sections. Click the Done button to submit your membership name. (You probably will want to clear the four check boxes at the bottom of the form so you do not receive unsolicited e-mail.) After your Member Name is confirmed, click the Excite Planner link on the confirmation page. You can then sign in.

3. Once you sign in, an empty calendar appears. Enter the following appointments in your own time zone:

Event	Date	Start Time	End Time	Repeating?
Meet Marvin from Bob Baker's	4/23/2001	9:00 AM	9:30 AM	No
Kearny Mesa Dodge parts mgr.	4/23/2001	12:30 PM	1:45 PM	No
Randy's Foreign Car; see Randy	4/23/2001	4:30 PM	5:00 PM	No
La Jolla Alarms; Susan Wickert	4/27/2001	7:30 AM	8:15 AM	No

Explore

4. You have a sales meeting every week. Add an appointment every Monday for the next six months from 8:00 AM until 10:00 AM. The weekly appointments occur beginning March 2001 and run through and including December 2001. (Excite.com calls this a repeating event.) In the Event textbox, type Weekly Sales Meeting.

5. View your appointments for April 23, 2001. Notice that there is a conflict. Reschedule the Marvin (from Baker Baker's) meeting to April 27, 2001, at 1:00 PM until 1:30 PM.

6. Display a printable view of your calendar for April 23, 2001.

7. Print the calendar.

8. Click the Excite Home link, and then click the Sign Out link in the upper left portion of the page to log out of your calendar. (Remember your Excite Member Name and password for future use.)

9. Close your browser.

Case 2. Dorm Lamps, Inc. Your friend Robin has invented a new high-intensity lamp that is an ideal product for college students who share dorm rooms. You have been selling the lamps for three months through word-of-mouth advertising on your campus. You would like to expand your sales to other college campuses. Robin suggests creating a Web page that will accept orders. The lamps are small and lightweight; therefore, they could be shipped to customers easily using a variety of methods. Because you are both college students with no business experience, you wonder who will trust you or your Web site to deliver quality merchandise. You would like to investigate the terms and conditions of several Web site assurance providers to determine which, if any, Robin should use for the proposed site.

Do the following:

1. Start your Web browser, go to the Student Online Companion (http://www.course.com/newperspectives/internet2), click the link for your book, click the Tutorial 10 link, and then click the Case Problems link in the left frame. Click the BBBOnline hyperlink to open that page.

2. Examine the Web site assurance criteria presented on this site and determine whether Dorm Lamps would qualify. Be sure to assess the approximate cost of obtaining this assurance.

3. Click the Back button on your browser to return to the Student Online Companion page, and then click the VeriSign hyperlink.

4. Examine the various Web site assurance services offered on this site, including the WebTrust assurance service, and evaluate the costs and benefits for Dorm Lamps to obtain each service.

5. Write a three-page summary of your findings. Be sure to recommend a specific assurance service or explain why none of the services you identified would be suitable for Dorm Lamps, Inc. Support your recommendation with facts and logical arguments.

6. Close your browser.

Case 3. *Sagamore Community College* Sagamore Community College (SCC) offers two-year associate degree programs in computer technologies. Because of its impressive array of computer laboratories and its state-of-the-art computer infrastructure, the college attracts students from a community that employs many high-tech workers. Unfortunately, SCC does not currently provide timely course and degree information on its Web site. Ernesto Cervantes, SCC's director of Academic Computing, wants to change the SCC home page so students can customize and use it as a portal site. Ernesto wants the portal to offer class lists, information about instructors, and course information. Ernesto would like to see examples of existing portal sites that can serve as examples for constructing SCC's home page.

Do the following:

1. Start your Web browser, go to the Student Online Companion (http://www.course.com/newperspectives/internet2), click the link for your book, click the Tutorial 10 link, and then click the Case Problems link in the left frame. Click the Personalized Lycos link.

2. Click the Sign up link under My Lycos – Personalize near the top of the page to open that Web page.

3. Enter your information into the required text boxes.

4. Return to the Lycos home page by entering the URL http://www.lycos.com and then click the My Lycos – Personalize link.

5. Indicate your interests by clicking the Edit bar above each section that you want to customize.

6. Click the appropriate check boxes in each section that you customize and then click the I'm Done button when you have finished customizing each section. At a minimum, customize the News, Stocks, and Weather sections.

Explore   7. Change the color scheme of your personal page to one that you like.

Explore   8. Change the layout of your personal page by clicking the Change Box Size in the My Page Setup section on the left of your page.

Explore   9. Remove the sports score displays from your Lycos personalized page.

10. Print all pages of your customized page.

11. Close your browser.

Case 4. *Battery World* You have been using electronic devices such as calculators, cameras, and portable CD players for years. Recently, you started using laptop computers in your job. One frustration you have experienced using all of these devices is replacing the batteries. You realize that, as more electronic devices need more and different kinds of batteries, a business that offers overnight shipments of batteries might be a good idea. After much research, you have decided to open a Web-based business, Battery World, that will stock a wide variety of batteries ready for overnight delivery. You have worked out many of the details of ordering and stocking your batteries, but you have not yet decided on how you might best ship them.

Do the following:

1. Start your Web browser, go to the Student Online Companion (http://www.course.com/newperspectives/internet2), click the link for your book, click the Tutorial 10 link, and then click the Case Problems link in the left frame. Click the FedEx hyperlink to open that page.

2. Examine the services provided on the Federal Express Web site for overnight shipments. Include the elements of package tracking, obtaining rate information, and pickup and delivery services information in your study.

3. Click the Back button on your browser to return to the Student Online Companion page, and then click the United Parcel Service hyperlink.

4. Examine the services provided on the United Parcel Service Web site for overnight shipments. Include the elements of package tracking, obtaining rate information, and pickup and delivery services information in your study.

5. Click the Back button on your browser to return to the Student Online Companion page, and then click the DHL Worldwide hyperlink.

6. Examine the services provided on the DHL Worldwide Web site for overnight shipments. Include the elements of package tracking, obtaining rate information, and pickup and delivery services information in your study.

7. Write a two-page summary that includes a comparison of how easy each company's site was to use as you searched it for the information you needed.

8. Close your browser.

Case 5. *Students for a Clean Environment* You have just been elected recording secretary for a student activist organization called Students for a Clean Environment. Your organization's goals encompass various activities that promote clean air, clean water, and environmental protection in general. Because you have so much experience using a personal computer, the organization's president, Stirling Leonard, has asked you to keep a list of members' names, addresses, telephone numbers, and e-mail addresses. Stirling suggests you use Excite to create the address book so you can access addresses and e-mail members from any computer on campus.

Do the following:

1. Start your Web browser, go to the Student Online Companion (http://www.course.com/newperspectives/internet2), click the link for your book, click the Tutorial 10 link, and then click the Case Problems link in the left frame. Click the Case Problem 5 Excite Planner hyperlink to open that page.

2. You will need an Excite Member Name and Password to complete this exercise. If you completed Case Problem 1 above, then you already have an Excite account and can skip the remainder of this step. Otherwise, click the Sign me up! hyperlink under the New User panel to sign up. Type a Member Name that you choose. (Append your four-digit birth year to your first and last names. That should provide an available member name.) Then type a password and fill in the text boxes in the Password Reminder Phrase and Personalization Information sections. Click the Done button to submit your membership name. (You probably will want to clear the four check boxes at the bottom of the form so you do not receive unsolicited e-mail.) After your Member Name is confirmed, click the Excite Planner link on the confirmation page. You can then sign in.

3. After you sign in with your Excite Member Name and Password, an empty address book appears. Enter the following names, e-mail addresses, and telephone numbers into your address book (start by clicking the New Contact button and then entering the first name):

First Name	Last Name	Email	Home Phone
Alice	Honyecutt	ahoneycutt@state.edu	555-2234
William	Bakalski	bakalski@state.edu	555-4321
Brenda	Skintik	brendas@state.edu	555-3345
Gary	Chin	gchin@state.edu	555-5567

4. Add your class instructor to your address book. Use his or her office phone in place of the Home Phone.

5. Add your own name, e-mail address, and campus phone number to your address book.

6. Display your address book in a printable form.

7. Print your address book.

8. Delete your address book entry for your instructor.

9. Display your address book in a printable form and print it again.

10. Click the Sign Out link to log out of your Excite account.

11. Close your browser.

QUICK CHECK ANSWERS

Session 10.1

1. The terms for measures commonly used are eyeballs and page view.

2. user name, password

3. False. You can only customize portal Web pages. "Normal" Web pages are fixed by the publisher and cannot be changed.

4. False. In addition, you must publish your calendar to make its public entries available to the public.

5. The main advantage of Web-based calendars is that you can access your calendar from any place that has a browser. Additionally, you can share the calendar with others. Neither of these is possible with a PDA.

Session 10.2

1. EDI occurs when one business transmits computer-readable data in a standard format to another business.

2. The VAN can provide third-party assurances and dispute resolution services.

3. distribute new products, deliver upgrades to existing products, and provide user support

4. to attract potential purchasers to the site

5. Customers often have specific titles or characteristics in mind, the products are easily identifiable, and the products have a high value-to-weight ratio.

6. misrepresented product, damaged product, seller does not deliver product

7. transaction security and buyer privacy

8. They provide some assurance that a Web site meets some criteria for conducting business in a secure and privacy-preserving manners for years.

LEVEL I

New Perspectives on

CREATING WEB PAGES WITH HTML,

2nd Edition

Read This Before You Begin

To the Student

Data Disks

To complete the Level I tutorials, Review Assignments, and Case Problems in this book, you need two Data Disks. Your instructor will either provide you with Data Disks or ask you to make your own.

If you are making your own Data Disks, you will need two blank, formatted high-density disks. You will need to copy a set of folders from a file server or standalone computer or the Web onto your disks. Your instructor will tell you which computer, drive letter, and folders contain the files you need. You could also download the files by going to **http://www.course.com**, clicking Data Disk Files, and following the instructions on the screen.

The following table shows you which folders go on your disks, so that you will have enough disk space to complete all the tutorials, Review Assignments, and Case Problems:

Data Disk 1

Write this on the disk label:
Data Disk 1: Level 1 Tutorial 1

Put these folders on the disk:
Tutorial.01

Data Disk 2

Write this on the disk label:
Data Disk 2: Level 1 Tutorial 2

Put these folders on the disk:
Tutorial.02

When you begin each tutorial, be sure you are using the correct Data Disk. See the inside front or inside back cover of this book for more information on Data Disk Files, or ask your instructor or technical support person for assistance.

Course Lab

Tutorial 1 features an interactive Course Lab to help you understand Web page concepts. There are Lab Assignments at the end of the tutorial that relate to this Lab. To start the Lab, Click the Start button on the Windows taskbar, point to Programs, point to Course Labs, point to New Perspectives Applications, and click creating Web Pages: HTML.

Using Your Own Computer

If you are going to work through this book using your own computer, you need:

- **Computer System** A text editor and a Web browser (preferably Netscape Navigator or Internet Explorer, versions 3.0 or higher) must be installed on your computer. If you are using a non-standard browser, it must support frames and HTML 3.2 or higher. Most of the tutorials can be completed with just a text editor and a Web browser. However, to complete the last sections of Tutorial 2, you will need an Internet connection and software that connects you to the Internet.

- **Data Disks** Ask your instructor or lab manager for details on how to get the Data Disk. You will not be able to complete the tutorials or exercises in this book using your own computer until you have Data Disks. The Data Disk Files may be obtained electronically over the Internet. See the inside back cover of this book for more details.

Visit Our World Wide Web Site

Additional materials designed especially for you are available on the World Wide Web. Go to **http://www.course.com**. For example, see our Student Online Companion that contains additional coverage of selected topics in the text. These topics are indicated in the text by an online companion icon located in the left margin.

To the Instructor

The Data Disk Files are available on the Instructor's Resource Kit for this title. Follow the instructions in the Help file on the CD-ROM to install the programs to your network or standalone computer. For information on creating Data Disks, see the "To the Student" section above.

You are granted a license to copy the Data Disk Files to any computer or computer network used by students who have purchased this book.

OBJECTIVES

In this tutorial you will:

- Explore the structure of the World Wide Web

- Learn the basic principles of Web documents

- Get to know the HTML language

- Create an HTML document

- View an HTML file in a Web browser

- Tag text elements, including headings, paragraphs, and lists

- Insert character tags

- Add special characters

- Insert horizontal lines

- Insert an inline graphic image

LAB

Web Pages & HTML

CREATING A WEB PAGE

Web Fundamentals and HTML

CASE

Creating an Online Resume

Mary Taylor just graduated from Colorado State University with a master's degree in telecommunications. Mary wants to explore as many employment avenues as possible, so she decides to post a copy of her resume on the World Wide Web. Creating an online resume offers Mary several advantages. The Web's skyrocketing popularity gives Mary the potential of reaching a large and varied audience. She can continually update an online resume, offering details on her latest projects and jobs. An online resume also gives a prospective employer the opportunity to look at her work history in more detail than is normal with a paper resume, because Mary can include links to other relevant documents. Mary asks you to help her create an online resume. You're happy to do so because it's something you wanted to learn anyway. After all, you'll be creating your own resume soon enough.

SESSION 1.1

In this session you will learn the basics of how the World Wide Web operates. Then you will begin to explore the code used to create Web documents.

Introducing **the World Wide Web**

The **Internet** is a structure made up of millions of interconnected computers whose users can communicate with each other and share information. The physical structure of the Internet uses fiber-optic cables, satellites, phone lines, and other telecommunications media that send data back and forth, as Figure 1-1 shows. Computers that are linked together form a **network**. Any user whose computer can be linked to a network that has Internet access can join the worldwide Internet community.

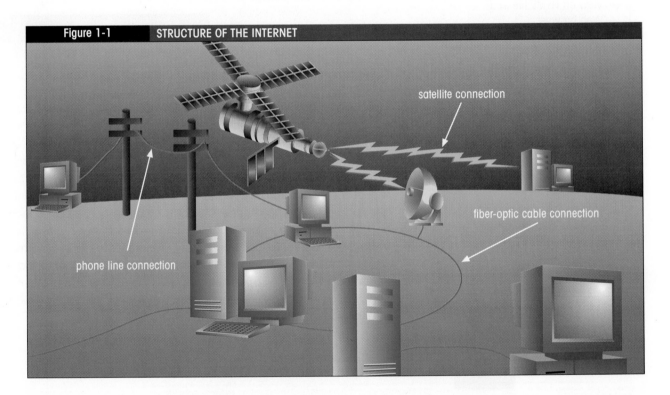

Figure 1-1   STRUCTURE OF THE INTERNET

satellite connection

fiber-optic cable connection

phone line connection

Before 1989, anyone with Internet access could take advantage of the opportunities the Internet offered, but not without some problems. New users often found their introduction to the Internet an unpleasant one. Many Internet tools required you to master a bewildering array of terms, acronyms, and commands before you could begin navigating the Internet. Navigation itself was a hit-and-miss proposition. A computer in Bethesda might have information on breast cancer, but if you didn't know that computer existed and how to reach it, the Internet offered few tools to help you get there. What Internet users needed was a tool that would be easy to use and would allow quick access to any computer on the Internet, regardless of its location. This tool would prove to be the World Wide Web.

The Development of the World Wide Web

The **World Wide Web** organizes the Internet's vast resources to give you easy access to information. In 1989, Timothy Berners-Lee and other researchers at the CERN nuclear research facility near Geneva, Switzerland, laid the foundation of the World Wide Web, or the Web. They wanted to create an information system that made it easy for researchers to locate and share data and that required minimal training and support. They developed a system of hypertext documents that made it very easy to move from one source of information to another. A **hypertext document** is an electronic file that contains elements that you can select, usually by clicking a mouse, to open another document.

Hypertext offers a new way of progressing through a series of documents. When you read a book, you follow a linear progression, reading one page after another. With hypertext, you progress through pages in whatever way is best suited to your goals. Hypertext lets you skip from one topic to another, following a path of information that interests you. Figure 1-2 shows how topics could be related in a hypertext fashion, as opposed to a linear fashion.

Figure 1-2	LINEAR VS. HYPERTEXT DOCUMENTS

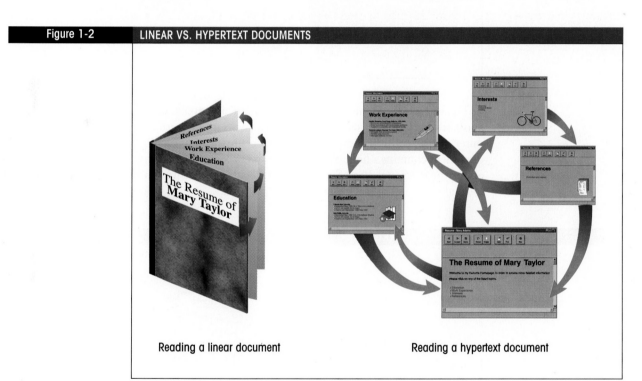

Reading a linear document   Reading a hypertext document

You might already be familiar with two common sources of hypertext: Windows Help files and Macintosh HyperCard stacks. In these programs, you move from one topic to another by clicking or highlighting a phrase or keyword known as a **link**. Clicking a link takes you to another section of the document, or it might take you to another document entirely. Figure 1-3 shows how you might navigate a link in a Help file.

Figure 1-3	CLICKING A LINK IN A HELP FILE

Hypertext as implemented by the CERN group involves jumping from one document to another on computers scattered all over the world. In Figure 1-4, you are working at a computer in Canada that shows a hypertext document on traveling in the United States. This document contains a link to another document located on a computer in Washington, D.C., about the National Park Service. That document in turn contains a link to a document located in California on Yosemite National Park.

Figure 1-4	NAVIGATING HYPERTEXT DOCUMENTS ON THE WEB

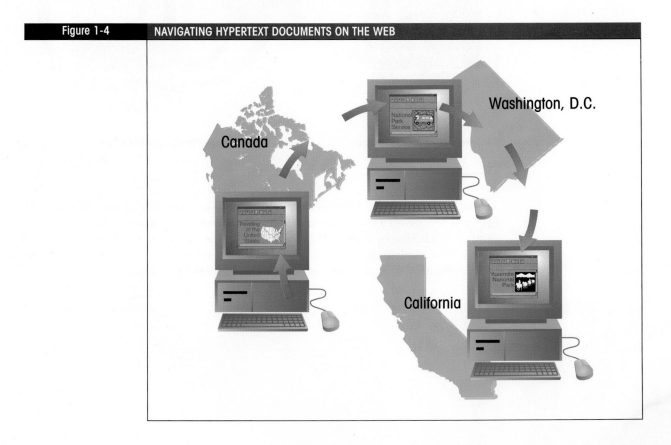

You move from document to document (and computer to computer) by simply clicking links. This approach makes navigating the Internet easy. It frees you from having to know anything about the document's location. The link could open a document on your computer or a document on a computer in South Africa. You might never notice the difference.

Your experience with the Web is not limited to reading text. Web documents, also known as **pages**, can contain graphics, video clips, sound clips, and, more recently, programs that you can run directly from the page. Moreover, as Figure 1-5 shows, Web pages can display text in a wide variety of fonts and formats. A Web page is not only a source of information, it can also be a work of art.

Figure 1-5 **WEB PAGE FEATURING INTERESTING FONTS, GRAPHICS, AND LAYOUT**

A final feature that contributes to the Web's popularity is that it gives users the ability to easily create their own Web pages. This is in marked contrast to other Internet tools, which often require the expertise of a computer systems manager. Figure 1-6 illustrates the growth of the world online population. In a space of six years, the online population is projected to more than triple in size. Is there any doubt why Mary sees the Web as a worthwhile place to post a resume?

Figure 1-6   GROWTH OF THE WORLD ONLINE POPULATION

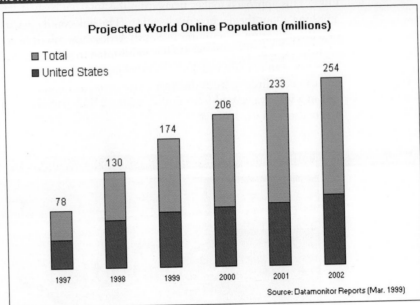

Web Servers and Web Browsers

The World Wide Web has the two components, shown in Figure 1-7. The **Web server** is the computer that stores the Web page that users access. The **Web browser** is the software program that accesses the Web document and displays its contents on the user's computer. The browser can locate a page on a server anywhere in the world and display it for you to see.

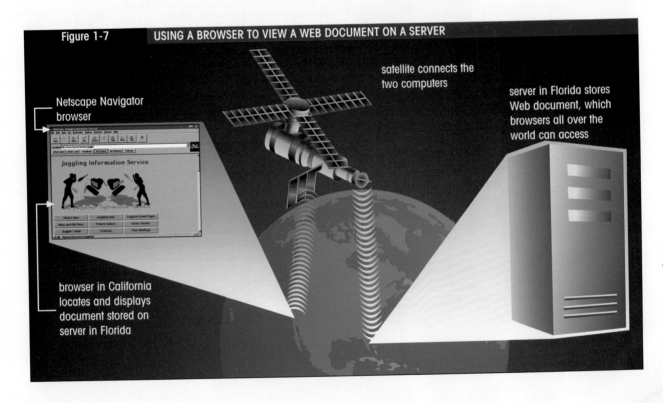

Figure 1-7   USING A BROWSER TO VIEW A WEB DOCUMENT ON A SERVER

Browsers can either be text-based, like the Lynx browser found on UNIX machines, or graphical, like the popular Internet Explorer and Netscape browsers. With a **text-based browser**, you navigate the Web by typing commands; with a **graphical browser** you can use the mouse to move from page to page. Browsers are available for virtually every computer platform. No matter what kind of computer you have, you can probably use it to navigate the Web.

HTML: **The Language of the Web**

When your browser locates a Web document on a server, it needs a way to interpret what it finds. To create a Web document, you use a special language called a **markup language**. The most common markup language is **Hypertext Markup Language** or **HTML**. HTML is one type of a more general markup language called **Standard Generalized Markup Language (SGML)**. SGML encompasses several types of markup languages called **Document Type Definitions (DTD)**. So if you want to engage in a little acronym overload, you can tell your friends that HTML is an SGML DTD used on the WWW.

HTML was designed to describe the contents of a Web page in a very general way. As you've seen in previous figures, a browser can display text on a Web page with a variety of fonts and styles. If you've used a word processor, you know that you can specify the appearance of text in terms of a font type (such as Arial or Times Roman) or an attribute (such as bold or italic). Basic HTML doesn't describe how text looks. Instead it uses a **code** that describes the function the text has in the document. Text appearing in the document heading is marked with a heading code. Text appearing in a bulleted list is marked with a list code. A Web browser interprets these codes to determine the text's appearance. Different browsers might make different choices. One browser might apply a Times Roman font to text in the document heading, while another browser might use an Arial font. Figure 1-8 shows how the same HTML file might appear on two different browsers.

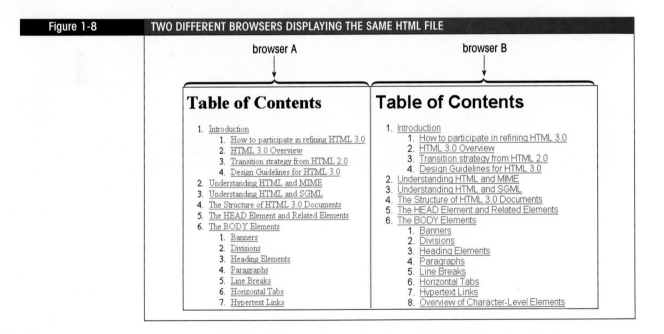

Figure 1-8   **TWO DIFFERENT BROWSERS DISPLAYING THE SAME HTML FILE**

There are a couple of reasons for the differences you see in Figure 1-8. The Web must work well with all kinds of computers (UNIX, Macintosh, Windows), a feature known as **portability**. Because each computer differs in terms of what, if any, fonts it can display, the browser determines how text is to be displayed. Portability frees Web page authors from worrying about making their pages compatible with the large variety of computers and operating systems on the Internet. HTML works with a wide range of devices, from clunky teletypes to high-end workstations. It also works with nonvisual media such as speech and Braille. Of course portability does limit your ability in defining the appearance of your document, so enhancements have been made to HTML to allow the Web page author to use **style sheets** to better control the fonts and styles on the Web page. Creating a Web page with style sheets should only be done after you've mastered basic HTML.

Another advantage of HTML is speed. Specifying the exact appearance of the Web page could dramatically increase both the size of the file and the time required to retrieve it. It is much quicker to render the document on the local computer, using local specifications. The downside of this approach is that you cannot be sure exactly how every browser will display the text on your page. It's essential that you test your code on several different browsers, and if possible, operating systems, before posting your pages on the Internet.

Versions of HTML

HTML has a set of rules under which it operates, called its **syntax**. There must be a consensus among creators of Web documents on the syntax used in HTML files. If there were not, you would have no guarantee that other browsers on the Internet would recognize the code in your Web document. It wouldn't do Mary much good to create a stunning online resume that her potential employers could not read. This consensus is referred to as the **specifications** or **standards** that have been developed by a consortium of Web authors, software companies, and interested users called the **World Wide Web Consortium**, or **W3C**. Figure 1-9 lists four versions of HTML; each follows a defined set of standards.

Figure 1-9		VERSIONS OF HTML
VERSION	**DATE**	**DESCRIPTION**
HTML 1.00	1989–1994	The first public version of HTML, which included browser support for inline images and text controls
HTML 2.00	1995	The version supported by all graphical browsers, including Netscape Communicator, Internet Explorer, and Mosaic. It supported interactive form elements such as option buttons and text boxes. A document written to follow 2.0 specifications would be readable by most browsers on the Internet.
HTML 3.20	1997	This version included more support for creating and formatting tables, and expanded the options for interactive form elements. It also allows for the creation of complex mathematical equations.
HTML 4.01	1999	This version adds support for style sheets, to give Web authors greater control over page layout. It adds new features to tables and forms and provides support for international features. This version also expands HTML's scripting ability and support for multimedia elements.

For more information on HTML standards and any updates, see the Web page at *http://www.w3.org/MarkUp/*.

Some browsers also support **extensions**, features that add new possibilities to HTML. The Netscape Navigator and Internet Explorer browsers employ the most well-known extensions. Because only these browsers can interpret those extensions, many people argue that extensions have undermined a fundamental advantage of the World Wide Web: the ability of a Web document to work on different platforms and browsers. On the other hand, Web authors clearly want these additional features. Moreover, these extensions foreshadowed many of the enhancements added in HTML 4.0, and others will no doubt become part of future HTML standards. If you plan to use extensions in your Web documents, you should indicate this on your page and identify the browsers that support those extensions.

Tools for Creating HTML Documents

HTML documents are simple text files. The only software package you need to create them is a basic text editor such as the Windows Notepad program. If you want a software package to do some of the work of creating an HTML document, you can use an HTML converter or an HTML editor.

An **HTML converter** takes text in one format and converts it to HTML code. For example, you can create the source document with a word processor such as Microsoft Word, and then have the converter save the document as an HTML file. Converters have several advantages. They free you from the occasionally laborious task of typing HTML code, and, because the conversion is automated, you do not have to worry about typographical errors ruining your code. Finally, you can create the source document using a software package that you might be more familiar with. Be aware that a converter has some limitations. As HTML specifications are updated and new extensions created, you will have to wait for the next version of the converter, to take advantage of these features. Moreover, no converter can support all HTML features, so for anything but the simplest Web page, you still have to work with HTML.

An **HTML editor** helps you create an HTML file by inserting HTML codes for you as you work. HTML editors can save you a lot of work. They have many of the same advantages and limitations as converters. They do let you set up your Web page quickly, but to create the finished document, you often still have to work directly with the HTML code.

Session 1.1 QUICK CHECK

1. What is hypertext?

2. What is a Web server? A Web browser? Describe how they work together.

3. What is HTML?

4. How do HTML documents differ from documents created with a word processor such as Word or WordPerfect?

5. What are the advantages of letting Web browsers determine the appearance of Web pages?

6. What are HTML extensions? What are some advantages and disadvantages of using extensions?

7. What software program do you need to create an HTML document?

SESSION 1.2

In this session you begin entering the text that will form the basis of your Web page. You will insert the appropriate HTML codes, creating a simple Web page that outlines Mary's work experience and qualifications.

Creating an HTML Document

It's always a good idea to plan the appearance of your Web page before you start writing code. In her final semester, Mary developed a paper resume that she distributed at campus job fairs. Half her work is already done, because she can use the paper resume as her model. Figure 1-10 shows Mary's hardcopy resume.

Figure 1-10   **MARY'S PAPER RESUME**

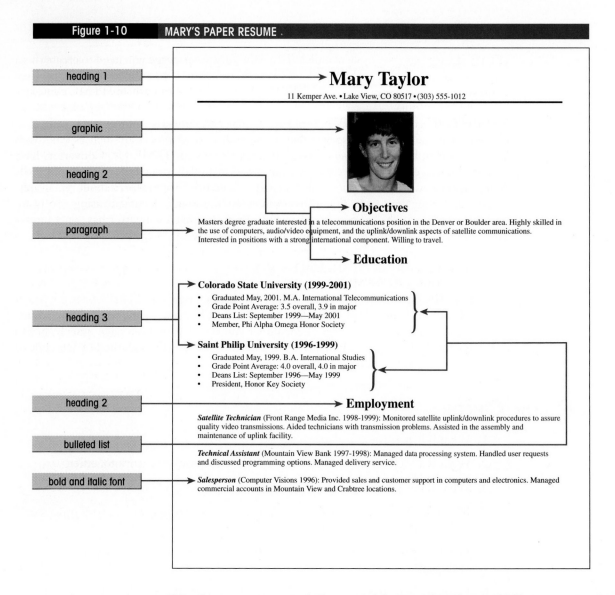

Mary's paper resume includes several features that she would like you to implement in the online version. A heading at the top prominently displays her name in a large font. Beneath the heading is her photo. Mary's resume is divided into three sections: Objectives, Education, and Employment. Within the Objectives section, a paragraph describes Mary's interests and future goals. Within the Education section, two smaller headings name the two universities she attended. Under each of these headings, a bulleted list details her accomplishments. The Employment section describes each position she's held, with the official title in boldface and italics. Mary's paper resume has three heading levels, bulleted lists, formatted characters, and graphics. When she creates her online resume with HTML, she wants to include these features. As you help Mary create this document for the World Wide Web, you will probably want to refer to Figure 1-10 periodically as the page develops.

HTML Syntax

An HTML document has two elements: document content and tags. **Document content** are those parts of the document that you want the user to see, such as text and graphics. **Tags** are the HTML codes that control the appearance of the document content.

The HTML syntax for creating the kinds of features that Mary wants in her page follows a very basic structure. You apply a tag to document content using the syntax:

```
<Tag Name Properties> Document Content </Tag Name>
```

You can always identify a tag by the brackets (< >) that enclose the tag name. Some tags can include **properties**, or additional information placed within the brackets that controls how the tag is used. Tags usually come in pairs: the **opening tag** is the first tag, which tells the browser to turn on the feature and apply it to the document content that follows. The browser applies the feature until it encounters the **closing tag**, which turns off the feature. Note that closing tags are identified by the slash (/) that precedes the tag name. Not every type of tag has an opening and closing tag. Some tags are known as **one-sided tags** because they require only the opening tag. **Two-sided tags** require both opening and closing tags.

For example, look at the first line of Mary's resume, the name Mary Taylor, in Figure 1-10. You could format this line with the two-sided HTML tag as follows:

```
<H1 ALIGN=CENTER>Mary Taylor</H1>
```

Here the <H1 ALIGN=CENTER > opening tag tells the browser that the text that follows, Mary Taylor, should be formatted with the H1 style (H1 stands for Heading 1; you'll learn what this means later). This tag also includes a property, the **alignment property** (ALIGN), which tells the browser how to align the text: in this case, centered. After the opening tag comes the content, Mary Taylor. The </H1> tag signals the browser to turn off the H1 style. Remember that each browser determines the exact effect of the H1 tag. One browser might apply a 14-point Times Roman bold font to Mary's text, whereas another browser might use 18-point italic Arial—but in each case, the font would be appropriately larger than the normal font of the document. Figure 1-11 shows how three different browsers might interpret this line of HTML code.

Figure 1-11	EXAMPLES OF HOW DIFFERENT BROWSERS MIGHT INTERPRET THE HTML <H1> TAG
BROWSER INTERPRETING THE H1 TAG	**APPEARANCE OF THE DOCUMENT CONTENT**
Browser A	Mary Taylor
Browser B	**Mary Taylor**
Browser C	*Mary Taylor*

Tags are not case sensitive. That means that typing "<H1>" has the same effect as typing "<h1>". Many Web authors like to use only uppercase for tags, to distinguish tags from document content. We'll follow that convention throughout this book.

Creating Basic Tags

When you create your Web page, you first enter tags that indicate the markup language used in the document, identify the document's key sections, and assign the page a title.

In the steps that follow, type the text exactly as you see it. The text after the steps explains each line. To start entering code, you need a basic text editor such as Notepad or WordPad.

To start creating an HTML file:

1. Place your Data Disk in drive A.

TROUBLE? If you don't have a Data Disk, you need to get one. Your instructor will either give you one or ask you to make your own. See the Read This Before You Begin page at the beginning of the tutorials for instructions.

TROUBLE? If your Data Disk won't fit in drive A, try drive B. If it fits in drive B, substitute drive B for drive A in every tutorial.

2. Open a text editor on your computer, and then open a new document.

TROUBLE? If you don't know how to locate, start, or use the text editor on your system, ask your instructor or technical support person for help.

3. Type the following lines of code into your document. Press the **Enter** key after each line (twice for a blank line).

```
<HTML>
<HEAD>
<TITLE>The Resume of Mary Taylor</TITLE>
</HEAD>

<BODY>
</BODY>

</HTML>
```

4. Save the file as **Resume.htm** in the Tutorial.01 folder on your Data Disk, but do not close your text editor. The text you typed should look something like Figure 1-12.

Figure 1-12	INITIAL HTML TAGS

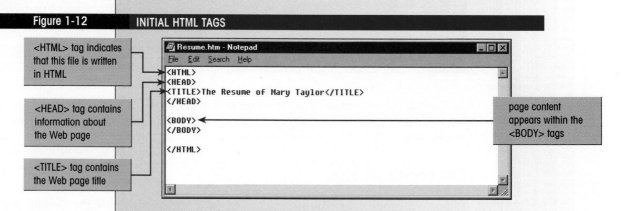

<HTML> tag indicates that this file is written in HTML

<HEAD> tag contains information about the Web page

<TITLE> tag contains the Web page title

page content appears within the <BODY> tags

TROUBLE? If you don't know how to save a file on your Data Disk, ask your instructor or technical support person for assistance.

TROUBLE? Don't worry if your screen doesn't look exactly like Figure 1-12. The text editor shown in the figures is the Windows Notepad editor. Your text editor might look very different. Just make sure you entered the text correctly.

TROUBLE? If you are using the Windows Notepad text editor to create your HTML file, make sure you don't save the file using the text document type (.txt), which Notepad automatically adds to the filename. This renders the file unreadable to the Netscape Navigator browser, which requires an .htm or .html file extension. So make sure you save the file using the All Files (*.*) type, and then add the .htm or .html extension to the filename yourself.

The opening and closing HTML tags bracket all the remaining code you'll enter in the document. This indicates to a browser that the page is written in HTML. While you don't have to include this tag, it is necessary if the file is to be read by another SGML application. Moreover, it is considered good style to include it.

The <HEAD> tag is used where you enter information about the Web page itself. One such piece of information is the title of the page, which appears in the title bar of the Web browser. This information is entered using the <TITLE> tag. The title in this example is "The Resume of Mary Taylor".

Finally, the portion of the document that Web users will see is contained between the <BODY> tags. At this point, the page is blank, with no text or graphics. You'll add those later. The <HEAD> and <BODY> tags are not strictly required, but you should include them to better organize your document and make its code more readable to others. The extra space before and after the BODY tags is also not required, but it will make your code easier to view as you add more features to it.

Displaying Your HTML Files

As you continue adding to Mary's HTML file, you should occasionally display the formatted page with your Web browser to verify that there are no syntax errors or other problems. You might even want to view the results on several browsers to check for differences between one browser and another. In the steps and figures that follow, the Internet Explorer browser is used to display Mary's resume page as it gradually unfolds. If you are using a different browser, ask your instructor how to view local files (those located on your own computer rather than on the Web).

To view the beginning of Mary's resume page:

1. Start your browser. You do not need to be connected to the Internet to view a file loaded on your computer.

   TROUBLE? If you try to start your browser and are not connected to the Internet, you might get a warning message. Netscape Navigator, for example, gives a warning message telling you that it was unable to create a network socket connection. Click OK to ignore the message and continue.

2. After your browser loads its home page, click **File** on the menu bar and then click **Open**.

   TROUBLE? If you're using Netscape Navigator, you will have to use a different command to open the file from your Data Disk. Talk to your instructor or technical support person to find out how to open the file.

3. Locate the **Resume.htm** file that you saved in the Tutorial.01 folder on your Data Disk, and then click Open. Your browser displays Mary's file, as shown in Figure 1-13. Note that the page title, which you typed earlier between the <TITLE> tags, appears in the browser's title bar.

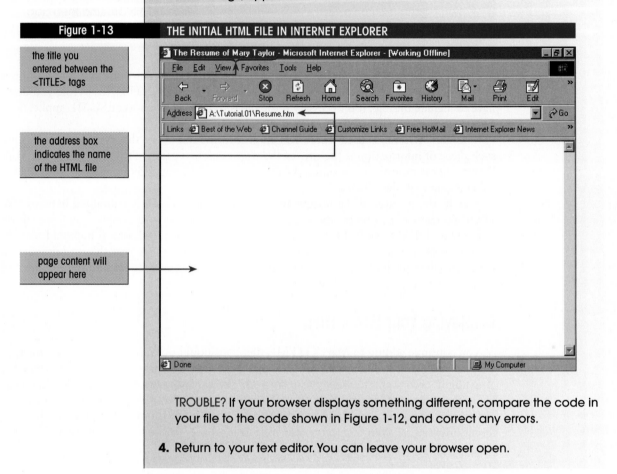

| Figure 1-13 | THE INITIAL HTML FILE IN INTERNET EXPLORER |

the title you entered between the <TITLE> tags

the address box indicates the name of the HTML file

page content will appear here

TROUBLE? If your browser displays something different, compare the code in your file to the code shown in Figure 1-12, and correct any errors.

4. Return to your text editor. You can leave your browser open.

Creating **Headers, Paragraphs, and Lists**

Now that the basic structure of Mary's page is set, you can start filling in the page content. One place to start is the headers for the various sections of her document. Her document needs a header for the entire page and headers for each of three sections: Objectives, Education, and Employment. The Education section has two additional headers that provide information about the two universities she attended. You can create all these headers using HTML heading tags.

Creating Header Tags

HTML supports six levels of headers, numbered <H1> through <H6>, with <H1> being the largest and most prominent, and <H6> being the smallest. Headers (even the smallest) appear in a larger font than normal text, and some headers are boldface. The general syntax for a header tag is:

```
<Hy>Heading Text</Hy>
```

where *y* is a header numbered 1 through 6.

Figure 1-14 illustrates the general appearance of the six header styles. Your browser might use slightly different fonts and sizes.

Figure 1-14	SIX HEADER LEVELS

This is an H1 Header

This is an H2 Header

This is an H3 Header

This is an H4 Header

This is an H5 Header

This is an H6 Header

REFERENCE WINDOW   **RW**

<u>Creating a Header Tag</u>
- Open the HTML file with your text editor.
- Type <Hy> where y is the header number you want to use.
- If you want to use a special alignment, specify the alignment property setting after y and before the closing symbol, >.
- Type the text that you want to appear in the header.
- Type </Hy> to turn off the header tag.

Starting with HTML 3.2, the header tag can contain additional properties, one of which is the alignment property. Mary wants some headers centered on the page, so you'll take advantage of this property. Although Mary's address is not really header text, you decide to format it with an <H5> tag, because you want it to stand out a little from normal paragraphed text.

To add headings to the resume file:

1. Return to your text editor, and then open the **Resume.htm** file, if it is not already open.

2. Type the following text between the <BODY> and </BODY> tags (type the address and phone number all on one line, as shown in Figure 1-15):

    <H1 ALIGN=CENTER>Mary Taylor</H1>

    <H5 ALIGN=CENTER>11 Kemper Ave. Lake View, CO 80517 (303) 555-1012</H5>

<H2 ALIGN=CENTER>Objectives</H2>

<H2 ALIGN=CENTER>Education</H2>

<H3>Colorado State University (1999-2001)</H3>

<H3>Saint Philip University (1996-1999)</H3>

<H2 ALIGN=CENTER>Employment</H2>

The revised code is shown in figure 1-15. To make it easier to follow the changes to the HTML file, new and altered text is highlighted in red. This will not be the case in your own text files.

| Figure 1-15 | ENTERING HEADER TAGS |

```
<BODY>
<H1 ALIGN=CENTER>Mary Taylor</H1>
<H5 ALIGN=CENTER>11 Kemper Ave. Lake View, CO 80517 (303) 555-1012</H5>
<H2 ALIGN=CENTER>Objectives</H2>
<H2 ALIGN=CENTER>Education</H2>
<H3>Colorado State University (1999-2001)</H3>
<H3>Saint Philip University (1996-1999)</H3>
<H2 ALIGN=CENTER>Employment</H2>
</BODY>
```

3. Save the revised Resume.htm file in the Tutorial.01 folder on your Data Disk. You can leave your text editor open.

The section headers all use the ALIGN=CENTER property to center the text on the page. The <H3> tags used for the two university headers, however, do not include that property and will be left-justified because that is the default alignment setting. If a browser that displays Mary's page does not support HTML 3.2 (or above) or does not support the alignment property through an extension, the headers will appear, but all of them will be left-justified.

To display the revised Resume.htm file:

1. Return to your Web browser.

2. If the previous version of the file still appears in the browser window, click **View** on the menu bar, and then click **Refresh**. If you are using Netscape, you will need to click **View** and then click **Reload**.

The updated Resume.htm file looks like Figure 1-16.

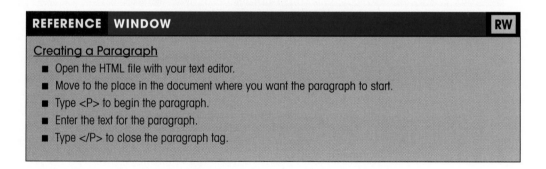

Figure 1-16   HEADERS AS THEY APPEAR IN THE BROWSER

Entering Paragraph Text

The next thing that you have to do is enter information for each section. If your paragraph does not require any formatting, you can enter the text without tags.

REFERENCE WINDOW   **RW**

__Creating a Paragraph__

- Open the HTML file with your text editor.
- Move to the place in the document where you want the paragraph to start.
- Type <P> to begin the paragraph.
- Enter the text for the paragraph.
- Type </P> to close the paragraph tag.

Mary's career objective, which appears just below the Objectives heading, does not require formatting, so you can enter that as paragraph text.

To enter paragraph text:

1. Return to your text editor, and then reopen the **Resume.htm** file, if it is not already open.

2. Type the following text directly after the line of code that specifies the Objectives heading:

   Masters degree graduate interested in a telecommunications position in the Denver or Boulder area. Highly skilled in the use of computers, audio/video equipment, and the uplink/downlink aspects of satellite communications. Interested in positions with a strong international component. Willing to travel.

Your text should be placed between the Objectives head and the Education head, as shown in Figure 1-17. Check your work for mistakes, and edit the file as necessary.

Figure 1-17   **ENTERING PARAGRAPH TEXT**

```
<BODY>
<H1 ALIGN=CENTER>Mary Taylor</H1>
<H5 ALIGN=CENTER>11 Kemper Ave. Lake View, CO 80517 (303) 555-1012</H5>
<H2 ALIGN=CENTER>Objectives</H2>
Masters degree graduate interested in a telecommunications position in
the Denver or Boulder area. Highly skilled in the use of computers,
audio/video equipment and the uplink/downlink aspects of satellite
communications. Interested in positions with a strong international
component. Willing to travel.
<H2 ALIGN=CENTER>Education</H2>
```

TROUBLE? If you are using a text editor like Notepad, the text might not wrap to the next line automatically. You might need to select the Word Wrap command on the Edit menu, or a similar command, so you can see all the text on your screen.

3. Save the changes you made to the Resume.htm file.

4. Return to your Web browser, and then reopen the **Resume.htm** file to view the text you've added. See Figure 1-18.

Figure 1-18   **PARAGRAPH TEXT IN THE BROWSER**

Mary Taylor

11 Kemper Ave. Lake View, CO 80517 (303) 555-1012

Objectives

Masters degree graduate interested in a telecommunications position in the Denver or Boulder area. Highly skilled in the use of computers, audio/video equipment, and the uplink/downlink aspects of satellite communications. Interested in positions with a strong international component. Willing to travel.

Education

5. Now enter the Employment paragraph text by returning to your text editor and reopening the **Resume.htm file**, if needed.

6. Go to the end of the file, and, in the line before the final </BODY> tag, type the following text:

Satellite Technician (Front Range Media Inc. 1998-1999): Monitored satellite uplink/downlink procedures to assure quality video transmissions. Aided technicians with transmission problems. Assisted in the assembly and maintenance of uplink facility.

Technical Assistant (Mountain View Bank 1997-1998): Managed data processing system. Handled user requests and discussed programming options. Managed delivery service.

Salesperson (Computer Visions 1996): Sales and customer support in computers and electronics. Managed commercial accounts in Mountain View and Crabtree locations.

Figure 1-19 shows the new code in Mary's resume file.

| Figure 1-19 | ENTERING EMPLOYMENT TEXT |

```
<H2 ALIGN=CENTER>Education</H2>
<H3>Colorado State University (1999-2001)</H3>
<H3>Saint Philip University (1996-1999)</H3>
<H2 ALIGN=CENTER>Employment</H2>
Satellite Technician (Front Range Media Inc. 1998-1999): Monitored
satellite uplink/downlink procedures to assure quality transmissions.
Aided technicians with transmission problems. Assisted in the assembly
and maintenance of uplink facility.

Technical Assistant (Mountain View Bank 1997-1998): Managed data
processing system. Handled user requests and discussed programming
options. Managed delivery service.

Salesperson (Computer Visions 1996): Sales and customer support in
computers and electronics. Managed commercial accounts in Mountain View
and Crabtree locations.
</BODY>
```

employment history

7. Save the changes you've made to the file.

8. Return to your Web browser, and then reopen the **Resume.htm** file.

9. Scroll down to see how the new text looks (see Figure 1-20).

| Figure 1-20 | THE EMPLOYMENT HISTORY DISPLAYED BY THE BROWSER |

Education

Colorado State University (1999-2001)

Saint Philip University (1996-1999)

Employment

employment history is not separated into paragraphs

Satellite Technician (Front Range Media Inc. 1998-1999): Monitored satellite uplink/downlink procedures to assure quality transmissions. Aided technicians with transmission problems. Assisted in the assembly and maintenance of uplink facility. Technical Assistant (Mountain View Bank 1997-1998): Managed data processing system. Handled user requests and discussed programming options. Managed delivery service. Salesperson (Computer Visions 1996): Sales and customer support in computers and electronics. Managed commercial accounts in Mountain View and Crabtree locations.

To your surprise, the text you typed into the HTML file looks nothing like what appeared on the browser, as you can see from Figure 1-20. Instead of being separated by blank lines, the three paragraphs are running together. What went wrong?

The problem here is that HTML formats text only through the use of tags. HTML ignores such things as extra blank spaces, blank lines, or tabs. As far as HTML is concerned, the following three lines of code are identical, so a browser interprets and displays each line just like the others, ignoring the extra spaces and lines:

```
<H1>To be or not to be. That is the question.</H1>
<H1>To be or not to be.   That is the question.</H1>
<H1>To be or not to be.
            That is the question.</H1>
```

At first glance, the Employment section seemed not to need any formatting; however, each paragraph needs to be separated by a blank line. To add this space between paragraphs, you need to use the **paragraph tag**, **<P>**, which adds a blank paragraph (the extra line you need) before text to separate it from any text that precedes it.

To add paragraph tags for blank lines:

1. Return to your text editor and the Resume.htm file.

2. Modify the Employment text, bracketing each paragraph between a **<P>** and **</P>** tag, so that the lines now read:

   <P>Satellite Technician (Front Range Media Inc. 1998-1999): Monitored satellite uplink/downlink procedures to assure quality video transmissions. Aided technicians with transmission problems. Assisted in the assembly and maintenance of uplink facility.</P>

   <P>Technical Assistant (Mountain View Bank 1997-1998): Managed data processing system. Handled user requests and discussed programming options. Managed delivery service. </P>

   <P>Salesperson (Computer Visions 1996): Sales and customer support in computers and electronics. Managed commercial accounts in Mountain View and Crabtree locations.</P>

3. Save the revised text file.

4. Return to your Web browser, and then reopen the **Resume.htm** file. The text in the Employment section is properly separated into distinct paragraphs, as shown in Figure 1-21.

Figure 1-21	EMPLOYMENT HISTORY SEPARATED INTO PARAGRAPHS

Colorado State University (1999-2001)

Saint Philip University (1996-1999)

the text is now separated into paragraphs

Employment

Satellite Technician (Front Range Media Inc. 1998-1999): Monitored satellite uplink/downlink procedures to assure quality transmissions. Aided technicians with transmission problems. Assisted in the assembly and maintenance of uplink facility.

Technical Assistant (Mountain View Bank 1997-1998): Managed data processing system. Handled user requests and discussed programming options. Managed delivery service.

Salesperson (Computer Visions 1996): Sales and customer support in computers and electronics. Managed commercial accounts in Mountain View and Crabtree locations.

If you start examining the HTML code for pages that you encounter on the Web, you might notice that the <P> tag is used in different ways on other pages. In the original version of HTML, the <P> tag inserted a blank line into the page. In HTML 1.0, <P> was placed at the end of each paragraph; no </P> tag was required. In versions 2.0 and 3.2, the paragraph tag is two-sided: both the <P> and </P> tags are used. Moreover, the <P> tag is placed at the beginning of the paragraph, not the end. Starting with HTML 3.2, you can specify the alignment property in a paragraph tag, but in HTML 1.0 and 2.0 you cannot; paragraphs are always assumed to be left justified. For the Web documents that you are creating in this book, you should use the style convention shown in the above example.

Creating Lists

You still need to enter the lists describing Mary's achievements at Colorado State University and Saint Philip University. HTML provides tags for such lists. HTML supports three kinds of lists: ordered, unordered, and definition.

An **ordered list** is a list in numeric order. HTML automatically adds the numbers once you display your Web page in a browser. If you remove an item from the list, HTML automatically updates the numbers to reflect the new order. For example, Mary might want to list her scholastic awards in order from the most important to the least important. To do so, you could enter the following code into her HTML document:

```
<H3>Scholastic Awards</H3>
<OL>
<LI>Enos Mills Scholarship
<LI>Physics Expo blue ribbon winner
<LI> Honor Key Award semifinalist
</OL>
```

This example shows the basic structure of an HTML list. The list text is bracketed between the <OL> and </OL> tags, where OL stands for ordered list. This tells the browser to present the text between the tags as an ordered list. Each list item is identified by a single <LI> tag, where LI stands for list item. There is no closing tag for list items.

A Web browser might display this code as:

Scholastic Awards

1. Enos Mills Scholarship

2. Physics Expo blue ribbon winner

3. Honor Key Award semifinalist

You can also specify the symbol used for the ordered list, using the **TYPE** property. The default, as you've seen, is a number. By setting the TYPE property to "a", you can use letters instead of numbers. For example, the code:

```
<OL TYPE=a>
<LI>Enos Mills Scholarship
<LI>Physics Expo blue ribbon winner
<LI> Honor Key Award semifinalist
</OL>
```

yields the following list:

a. Enos Mills Scholarship

b. Physics Expo blue ribbon winner

c. Honor Key Award semifinalist

Other values of the TYPE property are "A" for uppercase letters, "i" for lowercase Roman numerals, and "I" for uppercase Roman numerals. Be aware that the TYPE property is not supported by all browsers. It was not part of the HTML standards prior to HTML 3.0.

You can also create an **unordered list**, in which list items have no particular order. Browsers usually format unordered lists by inserting a bullet symbol before each list item. The entire list is bracketed between the <UL> and </UL> tags, where UL stands for unordered list. If Mary wants to display her awards without regard to their importance, you could enter the following code:

```
<H3>Scholastic Awards</H3>
<UL>
<LI>Enos Mills Scholarship
<LI>Physics Expo blue ribbon winner
<LI>Honor Key Award semifinalist
</UL>
```

A Web browser might display this code as:

Scholastic Awards

- Enos Mills Scholarship
- Physics Expo blue ribbon winner
- Honor Key Award semifinalist

As with the ordered list, you can use the TYPE property to specify the type of symbol used in the list. The default symbol is a bullet or "disc." Other values for the TYPE property are SQUARE for square bullets and CIRCLE for circles. This property was introduced with HTML 3.0, although Netscape has supported it since version 1.0. Internet Explorer does not support this property, although this may change with new versions. If symbol type is an important part of your document, you will probably want to test this feature on several different browsers.

A third type of list that HTML can display is a definition list. A **definition list** is a list of terms, each followed by a definition line, usually indented slightly to the right. The <LI> tag used in ordered and unordered lists for individual items is replaced by two tags: the <DT> tag used for each term in the list and the <DD> tag used for each term's definition. As with the <LI> tag, both of these tags are one-sided. The entire list is bracketed by the <DL> and </DL> tags, indicating to the browser that the list is a definition list. If Mary wants to create a list of her scholastic awards and briefly describe each, she can use a definition list, even though the items are not actually terms and definitions. To create a definition list for her awards, you could enter this code into her HTML file:

```
<H3>Scholastic Awards</H3>
<DL>
<DT>Enos Mills Scholarship<DD>Awarded to the outstanding
student in the senior class
<DT>Physics Expo blue ribbon winner<DD>Awarded for a research
 project on fiber optics
<DT>Honor Key Award semifinalist<DD>Awarded for an essay on
the information age
</DL>
```

A Web browser might display this code as:

Scholastic Awards

Enos Mills Scholarship

Awarded to the outstanding student in the senior class

Physics Expo blue ribbon winner

Awarded for a research project on fiber optics

Honor Key Award semifinalist

Awarded for an essay on the information age

Creating Lists
- Open the HTML file with your text editor.
- Move to the place in the document where you want the list to appear.
- Type <OL> to start an ordered list, <UL> to start an unordered list, and <DL> to start a definition list.
- For each item in an ordered or unordered list, type <LI> followed by the text for the list item. For each item in a definition list, type <DT> before the term and <DD> before the definition.
- To turn off the list, type </OL> for an ordered list, </UL> for an unordered list, and </DL> for a definition list.

On her paper resume (Figure 1-10), Mary's educational accomplishments are in a bulleted list. You can include this feature in Mary's online resume by using the <OL> and <LI> tags.

To add an unordered list to the resume file:

1. Return to your text editor and reopen the **Resume.htm file**, if it is not still open.

2. Type the following code and text between the headers "Colorado State University" and "Saint Philip University":

<UL>

<LI>Graduated May, 2001. M.A. International Telecommunications

<LI>Grade Point Average: 3.5 overall, 3.9 in major

<LI>Dean's List: September 1999-May 2001

<LI>Member, Phi Alpha Omega Honor Society

</UL>

3. Type these lines of code after the heading "Saint Philip University":

<UL>

<LI>Graduated May, 1999. B.A. International Studies

<LI>Grade Point Average: 4.0 overall, 4.0 in major

<LI>Dean's List: September 1996-May 1999

<LI>President, Honor Key Society

</UL>

The new lines in the resume file should look like Figure 1-22.

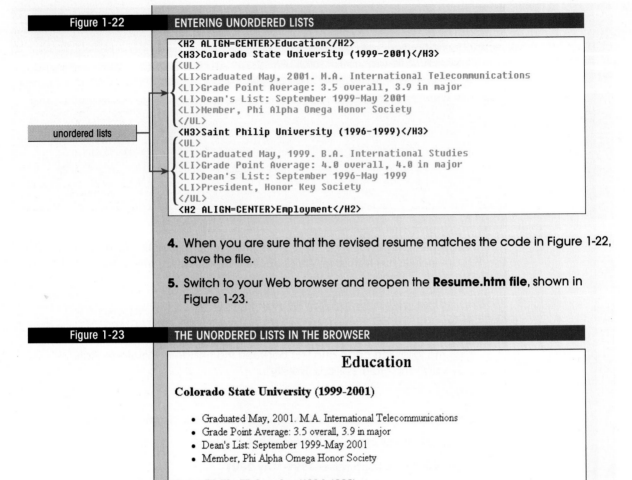

Figure 1-22   ENTERING UNORDERED LISTS

unordered lists

```
<H2 ALIGN=CENTER>Education</H2>
<H3>Colorado State University (1999-2001)</H3>
<UL>
<LI>Graduated May, 2001. M.A. International Telecommunications
<LI>Grade Point Average: 3.5 overall, 3.9 in major
<LI>Dean's List: September 1999-May 2001
<LI>Member, Phi Alpha Omega Honor Society
</UL>
<H3>Saint Philip University (1996-1999)</H3>
<UL>
<LI>Graduated May, 1999. B.A. International Studies
<LI>Grade Point Average: 4.0 overall, 4.0 in major
<LI>Dean's List: September 1996-May 1999
<LI>President, Honor Key Society
</UL>
<H2 ALIGN=CENTER>Employment</H2>
```

4. When you are sure that the revised resume matches the code in Figure 1-22, save the file.

5. Switch to your Web browser and reopen the **Resume.htm file**, shown in Figure 1-23.

Figure 1-23   THE UNORDERED LISTS IN THE BROWSER

Education

Colorado State University (1999-2001)

- Graduated May, 2001. M.A. International Telecommunications
- Grade Point Average: 3.5 overall, 3.9 in major
- Dean's List: September 1999-May 2001
- Member, Phi Alpha Omega Honor Society

Saint Philip University (1996-1999)

- Graduated May, 1999. B.A. International Studies
- Grade Point Average: 4.0 overall, 4.0 in major
- Dean's List: September 1996-May 1999
- President, Honor Key Society

Mary's resume file now includes lists formatted much like those on her paper resume. If your browser does not create a page that looks like Figure 1-23, return to the HTML file, and check for inconsistencies.

Creating **Character Tags**

Until now you've worked with tags that affect either the entire document or individual lines. HTML also lets you modify the characteristics of individual characters. A tag that you apply to an individual character is called a **character tag**. You can use two kinds of character tags: logical and physical. **Logical character tags** indicate how you want to use text, not necessarily how you want it displayed. Figure 1-24 lists some common logical character tags.

Figure 1-24	COMMON LOGICAL CHARACTER TAGS
TAG	**DESCRIPTION**
<EM>	Indicates that characters should be emphasized in some way. Usually displayed with italics.
<STRONG>	Emphasizes characters more strongly than <EM>. Usually displayed in a bold font.
<CODE>	Indicates a sample of code. Usually displayed in a Courier font or a similar font that allots the same width to each character.
<KBD>	Used to offset text that the user should enter. Often displayed in a Courier font or a similar font that allots the same width to each character.
<VAR>	Indicates a variable. Often displayed in italics or underlined.
<CITE>	Indicates short quotes or citations. Often italicized by browsers.

Figure 1-25 shows examples of how these tags might appear in a browser. Note that you can combine tags, allowing you to create boldface and italics text by using both the <EM> and the <STRONG> tags.

Figure 1-25	LOGICAL CHARACTER TAGS AS THEY APPEAR IN THE BROWSER

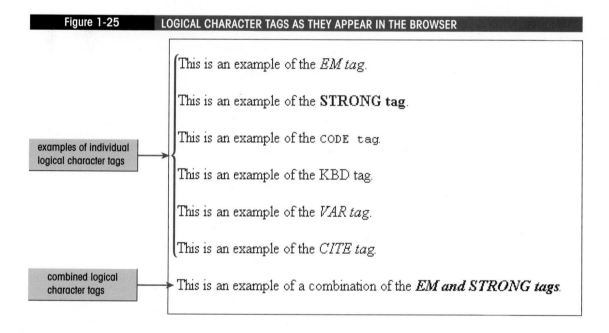

examples of individual logical character tags

combined logical character tags

HTML authors can also use **physical character tags** to indicate exactly how characters are to be formatted. Figure 1-26 shows common examples of physical character tags.

Figure 1-26	COMMON PHYSICAL CHARACTER TAGS
TAG	**DESCRIPTION**
<B>	Indicates that the text should be bold.
<I>	Indicates that the text should be italic.
<TT>	Indicates that the text should be used with a font such as Courier that allots the same width to each character.
<BIG>	Indicates that the text should be displayed in a big font. Available only in HTML 3.0.
<SMALL>	Indicates that the text should be displayed in a small font. Available only in HTML 3.0.
<SUB>	The text should be displayed as a subscript, in a smaller font if possible. Available only in HTML 3.0.
<SUP>	The text should be displayed as a superscript, in a smaller font if possible. Available only in HTML 3.0.

Figure 1-27 shows examples of how these tags might appear in a browser. Some browsers also support the <U> tag for underlining text, but other browsers might not show underlining, so use it cautiously.

Figure 1-27	PHYSICAL CHARACTER TAGS AS THEY APPEAR IN THE BROWSER

This is an example of the **B tag**.

This is an example of the *I tag*.

This is an example of the TT tag.

This is an example of the **BIG tag**.

This is an example of the SMALL tag.

This is an example of the $_{SUB\ tag}$

This is an example of the $^{SUP\ tag}$.

Given the presence of both logical and physical character tags, which should you use to display some text in an italicized font: <EM> or <I>? Some older versions of browsers are text-based and cannot display italics. These older browsers ignore the <I> tag, so the emphasis you want to place on a certain piece of text is lost. If this a concern, you should use a logical tag. On the other hand, the physical character tags are more commonly used today and are easier to interpret. Some Web page authors believe that the use of logical character tags such as <EM> and <STRONG> is archaic and confusing.

Only one part of Mary's resume requires character tags: the Employment section, where Mary wants to emphasize the title of each job she has held. She decides to use a combination of the <B> and <I> tags to display the titles in boldface and italics.

To add character tags to the resume file:

1. Return to your text editor, and reopen the **Resume.htm** file if necessary.

2. Type the **<I>** and **<B>** tags around the job titles in the Employment section of the resume (just after the <P> tags), so that they read:

   <I><B>Satellite Technician</B></I>

   <I><B>Technical Assistant</B></I>

   <I><B>Salesperson</B></I>

   See Figure 1-28.

Figure 1-28	APPLYING CHARACTER TAGS

use the <B> and <I> tags to display this text in boldface and italics

```
<H2 ALIGN=CENTER>Employment</H2>
<P><I><B>Satellite Technician</B></I> (Front Range Media Inc. 1998-
1999): Monitored satellite uplink/downlink procedures to assure quality
transmissions. Aided technicians with transmission problems. Assisted
in the assembly and maintenance of uplink facility.</P>

<P><I><B>Technical Assistant</B></I> (Mountain View Bank 1997-1998):
Managed data processing system. Handled user requests and discussed
programming options. Managed delivery service.</P>

<P><I><B>Salesperson</B></I> (Computer Visions 1996): Sales and
customer support in computers and electronics. Managed commercial
accounts in Mountain View and Crabtree locations.</P>
</BODY>
```

3. Save the changes to your Resume file.

4. Return to your Web browser, and reopen the Resume file. The updated Employment section of Mary's page should look like Figure 1-29.

Figure 1-29	THE EFFECT OF THE CHARACTER TAGS IN THE BROWSER

boldface and italics

Employment

Satellite Technician (Front Range Media Inc. 1998-1999): Monitored satellite uplink/downlink procedures to assure quality transmissions. Aided technicians with transmission problems. Assisted in the assembly and maintenance of uplink facility.

Technical Assistant (Mountain View Bank 1997-1998): Managed data processing system. Handled user requests and discussed programming options. Managed delivery service.

Salesperson (Computer Visions 1996): Sales and customer support in computers and electronics. Managed commercial accounts in Mountain View and Crabtree locations.

5. If you are continuing to Session 1.3, you can leave your text editor and browser open. Otherwise, close your browser and text editor.

When you apply two character tags to the same text, you should place one set of tags completely within the other. For example, you would combine the <I> and <B> tags like this:

```
<I><B>Satellite Technician</B></I>
```

and not like this:

```
<I><B>Satellite Technician</I></B>
```

Although many browsers interpret both sets of code the same way, nesting tags within each other rather than overlapping them makes your code easier to read and interpret.

You have finished adding text to Mary's online resume. In Session 1.3, you will add special formatting elements such as lines and graphics.

Session 1.2 QUICK CHECK

1. Why should you include the <HTML> tag in your Web document?

2. Describe the syntax for creating a centered heading 1.

3. Describe the syntax for creating a paragraph.

4. If you want to display several paragraphs, why can't you simply type an extra blank line in the HTML file?

5. Describe the syntax for creating an ordered list, an unordered list, and a definition list.

6. Give two ways of italicizing text in your Web document. What are the advantages and disadvantages of each method?

SESSION 1.3

In this session you will insert three special elements into Mary's online resume: a special character, a line separating Mary's name and address from the rest of her resume, and a photograph of Mary.

Adding Special Characters

Occasionally you will want to include special characters in your Web page that do not appear on your keyboard. For example, a math page might require mathematical symbols such as β or μ. As Mary views her resume file, she notices a place where she could use a special symbol. In the address information under her name, she finds that the street address, city, and phone numbers all flow together. She decides to look into special characters that could separate the information.

HTML supports several character symbols that you can insert into your page. Each character symbol is identified by a code number or name. To create a special character, type an ampersand (&) followed either by the code name or the code number, and then a semicolon. Code numbers must be preceded by a pound symbol (#). Figure 1-30 shows some HTML symbols and the corresponding code numbers or names. A fuller list of special characters is included in Appendix B.

Figure 1-30   SPECIAL CHARACTERS AND CODES

SYMBOL	CODE	CODE NAME	DESCRIPTION
©	&#169;	&copy;	Copyright symbol
®	&#174;	&reg;	Registered trademark
•	&#183;	&middot;	Middle dot
°	&#186;	&ordm;	Masculine ordinal
TM	&#153;	&trade;	Trademark symbol
			Nonbreaking space, useful when you want to insert several blank spaces, one after another
<	&#60;	&lt;	Less than symbol
>	&#62;	&gt;	Greater than symbol
&	&#39;	&amp;	Ampersand

One solution for Mary's resume is to insert several **nonbreaking spaces** using the   character code. However, Mary decides it would look better to insert a bullet (•) between the street address and the city, and another bullet between the zip code and the phone number.

To add a character code to the resume file:

1. Make sure the **Resume.htm** file is open in your text editor.

2. Revise the address line at the beginning of the file, inserting the code for a middle dot, **·**, between the street address and the city, and between the zip code and the phone number, so that the line reads:

   <H5 ALIGN=CENTER>11 Kemper Ave. · Lake View, CO 80517 · (303) 555-1012</H5>

   TROUBLE? In your text editor this line probably appears as a single line.

3. Save the changes to your Resume file.

4. Return to your Web browser and reopen the Resume file. Figure 1-31 shows Mary's resume with the bullets separating the address elements.

Figure 1-31   SPECIAL CHARACTERS IN THE BROWSER

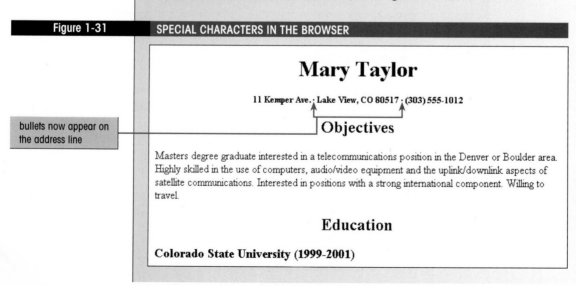

bullets now appear on the address line

Mary Taylor

11 Kemper Ave. • Lake View, CO 80517 • (303) 555-1012

Objectives

Masters degree graduate interested in a telecommunications position in the Denver or Boulder area. Highly skilled in the use of computers, audio/video equipment and the uplink/downlink aspects of satellite communications. Interested in positions with a strong international component. Willing to travel.

Education

Colorado State University (1999-2001)

The next thing Mary wants in her resume is a horizontal line separating the name and address information from the rest of her resume.

Inserting **Horizontal Lines**

The horizontal line after Mary's name and address in Figure 1-10 lends shape to the appearance of her paper resume. She'd like you to duplicate that in the online version. You use the **<HR>** tag to create a horizontal line, where HR stands for horizontal rule. The <HR> tag is one-sided. When a text-based browser encounters the <HR> tag, it inserts a line by repeating an underline symbol across the width of the page. A graphical browser inserts a graphical line.

To add a horizontal line to the Resume file:

1. Return to your text editor and reopen the **Resume.htm** file if necessary.

2. At the end of Mary's address line, press the **Enter** key to insert a new blank line.

3. In the new line, type **<HR>**.

4. Save the changes to your Resume file.

5. Return to your Web browser and reopen the Resume file. The Resume file with the new horizontal line appears in Figure 1-32.

Figure 1-32	HORIZONTAL LINE AS IT APPEARS IN THE BROWSER

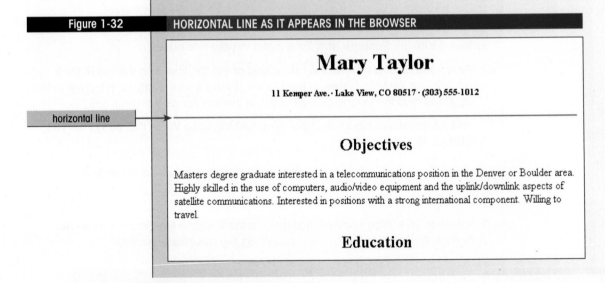

horizontal line

Mary Taylor

11 Kemper Ave. · Lake View, CO 80517 · (303) 555-1012

Objectives

Masters degree graduate interested in a telecommunications position in the Denver or Boulder area. Highly skilled in the use of computers, audio/video equipment and the uplink/downlink aspects of satellite communications. Interested in positions with a strong international component. Willing to travel.

Education

The <HR> tag has several properties that you may want to use in your Web page. The ALIGN property can be set to left, right, or center to place the line on the page (the default is center). You can also use the WIDTH property to tell the browser what percentage of the width of the page the line should occupy. For example, WIDTH=50% tells the browser to place the line so that its length covers half of the page. You can use the SIZE property to specify the line's thickness in pixels. A pixel, short for picture element, is ½-inch wide. Figure 1-33 shows how a browser would interpret the following lines of HTML code:

```
<HR ALIGN=CENTER SIZE=12 WIDTH=100%>
<HR ALIGN=CENTER SIZE=6 WIDTH=50%>
<HR ALIGN=CENTER SIZE=3 WIDTH=25%>
<HR ALIGN=CENTER SIZE=1 WIDTH=10%>
```

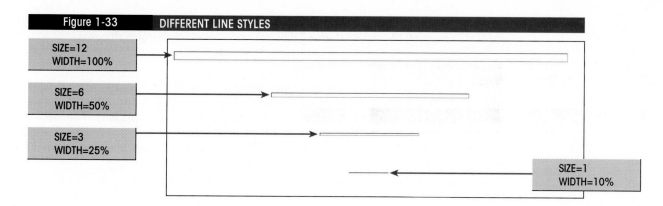

Figure 1-33   DIFFERENT LINE STYLES

SIZE=12
WIDTH=100%

SIZE=6
WIDTH=50%

SIZE=3
WIDTH=25%

SIZE=1
WIDTH=10%

Netscape Navigator and Internet Explorer also support properties specific to those browsers. As always, you should remember that using browser-specific extensions might produce wildly different results on browsers that do not support the extensions.

Inserting a Graphic

One feature of Web pages that has made the World Wide Web so popular is the ease of displaying a graphic image. The Web supports two methods for displaying a graphic: as an inline image and as an external image.

An **inline image** appears directly on the Web page and is loaded when the page is loaded. Two of the more commonly supported image types are GIF (Graphics Interchange Format) and JPEG (Joint Photographic Experts Group). Before you display a graphic image, you should convert it to one of these two types.

An **external image** is not displayed with the Web page. Instead, the browser must have a **file viewer,** a program that the browser loads automatically, whenever it encounters the image file, and uses to display the image. You can find file viewers at several Internet Web sites. Most browsers make it easy to set up viewers for use with the Web. External images have one disadvantage: you can't actually display them on the Web page. Instead they are represented by an icon that a user clicks to view the image. However, external images are not limited to the GIF or JPEG formats. You can set up virtually any image format as an external image on a Web page, including video clips and sound files.

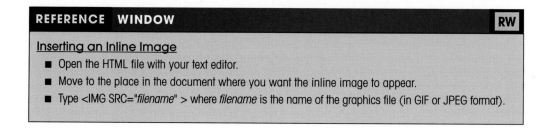

REFERENCE   WINDOW   **RW**

Inserting an Inline Image
- Open the HTML file with your text editor.
- Move to the place in the document where you want the inline image to appear.
- Type <IMG SRC="*filename*" > where *filename* is the name of the graphics file (in GIF or JPEG format).

Mary is more interested in using an inline image than an external image. **<IMG>** is the tag used for displaying an inline image. You can place inline images on a separate line in your document, or you can place the image within a line of text (hence the term "inline").

To access the image file, you need to include the filename within the tag. You do this using the SRC property, short for "source." The general syntax for an inline image is:

```
<IMG SRC="filename">
```

If the image file is located in the same folder as the HTML file, you do not need to include any folder information. However, if the image file is located in another folder or on another computer, you need to include the full path with the SRC property. Tutorial 2 discusses directory paths and filenames in more detail. For now, assume that Mary's image file is placed in the same folder as the HTML file. The image file that Mary has created is a photograph of herself in JPEG format. The name of the file is Taylor.jpg.

You'd also like to center the image on the page. There is no property in the <IMG> tag that would allow you to center it on a page, but you can nest the <IMG> tag within a paragraph tag, <P>, and then center the paragraph on the page using the ALIGN=CENTER property for the <P> tag. This has the effect of centering all of the text in the paragraph, including any inline images. Note that the ALIGN property was introduced in HTML 3.2; in browsers that do not support this convention, Mary's image may be left-justified.

To add Mary's photo to the online resume:

1. Look in the Tutorial.01 folder on your Data Disk and verify that both the Resume.htm file and Taylor.jpg file are there.

2. Return to your text editor with the Resume.htm file open.

3. At the end of the line with the <HR> tag that you just typed, press the **Enter** key to create a new line.

4. Type **<P ALIGN=CENTER><IMG SRC="Taylor.jpg"></P>** and then save the changes to the Resume file.

5. Print a copy of your completed Resume.htm file, and then close your text editor, unless you are continuing to the Review Assignments.

6. Return to your Web browser, and reopen the Resume file. Mary's online resume now includes an inline image. See Figure 1-34 for a view of the entire page.

Figure 1-34 | **MARY'S COMPLETED RESUME PAGE**

Mary Taylor

11 Kemper Ave. · Lake View, CO 80517 · (303) 555-1012

Objectives

Masters degree graduate interested in a telecommunications position in the Denver or Boulder area. Highly skilled in the use of computers audio/video equipment, and the uplink/downlink aspects of satellite communications. Interested in positions with a strong international component. Willing to travel.

Education

Colorado State University (1999-2001)

- Graduated May, 2001. M.A. International Telecommunications
- Grade Point Average: 3.5 overall, 3.9 in major
- Dean's List: September 1999-May 2001
- Member, Phi Alpha Omega Honor Society

Saint Philip University (1996-1999)

- Graduated May, 1999. B.A. International Studies
- Grade Point Average: 4.0 overall, 4.0 in major
- Dean's List: September 1996-May 1999
- President, Honor Key Society

Employment

Satellite Technician (Front Range Media Inc. 1998-1999): Monitored satellite uplink/downlink procedures to assure quality transmissions. Aided technicians with transmission problems. Assisted in the assembly and maintenance of uplink facility.

Technical Assistant (Mountain View Bank 1997-1998): Managed data processing system. Handled user requests and discussed programming options. Managed delivery service.

Salesperson (Computer Visions 1996): Sales and customer support in computers and electronics. Managed commercial accounts in Mountain View and Crabtree locations.

7. Use your browser to print a copy of Mary's online resume.

Compare the printout of the code, shown below, to the online resume on your browser. When you finish, you can exit your browser unless you're continuing to the Review Assignments.

```
<HTML>
<HEAD>
<TITLE>The Resume of Mary Taylor</TITLE>
</HEAD>
<BODY>
<H1 ALIGN=CENTER>Mary Taylor</H1>
<H5 ALIGN=CENTER>11 Kemper Ave. &#183; Lake View, CO 80517
&#183; (303) 555-1012</H5>
<HR>
<P ALIGN=CENTER><IMG SRC="Taylor.jpg"></P>
<H2 ALIGN=CENTER>Objectives</H2>
Masters degree graduate interested in a telecommunications
position in the Denver or Boulder area. Highly skilled in
the use of computers, audio/video equipment, and the uplink/
downlink aspects of satellite communications. Interested in
positions with a strong international component. Willing to
travel.
<H2 ALIGN=CENTER>Education</H2>
<H3>Colorado State University (1999-2001)</H3>
<UL>
<LI>Graduated May, 2001. M.A. International Telecommunications
<LI>Grade Point Average: 3.5 overall, 3.9 in major
<LI>Dean's List: September 1999-May 2001
<LI>Member, Phi Alpha Omega Honor Society
</UL>
<H3>Saint Philip University (1996-1999)</H3>
<UL>
<LI>Graduated May, 1999. B.A. International Studies
<LI>Grade Point Average: 4.0 overall, 4.0 in major
<LI>Dean's List: September 1996-May 1999
<LI>President, Honor Key Society
</UL>
<H2 ALIGN=CENTER>Employment</H2>
<P><I><B>Satellite Technician</B></I> (Front Range Media Inc.
1998-1999): Monitored satellite uplink/downlink procedures
to assure quality video transmissions. Aided technicians
with transmission problems. Assisted in the assembly and
maintenance of uplink facility.</P>
<P><I><B>Technical Assistant</B></I> (Mountain View Bank 1997
-1998): Managed data processing system. Handled user requests
and discussed programming options. Managed delivery
service. </P>
<P><I><B>Salesperson</B></I> (Computer Visions 1996): Sales
and customer support in computers and electronics. Managed
commercial accounts in Mountain View and Crabtree
locations.</P>
</BODY>
</HTML>
```

You show the completed online resume file to Mary; she thinks it looks great. You tell her that the next step is adding hypertext links to other material about herself for interested employers. You take a break while she heads to her desk to start thinking about what material she'd like to add. You'll learn about hypertext links in Tutorial 2.

Session 1.3 QUICK CHECK

1. How would you insert a copyright symbol, ©, into your Web page?

2. What is the syntax for inserting a horizontal line into a page?

3. What is the syntax for creating a horizontal line that is 70% of the display width of the screen and 4 pixels high?

4. What is an inline image?

5. What is an external image?

6. What is the syntax for inserting a graphic named Mouse.jpg into a Web document as an inline image?

7. What are two graphic file formats you can use for inline images?

REVIEW ASSIGNMENTS

After thinking some more about her online resume, Mary Taylor decides that she wants you to add a few more items. In the Education section, she wants you to add that she won the Enos Mills Scholarship contest as a senior at St. Philip University. She also wants to add that she worked as a climbing guide for The Colorado Experience touring company from 1994 to 1995. She would like to add her e-mail address, mtaylor@tt.gr.csu.edu, in italics at the bottom of the page. You tell her that adding a horizontal line to separate it from the rest of the resume might look nice. She agrees, so you get to work.

1. Open the **Resume.htm** file located in the Tutorial.01 folder on your Data Disk. This is the file you created over the course of this tutorial.

2. Save the file on your Data Disk in the Tutorial.01/Review folder with a new name: Resume2.htm, so that you will leave your work from the tutorial intact.

3. After the HTML line reading "President, Honor Key Society," enter a new line, "Winner of the Enos Mills Scholarship."
   Use the <LI> tag to format this line as an addition to the existing list.

4. Move to the Employment section of the Resume2.htm file.

5. After the paragraph describing Mary's experience as a salesperson, insert a new paragraph, "Guide (The Colorado Experience 1994-1996): Climbing guide for private groups and schools." Make sure you mark the text with the correct code for a two-sided paragraph tag.

6. Using the <I> and <B> tags, bracket the word "Guide" in the line you just entered to make it both bold and italic.

7. After the paragraph on Mary's climbing guide experience, insert a horizontal line using the <HR> tag. Set the thickness of the line to 6 pixels.

8. After the horizontal line, insert a new line with Mary's e-mail address.

Explore 9. Use the <CITE> tag to format her e-mail address as a citation:
   <CITE>mtaylor@tt.gr.csu.edu</CITE>

10. Save the changes to your Resume2.htm file and print it.

11. View the file with your Web browser.

12. Print a copy of the page as viewed by your browser.

PROJECTS

1. Creating a Web Page at the University Music Department   You are an assistant to a professor in the Music Department who is trying to create Web pages for topics in classical music. He wants to create a page showing the different sections of the fourth movement of Beethoven's Ninth symphony. The page should appear as shown in Figure 1-35.

Figure 1-35

Beethoven's Ninth Symphony

The Fourth Movement

Sonata-Concerto Form

1. Open Ritornello
2. Exposition
    1. Horror/Recitative
    2. Joy Theme
    3. Turkish Music
3. Development
4. Recapitulation
    1. Joy Theme
    2. Awe Theme
5. Coda Nos. 1 2 3

The page needs an inline image, three headings, and a list of the fourth movement's different sections. Several of the sections also have sublists. For example, the Recapitulation section contains both the Joy and Awe themes. You can create lists of this type with HTML by inserting one list tag within another. The HTML code for this is:

```
<OL>
<LI>Recapitulation
         <OL>
         <LI>Joy Theme
         <LI>Awe Theme
         </OL>
</OL>
```

1. Open a text editor program.

2. Type the <HTML>, <HEAD>, and <BODY> tags to identify different sections of the page.

3. Within the HEAD section, insert a <TITLE> tag with the text: "Beethoven's Ninth Symphony, 4th Movement".

4. Within the BODY section, create an <H1> header with the text "Beethoven's Ninth Symphony" and center the heading on the page with the ALIGN property.

5. Below the <H1> header, create an <H2> header with the text "The Fourth Movement" and then center the header on the page.

6. Below the <H2> header, create an <H3> header with the text "Sonata-Concerto Form", but this time do not center the header.

7. Create an ordered list using the <OL> tag, with the list items "Open Ritornello", "Exposition", "Development", "Recapitulation", and "Codas Nos. 1 2 3".

Explore ▶ 8. Within the Exposition list, create an ordered list with the items "Horror/Recitative", "Joy Theme", and "Turkish Music".

Explore ▶ 9. Within the Recapitulation list, create an ordered list with the items "Joy Theme" and "Awe Theme".

10. Before the <H1> header, insert the inline image LVB.jpg (located in the Projects folder of the Tutorial.01 folder on your Data Disk) centered on the page.

11. After the <H2> header, insert a horizontal line that extends the width of the page and is 1 pixel in height.

12. Save the file as Ludwig.htm in the Cases folder of the Tutorial.01 folder on your Data Disk, print it, and then close your text editor.

13. View the file with your Web browser, print it, and then close your browser.

2. Creating a Web Page for the Mathematics Department   Professor Laureen Coe of the Mathematics Department is preparing material for her course on the history of mathematics. As part of the course, she has written short profiles of famous mathematicians. Using content she's already written, Laureen would like you to create several Web pages to be placed on the university's Web server. You'll create the first one in this exercise. A preview of one of the pages about the mathematician Leonhard Euler is shown in Figure 1-36.

Figure 1-36

Euler, Leonhard

(1707-1783)

The greatest mathematician of the eighteenth century, **Leonhard Euler** was born in Basel, Switzerland. There, he studied under another giant of mathematics, **Jean Bernoulli**. In 1731 Euler became a professor of physics and mathematics at St. Petersburg Academy of Sciences. Euler was the most prolific mathematician of all time, publishing over *800 different books and papers*. His influence was felt in physics and astronomy as well. Euler's work on mathematical analysis, <u>Introductio in analysin infinitorum</u> (1748) remained a standard textbook for well over a century. For the princess of Anhalt-Dessau he wrote *Lettres à une princesse d'Allemagne* (1768-1772), giving a clear non-technical outline of the main physical theories of the time.

One can hardly write mathematical equations without copying Euler. Notations still in use today, such as *e* and *π*, were developed by Euler. He is perhaps best known for his research into mathematical analysis. Euler's formula:

$$\cos(x) + i\sin(x) = e^{(ix)}$$

demonstrates the relationship between analysis, trignometry and imaginary numbers, in one beautiful and elegant equation.

Leonhard Euler died in 1783, leaving behind a legacy perhaps unmatched, and certainly unsurpassed, in the annals of mathematics.

Math 895: The History of Mathematics

1. Start your text editor and then open the file **Eulertxt.htm**, located in the Cases folder of the Tutorial.01 folder on your Data Disk, and save it as Euler.htm.

2. Add the opening and closing <HTML>, <HEAD>, and <BODY> tags to the file in the appropriate locations.

3. Insert "Leonhard Euler" as a page title in the Head section of the document.

4. Insert the inline image **Euler.jpg** (located in the Tutorial 1 Projects folder on your Data Disk) at the top of the body of the document.

5. Format the first line of the page's body, "Euler, Leonhard", with the <H1> tag, and format the second line of the page's body, "(1707-1783)", with the <H3> tag.

6. Add the appropriate paragraph tags, <P>, to the document to separate the paragraphs.

7. Within the first paragraph, display the names, "Leonhard Euler" and "Jean Bernoulli" in boldface. Italicize the phrase "800 different books and papers", and underline the publication "Introductio in analysin infinitorum".

8. Replace the one-letter word "a" in "Lettres a une princesse d'Allemagne" with an *à*, using the character code &agrave, and then italicize the entire name of the publication.

9. In the second paragraph, italicize the notation "e" and replace the word "pi" with the inline image "**pi.jpg**" located in the Cases folder on your Data Disk.

Explore ▷ 10. Center the equation and italicize the letters "x", "i", and "e" in the equation. Display the term "*(ix)*" as a superscript, using the <SUP> tag.

Explore ▷ 11. Format the name of the course at the bottom of the page using the <CITE> tag.

12. Add horizontal lines before and after the biographical information.

13. Save the Euler.htm file, and then print it from your text editor.

14. View the file in your Web browser, and then print a copy of the page as displayed by the browser.

3. Chester the Jester   A friend of yours who performs as a clown named "Chester the Jester" wants to advertise his services on the World Wide Web. He wants his Web page to be bright and colorful. One way of doing this is to create a colorful background for the page. You create a background using a graphic image. Such backgrounds are called tile-image backgrounds because the graphic image is repeated over and over again, like tiles, until it covers the entire page. To create a tile-image background, you must have a graphic image in either GIF or JPEG file format. You insert the file in the background by adding the BACKGROUND property to the <BODY> tag with the syntax:

```
<BODY BACKGROUND= "filename">
```

Your friend gives you a JPEG file named Diamonds.jpg, which contains the pattern he uses in his clown costume. He also has a JPEG file named Chester.jpg, which shows him in his clown outfit. A preview of the page you'll create is shown in Figure 1-37.

Figure 1-37

1. Start your text editor, open the file **Chestertxt.htm** from the Cases folder of the Tutorial.01 folder on your Data Disk, and save it as Chester.htm.

2. Insert the <HTML>, <HEAD>, and <BODY> tags in the appropriate locations.

3. Insert a <TITLE> tag in the Head section, giving the Web page the title "Chester the Jester".

Explore

4. Modify the <BODY> tag to read:

```
<BODY BACKGROUND="Diamonds.jpg">
```

5. Format the text "Chester the Jester" with the <H1> tag and center it on the Web page.

6. Format the text "Clown Juggler Magician" with the <H3> tag and center it on the page. Insert a middle dot, character symbol •, between each word.

7. Insert the inline image **"Chester.jpg"** (located in the Projects folder of the Tutorial.01 folder on your Data Disk) after the <H3> header. Center it on the page.

8. Format the text "Hire him for your child's party today!" with the <H3> tag, centered on the page.

9. Insert a horizontal line after the <H3> header.

10. Format the next three lines as an unordered list.

11. Format the text in the last line of document text, using the <I> tag.

12. Save the Chester.htm file and then print it from your text editor.

13. View the file in your Web browser and then print it in your browser.

4. Create Your Own Resume   After completing Mary Taylor's resume, you are eager to make your own. Using the techniques from this tutorial, design and create a resume for yourself. Make sure to include these features: section headers, bulleted or numbered lists, bold and/or italic fonts, paragraphs, special characters, inline graphic images, and horizontal lines.

1. Start your text editor, and then create a file called MyResume.htm in the Cases folder of the Tutorial.01 folder on your Data Disk. Type the appropriate HTML code and content.

2. Add any other tags you think will improve your document's appearance.

3. You could take a picture of yourself to your lab or a local office services business and scan it. If you do, save it as a GIF or JPEG file. Then place the graphic file in the Projects folder of the Tutorial.01 folder on your Data Disk. Add the appropriate code in your MyResume.htm file. If you don't have your own graphic file, use the file **Kirk.jpg** located in the Projects folder of the Tutorial.01 folder on your Data Disk.

4. You could use a graphics package that can store images in GIF or JPEG format to create a background image that you could insert as you did in Case Problem 3. If you do, use light colors so the text you place on top is readable. Add the appropriate code to your MyResume.htm file, using the steps in Case Problem 3.

5. Test your code as you develop your resume, by viewing MyResume.htm in your browser.

6. When you finish entering the code, save and print the MyResume.htm file from your text editor.

7. View the final version in your browser, print the Web page, and then close your browser and text editor.

LAB ASSIGNMENTS

Web Pages & HTML

This Lab Assignment is designed to accompany the interactive Course Lab called The Internet World Wide Web. To start the Internet World Wide Web Course Lab, click the Start button on the Windows taskbar, point to Programs, point to Course Labs, point to New Perspectives Applications, and click The Internet World Wide Web. If you do not see Course Labs on your Programs menu, see your instructor or technical support person.

The Internet World Wide Web Lab Assignment   One of the most popular services on the Internet is the World Wide Web. This Lab is a Web simulator that teaches you how to use Web browser software to find information. You can use this Lab whether or not your school provides you with Internet access.

1. Click the Steps button to learn how to use Web browser software. As you proceed through the Steps, answer all of the Quick Check questions that appear. After you complete the Steps, you will see a Quick Check Summary Report. Follow the instructions on the screen to print this report.

2. Click the Explore button on the Welcome screen. Use the Web browser to locate a weather map of the Caribbean Virgin Islands. What is its URL?

3. A scuba diver named Wadson Lachouffe has been searching for the fabled treasure of Greybeard the pirate. A link from the Adventure Travel Web site leads to Wadson's Web page, called "Hidden Treasure". In Explore, locate the Hidden Treasure page and answer the following questions:
   a. What was the name of Greybeard's ship?
   b. What was Greybeard's favorite food?
   c. What does Wadson think happened to Greybeard's ship?

4. In the Steps, you found a graphic of Jupiter from the photo archives of the Jet Propulsion Laboratory. In the Explore section of the Lab, you can also find a graphic of Saturn. Suppose one of your friends wanted a picture of Saturn for an astronomy report. Make a list of the blue, underlined links your friend must click to find the Saturn graphic. Assume that your friend will begin at the Web Trainer home page.

5. Enter the URL *http://www.atour.com* to jump to the Adventure Travel Web site. Write a one-page description of this site. In your paper include a description of the information at the site, the number of pages the site contains, and a diagram of the links it contains.

6. Chris Thomson is a student at UVI and has his own Web pages. In Explore, look at the information Chris has included on his pages. Suppose you could create your own Web page. What would you include? Use word-processing software to design your own Web pages. Make sure you indicate the graphics and links you would use.

QUICK | CHECK ANSWERS

Session 1.1

   1. Hypertext refers to text that contains points called links that allow the user to move to other places within the document, or to open other documents, by activating the link.

   2. A Web server stores the files used in creating World Wide Web documents. The Web browser retrieves the files from the Web server and displays them. The files stored on the Web server are described in a very general way; it is the Web browser that determines how the files will eventually appear to the user.

   3. HTML, which stands for Hypertext Markup Language, is used to create Web documents.

4. HTML documents do not exactly specify the appearance of a document; rather they describe the purpose of different elements in the document and leave it to the Web browser to determine the final appearance. A word processor like Word exactly specifies the appearance of each document element.

5. Documents are transferred more quickly over the Internet and are available to a wider range of machines.

6. Extensions are special formats supported by a particular browser, but not generally accepted by all browsers. The advantage is that people who use that browser have a wider range of document elements to work with. The disadvantage is that the document will not work for users who do not have that particular browser.

7. All you need is a simple text editor.

Session 1.2

1. The <HTML> tag identifies the language of the file as HTML to packages that support more than one kind of generalized markup language.

2. <H1 ALIGN=CENTER> *Header text* </H1>

3. <P> *Paragraph text* </P>

4. HTML does not recognize the blank lines as a format element. A Web browser will ignore blank lines and run the paragraphs together on the page.

5. Unordered list:
```
<UL>
    <LI> List item
    <LI> List item
</UL>
```
Ordered list:
```
<OL>
    <LI> List item
    <LI> List item
</OL>
```
Definition list:
```
<DL>
    <DT> List term <DD> Term definition
    <DT> List term <DD> Term definition
</DL>
```

6. <EM> *Italicized text* </EM>
   and
   ```
   <I> Italicized text </I>
   ```
   The advantage of using the <EM> tag is that it will be recognized even by older browsers that do not support italics (such as a terminal connected to a UNIX machine), and those browsers will still emphasize the text in some way. The <I> tag, on the other hand, will be ignored by those machines. Using the <I> tag has the advantage of explicitly describing how you want the text to appear.

Session 1.3

1. ©

2. <HR>

3. <HR WIDTH=70% SIZE=4>

4. An inline image is a GIF or JPEG that appears on a Web document. A browser can display it without a file viewer.

5. An external image is a graphic that requires the use of a software program, called a viewer, to be displayed.

6. <IMG ALIGN=LEFT SRC="Mouse.jpg">

7. GIFs and JPEGs

OBJECTIVES

In this tutorial you will:

- Create hypertext links between elements within a document

- Create hypertext links between one document and another

- Review some basic Web page structures

- Create hypertext links to pages on the Internet

- Understand the difference between and use absolute and relative pathnames

- Learn to create hypertext links to various Internet resources, including FTP servers and newsgroups

ADDING
HYPERTEXT LINKS
TO A WEB PAGE

Developing an Online Resume with Hypertext Links

CASE

Creating an Online Resume, continued

In Tutorial 1 you created the basic structure and content of an online resume for Mary Taylor. Since then Mary has made a few changes to the resume, and she has ideas for more content. The two of you sit down and discuss her plans. Mary notes that although the page contents reflect the paper resume, the online resume has one disadvantage: prospective employers must scroll around the document window to view pertinent facts about Mary. Mary wants to make it as easy to jump from topic to topic in her online resume as it is to scan through topics on a one-page paper resume.

Mary also has a few references and notes of recommendation on file that she wants to make available to interested employers. She didn't include all this information on her paper resume because she wanted to limit that resume to a single page. With an online resume, Mary can still be brief, but at the same time she can make additional material readily available.

In this session you will create anchors on a Web page that let you jump to specific points in the document. After creating those anchors, you will create and then test your first hypertext link to another document.

Creating a Hypertext Document

In Tutorial 1 you learned that a hypertext document contains **hypertext links**, items that you can select, usually by clicking a mouse, to instantly view another topic or document, often called the **destination** of the link. These links can point to another section in the same document, to an entirely different document, to a different Web page, and to a variety of other Web objects, which you'll learn about later in this tutorial.

In addition to making access to other documents easy, hypertext links provide some important organizational benefits. They indicate what points or concepts you think merit special attention or further reading. You can take advantage of these features by adding hypertext links to Mary's online resume.

At the end of Tutorial 1, the resume had three main sections: Objectives, Education, and Employment. You and Mary have made some additions and changes since then, including adding a fourth section, Other Information, which provides additional information about Mary that employers might find helpful in their job searches. However, because of the document window's limited size, the opening screen does not show any of the main sections of Mary's resume. The browser in Figure 2-1 shows Mary's name, address, and photograph, but nothing about her education or employment history. Employers have to scroll through the document to find this information.

Figure 2-1   OPENING SCREEN OF MARY'S ONLINE RESUME

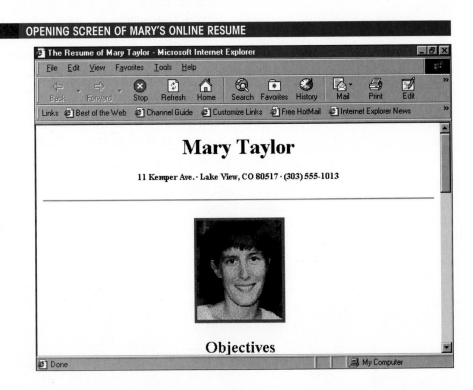

Without using hypertext links, you can do little to show more of Mary's resume in the browser except remove the image file or move it to the end of the resume, which Mary doesn't want you to do. However, you could place text for the four headings (Objectives,

Education, Employment, and Other Information) at the top of the document and then turn these headings into hypertext links. When readers open Mary's resume, they'll see not only her name, address, and photo, but also links to the main parts of her resume. They can then click any of the headings, and they will immediately see that section of the document. The hypertext links that you create here point to sections within the same document. You'll create such hypertext links in Mary's resume using three steps:

1. Type the headings into the HTML file.

2. Mark each section in the HTML file using an anchor. (You'll learn what this is shortly.)

3. Link the text you added in Step 1 to the anchors you added in Step 2.

You can accomplish the first step using techniques you learned in Tutorial 1. You need to open the Resume.htm text file in your text editor and then enter the text. You want the text to appear on the same line as Mary's photo in the browser, as in Figure 2-2.

| Figure 2-2 | ADDING TEXT FOR LINKS TO LATER SECTIONS IN THE RESUME |

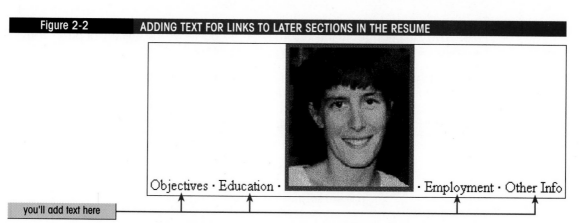

you'll add text here

Objectives · Education ·   · Employment · Other Info

To achieve this, you place the text within the paragraph tags that already encompass the Taylor.jpg graphics file. You could type all the text into the HTML file on the same line, but to keep the HTML file as legible as possible, add the text in two lines instead. This way, when you add more tags to the text later, it will still be easy to read. Remember that because you format with markup tags in HTML, putting the text on different lines does not affect its appearance in the browser.

To add text to the document, indicating the different sections of the resume:

1. Open your text editor.

2. Open the file **Resumetxt.htm** from the Tutorial.02 folder on your Data Disk, and then save it as **Resume.htm** in the Tutorial.02 folder so you still have a copy of the original.

   TROUBLE? If you can't locate the Resumetxt.htm file in the Tutorial.02 folder in your text editor's Open dialog box, you might need to set the file type to All Files.

3. Before "<IMG SRC="Taylor.jpg">", type **Objectives · Education ·** (be sure to type the semicolons), and then press the **Enter** key so this new entry is on its own line.

4. Create a new line directly after "<IMG SRC="Taylor.jpg">" and then type **· Employment · Other Info** so this new entry is on its own line. See Figure 2-3. The new lines include the special character code · which inserts a bullet into the text to separate section headings.

| Figure 2-3 | INSERTING NEW TEXT IN THE RESUME PAGE |

```
<BODY>
<H1 ALIGN=CENTER>Mary Taylor</H1>
<H5 ALIGN=CENTER>11 Kemper Ave. &#183 Lake View, CO 80517 &#183 (303) 555-
1013</H5>
<HR>

<P ALIGN=CENTER>
Objectives &#183; Education &#183;
<IMG SRC="Taylor.jpg">
&#183; Employment &#183; Other Info
</P>

<H2 ALIGN=CENTER>Objectives</H2>
```

5. Save the changes to the Resume.htm file, but leave the text editor open. You will revise this document throughout this tutorial.

6. Start your Web browser (you do not have to connect to the Internet), and open **Resume.htm** to verify the change. See Figure 2-4.

| Figure 2-4 | NEW RESUME PAGE TEXT |

Mary Taylor

11 Kemper Ave. · Lake View, CO 80517 · (303) 555-1013

Objectives · Education ·   · Employment · Other Info

Creating **Anchors**

Now that you've created the text describing the resume's different sections, you need to locate each header and mark it in the document, using the <A> tag. The **<A> tag** creates an **anchor**, text that is specially marked so that you can link *to* it from other points in the document. Text that is anchored will become the *destination* of a link; it is *not* the text you click. You assign each anchor its own anchor name, using the NAME property. For example, if you want the text "Employment" to be an anchor, you could assign it the anchor name "EMP":

```
<A NAME="EMP">Employment</A>
```

Later, when you create a link to this anchor from the headings you just inserted at the beginning of Mary's resume, the link will point to this particular place in the document, using the anchor name, EMP. Figure 2-5 illustrates how the anchor you create will work as a reference point to a link.

Figure 2-5	ANCHORING TEXT

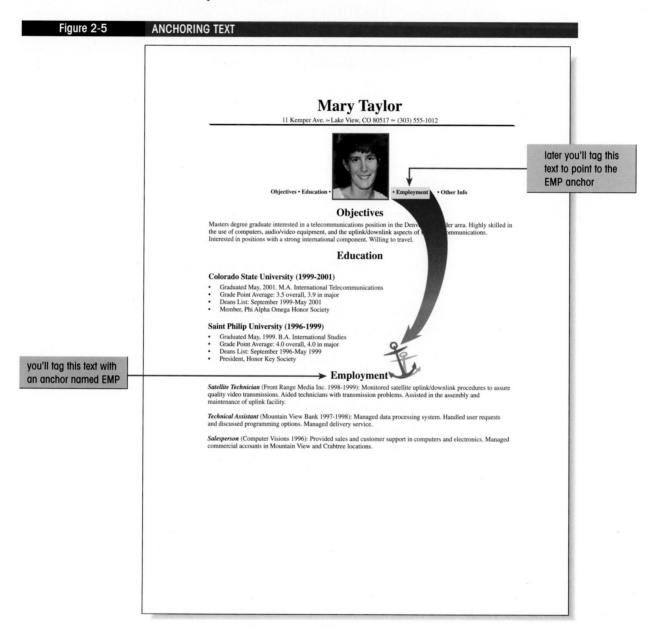

An anchor doesn't have to be just text. You can also mark an inline image using the same syntax:

```
<A NAME="PHOTO"><IMG SRC="Taylor.jpg"></A>
```

In this example, you anchor a photo. You can create a link to this photo from other points in the document by using the anchor name PHOTO. As you'll see, adding an anchor does not change your document's appearance in any way.

REFERENCE **WINDOW** **RW**

Creating Anchors
- Locate the text or graphic you want to anchor.
- Before the text or graphic, place the tag
  <A Name="*anchor_name*"> where *anchor_name* is the name you choose for your anchor.
- After the text or graphic, place a closing </A> tag to turn off the anchor.

For Mary's resume file, you decide to create four anchors named OBJ, ED, EMP, and OTHER for the Objectives, Education, Employment, and Other Information sections.

To add anchors to the resume's section headings:

1. Return to your text editor and open the **Resume.htm** file, if it is not already open.

2. Locate the H2 header for the Objectives section. This line currently reads:

   `<H2 ALIGN=CENTER>Objectives</H2>`

3. Add an anchor tag around the Objectives heading so that it reads:

   `<H2 ALIGN=CENTER><A NAME="OBJ">Objectives</A></H2>`

4. Locate the H2 header for the Education section. This line currently reads:

   `<H2 ALIGN=CENTER>Education</H2>`

5. Add an anchor tag around the Education heading so that it reads:

   `<H2 ALIGN=CENTER><A NAME="ED">Education</A></H2>`

6. Locate the H2 header for the Employment section, which reads:

   `<H2 ALIGN=CENTER>Employment</H2>`

   and add an anchor tag so that it reads:

   `<H2 ALIGN=CENTER><A NAME="EMP">Employment</A></H2>`

7. Locate the H2 header for the Other Information section, which reads:

   `<H2>Other Information</H2>`

   and add an anchor tag so that it reads:

   `<H2><A NAME="OTHER"> Other Information</A></H2>`

8. Save the changes you made to the Resume file.

9. Open your Web browser, reload the **Resume.htm** file, then scroll through Resume.htm to confirm that the Resume file appears unchanged. Remember that the marks you placed in the document are reference points and should not change the appearance of the resume in your browser.

   TROUBLE? If you see a change in the document, check to make sure that you used the NAME property of the <A> tag.

You created four anchors in the Web page. The next step is to create links to those anchors from the text you added around Mary's picture.

Creating **Links**

After you anchor the text that will be the destination for your links, you create the links themselves. For Mary's resume, you want to link the text you entered around her photograph to the four sections in her document. Figure 2-6 shows the four links you want to create.

Figure 2-6 | **LINKS YOU NEED TO CREATE**

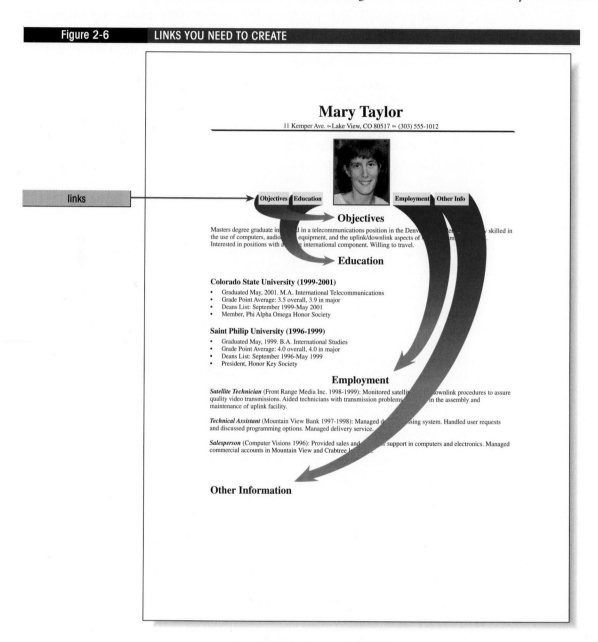

To create a link to an anchor, you use the same [A] tag you used to create the anchor. The difference is that instead of using the NAME property to define the anchor, you use the **HREF** property, short for Hypertext Reference, to indicate the location to jump to. HREF can refer to an anchor that you place in the document, or, as you'll see later, to a different Web page or a resource on the Internet. <A> tags that create links are called **link tags**.

You link to an anchor using the anchor name preceded by a pound (#) symbol. For example, to create a link to the Employment heading in Mary's resume, you use the anchor name EMP and this HTML tag:

```
<A HREF="#EMP">Employment</A>
```

In this example, the entire word "Employment" becomes a hypertext link. When you open the resume in your Web browser and click any part of that word, you jump to the location of the EMP anchor.

You can also designate an inline image as a hypertext link. To turn an inline image into a hypertext link, place it within link tags, as in:

```
<A HREF="#OTHER"><IMG SRC="Taylor.jpg"></A>
```

REFERENCE WINDOW   **RW**

Linking to Text Within a Document

- Mark the destination text with an anchor.
- Locate the text or graphic you want to designate as the link.
- Before the text or graphic, place the tag
  <A HREF="#anchor_name"> where *anchor_name* is the name of the anchor.
- Close the link tag with the </A> closing tag after the text or graphic you designated as the link.

Sometimes a link does not work as you expect. One common source of trouble is the case of the anchor. The HREF property is case sensitive. The anchor name "EMP" is not the same as "emp". You should also remember to make each anchor name unique within a document. If you use the same anchor name for different text, your links won't go where you expect.

In the current HTML document, you've created four anchors to which you can link. You're ready to place the link tags around the appropriate text in the HTML file.

To add link tags to the Resume.htm file:

1. Return to your text editor and make sure the Resume.htm file is open.

2. Locate the paragraph containing the four section headings and Mary's photograph at the top of the page. Within that paragraph you need to bracket each section heading with a link tag and the HREF property.

3. Change the line reading "Objectives · Education ·" to

   ```
   <A HREF="#OBJ">Objectives</A> &#183;
   <A HREF="#ED">Education</A> &#183;
   ```

4. Change the line reading "· Employment · Other Info" to

   ```
   &#183; <A HREF="#EMP">Employment</A> &#183;
   <A HREF="#OTHER">Other Info</A>
   ```

5. Compare your HTML file to Figure 2-7.

Figure 2-7 | ADDING LINK TAGS

```
<BODY>
<H1 ALIGN=CENTER>Mary Taylor</H1>
<H5 ALIGN=CENTER>11 Kemper Ave. &#183 Lake View, CO 80517 &#183 (303) 555-
1013</H5>
<HR>

<P ALIGN=CENTER>
<A HREF="#OBJ">Objectives</A> &#183; <A HREF="#ED">Education</A> &#183;
<IMG SRC="Taylor.jpg">
&#183; <A HREF="#EMP">Employment</A> &#183; <A HREF="#OTHER">Other Info</A>
</P>

<H2 ALIGN=CENTER><A NAME="OBJ">Objectives</A></H2>
```

6. Save the changes you made to Resume.htm.

7. Open your Web browser and reload the **Resume.htm** file. The headings should now be a different color and be underlined—the standard formatting for links in most browsers. See Figure 2-8.

Figure 2-8 | TEXT LINKS AS THEY APPEAR IN THE BROWSER

Mary Taylor

11 Kemper Ave. · Lake View, CO 80517 · (303) 555-1013

Objectives · Education · · Employment · Other Info

text links

TROUBLE? If the headings do not appear as text links, check your code and make sure that you are using the <A> tag around the text and the HREF property within the tag.

Before continuing, you should verify that the links work properly. To test a link, you click it.

To test your links:

1. Click one of the links. You should jump to the section of the document indicated by the link. If not, check your code for errors by comparing it to Figure 2-7.

2. Click each of the other links, scrolling back to the top of the page each time.

3. If you are continuing to Session 2.2, you can leave your browser and text editor open. Otherwise, close them.

If you still have problems, make sure you used the correct case and that you coded the anchor and link tags correctly. When you add an anchor to a large section of text, such as a section heading, make sure to place the anchor within the header tags. For example, you should write your tag as:

```
<H2><A NAME="EMP">Employment</A></H2>
```

not as:

```
<A NAME="EMP"><H2>Employment</H2></A>
```

The latter could confuse some browsers. The general rule is to always place anchors within other tag elements. Do not insert any tag elements within an anchor, except for tags that create document objects such as inline graphics.

You show the new links to Mary. She is excited to see how they work. She thinks they will quickly inform interested employers about her resume's contents and help them quickly find the information they want. In the next session, you'll create links that jump to other HTML documents.

Session 2.1 QUICK CHECK

1. What is the HTML code for marking the text "Colorado State University" with the anchor name CSU?

2. What is the HTML code for linking the text "Universities" to an anchor that is named CSU?

3. What is wrong with the following statement?

   ```
   <A NAME="INFO"><H3>For more information</H3></A>
   ```

4. What is the HTML code for marking an inline image, Photo.jpg, with the anchor name PHOTO?

5. What is the HTML code for linking the inline image Button.jpg to an anchor with the name LINKS?

6. True or False: Anchor names are case insensitive.

SESSION 2.2

In Session 2.1 you created hypertext links to other points within the same document. In this session you will create links to other HTML documents.

Mary wants to add two more pages to her online resume: a page of references and a page of comments about her work from former employers and teachers. She then wants to add links on her resume that point to both these pages. Figure 2-9 shows what she has in mind.

Figure 2-9 | **MARY'S THREE WEB DOCUMENTS**

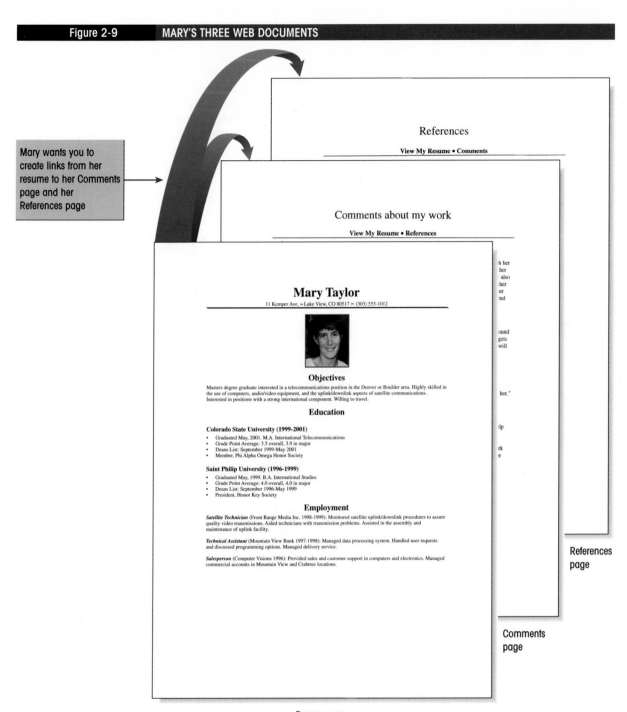

Mary wants you to create links from her resume to her Comments page and her References page

Resume page

You tell Mary that her ideas are good, but that before she starts thinking about how the documents will link to each other, she should understand the basics of Web page structures.

Web **Page Structures**

The three pages that will make up Mary's online resume—Resume, Comments, and References—are part of a system of Web pages. Before you set up links for navigating a group of Web pages, it's worthwhile to map out exactly how you want the pages to relate, using a technique known as storyboarding. **Storyboarding** your Web pages before you create links helps you determine which structure works best for the type of information you're presenting. You want to make sure readers can navigate easily from page to page without getting lost.

Linear Structures

You'll encounter several Web structures as you navigate the Web. Examining these structures can help you decide how to design your own system of Web pages. Figure 2-10 shows one common structure, the **linear structure**, in which each page is linked to the next and to previous pages, in an ordered chain of pages.

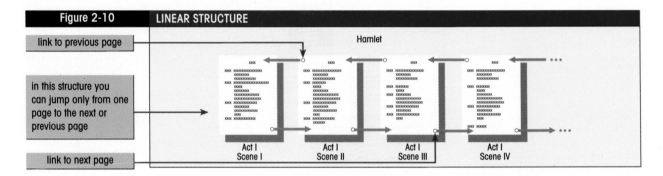

You could use this type of structure in Web pages that have a defined order. Suppose that a Web site of Shakespeare's *Hamlet* has a single page for each scene. If you use a linear structure for these pages, you assume that users want to progress through the scenes in order.

You might, however, want to make it easier for users to return immediately to the opening scene, rather than backtrack through several scenes. Figure 2-11 shows an **augmented linear structure**, in which you include a link in each page that jumps directly back to the first page, while keeping the links that allow you to move to the next and previous pages. This kind of storyboarding can reveal approaches to organizing the Web site that otherwise might not be noticed.

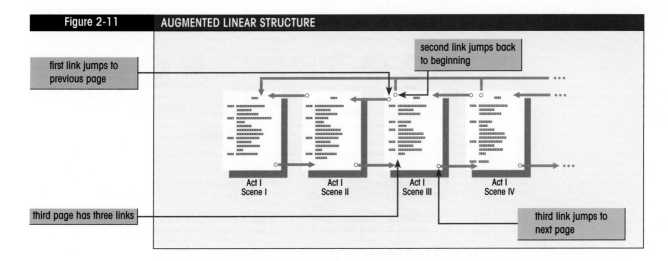

Figure 2-11   AUGMENTED LINEAR STRUCTURE

Hierarchical Structures

Another popular structure is the hierarchical structure of Web pages shown in Figure 2-12. A **hierarchical structure** starts with a general topic that includes links to more specific topics. Each specific topic includes links to yet more specialized topics, and so on. In a hierarchical structure, users can move easily from general to specific and back, but not from specific to specific.

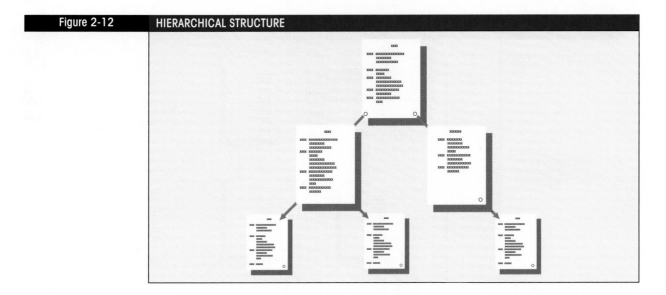

Figure 2-12   HIERARCHICAL STRUCTURE

As with the linear structure, including a link to the top of the structure on each page gives users an easy path back to the beginning. Subject catalogs such as the Yahoo! directory of Web pages often use this structure. Figure 2-13 shows this site, located at *http://www.yahoo.com*.

| Figure 2-13 | HIERARCHICAL STRUCTURE ON YAHOO! WEB PAGE |

Mixed Structures

You can also combine structures. Figure 2-14 shows a hierarchical structure in which each level of pages is related in a linear structure. You might use this system for the *Hamlet* Web site to let the user move from scene to scene linearly, or from a specific scene to the general act to the overall play.

| Figure 2-14 | COMBINATION OF LINEAR AND HIERARCHICAL STRUCTURES |

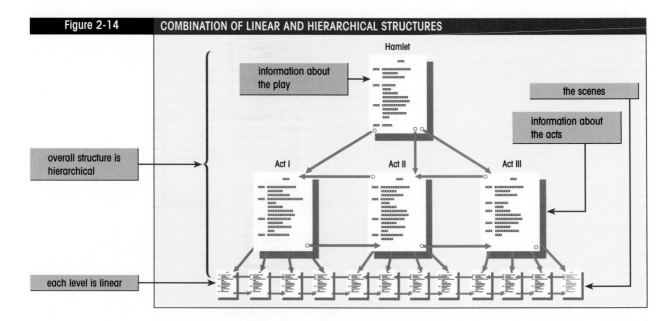

As these examples show, a little foresight can go a long way toward making your Web pages easier to use. The best time to organize a structure is when you first start creating multiple pages and those pages are small and easy to manage. If you're not careful, your structure might look like Figure 2-15.

Figure 2-15	MULTIPAGE DOCUMENT WITH NO COHERENT STRUCTURE

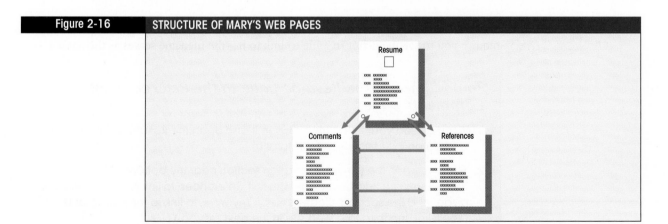

This structure is confusing, and it makes it difficult for readers to grasp the contents of the entire Web site. Moreover, a user who enters this structure at a certain page might not even be aware of the presence of other pages at the far end of the chain.

Creating Links Between Documents

Mary and you discuss the type of structure that will work best for her online resume. She wants employers to move effortlessly among the three documents. Because there are only three pages, all focused on the same topic, you decide to include links within each document to the other two. If Mary later adds other pages to her resume, she will need to create a more formal structure involving some principles discussed in the previous sections.

For her simple three-page site, the structure shown in Figure 2-16 works just fine.

Figure 2-16	STRUCTURE OF MARY'S WEB PAGES

Mary has given you the information to create two additional HTML files: Refertxt.htm, a page with the names and addresses of previous employers and professors; and Comtxt.htm, a page with comments from previous employers and teachers. You suggest that Mary include a graphic—a check mark–on the Comments page. You have just the file for her, Check.jpg. These three files are in the Tutorial.02 folder on your Data Disk. You should save these files with new names: Refer.htm and Comments.htm, to keep the originals intact.

> *To rename the Refertxt.htm and Comtxt.htm files:*
>
> **1.** Using your text editor, open **Refertxt.htm** from the Tutorial.02 folder on your Data Disk, and save it as **Refer.htm**.
>
> **2.** With your text editor, open the file **Comtxt.htm** in the Tutorial.02 folder, and save it as **Comments.htm**.

Linking to a Document

You begin by linking Mary's Resume page to the References and Comments pages. You use the same <A> tag that you used earlier. For example, let's say you wanted a user to be able to click the phrase "Comments on my work" to jump to the Comments.htm file. You could enter this HTML command in your current document:

```
<A HREF="Comments.htm">Comments on my work</A>
```

In this example, the entire text "Comments on my work" is linked to the HTML file, Comments.htm. In order for the browser to be able to locate and open the Comments.htm file, it must be in the same folder as the Resume.htm file, the document containing the links.

REFERENCE WINDOW   **RW**

Linking to a Document on Your Computer
- Locate the link text or graphic (that is, the text or image you want to click to jump to the destination of the link).
- Before the text or graphic, place the tag
  <A HREF="*filename*">
  where filename is the name of the destination document.
- After the link text or graphic, place the tag </A>.

Unlike creating hypertext links between elements on the same page, this process does not require you to set an anchor in a file to link to it—the filename serves as the anchor.

> *To add links in the Resume page to the References and Comments pages:*
>
> **1.** If you closed your text editor, reopen it and open the **Resume.htm** file that you worked on in Session 2.1 of this tutorial.
>
> **2.** Scroll down to the Other Information section near the bottom of the page. Three items are listed; you want the first, References, to link to the References page, and the second, Comments on my work, to link to the Comments page. (You'll link the third to a Web site in the next session.)
>
> **3.** Change the line reading "<LI>References" to:
>
> ```
> <LI><A HREF="Refer.htm">References</A>
> ```
>
> **4.** Change the line reading "<LI> Comments on my work" to read:
>
> ```
> <LI><A HREF="Comments.htm">Comments on my work</A>
> ```

See Figure 2-17.

| Figure 2-17 | TEXT LINKED TO OTHER FILES |

<A> tag creating a link to another file

```
<H2><A NAME="OTHER">Other Information</A></H2>
<UL>
<LI><A HREF="Refer.htm">References</A>
<LI><A HREF="Comments.htm">Comments on my work</A>
<LI>Go to Colorado State
</UL>

<H3> Interested? </H3>
Contact Mary Taylor at mtaylor@tt.gr.csu.edu

</BODY>
```

5. Save the changes to the Resume file.

6. Open your Web browser, if it is not open already, and view Resume.htm. The items in the Other Information section now appear as the text links shown in Figure 2-18.

| Figure 2-18 | NEW LINKS |

Technical Assistant (Mountain View Bank 1996-1998): Managed data processing system. Trained users on data entry and report generation. Managed delivery service.

Salesperson (Computer Visions 1995): Sales and customer support in computers and electronics. Managed commercial accounts in Lake View and Crabtree locations.

Other Information

links in Mary's resume to other files

- References
- Comments on my work
- Go to Colorado State

Interested?

Contact Mary Taylor at mtaylor@tt.gr.csu.edu

7. Click the **References** link to verify that you jump to the References page shown in Figure 2-19.

TROUBLE? If the link doesn't work, check to see that Resume.htm and Refer.htm are in the same folder on your Data Disk.

Figure 2-19   REFERENCES PAGE

References

View My Resume · Comments

Lawrence Gale, Telecommunications Manager

Front Range Media Inc.
1000 Black Canyon Drive
Fort Tompkins, CO 80517
(303) 555-0103

Karen Carlson, Manager

Mountain View Bank
2 North Maple St.
Lake View, CO 80517
(303) 555-8792

Trent Wu, Sales Manager

Computer Visions
24 Mall Road
Lake View, CO 80517
(303) 555-1313

Robert Ramirez, Prof. Electrical Engineering

Colorado State University
Kleindist Hall
Fort Collins, CO 80517

8. Go back to the Resume page (usually by clicking a Back button on the tool-bar of your browser), and then click the **Comments on my work** link to verify that you jump to the Comments page shown in Figure 2-20.

Figure 2-20	COMMENTS PAGE

Comments about my work

View My Resume · References

 Lawrence Gale, Telecommunications Manager, *Front Range Media Inc.*

"Mary is a highly professional technician who takes much pride in her work. She impressed me with her ability to learn the details of our sophisticated and complex hardware and software, especially given her lack of telecommunications experience when she first started with us. Mary works well in a team but also has the ability to take my suggestions and finish a project in a highly competent manner without further direction. As she closes out her work here, I find her to be an excellent and essential component in our operations. I have complete confidence that you will be very pleased with Mary's work and recommend her very highly."

 Karen Carlson, Manager, *Mountain View Bank*

"Mary assisted in the operations and development of a new database program we were setting up. I found Mary to be an enthusiastic and hard-working addition to our team. Mary is one of those people who gets things done and done right. She will excel in whatever she does. I think any company that hires her will be very happy that they did."

Next you want to add similar links in the Refer.htm and Comments.htm files that point to the other two pages. Specifically, in Refer.htm, you need to add one link to Resume.htm and another to Comments.htm; in Comments.htm you need one link to Resume.htm and another to Refer.htm. This way, each page will have two links on it that point to the other two pages.

To add links in the References page to the Resume and Comments pages:

1. Return to your text editor and then open the file **Refer.htm** from the Tutorial.02 folder on your Data Disk.

2. Locate the H4 header at the top of the page.

3. Change the text "View My Resume" to:

    `<A HREF="Resume.htm">View My Resume</A>`

4. Locate the text "Comments" on the same line. Change "Comments" to:

    `<A HREF="Comments.htm">Comments</A>`

5. Compare your code to Figure 2-21.

Figure 2-21	ADDING LINKS TO THE REFERENCES PAGE

new links

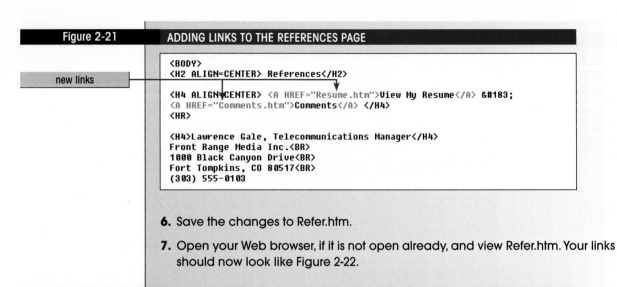

```
<BODY>
<H2 ALIGN=CENTER> References</H2>

<H4 ALIGN=CENTER> <A HREF="Resume.htm">View My Resume</A> &#183;
<A HREF="Comments.htm">Comments</A> </H4>
<HR>

<H4>Lawrence Gale, Telecommunications Manager</H4>
Front Range Media Inc.<BR>
1000 Black Canyon Drive<BR>
Fort Tompkins, CO 80517<BR>
(303) 555-0103
```

6. Save the changes to Refer.htm.

7. Open your Web browser, if it is not open already, and view Refer.htm. Your links should now look like Figure 2-22.

Figure 2-22	LINKS ON THE REFERENCES PAGE

new links

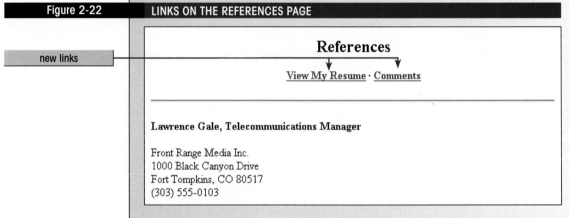

References

View My Resume · Comments

Lawrence Gale, Telecommunications Manager

Front Range Media Inc.
1000 Black Canyon Drive
Fort Tompkins, CO 80517
(303) 555-0103

8. Test the two links to verify that you jump to the Resume and Comments pages.

TROUBLE? If the links do not work, check the spelling of the filenames in the HREF property of the <A> tag. For some Web servers, the case (upper or lower) is also important, so you should make sure that the case matches as well.

Now you need to follow similar steps so that the Comments page links to the two other pages.

To add links in the Comments page to the Resume and References pages:

1. Return to your text editor, and then open the file **Comments.htm** from the Tutorial.02 folder on your Data Disk (you can close Refer.htm).

2. Locate the H4 heading at the top of the page.

3. Change the text "View My resume" to:

```
<A HREF="Resume.htm">View My Resume</A>
```

4. Change "References" on the same line to:

```
<A HREF="Refer.htm">References</A>
```

5. Save the changes to Comments.htm.

6. Open your Web browser, if it is not open already, and view Comments.htm. You should see the links shown in Figure 2-23.

| Figure 2-23 | **LINKS ON THE COMMENTS PAGE** |

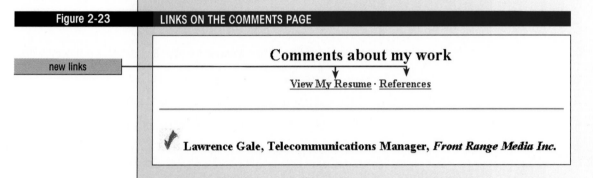

new links

7. Click the two links to verify that you jump to the Resume and References pages.

Now that all the links among the three pages are set up, you can easily move among the three documents.

Linking to a Section of a Document

You might have noticed in testing your links that you always jump to the top of the destination page. What if you'd like to jump to a specific location elsewhere in a document, rather than the beginning? To do this, you can set anchors as you did in Session 2.1 and link to an anchor you create within the document. For example, to create a link to a section in the file Home.htm marked with an anchor name of "Interests," you would create an anchor in the Home.htm file at the section on Interest, and then you would enter this HTML code in your current document:

```
<A HREF="Home.htm#Interests">View my interests</A>
```

In this example, the entire text, "View my interests," is linked to the Interests section in the Home.htm file. Note that the pound (#)symbol in this tag distinguishes the filename from the anchor name (that is why you included the # symbol earlier when linking to anchors within the same document).

Mary wants to link the positions listed in the Employment section of her resume to specific comments from employers on the Comments page. The Comments.htm file already has these anchors in place:

- **GALE**, for comments made by Lawrence Gale, Mary's telecommunications manager
- **CARLSON**, for comments made by Karen Carlson, manager of Mountain View Bank
- **WU**, for comments made by Trent Wu of Computer Visions

Now you need to link the names listed in the Resume file to these three anchors in the Comments page.

To add links to the Resume page that jump to anchors on the Comments page:

1. With your text editor, reopen the **Resume.htm** file (you can close the Comments file).

2. Locate the Employment section in the middle of the Resume file. You need to bracket each job title with link tags that point to the appropriate comment in the Comments page. Leave in place any tags that format the text, such as the <P>, <I>, and <B> tags.

3. Move to the first job description and replace the title "Satellite Technician" with:

   `<A HREF="Comments.htm#GALE">Satellite Technician</A>`

4. Move to the next job description and replace the title "Technical Assistant" with:

   `<A HREF="Comments.htm#CARLSON">Technical Assistant </A>`

5. Move to the final job description, and replace the title "Salesperson" with:

   `<A HREF="Comments.htm#WU">Salesperson</A>`

6. Save the changes to the Resume file.

7. Open your Web browser and open **Resume.htm**. The job titles in the Employment section should appear as text links, as shown in Figure 2-24.

| Figure 2-24 | LINKS TO SPECIFIC LOCATIONS WITHIN THE COMMENTS PAGE |

links in the resume that point to specific locations within the Comments page

Employment

Satellite Technician (Front Range Media Inc. 1998-1999): Monitored satellite uplink/downlink procedures to assure quality video transmissions. Aided technicians in the diagnoses and repair of transmission errors. Assisted in the assembly and maintenance of uplink facility.

Technical Assistant (Mountain View Bank 1996-1998): Managed data processing system. Trained users on data entry and report generation. Managed delivery service.

Salesperson (Computer Visions 1995): Sales and customer support in computers and electronics. Managed commercial accounts in Lake View and Crabtree locations.

Other Information

- References
- Comments on my work
- Go to Colorado State

8. Click the three links to verify that you jump to the appropriate places in the Comments page.

   TROUBLE? If you have a problem with your links, remember that anchors are case sensitive. Make sure you typed GALE, CARLSON, and WU in all uppercase letters.

9. If you are continuing to Session 2.3, you can leave your browser and text editor open. Otherwise, close them.

With these last hypertext links in place, you have given readers of Mary's online resume access to additional information. In the next session, you will learn how to point your hypertext links to documents and resources on the Internet.

Session 2.2 QUICK CHECK

1. What is storyboarding? Why is it important in creating a Web page system?

2. What is a linear structure?

3. What is a hierarchical structure?

4. You are trying to create a system of Web pages for the play *Hamlet* in which each scene has a Web page. On each page you want to include links to the previous and next scenes of the play, as well as to the first scene of the play and the first scene of the current act. Draw a diagram of this multipage document. (Just draw enough acts and scenes to make the structure clear.)

5. What code would you enter to link the text "Sports info" to the HTML file Sports.htm?

6. What code would you enter to link the text "Basketball news" to the HTML file Sports.htm at a place in the file with the anchor name BBALL?

SESSION 2.3

In Session 2.2 you created links to other documents within the same folder as the Resume.htm file. In this session you will learn to create hypertext links to documents located in other folders and in other computers on the Internet.

Mary wants to add a link to her Resume page that points to the Colorado State University home page. The link gives potential employers an opportunity to learn more about the school she attended and the courses it offers. Before creating this link for Mary, you need to review the way HTML references files in different folders and computers.

Linking to Documents in Other Folders

Until now you've worked with documents that were all in the same folder. When you created links to other files in that folder, you specified the filename in the link tag, but not its location. Browsers assume that if no folder information is given, the file is in the same folder as the current document. In some situations you might want to place different files in different folders, particularly when working with large multidocument systems that span several topics, each topic with its own folder.

When referencing files in different folders in the link tag, you must include each file's location, called its **path**. HTML supports two kinds of paths: absolute paths and relative paths.

Absolute Pathnames

The **absolute path** shows exactly where the file is on the computer. In HTML you start every absolute pathname with a slash (/). Then you type the folder names on the computer, starting with the topmost folder in the folder hierarchy and progressing through the different levels of subfolders. You separate each folder name from the next with a slash. The pathname, from left to right, leads down through the folder hierarchy to the folder that contains the file. After you type the name of the folder that contains the file, you type a final slash and then the filename.

For example, consider the folder structure shown in Figure 2-25.

Figure 2-25	FOLDER TREE

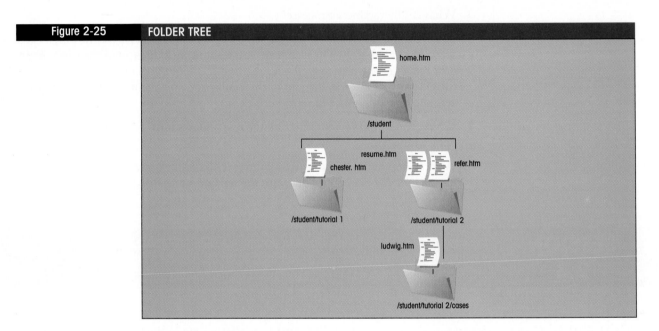

Figure 2-25 shows five HTML files contained in four different folders. The topmost folder is the student folder. Within the student folder are the tutorial1 and tutorial2 folders, and within the tutorial2 folder is the cases folder. Figure 2-26 shows absolute pathnames for the five files.

Figure 2-26	ABSOLUTE PATHNAMES

ABSOLUTE PATHNAME	INTERPRETATION
/student/home.htm	The home .htm file in the student folder
/student/tutorial1/chester.htm	The chester.htm file in the tutorial1 folder, a subfolder of the student folder
/student/tutorial2/resume.htm	The resume.htm file in the tutorial2 folder, another subfolder of the student folder
/student/tutorial2/refer.htm	The refer.htm file in the same folder as the resume.htm folder
/student/tutorial2/cases/ludwig.htm	The ludwig.htm file in the cases folder, a subfolder of the /student/tutorial2 folder

Even the absolute pathnames of files located on different hard disks begin with a slash. To differentiate these files, HTML requires you to include the drive letter followed by a vertical bar (|). For example, a file named "resume.htm" in the student folder on drive A of your computer has the absolute pathname "/A | /student/resume.htm".

Relative Pathnames

If a computer has many folders and subfolders, absolute pathnames can be long, cumbersome, and confusing. For that reason, most Web authors use relative pathnames in their hypertext links. A **relative path** gives a file's location in relation to the current Web document. As with absolute pathnames, folder names are separated by slashes. Unlike absolute pathnames, a relative pathname does not begin with a slash. To reference a file in a folder above the current folder in the folder hierarchy, relative pathnames use two periods (..).

For example, if the current file is resume.htm, located in the /student/tutorial2 folder shown in Figure 2-25, the relative pathnames and their interpretations for the other four files in the folder tree appear as in Figure 2-27.

Figure 2-27	RELATIVE PATHNAMES

RELATIVE PATHNAME	INTERPRETATION
../home.htm	The home.htm file in the folder one level up in the folder tree from the current file
../tutorial1/chester.htm	The chester.htm file in the tutorial1 subfolder of the folder one level up from the current file
refer.htm	The refer.htm file in the same folder as the current file
cases/ludwig.htm	The ludwig.htm file in the cases subfolder, one level down from the current folder

A second reason to use relative pathnames is that they make your hypertext links portable. If you have to move your files to a different computer or server, you can move the entire folder structure and still use the relative pathnames in the hypertext links. If you use absolute pathnames, you need to painstakingly revise each and every link.

Linking **to Documents on the Internet**

Now you can turn your attention to creating a link on Mary's resume to Colorado State University. To create a hypertext link to a document on the Internet, you need to know its URL. A **URL**, or **Uniform Resource Locator**, gives a file's location on the Web. The URL for Colorado State University, for example, is *http://www.colostate.edu/*. You can find the URL of a Web page in the Location or Address box of your browser's document window.

After you know a document's URL, you are ready to add the code that creates the link—again, the <A> code with the HREF property that creates links to documents on your computer. For example, to create a link to a document on the Internet with the URL *http://www.mwu.edu/course/info.html*, you use this HTML code:

```
<A HREF="http://www.mwu.edu/course/info.html"> Course
Information</A>
```

This example links the text "Course Information" to the Internet document located at *http://www.mwu.edu/course/info.html*. As long as your computer is connected to the Internet, clicking the text within the tag should make your browser jump to that document.

REFERENCE WINDOW   **RW**

Linking to a Document on the Internet
- Locate the text or graphic you want to designate as the link.
- Before the text or graphic, place the tag <A HREF="*URL*"> where *URL* is the URL of the Web page you want to link to.
- After the text or graphic, insert the </A> closing tag.

In the Other Information section of Mary's resume, she wants to link the text "Go to Colorado State" to the CSU home page. You're ready to add that link.

To add a link to the Colorado State University page from Mary's Resume page:

1. If necessary, open your text editor, and then open the **Resume.htm** file that you worked on in Session 2.2 of this tutorial.

2. Locate the Other Information section near the bottom of the page.

3. Change the line "<LI>Go to Colorado State" to:

   ```
   <LI><A HREF="http://www.colostate.edu/"> Go to Colorado
   State</A>
   ```

4. Save the changes to the Resume file.

5. If necessary, open your Web browser and connect to the Internet.

6. Open the file **Resume.htm**. The Go to Colorado State entry should look like the text link shown in Figure 2-28.

| Figure 2-28 | **LINK TO ANOTHER PAGE ON THE WEB** |

Other Information

- References
- Comments on my work
- Go to Colorado State

link to Colorado State
home page

Interested?

Contact Mary Taylor at mtaylor@tt.gr.csu.edu

7. Click the **Go to Colorado State** link. The Colorado State University home page shown in Figure 2-29 appears.

   TROUBLE? If the CSU home page doesn't appear right away, it might just be loading slowly on your system because it contains a large graphic. If the CSU home page still doesn't appear, verify that your computer is connected to the Internet.

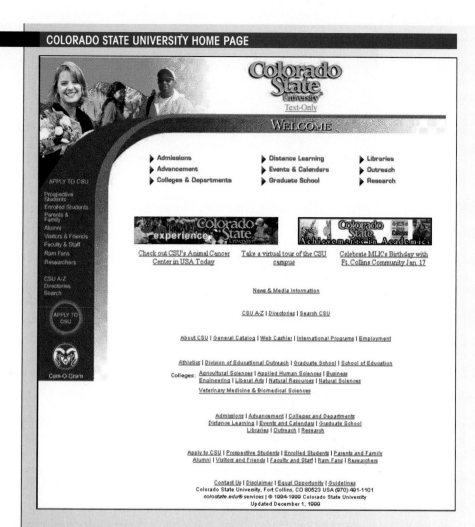

| Figure 2-29 | COLORADO STATE UNIVERSITY HOME PAGE |

8. Click the **Back** button in your browser to return to Mary's resume.

Linking **to Other Internet Objects**

Occasionally you see a URL for an Internet object other than a Web page. Recall that one reason for the World Wide Web's success is that it lets users access several types of Internet resources using the same program. The method you used to create a link to the Colorado State University home page is the same method you use to set up links to other Internet resources, such as FTP servers to Usenet newsgroups (you'll learn what these are below). Only the proper URL for each object is required.

Each URL follows the same basic format. The first part identifies the **communication protocol**, the set of rules governing how information is exchanged. Web pages use the communication protocol **HTTP**, short for **Hypertext Transfer Protocol**. All Web page URLs begin with the letters "http". Other Internet resources use different communication protocols. After the communication protocol there is usually a separator, like a colon followed by a slash or two (://). The exact separator depends on the Internet resource. The rest of the URL identifies the location of the document or resource on the Internet. Figure 2-30 interprets a Web page with the URL:

```
http://www.mwu.edu/course/info.html#majors
```

Figure 2-30 | **INTERPRETING PARTS OF A URL**

PART OF URL	INTERPRETATION
http://	The communication protocol
www.mwu.edu	The Internet host name for the computer storing the document
/course/info.html	The pathname and filename of the document on the computer
#majors	An anchor in the document

Notice that the URL for the Colorado State home page doesn't seem to have any path or file information. By convention, if the path and filename are left off the URL, the browser searches for a file named "index.html" or "index.htm" in the root folder of the Web server. Note that the path can be expressed in relative or absolute terms. This is the file displayed in Figure 2-29.

Before you walk Mary through the task of creating her final link, you take a quick detour to show her how to create links to other Internet resources, if needed. You might not be familiar with all the Internet resources discussed in these next sections. This tutorial doesn't try to teach you about these resources in detail; it just shows you how to reference them in your HTML files.

Linking to FTP Servers

FTP servers store files that Internet users can download, or transfer, to their computers. **FTP**, short for **File Transfer Protocol**, is the communications protocol these file servers use to transfer information. URLs for FTP servers follow the same format as those for Web pages, except that they use the FTP protocol rather than the HTTP protocol: ftp://*FTP_Hostname*. For example, to create a link to the FTP server located at ftp.microsoft.com, you could use this HTML code:

```
<A HREF="ftp://ftp.microsoft.com">Microsoft FTP server</A>
```

In this example, clicking the text "Microsoft FTP server" jumps the user to the Microsoft FTP server page shown in Figure 2-31. Note that different browsers will show the contents of the FTP site in different ways. Figure 2-31 shows what it might look like with Internet Explorer.

Figure 2-31   **FTP SERVER AT FTP.MICROSOFT.COM**

Name	Size	Type	Modified	
bussys		File Folder	11/21/99 12:00 AM	
deskapps		File Folder	6/8/99 12:00 AM	
developr		File Folder	4/20/99 12:00 AM	
kbhelp		File Folder	3/26/99 12:00 AM	
misc		File Folder	1/14/00 5:00 AM	
peropsys		File Folder	9/8/99 12:00 AM	
products		File Folder	8/11/99 12:00 AM	
reskit		File Folder	12/9/99 12:00 AM	
services		File Folder	12/8/99 12:00 AM	
softlib		File Folder	10/1/99 12:00 AM	
solutions		File Folder	12/11/98 12:00 AM	
dirmap.htm	7.79 KB	Internet Document (...	1/28/99 12:00 AM	
dirmap.txt	4.23 KB	Text Document	1/28/99 12:00 AM	
disclaim1.txt	710 bytes	Text Document	4/12/93 12:00 AM	
disclaimer.txt	712 bytes	Text Document	8/25/94 12:00 AM	
homemm.old	1.18 MB	OLD File	10/7/98 12:00 AM	
ls-lr.txt	24.8 MB	Text Document	1/14/00 3:37 AM	
ls-lr.z	4.95 MB	WinZip File	1/14/00 3:37 AM	
ls-lr.zip	2.66 MB	WinZip File	1/14/00 3:37 AM	

Linking to Usenet News

Usenet is a collection of discussion forums, called **newsgroups**, that lets users send and retrieve messages on a wide variety of topics. The URL for a newsgroup is news:*newsgroup*. To access the surfing newsgroup, alt.surfing, you place this line in your HTML file:

```
<A HREF="news:alt.surfing">Go to the surfing newsgroup</A>
```

When you click a link to a newsgroup, your computer starts your newsgroup software and accesses the newsgroup. For example, if you have the Outlook Newsreader program installed, clicking the above link will open the window shown in Figure 2-32.

Figure 2-32   **ACCESSING THE ALT.SURFING NEWSGROUP**

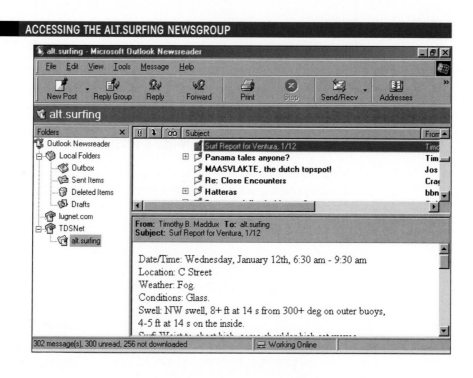

Linking to E-mail

Many Web authors include their e-mail addresses on their Web pages so that users who access these pages can easily send feedback. You can set up these e-mail addresses to act as hypertext links. When a user clicks the e-mail address, the browser starts a mail program and automatically inserts the author's e-mail address into the outgoing message. The user then types the body of the message and mails it. The URL for an e-mail address is mailto:*e-mail_address*. To create a link to the e-mail address davis@mwu.edu, for example, you enter the following into your Web document:

```
<A HREF="mailto:davis@mwu.edu">davis@mwu.edu</A>
```

If you click the text davis@mwu.edu and you have Microsoft Outlook installed as your default e-mail program, the window shown in Figure 2-33 appears.

Figure 2-33	SENDING MAIL TO DAVIS@MWU.EDU

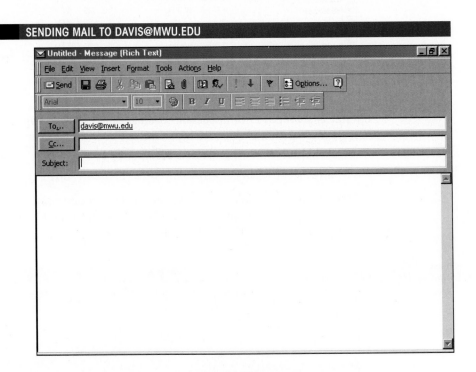

Adding an E-mail Link to Mary's Resume

Mary wants a final addition to her resume: a link to her e-mail address. With this link, an interested employer can quickly send Mary a message through the Internet. Mary placed her e-mail address at the bottom of the Resume page. Now you need to designate that text as a link so that when an employer clicks it, a window similar to the one shown in Figure 2-33 will open.

To add an e-mail link to Mary's resume:

1. Return to the Resume.htm file in your text editor.

2. Go to the bottom of the page.

3. Change the text "mtaylor@tt.gr.csu.edu" to

```
<A HREF="mailto:mtaylor@tt.gr.csu.edu">
mtaylor@tt.gr.csu.edu</A>
```

4. Save the changes to the Resume file.

5. Return to your Web browser and reload Resume.htm.

6. Move to the bottom of the page. Mary's e-mail address should look like the hypertext link shown in Figure 2-34.

   TROUBLE? Some browsers do not support the mailto URL. If you use a browser other than Netscape Navigator or Internet Explorer, check to see if it supports this feature.

Figure 2-34   MARY TAYLOR'S E-MAIL ADDRESS AS A HYPERLINK

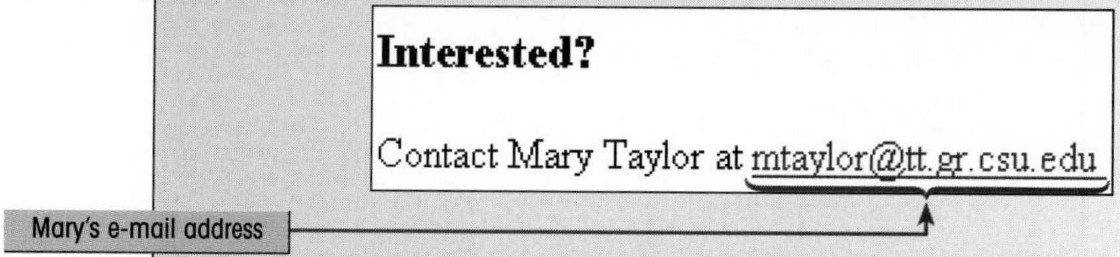

Mary's e-mail address

7. Click the hypertext link to Mary's e-mail address. See Figure 2-35.

Figure 2-35   MAIL MESSAGE WITH MARY TAYLOR'S E-MAIL ADDRESS AUTOMATICALLY INSERTED

   TROUBLE? Your e-mail window might look different, depending on the mail program installed on your computer.

8. Cancel the mail message by clicking the Close button in the upper-right corner of the window. Mary's e-mail address is fictional, so you can't send her mail anyway.

9. Close your Web browser and text editor.

You show Mary the final form of her online resume. She's really thrilled with the result. You tell her the next thing she needs to do is contact an Internet service provider and transfer the files to an account on their machine. When that's done, Mary's resume becomes available online to countless employers across the Internet.

Session 2.3 QUICK CHECK

1. What's the difference between an absolute path and a relative path?

2. Refer to the diagram in Figure 2-25: If the current file is ludwig.htm in the /student/tutorial2/cases folder, what are the relative pathnames for the four other files?

3. What tag would you enter to link the text "Washington" to the FTP server at *ftp.uwash.edu*?

4. What tag would you enter to link the text "Boxing" to the newsgroup *rec.sports.boxing.pro*?

5. What tag would you enter to link the text "President" to the e-mail address *president@whitehouse.gov*?

REVIEW ASSIGNMENTS

Mary Taylor decides that she wants you to add a few more items to her resume. She wants to add a link at the bottom of her resume page that returns readers to the top. Also, in the Employment section, she wants to add the information that she worked as a tutor for Professor Ramirez at Colorado State University and link that job title to comments Professor Ramirez made about her in the Comments page. Finally, she wants to add a link to Colorado State's Department of Electrical and Computer Engineering, where she did a lot of her graduate work.

1. Open the **Resume.htm** file located in the Tutorial.02 folder on your Data Disk. You worked with this file over the course of this tutorial.

2. Save the file on your Data Disk in the Review folder with the same name, Resume.htm. This will leave intact the version that is in the Tutorial.02 folder.

3. Add an anchor tag around the H1 header at top of the page (Mary's name). Give the anchor the name TOP.

4. After the HTML line at the bottom of the page containing Mary's e-mail address, and before the </BODY> tag, enter a new paragraph with the line "Go to the top of the page." Change this text to a hyperlink, pointing to the TOP anchor you created in Step 3.

5. Move to the Employment section. After the paragraph describing Mary's experience as a salesperson, insert this paragraph: "Tutor (Colorado State): Tutored students in electrical engineering and mathematics." Format this paragraph using the same <P>, <B>, and <I> tags you used for the other job descriptions in the resume.

6. Change the text "Tutor" to a hyperlink pointing to the RAMIREZ anchor in the Comments page (this anchor already exists).

7. Move to the Other Information section, and add a new list item to the unsorted list: "Go to Colorado State Department of Electrical and Computer Engineering."

8. Change the new list item to a hyperlink pointing to the URL: *http://www.lance.colostate.edu/depts/ee/*.

9. Save the Resume.htm file and print it.

10. View the Resume.htm file with your Web browser. Make sure you open Resume.htm in the Review folder of the Tutorial.02 folder. Verify that all of the new links work correctly.

11. Print a copy of the Resume page as displayed by the browser.

CASE PROBLEMS

Case 1. Creating Links to Federal Departments As a librarian at the city library, you are creating a Web page to help people access the home pages for several federal government departments. Figure 2-36 lists each department's URL.

Figure 2-36

DEPARTMENT	URL
Department of Agriculture	*http://www.usda.gov/*
Department of Commerce	*http://www.doc.gov/*
Department of Defense	*http://www.defenselink.mil/*
Department of Education	*http://www.ed.gov/*
Department of Energy	*http://www.doe.gov/*
Department of Health and Human Services	*http://www.dhhs.gov/*
Department of Housing and Urban Development	*http://www.hud.gov/*
Department of Interior	*http://www.doi.gov/*
Department of Justice	*http://www.usdoj.gov/*
Department of Labor	*http://www.dol.gov/*
Department of State	*http://www.state.gov/*
Department of Transportation	*http://www.dot.gov/*
Department of Treasury	*http://www.ustreas.gov/*
Department of Veteran Affairs	*http://www.va.gov/*

You'll create an unsorted list containing department names, and then make each name a text link to the department's home page.

1. Start the text editor on your computer and open a new document.

2. Enter the <HTML>, <HEAD>, and <BODY> tags to identify different sections of the page.

3. Within the HEAD section, insert a <TITLE> tag with the text "Federal Government Departments".

4. Within the BODY section, create a centered H1 header with the text "A list of federal departments".

5. Create an unordered list of the department names shown in the first column of Figure 2-36. You can save yourself a lot of typing by using the Copy and Paste commands in your text editor (so that you don't have to type "Department of " each time).

6. Link each department name with its URL (shown in the second column of Figure 2-36).

7. Save the file as Depart.htm in the Cases subfolder of the Tutorial.02 folder on your Data Disk, print the file, and then close your text editor.

8. View the file with your Web browser, create a printout, and then close your browser.

Case 2. Using Graphics as Hypertext Links   You are an assistant to a professor in the Music Department who is trying to create Web pages for topics in classical music. Previously you created a Web page for her that showed the different sections of the fourth movement of Beethoven's Ninth symphony. Now that you've learned to link multiple HTML files together, you have created pages for all four movements.

Explore

The four pages are in the Cases folder of the Tutorial.02 folder on your Data Disk. Their names are: Move1A.htm, Move2A.htm, Move3A.htm, and Move4A.htm. You'll rename them Move1.htm, Move2.htm, Move3.htm, and Move4.htm so that you'll have the originals if you want to work on them later. Figure 2-37 shows the page for the third movement.

Figure 2-37

Beethoven's Ninth Symphony

☜ The Third Movement ☞

Sectional Form

1. A-Section
2. B-Section
3. A-Section varied
4. B-Section
5. Interlude
6. A-Section varied
7. Coda

View the Classical Net Home page.

You now need to link the pages. You've already placed graphic elements—the hands pointing to the previous or next movement of the symphony—in each file. You decide to mark each graphic image as a hypertext link that jumps the user to the previous or next movement.

1. Start your text editor and then open the **Move1A.htm — Move4A.htm** files in the Tutorial.02/Cases folder on your Data Disk, and save them as Move1.htm — Move4.htm in the Cases folder.

2. Within each of the HTML files you created in Step 1, edit the inline images, Right.jpg and Left.jpg, so that the Right.jpg inline image is a hyperlink pointing to the next movement in the symphony, and Left.jpg points to the previous movement in the symphony.

3. Within each of the four HTML files, change the text "View the Classical Net Home page." to a hyperlink pointing to the URL *http://www.classical.net/*. Save and print all four HTML files and then close your text editor.

4. Open the pages in your Web browser and verify that all of the links work correctly.

5. Print each page in the Web browser, and then close your browser.

Case 3. Creating a Product Report Web Site   You work for Jackson Electronics, an electronics firm in Seattle, Washington. You've been asked to create a Web site describing the company's premier flatbed scanner, the ScanMaster. There are three Web pages in the site: a product report, a fact sheet, and a sheet of frequently asked questions (FAQs). Your job is to add the links connecting the pages.

1. Start your text editor and then open the files **SMtxt.htm**, **Factstxt.htm**, and **FAQtxt.htm** in the Tutorial.02/Cases folder of your Data Disk and save the files as: Scanner.htm, Facts.htm and FAQ.htm, in the Cases folder.

2. Open the **Scanner.htm** file in your text editor, and add anchor names to the five H1 headers after the table of contents. Use the following anchor names: PR, SALES, STANDARD, PLAN, and LINKS.

3. Link the entries in the table of contents to the anchors that you created in Step 2.

4. Change the text "e-mail" in the second paragraph of the "Products Report Go Online" section to a hyperlink pointing to the e-mail address "jbrooks@Jckson_Electronics.com".

5. Go to the Links section of the document, and link the text "View the ScanMaster fact sheet" to the Facts.htm file. Link the text "View the Product Summary" to an anchor named SUMMARY in the Facts.htm file. Link "View the Features List" to the FEA-TURES anchor in Facts.htm. Link "View Ordering Information" to the INFO anchor in Facts.htm. Finally, link the text "View the FAQ sheet" to the FAQ.htm file. Save your changes to Scanner.htm file. Print the Scanner.htm file from your text editor.

6. Open the Facts.htm file in your text editor. Create anchors for each of the H2 headers with the names SUMMARY, FEATURES, and INFO.

7. Change the text "Return to the product report." at the bottom of the page to a hyperlink pointing to the Scanner.htm file. Save your changes. Print the Facts.htm file from your text editor.

8. Open the FAQ.htm file in your text editor. Change the last line to a hyperlink pointing to the Scanner.htm file. Print the FAQ.htm file from your text editor.

9. Open the Scanner.htm file in your Web browser and verify that all of your links work correctly.

10. Print each of the three resulting Web pages from your browser.

Case 4. Create Your Own Home Page   Now that you've completed this tutorial, you are ready to create your own home page. The page should include information about you and your interests. If you like, you can create a separate page devoted entirely to one of your favorite hobbies. Include the following elements:

- section headers
- bold and/or italic fonts
- paragraphs
- an ordered, unordered, or definition list

Explore
- an inline graphic image that is either a link or the destination of a link
- links to some of your favorite Internet pages
- a hypertext link that moves the user from one section of your page to another

1. Create a file called Myhome.htm in the Cases folder of the Tutorial.02 folder on your Data Disk, and enter the appropriate HTML code.

2. Add any other tags you think will improve your document's appearance.

3. Insert any graphic elements you think will enhance your document.

Explore ▶ 4. Use at least one graphic element as either a link or the destination of a link.

5. Use your Web browser to explore other Web pages. Record the URLs of pages that you like, and list them in your document. Then create links to those URLs.

6. Test your code as you develop your home page by viewing Myhome.htm in your browser.

7. When you finish entering your code, save and print the Myhome.htm file, and then close your text editor.

9. View the final version in your browser, print the Web page, and then close your browser.

QUICK | CHECK ANSWERS

Session 2.1

1. <A NAME="CSU">Colorado State University</A>

2. <A HREF="#CSU">Universities</A>

3. Anchor tags should be placed within style tags such as the <H3> header tag.

4. <A NAME="PHOTO"> <IMG SRC="Photo.jpg"> </A>

5. <A HREF="#LINKS"> <IMG SRC="Button.jpg"> </A>

6. False. Anchor names are case-sensitive.

Session 2.2

1. Storyboarding is diagramming a series of related Web pages, taking care to identify all hypertext links between the various pages. Storyboarding is an important tool in creating Web sites that are easy to navigate and understand.

2. A linear structure is one in which Web pages are linked from one to another in a direct chain. Users can go to the previous page or next page in the chain, but not to a page in a different section of the chain.

3. A hierarchical structure is one in which Web pages are linked from general to specific topics. Users can move up and down the hierarchy tree.

4. A company might use such a structure to describe the management organization.

5. <A HREF="Sports.htm">Sports info</A>

6. <A HREF="Sports.htm#BBALL">Basketball news</A>

Session 2.3

1. An absolute path gives the location of a file on the computer's hard disk. A relative path gives the location of a file relative to the active Web page.

2. ../../home.htm

../../tutorial1/chester.htm

../resume.htm

../refer.htm

3. <A HREF="ftp://ftp.uwash.edu">Washington</A>

4. <A HREF=news:rec.sports.boxing.pro>Boxing</A>

5. <A HREF=mailto:president@whitehouse.gov>President</A>

HTML Extended Color Names

The following is a list of extended color names and their corresponding hexadecimal triplets supported by most Web browsers. To view these colors, you must have a video card and monitor capable of displaying up to 256 colors. As with other aspects of Web page design, you should test these color names on a variety of browsers before committing to their use. Different browsers may render these colors differently, or not at all.

Extended Color Names

COLOR NAME	HEXADECIMAL VALUE	PREVIEW
ALICEBLUE	#F0F8FE	
ANTIQUEWHITE	#FAEBD7	
AQUA	#00FFFF	
AQUAMARINE	#70DB93	
AZURE	#F0FFFF	
BEIGE	#F5F5DC	
BLACK	#000000	
BLUE	#0000FF	
BLUEVIOLET	#9F5F9F	
BRASS	#B5A642	
BRIGHTGOLD	#D9D919	
BRONZE	#8C7853	
BROWN	#A52A2A	
CADETBLUE	#5F9F9F	
CHOCOLATE	#D2691E	
COOLCOPPER	#D98719	
COPPER	#B87333	
CORAL	#FF7F50	
CRIMSON	#DC143C	
CYAN	#00FFFF	
DARKBLUE	#00008B	
DARKBROWN	#5C4033	
DARKCYAN	#008B8B	
DARKGOLDENROD	#B8860B	
DARKGRAY	#A9A9A9	
DARKGREEN	#006400	
DARKKHAKI	#BDB76B	
DARKMAGENTA	#8B008B	
DARKOLIVEGREEN	#4F4F2F	
DARKORANGE	#FF8C00	
DARKORCHID	#9932CD	

COLOR NAME	HEXADECIMAL VALUE	PREVIEW
DARKPURPLE	#871F78	
DARKSALMON	#E9967A	
DARKSLATEBLUE	#6B238E	
DARKSLATEGRAY	#2F4F4F	
DARKTAN	#97694F	
DARKTURQUOISE	#7093DB	
DARKVIOLET	#9400D3	
DARKWOOD	#855E42	
DIMGRAY	#545454	
DUSTYROSE	#856363	
FELDSPAR	#D19275	
FIREBRICK	#8E2323	
FORESTGREEN	#238E23	
GOLD	#CD7F32	
GOLDENROD	#DBDB70	
GRAY	#C0C0C0	
GREEN	#00FF00	
GREENCOPPER	#527F76	
GREENYELLOW	#93DB70	
HOTPINK	#FF69B4	
HUNTERGREEN	#215E21	
INDIANRED	#4E2F2F	
INDIGO	#4B0082	
IVORY	#FFFFF0	
KHAKI	#9F9F5F	
LAVENDER	#E6E6FA	
LIGHTBLUE	#C0D9D9	
LIGHTCORAL	#F08080	
LIGHTCYAN	#E0FFFF	
LIGHTGRAY	#A8A8A8	
LIGHTGREEN	#90EE90	

COLOR NAME	HEXADECIMAL VALUE	PREVIEW
LIGHTPINK	#FFB6C1	
LIGHTSTEELBLUE	#8F8FBD	
LIGHTWOOD	#E9C2A6	
LIME	#00FF00	
LIMEGREEN	#32CD32	
MAGENTA	#FF00FF	
MANDARINORANGE	#E47833	
MAROON	#8E236B	
MEDIUMAQUAMARINE	#32CD99	
MEDIUMBLUE	#3232CD	
MEDIUMFORESTGREEN	#6B8E23	
MEDIUMGOLDENROD	#EAEAAE	
MEDIUMORCHID	#9370DB	
MEDIUMSEAGREEN	#426F42	
MEDIUMSLATEBLUE	#7F00FF	
MEDIUMSPRINGGREEN	#7FFF00	
MEDIUMTURQUOISE	#70DBDB	
MEDIUMVIOLETRED	#DB7093	
MEDIUMWOOD	#A68064	
MIDNIGHTBLUE	#2F2F4F	
MINTCREAM	#F5FFFA	
MISTYROSE	#FFE4E1	
NAVYBLUE	#23238E	
NEONBLUE	#4D4DFF	
NEONPINK	#FF6EC7	
NEWMIDNIGHTBLUE	#00009C	
NEWTAN	#EBC79E	
OLDGOLD	#CFB53B	
OLIVE	#808000	
ORANGE	#FF7F00	
ORANGERED	#FF2400	
ORCHID	#DB70DB	
PALEGOLDENROD	#EEE8AA	
PALEGREEN	#8FBC8F	
PALETURQUOISE	#AFEEEE	

COLOR NAME	HEXADECIMAL VALUE	PREVIEW
PINK	#BC8F8F	
PLUM	#EAADEA	
POWDERBLUE	#B0E0E6	
PURPLE	#800080	
QUARTZ	#D9D9F3	
RED	#FF0000	
RICHBLUE	#5959AB	
ROYALBLUE	#4169E1	
SADDLEBROWN	#8B4513	
SALMON	#6F4242	
SANDYBROWN	#F4A460	
SCARLET	#8C1717	
SEAGREEN	#238E68	
SIENNA	#8E6B23	
SILVER	#E6E8FA	
SKYBLUE	#3299CC	
SLATEBLUE	#007FFF	
SNOW	#FFFAFA	
SPICYPINK	#FF1CAE	
SPRINGGREEN	#00FF7F	
STEELBLUE	#236B8E	
SUMMERSKY	#38B0DE	
TAN	#DB9370	
TEAL	#008080	
THISTLE	#D8BFD8	
TOMATO	#FF6347	
TURQUOISE	#ADEAEA	
VERYDARKBROWN	#5C4033	
VERYDARKGRAY	#CDCDCD	
VIOLET	#4F2F4F	
VIOLETRED	#CC3299	
WHEAT	#D8D8BF	
WHITE	#FFFFFF	
YELLOW	#FFFF00	
YELLOWGREEN	#99CC32	

HTML Special Characters

The following table lists the extended character set for HTML, also known as the ISO Latin-1 Character set. Characters in this table can be entered either by code number or code name. For example, to insert the registered trademark symbol, ®, you would use either &reg or &#174.

Not all code names are recognized by all browsers. Some older browsers that support only the HTML 2.0 standard will not recognize the code name &times, for instance. Code names that may not be recognized by older browsers are marked with an asterisk. If you are planning to use these symbols in your document, you may want to use the code number instead of the code name.

CHARACTER	CODE	CODE NAME	DESCRIPTION
	&#00 - &#08		Unused
	&#09		Tab
	&#10		Line feed
	&#11 - &#31		Unused
	&#32		Space
!	&#33		Exclamation mark
"	&#34	&quot	Double quotation mark
#	&#35		Pound sign
$	&#36		Dollar sign
%	&#37		Percent sign
&	&#38	&amp	Ampersand
'	&#39		Apostrophe
(	&#40		Left parenthesis
)	&#41		Right parenthesis
*	&#42		Asterisk
+	&#43		Plus sign
,	&#44		Comma
-	&#45		Hyphen
.	&#46		Period
/	&#47		Forward slash
0 - 9	&#48 - &#57		Numbers 0 - 9
:	&#58		Colon
;	&#59		Semicolon
<	&#60	&lt	Less than sign
=	&#61		Equals sign
>	&#62	&gt	Greater than sign
?	&#63		Question mark
@	&#64		Commercial at
A - Z	&#65 - &#90		Letters A - Z
[	&#91		Left square bracket

CHARACTER	CODE	CODE NAME	DESCRIPTION
\	&#92		Back slash
]	&#93		Right square bracket
^	&#94		Caret
_	&#95		Horizontal bar
`	&#96		Grave accent
a - z	&#97 - &#122		Letters a - z
{	&#123		Left curly brace
|	&#124		Vertical bar
}	&#125		Right curly brace
~	&#126		Tilde
	&#127 - &#129		Unused
‚	&#130		Low single comma quotation mark
ƒ	&#131		Function sign
„	&#132		Low double comma quotation mark
…	&#133		Ellipses
†	&#134		Dagger
‡	&#135		Double dagger
ˆ	&#136		Caret
‰	&#137		Per mile sign
Š	&#138		Capital S with hacek
<	&#139		Less than sign
Œ	&#140		Capital OE ligature
	&#141 - &#144		Unused
`	&#145		Single beginning quotation mark
'	&#146		Single ending quotation mark
"	&#147		Double beginning quotation mark
"	&#148		Double ending quotation mark
•	&#149		Middle dot
–	&#150		En dash
—	&#151		Em dash
~	&#152		Tilde
™	&#153	&trade*	Trademark symbol
š	&#154		Small s with hacek
›	&#155		Greater than sign
œ	&#156		Small oe ligature
	&#157 - &#158		Unused
Ÿ	&#159		Capital Y with umlaut

CHARACTER	CODE	CODE NAME	DESCRIPTION
		*	Non-breaking space
¡	&#161	&iexcl*	Inverted exclamation point
¢	&#162	&cent*	Cent symbol
£	&#163	&pound*	Pound sterling
¤	&#164	&curren*	General currency symbol
¥	&#165	&yen*	Yen sign
¦	&#166	&brvbar*	Broken vertical bar
§	&#167	&sect*	Section sign
¨	&#168	&uml*	Umlaut
©	&#169	&copy*	Copyright symbol
ª	&#170	&ordf*	Feminine ordinal
«	&#171	&laquo*	Left angle quotation mark
¬	&#172	&not*	Not sign
	&#173	&shy*	Soft hyphen
®	&#174	&reg*	Registered trademark
¯	&#175	&macr*	Macron
°	&#176	&deg*	Degree sign
±	&#177	&plusmn*	Plus/minus symbol
²	&#178	&sup2*	Superscript 2
³	&#179	&sup3*	Superscript 3
´	&#180	&acute*	Acute accent
µ	&#181	&micro*	Micro symbol
¶	&#182	&para*	Paragraph sign
·	&#183	&middot*	Middle dot
¸	&#184	&cedil*	Cedilla
¹	&#185	&sup1*	Superscript 1
º	&#186	&ordm*	Masculine ordinal
»	&#187	&raquo*	Right angle quotation mark
¼	&#188	&frac14*	Fraction one-quarter
½	&#189	&frac12*	Fraction one-half
¾	&#190	&frac34*	Fraction three-quarters
¿	&#191	&iquest*	Inverted question mark
À	&#192	&Agrave	Capital A, grave accent
Á	&#193	&Aacute	Capital A, acute accent
Â	&#194	&Acirc	Capital A, circumflex accent
Ã	&#195	&Atilde	Capital A, tilde
Ä	&#196	&Auml	Capital A, umlaut

CHARACTER	CODE	CODE NAME	DESCRIPTION
Å	&#197	&Aring	Capital A, ring
Æ	&#198	&Aelig	Capital AE ligature
Ç	&#199	&Ccedil	Capital C, cedilla
È	&#200	&Egrave	Capital E, grave accent
É	&#201	&Eacute	Capital E, acute accent
Ê	&#202	&Ecirc	Capital E, circumflex accent
Ë	&#203	&Euml	Capital E, umlaut
Ì	&#204	&Igrave	Capital I, grave accent
Í	&#205	&Iacute	Capital I, acute accent
Î	&#206	&Icirc	Capital I, circumflex accent
Ï	&#207	&Iuml	Capital I, umlaut
Ð	&#208	&ETH*	Capital ETH, Icelandic
Ñ	&#209	&Ntilde	Capital N, tilde
Ò	&#210	&Ograve	Capital O, grave accent
Ó	&#211	&Oacute	Capital O, acute accent
Ô	&#212	&Ocirc	Capital O, circumflex accent
Õ	&#213	&Otilde	Capital O, tilde
Ö	&#214	&Ouml	Capital O, umlaut
×	&#215	&times*	Multiplication sign
Ø	&#216	&Oslash	Capital O slash
Ù	&#217	&Ugrave	Capital U, grave accent
Ú	&#218	&Uacute	Capital U, acute accent
Û	&#219	&Ucirc	Capital U, circumflex accent
Ü	&#220	&Uuml	Capital U, umlaut
Ý	&#221	&Yacute	Capital Y, acute accent
þ	&#222	&THORN	Capital THORN, Icelandic
ß	&#223	&szlig	Small sz ligature
à	&#224	&agrave	Small a, grave accent
á	&#225	&aacute	Small a, acute accent
â	&#226	&acirc	Small a, circumflex accent
ã	&#227	&atilde	Small a, tilde
ä	&#228	&auml	Small a, umlaut
å	&#229	&aring	Small a, ring
œ	&#230	&aelig	Small AE ligature
ç	&#231	&ccedil	Small C, cedilla
è	&#232	&egrave	Small e, grave accent
é	&#233	&eacute	Small e, acute accent

CHARACTER	CODE	CODE NAME	DESCRIPTION
ê	&#234	&ecirc	Small e, circumflex accent
ë	&#235	&euml	Small e, umlaut
ì	&#236	&igrave	Small i, grave accent
í	&#237	&iacute	Small i, acute accent
î	&#238	&icirc	Small i, circumflex accent
ï	&#239	&iuml	Small i, umlaut
ð	&#240	&eth	Small ETH, Icelandic
ñ	&#241	&ntilde	Small N, tilde
ò	&#242	&ograve	Small o, grave accent
ó	&#243	&oacute	Small o, acute accent
ô	&#244	&ocirc	Small o, circumflex accent
õ	&#245	&otilde	Small o, tilde
ö	&#246	&ouml	Small o, umlaut
÷	&#247	&divide*	Division sign
ø	&#248	&oslash	Small o slash
ù	&#249	&ugrave	Small u, grave accent
ú	&#250	&uacute	Small u, acute accent
û	&#251	&ucirc	Small u, circumflex accent
ü	&#252	&uuml	Small u, umlaut
ý	&#253	&yacute	Small y, acute accent
þ	&#254	&thorn	Small thorn, Icelandic
ÿ	&#255	&yuml	Small y, umlaut

Putting a Document on the World Wide Web

Once you've completed your work on your HTML file, you're probably ready to place it on the World Wide Web for others to see. To make a file available to the World Wide Web, you have to transfer it to a computer connected to the Web called a **Web server**.

Your **Internet Service Provider (ISP)**—the company or institution through which you have Internet access—usually has a Web server available for your use. Because each Internet Service Provider has a different procedure for storing Web pages, you should contact your ISP to learn its policies and procedures. Generally you should be prepared to do the following:

- Extensively test your files under a variety of browsers and under different display conditions. Weed out any errors and design problems before you place the page on the Web.

- If your HTML documents have a three-letter "HTM" extension, rename those files with the four-letter extension "HTML." Some Web servers will require the four-letter extension for all Web pages.

- Check the hyperlinks and inline objects in each of your documents to verify that they point to the correct filenames. Verify the filenames with respect to upper and lower cases. Some Web servers will distinguish between a file named "Image.gif" and one named "image.gif." To be safe, match the uppercase and lowercase letters.

- If your hyperlinks use absolute pathnames, change them to relative pathnames.

- Find out from your ISP the name of the folder into which you'll be placing your HTML documents. You may also need a special user name and password to access this folder.

- Use **FTP**, a program used on the Internet that transfers files, or e-mail to place your pages in the appropriate folder on your Internet Service Provider's Web server. Some Web browsers, like Internet Explorer and Netscape Navigator, have this capability built in, allowing you to transfer your files with a click of a toolbar button.

- Decide on a name for your site on the World Wide Web (such as "http://www.jackson_electronics.com"). Choose a name that will be easy for customers and interested parties to remember and return to.

- If you select a special name for your Web site, you may have to register it. Registration information can be found at http://www.internic.net. This is a service your ISP may also provide for a fee. Registration is necessary to ensure that any name you give to your site is unique and not already in use by another party. Usually you will have to pay a yearly fee to keep control of a special name for your Web site.

- Add your site to the indexes of search pages on the World Wide Web. This is not required, but it will make it easier for people to find your site. Each search facility has different policies regarding adding information about Web sites to its index. Be aware that some will charge a fee to include your Web site in their list.

Once you've completed these steps, your work will be available on the World Wide Web in a form that is easy for users to find and access.

HTML Tags and Properties

The following is a list of the major HTML tags and properties. The three columns at the right indicate the earliest HTML, Netscape, and Internet Explorer versions that supported these tags. For example, a version number of "3.0" for Internet Explorer indicates that versions of Internet Explorer 3.0 *and above* will support the tag or attribute. Both opening and closing tags are displayed where they are required (e.g., <TABLE> … </TABLE>). A single tag means that no closing tag is needed.

You can view more detailed information about the latest HTML specifications at *http://www.w3.org*. Additional information about browser support for different HTML tags is available at *http://www.htmlcompendium.org/*.

Because the World Wide Web is in a constant state of change, you should check this information against the current browser versions.

Properties are of the following types.

- *Color* A recognized color name or color value
- *Document* The filename or URL of a file
- *List* List of items separated by commas; usually enclosed in double quotes
- *Options* Limited to a specific set of values (values are shown below the property)
- *Text* Any text string
- *URL* The URL for a Web page or file
- *Value* A number, usually an integer

TAGS AND PROPERTIES	DESCRIPTION	HTML	NETSCAPE	IE
Block-Formatting Tags	Block-formatting tags are used to format the appearance of large blocks of text			
<ADDRESS> … </ADDRESS>	The <ADDRESS> tag is used for information such as addresses and authorship. The text is usually italicized, and in some browsers it is indented.	2.0	1.0	1.0

TAGS AND PROPERTIES	DESCRIPTION	HTML	NETSCAPE	IE
<BASEFONT>	The <BASEFONT> tag specifies the default font size, in points, for text in the document. The default value is 3.	3.2	1.0	2.0
SIZE=*Value*	*Value* is the size (in points) of the text font.	3.2	1.1	2.0
<BLOCKQUOTE> ...</BLOCKQUOTE>	The <BLOCKQUOTE> tag is used to set off long quotes or citations, usually by indenting the enclosed text on both sides. Some browsers italicize the text as well.	2.0	1.0	2.0
 	The tag forces a line break in the text.	2.0	1.0	2.0
CLEAR=*Option* (LEFT | RIGHT | ALL | NONE)	Causes the next line to start at the spot in which the specified margin is clear.	3.0	1.0	2.0
<CENTER> ... </CENTER>	The <CENTER> tag centers the enclosed text or image horizontally.	3.2	1.1	2.0
<DFN> ... </DFN>	The <DFN> tag is used for the defining instance of a term, i.e., the first time the term is used. The enclosed text is usually italicized.	2.0		2.0

TAGS AND PROPERTIES	DESCRIPTION	HTML	NETSCAPE	IE
<DIV> ... </DIV>	The <DIV> tag is to set the text alignment of blocks of text or images. Supported by older browsers, it has been made obsolete by newer tags.	3.0	2.0	3.0
<HR>	The <HR> tag creates a horizontal line.	1.0	1.0	2.0
ALIGN=*Option* (LEFT | CENTER | RIGHT)	Alignment of the horizontal line. The default is CENTER.	3.2	1.1	2.0
COLOR=*Color*	Specifies a color for the line.			3.0
NOSHADE	Removes 3-D shading from the line.	3.0	1.1	3.0
SIZE=*Value*	The size (height) of the line in pixels.	3.2	1.1	2.0
WIDTH=*Value*	The width (length) of the line either in pixels or as a percentage of the display area.	3.2	1.1	2.0
<H1> ... </H1> <H2> ... </H2> <H3> ... </H3> <H4> ... </H4> <H5> ... </H5> <H6> ... </H6>	The six levels of text headings, ranging from the largest (<H1>) to the smallest (<H6>). Text headings appear in a boldface font	1.0	1.0	1.0
ALIGN=*Option* (LEFT | RIGHT | CENTER)	The alignment of the heading.	3.0	4.0	2.0
<LISTING> ... </LISTING>	The <LISTING> tag displays text in a fixed-width font resembling a typewriter or computer printout. This tag has been rendered obsolete by some newer tags.	2.0	1.0	3.0

TAGS AND PROPERTIES	DESCRIPTION	HTML	NETSCAPE	IE
\<NOBR\> ... \</NOBR\>	The \<NOBR\> tag prevents line breaks for the enclosed text. This tag is not often used.		1.1	2.0
\<P\> ... \</P\>	The \<P\> tag defines the beginning and ending of a paragraph of text.	1.0	1.0	1.0
ALIGN=*Option* (LEFT | CENTER | RIGHT)	The alignment of the text in the paragraph.	1.0	1.1	3.0
\<PLAINTEXT\> ... \</PLAINTEXT\>	The \<PLAINTEXT\> tag displays text in a fixed-width font. An obsolete tag that authors should avoid using, it is supported by some earlier versions of Netscape, but in an erratic way.	2.0	4.0	2.0
\<PRE\> ... \</PRE\>	The \<PRE\> tag retains the preformatted appearance of the text in the HTML file, including any line breaks or spaces. Text is usually displayed in a fixed-width font.	1.0	1.0	1.0
\<WBR\> ... \</WBR\>	The \<WBR\> tag overrides other tags that may preclude the creation of line breaks and directs the browser to insert a line break if necessary. Used in conjunction with the \<NOBR\> tag. This tag is not often used.		1.1	2.0
\<XMP\> ... \</XMP\>	The \<XMP\> tag displays blocks of text in a fixed-width font. The tag is obsolete and should not be used.	3.2	4.0	5.0

TAGS AND PROPERTIES	DESCRIPTION	HTML	NETSCAPE	IE
Character Tags	Character tags modify the appearance of individual characters, words, or sentences to distinguish them from the surrounding text. Character tags usually appear nested within block-formatting tags.			
<ABBR> ... </ABBR>	The <ABBR> tag indicates text in an abbreviated form (e.g., WWW, HTTP, and URL).	4.0		
<ACRONYM> ... </ACRONYM>	The <ACRONYM> tag indicates a text acronym (e.g., WAC, radar).	4.0		4.0
<B> ... </B>	The <B> tag displays the enclosed text in boldface type.	1.0	1.0	1.0
<BIG> ... </BIG>	The <BIG> tag increases the size of the enclosed text. The exact appearance of the text depends on the browser and the default font size.	3.0	2.0	3.0
<BLINK> ... </BLINK>	The <BLINK> tag causes the enclosed text to blink on and off.		1.0	
<CITE> ... </CITE>	The <CITE> tag is used for citations. The enclosed text is usually displayed in italics.	1.0	1.0	2.0

TAGS AND PROPERTIES	DESCRIPTION	HTML	NETSCAPE	IE
<CODE> ... </CODE>	The <CODE> tag is used for text taken from the code for a computer program. It is usually displayed in a fixed-width font.	1.0	1.0	1.0
<EM> ... </EM>	The <EM> tag is used to emphasize text. The enclosed text is usually displayed in italics.	1.0	1.0	2.0
<FONT> ... </FONT>	The <FONT> tag is used to control the appearance of the text it encloses.	3.0	1.1	2.0
COLOR=*Color*	The color of the enclosed text.	3.0	2.0	2.0
FACE=*List*	The font face of the text. Multiple font faces can be specified, separated by commas. The browser will try to render the text in the order specified by the list.	3.0	3.0	2.0
SIZE=*Value*	Size of the font in points. It can be absolute or relative. Specifying SIZE=5 sets the font size to 5 points. Specifying SIZE=+5 sets the font size 5 points larger than that specified in the <BASEFONT> tag.	3.0	4.0	2.0
<I> ... </I>	The <I> tag italicizes the enclosed text.	1.0	1.0	1.0
<KBD> ... </KBD>	The <KBD> tag is used for text made to appear as if it came from a typewriter or keyboard. Text is displayed with a fixed-width font.	1.0	1.0	2.0

TAGS AND PROPERTIES	DESCRIPTION	HTML	NETSCAPE	IE
<SAMP> ... </SAMP>	The <SAMP> tag displays text in a fixed-width font.	1.0	1.0	2.0
<SMALL> ... </SMALL>	The <SMALL> tag decreases the size of the enclosed text. The exact appearance of the text depends on the browser and the default font size.	3.0	2.0	3.0
<STRIKE> ... </STRIKE>	The <STRIKE> tag displays the enclosed text with a horizontal line through it. (*Note:* future revisions to HTML may phase out STRIKE in favor of the more concise S tag from HTML 3.0.)	3.2	3.0	2.0
<STRONG> ... </STRONG>	The <STRONG> tag is used to strongly emphasize the enclosed text, usually in a boldface font.	1.0	1.0	1.0
_{...}	The <SUB> tag displays the enclosed text as a subscript.	1.0	2.0	3.0
^{...}	The <SUP> tag displays the enclosed text as a superscript.	1.0	2.0	3.0
<TT> ... </TT>	The <TT> tag displays text in a fixed-width, teletype-style font.	1.0	1.0	1.0

TAGS AND PROPERTIES	DESCRIPTION	HTML	NETSCAPE	IE
<U> ... </U>	The <U> tag underlines the enclosed text. The <U> tag should be avoided because users may confuse the underlined text with hypertext, which is typically underlined.	1.0	3.0	2.0
<VAR> ... </VAR>	The <VAR> tag is used for text that represents a variable and is usually displayed in italics.	1.0	1.1	1.0

Document Tags

Document tags are tags that specify the structure of the HTML file or control its operations and interactions with the Web server.

TAGS AND PROPERTIES	DESCRIPTION	HTML	NETSCAPE	IE
<!>	The <!> tag is used for comments that document the features of your HTML file.	1.0	1.0	1.0
<BASE>	The <BASE> tag allows you to specify the URL for the HTML document. It is used by some browsers to interpret relative hyperlinks.	1.0	1.0	2.0
HREF=*URL*	Specifies the URL that forms the base for all relative hyperlinks.	1.0	4.0	2.0
TARGET=*Text*	Specifies the default target window or frame for every hyperlink in the document.	4.0	2.0	3.0

TAGS AND PROPERTIES	DESCRIPTION	HTML	NETSCAPE	IE
<BODY> ... </BODY>	The <BODY> tag encloses all text, images, and other elements that will be visible to the user on the Web page.	1.0	1.0	1.0
ALINK=Color	Color of activated hypertext links, which are links that have been clicked by a user who has not yet released the mouse button.	1.0	1.1	2.0
BACKGROUND=Document	The graphic image file used for the Web page background.	1.0	1.1	2.0
BGCOLOR=Color	The color of the Web page background.	3.2	1.1	2.0
BGPROPERTIES=FIXED	Keeps the background image fixed so that it does not scroll with the Web page.			2.0
LEFTMARGIN=Value	Indents the left margin of the page by the number of pixels specified in value.			2.0
LINK=Color	Color of all unvisited links.	1.0	1.1	2.0
TEXT=Color	Color of all text in the document.	1.0	1.1	2.0
TOPMARGIN=Value	Indents the top margin of the page by the number of pixels specified in value.			2.0
VLINK=Color	Color of previously visited links.	1.0	1.1	2.0
<HEAD> ... </HEAD>	The <HEAD> tag encloses code that provides information about the document.	1.0	1.0	1.0

TAGS AND PROPERTIES	DESCRIPTION	HTML	NETSCAPE	IE
<HTML> ... </HTML>	The <HTML> tag indicates the beginning and end of the HTML document.	1.0	1.0	1.0
<ISINDEX>	The <ISINDEX> tag identifies the file as a searchable document.	1.0	1.0	2.0
ACTION=*CGI Program*	Sends the submitted text to the program identified by *CGI Program*.			2.0
PROMPT=*Text*	The text that should be placed before the index's text-input field.	3.0	1.1	2.0
<LINK>	The <LINK> tag specifies the relationship between the document and other objects.	1.0	3.0	2.0
HREF=*URL*	The URL of the <LINK> tag hotlinks the user to the specified document.	1.0	4.0	2.0
ID=*Text*	The file, URL, or text that acts as a hypertext link to another document.	1.0	3.0	3.0
REL=*URL*	Directs the browser to link forward to the next page in the document.	1.0	4.0	2.0
REV=*URL*	Directs the browser to go back to the previous link in the document.	2.0		2.0
TITLE=*Text*	The title of the document named in the link.	1.0		2.0
<META>	The <META> tag is used to insert information about the document not defined by other HTML tags and properties. It can include special instructions for the Web server to perform.	1.0	1.0	1.0

TAGS AND PROPERTIES	DESCRIPTION	HTML	NETSCAPE	IE
CONTENT=*Text*	Contains information associated with the NAME or HTTP-EQUIV properties.	1.0	1.1	2.0
HTTP-EQUIV=*Text*	Directs the browser to request the server to perform different HTTP operations.	2.0	1.1	2.0
NAME=*Text*	The type of information specified in the CONTENT property.	2.0	1.1	2.0
<TITLE> … </TITLE>	The <TITLE> tag is used to specify the text that appears in the Web browser's title bar.	2.0	1.1	2.0

Graphic and Link Tags

Graphic and link tags are used for hypertext links and inline images.

TAGS AND PROPERTIES	DESCRIPTION	HTML	NETSCAPE	IE
<A> … </A>	The <A> tag marks the beginning and end of a hypertext link.	1.0	1.0	1.0
HREF=*URL*	Indicates the target, filename, or URL that the hypertext points to.	1.0	1.0	1.0
NAME=*Text*	Specifies a name for the enclosed text, allowing it to be a target of a hyperlink.	1.0	1.0	2.0
REL=*Text*	Specifies the relationship between the current page and the link specified by the HREF property.	1.0		2.0
REV=*Text*	Specifies a reverse relationship between the current page and the link specified by the HREF property.	1.0		2.0
TABINDEX=*Value*	Specifies the tab order in the form.	4.0		4.0

TAGS AND PROPERTIES	DESCRIPTION	HTML	NETSCAPE	IE
TARGET=*Text*	Specifies the default target window or frame for the hyperlink.	4.0	1.0	3.0
TITLE=*Text*	Provides a title for the document whose address is given by the HREF property.	1.0		2.0
<AREA>	The <AREA> tag defines the type and coordinates of a hotspot within an image map.	3.2	1.0	2.0
COORDS=*Value 1, value 2…*	The coordinates of the hotspot. The coordinates depend upon the shape of the hotspot: Rectangle: COORDS=*x_left, y_upper, x_right, y_lower* Circle: COORDS= *x_center, y_center, radius* Polygon: COORDS= $x_1, y_1, x_2, y_2, x_3, y_3, …$	3.2	1.0	2.0
HREF=*URL*	Indicates the target, filename, or URL that the hotspot points to.	3.2	1.0	2.0
SHAPE=*Option* (RECT | CIRCLE | POLY)	The shape of the hotspot.	3.2	1.0	2.0
TABINDEX=*Value*	Specifies the tab order in the form.	4.0		4.0
TARGET=*Text*	Specifies the default target window or frame for the hotspot.	4.0	2.0	3.0
<IMG>	The <IMG> tag is used to insert an inline image into the document.	1.0	1.0	2.0

TAGS AND PROPERTIES	DESCRIPTION	HTML	NETSCAPE	IE
ALIGN=*Option* (LEFT | RIGHT | TOP | TEXTTOP | MIDDLE | ABSMIDDLE | BASELINE | BOTTOM | ABSBOTTOM)	Specifies the alignment of the image. Specifying an alignment of LEFT or RIGHT aligns the image with the left or right page margin. The other alignment options align the image with surrounding text.	1.0	1.1	2.0
ALT=*Text*	Text to display if the image cannot be displayed by the browser.	2.0	1.1	2.0
BORDER=*Value*	The size of the border around the image, in pixels.	3.2	1.1	2.0
CONTROLS	Displays VCR-like controls under moving images. Used in conjunction with the DYNSRC property.			2.0
DYNSRC=*Document*	Specifies the file of a video, AVI clip, or VRML world displayed inside the page.			2.0
HEIGHT=*Value*	The height of the image, in pixels.	3.0	1.1	2.0
HSPACE=*Value*	The amount of space to the left and right of the image, in pixels.	3.0	1.1	2.0
ISMAP	Identifies the graphic as an image map. For use with server-side image maps.	3.0	2.0	2.0
LOOP=*Value*	Specifies the number of times a moving image should be played. The value must be either a digit or INFINITE.			2.0
LOWSRC=*Document*	A low-resolution version of the graphic that the browser should initially display before loading the high-resolution version.		1.0	4.0
SRC=*Document*	The source file of the inline image	1.0	1.0	2.0
START=*Item* (FILEOPEN | MOUSEOVER)	Tells the browser when to start displaying a moving image file. FILEOPEN directs the browser to start when the file is open. MOUSEOVER directs the browser to start when the mouse moves over the image.			2.0

TAGS AND PROPERTIES	DESCRIPTION	HTML	NETSCAPE	IE
USEMAP=#Map_Namet	Identifies the graphic as an image map and specifies the name of the image map definition to use with the graphic. For use with client-side image maps.	3.2	2.0	2.0
VSPACE=Value	The amount of space above and below the image, in pixels.	3.2	1.1	2.0
WIDTH=Value	The width of the image, in pixels.	3.0	1.1	2.0
<MAP> ... </MAP>	The <MAP> tag specifies information about a client-side image map. (Note: It must enclose <AREA> tags.)	3.2	1.0	2.0
NAME=Text	The name of the image map.	3.2	2.0	2.0

List Tags

	List tags are used to create a variety of different kinds of lists			
<DD>	The <DD> tag formats text to be used as relative definitions in a<DL> list.	1.0	1.0	2.0
<DIR> ... </DIR>	The <DIR> tag encloses an unordered list of <LI> items, formatted in narrow columns.	1.0	1.0	2.0
TYPE=Option (CIRCLE I DISK I SQUARE)	Specifies the type of bullet used for displaying each <LI> item in the <DIR> list.		2.0	

TAGS AND PROPERTIES	DESCRIPTION	HTML	NETSCAPE	IE
<DL> ... </DL>	The <DL> tag encloses a definition list in which the <DD> definition term is left-aligned and the <DT> relative definition is indented.	1.0	1.0	2.0
<DT>	The <DT> tag is used to format the definition term in a <DL> list.	1.0	1.0	2.0
<LI>	The <LI> tag identifies list items in a <DIR>, <MENU>, <OL>, or <UL> list.	1.0	1.0	2.0
<MENU> ... </MENU>	The <MENU> tag encloses an unordered list of items, similar to a <UL> or <DIR> list.	1.0	1.0	2.0
<OL> ... </OL>	The <OL> tag encloses an ordered list of <LI> items. Typically, ordered lists are rendered as numbered lists.	1.0	1.0	1.0
START=*Value*	The value of the starting number in the ordered list.	3.2	2.0	2.0
TYPE=*Option* (A l a l I l i l 1)	Specifies how ordered items are to be marked. A = uppercase letters. a = lowercase letters. I = uppercase Roman numerals. i = lowercase Roman numerals. 1 = Digits. The default is 1.	3.2	2.0	2.0

TAGS AND PROPERTIES	DESCRIPTION	HTML	NETSCAPE	IE
<UL>	The <UL> tag encloses an unordered list of <LI> items. Typically, unordered lists are rendered as bulleted lists.	1.0	1.0	1.0
Type=*Option* (CIRCLE | DISK | SQUARE)	Specifies the type of bullet used for displaying each <LI> item in the <UL> list.	3.2	2.0	

New Perspectives on

THE INTERNET

2ⁿᵈ Edition

EUDORA

Eudora E-Mail Client

Eudora is an e-mail client program that runs on your computer, either a Windows or a Macintosh operating system, and communicates with the mail server that is on the Internet. You can use Eudora only if you are connected directly to the Internet on a university network (usually in a lab) or have a PPP or SLIP connection through an Internet service provider (ISP).

Qualcomm, the company that publishes Eudora, offers a free, downloadable version of Eudora, called Eudora Light, on its Web site. You can download the free version of Eudora Light to complete these steps, or your school might have the complete Eudora Pro package installed in the lab. (The steps will be slightly different depending on which version of Eudora Light you are using, but they should work the same.) A link to the Qualcomm Corporation home page appears in the Student Online Companion Web page for Appendix E.

Note: The steps in this appendix assume that you have read and understand Session 2.1 in Tutorial 2, which covers introductory e-mail concepts.

To start and initialize Eudora for use on a public computer:

1. Click the **Start** button on the taskbar, point to **Programs**, point to **Eudora Pro**, and then click **Eudora Pro**. Eudora starts on your computer.

   TROUBLE? If you do not see Eudora Pro on your Programs menu, then Eudora is not installed on your computer, or it is installed in a different location. Ask your instructor or technical support person for help.

   TROUBLE? If a Note dialog box opens and asks if you want to change Eudora to your default mail program, click the No button.

   TROUBLE? If the Tip of the Day dialog box opens, click the Close button to close it.

   TROUBLE? If the New Account Wizard dialog box opens, click the Cancel button to close it.

2. Click **Tools** on the menu bar, and then click **Options** to open the Options dialog box. If necessary, click the **Getting Started** category button to display the start-up options.

   TROUBLE? If you are using Eudora Light, your steps might differ. Ask your instructor or technical support person for help.

3. Click in the Real name text box, and then type your first and last name, separated by a space.

   TROUBLE? If your account information already appears in the Options dialog box, skip to Step 8.

4. Press the **Tab** key to move to the Return address text box, and then type your full e-mail address (such as barbgoldberg@yahoo.com).

5. Press the **Tab** key to move to the Mail Server (Incoming) text box, and then type the address of your incoming mail server. Usually, the mail server address is the word *mail* or *pop*, followed by a period, and then the remainder of your domain address (such as pop.yahoo.com). Ask your instructor or technical support person for the correct incoming mail server name to use.

6. Press the **Tab** key to move to the Login Name text box, and then type your login name, which is the same as your username or user ID. Type only your login name (such as barbgoldberg), and not the domain name. See Figure E-1.

Figure E-1 ACCOUNT INFORMATION FOR BARBARA GOLDBERG

7. Press the Tab key to move to the SMTP Server (Outgoing) text box, and then type the address of your outgoing mail server. Usually, the mail server address is the word *mail* or *smtp* followed by a period, and then the remainder of your domain address (such as mail.yahoo.com). Ask your instructor or technical support person for the correct outgoing mail server name to use.

8. Click the **Checking Mail** category button.

9. Click the **Save password** check box, if necessary, to clear it. Clearing the Save password check box prevents Eudora from remembering your password so other users on this computer cannot access your account information after you exit the program.

10. Click the **Incoming Mail** category button.

11. Click the **Leave mail on server** check box, if necessary, to place a check mark in it. When checked, any mail you download and read also stays on the main server so you can reread the mail from **any** computer. If you leave the Leave mail on server check box cleared, then the mail is deleted the first time you read your mail on any PC. It is available only on the original PC on which you read it.

12. Click the **OK** button to save the new settings and close the Options dialog box.

Now, you have created your user account. If you are using a public computer, you can click the Forget Password(s) command on the Special menu to erase your password so no one can use it to access your e-mail account.

Creating a Message in Eudora

You use the **Composition window**, which includes a title bar, toolbar, the message header, and the message body, to send a message.

The title bar first displays the text "No Recipient, No Subject" until you enter information into the message. The title bar then displays the recipient's e-mail address and the subject of the message. The Composition window toolbar includes buttons that allow quick access to many message features, such as the priority (importance) of your message, text styles, and the ability to send your message.

The message header in the Composition window contains the To, From, Subject, Cc, Bcc, and Attached lines. The message body appears below the message header, and it contains your message.

To send a message using Eudora:

1. Click the **New Message** button on the toolbar. Eudora opens the Composition window.

2. Click the To line, and then type **barbgoldberg@yahoo.com**, which is the recipient's full e-mail address consisting of a user name and domain name separated by the @ sign. Notice that the From line already contains your full e-mail address.

   Note: For these steps, you will send an e-mail message to a real mailbox owned by Barb Goldberg. However, please note that all messages sent to this account are deleted without being read. If you have questions, then you should e-mail your instructor or technical support help at your institution.

3. Press the **Tab** key to move to the Subject line, and then type **Sample Eudora Message**.

4. Press the **Tab** key to move to the Cc line, and then type your full e-mail address so you will receive a copy of the message that you send.

   TROUBLE? If you make a typing mistake, use the arrow keys to move the insertion point to a previous line, or within a line, and then correct the mistake. If the arrow keys do not move the insertion point up or down in the message header, press Shift + Tab or the Tab key to move the insertion point up or down, respectively.

5. Press the **Tab** key twice to move the insertion point to the message body, and then type **Please let me know that you received this message. I am testing the Eudora mail client program.**

6. Press the **Enter** key twice to insert a blank line, and then type your first and last names to sign the message. See Figure E-2.

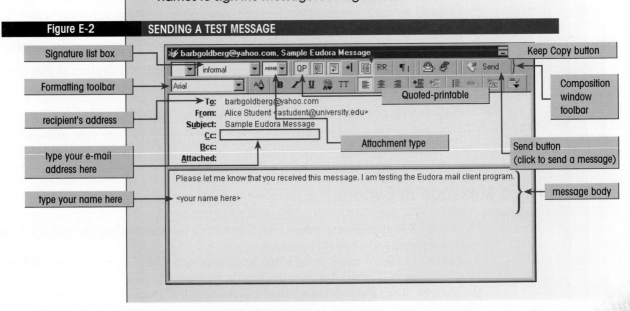

Figure E-2	SENDING A TEST MESSAGE

Now, you can send the message. Be sure to double-check the message body, the recipient's address, and the Cc address to ensure they are correct.

To check your mail send options and send your message:

1. Click **Tools** on the menu bar, and then click **Options** to open the Options dialog box. Click the **Sending Mail** category button to display the options shown in Figure E-3.

Figure E-3   CHECKING SENDING MAIL PREFERENCES

Your message might not be sent to the mail server immediately, depending on how Eudora is configured on your computer. Eudora might queue the message and send it later at your command, or it might send the message when you exit the program. Clicking the Immediate send check box will send mail immediately when you click the Send button. If you clear this check box, then mail will be sent only when you check for incoming mail. You will configure your program to send mail immediately after clicking the Send button.

2. If necessary, click the **Immediate send** check box so it contains a check mark, and then click the **OK** button to close the Options dialog box.

3. Click the **Send** button on the Composition window toolbar to send the message.

Receiving Mail

Eudora can save delivered mail in any of several standard or custom mailboxes on your PC. Depending on your configuration, Eudora periodically communicates with the mail server to see if you have new mail. When you start Eudora, it checks to see if you have any new mail messages. Before Eudora can check for new e-mail, you must enter a password. When you enter your password, asterisks display for each character you type to keep your password hidden. After clicking the OK button, Eudora requests that the mail server deliver your new mail to your PC. Within a few seconds, any new messages appear in the In box and their summary information displays in a window.

To manually check for mail:

1. Click the **Check Mail** button on the Composition window toolbar to retrieve all new mail messages. After a few moments, any new mail messages are transferred to your PC and appear in your In box. See Figure E-4.

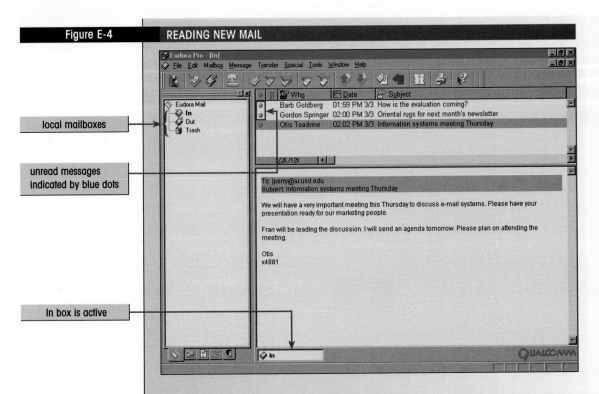

Figure E-4   READING NEW MAIL

TROUBLE? If the Enter Password dialog box opens, type your password in the Password text box, and then click the OK button to continue. If you do not know your password, ask your instructor or technical support person for help.

TROUBLE? If you do not see the In box, double-click the In folder in the left panel of the window to open it.

Notice several features of the In box. Unread messages contain a dot to their left in the message header pane. On the left side of the display is a list of available mailboxes. You can create, delete, or rename mailboxes. Mailboxes let you organize your mail by type; you might create different mail folders to store messages from different individuals or to group messages by project.

You should receive a copy of your **Sample Eudora Message** message when you check for new mail. Wait until you see this message summary line in the upper panel, and then continue with Step 2.

2. Double-click the **Sample Eudora Message** message summary line to open the message into a larger content pane with a title bar, toolbar, and a message body. If the message already appears highlighted, then press the spacebar or the Enter key to open the message.

3. Read the message, and then click the message close button to redisplay the message summary lines. Double-click any other message summary lines you received to read them.

You can save new messages in different mailboxes by right-clicking the message summary line and then clicking Transfer on the shortcut menu. You then click the destination mailbox to move the message to its new location. For now, you will leave the new messages in your In mailbox and close it.

4. Click the **Close** button for the In box window to close it. (Be careful not to click the Eudora application close button, which will close the entire program, not just the In box.)

After you receive new mail, you can leave it in your In box and on the server, or you can treat it like other documents (that is, printing, deleting, or filing it).

Printing **a Message**

To print an e-mail message, select the message summary line that you want to print, click the Print button, and then use the Print dialog box to select the desired print options.

To print an e-mail message:

1. Double-click the **In box** to open it.

2. Click the **Sample Eudora Message** message summary line in the upper panel again, if necessary, to select it. The top few lines of the message appear in the content pane.

3. Click the **Print** button on the toolbar. The Print dialog box opens. You can use this dialog box to change the default printer, the number of copies to print, or the pages to print, if necessary. The default settings are correct, so click the **OK** button to print the message summary line and body.

Your message prints. Now, file the message into a mailbox that you will create.

Filing **a Message**

Eudora mailboxes provide a convenient way to file your e-mail messages by category. If the mailboxes do not appear on the screen, click Mailboxes on the Tools menu. Normally, the Mailboxes window will appear on the left side of the screen. You can move mail from the In mailbox to any other mailbox or folder to file it.

To create a new mailbox:

1. Click **Mailbox** on the menu bar, and then click **New**. The New Mailbox dialog box opens.

2. Type **Marketing** in the Name the new mailbox text box, and then click the **OK** button to create the new Marketing mailbox. When you create a new mailbox, a menu command is also added to the Transfer menu.

3. Click **Transfer** on the menu bar. Notice that →**Marketing** appears on the menu.

4. Press the **Esc** key to close the Transfer menu without taking any action.

After you create the Marketing mailbox, you can transfer mail to it. Besides copying or transferring mail from the In box, you can select and transfer any message to another box. The only difference between transferring a message and copying it is that a transferred message is removed from its original mailbox and is moved to its new location. When you copy a message, it remains in its original mailbox, and a copy is placed in another mailbox. Copying a message is useful when you need to file a message in more than one mailbox.

You also can create a new mailbox and transfer mail to it in one step by selecting New from the Transfer menu and then entering a new mailbox name. After you click the OK button, Eudora automatically transfers the selected messages to the new mailbox.

To transfer a message to a mailbox:

1. If necessary, open your In box by double-clicking the **In** mailbox on the left side of the screen, and then click the **Sample Eudora Message** message summary line to select it.

2. Click **Transfer** on the menu bar (see Figure E-5), and then click →**Marketing**. Eudora transfers the selected message to the Marketing mailbox.

Figure E-5   TRANSFERRING A MESSAGE TO ANOTHER MAILBOX

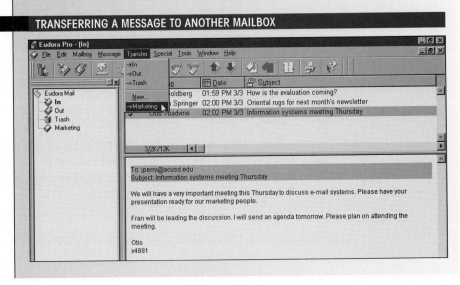

If you transfer one or more messages to the wrong mailbox, you can cancel the transfer by clicking Undo on the Edit menu immediately after the transfer. The Undo command text will reflect the exact transfer and actually be Undo Transfer from In to Marketing.

If you want to copy a message into a separate mailbox, click Transfer on the menu bar, and then hold down the Shift key and click the mailbox name in which to store the copy of the message.

Forwarding **a Message**

You can forward any message that you receive to one or more recipients. To forward an existing mail message to another user, open the mailbox containing the message, select the message, and then click the **Forward** button on the toolbar. Your e-mail address and name automatically appear in the From line of the message header, and the Subject line is amended with the text **Fwd** or **Forward** to indicate that the message is being forwarded. Simply fill in the To line and then click the Send button in the Composition window to send the message.

Replying **to a Message**

When you reply to a message, Eudora automatically formats a new, blank message and addresses it to the sender. To reply to a message, select a message in any mailbox, and then click the **Reply** button on the toolbar. Eudora will open a new message window and place the original sender's address in the To line and your address in the From line. You can leave the Subject line as is or modify it.

Deleting **a Message**

To prevent you from inadvertently deleting important messages, Eudora requires you to complete two steps to delete a message from your PC. First, you temporarily delete a message by placing it in the Trash, which is a special mailbox on your system. You then permanently delete a message by emptying the trash.

To delete a message and a mailbox:

1. Double-click the **Marketing** mailbox to open it, and then click the **Sample Eudora Message** message summary line in your Marketing mailbox to select it. You can select more than one message by holding down the Ctrl key and then clicking each message's summary line.

2. Click the **Delete Message(s)** button on the toolbar. You also can press the Delete key to delete selected message(s). The deleted message is sent to the Trash mailbox.

   TROUBLE? If you accidentally send a message to the Trash mailbox, double-click the Trash mailbox folder to open it, select the message that you need to restore, click Transfer on the menu bar, and then click →In. The message is transferred to your In mailbox, where you can access it and file it into another folder as necessary.

3. Repeat Steps 1 and 2 to delete any other messages that you received or filed during this session.

4. Right-click the **Marketing** mailbox, and then click **Delete** on the shortcut menu to delete the Marketing mailbox that you created.

5. To delete all messages in the Trash mailbox and permanently remove them from your PC, click **Special** on the menu bar and then click **Empty Trash**. Click **Yes** to empty the trash. After you empty the trash, you cannot recover the deleted messages.

Even after you delete a message, the deleted message still occupies space. Normally, Eudora recovers this space automatically. However, you can force this space recovery to happen by clicking the Compact Mailboxes command on the Special menu.

You can set up Eudora to warn you whenever you are about to transfer unread, queued, or unsent messages to the Trash mailbox. If you hear a warning sound or see a warning message box when you attempt to empty the Trash mailbox, check to make sure you have read all the messages before permanently deleting them. When Eudora finds unread mail in the Trash mailbox, the mailbox name appears in bold type. If this occurs, open the Trash mailbox and read any bolded messages.

Maintaining **an Address Book**

You can use an address book to create individual and group addresses.

To create an address book entry:

1. Click the **Address Book** button on the toolbar to open the Address Book window.

2. Click the **New** button in the left panel of the Address Book window.

3. Type your first name in the What do you wish to call it? text box in the New Nickname dialog box, and then click the **OK** button.

4. Click the **Address(es)** tab, and then type your e-mail address in the large panel on the right.

5. Click the **Info** tab, and then type your first and last names in the Name text box.

6. Click **File** on the menu bar, and then click **Save** to save the new entry.

7. Click the **Close** button on the Address Book title bar. The Address Book closes.

When you want to send a message to someone listed in your address book, you can type that person's nickname or his or her full name, and Eudora will address the message automatically.

You also can use Eudora to create a distribution list (or a group mailing list). A distribution list is a single nickname that represents more than one individual e-mail address. To create a distribution list, open the address book, click the New button, type the list's nickname in the New Nickname text box, click the OK button, click the Addresses tab, and then type the e-mail addresses for each person in the group and separate them with a comma. To save your list, click File on the menu bar, and then click Save.

You also can create individual nicknames for everyone on the distribution list, and then use each person's nickname, and *not* his or her individual e-mail address, to create the distribution list. That way, if a person's e-mail address changes, you can change it in one place so all the distribution lists that include that person's e-mail address will be updated automatically. This technique is the best way to enter distribution list names in the address book.

Exiting Eudora

Before you leave the computer on which you are working, be sure to exit Eudora. If you are using a public computer, it is *very* important to erase your name and account from selected Eudora text boxes.

To erase your name and account from Eudora text boxes:

1. Click **Tools** on the menu bar, and then click **Options**. The Options dialog box opens.

2. Click the **Getting Started** icon, and then drag your mouse pointer across the Real name text to select it.

3. Press the **Delete** key to erase the contents of the text box.

4. Repeat Steps 2 and 3 for the Return address text box and for the Login Name text box.

5. Click the **OK** button to save your changes and close the Options dialog box.

After deleting your personal information, you can exit Eudora.

To exit Eudora:

1. Click **File** on the menu bar, and then click **Exit**. Eudora closes.

PINE

Pine E-Mail Client

Pine, or **Program for Internet News and E-mail**, is a popular e-mail client program developed for UNIX computers. It is also available on Windows 95/98 PCs. Originally, Pine was conceived and developed by the University of Washington in Seattle in 1989 as a simple mailer that runs on minicomputers. Since then, Pine has been refined and improved for use on the PC. Pine has a simple character-based interface that is easy to learn and use. It also is one of the most widely used e-mail programs in colleges and universities. Because you are likely to use Pine at your school, it is helpful to understand how to use it.

Using Pine to Send a Message

Your instructor or technical support person will give you specific instructions for starting the Pine program on your system. Normally, you log on to a computer system with your user name and password, and then you type "pine" on UNIX-based systems to start it. After starting the program, the Pine Main Menu window appears, as shown in Figure F-1. The first line indicates the Pine version number, screen name, and other useful information, such as the current folder and the number of new messages. The main part of the Pine window is the work area, and the message and prompt line appear at the bottom of the window. Menu commands for using Pine appear as the last two lines on the screen.

Figure F-1	PINE MAIN MENU

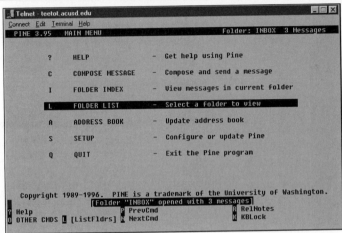

The Main Menu window is the starting point for all Pine e-mail activities. You can use the Main Menu window to seek help, compose and send a message, read incoming mail, manage your mail folders, maintain an address book, perform Pine system setup activities, and exit the Pine program. Every action in Pine springs from one or two keystrokes—the mouse is of little use while you are using Pine.

The first screen Pine displays should look similar to Figure F-1. The key you type to invoke any of the menu commands appears to the left of each option or command name. You can type either uppercase or lowercase letters. However, do *not* press the Enter key after typing a menu command key. You will send a message next.

Note: The steps in this appendix assume that you have read and understand Session 2.1 in Tutorial 2, which covers introductory e-mail concepts.

To create a message:

1. Start Pine, and then if necessary, type **M** to go to the Main Menu window.

   TROUBLE? If you press the Enter key after typing a menu command key (such as M), an error will occur. Do not press the Enter key after typing menu command keys.

2. Type **C** to open the Compose Message window.

3. Type **barbgoldberg@yahoo.com** on the To line. Press the **Enter** key to move to the Cc line.

Note: For these steps, you will send an e-mail message to a real mailbox. However, please note that all messages sent to the barbgoldberg account are deleted without being read.

TROUBLE? If you make a typing mistake, use the arrow keys to move the insertion point to the character following the one that you need to delete, and then press the Backspace key to delete the character. The Delete key sometimes does not work on character-based systems.

4. Type your full e-mail address on the Cc line, and then press the **Enter** key. You won't send an attachment with your message, so press the **Enter** key again to go to the Subject line.

5. Type **Sample Pine Message** in the Subject line, and then press the **Enter** key to move to the Message Text line.

6. Type the simple message **I am using Pine to compose and send this e-mail message.**

7. Press the **Enter** key twice to move down two lines in the message body.

8. Type your first and last names to sign your message. See Figure F-2.

Figure F-2	SENDING A MESSAGE WITH PINE

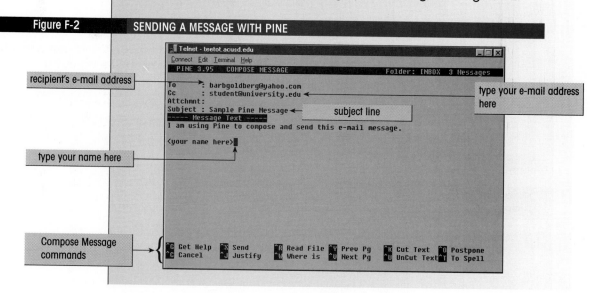

Notice the commands at the bottom of the Compose Message window. The command ^X stands for Ctrl + X, which sends the message.

Once you are satisfied that the message is complete—check the recipient's e-mail address—and that the message body is correct, then you can send the message.

To send the message:

1. With the Compose Message window still open, press **Ctrl + X**. A prompt line asks if you want to send the message.

2. Type **Y** to send the message. The message is sent to the recipient(s), and the Compose Message window closes.

When you need to send the same message to several people, type all of the e-mail addresses in the To line and separate them with commas.

Pine is different from other e-mail clients because it sends mail immediately without queuing it first. Your only opportunity to cancel sending a message is to type N at the prompt when asked to send the message. If you want to cancel your message, press Ctrl + C. Pine asks you to confirm the cancel operation with a prompt beginning with "Cancel message…". Confirm you want to cancel the message by typing C. Pine closes the Compose Message window.

Using Pine to Receive Mail

Pine helps manage your mail by saving messages in a folder. Pine supplies several folders including those named INBOX, received, and sent. The INBOX folder holds all unread received mail. The sent mailbox holds mail you have sent, and the received folder holds mail you have received and read. You can add folders at any time and name them anything you want.

Mail arrives at the server, and Pine retrieves it. Pine does not always signal you when new mail arrives if you are using Pine, so check your mail regularly so you don't miss important messages while you are online.

To read new mail messages using Pine:

1. If necessary, type **M** to open the Main Menu window.

2. Type **I** to open the INBOX folder. The Folder Index window shows new and read messages and messages that are marked for deletion. See Figure F-3.

Figure F-3 | FOLDER INDEX WINDOW

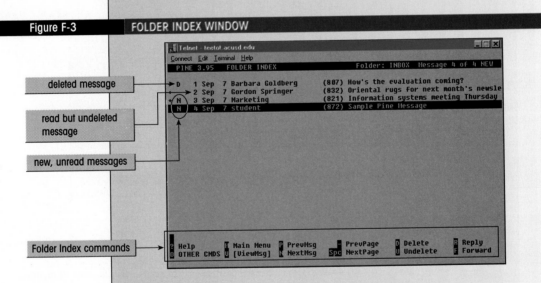

deleted message

read but undeleted message

new, unread messages

Folder Index commands

Examine Figure F-3 carefully. Each message in the INBOX is numbered. The letters to the left of each message number in the INBOX indicate something about the status of each message. The first message has a "D" indicator, which means that you have read and marked the message for deletion. The second message has no indicator to its left, which indicates that you have read the message but not deleted it. The last two messages shown in Figure F-3 have an "N" status indicator, which indicates the messages are both new and that you have not read them yet.

3. Your Sample Pine Message should be selected—if it is not, use the arrow keys to select it, and then press the **Enter** key to open the selected message summary in its own window. The message opens so you can read its contents. See Figure F-4.

| Figure F-4 | READING A MESSAGE |

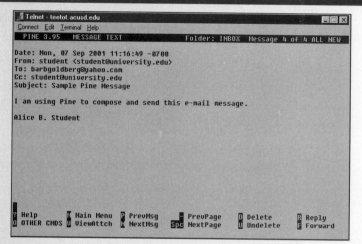

After you read a message, you have many options. For now, you will exit Pine.

4. Type **Q** to quit Pine. The message "Really quit pine?" appears near the bottom of the display.

5. Type **Y** to confirm your intent to leave Pine. The message "Save the 1 read message in "received"?" appears in the message line near the bottom of the display. (Your message might be different.)

6. Type **Y** to save the message you just read in the received folder. The message "Expunge the 1 deleted message from the "INBOX"?" appears. The deleted message is the one you just read.

7. Type **Y** to remove the message from the INBOX permanently. Pine closes, and you return to the system from which you invoked Pine.

Keep in mind a subtle point. Pine stores received messages in the INBOX. Messages remain in the INBOX until you delete them or save them in another folder. That is why Pine deletes the message that you moved to the received folder. Had you chosen *not* to send the message you read in the received folder, then Pine would automatically remove it from the INBOX. Pine removes the "N" status mark from messages you have read but have not yet moved to other folders. These messages remain in the INBOX.

Printing a Message Using Pine

Pine provides three options for printing messages. The first option assumes you have a printer attached to your computer or workstation, whereas another assumes you are using a standard UNIX workstation. Use this option if you are using a dial-up connection to a remote host computer running Pine. The last option provides printing using a predefined print command. Ask your instructor or technical support person for help using this option. If you are using Pine in a university computer lab, the best option is to print to a network printer. Ask your lab administrator to help check your printer setup before you print your e-mail.

To print a message using Pine:

1. Start Pine, and then type **I** to open the Folder Index window and the INBOX.

2. Use the Up and Down arrow keys to select the Sample Pine Message summary line.

3. Press the **Enter** key if you want to open the message to check its contents before printing. (You do not need to open a message in order to print it.)

4. Type **Y** to print the message. The message "Print message <#> using" followed by the printer selection appears on the message line.

   TROUBLE? The print command might not be visible on the first screen of menu commands. Type OK to see other commands in the command lines at the screen's bottom edge.

5. Type **Y** to print the message. If you need to cancel the print operation, either press Ctrl + C or type N for no. Either choice cancels the print command.

6. Type **Q** to quit pine. Respond appropriately to any messages that appear in the message line as you are leaving Pine.

Filing a Pine Message

You can organize your e-mail into different folders by topic, date, or any other category that makes sense to you. Pine even helps keep your INBOX organized chronologically. At the end of every month, Pine prompts you about your folders holding sent mail. Pine first asks if you want to rename your current sent folder. Doing so preserves that month's messages in a uniquely named folder. Second, Pine asks if you want to delete the previous month's sent mail folders and the current month's sent mail folder. You can choose to respond no by typing N to any question or yes by typing Y.

To view your current folders, type L in the Pine Main Menu window. At least three mail folder names appear. They are INBOX, received, and sent. You can move mail from any folder to any other folder. You also can create any new folders you would like and call them any name except an existing folder's name.

To create a new Pine folder:

1. Start Pine and type **L** (ListFldrs) in the Main Menu window to open the Folder List window.

2. Type **A** to add a folder. The prompt "Name of folder to add:" appears at the bottom of the screen.

3. Type **Marketing** to name the new folder, and then press the **Enter** key. Pine creates a new folder and selects it. See Figure F-5.

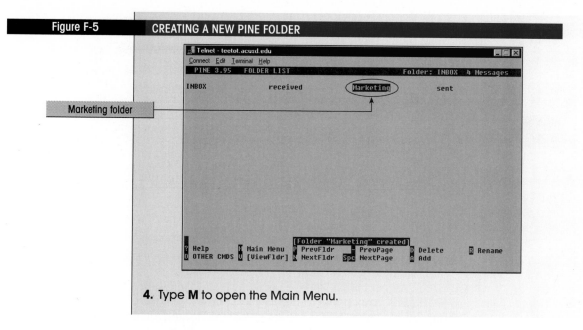

Figure F-5 CREATING A NEW PINE FOLDER

Marketing folder

4. Type **M** to open the Main Menu.

After creating the Marketing folder, you can save messages into it. When you save a message from one folder into another folder, Pine marks the original message for deletion and then moves it to the new folder. If you want to copy a message from one folder into another folder, then you must undelete the message in the original folder by selecting it and typing U for undelete. If you do not undelete the original message, it will be expunged when you exit Pine. Copying a message to different folders is useful if you want to file a message in several folders corresponding to different message categories. Next, you will save a message in the Marketing folder.

To save a message into another folder:

1. Start Pine, and then open the INBOX folder.

   TROUBLE? To open the INBOX, type M to open the Main Menu window and then type I to open the INBOX.

2. Use the Up and Down arrow keys to select the Sample Pine Message summary line in the Folder List.

3. Type **S** to save the highlighted message. The prompt "SAVE to folder (received):" appears at the bottom of the screen.

4. Type **Marketing**, the name of the folder to which you want to transfer the message. See Figure F-6.

Figure F-6	SAVING A MESSAGE TO ANOTHER FOLDER

message being saved in the Marketing folder

folder to which highlighted message is saved

TROUBLE? If you cannot remember the name of the new folder, press Ctrl + T to display a list of all folder names, select the desired folder, and then press the Enter key.

5. Press the **Enter** key to save the message. Pine displays a message indicating that the message was transferred to the Marketing folder and the original message was marked for deletion.

TROUBLE? If you transfer a message to the wrong folder, just repeat the preceding steps by opening the folder containing the message you transferred. Then, save it to the correct folder.

6. Type **Q** to exit Pine. Pine will ask if you want to expunge messages marked for deletion—including the one you just saved in the Marketing folder—from the INBOX. Because you have a copy of the message in the Marketing folder, you will expunge the original message and any others marked.

7. Type **Y** to expunge messages marked for deletion, including the one you transferred to the Marketing folder.

Forwarding a Message Using Pine

When you forward a message, Pine sends the entire message you received (including the header lines and the body of the message) and adds a line above the entire message indicating that it is a forwarded message. After you add the e-mail address of the person to forward the message to and a subject line and send the message, it is delivered to the addressee just like any other mail message. The original message remains in your INBOX unless you delete it.

To forward an existing mail message to another user, open the INBOX containing the message, highlight the message in the Folder Index window (the INBOX), and then type F to invoke the Forward command. Enter the recipient's e-mail address in the To field, type a short subject, and then enter a brief explanation of why you are forwarding the message in the Message Text area, if necessary. Press Ctrl + X to send the message.

Replying to a Message Using Pine

You use the Pine Reply command to reply to a sender's message. Open the INBOX message to which you want to respond and type R to execute the Reply command. Pine asks you if you want to include the original message in the reply. Type Y to include it, or type N to omit it. If the sender's message has Cc or Bcc recipients, Pine will ask if you want to reply to all recipients. Again, type either Y or N to answer yes or no, respectively. The Compose Message Reply window opens with the header completed, and the insertion point appears in the first position of the Message Text area. Pine automatically inserts the original message sender's e-mail address in the To line of the response. The greater than symbol (>) appears to the left of each line of the original message to distinguish it from the text you supply in response. In addition to writing response lines, you can modify any portion of the sender's message in your response. Often, a responder will delete much of the sender's text, leaving only a snippet of the original message—just enough to provide a context for the response.

Deleting a Message Using Pine

To prevent you from inadvertently deleting important messages, Pine requires you to take two steps to delete an e-mail message. First, you delete a message, which simply marks the message for permanent removal. Second, you permanently remove a message by expunging all messages marked for deletion.

To delete a message using Pine:

1. Start Pine, and then type **L** to display your e-mail folders.

2. Press the right arrow key enough times to select the Marketing folder.

3. Press the **Enter** key to open the Marketing folder to reveal the message you saved.

4. Use the Up and Down arrow keys to select your Sample Pine Message summary line, and then type **D** to mark the highlighted record for deletion. The letter "D" appears in the left column of the message line and the next message summary line, if there is one, is selected. See Figure F-7.

| Figure F-7 | MARKING A MESSAGE FOR DELETION |

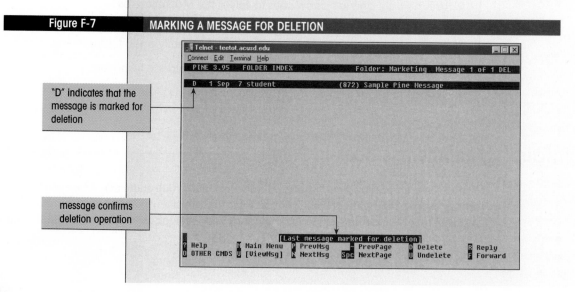

"D" indicates that the message is marked for deletion

message confirms deletion operation

TROUBLE? If you mark the wrong message for deletion, type U to send the Undelete command and remove the deletion mark. You can undelete a message any time before you expunge all messages.

5. Repeat Step 4 to delete any other messages that you received during this session.

6. Type **M** to return to Pine's Main Menu window. If you want to quit Pine at this point and do not want to delete marked messages permanently, type N when Pine asks if you want to expunge the deleted messages.

You can mark a message in any folder for deletion. Next, you will expunge all messages marked for deletion.

To expunge a Pine message:

1. Type **Q** to quit Pine.

2. Type **Y** at the "Really quit pine?" prompt.

3. If Pine asks you if you want to save a message or messages in the received folder, type Y if you want to move messages from the INBOX folder to the received folder. Otherwise, type N and the group of messages—unmarked ones—will remain in the INBOX.

4. Type **Y** to expunge all marked messages at the "Expunge the 1 deleted message from "INBOX"?" prompt. All messages marked for deletion disappear, and control returns to the program from which you started Pine.

Besides deleting individual e-mail messages, you can delete entire e-mail folders. Next, you will delete the Marketing folder.

To delete a Pine e-mail folder:

1. Start Pine, if necessary, and type **L** to open the FOLDER LIST.

2. Use the right and left arrow keys to select the Marketing folder.

3. Type **D** to delete the Marketing folder. A message displays near the bottom of the display: Really delete "Marketing" (the currently open folder)?

4. Type **Y** to confirm the deletion. The Marketing folder is removed.

5. Type **M** to return to Pine's Main Menu window.

Maintaining an Address Book in Pine

You can use an address book to create individual and group addresses. After you have a few entries in your Pine address book, you can refer to them at any point while you are composing, replying to, or forwarding a message. Pine sorts address book entries in order by full name.

To create an address book entry:

1. Start Pine, and make sure that you are in the Main Menu window.

2. Type **A** to open the Address Book window.

   TROUBLE? If you see the message "(Empty)" in the Address Book window, don't worry. That simply means that you do not yet have any e-mail addresses stored in your address book.

3. Type **A** to add a new entry.

4. Type your first name on the Nickname line, and then press the **Enter** key.

5. Type your last name, a comma, a space, and your first name (such as Goldberg, Barbara) on the Fullname line, and then press the **Enter** key three times to move to the Addresses line.

6. Type your full e-mail address in the Addresses line. Notice the instructions below the entry to help you save it. See Figure F-8.

| Figure F-8 | CREATING A NEW ADDRESS BOOK ENTRY |

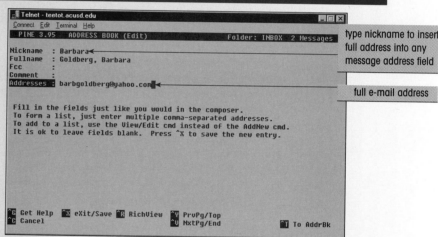

TROUBLE? If you make a mistake in any entry, use the arrow keys to move to the line and correct the mistake.

7. Press **Ctrl + X** to save the new entry, and then type **Y** to confirm exiting and saving the new entry. The address book shows the new entry in alphabetical order by the Fullname field.

   TROUBLE? If you change your mind and do not want to save the entry, press Ctrl + C to cancel saving the entry, and then type Y to confirm cancellation.

8. Type **M** to go to the Main Menu window.

When you want to send a message to someone who is listed in your address book, you can type that person's nickname or his or her full name, and Pine will address the message automatically.

You also can use Pine to create a distribution list of e-mail addresses. To do this, type A to open the Address Book window, type A to add a new address, type the list's name on the Nickname line and press the Enter key to move to the Addresses line, and then type the individual e-mail addresses and separate them with commas. Press Ctrl + X to save the new entry, and then type Y to exit and save changes. The address book reappears with the distribution list address visible. You can see the individual addresses in the group address by selecting the entry.

Exiting Pine

When you are finished using Pine, you should exit the program. Furthermore, if you have used Telnet to log into a UNIX system running Pine, be sure to log out of your account. The next steps illustrate how to exit the Pine e-mail system. Consult with your instructor about logging off the system at your school.

To exit Pine:

1. Type **Q**, and then respond to any prompts to exit Pine and return to the system from which you started.

2. Type **Y** when the "Really quit pine?" message appears.

3. If additional messages appear near the bottom of the display (they are easy to overlook), respond by typing Y (for yes) or N (for no) as appropriate. Example messages include "Save read message in "received"?" or "Expunge the deleted message from "INBOX"?" The "Pine finished" message confirms you exited the program.

TASK	PAGE #	RECOMMENDED METHOD	WHERE USED
FTP AND WINDOWS TASKS			
Anonymous login using command-line FTP	WEB 6.38	Type anonymous, press Enter	FTP
Download file using command-line FTP	WEB 6.37	See Reference Window "Downloading a file using command-line FTP"	FTP
Downloading a file	WEB 6.11	See Reference Window "Downloading a file using an FTP client program"	FTP
End session using command-line FTP	WEB 6.39	Type quit, press Enter	FTP
List files and folders using command-line FTP	WEB 6.40	Type dir, press Enter	FTP
Open a connection using command-line FTP	WEB 6.38	Type open followed by connection URL, press Enter	FTP
Route, trace Internet	WEB 6.41	Click the Start button, click Run, type c:\windows\tracert, type the destination URL following the command, click OK	Windows
Uploading a file	WEB 6.15	See Reference Window "Uploading a file using an FTP client program"	FTP
Use Windows built-in FTP	WEB 6.37	Click the Start button, click Run, type c:\windows\ftp, click OK	Windows
NETSCAPE NAVIGATOR TASKS			
Address book entry, create	WEB 2.29	See Reference Window "Adding an address to the address book"	Messenger
Address book group, create	WEB 2.31	See Reference Window "Creating a mailing list"	Messenger
Attached file, save in Netscape Message window	WEB 2.22	See Reference Window "Saving an attached file"	Messenger
Bookmark folder, create	WEB 3.24	See Reference Window "Creating a Bookmarks folder"	Navigator
Bookmark, create	WEB 3.25	Click the Bookmarks button, click Add Bookmark	Navigator
Bookmark, create in a specific folder	WEB 3.25	See Reference Window, "Creating a bookmark in a bookmarks folder"	Navigator
Bookmarks file, save to floppy disk	WEB 3.26	See Reference Window, "Saving a bookmark to a floppy disk"	Navigator
Bookmarks window, open	WEB 3.24	Click the Bookmarks button, click Edit Bookmarks	Navigator
E-mail name, set up your	WEB 2.17	Click Edit, click Preferences, click Identity in the Mail & Newsgroups category, type your first and last names, type your full e-mail address, click OK	Messenger
File, attach in Composition window	WEB 2.19	Click the Attach button, click File, locate the file, click Open	Messenger

TASK	PAGE #	RECOMMENDED METHOD	WHERE USED
Font size of a Web page, change	WEB 3.33	Click Edit, click Preferences, click the Fonts category, use the Size list arrow to change font size, click OK	Navigator
Help, get	WEB 3.35	See Reference Window "Opening the NetHelp - Netscape window"	Navigator
History list, open	WEB 3.29	Click Communicator, point to Tools, click History	Navigator
Home page, change default	WEB 3.30	See Reference Window "Changing the default home page"	Navigator
Home page, return to	WEB 3.30	Click the Home button	Navigator
Mail folder, create	WEB 2.26	Click File, click New Folder	Messenger
Mail folder, delete	WEB 2.28	Click the folder to select, right-click the folder, click Delete Folder, click OK	Messenger
Mail preferences, set servers	WEB 2.16	Click Edit, click Preferences, click Mail & Newsgroups category, click Mail Servers, type SMTP and POP server names, click OK	Messenger
Mail, attach file	WEB 7.23	See Reference Window "Attaching a file to an e-mail message"	Messenger
Mail, compose	WEB 2.19	Click the New Msg button	Messenger
Mail, copy to another folder in Message List window	WEB 2.26	Click Message, point to Copy Message, click destination folder	Messenger
Mail, delete	WEB 2.27	Right-click the message summary, click Delete Message	Messenger
Mail, delete permanently	WEB 2.28	Click File, click Empty Trash on Local Mail	Messenger
Mail, forward from Message List window	WEB 2.24	Click the Forward button	Messenger
Mail, move to another folder in Message List window	WEB 2.27	Click File button, click destination folder	Messenger
Mail, open attached file	WEB 7.25	See Reference Window "Viewing and detaching a file from an e-mail message"	Messenger
Mail, print message	WEB 2.27	Right-click the message summary, click Print Message	Messenger
Mail, read in Message List window	WEB 2.21	Click the message summary line	Messenger
Mail, receive messages in Message List window	WEB 2.21	Click the Get Msg button, type your user name and password, click OK	Messenger
Mail, reply to all recipients in Message List window	WEB 2.23	Click the message summary line, click the Reply All button	Messenger

TASK	PAGE #	RECOMMENDED METHOD	WHERE USED
Mail, reply to sender in Message List window	WEB 2.23	Click the message summary line, click the Reply button	Messenger
Mail, send from Composition window	WEB 2.20	Click the Send button	Messenger
Mail, spell check in Composition window	WEB 2.20	Click the Spelling button	Messenger
Mailing list, conceal your name on a LISTSERV list	WEB 7.15	See Reference Window "Concealing your name on a mailing list"	Messenger
Mailing list, leave	WEB 7.16	See Reference Window "Leaving a mailing list"	Messenger
Mailing list, post a message to	WEB 7.11	See Reference Window "Posting a message to a mailing list"	Messenger
Mailing list, retrieve archive file	WEB 7.12	See Reference Window "Retrieving an archive filename list"	Messenger
Mailing list, retrieve membership list	WEB 7.14	See Reference Window "Retrieving member information from a mailing list"	Messenger
Mailing list, subscribe to	WEB 7.07	See Reference Window "Subscribing to a mailing list"	Messenger
Messenger, start	WEB 2.15	Click the Start button, point to Programs, point to Netscape Communicator, click Netscape Messenger	
Navigator window, maximize	WEB 3.17	Click the Maximize button	Navigator, Messenger
Navigator window, minimize	WEB 3.11	Click the Minimize button	Navigator, Messenger
Navigator window, restore maximized	WEB 3.11	Click the Restore button	Navigator, Messenger
Navigator, close	WEB 3.11	Click the Close button	Navigator, Messenger
Navigator, start	WEB 3.17	Click the Start button, point to Programs, point to Netscape Communicator, click Netscape Navigator	
News articles, read and send	WEB 8.26	See Reference Window "Reading and sending articles using Messenger"	Messenger
Newsreader, start	WEB 8.24	See Reference Window "Starting the Netscape Messenger newsreader"	Messenger
Page print settings, change	WEB 3.32	Click File, click Page Setup	Navigator
Security, strengthen in Navigator	WEB 9.37	Click Edit, click Preferences, click Advanced, adjust security settings	Navigator
Start page, return to	WEB 3.30	Click the Home button	Navigator

TASK REFERENCE

TASK	PAGE #	RECOMMENDED METHOD	WHERE USED
Toolbar, hide	WEB 3.20	Click View, point to Show, deselect toolbar to hide	Navigator
Toolbar, show	WEB 3.20	Click View, point to Show, select toolbar to show	Navigator
URL, enter and go to	WEB 3.21	See Reference Window "Entering a URL in the Location field"	Navigator
Web page graphic, save	WEB 3.40	See Reference Window "Saving an image from a Web page on a floppy disk"	Navigator
Web page in history list, move forward to previous	WEB 3.19	Click the Forward button	Navigator
Web page in history list, return to previous	WEB 3.27	Click the Back button	Navigator
Web page text, save	WEB 3.38	See Reference Window "Copying text from a Web page to a WordPad document"	Navigator
Web page, print all pages	WEB 3.31	Click the Print button	Navigator
Web page, print one or a few pages	WEB 3.32	See Reference Window "Printing the current Web page"	Navigator
Web page, reload	WEB 3.30	Click the Reload button	Navigator
Web page, save to floppy disk	WEB 3.37	See Reference Window "Saving a Web page to a floppy disk"	Navigator
Web page, stop loading	WEB 3.15	Click the Stop button	Navigator

MICROSOFT INTERNET EXPLORER TASKS

TASK	PAGE #	RECOMMENDED METHOD	WHERE USED
Address book entry, create	WEB 2.47	See Reference Window "Entering a new e-mail address in the address book"	Outlook Express
Address book group, create	WEB 2.49	See Reference Window "Creating a group address entry"	Outlook Express
Attached file, save	WEB 2.41	See Reference Window "Saving an attached file"	Outlook Express
Favorite, move to a new folder	WEB 3.50	See Reference Window "Moving an existing favorite into a new folder"	Internet Explorer
Favorites folder, create	WEB 3.48	See Reference Window "Creating a new Favorites folder"	Internet Explorer
Favorites frame, open	WEB 3.47	Click the Favorites button	Internet Explorer
File, attach in New Message window	WEB 2.38	Click the Attach button, locate the file, click Attach	Outlook Express
Font size of Web page, change	WEB 3.57	Click View, point to Text Size, click the desired size option	Internet Explorer
Help, get	WEB 3.58	See Reference Window "Getting Help in Internet Explorer"	Internet Explorer

TASK	PAGE #	RECOMMENDED METHOD	WHERE USED
History list, open	WEB 3.53	Click the History button	Internet Explorer
Home page, change default	WEB 3.55	See Reference Window "Changing the Home toolbar button settings"	Internet Explorer
Home page, return to	WEB 3.54	Click the Home button	Internet Explorer
Internet Explorer window, maximize	WEB 3.42	Click the Maximize button	Internet Explorer, Outlook Express
Internet Explorer window, minimize	WEB 3.11	Click the Minimize button	Internet Explorer, Outlook Express
Internet Explorer window, restore maximized	WEB 3.11	Click the Restore button	Internet Explorer, Outlook Express
Internet Explorer, close	WEB 3.11	Click the Close button	Internet Explorer, Outlook Express
Internet Explorer, start	WEB 3.41	Click the Start button, point to Programs, click Internet Explorer	
Mail account, set up	WEB 2.35	Click Tools, click Accounts, click the Mail tab, click the Add button, click Mail, follow steps in the Internet Connection Wizard	Outlook Express
Mail folder, create	WEB 2.44	Click File, point to Folder, click New	Outlook Express
Mail folder, delete	WEB 2.47	Right-click the folder, click Delete	Outlook Express
Mail, compose	WEB 2.37	Click the New Mail button	Outlook Express
Mail, copy to another folder	WEB 2.45	Click the message summary, click Edit, click Copy to Folder	Outlook Express
Mail, delete	WEB 2.46	Click the message summary, click the Delete button	Outlook Express
Mail, delete permanently	WEB 2.46	Open Deleted Items folder, click the message summary of message to delete, click the Delete button	Outlook Express
Mail, forward from Inbox window	WEB 2.43	Click the Forward button	Outlook Express
Mail, move to another folder	WEB 2.45	Click the message summary, drag the message to destination folder	Outlook Express
Mail, print	WEB 2.45	Click the message summary, click the Print button	Outlook Express
Mail, read	WEB 2.39	Click the message summary	Outlook Express
Mail, reply to author from Inbox window	WEB 2.42	Click the message summary, click the Reply button	Outlook Express
Mail, send and receive	WEB 2.39	Click the Send/Recv button	Outlook Express
Mail, send from New Message window	WEB 2.39	Click the Send button	Outlook Express

TASK	PAGE #	RECOMMENDED METHOD	WHERE USED
Mail, spell check in New Message window	WEB 2.39	Click Tools, Spelling	Outlook Express
Mailing list, conceal your name on a LISTSERV list	WEB 7.15	See Reference Window "Concealing your name on a mailing list"	Outlook Express
Mailing list, leave	WEB 7.16	See Reference Window "Leaving a mailing list"	Outlook Express
Mailing list, post a message to	WEB 7.11	See Reference Window "Posting a message to a mailing list"	Outlook Express
Mailing list, retrieve archive file	WEB 7.12	See Reference Window "Retrieving an archive filename list"	Outlook Express
Mailing list, retrieve membership list	WEB 7.14	See Reference Window "Retrieving member information from a mailing list"	Outlook Express
Mailing list, subscribe to	WEB 7.07	See Reference Window "Subscribing to a mailing list"	Outlook Express
News articles, read and send	WEB 8.28	See Reference Window "Reading and sending articles using Outlook Express"	Outlook Express
Newsreader, start	WEB 8.27	See Reference Window "Starting the Microsoft Outlook Express newsreader"	Outlook Express
Outlook Express, start	WEB 2.34	Click the Start button, point to Programs, click Outlook Express	
Page print settings, change	WEB 3.56	Click File, click Page Setup	Internet Explorer
Security, strengthen in Internet Explorer	WEB 9.37	Click Tools, click Internet Options, click Security tab, adjust security settings	Internet Explorer
Start page, return to	WEB 3.54	Click the Home button	Internet Explorer
Toolbar, hide or show	WEB 3.44	See Reference Window "Hiding and restoring the toolbars"	Internet Explorer
URL, enter and go to	WEB 3.45	See Reference Window "Entering a URL in the Address Bar"	Internet Explorer
Web page graphic, save	WEB 3.63	See Reference Window "Saving an image from a Web page on a floppy disk"	Internet Explorer
Web page in history list, move forward to previous	WEB 3.48	Click the Forward button	Internet Explorer
Web page in history list, return to previous	WEB 3.47	Click the Back button	Internet Explorer
Web page text, save	WEB 3.61	See Reference Window "Copying text from a Web page to a WordPad document"	Internet Explorer
Web page, print all pages	WEB 3.56	Click the Print button	Internet Explorer
Web page, print one or a few pages	WEB 3.56	See Reference Window "Printing the current Web page"	Internet Explorer

TASK	PAGE #	RECOMMENDED METHOD	WHERE USED
Web page, refresh	WEB 3.54	Click the Refresh button	Internet Explorer
Web page, save to floppy disk	WEB 3.60	See Reference Window "Saving a Web page to a floppy disk"	Internet Explorer
Web page, stop loading	WEB 3.15	Click the Stop button	Internet Explorer
WEB CALENDAR TASKS			
Appointment, create	WEB 10.19	Click appropriate year, month, and day links, click time link, type title, select type of appointment, click appropriate option in Sharing category, set duration, click Save	My Yahoo!
Appointment, create recurring	WEB 10.21	Click appropriate year, month, and day links, click time link, type title, select type of appointment, click appropriate option in Sharing category, set duration, set repeating information, click Save	My Yahoo!
Appointment, deleting	WEB 10.25	Click appointment link, click the Delete button	My Yahoo!
Calendar, clear	WEB 10.26	On calendar page click Options link, click Advanced Options link, click Delete all events and To Do items from your calendar link, click Reset	My Yahoo!
Calendar, publishing	WEB 10.23	On calendar page click Options link, click Calendar Sharing link, click appropriate option in Active Sharing section, click Save, click Activate Sharing if necessary	My Yahoo!
EUDORA TASKS			
Eudora, exit	WEB E.12	Click File on the menu bar, click Exit	
Eudora, start	WEB E.04	Click the Start button, point to Programs, point to Eudora Pro, click Eudora Pro	
Mail, create address book entry	WEB E.11	Click the Address Book button, click the New button, type nickname, click OK, click Address(es) tab, type e-mail address, click Info tab, type first and last names, click File, click Save	
Mail, delete message	WEB E.11	Select the message, click the Delete Message(s) button	
Mail, forward	WEB E.10	Select the message, click the Forward button	
Mail, print	WEB E.09	Select the message, click the Print button	
Mail, reply to message	WEB E.10	Select the message, click the Reply button	
Mail, retrieve and read	WEB E.07	Click the Check Mail button, enter password, double-click the message summary	

TASK	PAGE #	RECOMMENDED METHOD
Mail, send message	WEB E.07	Click the Send button
Mail, transfer message to another mailbox	WEB E.10	Select the message, click Transfer on the menu bar, click the target mailbox
Mailbox, create	WEB E.09	Click Mailbox on the menu bar, click New, type the new mailbox name, click OK

PINE TASKS

TASK	PAGE #	RECOMMENDED METHOD
Mail, compose	WEB F.02	Type C at the Main menu
Mail, create a folder	WEB F.06	From the Main menu, type A, type the name of the folder, press Enter
Mail, create address book entry	WEB F.11	From the Main menu, type A, type A again, enter address information in the appropriate lines, press Ctrl + X, type Y
Mail, delete message	WEB F.09	Open a mail folder, select a message summary line, type D
Mail, expunge message	WEB F.10	From the Main menu, type Q, type Y, type Y again
Mail, forward	WEB F.08	Open a message, type F, fill in recipient's address, press Ctrl + X, then press Y
Mail, print	WEB F.06	Open a message, press Y twice
Mail, quit	WEB F.12	From the Main Menu type Q, type Y
Mail, retrieve and read	WEB F.04	From the Main menu, type I, use arrow keys to select the message summary, press Enter
Mail, send	WEB F.03	With the Compose Message window open, press Ctrl + X